THE BEGINNING OF PRINT CULTURE *in Athabasca Country*

ᒪᓇᒋᐊᑕᐠ ᑭᓭ ᒪᓂᑐ

manâcihâtâhk kisê-manitow Let Us Respect God

ᑕᐍᑕᐘᑕᐠ ᑭᓭ ᒪᓂᑐ

tâpwêtawâtâhk kisê-manitow Let Us Believe in God

ᒪᒥᓯᑐᑕᐘᑕᐠ ᑭᓭ ᒪᓂᑐ

mamisîtotawâtâhk kisê-manitow Let Us Trust in God

ᓴᑭᐊᑕᐠ ᑭᓭ ᒪᓂᑐ

sâkihâtâhk kisê-manitow Let Us Love God

ᑲᑿᑕᑫᔨᒧᑕᐠ

kakwâtakêyimotâhk Let Us Suffer for It

ᓇᓇᐢᑯᒪᑕᐠ ᑭᓭ ᒪᓂᑐ

nanâskomâtâhk kisê-manitow Let Us Thank God

THE BEGINNING OF

PRINT CULTURE

in Athabasca Country

A Facsimile Edition & Translation of a Prayer Book in Cree Syllabics
by Father Émile Grouard, OMI
Prepared and Printed at Lac La Biche in 1883
with an Introduction by Patricia Demers

TRANSLATED BY PATRICIA DEMERS
NAOMI MCILWRAITH
AND DOROTHY THUNDER

Published by
THE UNIVERSITY OF ALBERTA PRESS
Ring House 2
Edmonton, Alberta, Canada T6G 2E1

LIBRARY AND ARCHIVES CANADA
CATALOGUING IN PUBLICATION

The beginning of print culture in Athabasca country : a facsimile edition and translation of a prayer book in Cree syllabics / Patricia Demers, with Naomi L. McIlwraith, Dorothy Thunder.

Includes a reproduction of the original text written in Cree syllabics by Father Grouard, printed 1883.
ISBN 978-0-88864-515-9

1. Catholic Church – Prayers and devotions.
2. Cree language – Texts.
3. Cree Indians – Prayers and devotions.
4. Grouard, mgr. (Émile-Jean-Baptiste-Marie), 1840–1931.
5. Printing – Alberta – History.
6. Prayer books – Alberta – History.
I. Demers, Patricia.
II. McIlwraith, Naomi L.
III. Thunder, Dorothy.
IV. Grouard, mgr. (Émile-Jean-Baptiste-Marie), 1840–1931.

BX2128.C7B43 2009   242'.802
C2009-902155-2

First edition, first printing, 2010.
Printed and bound in Canada by Friesens, Altona, Manitoba.
Copyediting and Proofreading by Meaghan Craven.
Map by Wendy Johnson.

The University of Alberta Press is committed to protecting our natural environment. As part of our efforts, this book is printed on Enviro paper: it contains 100% post-consumer recycled fibres and is acid- and chlorine-free.

The University of Alberta Press gratefully acknowledges the support received for its publishing program from The Canada Council for the Arts. The University of Alberta Press also gratefully acknowledges the financial support of the Government of Canada through the Book Publishing Industry Development Program (BPIDP), the Alberta Foundation for the Arts, and the Alberta Historical Resources Foundation for its publishing activities.

This book has been published with the help of a grant from the Canadian Federation for the Humanities and Social Sciences, through the Aid to Scholarly Publications Program, using funds provided by the Social Sciences and Humanities Research Council of Canada.

Canadä

CONTENTS

FOREWORD

This book was a very long time in the making: it began in 1883 as one of the earliest documents ever printed in northern Alberta and evolved into the book you now hold. Its appearance is testament to dedicated work and study conducted at two very different periods of time in the history of western Canada. But these two periods of time, and the two works encompassed within these pages, for all their differences, share common ground. This book's existence is testament to the importance of the Cree language, in both the late nineteenth century and today.

The Cree language was not Father Émile Grouard's primary inspiration, but as the means to his work, it was inspiring nonetheless. He wrote that he found "incomparable perfection" within the language, which shows exactly how he felt about Cree, *nēhiyawēwin*. It is also clear that he held a high level of respect for all the languages he worked with, as well as for the speakers of those languages whom he had the privilege to serve. For Father Grouard, Cree, Montagnais (Dene), Loucheux (Gwich'in), and other First Nations languages were not an impediment to his work but a means for further learning and understanding. The inclusion of language lessons at the mission schools under his care illustrates the importance he attached to learning in the Native languages.

Grouard's position relative to Native languages and their speakers represents an enlightened and advanced attitude in comparison to the negative treatment that speakers of First Nations languages received under the residential school system. Through much of the twentieth century, misguided monolingual policies contributed to the diminished use, serious endangerment and even complete loss of many Indigenous languages. Had Grouard been ruled by such policies, the original document upon which the current study is based would never have been. Further, if those policies of linguistic persecution had fully won out, the current study would never have been attempted. It is only in the returning enlightenment of the recent decades that we have become freer to listen to the Elders' wisdom regarding the importance of a people's first language. In today's climate of language revival and growing interest in literary documentation, reviews of missionary translations have not only become possible but also desirable for the many levels of information they might yield.

If the task that Grouard took on was daunting, yet more difficult is the task that Demers, McIlwraith, and Thunder have set themselves, and they are to be applauded for meeting such a challenge. On the surface, it might appear that modern scholars need only assess Grouard's translation for accuracy with respect to a native speaker's fluency in Cree. However, the potential sources for error and misunderstanding are far greater, especially given the temporal distance between Grouard's work and this modern study. Certainly, Grouard had to deal with the potential for miscommunication between the two primary languages involved (French and Cree) not to mention influences from Hebrew, Greek, Latin, and English, and his own ability to accurately interpret the tenets of one culture's belief to another. Then his translation was communicated through the medium of print in a very different type of writing system: the Cree Syllabary. The authors of the current volume arrived at this literary material from cultural and linguistic perspectives that differ again from Grouard's and that of his intended audience. Many questions arose during the process of examining Grouard's text. For example, were apparent errors to be attributed solely to Grouard's original work in understanding and translation? Have the limitations of the underspecified Syllabic script, or mere errors in the original typesetting, introduced new sources of misunderstanding and further obscured Grouard's intent? Has change in the Cree language over the past century affected a modern reading of the material? And, finally, can we know if Grouard's original audience experienced all, some, or none of the same difficulties that the authors uncovered today?

The two works within these pages share common ground. Together they make a significant and interesting contribution to Cree language studies and Cree literature. In presenting this material anew in the current edition, Demers, McIlwraith, and Thunder have provided a valuable resource both through their own interpretations and analyses and also through the wealth of material that they have uncovered for future research.

This book was a very long time in the making. I hope it is just the beginning.

Arok Wolvengrey
First Nations University of Canada

PREFACE

In our critical climate few topics provoke such heated and polarized responses as the need to retain First Nations languages and to examine missionary work within Aboriginal communities. The first is endorsed and warmly promoted; the other is scrutinized with a minefield of accusations—from suspicion to denunciation. This project proposes to fill a gap in awareness and documentation by reproducing, translating, and commenting on a missionary text in a First Nations language. Rather than attempt to bring the poles together in a sort of rhetorical vice, it aims to chart the territory now so vehemently contested from the point of view of pioneer conditions and aspirations. Of course any re-creation of the recoverable past is undeniably filtered through our own twenty-first-century reality. Even if we align ourselves with the position of the irrecoverable past, seeing the past solely through a contemporary or presentist lens diminishes its ideological particularity, zeal, and commitment.

Mapping the terrain and influence of the nineteenth-century missionary press is a daring task for several reasons. The scarcity of documentation and depletion of the once widely circulated archives make finding a text or commentary a cause for celebration. Speculating about the possibilities of give and take in the indigenization of missionary catechetics through transformations to fit local culture provides an opportunity to explore the linkages between "a naturized church and a recontextualized Christianity."[1] The advent of a printing press in a largely oral culture also showcases the hybridity "of the oral and written, the past and present, the Aboriginal and the Western."[2] Such a moment of blending prompts us to acknowledge the foundational importance of oral traditions "connecting speaker and listener in communal experience and uniting past and present in memory."[3] In fact, learning about "oral aesthetics" entails "respectful and appreciative reception"[4] of a living, changing, non-static tradition. The convergence of the oral and the written, crystallized by the introduction of the printing press in Athabasca Country, highlights the interaction between orality and literacy. It is the oral word, the first illuminator of consciousness, that "ties human beings to one another in society."[5] The imprints of the mission press might be considered documents of "textualized orality" in which a writer represents the "speech habits and oral strategies of communication."[6] Moreover, following the paths of communication in a Syllabics text challenges us with the immeasurably vast possibilities of language. As neuroscientists continue to discover, writing and reading are the ultimate cognitive workout, supplying "the neuronal basis for new thoughts" and intensifying a grasp of "the different properties of words...that allow new words to be formed from existing stems and morphemes."[7]

A previously widespread but now rare text from the formative stage of missionary activity in the Great North-West is our focus and platform for historical and linguistic examination, for parsing the language of fervently held beliefs in faith, justice, mercy, and peace. While we are not mitigating the reports of direct and collateral damages, or the over 60,000 complaints presented to the Royal Commission on Aboriginal Peoples (1993), or the searing indictment of residential schools (in Tomson Highway's autobiographical novel, *Kiss of the Fur Queen*, as but one example), we are directing attention to an earlier and arguably idealistic phase. During this period in Athabasca Country, when the reality of print culture affected the whole community, speaking—not silencing—the language of the people was of vital importance. Strangely, the missionary author who championed the knowledge of Indigenous languages, Émile Grouard (1840–1931), remains almost unknown.

The intellectual scene today is very promising for the retrieval and study of an early Syllabics document, when interest is widespread in rescuing Aboriginal languages from neglect, and in restoring and teaching them. Equally prominent are explorations of literacy and language practice that blend oral and written traditions. The first edition of the poetry and other writing of Jane Johnston Schoolcraft (1800–1842) or Bamewawagezhikaquay, as she was known in Ojibwe, introduces her "unprecedented" and "bicultural" work as "its own evolving and mobile space in the cultural landscape."[8] According to the book's editor, Robert Dale Parker, she brought together Ojibwe and American worlds by "writing poetry in an Indian language, writing out English-language versions of Indian oral stories and songs on a large scale, and knowledgeably integrating Indian language into English-language literary writing."[9] The integration of Cree and French languages, along with Latin texts, makes the work of Émile Grouard, OMI, presented here, a *multi*-cultural lens through which to view a specific historical epoch of immense importance for the cultural diversity of the Canadian North-West. Similarly, the first edition of the published works and manuscripts of the eighteenth-century Mohegan missionary and "intertribal political and spiritual leader," Samson Occom (1723–1792), is another landmark in "intellectual and cultural repatriation."[10] Grouard's catechetical texts are also milestone events, allowing readers a latter-day access to the sounds and rhetoric of nineteenth-century Cree discourse. Our hope is that this facsimile edition and translation will contribute to the burgeoning, hybridized field of Aboriginal language studies and social history, illuminating a generative period in the dissemination of print culture in western Canada, along with remarkable fusions of Cree, French, and Latin linguistic patterns.

The importance of mission presses producing material in Native Syllabics in the 1870s and 1880s in the Great North-West is an understudied and largely forgotten piece of western Canadian history. English-language periodicals funded by commercial advertisements in growing urban centres from the same period, however, have received more attention in the public record; thanks to digitization and scholarly scrutiny, their development and expansion are easier to recognize and chart.[11] In contrast to this steady entrepreneurial march, the untold story of the mission press is punctuated by paradox and reversal. Phenomenal numbers of texts, painstakingly produced in isolated mission outposts, have dwindled to a precious residue. The small, cast-iron, Stanhope hand press, its platen printing a whole sheet at a single pull, produced thousands of copies of books, stitched and bound for wide distribution in the North; from this huge output a few samples are now preserved as rare artifacts.

Unlike the boosterism of the secular press, the missionary work of catechizing is often consigned—and condemned—to a colonialist past. Yet these ephemeral texts hold fascinating stories of linguistic transformation and borrowing, stories that have remained hidden to nonreaders of Syllabics. We think a closer look at the pioneering imprints of Oblate missionaries, especially the books in five Native languages written by Father Émile Grouard, yields significant insights into the characterization and expression of Indigenous culture and identity, as well as the extraordinary earnestness of missionaries in learning Syllabics. Such observation could also inform an agenda for continuing critical investigation of the broadly understood missionary enterprise, which influenced all aspects of community life, education, and politics.

A limited number of Natives, usually those closely associated with Elders, and very few non-Natives can actually read Syllabics. The Plains Cree text reproduced here, a classic mission press imprint, provides both a primer in this shorthand script of geometric characters representing syllables and a window on the world of nineteenth-century communities and devotions. Admittedly, some mission publications (Catholic, Anglican, and Wesleyan) predated Grouard's efforts, but they were published elsewhere—in Rupert's Land (Saint Boniface and Rossville Mission, Norway House), Montreal, Paris, and London—and imported back to the North-West. Grouard's texts were the first publications produced in Athabasca Country. More fascinating still is the existence of his original Paris-made printing press, with many of the Syllabics fonts and copperplates he ordered in Belgium, housed in the Oblate Collection at the Provincial Archives of Alberta.

Painter, writer, builder, innovator, tireless pastor, and, later, bishop—Grouard's prodigious energy and accomplishments usually prompt association with the better-known Oblate Father Albert Lacombe (1827–1916). Lacombe's phonetic Cree–French dictionary and grammar, *Dictionnaire de la langue des Cris* and *Grammaire de la langue des Cris* (Montreal, 1874), compiled mainly by Brother Constantine Scollen, provided a substantial basis for further Oblate texts. Always curious, adaptive, and venturesome, Grouard was a man of letters and action. The range of his career, its mixture of spirituality and practicality, other-worldliness and acute observations of his place and time, also suggest comparison with the Italian-born missionary a generation earlier, Father Anthony Ravalli, SJ (1812–1884), the first medical doctor in Montana. Priest, physician, artist, sculptor, and architect, this Jesuit planted the first wheat and oats, taught the first classes, and decorated the chapel at St. Mary's Mission in Stevensville, Montana, where he ministered to the spiritual and physical needs of Flathead and Nez Perce nations. Unlike Ravalli, though, Grouard delighted in writing, creating catechetical texts to assist and extend his evangelizing ministry.

This book focuses on one of the primary texts that comprise Grouard's legacy. His use of Syllabics locates *kâtolik ayamihêwi-masinahikan* as both Cree and Oblate, blending Indigenous (Syllabics) and European (French and Latin) languages. In addition to the hybridity of these identifying markers, the language of the text has a contentious history. Understanding the power and provenance of Syllabics depends very much on which source you consult. The Reverend James Evans (1801–1846), Methodist missionary, is often cited as the "inventor of the Syllabic system of the Cree language," in the title given him by another missionary, John MacLean in his published biography.[12] In Evans's sixteen-page Cree Syllabary, a booklet first printed at Norway House in October 1840 on a homemade device fashioned from an old fur-bale press, he manoeuvred basic shapes through four different positions to create thirty-six distinct sounds. Evans's system was quickly taken up and disseminated by three associates: "Reverend George Barnley at Moose Factory and along the Albany River; Reverend Robert Rundle through the foothills of the Rockies and Reverend William Mason around Norway House."[13] Those who accept Evans as the originator see him as a student of languages, who used the 1838–1839 winter spent at Michipicoten in examining Greek and Hebrew comparative models as, according to Paul Hengstler, a time of "research, innovation, and invention."[14] Most Aboriginal views, however, contest this attribution. In the argument of the Montana Cree philosopher, Raining Bird, the universal first language was Cree, a gift of the Creator *Ki-sei-men'-to*, in a birchbark book teaching people to live properly. The book fell into the hands of "a half breed," who "took it to the missionaries, and read the material in it to them."[15] First Nations' theories emphasize the mysterious, numinous, secret, and direct nature of this gift. While we acknowledge the real distinction between invention and appropriation, we are willing to let both views coexist, though conceding that they are rarely harmonious. Our approach to the coexistence of missionary and Aboriginal accounts subscribes to the appeal by Native feminist scholar Devon Abbott Mihesuah for the appreciation of "heterogeneity...and the necessity for more sensitivity in studying and writing about individuals outside one's racial and cultural group."[16]

For us this sensitivity to nuance, audience, and context informs our undertaking as translators. The transcription, transliteration, and English translation of Grouard's *kâtolik ayamihêwi-masinahikan* have been a daunting rescue mission and an exciting opportunity for discovery. Working with both the phonemic system of the sound and word patterns of Cree Syllabics, organized according to syllables, and the alphabetic symbols of English sounds used in the transcription and transliteration to Standard Roman Orthography (SRO) and in the idiomatic English has presented special challenges. We kept as our mantra the observation of the editors prefacing the invaluable dictionary, *Cree: Words*, that "sounds, word formation, sentence patterns and meanings all change over time."[17] Because standards for the representation of Cree sounds have altered considerably from the nineteenth century to the present, we have decided to include both a direct *transcription* of Grouard's Syllabics in Roman font and, in italics, a *transliteration* of the Cree, which conforms to current linguistic practice. Each line of text, therefore, will have three avenues of access: a transcription of the Syllabics, a transliteration in contemporary SRO, and an English translation.

In poring over the text, we found ourselves viewing Syllabics from many angles, often weighing the context to arrive at an understanding of the meaning. Our attempts to enter the nineteenth-century scene in the Great North-West have involved sustained attentiveness, a few conjectures, and some educated guesswork. The closer we looked, the more engaged we became in what a character, who works as a translator, in Michael Ondaatje's *Divisadero*, refers to as "some modest contrapuntal dance."[18] Without sounding immodest, we believe that our dance with this important but neglected text could actually be choreographing moves for others—linguists, social historians, Aboriginal language specialists.

We must also admit that our grappling with meaning, with the vexing questions of the interpretability of language, brought home to us forcefully how much writing is a matter of difference, of great difference often discovered in small differences. Our direct transcription of the underspecified Cree Syllabics into an alphabetic equivalent and transliteration in Standard Roman Orthography familiar to modern Cree scholars involved reconstruction at virtually every turn. Some aspects of our SRO may not appear to be as "standard" as Cree experts would wish. Moreover, our back translation into English might on occasion still miss Grouard's intent, but honestly so. The misconstruals that may exist in our text have resulted from a whole menu of possibilities: among them, misreading of Grouard's underspecified Syllabics, periodic inconsistency within the Syllabics, and misinterpreting Grouard's intent due to changes in language and usage over time and differences in cultural perspectives. Occasionally in the process of transcribing and translating, we have silently added the concluding quotation mark (guillemet), an inadvertent omission in Grouard's large and challenging text. Although not rationalizing, we think our efforts and conjectures net some positive results. As well as underscoring the challenges today's Cree readers face in understanding this material, our project also illustrates the difficulties Grouard's contemporary Cree readers would have faced in dealing with the underspecification of important Cree sounds and in following catechetical material apparently so removed from their traditions.

Our concern is with the meaning and resonance of the Syllabics, which itself allows for the joint influence of Native and missionary impulses. Such a conjunction necessarily highlights the differences between nineteenth-century outlooks and our own, and hence distinguishes "between the motive of mission and the consequences."[19] That is, while we recognize that, as instructors and guides, leaders in Native communities were active participants in the missionaries' linguistic studies, we also recognize that, in the missionaries' intention "of radically transforming Indigenous societies," they "knowingly or not, provided the religious and ideological rationale for the larger colonial enterprise."[20] The telling coincidence that the date of this second printing of Grouard's text corresponds with the federal establishment of residential schools in western Canada has not been lost on us. In the case of the Lac La Biche mission, where Grouard ministered at the time, a boarding school already existed. Through the lens of contemporary understanding, testimonials, studies, plays, novels, and nationwide apologies bear evidence of the schools' "assimilative policies" that constituted what has been called "the lethal legacy Canadians face in the twenty-first century."[21]

With our eyes wide open and an awareness of the subsequent results (unforeseen or not), we have pursued this translation/edition with undiminished, actually increasing, vigour. Our work has reminded us that there is an intimate connection between meaning and use, that "textuality is a social condition of various times, places, and persons," and that editing is "more an act of translation than of reproduction."[22] What the undertaking continues to offer us is an illustration of how a religious impulse can in fact gesture toward a horizon of change, of possibility. Yes, it means that we make an effort to recalibrate our understanding of the missionary—in this case, a nineteenth-century evangelist, teacher, writer, painter, correspondent, ecclesiastical administrator, and compassionate observer. The idealistic zeal of the early missionary enterprise is the core of this rigorous entry (or re-entry) into Cree Syllabics. The recognition and respect we have gained through this sustained study of the other—in the intricacies of Syllabics and the enabling faith of the catechist—have allowed us to perceive the worth of "a fused horizon of standards, where we have been transformed by the study of the other, so that we are not simply judging by our old familiar standards."[23] We hope our readers will share this openness.

By concentrating on textual evidence and situating the text within the mission environs and its economic reality, this edition aims to shine light on the highest aspirations and beneficent ardour of the ministry. As a starting point, it seems to us important not to belittle or demonize the missionary, but to try to enter his mind. If we attend to its nuance, his text becomes an almost-speaking document, in which, curiously, we can hear both the speaker and his audience.

NOTES TO PREFACE

1. Linda Hutcheon, *A Theory of Adaptation* (New York: Routledge, 2006), 150.
2. Armand Garnet Ruffo, *(Ad)dressing Our Words: Aboriginal Perspectives in Aboriginal Literatures* (Penticton, BC: Theytus, 2001), 6.
3. Renée Hulan and Renate Eigenbrod, "Introduction: A Layering of Voices: Aboriginal Oral Traditions," In *Aboriginal Oral Traditions: Theory, Practice, Ethics*, Renée Hulan and Renate Eigenbrod, eds. (Halifax and Winnipeg: Fernwood Publishing with the Gorsebrook Research Institute, 2008), 7.
4. Kimberly Blaeser, "Writing Voices Speaking: Native Authors and an Oral Aesthetic," In *Talking on the Page: Editing Aboriginal Oral Texts*, Laura J. Murray and Keren Rice, eds. (Toronto: University of Toronto Press, 1999), 55.
5. Walter Ong, SJ, *Orality and Literacy* (London: Methuen, 1982), 178.
6. Susan Gingell, "Teaching the Talk That Walks on Paper: Oral Traditions and Textualized Orature in the Canadian Literature Classroom," In *Home-Work: Postcolonialism, Pedagogy, and Canadian Literature*, Cynthia Sugars, ed. (Ottawa: University of Ottawa Press, 2004), 286.
7. Maryanne Wolf, *Proust and the Squid: The Story and Science of the Reading Brain* (New York: Harper Perennial, 2007), 217–18.
8. Robert Dale Parker, ed., *The Sound the Stars Make Rushing Through the Sky: The Writings of Jane Johnston Schoolcraft* (Philadelphia: University of Pennsylvania Press, 2007), 3, 4.
9. Parker, *Sound the Stars Make*, 3.
10. Joanna Brooks, ed., *The Collected Writings of Samson Occom, Mohegan: Leadership and Literature in Eighteenth-Century Native America* (New York: Oxford University Press, 2006), xx.
11. See Merrill Distad, "Print and the Settlement of the West" and "Newspapers and Magazines," In *History of the Book in Canada, 1849–1918*, Yvan Lamonde, Patricia Lockhart Fleming, and Fiona A. Black, eds. (Toronto: University of Toronto Press, 2005), 62–71, 293–303; Aegidius Fauteux, *The Introduction of Printing into Canada* (Montreal: Rolland Paper Co., 1930), chapter six. For condensed biographies of Syllabics innovators, missionaries James Evans, John Horden, and Edmund Peck, along with facsimile samples of their work, see the website of Vancouver-based Tiro Typeworks: www.tiro.com (accessed 30 June 2008).
12. John MacLean, *James Evans, Inventor of the Syllabic System of the Cree Language* (Toronto: William Briggs, 1890). For more commentary on the legend and accomplishment of Evans, see Joyce Banks, "The Church Missionary Society and the Rossville Mission Press," *Papers of the Bibliographical Society of Canada* 32.1 (1994): 31–44; Bruce Peel, "Rossville Mission Press: Press, Prints and Translators," *Papers of the Bibliographical Society of Canada* 1 (1962): 28–43; and, Nan Shipley, *The James Evans Story* (Toronto: The Ryerson Press, 1966).
13. T.C.B. Boon, "The Use of Catechisms and Syllabics by the Early Missionaries of Rupert's Land," *The Bulletin of the United Church of Canada* 13 (1960): 10.
14. Paul Michael Hengstler, "A Winter's Research and Invention: Reverend James Evans's Exploration of Indigenous Language and the Development of Syllabics, 1838–1839," M.A. Thesis, Department of History and Classics, University of Alberta, 2003, 147.
15. Verne Dusenberry, *The Montana Cree: A Study in Religious Persistence* (Stockholm: Stockholm Studies in Comparative Religion, Almquist & Wiksells, 1962; rpt Norman: University of Oklahoma Press, 1998), 268.
16. Devon Abbott Mihesuah, *Indigenous American Women: Decolonization, Empowerment, Activism* (Lincoln: University of Nebraska Press, 2003), 5.
17. Arok Wolvengrey, compiler, and Freda Ahenakew, editor, et al., *Cree: Words*, 2 vols (Regina: Canadian Plains Research Center, University of Regina, 2001), I: ix.
18. Michael Ondaatje, *Divisadero* (Toronto: McClelland & Stewart, 2007), 63.
19. Lammin Sanneh, *Translating the Message: The Missionary Impact on Culture* (New York: Orbis Books, 1989), 53.
20. Winona Stevenson, "The Journals and Voices of a Church of England Native Catechist: Askenootow (Charles Pratt), 1851–1884," In *Reading Beyond Words: Contexts for Native History*, Jennifer Brown and Elizabeth Vibert, eds. (Peterborough, ON: Broadview Press, 1996), 310.
21. J.R. Miller, *Lethal Legacy: Current Native Controversies in Canada* (Toronto: McClelland & Stewart, 2004), 264.
22. Jerome J. McGann, *The Textual Condition* (Princeton: Princeton University Press, 1991), 16, 53.
23. Charles Taylor, "The Politics of Recognition," In *New Contexts of Canadian Criticism*, Ajay Heble, Donna Palmateer Pennee, J.R. (Tim) Struthers, eds. (Peterborough, ON: Broadview Press, 1997), 125.

ACKNOWLEDGEMENTS

This project has been a collaboration every step of the way. My fellow translators, Naomi McIlwraith and Dorothy Thunder from the Faculty of Native Studies at the University of Alberta, continue to be sources of real support and inspiration. The richly detailed reader's reports we received from Arok Wolvengrey, who allowed himself to be identified, were amazing documents of advice and truly generous, insightful expressions of scholarly expertise. Librarians and archivists have opened doors and, in some cases, vaults and churches for me. I am especially grateful to: Matthew Wangler, of the former Folk Life division of the Royal Alberta Museum; Linda Tzang, director of the Living Communities division of the Royal Alberta Museum; Soeur Marie-Rose Hurtubise, sgm, and Soeur Bernadette Poirier, sgm, of the Grey Nuns Regional Centre in Edmonton; Père André Dubois, OMI, at Archives Deschâtelets in Ottawa; Jacinthe Duval at the Centre du Patrimoine de la Société Historique de Saint-Boniface; Diane Lamoureux, archivist at the Oblate Collection of the Provincial Archives of Alberta; Christopher Kotecki at the Hudson's Bay Company Archives in Winnipeg; Jeannine Green of the Bruce Peel Special Collections Library at the University of Alberta; David Jones of the William C. Wonders Map Collection at the University of Alberta Libraries; and Victoria Barsalou, Thea Kachuk, and Simon Willier, curators at the Native Cultural Arts Museum at the Grouard Campus of Northern Lakes College. Early assistance in translation came from Clifford Cardinal, Trevor Cardinal, and Marjorie Memnook. More recently, Mrs. Florida Thunder provided valuable insights about several uncertainties in the text. In digitizing and formatting, Nuno Luzio, Jeff Papineau, Mary Pinkoski, Lana Sinclair, and Charlene Sorken have been delightfully energetic and precise collaborators. Amy Stafford and Katie McConchie joined me in the hunt at the Royal Alberta Museum warehouse, which stores Grouard's press, and took expert photos. Grants from the Faculty of Arts and the Central Research Fund at the University of Alberta helped to begin and sustain the research, and the generous support of the Killam Research Fund has carried the project through to publication. The unflagging support and attentive, intuitive care of editors Peter Midgley and Mary Lou Roy, designers Jason Dewinetz and Alan Brownoff, and the whole University of Alberta Press team have been supreme gifts. My colleague, Robert Wilson, shared many journeys to Lac La Biche, Grouard, and Girouxville, and I thank him for his photographs, his wit, and his presence.

Over many visits, the docents at the Lac La Biche Mission Interpretive Centre were always welcoming and genial. News of the shocking arson at the Mission on September 30, 2009, which destroyed the rectory, the hub of activity this volume celebrates, has been terribly saddening.

Although my fellow translators and I have sought advice and direction in many excellent dictionaries, especially *nēhiyawēwin: itwēwina Cree: Words*, we acknowledge that the misconstruals possibly remaining in our text are our own responsibility.

A NOTE ON THE TEXT

This facsimile edition is taken from the copy of *kâtolik ayamihêwi-masinahikan* housed in the Collection of the Missionary Oblates of Grandin Province at the Provincial Archives of Alberta, in Edmonton. I am very grateful to the Oblates for the extended loan of this rare text. The 224-page book has a black hard cover and a taped spine. It measures 9 × 14.5 centimetres (3.5 × 5.5 inches).

INTRODUCTION

Émile Grouard, OMI, and Print Culture in Athabasca Country

It may surprise some readers to learn that the first books printed in Athabasca Country emerged from a Paris-made press located at the Oblate mission of Notre Dame des Victoires at Lac La Biche. More intriguing yet may be the discovery that these early imprints, often decorated with hand-carved chapter headings and copperplate illustrations, were created in the Syllabics of five distinct Indigenous peoples. These texts are anything but inert religious objects. Conduits to our past and results of a precise knowledge of Native languages, undoubtedly conveyed and polished by conversation with Elders, the stories of these now-rare books reveal the conditions of their collaborative production and wide distribution. They promote an understanding of the ways words on the printed page can move minds and imaginations. Moreover, they testify to the zeal of their primary author, Father Émile Grouard, in his determination to speak and write in the languages of the peoples he was evangelizing. This book introduces Grouard, the forgotten pioneer of print culture in Alberta, and one of his earliest texts.

ABOVE: Grouard as a young priest. [Courtesy Archives Deschâtelets]

ABOVE RIGHT: Grouard's Paris-made Stanhope printing press. [Courtesy Royal Alberta Museum]

Émile-Jean-Baptiste-Marie Grouard (1840–1931) was born in Brûlon, in the historic region of Maine, in northwest France.[1] One of six children of André and Anne (Ménard) Grouard, and the greatest challenge to his devout parents, young Émile delighted in truancy; he preferred roaming the countryside to sitting in a classroom. He and his two brothers, both of whom died young, became priests. In 1859, while he was in the third year of study at the Grand Séminaire in the capital, Le Mans, the visit of his cousin, Monsignor Vital-Justin Grandin, changed the direction of Grouard's vocation. Grandin, an Oblate, was in France to be consecrated a bishop (the first bishop of St. Albert) by the founder and Superior General of the Congregation of the Order of Mary Immaculate, Eugène de Mazenod, bishop of Marseilles. Grandin prompted the venturesome Émile to consider life as an Oblate missionary. In April 1860, Grouard left France to continue his studies at the Grand Séminaire in Quebec City, where he soon felt at home. Thanks to seminarians from Prince Edward Island, Grouard also picked up a working knowledge of English before being ordained by Monsignor Alexandre-Antonin Taché in Boucherville in April 1862. As Grouard discovered during his novitiate and throughout his lengthy apostolate in the Athabasca missions, the Oblate imperative to spread the good news to the poor—conveyed in their emblematic motto, *Evangelizare pauperibus misit me; pauperes evangelizantur,* encircling a cross crowned with thorns—called for an original understanding of ways of reaching an Indigenous congregation and readership.

Grouard's early letters in French and English from northern mission posts pulse with his robust eagerness and wry humour. Writing to his superior, Bishop Taché, from the Mission of the Nativity at Fort Chipewyan on Lake Athabasca, the young novice affirms that his principal task is learning "Montagnais" (one of the Athapaskan-speaking peoples called Dene Suline today).[2] He plunges in, in August 1862, and reports that he is making some progress in September ("J'avance à petits pas dans le Montagnais"), profiting from the help of the Montagnais themselves "pour apprendre leur langue"; by May 1863, he is carrying on conversations and delivering three or four sermons ("Trois ou quatre fois je les prêchai moi-même").[3] Writing to his parents from Mission St-Paul at Fort Nelson in 1868, he coyly downplays his sense of amazement in a land rich in exciting variety ("notre vie dans ce pays est si uniforme dans sa variété que l'on s'accoutume à ne regarder que d'un oeil indifférent des choses qui au premier abord excitent la curiosité").[4] He regales them in this ten-page document with the unswerving Catholic faith of the Loucheux ("Squint-Eye") at Fort de Liards, whose language he also learned. Despite the efforts of the Protestant missionary with his Greek Bible, Grouard assures his parents, local faith remains unshaken, and his own health stays fortified by a diet of fish, potatoes, and turnips. To the Hudson's Bay Company factor at Fort Chipewyan, Roderick McFarlane, Grouard sends a polished, gentlemanly request for thirty pounds of nails and four hundred pounds of grease, explaining "the reason why so much grease is wanted is the incredible expense made of it here and occasioned by the large quantity of soap which the sisters waste every year"; picturing Fort Chipewyan in 1872 as "a land flowing, not with milk & honey, but with marrow & grease," he notes, more likely in playfulness than real exasperation, that the sisters "are constantly washing & you would say they are come for nothing else."[5] But health and diet, climate and rigour, wit and humour all are subservient to his serious, primary job of evangelization.

The books Grouard and fellow Oblates Henri Faraud, Albert Lacombe, Émile Petitot, and Valentine Végréville among them composed and printed enlarge our own understanding of the history of the book in Canada and, particularly, the development of print culture in the West. Books are, as the bibliographer D.F. McKenzie has reminded us, "ineluctably, social products whose true value can rarely be stated only in monetary terms";[6] they testify to the connectedness of most known forms of communication, whether gesture, performance, speech, drawing, writing, or print. In fact, the narrative of this overlooked textual archive touches on all aspects of communication. Offering a unique double perspective on the missionary project, the books themselves, located in the contexts of the 1870s, '80s, and '90s, are the subjects of intense, vocational commentary by the missionaries. But they also pass beyond the measures of "clerical calculus."[7] For contemporary First Nations translators, who grapple with both the formal correctness of this representation of their language and its daring transcription of sacred speech about the Creator, the books' "New World sign systems" highlight the question of "what constitutes the 'written'"[8] in arresting ways. What was understood and is here reproduced as phonemic writing differs radically from the alphabetic scripts of the dominant colonial languages. The "shorthand-based script" and "geometric characters"[9] of Syllabics (named because the characters denote syllables, not letter sounds as in the alphabet) are captured in these texts as a distinctive language, that is, "a system of more or less permanent marks used to represent an utterance."[10] In this archive, language—both speech and writing—is in the service of religion; it invites us to consider the processes of instruction and affirmation. The lessons and hymns about a compassionate God and resourceful tempter, the discontents of sin and pleasures of the right way or good path, are conveyed in forceful, direct, insistent language reinforced, as is the catechetical norm, through repetition. This facsimile edition and translation, itself a combination of Indigenous and colonial languages, strives to uncover the layers of perception that allow us to grasp the original utterance. In the process it also explores a series of double perspectives: then and now, the spoken and the written, beliefs known and doctrine imparted.

THE ESTABLISHMENT AND IMPORTANCE OF THE LAC LA BICHE MISSION

The account of the first books printed in Alberta is a fabric of woven narratives. In the last decades of the nineteenth century in Athabasca Country or the Great North-West, as the increasingly colonized future province was called, the work of commerce and catechesis often intersected. Both merchants and missionaries desired contact with Indigenous peoples; both valued and sought out transportation routes; both felt the effects of competition in the fur trade and the expansion of the railroad. But, then as now, traders in the employ of large corporations and ordained or consecrated volunteers offering their lives in the vocation of evangelization have fundamentally different perspectives on the land and its inhabitants. Such differences supply some of the underlying tensions for the opening scene of this story: the community of Lac La Biche, with Cree, Métis, Saulteux, and Montagnais residents, where by the 1850s both a Hudson's Bay Company post and an Oblate mission had been established (re-established in the case of the Hudson's Bay Company).[11]

Sometimes referred to as Red Deer's Lake, Lac La Biche derives its name from the red deer or wapiti (North American elk) called—without designating sex—"biche." In 1854, the Oblate bishop of Saint Boniface, Monsignor Taché, visited the mission, approximately 250 kilometres northeast of Edmonton, dedicating it to Notre Dame des Victoires—as much to recall the cathedral in Quebec City and signal the mission's undertaking as different from that

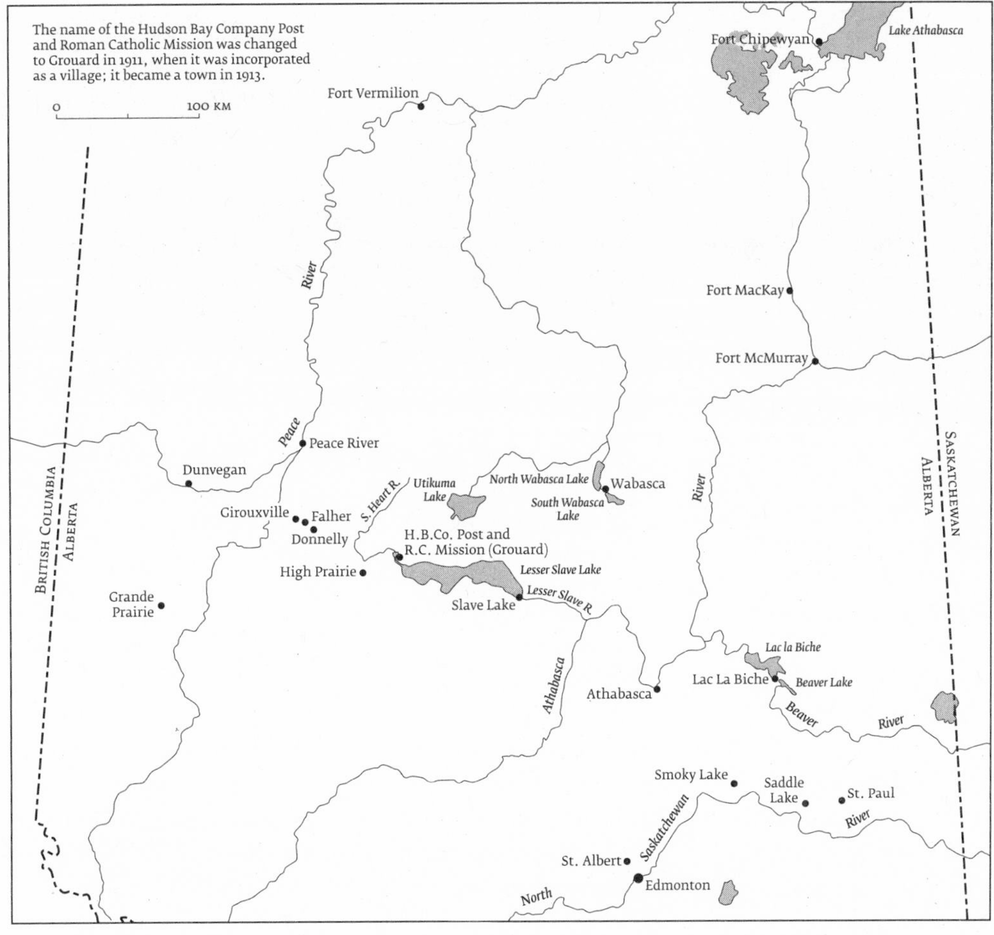

Detail from a general map of the northwestern part of the Dominion of Canada. [Courtesy William C. Wonders Map Collection, University of Alberta Libraries]

of the post as to fence off its ministry from the endeavours of the Ojibwe Wesleyan missionary, Henry Bird Steinhauer. The first long-term resident Oblates, Fathers Jean Tissot and Augustin Maisonneuve, expended their energies in relocating the mission's log cabin to a site ten kilometres removed from its original position close to the fort and in constructing a house and a two-storey structure, which would serve eventually as the home for the Grey Nuns (les Soeurs Grises de Montréal), their partners in the missionary enterprise. In addition to evangelizing the Indians and Métis, who had until that point been served by the Lac Sainte Anne mission, the establishment of a mission at Lac La Biche was a strategic move. Notre Dame des Victoires pre-empted the plans of the Anglicans, who enjoyed the protection of the Hudson's Bay Company, and secured a better location for fishing and agriculture, activities at which the missionaries excelled. It led to the erection of a warehouse for the northern missions at a location that provided ideal navigational access to Lake Athabasca and thus to sites in the immense Athabasca–Mackenzie region.

Though it was known to Indian and Métis trappers for generations, Nor'wester David Thompson's charting of Portage La Biche in 1798 (along with his later discovery of the Athabasca Pass with linkage to the Columbia River) consolidated the importance of Lac La Biche as a vital hinge between Rupert's Land and Athabasca Country. In a world of pre-railway transportation, the geological particularity of Portage La Biche involved glacial meltwaters that had formed "an alluvial fan...creating the height of land which narrowly separates the Athabasca and Churchill River drainages."[12] This soil deposit formed Field Lake, which discharged into the Beaver River. The North West Company's charting of this passageway meant that traders and carriers of freight could travel by scow or barge west on the North Saskatchewan, or by Red River cart across the prairie, and then sail on the Beaver River, traverse the short and long wetland portages to arrive at Lac La Biche, which discharges into the Athabasca River, and hence reach Athabasca Country.

THE GREY NUNS AT THE LAC LA BICHE MISSION

Because the presence of the Grey Nuns was an integral factor in the success and duration of the Lac La Biche mission, their story must be included in any account of Notre Dame des Victoires. The first missionaries, Sisters Delphine Guénette, the twenty-seven-year-old superior, Adélaïde Daunais, and Marie Tisseur, arrived in late August 1862. Their three-month trek from Montreal had included a train journey to St. Paul, Minnesota, a bus trip to Georgetown, passage by steamer to Saint Boniface, and forty-nine days of travelling by ox cart across the prairie. Isolation and deprivation awaited these city-bred young women, who were willing to share with the missionary priests "fortune et privation."[13] Although a dwelling was prepared, with a chapel, kitchen, and refectory, the new arrivals had no furniture: their trunk became a table at which they knelt to eat. The details of the Grey Nuns' thirty-six-year stay at Lac La Biche, as related in the reports and correspondence of *Chroniques Historiques de la mission du Lac La Biche* and *Hospice Saint-Joseph Lac La Biche: Mémoire sur les 20 premières années de son Histoire 1862–*

1882, and narrated by Sister Thérèse Castonguay, sgm, in *A Leap of Faith*, provide insights to the joys and sorrows of offering all "pour y faire quelque bien à la gloire de Dieu."[14]

As well as establishing a school where they taught reading, writing, grammar, geography, and religious instruction in English and French and a hospice (Hospice Saint-Joseph served as both orphanage and school) where they clothed, fed and, in some cases, raised children, the nuns were responsible for the gardens, planting, fields and harvests, the preservation of fruit and fish, the preparation of all meals, the care of the sick within the mission and the community, the repair, renewal and re-making of the missionaries' soutanes and travelling outfits, the bleaching and ironing of altar linens, and the making of hosts for all missions. They were definitely more than the ferocious cleaners about whom the young Father Grouard quipped! Small wonder that these workhorses toiled night and day, or that the superior at the mission, Monsignor Henri Faraud, was so visibly upset at the delicate appearance of the newly arrived Sister Saint Michael.[15] The superior general in Montreal, Mother Julie Deschamps, in noting that she had not received the regular letter from Lac La Biche in June 1878, nevertheless commented on reports of significant progress and excellent instruction, subtly relaying her encouragement by observing that these instructresses are not really "Samsons."[16] The missionary nuns at Lac La Biche may not have been super-powerful giants, but their third superior at the mission, Sister Marie-Hélène Beaubien Youville, recognized that her sisters were "courageuses athlètes dans l'arène du sacrifice."[17]

For readers today, the sisters' highs and lows—the latter scarcely articulated in their annals—supply an approachable perspective on the close-to-foreign notion of sacrifice. Where else but in the Grey Nuns' *Chroniques* could we encounter such a vivid depiction of the active engagement of missionary service as in the use of "missioning"[18] as a verb? Poverty and deprivation led to practical solutions and enforced frugality: shipping crates were refashioned as wardrobes; fish parts yielded soap; fruit was preserved under layers of grease rather than wax. When Monsignor Faraud built a loom, the first in the North-West, the sisters spun metres of wool to make shawls and blankets for their young students and clothing for the travelling priests, items that were considerably cheaper and warmer than comparable articles sold by the Hudson's Bay Company.

The school they launched with such optimism in May 1863, boasting forty students in classes by 1864, was a barometer of circumambient conditions. Closed by a fever epidemic in 1865, with enrolments hovering between two and five for a few weeks or months at a time during the next five years, it was closed again during the smallpox outbreak of 1870. In 1871, they reopened the school and established the Hospice Saint-Joseph, a combination residence and orphanage, which originally admitted fifteen children. As student numbers dwindled, the school was discontinued the following year, but it started again in 1873.

Fluctuations in attendance at the school and the hospice were bitter lessons for the sisters, hinted at in *Mémoire*. As they saw their small troop scattering ("la troupe enfantine s'éparpilla"), they tried to set up conditions to ensure the presence of youngsters to teach, namely, that children would only be accepted at the hospice if their parents agreed to allow them to stay under the nuns' tutelage until the age of eighteen.[19] This feature of the missionary project that is so questionable and troubling for readers today was a fundamental—however wrong-headed—part of the plan, one that is now construed as uniformly assimilationist and oppressive. Because we do not know enough about the day-to-day conduct and general atmosphere of the hospice and because we only have comments from one perspective, that of the missionaries, it would be erroneous to conclude that this kind of schooling was foreign or hostile to the Aboriginal "approach to instruction that relied on looking, listening and learning—the three Ls."[20] As the major historian of the residential schools, James Miller, has observed, "the degree of attachment to coercive assimilation by different groups and in different eras makes blanket summaries misleading."[21]

Without question the documented Native experiences of radical jolts—from a nomadic family setting of little coercion to a settled, institutional milieu where different, invariably Euro-Canadian, concepts of learning and discipline prevailed—are heart-wrenching accounts of loneliness and abuse. Yet it seems to me that a quite distinct sense of inculcation existed in the early period of the Lac La Biche mission. There was no attempt to suppress Native language; as a matter of fact, the advent of the printing press underscored the value placed on communication in Indigenous languages. Deprivation and need were realities shared by Native and Métis residents, as well as the recently arrived missionaries. Numerous instances in the reports filed in *Missions de la Congrégation des Oblats de Marie Immaculée* attest to the pleas from Native communities that the Oblates visit and minister to them. In relating the events of the annual retreat at the Lac La Biche mission in February 1877, Father Hipploybte Leduc's letter closes with enthusiastic praise of the nuns' instruction in English and French at the school and orphanage. The assembled Oblate clergy were surprised and enchanted ("surpris et enchanté") by the students' performance at an examination. In the evening the children presented two plays, one in English and the other in French, for an invited audience of "tous les notables de la place, catholiques et protestants." Leduc goes as far as to call the school "une vraie maison d'étude," with fifteen to twenty classes per week, and "une véritable université," where marks are awarded for Cree, Montagnais, English, theology, drawing, painting, and mathematics.[22]

Another indication of the positive influence of the sisters' presence emerges from a more secular setting. The sudden outbreak of scarlet fever in 1878 almost devastated the family of the Hudson's Bay Company's junior chief trader, William Traill. An Anglican with little time for the nuns, Traill, who was the son of the Upper Canada author, Catharine Parr Traill, resented the primitiveness of the post. He initially resisted his almost-dying wife's plea to call for one of the Grey Nuns; however, he relented, and a sister hurried to Harriet Traill's aid. Despite the highly contagious nature of the disease, the nun returned to the Traill home, this time as a result of Traill's urgent note addressed to "Kindest of Sisters," signed "Yours in affliction," and assuring the recipient: "Your presence in the house is as the presence of an Angel of mercy."[23] On Mrs. Traill's recovery, the mission was showered with gifts—clothing for the children, and such delicacies as plum pudding, raisins, and chocolate. Patrick ("Piché") Pruden, a free trader, showed his gratitude for the nuns' care of his family during the epidemic by giving them a sleigh and a fine fur coat; the little sisterhood at Notre Dame des Victoires, judging the coat too elegant for them ("trop précieuse pour leur usage"), offered it to their superior in Montreal.

Grouard on steamer *Madonna*, 1906. [Courtesy Archives Deschâtelets]

The gifts recorded in *Mémoire* are a wonderful blend of the practical and the aesthetic, the gustatory and the spiritual. When a French priest who had been staying at Notre Dame des Victoires returns to France, he not only leaves his library of ascetic writing to the sisters but also gives them hinges, sashes, and screws as window fittings. A crate from France that the nuns receive the next year contains a five-octave harmonium for their private chapel, along with Belgian chocolates and ten pounds of tapioca. Naive exuberance reigns during the ceremonial opening of such deliveries. Sisters stand armed with crowbar, scissors, hammer, and screwdriver; each object uncovered in turn

Grouard with Legion of Honour Medal, 1925. [Courtesy Archives Deschâtelets]

elicits shouts of joy and a few tears of gratitude for the contents and the care with which they were packed.

Ironically, although the Grey Nuns were vital to the outreach of Notre Dame des Victoires, their *Chroniques* and *Mémoire* disclose, albeit briefly and guardedly, feelings of being undervalued or taken for granted. They prepared their students for their first confessions and communions; in addition to academic subjects, they taught them the domestic skills of cooking, sewing, washing, and ironing, everything that contributes to the running of a household ("tout ce qui touche à la direction d'un ménage"). Yet they themselves felt that they were "pauvres servantes, pas maîtresses chez-elles."[24] The food they worked so tirelessly to prepare and preserve was occasionally removed without their knowledge. Whether it was Monsignor Faraud's plan to cut a road from Lac La Biche to the Athabasca River and to provision the team of Oblate and lay workers in 1871, or Monsignor Clut's embarking for the Mission of the Nativity at Fort Chipewyan in 1874 and taking all the provisions and utensils from Lac La Biche with him, the sisters were often not only disregarded but also left destitute.

They endured threats of violence, too. Terrorized by the news of the murder of two Oblates at Frog Lake and the intended pillaging of the mission at Lac La Biche by Cree and Métis peoples loyal to Chief Big Bear, the sisters felt the effects of the 1885 Rebellion. With the disappearance of the buffalo, the increasing waves of European settlers, and government surveys and treaties impoverishing Indigenous peoples and destroying their traditional ways of life, mounting Aboriginal frustration erupted in tense standoffs and bloodshed. Facing the threat of a raid, the Grey Nuns and their charges took refuge in April 1885 by travelling across the frozen lake to an ice-fishing hut on one of the islands until it was safe to return to Notre Dame des Victoires.

Thirteen years later, as the sisters prepared to leave for their next posting at Saddle Lake, their annals refer poignantly to the unobserved and veiled aspect of their lives. The entry in *Chroniques* for May 1898 acknowledges the difficulty of leaving behind the walls of their convent, silent witnesses to so much self-denial, while *Mémoire* remarks on the prosaic and little-appreciated martyr who, known only to God and others who suffer, nevertheless opens a way to Heaven.[25]

FATHER GROUARD AND HIS PROJECTS

The arrival of Father Émile Grouard at Notre Dame des Victoires in September 1876, as noted in the Grey Nuns' *Mémoire*, signals the real beginning of print culture in Athabasca Country. This was not, however, the start of Grouard's missionary work, since he had already spent thirteen years (1862–1874) in the North-West serving the Dene at missions in Fort Chipewyan, Fort Providence (on the northwest corner of Great Slave Lake), and Fort Liard (also in the Mackenzie in what is now the Northwest Territories, bordered by Nunavut to the east and Yukon to the west), until the rare disease of voicelessness ("l'aphonie") caused him to return to France for medical attention. During his two-year health cure, Grouard studied the first principles and elementary practices of painting and became reacquainted with the missionary

Bishop Émile Grouard. Painting by Emile Vanderaegen, commissioned on the occasion of the sixtieth anniversary of Grouard's ordination, 1922. [Courtesy Musée de Girouxville, AB]

artist and linguist Father Émile Petitot, OMI, with whom he had originally journeyed into the Great North-West and who was working on his polyglot dictionary of Montagnais, Loucheux, and Peau-de-Lièvre (Hareskin) languages at the same time. Grouard also taught himself the art of printing to produce the collection of Old and New Testament stories prepared in Syllabics by Monsignor Faraud, which was published in Paris in 1876. This period of recuperation, so characteristically full of the intellectual energies of a gifted autodidact, is seminal for the rest of Grouard's remarkable sixty-year apostolate.

Although his works may not be as well-known as those of fellow Oblate, Father Albert Lacombe, who reached close-to-nonagenarian status, the even longer-lived Émile Grouard's studies and writings offer an unmined vein of information about the missionary influence in opening up and extending literacy throughout Athabasca Country. Despite his virtual obscurity today, Grouard's native France awarded him the cross of the Legion of Honour in 1925. Calling him "le pionnier le plus intrépide du Grand Nord," the citation catalogued his activity as priest, missionary, navigator, geographer, explorer, builder of towns, architect, painter, writer, printer, and agriculturalist.[26] A man of immense charisma, vigour, intelligence, tenacity, and indefatigable energy, Grouard has left an amazingly varied legacy. In addition to maintaining, visiting, and superintending missions in the vast Athabasca–Mackenzie vicariate, provisioning and financing these far-flung posts, and introducing such advances as grist mills and steamboats to the northern settlements, Grouard was an artist: a writer and a painter. In addition to the catechetical texts he composed and printed in Indigenous languages; he wrote detailed, poetic reports for the *Missions*, humane and witty letters in English and French, and, in his eighties, a candid autobiography, *Souvenirs de mes Soixante ans d'Apostolat dans l'Athabaska-Mackenzie*.

He put his Parisian painting skills to work by creating large altar panels, all featuring titles or signage in Cree or Montagnais Syllabics, to decorate the churches of Notre Dame des Victoires at Lac La Biche, St. Bernard in the village that eventually bore his name, and St. Charles in Dunvegan; the latter two decorated altars still exist. For each of these churches he created three panels: a large central depiction of the Crucifixion and side panels representing various saints and patriarchs. At St. Bernard's

in Grouard, now designated an historic site, the arched top of the Crucifixion panel is encircled in a biblical pericope in Cree Syllabics about God's love of the world; on the right, Moses is depicted elevating the tablets with the two great commandments marked out in Cree Syllabics, while on the left, St. Bernard of Clairvaux, the twelfth-century Cistercian theologian, reformer, preacher, and Doctor of the Church, who laid the foundations for one of the best monastic libraries of the Middle Ages, is garbed as a bishop with mitre and crozier.

Grouard's own attitude toward his painting was self-deprecatory; he likened his talent to the French proverb about a one-eyed man being king in the land of the blind, "un borgne est roi au pays des aveugles"—perhaps

Altar triptych by Monsignor Émile Grouard, OMI, Église Saint-Bernard, Grouard, AB.

LEFT PANEL: St. Bernard of Clairvaux

CENTRE PANEL: Crucifixion ("God sent His only begotten Son" I John 4.9)

RIGHT PANEL: Moses with the Two Great Commandments (Love God and Love Neighbour, based on Exodus 20) in Syllabics.

remembered from his childhood reading of Balzac.[27] The missionary's contemporaries, lay and clerical, disagreed with this self-assessment. Native parishioners at Notre Dame des Victoires were transfixed and moved by the altar paintings, and Bishop Faraud was so impressed that he wanted the tableaux reproduced in all their churches. When the news was circulated at St. Charles Church that the missionary-artist had no canvas for an altar triptych, a hunter promptly supplied an intact moosehide skin, which Grouard proceeded to soak, stretch, and frame for his panels. According to a tribute in *L'Illustration*, which featured a cover photograph of the eighty-five-year-old missionary sawing wood for a new school, Grouard's *Calvary* was his "masterpiece."[28]

His work as a printer, a craft learned in Paris and transferred to Athabasca Country, is actually a resumé of Grouard's ministry, for he transported the press to every one of his mission posts. As he relates in *Souvenirs*, when the Syllabic fonts that had been cast in Brussels first arrived in Paris, the police, acting on a tip from customs officers, seized the boxes and interrogated Grouard as a revolutionary. It was a charged time, Grouard observes, only four years after the Commune, a popular revolution that had resulted in the murders of up to 30,000 Parisians and the imprisonment and deportation of many more thousands; by 1875 activists who had sought refuge in Belgium were beginning to slip back into Paris.[29] After clearing this hurdle by explaining his position as a missionary priest and taking from his pocket a copy of a Montreal-printed catechism in Syllabics to satisfy his interrogator, Grouard advanced to the next challenge.

Grouard presented Bishop Faraud's Syllabic manuscript of Old and New Testament stories to the head of a large publishing company, A[chille]. Hennuyer, which agreed to publish the book on the condition that Grouard himself do the typesetting. After a few lessons in typography and page design from an employee of the firm, Grouard's apprenticeship as a printer began. He worked alone in his room, printing the first drafts from a hand-operated press and making corrections; when the first copy of pages was ready, Grouard accompanied an employee to the publishing house to typeset individual sheets and to make the necessary corrections before a machine printed 3,000 copies. After the multiple printing of each sheet, Grouard would wash the characters and proceed to typeset the next set of pages. Finally he assisted in the correct assembling, folding, stitching, and binding of these sheets. Grouard remarks self-deprecatingly that thus he learned "tant bien que mal"—the *métier* of printing.[30] In palpable ways Grouard had learned not only about the physical and intellectual effort necessary to produce the printed page but also about the power of the textual document and its reception through the politics of culturally specific lenses.

Grouard's period in France also brought the principles of his vocation into sharp focus. When the president of the Society for the Apostolic Work of the Missions, Mademoiselle Berrod, who had heard of Grouard's promise as a painter, offered him a trip to Rome to study painting more intensively, he found himself conflicted between duty and pleasure. Sounding very much like a controlled classical hero of Corneille, he announced that, on reflection, duty won ("Après quelques réflexions, le devoir l'emporta").[31] Instead of accepting the offered trip to Rome, he secured his benefactor's consent to use the funds to buy copperplates to illustrate the book he was printing. In his autobiography, Grouard makes a special point of mentioning his own careful wrapping and packaging of these plates and the Syllabic fonts, along with the hand press that he purchased in Paris and his brushes and paints, for the return journey to the North-West. The press and a selection of fonts and copperplates now reside in the Oblate Collection of the Provincial Archives of Alberta.

At Notre Dame des Victoires, Grouard put to use the lessons he had learned about the theory and practice of

Grouard (right) cutting wood. *L'Illustration*, 13 February 1926. [Courtesy Archives Deschâtelets]

printing. As a newly ordained missionary, in his mid-twenties serving at Fort Liard, he had acquired valuable pointers about rote-learned instruction and the importance of a hand-held depiction of language. Following the example of Monsignor Faraud, Grouard taught the Our Father, Hail Mary, and Creed by distributing to his Native parishioners little pieces of paper on which he had made signs—what he calls "hieroglyphics"—indicating the phrases of these prayers. This experiment in devising *aides-mémoire* was a great success because it recognized and relied upon the Natives' highly developed vision and hearing (senses that made them expert hunters) and also contributed to their eager learning. So successful were the lessons that the little slips of paper never left his students' hands, and when Grouard ran out of paper, they quickly supplied parchment or moosehide to continue the process. He remarks proleptically that the Montagnais held onto these papers until the day when he could give them books printed in Syllabics.[32]

Grouard's apprenticeship in Paris working on Monsignor Faraud's text had also heightened his awareness of the incontestable value of direct communication in Native languages, which became the salient feature of his whole ministry. Since he had learned Dene in his earlier postings, his first task upon arrival in Lac La Biche was to continue printing while he learned Cree. His earliest publications at the mission were two texts in Montagnais Syllabics (1877, 1878) and another prayer book in Loucheux Syllabics (1879).[33] The 1883 text reproduced in facsimile and translated into Standard Roman Orthography (both in accord with Grouard's text and with modern practice) and idiomatic English in this edition is the most extensive text in Cree Syllabics Grouard prepared and printed at Lac La Biche. It illustrates his quickness and receptivity as a student of the language.

When Grouard was learning Cree, Monsignor Faraud and local inhabitants were his teachers. The earnest student admitted to Bishop Taché that he had spent every spare minute during the winter studying Cree: "afin de me rendre propre à exercer le saint ministère dans cette langue"; he re-read Father Lacombe's text of sermons three or four times; and he repeated Faraud's extravagant praise of their Oblate colleague as an equal of Fénélon: "Fénélon n'a pas mieux écrit en français que le Père Lacombe en cris!"[34] As much as he adapted biblical narratives from Faraud and lessons and hymns from Lacombe, Grouard himself had a great capacity for absorbing languages and nuance quickly. An indication of his perfectionism in mastering this language emerges in his admission that for ten years he wrote each sermon in Cree and, in advance of delivery, had it corrected by local people ("les gens du pays"). Recognizing the universality and transportability of Cree, its role as a *lingua franca* among First Nations in North America, Grouard commented on the forms and rules of the language in ways that reflect an insider's familiarity with its syntax and an appreciation of its beauty.

> If the pronunciation of Cree is gentle and pleasant, the grammar clear and precise, the formation of words simple and natural, by contrast, the conjugation of verbs presents such

a complexity, with so many changes, that you think yourself in a labyrinth, where innumerable passageways intersect to infinity and expose you to perpetual bewilderment. However, with time, reflection and a determined will, you succeed in grasping the thread. Thus you cannot help but admire the incomparable perfection of this language.[35]

During Grouard's first period at Lac La Biche, from September 1876 until February 1883, when he was ordered to the St. Charles Mission at Dunvegan to replace the ailing Father Tissier, he reported on the progress of the press regularly to Bishop Taché, to whom he sent copies of all his imprints. In the winter of 1879, with the assistance of Father Blanchet, he printed 2,000 copies in Syllabics of "un petit livre cris,"[36] consisting of prayers, Lacombe's short catechism, and hymns, along with the collection in Loucheux. The physical realities of the hand-printing process enter his letters, too. Well before the advent of photocopiers and electronic files, the 1887 reprinting of 3,000 copies of the early Montagnais collection, to correspond with the size and format of the Cree volumes, involved prolonged labour ("Ça a été une besogne longue et fatiguante")[37] from September to May, complicated by a lack of paper when he had reached page 160. Grateful as he was for his superior's approval, which fed the hope that his work was worthwhile ("Il me fait espérer que mon travail et ma peine ne seront pas tout à fait inutiles"),[38] he also admitted that additional collections in Beaver, Hareskin, and Squint-Eye had so filled his head with turns, roots, and idioms that he found it almost impossible to think of other things.[39]

During his time at Lac La Biche, Grouard produced two editions of the Cree text presented in this book. This facsimile edition is based on the second imprint, which he finished just before taking up his new post, as he outlines in his first correspondence from Dunvegan. The richly detailed letter from Dunvegan is much more than a year-end report; it provides a checklist of the major themes of his missionary work: a mantra-like need to preach and speak in the language of the people; a desire—often expressed as frustration—to balance physical and mental activity; a drive to be responsive to the needs of Native communities; a strong resolve to reach his destination despite the challenge of weather and geography; and an alert, informed observation of the beauties, dangers, and changing economy of the land.

Foremost for Grouard was the primacy of communication. How can you preach, he asked in this letter, without knowing the language of the people you are talking to? And how do you come to know a Native language without studying it?[40] The letter writer himself was one of the most knowledgeable and experienced sources of answers to these fundamental questions. He knew that the rhythms and necessities of mission life meant that the winter months were the only time to devote wholeheartedly to language study and to printing and binding books. As he acknowledged, all spare moments had been given over to the press at Lac La Biche, where his latest work, a reprinting of the collection of prayers, instructions, and hymns in Cree, was produced with the help of an enthusiastic apprentice, Monsignor Faraud himself.[41]

Missionary work, his letter makes clear, involves availability, despite distances, inconvenience, or the challenge of travelling without map or globe ("ni carte, ni sphere"). When two Montagnais arrived at Notre Dame des Victoires from the Île à la Crosse Mission (situated in present-day Saskatchewan), asking Father Grouard to minister to a dying father and son in their community, he snowshoed the 300-mile (480-kilometre) round trip; although he only arrived in time to preside at the funeral, Grouard did hear confessions before heading back to Lac La Biche. Grouard's journey to his new post at Dunvegan began in late February. Driving dog teams, snowshoeing, and camping in the snow were common experiences for him, as he recorded matter-of-factly the nine-day snowshoe trek to St. Bernard's mission (that is, the town of Grouard) from which point, after a day's rest, he completed the trek to Dunvegan by March 15. At St. Charles Mission he not only gave lessons in Cree to another Oblate and taught classes each day to the Catholic children at the Fort, but he also took lessons himself in the Beaver language from a local member of this tribe who knew Cree. Thus Grouard was equipping himself to translate his catechetical manual into Beaver, which he did by 1888 when he had returned to Lac La Biche,[42] more immediately to respond to the call of the Native community in Grande Prairie, who asked him to visit shortly after his arrival in Dunvegan. Grouard relates making the fifty-mile (eighty-kilometre) journey on a horse with a wooden saddle provided by his hosts. This was a form of horsemanship he was not used to, he notes in an understatement; however, undeterred by sore muscles or a rudimentary knowledge of Beaver, he went on to deliver a week-long mission, preaching morning and evening, instructing children at midday, and by the end of the week hearing confessions in a blend of the two languages: "moitié cris, moitié castor."[43]

Grouard's posting to Dunvegan opened his eyes to the luxuriance and fertility of the land, an image fragile and evanescent. Despite protestations about his unskilful pen ("ma plume inhabile"), he proceeded to describe the land rippling like the movement of the sea ("terrain ondulé comme une mer en movement") and vast prairie dotted here and there with clusters of trees together in a little dip of land, like flowers in a basket ("des prairies immenses, parsemées çà et là de bouquets d'arbres groupés ensemble dans une légère dépression du sol, comme des fleurs dans une corbeille"). Grouard's perception of rich vegetation ("une végétation luxuriante") takes into account both the disappearance of roaming herds of buffalo ("de nombreux troupeaux de buffles y passaient en liberté; aujourd'hui, ils ont disparu") and their replacement by brigades of government surveyors staking lots for future immigrants ("des brigades d'arpenteurs qui ont employé tout l'été à tracer des lignes destinées à indiquer la distribution des terres aux émigrants de l'avenir").

All Grouard's reports are remarkably full of detail, vigorous, yet introspective, in tone. In prose whose energy connotes strenuousness and zeal, he recounts the exertions at Dunvegan of clearing land, hewing wood, harnessing himself to the plow, planting wheat and barley, enclosing pasture land, and fraternizing with a Protestant minister, who helped him harvest his crops. He was a perceptive observer, especially alert to the impoverishment of the once-flourishing Beaver people, brought low by several epidemics and the rivalry for furs with other Native trappers, which was actually exterminating fur-bearing animals ("une guerre d'extermination aux animaux à fourrures"). As he catalogued necessary, material concerns, Grouard was always aware of the ironies of the position of the missionary administrator, who must attend to "tout ce cortège d'occupations et de préoccupations matérielles." When, in 1890, Grouard moved to the Mission of the Nativity, after having spent two years at Lac La Biche, where he had produced texts in Montagnais, Beaver, and Hareskin, he paused to consider the dimensions of responsibility that Gutenberg's invention entails. Crating the press, fonts, and copperplates, such potent sources of unfailing light ("sources fécondes d'où jaillissent, dit-on, des flots de lumière intarissables"),[44] prompted him to wonder about the meeting ground of the artistic and the practical, the aesthetic and the quotidian, in his didactic undertaking. He interrogated himself about the nutritional value of his intellectual kitchen utensils ("mes ustensiles de cuisine intellectuelle") printing a scribbled Dene ("ma qualité d'imprimeur en barbouillages Montagnais") in a region suffering from famine ("dans un lieu exposé à la famine").

Along with such unvarnished assessment, the strongest feature of Grouard's ministry is its ardour. He did not close his eyes to poverty or want. But his overarching missionary faith meant that he perceived this reality doubly: as physical and spiritual, tangible and immaterial need.

NOTES TO INTRODUCTION

1. Bordered by Normandy to the north, Brittany to the west, Anjou to the south, and Orléans to the east, Maine (or Le Maine) had been held alternately by English and French Crowns, until it was claimed and declared a duchy by Louis XIV at the end of the fifteenth century.
2. Grouard's reference to the Native people at Fort Chipewyan as "Montagnais," although they lived on flat country removed from the Rocky Mountains, requires some explanation. He is likely following the practice of the early Oblate anthropologist, his friend Father Émile Petitot, in using the term "Montagnais." I have retained Grouard's usage throughout. See Kerry Abel, *Drum Songs: Glimpses of Dene History*, Second Edition (Montreal and Kingston: McGill-Queen's University Press, 2005), 11.
3. "Monseigneur et bien-cher Père," Lettres à Mgr Taché, Archives Deschâtelets, Ottawa, HE 2221. T. 2Z. 104–07.
4. "Mes très chers Parents," Archives Deschâtelets, Ottawa, G LPP 1777.
5. "My Dear Sir," letter 30 November 1872, Archives Deschâtelets, Ottawa, HE 1864.G87L.
6. D.F. McKenzie, "Printing and Publishing 1557–1700: Constraints on the London Book Trades," In *The Cambridge History of the Book in Britain*, Vol IV 1557–1695, J. Barnard and D.F. McKenzie, eds. (Cambridge: Cambridge University Press, 2002), 553.
7. James Axtell, "Some Thoughts on the Ethnohistory of Missions," *Ethnohistory* 19 (1982): 35.
8. Germaine Warkentin, "Aboriginal Sign Systems and the History of the Book in Canada," *Book History* 2 (1999): 5.
9. John D. Nichols, "The Cree Syllabary," In *The World's Writing Systems*, Peter T. Daniels and William Bright, eds. (New York: Oxford University Press, 1996), 599.
10. Peter T. Daniels, "The Study of Writing Systems," *The World's Writing Systems*, 3.
11. Portage La Biche was a vital link in the Hudson's Bay Company transportation system. The company's amalgamation with the North West Company and the use of a more direct route on the North Saskatchewan with a trail linking Fort Edmonton to the Athabasca River, the route favoured by HBC governor, Sir George Simpson, resulted in the closure of the HBC post at Lac La Biche, which was originally called Greenwich House. However, by 1853, "competition from free traders prompted the Hudson's Bay Company to re-establish a post at Lac La Biche." See Mike Maccagno, *Rendezvous Notre-Dame des Victoires* (Lac La Biche: Mission Historical Preservation Society, 1988).
12. Edward J. McCullough and Michael Maccagno, *Lac La Biche and the Early Fur Traders* (Canadian Circumpolar Institute, Alberta Vocational College: Lac La Biche, 1991), 26.
13. "Les soeurs missionaires partageraient avec les prêtres missionaires fortunes et privations," *Hospice Saint-Joseph Lac La Biche: Mémoire sur les 20 premières années de son histoire 1862–1882*, 2 (Grey Nuns Regional Centre Archives, Edmonton).
14. In July 1880, Mother Deschamps wrote: "Sept Soeurs Grises sur la route, dans ces vastes déserts du Nord, non pour y chercher l'or et les faux biens de ce monde, mais pour y faire quelque bien à la gloire du Dieu qu'elles aiment et qu'elles veulent servir dans les pauvres, les ignorants et les plus abandonnés." *Chroniques historiques de la mission du Lac La Biche*, 10 (Grey Nuns Regional Centre Archives, Edmonton).
15. The account in *Mémoire* makes clear Faraud's displeasure with the newly arrived sister and her two assistants, whom he greeted coolly: "Mgr Faraud parut fort contrarié de leur mine fatiguée et délicate. Il les reçut assez froidement pour leur faire sentir qu'elles n'étaient pas les bienvenues." *Mémoire*, 13.
16. In *Chroniques* Mother Deschamps observed, "nous souhaitons plus de forces aux maîtresses que nous savons n'être point des *samsons*." *Chroniques*, 6.
17. Sister Youville's letter of May 1881 refers to her fellow missionaries as brave athletes in the arena of sacrifice. *Chroniques*, 15.
18. When Sister Daunais was moved from Lac La Biche to St. Albert, the *Chroniques* records: "cette dernière missionera à S. Albert." *Chroniques*, July 1879, 7.
19. "Pour obvier aux inconvénients de tant d'inconstance qui paralysait le dévouement des soeurs, La Supérieure proposa au Rev. Père Directeur de ne plus accepter d'enfants à élever et instruire, sans que leurs parents signassent un engagement certifiant qu'ils abandonnaient aux soeurs leurs enfants jusqu'à l'âge de 18 ans révolus. Ce plan fut accepté." *Mémoire*, 24.
20. James R. Miller, *Shingwauk's Vision: A History of Native Residential Schools* (Toronto: University of Toronto Press, 1996), 16.
21. Miller, *Shingwauk's Vision*, 427.
22. "Lettre du R.P. Leduc au R.P. Aubert," *Missions de la congrégation des oblats de Marie Immaculée* (Paris: A. Hennuyer, 1877), No. 59: 305–06.
23. *Mémoire*, 43.

24. *Mémoire*, 36, 23.
25. "Il est pénible, je le sais,...de laisser les murs, témoins de tant d'abnegation." *Chroniques*, 48. "Ce martyre sera des plus prosaiques, connu de Dieu seul et celle qui souffre. Ce martyre est ordinairement peu apprécié, et pourtant, il ouvre le ciel, tout aussi bien que les tortures des tyrans ou la lance des bourreaux." *Mémoire*, 53.
26. As quoted from "Lettre de l'Evêque du Mans à ses diocésains," *La Croix* de Paris, 26 mars 1931, in "Derniers hommages à Mgr Grouard," *Missions* (Paris: A. Hennuyer, 1931), No. 243: 442–45.
27. Grouard continues that "there where no one had ever held a brush, I was regarded as a great artist" ("là où personne n'avait jamais manié le pinceau, on me regardait comme un grand artiste"). See *Souvenirs de mes Soixante ans d'Apostolat dans l'Athabaska-Mackenzie* (Lyon: Œuvre Apostolique de M.I., 1923), 210. The version of the proverb alluded to by Balzac in *Les Illusions perdues* (1843) is "dans le royaume des aveugles les borgnes sont rois." See *Trésor de la Langue Française*, tome iv, publié sous la direction de Paul Imbs (Paris: Éditions du centre national de la recherche scientifique, 1975).
28. As quoted from *La Bonne Nouvelle* (1920): 32: "Le Calvaire de Grouard est son chef d'oeuvre," in *L'Illustration* (le 13 février 1926): 133. The photo has this caption: "Deux missionaries Oblats—dont l'un, à droite, Mgr Grouard, âgé de quatre-vingts-cinq ans, a été récemment décoré de la Légion d'honneur—sciant des arbres pour la construction d'une école destinée à de petits Indiens."
29. The Paris Commune (1871) was sparked by the defeat of France by Prussia that year; the prospect of victorious Prussian troops marching through Paris was intolerable for the working class and most members of the National Guard, who set up guns to oppose the march. The Fédérés united in socialist causes to control rents, improve working conditions, set up day nurseries close to factories, and advocate the education of women. A six-week siege involving the Fédérés and the Versaillists, forces loyal to the head of the national government, Adolph Thiers, resulted in mass executions; many Parisians sympathetic to the Fédérés fled to neighbouring Belgium. In 1875, customs officers were still vigilant about suspicious potential contraband, and hence the interrogation of Émile Grouard was ordered.
30. "C'est ainsi que j'appris tant bien que mal le métier de typographe." *Souvenirs*, 163.
31. *Souvenirs*, 167.
32. "Ils les ont gardés jusqu'au jour où l'on peut donner des livres en caractères syllabiques," *Souvenirs*, 102.
33. See *Peel's Bibliography of the Canadian Prairies to 1953*. Revised and enlarged. Ernie E. Ingles and N. Merrill Distad, eds. (Toronto: University of Toronto Press, 2003), 1876–1922, especially 808, 846, 874, 875, 1143.
34. "Monseigneur et très-cher Père," Lac La Biche, le 30 avril 1878, Archives Archevêché de Saint-Boniface, Manitoba, T 20325–6.
35. "Si la pronunciation du cris est douce et agréable, les règles de la grammaire claires et précises, la formation des mots simple et naturelle; par contre les conjugaisons présentent une telle complexité, de si nombreuses transformations, que l'on croirait dans un labyrinthe, où des chemins sans nombre se croisent à l'infini et vous exposent à des égarements perpétuels. Cependant avec le temps, la réflexion et une bonne volonté persévérante, vous parvenez à saisir le fils. Alors, vous ne pouvez vous empêcher d'admirer la perfection incomparable de cette langue." *Souvenirs*, 182–83.
36. "Monseigneur et très-cher Père," Lac La Biche, le 29 mai 1880, Archives Archevêché de Saint-Boniface, Manitoba, T. 23937–8. After noting that the next task is to produce a collection in Peau-de-Lièvre, Grouard observes: "vous voyez que nous ne perdons pas absolumment notre temps" (T. 23938). The "assistant" referred to may be Father Francis Norbert Blanchet (1795–1883), a missionary active in the Pacific Northwest, first vicar apostolic of Oregon Territory, and later archbishop of Oregon City, whose vast experience with the catechetical teaching device known as the Catholic Ladder, would have been invaluable. Since Blanchet resigned in 1880, he may have been visiting in St. Albert, when Bishop Grandin suggested that help was needed in Lac La Biche. See Philip M. Hanley, *History of the Catholic Ladder*. E.J. Kowrach, ed. (Fairfield, Washington: Ye Galleon Press, 1993).
37. "Monseigneur et très-cher Père," Lac La Biche, le 9 mai 1887, Archives Archevêché de Saint-Boniface, Manitoba, T. 35800.
38. "Monseigneur et très-cher Père," Lac Athabaska, le 29 décembre 1888, Archives Archevêché de Saint-Boniface, Manitoba, T. 38791. "L'approbation que vous donnez aux livres sauvages sorties de notre presse m'est aussi bien précieuse."
39. "Révérendissme et bien Aimé Père," Lac La Biche, le 16 juin 1888, Archives Deschâtelets, Ottawa, G LPP 1786. "D'ailleurs j'ai la tête si remplie de tournures, racines, locutions, etc.... sauvages, par suite des réflexions forcées sur les ouvrages que

je viens d'imprimer qu'il me semble presque impossible de penser à autre chose."

40. "Comment prêcher sans connaître la langue de ceux à qui l'on parle? et comment connaître une langue sauvage sans l'étudier?" "Lettre du R.P. Grouard," le 5 décembre 1883, *Missions* (Paris: A. Hennuyer, 1884), No. 86: 151.
41. "Notre dernier travail en ce genre a été la réimpression du receuil de prières, instructions et cantiques à l'usage des Cris....Cet apprenti était bel et bien Mgr Faraud lui-même qui se mit à l'œuvre avec une ardeur toute juvénile, sans se laisser décourager par quelques coquilles, inévitables au début," *Missions*, 145–46.
42. The title page of *Prières Catéchisme et Cantiques dans la Langue des Indiens Castors*, dated 1888 and identified as printed at Lac La Biche, is on display at the Interpretive Centre at Notre Dame des Victoires mission in Lac La Biche.
43. "Lettre du R.P. Grouard," *Missions*, No. 86 (1884): 155.
44. "Lettre du R.P. Grouard," *Missions*, No. 112 (1890): 84–85.

ᑲᑐᓂᐠ
ᐊᔭᒥᐁᐃᐧᒪᓯᓇᐃᑲ

ᑲᑐᓂᐠ
ᐊᔭᒥᐁᐃᐧᒪᓯᓇᐃᑲ

CATHOLIC
PRAYER BOOK

KATOLIK
KÂTOLIK

AYAMIEWI MASINAIKAN
AYAMIHÊWI-MASINAHIKAN

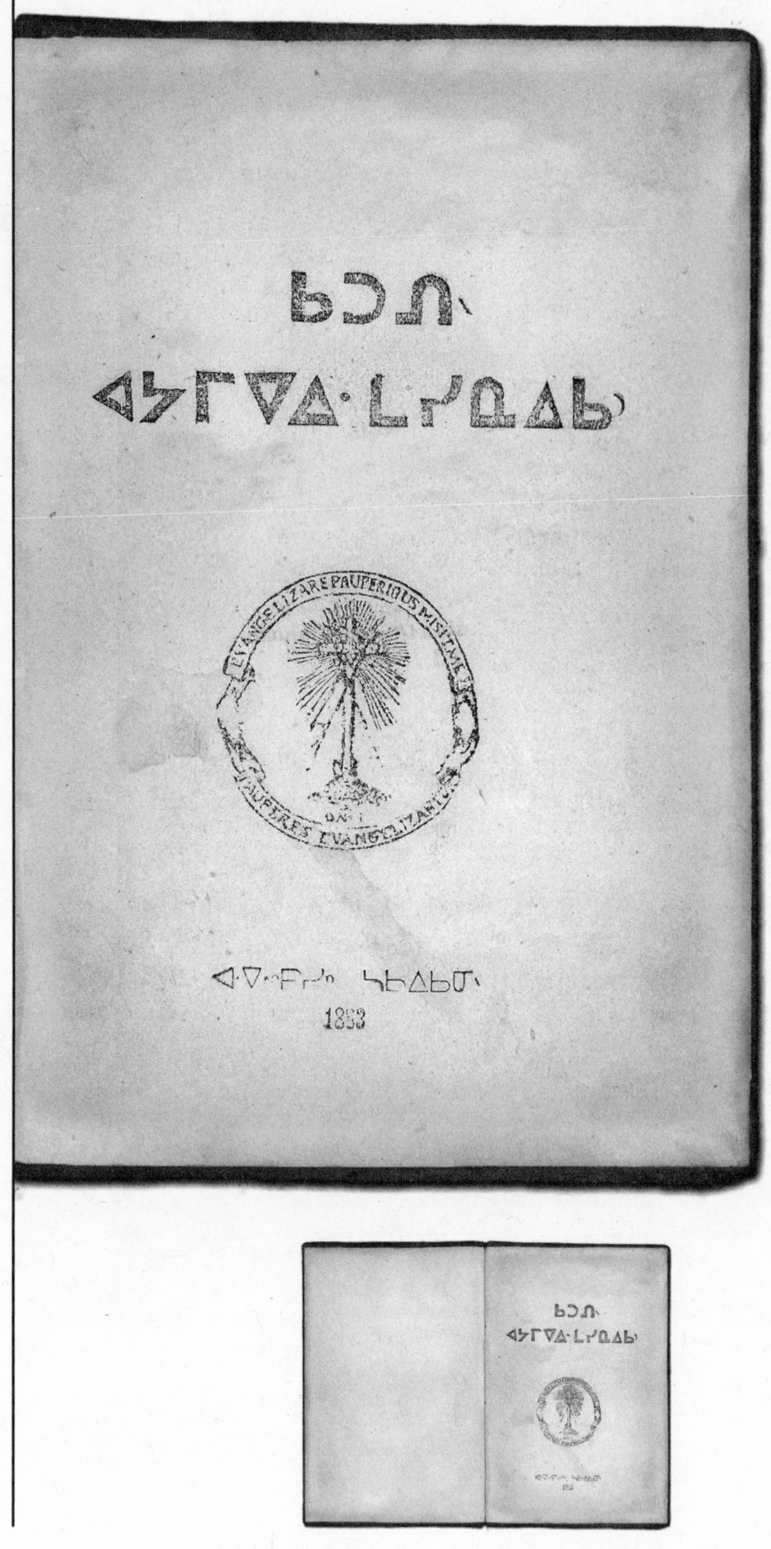

CATHOLIC PRAYER BOOK

[OBLATE EMBLEMATIC MOTTO]

ELK LAKE (LAC LA BICHE)

1883

KATOLIK
KÂTOLIK

AYAMIEWI MASINAIKAN
AYAMIHÊWI-MASINAHIKAN

[OBLATE EMBLEMATIC MOTTO]

WAWASKISIW SAKAIKANIK
WÂWÂSKÊSIW SÂKAHIKANIHK
1883

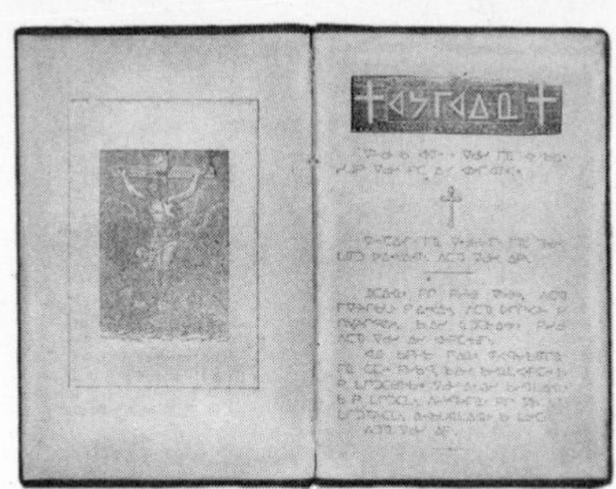

PRAYERS

When one wakes up and also when one goes to bed, this is how everyone will pray.

God, the Father and the Son of God and the Holy Spirit wish this to happen.

Our Father, You are in Heaven, Your name is revered. May Your name be honoured.

Today give us our bread and every day forgive those who did evil to us so that we do not think evil thoughts, and in this way forgive us our sins, the evil that we did. Take care of us, great and evil, take away from us that which is evil.

So let it be.

AYAMIAWINA
AYAMIHÂWINA

eyikok ka waniskak ekosi mina wa kawisimoki ekosi
iyikohk kâ-waniskâhk êkosi mîna wâ-kawisimohki êkosi

kita isi ayami aniwan.
kita-isi-ayamihâniwan.

weyotawimit mina wekosisimit mina meyosit
wiyôhtâwîmit mîna wêkosisimit mîna (ê-)miyosit

manito owiyowinik. pitane ekosi ikik.
manitow owihowinihk. pitanê êkosi ihkik.

---

notawinan kici kisikok eyayan, pitane
nôhtâwînân kihci-kîsikohk (ê-)ayâyan, pitanê

miweyicikatek ki wiyowin, pitane ocicipayik ki
miywêyihcikâtêk kiwîhowin, pitanê ocihcipayik

tipeyicikewin, ka isi natotakawiyan kisikok pitane ekosi
kitipêyihcikêwin, kâ-isi-natohtâkawiyan kîsikohk pitanê êkosi

isi waskitaskamik.
isi waskitaskamik.

anoc kakisikak miinan nipakwesikaniminan mina
anohc kâ-kîsikâk miyinân nipahkwêsikaniminân mîna

tatwaw kisikake, kaisi kasinamawakitwaw ka ki
tahtwâw kîsikâki, kâ-isi-kâsînamawakihtwâw kâ-kî-

macitotakoyakwaw ekosi wi isi kasinamawinan ka ki
maci-itôtâkoyâhkwâw êkosi wî-isi-kâsînamawinân kâ-kî-

macitotamak, pisiskeyiminan kici eka maci
maci-itôtamâhk, pisiskêyiminân kici êkâ maci-

mamitoneyitamak, iyekatenamawinan ka mayatak.
mâmitonêyihtamâhk, iyîkatênamawinân kâ-mâyâtahk.

pitane ekosi ikik.
pitanê êkosi ihkik.

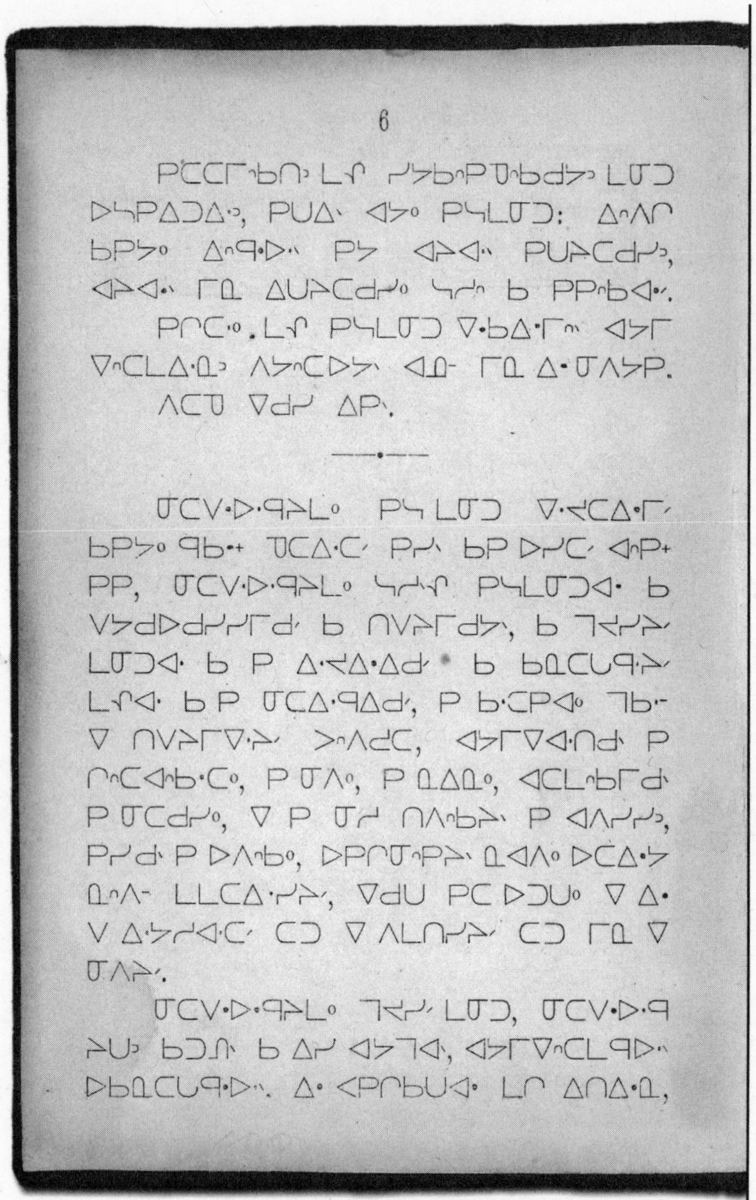

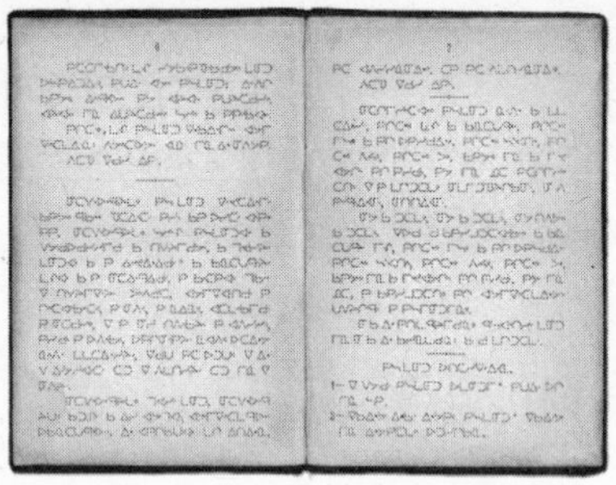

6 I greet you Mary. God is in your heart. Of all women you are more blessed than they because you bore Jesus.

Holy Mary, God takes you as a mother. Pray for us, we have sinned today and at the time when we die.

So let it be.

I believe in God, He is my Father. He created everything; He made the Heavens and the land and I believe in Jesus Christ, the One whom God took as His Son, the One who owns us. The good Lord gave Him His name, the One with the clean spirit. Mary, who gave birth to Him, suffered at the time when Pontius Pilate was leader. Jesus was nailed to the cross. He died. He was buried, He descended into the underworld, and after two nights He arose from death. He rose into Heaven and He sits at the right hand of His Father, the supernatural. He will come from Heaven; He is going to come and place judgement on all those who are living and also on all those who are dead.

I believe in Him, He is a good God. I believe in it, the Catholic ways of praying; they pray for all the clean spirits. All the bad words are going to be released.

kitatamiskatin mari siyakaskineskakoyan Manito
kitatamiskâtin Mari (ê-)sâkaskinêskâkoyan manitow

osakiitowin, kiteik ayaw kisemanitow: ispici kakiyaw
osâkihitowin, kitêhihk ayâw kisê-manitow: ispîhci kahkiyaw

iskwewak kiya ayiwak kiteyitakosin, ayiwak mina
iskwêwak kîya ayiwâk kitêyihtâkosin, ayiwâk mîna

iteyitakosiw sesos ka kikiskawat.
itêyihtâkosiw Sesos kâ-kikiskawat.

kicitwaw mari kise manito wekawimisk
kihcitwâw Mari kisê-manitow wêkâwîmisk

ayamiestamawinan piyastaoyak anoc mina winipiyaki.
ayamihêstamawinân pâstâhoyâhk anohc mîna wî-nipiyâhko.

pitane ekosi ikik.
pitanê êkosi ihkik.

---

nitapwewokeyimaw kise manitow weyotawimit kakiyaw
nitâpwêwakêyimâw kisê-manitow wiyôhtâwîmit kahkiyaw

kekway netawitat kisik kaki ositat askiy kiki,
kîkway nihtâwihitât kîsik kâ-kî-osîhtât askiy kiki,

nitapwewokeyimaw sesokri kise manitowa ka
nitâpwêwakeyimâw Sesokri kisê-manitowa kâ-

peyakookosisimikot ka tipeyimikayak, ka meyosiyit
pêyakôkosisimikot kâ-tipêyimikoyâhk, kâ-miyosiyit

manitowa ka ki wiyowiikot ka kanatacakweyit mariwa
manitowa kâ-kî-wîhowihikot kâ-kanâtahcahkwêyit Mariwa

ka ki nitawikeikot, ki kwatakiaw mekwac e tipeyimiweyit
kâ-kî-nihtâwikihikot, kî-kwâtakihâw mêkwâc ê-tipêyimiwêyit

pospilata, ayamiewawatikok ki cistaaskwataw, ki nipiw,
Pospilata, ayamihêwahtikohk kî-cîstahâskwatâw, kî-nipiw,

ki nainaw, atamaskamikok ki nitakosiw, e ki niso
kî-nahinâw, atâmaskamikohk kî-nîhtakosîw, ê-kî-nîso-

tipiskayik ki apisisin, kisikok ki opiskaw, okiciniskiyik
tipiskâyik kî-âpisisin, kîsikohk kî-ohpîskâw, okihciniskiyihk

naapiw otawiya naspic mamatawisiyit, ekote kita ototew
nahapiw ohtâwiya nâspic mamâhtâwisiyit, êkotê kita-otohtêw

e wi pe wiyasowatat tato e pimatisiyit tato mina e nipiyit.
ê-wî-pê-wîyasiwâtât itahto ê-pimâtisiyit itahto mîna ê-nipiyit.

e wi pe wiyasowatat tato e pimatisiyit tato mina e nipiyit.
ê-wî-pê-wiyasiwâtât itahto ê-pimâtisiyit itahto mîna ê-nipiyit.

nitapwewokeyimaw meyosit manitow,
nitâpwêwakêyimâw (ê-)miyosit manitow,

nitapwewokeyiten katolik ka isi ayameak,
nitâpwêwakêyihtên kâtolik ka-isi-ayimihâk,

ayamiestamakewok okanatacakwewok. wi pakicikatewa
ayamihêstamâkêwak okanâtahcahkwêwak. wî-pakiçîkâtêwa

maci itiwina,
macihtiwina,

7

ᑭᑕ ᐊᐱᓯᓯᓇᒋᐃᐧᐣ, ᑕᑭ ᑭᑕ ᐱᒪᑎᓯᓇᒋᐃᐧᐤ.
ᐱᑕᒋ ᐁᑯᓯ ᐃᑭᐠ.

——o——

ᒋᑕᑎᒥᓱᐣᑕᐊᐧᐤ ᑭᓭᒪᒋᑐ ᐧᓇᐣᐱ ᑲ ᒪᒪ ᑕᐃᐧᓯᐟ, ᑭᑎᑕᐧᐤ ᒫᕆ ᑲ ᑲᓇᑕᐧᑫᐠ, ᑭᑎᑕᐧᐤ ᒥᓭᔅ ᑲ ᑭᑎ ᐅᑭᓯᑯᐃᐧᐟ, ᑭᑎᑕᐧᐤ ᓵᐠᐸᑎᐣ, ᑭᑎᑕᐧᐤ ᐱᔦᕑ, ᑭᑎᑕᐧᐤ ᐴᔅ, ᑲᑭᔭᐤ ᒥᓇ ᑲ ᒥᔦ ᐊᔭᒥᐠ ᑭᑎ ᑭᓯᑰ, ᑭᔭ ᒥᓇ ᓅᑕ ᑭᑕᑎᒥᓱᐣ ᑕᑎᐣ ᐁ ᑭ ᒪᒋᑐᑕᒪᐣ ᒋᒪᒥᑐᒍᔦᑎᑲᒋᐠ, ᒋ ᐱ ᑭᐢᑫᐧᐃᐧᒋᐠ, ᒋᑎᑎᐃᐧᒋᐠ.

ᒋᔭ ᑲ ᑐᑕᒪᐣ, ᒋᔭ ᑲ ᑐᑕᒪᐣ, ᒋᔭ ᑎᐱᔭᐤ ᑲ ᑐᑕᒪᐣ. ᐁᐅᑯ ᑯ ᑲᑭᓯᒧᑐᑕᐊᐧᑳᐤ ᑲ ᑲᓇᑕᐧᑫᐠ ᒥᕆ, ᑭᑎᑕᐧᐤ ᒥᓭᔅ ᑲ ᑭᑎ ᐅᑭᓭᑯᐃᐧᐟ ᑭᑎᑕᐧᐤ ᓵᐠᐸᑎᐣ, ᑭᑎᑕᐧᐤ ᐱᔦᕑ, ᑭᑎᑕᐧᐤ ᐴᔅ, ᑲᑭᔭᐤ ᒥᓇ ᑲ ᒥᔦᐊᔭᒥᐠ ᑭᑎ ᑭᓯᑰ, ᑭᔭ ᒥᓇ ᓅᑕ, ᑭ ᑲᑭᓯᒧᑐᑕᐣ ᑭᑎ ᐊᔭᒥᐁᐣᑕᒪᐃᐧᔭᐣ ᑌᐯᔨᒋᑫᐤ ᑭ ᑭᓭᒥᒋᑐᒥᓇᐤ.

ᒋ ᑲ ᐃᐧ ᑭᑎᒪᑫᔨᒥᑯᓇᐣ ᑫᓭᐊᐧᑎᓯᐤ ᒪᒋᑐ ᒥᓇ ᒋ ᑲ ᐃᐧ ᑲᓯᓇᒪᑯᓇᐣ ᑲ ᑯ ᒪᒋᑐᑕᒪᐠ.

——•——

ᑭᓭᒪᒋᑐ ᐅᑎᑕᓯᐁᐧᐃᐧᓇ.

1— ᐁ ᐯᔭᑯ ᑭᓭᒪᒋᑐ ᐅᒪᒋᑐᒥ* ᑭᑌᐃᐠ ᐅᑎ ᒥᓇ ᓴᑭ.

2— ᐁᑲᐃᐧᔭ ᐃᐧᑳ ᐃᐧᔭᑭᐨ ᑭᓭᒪᒋᑐ* ᐁᑲᐃᐧᔭ ᒥᓇ ᐃᐧᔭᑭᑕᒪᐤ ᐅᑐᓯᑎᑲᓇ.

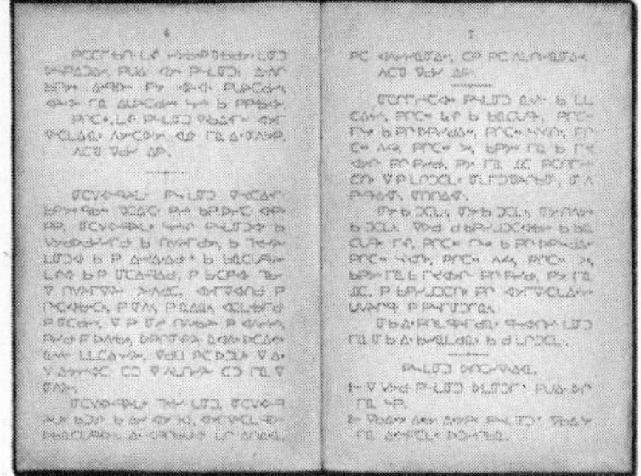

7 They will humble themselves, all the time, all who are living.

So let it be.

——o——

I confess God, the forever powerful, to Holy Mary, the one with the clean spirit, Saint Michael in Heaven, Saint Patrick, the great Saint Pierre, Saint Paul, and to all those holy ones who are in Heaven. To You also my Father, I confess to You that I did evil in my thoughts, in my speech, in my words.

Me, I did it, I did it, I myself, I did it. This I pray for, the clean spirit of Holy Mary, the Great One Michael, the Archangel, Saint Patrick, Saint Pierre, Saint Paul, and those holy ones in Heaven. You also, my Almighty Father, I pray to You so that You will pray for me. Our God rules everything.

He will have pity on us; He is a very kind God and He will forgive the sins that we did.

——•——

GOD'S COMMANDMENTS.

1– He is one God. Believe in Him in your heart and also love Him.

2– Do not ever criticize God. Also do not criticize His creations.

7 kita apisisinaniwiw, taki kita pimatisinaniwiw.
kita-âpisisinâniwiw, tahki kita-pimâtisinâniwiw.

pitane ekosi ikik.
pitanê êkosi ihkik.

——o——

nitacimisostawaw kise manitow naspic ka mamatawisit,
nitâcimisostâwâw kisê-manitow nâspic kâ-mamâhtâwisit,

kicitwaw mari ka kaṇatacakwet, kicitwaw misel ka
kihcitwâw Mari kâ-kanâtahcahkwêwêt, kihcitwâw Misel kâ-

kici okisikowit, kicitwaw sakpatis, kicitwaw piyer,
kihci-okîsikowit, kihcitwaw Sakpatis, kihcitwâw Piyer,

kicitwaw pal, kakiyaw mina ka miyoayacik kici kisikok,
kihcitwâw Pal, kahkiyaw mîna kâ-mîyo-ayâcik kihci-kîsikohk,

kiya mina nota kitacimisostatin e ki maci-totaman
kîya mîna nôhtâ kitâcimisostâtin ê-kî-maci-itôtamân

nimamitoneyicikanik, ni pikiskwewinik, nititiwinik.
nimâmitonêyihcikanihk, nipîkiskwêwinihk, nititiwinihk.

niya ka totaman, niya ka totaman, niya tipiyaw ka
niya kâ-itôtamân, niya kâ-itôtamân, niya tipiyâw kâ-

totaman. eoko kokakisimototawakwaw ka
itôtamân. êwako kikâkîsimototawakwâw kâ-

kanatacakwet mari, kicitwaw misel ka kici okisekowit
kanâtahcahkwêwêt Mari, kiheitwâw Misel kâ-kihci-okîsikowit

kicitwaw sakpatis, kicitwaw piyer, kicitwaw pal,
kihcitwâw Sakpatis, kihcitwâw Piyer, kihcitwâw Pal,

kakiyaw mina ka miyoayacik kici kisikok, kiya mina
kahkiyaw mîna kâ-miyo-ayâcik kihci-kîsikohk, kiya mîna

nota, ki kakisimototatin kici ayamiestamawiyan
nôhtâ, kikâkîsimototâtin kici-ayamihêstamawiyan

tepeyiciket ki kise minitominaw.
(ê-)tipêyihcikêt kikisê-manitôminaw.

ni ka wi kitimakeyimikonan kesewatisit manito mina
nika-wî-kitimâkêyimikonân kâ-kisêwâtisit manitow mîna

ni ka wi kasinamakonan ka ko macitotamak.
nika-wî-kasînamâkonân kâ-kî-maci-itôtamahk.

——•——

KISE MANITO OTITASIWEWINA.
KISÊ-MANITOW OTITASIWÊWINA.

1–e peyakot kise manitow omanitomi kiteik oci mina saki.
1–ê-pêyakot kisê-manitow omanitômi kitêhik ohci mîna sâkih.

2–ekawiya wikac wiyakim kise manito ekawiya mina
2–êkâwiya wîhkâc wîyakim kisê-manitow êkâwiya mîna

wiyakitamaw otosicikana.
wîyakihtamaw otôsîhcikana.

8

3– Do not work on the praying day, Sunday: pray carefully.

4– Respect your parents and you will live a long life.

5– Do not kill. Do not even think about how to kill.

6– Do not commit adultery. Do not even think about adultery.

7– Do not steal from anyone. And also, do not keep something that was stolen.

8– Do not ever lie. Also do not speak badly about anyone.

9– Depend only on one another, you who are married; do not desire different partners.

10– Do not be covetous.

——o——

[PRECEPTS OF THE CHURCH]

1– Respect the holy days.

2– On praying day [Sunday], especially Christmas Day, pray with the priest when he says Mass.

3– Tell the priest about all your sins, at least one time, every year.

4– Each time you confess you will earn for yourself the grace to receive Communion.

5– When you rise, fast and from morning to the holy day, as you are told. Pray also, every day at dawn, and for

8 3–ekawiya osicike eyamiekisikake peyatik ayamia.
3–êkâwiya osîhcikê ayamihêwi-kîsikâki pêyâhtik ayamihâ.

4–ki nikiikwok manacitotawik kinowes kici pimatisiyan.
4–kinîkihikwak manâcihtotawik kinwês kici-pimâtisiyân.

5–ekawiya nipatake ekawiya apo mamitoneyita kici
5–êkâwiya nipâtâkê êkâwiya ahpô mâmitonêyihta kici-

nipatakeyan.
nipâtâkêyan.

6–ekawiya pisikwatisi ekawiya apo
6–êkâwiya pisikwâtisi êkâwiya ahpô

pisikwacimamitoneyita.
pisikwâcimâmitonêyihta.

7–ekawiya kimotamaw awiyak otayana ekawiya mina
7–êkâwiya kimotamaw awiyak otayana êkâwiya mîna

kanaweyita kekway e ki kimotinaniwik.
kanawêyihta kîkway ê-kî-kimotinâniwik.

8–ekawiya wikac kiyaski ekawiya mina maci ayimom
8–êkâwiya wîhkâc kiyâski êkâwiya mîna maci-âyimôm

awiyak.
awiyak.

9–peyakoitok wiyekitoyek ekawiya petos awiyak
9–pêyakohitok (ê-)wîkihtoyêk êkâwiya pîtos awiyak

mositawinawik.
môsitawinawik.

10–ekawiya kakayesinaike.
10–êkâwiya kakayêsinahikê.

——o——

1–manacita kici kisikawa.
1–manâcihtâ kihci-kîsikâwa.

2–eyamiewikisikake wawac kici kisikake wici
2–(ê-)ayamihewi-kîsikâki wâwâc kihci-kîsikâki wîci-

ayamiamakan ayamiewiyiniw Lames itweci.
ayamihamâkan ayamihêwiyiniw Lames itwêci.

3–kakiyaw ki maci itiwina acimostawakan
3–kahkiyaw kimacihtiwina âcimostawahkan

ayamiewiyiniw seyakes peyakwaw tatwaw askiwiki.
ayamihêwiyiniw sêyâkês pêyakwâw tahtwâw askîwiki.

4–tatwaw apisisinokisikake kikawikaskitamason kici
4–tahtwâw apisisinowi-kîsikâki kika-wî-kaskîhtamâson kici-

saskamoikawiyan.
saskamonahikawiyan.

5–tatwaw paskiwiki newas kicipayiki iyewanisiisokan
5–tahtwâw pâskiwiki nêwas kihcipayiki iyêwanisîhisôkan

mina nemitanaw kisikaw mayawes ispayik
mîna nêmitanaw kîsikâw mayawês ispayik

9 forty days [Lent] before it [Easter] happens.

6– Do not eat meat on a fast day.

7– You will give something to the priest so that he will be able to live and continue his work.

GLORY BE TO THE FATHER, THE SON, AND THE HOLY SPIRIT.

In the beginning He was praiseworthy, is, and ever shall be praiseworthy. Today, in this way, He is also praiseworthy all the time. So let it be.

LET US RESPECT GOD.

You are my God; I respect You, the One. I know this; I remember all this; You own me and You own everything.

LET US BELIEVE IN GOD.

My God, I truly believe. God will believe in you also. He will teach you to pray properly to help the people. Your prayer will come true.

LET US TRUST IN GOD.

I greatly trust in your kindness, my God. To have a strong heart here in this land. Your plans are to take care of it in Heaven, to take me to Heaven with You.

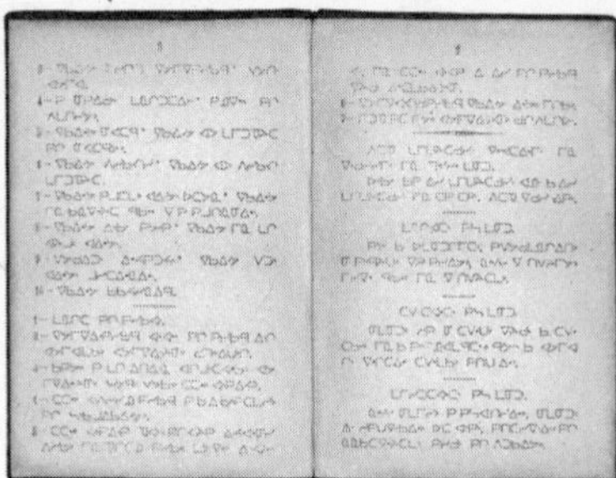

9 pak, mina tatwaw wapaki i isi kici kisikake eyikok
pak, mîna tahtwâw wâpâhki isi kihci-kîsikâki iyikohk

witamakawiyani.
wîtamâkawiyani.

6–eyamiewatikokisikake ekawiya wiyas micikan.
6–ayamihêwâhtikowi-kîsikâki êkâwiya wîyâs mîcîhkan.

7–mitone kita miyaw ayamiewiyiniw koci pimaciot.
7–mitonê kita-mîyaw ayamihêwiyiniw koci-pimâcihot.

PITANE MAMITEYITAKOSIT WEYOTAWIMIT
PITANÊ (Ê-)MÂMITÊYIHTÂKOSIT WIYÔHTÂWÎMIT

MINA WEKOSISIMIT MINA MEYOSIT MANITO.
MÎNA WÊKOSISIMIT MÎNA (Ê-)MIYOSIT MANITOW.

oskac kaki isi mamiteyitakosit anoc ka isi
oskac kâ-kî-isi-mâmihtêyihtâkosit anohc kâ-isi-

mamiteyitakosit mina taki taki. pitane ekosi ikik.
mâmihtêyihtâkosit mîna tahki tahkî. pitanê êkosi ihkik.

MANACIATAK KISE MANITO.
MANÂCIHÂTÂHK KISÊ-MANITOW.

kiya ka omanitomimitan, kipeyakomaniciitin ni
kiya kâ-omanitômimitân, kipêyako-manâcihitin

kiskeyiten eki kisiiyan, naspic e tipeyimiyan misiwe
nikiskêyihtên ê-kî-kiskisiyan, naspic ê-tipêyimiyan misiwê

kekway mina e tipeyitaman.
kîkway mîna ê-tipêyihtaman.

TAPWETAWATAK KISE MANITO.
TÂPWÊTAWÂTÂHK KISÊ-MANITOW.

ni manitom soki ni tapweten eyikok ka tapwetakwaw
nimanitôm sôhki nitâpwêhtên iyikohk ka-tâpwêhtakwâw

mina ka kiskinoamaketwaw kweyask ka ayamiacik
mîna ka-kiskinohamâkihtwâw kwâyask ka-ayamihâcik

wecitawi tapwemakan kititwewin.
wîcitwâwi tâpwemakan kititwêwin.

MAMISITOTAWATAK KISE MANITO.
MAMISÎTOTAWÂTÂHK KISÊ-MANITOW.

naspic nimamisin ki kisewatisiwin, nimanitom wi
nâspic nimamisîn kikisêwâtisiwin, nimanitôm wî-

sokiteiskawin ota askik, kititasiwewin kici
sôhkitêhêskawin ôta askîhk, kititasiwêwin kici-

nanakataweyitaman kisikok kici pitokaiyan.
nânâkatawêyihtaman kîsikohk kici-pîhtokwahiyan.

10

ᓴᑭᐊᑕᐠ ᑭᓭ ᒪᓂᑐ.

ᓂᒪᓂᑐᐣ ᐃᐢᐱ- ᐅᑌᐃᔭᐣ ᑭᓴᑭᐃᑎᐣ, ᓂᒋ ᐊᔨᓯᔨᓂᐅᐦ ᐊᐧᐊᐧ- ᑳᑭᔭᐤ ᐃᐢᐱᑌᔨᒥᓱᔭᐣ ᓂ ᑎᐢᐱᑌᔨᒪᐅᐦ ᑭᔭ ᐅᒋ.

ᑳᑳᐧᑕᑫᔨᒧᑕᐠ.

ᓇᐢᐱ- ᓂ ᑳᑳᐧᑕᑫᔨᒧᐣ, ᑭᓭ ᒪᓂᑐ ᓄᑕ, ᐁ ᑭ ᑭᓯᐋᐧᐃᑕᐣ ᑭᔭ ᐁ ᑭᓭᐋᐧᑎᓯᔭᐣ ᒥᓇ ᐁ ᓴᑭᐃᑯᓯᔭᐣ ᒪᒪᐃᐧᔦᐢ, ᐃᔦᐱᑏ ᐁ ᐸᑳᐧᑕᐟ ᐊᐃᐧᔭᐠ ᐁ ᒪᒋ ᐃᓯᑕᐦ ᓂ ᑭᐢᑫᔨᑕᐣ, ᑭᐢᑭᓯ ᒪᑲ ᑭᑯᓯᐢ ᓭᓱᐢ ᑲ ᑭ ᑳᐧᑕᑭᑕᐟ ᐁ ᐃᐧ ᑳᑭᒋᐃᐢ ᓂᔭ ᐅᒋ. ᐊᐤ! ᑭᑎᒪᑫᔨᒥᐣ ᐃᐧᔭ ᐅᒋ, ᓇᒪᐃᐧᔭ ᐊᔪᐊᐧᐦ ᑭ ᑲ ᑭᓯᐋᐧᐃᑎᐣ ᓂᓱᑲᒪᐃᐧᔭᓂ ᓂ ᑲ ᐃᐧ ᐅᒋ ᑳᐧᑕᑭᐃᓯᐣ.

ᓇᓇᐢᑯᒪᑕᐠ ᑭᓭ ᒪᓂᑐ.

ᐅᓭᐨ ᐁ ᑭ ᒥᔻᑐᑕᐃᐧᔭᐣ, ᓂ ᒪᓂᑐᐨ. ᐁ ᑭ ᐊᔨᓯᔨᓂᐃᐧᐃᔭᐣ ᐁ ᑭ ᐯ ᐃᑎᓴᐦᐊᒪᐃᐧᔭᐣ ᑭ ᑯᓯᐢ ᑭᒋᐱᑯᐃᐧ ᐁᑳᐧ ᒥᓇ ᐁ ᑭᐃᑌᔨᒥᔭᐣ ᑭᒋ ᐃᐧᒋ ᐃᐁᐧᔭᐣ ᑭᑎᓯᑕᐃᐧᓂᐤ ᑭᓇᓇᐢᑯᒥᑎᐣ ᐃᐢᐱ- ᐅᑌ ᐃᔭᐣ.

ᐸᑭᑎᓇᒧᐊᐧᑕᐠ ᑭᓭ ᒪᓂᑐ ᐁᑎᔭᐠ.

ᓂ ᒪᓂᑐᐨ, ᑭ ᐸᑭᑎᓇᒪᑎᐣ ᓂ ᒥᑐᓂᔨᒋᑲᐣ

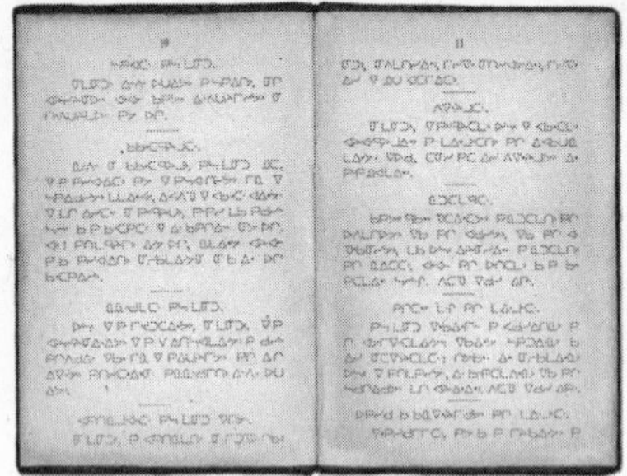

10 LET US LOVE GOD.

My God, I know You are here, I love You. My people, all of them think highly of You. You are Lord.

LET US SUFFER FOR IT.

I greatly suffered distress from it, God, my Father, I upset you. You are kind, and You are very much loved above all else. You hate anyone being evil. I know, I remember Your Son Jesus that He suffered. He went to comfort You for my sins. Have pity on me for Him. I will anger You no more. Work together with me. I will make myself suffer for this.

LET US THANK GOD.

Because You did me good, my God, You made me into a human. You sent Your Son to me, who saved me, and also You thought of me, to accompany You in Your way of worship. I thank You, for You are here within me.

LET US WELCOME GOD.

My God, I welcome You into my mind.

SAKIATAK KISE MANITO.
SÂKIHÂTÂHK KISÊ-MANITOW.

ni manitom ispic oteiyan ki sakiitin, nici ayisiyiniwok
nimanitôm ispic otêhiyan kisâkihitin, nîcâyisiyiniwak

wawac kakiyaw ispiteyimisoyan ni tispiteyimawok
wâwâc kahkiyaw (ê-)ispîhtêyimisoyan nitispîhtêyimâwak

kiya oci.
kiya ohci.

KAKWATAKEYIMOTAK.
KAKWÂTAKÊYIMOTÂHK.

naspic ni kakwatakeyimon, kise manito nota, e ki
nâspic nikakwâtakêyimon, kisê-manitow nôhtâ, ê-kî-

kisiwaitan kiya e kisewatisiyan mina e sakiikosiyan
kisiwâhitân kiya ê-kisêwâtisiyan mîna ê-sâkihikôsiyan

mamawiyes, iyepine e pakwatat awiyak e maci isitwat
mâmawiyês, iyêpinê ê-pakwâtat awiyak ê-maci-isihtwât

ni kiskeyiten, kiskisi maka kikosis sesos ka ki kwatakitat
nikiskêyihtên, nikiskisin mâka kikosis Sesos kâ-kî-kwâtakîtât

e wi kakiciisk niya ohci. aw! kitimakeyimin wiya ohci,
ê-wî-kâkîcihisk niya ohci. aw! kitimâkêyimin wiya ohci,

namawiya ayiwak ki ka kisiwaitin ni sokamawiyani ni ka
namâwiya ayiwâk kikâ-kisiwahitin nîsohkamawiyani nika-

wi oci kwatakiisos.
wî-ohci-kwâtakihison.

NANASKOMATAK KISE MANITO.
NANÂSKOMÂTÂHK KISÊ-MANITOW.

osam e ki miyototawiyan, ni manitom. e ki
osâm ê-kî-miyotôhtawiyan, nimanitôm. ê-kî-

ayisiyiniwiiyan e ki pe itisaamawiyan ki kosis kici pikoit
ayisiyiniwihiyan ê-kî-pê-itisahamawiyan kikosis kici-pihkohit

ekwa mina e ki iteyimiyan kici wici iweyan kitisitwawinik
êkwa mîna ê-kî-itêyimiyan kici-wîcihiwêyan kitisihtwâwinik

kinanaskomitin ispic oteiyan.
kinanâskomitin ispic otêhiyan.

PAKITINAMOWATAK KISE MANITO E TIYAK.
PAKITINAMAWÂTÂHK KISÊ-MANITOW Ê-TIYAK.

ni manitom, ki pakitinamatin ni mitoneyicikan
nimanitôm kipakitinamâtin nimitonêyihcikan

11 My mouth, my life, all my actions, with all of these I want to satisfy You.

YOU DESPISE SINNERS.

My God, You know it, because You dislike someone to think highly of himself. I pray to You to remove this from me: how I treat others as worthless. Teach me to know You.

LET US LISTEN TO IT.

You are able to do everything. I ask it of you: to make a good living, not to be sick, not to worry, but because I ask of you wisdom, to be able to listen to you, especially to be able to reach you. You did a good deed for me Jesus Christ. So let it be.

HOW TO PRAY TO HOLY MARY.

Merciful God we hope to get something from You, for You to pray for us. Do not forget our love for You. Help us with this because we are pitiful. Do a good deed for us not to be overpowered by evil. So let it be.

In Heaven You are protecting us. In this way we pray to Him. You are here with us.

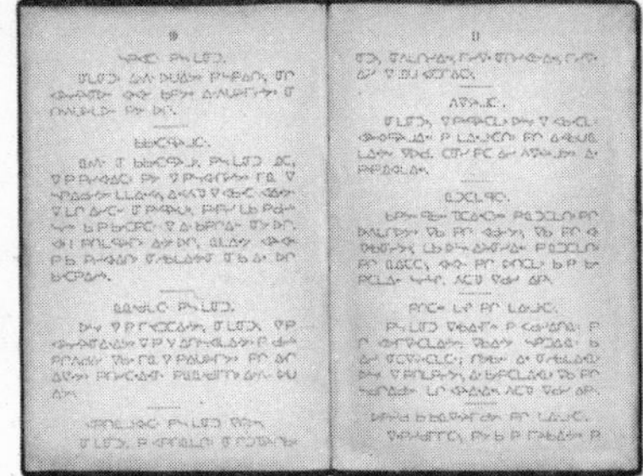

11 niton, ni pimatisiwin, misiwe nitisiayawin, misiwe isi e
nitôn, nipimâtisiwin, misiwê nitisâyâwin, misiwê isi ê-

note atamiitan.
nôhtê-atamihitân.

PIWEYIMOTAK.
PIWÊYIMOTÂHK.

ni manitom, e kiskeyitaman osam e pakwataman
nimanitôm ê-kiskêyihtaman osâm ê-pâkwâtaman

ayiwakeyimowin ki mawimostatin kici iyikatenamawiyan
ayiwâkêyimowin kimawimostâtin kici-iyîkatênamawiyan

eoko, tanisi kita isi piweyimoyan wi kiskinoamawin.
êwako, tânisi kita-isi-piwêyimoyan wî-kiskinohamâwin.

NATOTAMAKETAK.
NATOHTAMÂKÊTÂHK.

kakiyaw kekway netawitayan ki natotamatin kici
kahkiyaw kîkway nêtawîtayan kinatohtamâtin kici-

o pimacioyan eka kici akosiyan, eka kici waneskanisiyan,
opimâcihoyân êkâ kici-âhkosiyan, êkâ kici-wânêskanisiyân,

maka osam iyinisiwin ki natotamatin kici naitatan,
mâka osâm iyinîsiwin kinatohtamâtin kici-nahihtâtân,

wawac kici otitaman ka ki kaskitamawik sesokri. pitane
wâwâc kici-otihtamân kâ-kî-kaskîhtamawik Sesokri. pitanê

ekosi ikik.
êkosi ihkik.

KICITWAW MARI KICI MAWIMOSTAT.
KIHCITWÂW MARI KICI-MAWIMÔSTÂT.

kise manito wekawimisk ki pakosiitinan kici
kisê-manitow wêkâwîmisk kipâkosihitinân kici-

ayamiestamawiyak: ekawiya sakitowinan ka isi
ayamihêstamawiyâhk: êkâwiya sâkihitowinân ka-isi-

nitaweyitamatak; tiyakwac wi nisokamawinan
nitawêyihtâmâhk; tiyakwac wî-nîsôhkamawinân

osam e kitimakisiyak, wi kaskitamawinan eka kici
osâm ê-kitimâkisiyâhk, wî-kaskihtamawinân ekâ kici-

sakociikoyak maci ayiwiwin. pitane ekosi ihkik.
sâkocihikoyâhk maci-ayiwin. pitanê êkosi ihkik.

OKISIKO KA KANAWEYIMIKOYAK KICI MAWIMOSTAT.
OKÎSIKOHK KÂ-KANAWÊYIMIKOYÂHK KICI-MAWIMÔSTÂT.

wekisikomimitan, kiya ka ki miyikawiyan ki
wêkîsikômimitân, kiya kâ-kî-miyikawiyan ki

12

ᑎ ᑳᓇ ᐁᐧᔨᒥᔮᐣ, ᐃᐧ ᐃᐧᑎᐃᐧᐤ ᑳᑭᑫ ᐃᐧ ᑭᐢᑭᓄ
ᑕᐃᐣ ᑭᑎ ᒥᔭ ᑕᑯᔨᑌᔮᐣ ᐁᑕ ᑲ ᐣᑕᐁᐧᔨᒥᑲᐃᐧᔮᐣ
ᐱᑕᑌ ᐁᑯᓯ ᐃᑭᐠ

ᐊᐧ ᒣᑎᓯᑭ.

ᑭᓭ ᒪᓂᑐ ᓄᑕ, ᓂ ᑲ ᐃᐧ ᒥᔭᐢᑲᑯᐤ ᐅᒪ ᐊᓄ- ᑲ ᐃᐧ ᐊᓭᒥᔮᐣ. ᐱᑕᑌ ᐁᑫᓯ ᐃᑭᐠ.

ᐱᔭᑌ ᒣᑎᓯᑭ.

ᑫᓴᐊᐧᑎᓯᔮᐣ ᒪᓂᑐ ᑭ ᓇᓇᐢᑯᒥᑎᐣ ᐁ ᑭ ᐊᓴᒥᔮᐣ ᐊᓄ- ᑭᑎ ᐅᐱᒪᑎᐅᔮᐣ. ᐱᑕᑌ ᐁᑯᓯ ᐃᑭᐠ.

ᑯᓯᑲᐊᑎᑲᓯᐠ ᐊᔮᒥᐊᐃᐤ.

ᑭ ᓯᑲᐊᑕᑎᐣ ᐁᐧᔭᑕᐃᐧᒥᐠ ᒥᓇ ᐁᐧᑯᔨᓯᒥᐠ ᒥᓇ ᒣᔭᓯᐠ ᒪᓂᑐ ᐅᐃᐧᔭᐃᐧᓂᐠ.
ᐱᑕᑌ ᐁᑯᓯ ᐃᑭᐠ.

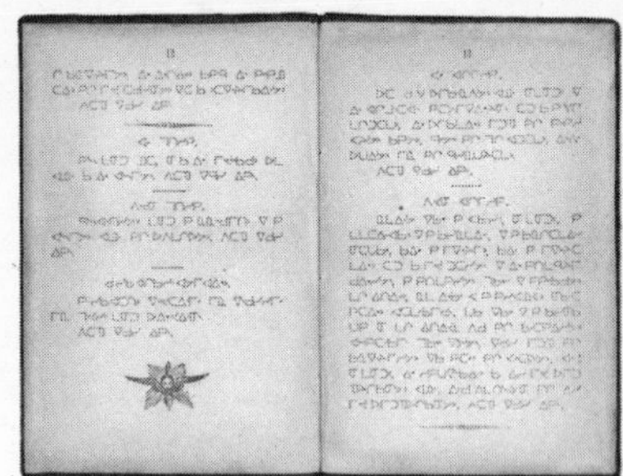

12 Keep me holy. Be with me all the time. Guide me to arrive there safely where I am wanted.

So let it be.

WHEN EATING.

God, my Father, this will make me feel good today, that You are going to feed me. So let it be.

AFTER EATING.

You are a kind God. I thank You that You fed me today. In this way I live a good life. So let it be.

PRAYER FOR BAPTISM.

I baptize you. I walk with you. In the name of the Good Lord. So let it be.

[ANGEL COPPERPLATE]

12 ci kanaweyimiyan, wi wiciwin kakike wi kiskinotain kici
ci-kanawêyimiyan, wî-wîciwin kâkikê wî-kiskinohtahin kici-

miyo-takosiniyan eta ka ntaweyimikawiyan
miyo-takosiniyân êta kâ-nitawêyimikawiyân

pitane ekosi ikik.
pitanê êkosi ihkik.

WA METISOKI.
WÂ-MÎCISOKI.

kise manito nota, ni ka wi miyoskakon oma anoc ka wi
kisê-manitow nôhtâ, nika-wî-miyôskâkon ôma anohc kâ-

asamiyan. pitane ekosi ihkik.
wî-asamiyan. pitanê êkosi ihkik.

PIYONI METISOKI.
PIYONI MÎCISOKI.

kesewatisiyan manito ki nanaskomitin e ki asamiyan
(ê-)kisêwâtisiyan manitow kinanâskomitin ê-kî-asamiyan

anoc kici opimacioyan. pitane ekosi ikik.
anohc (ê-)kici-opimâcihoyân. pitanê êkosi ihkik.

KO SIKAACIKASOK AYAMIAWIN.
KÔ-SIKAHÂHCIKÂSOK AYAMIHÂWIN.

ki sikaatatin weyotawimit mina wekosisimit mina
kisîkahâhtâtin wiyôhtâwîmit mîna wêkosisimit mîna

meyosit manito owiyowinik. pitane ekosi ikik.
(ê-)miyosit manitow owîhowinihk. pitanê êkosi ihkik.

[ANGEL COPPERPLATE]

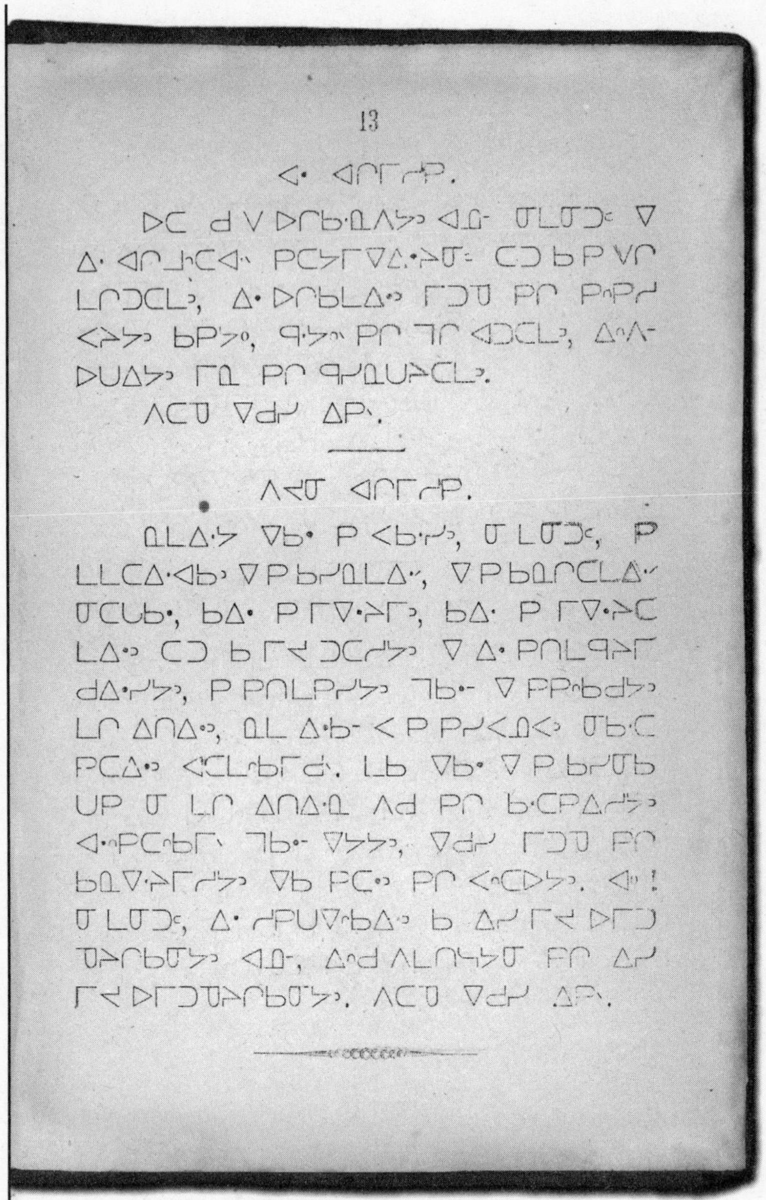

13 WHEN YOU ARE TALKING ABOUT YOURSELF.

I come here to kneel down. Today my Good Lord I am going to tell him, Your priest, those things that I did wrong. Help me very much to remember well everything that I spoke badly about. Here you are to be contrite.

So let it be.

CONFESSION.

You do not hate me any more, My Lord God, You are supernatural. God forgave my sins. He cleans my spirit for me. Once again You are pleased with me. You will be pleased with me for doing everything well for myself. I am going to be looked upon with compassion. I was poor. Right now I am bearing evil. Never will I bear my suffering to the underworld but now my evil deeds have been removed. You must suffer here on top of the earth right now. You are here and I care so very much to follow You. I am not going to sin again. My God, make me strong-hearted, to have a clear mind today, as long as I live, to have a good clear mind. So let it be.

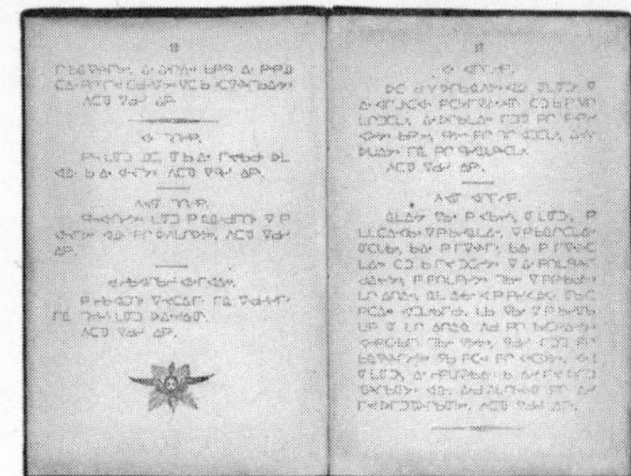

13

PWA ACIMISOKI.

PWA ÂCIMISÔKI.

ota ko pe ocikwanapiyan anoc ni manitom e wi
ôta kô-pê-ocihkwanapiyân anohc nimanitôm ê-wî-

acimostawak kitayamiewiyinic tato ka ki peci
âcimostawak kitayamihêwiyiniw tahto ka-kî-pêci-

macitotaman, wi ocikamawin mitone kici kiskisopayiyan
maci-itôtamân, wîcikamawin mitonê kici-kiskisopayiyân

kakiyaw, kweyask kici meci atotaman, ispic oteiyan mina
kahkiyaw, kwêyask kici-maci-âtotamân, ispic otêhiyân mîna

kici kesinateyitaman.
kici-kêsinatêyihtamân.

pitane ekosi ikik.
pitanê êkosi ihkik.

PIYONI ACIMISOKI.

PIYONÊ ÂCIMISÔKI.

namawiya ekwa ki pakwasin, ni manitom,
namâwiya êkwa kipakwâsin, nimanitôm,

ki mamatawiakan e ki kasinamawit, e ki kanacitamawit
kimâmâtâwihakan ê-kî-kâsînamawit, ê-kî-kanâcîtamawit

nitacakwa, kawi ki miweyimin, kawi ki miweyitamawin
nitahcâhkwa, kâwi kimiywêyimin, kâwi kimiywêyihtamawin

tato ka miyo totasoyan e wi kitomakeyimikowisiyan, ki
tahto kâ-miyo-itôtâsoyân ê-wî-kitimâkêyimikowisiyân, kî-

kitimakisiyan mekwac e kikiskakoyan maci itiwin, nama
kitimâkisiyân mêkwâc ê-kikiskâkoyân macihtiwin, nama

wikac pa ki kisipanopan nikwatakitawin atamaskamikok.
wihkâc pa-ki-kisipanopan nikwâtakihtâwin atamaskamikohk.

maka ekwa e ki kasinikateki ni maci itiwina piko kici
mâka êkwa ê-kî-kâsînikâtêki nimacihtiwina piko kici-

kwatakiisoyan waskitaskamik mekwac eyayan,
kwâtakihisoyân waskitaskamik mêkwâc (ê-)ayâyan,

ekosi mitone kici kanaweyimisoyan eka kitwan kici
êkosi mitonê kici-kanawêyimisoyân êkâ kîhtwâm (ê-)kici-

pastaoyan. aw! ni manitom, wi sokiteeskawin ka isi miyo
pâstâhoyân. aw! nimanitôm, wî-sôhkitêhêskawin ka-isi-

omitoneyicikaniyan anoc, isko pimatiweyani kici isi miyo
miyo-omitonêyicikaniyan anohc, isko pimâtisiyâni kici-miyo-

omitoneyicikaniyan. pitane ekosi ikik.
omitonêyihcikaniyân. pitanê êkosi ihkik.

14

ᐊ· ᓭᐢᑲᒧᑭ.

ᑫᓭᐊ·ᑎᓯᔮᐤ ᓭᓯᐢ, ᐁ ᐊᑕ ᐁᑲ ᒧᓯᐢ ᐊ·ᐸ ᒥᑕᐤ, ᑫᔦᐁ·ᐣ ᑭ ᑕᐯ·ᐅ·ᑫᔦᒥᑎᐤ ᐁᐤᑲᓱᐢᑎᐃ·ᓂ· ᑭᔮ ᑲ ᒧᐃ·ᑕᐤ ᓯᔮᐢᑲᒧᐃᑲᐃ·ᔮᓂ ᓂ ᑫᑎᓇᐅᐤ ᑕᓯᐸ· ᒥᔭᒪᐢᑲᑕᒪᐤ ᐁᓯ ᑭᓭᐊ·ᑎᓯᔮᐤ ᐁ ᐃ· ᐃᓯ ᒥᔪ ᑐᑕᐃ·ᔮᐤ ᐁ ᐊᑕ ᐱᐁ·ᔦᑕᑯᓯᔮᐤ, ᐊᔦᐊ·ᐣ ᒪᓇ ᐁ ᓃᐯᐃ·ᓯᔮᐤ ᒥᔭᒥᑐᓃᔦᑕᒪᓂ ᑲ ᑭ ᐯ ᐃᓯᐁ·ᐱᓯᔮᐤ; ᑭ ᒪᐃ·ᒨᐢᑕᑎᐤ ᑫᓭᐊ·ᑎᓯᔮᐤ ᑭᑎ ᐃ· ᑲᓯᓇᒪᐃ·ᔮᐤ, ᓇᐢᐱ- ᑭ ᓂᑕᐁ·ᔦᒥᑎᐤ ᓂ ᑌᐱ· ᑕᑭ ᑭᑎ ᐊᔮᔮᐤ. ᐱᑕᓃ ᐁᑯᓯ ᐃᑭ·.

—o—

ᐱᔪᓂ ᓭᐢᑲᒧᑭ.

ᐸᐢᑲ- ᑭ ᑭ·ᑕᑌ ᐃᓯ ᓇᓇᐢᑯᒥᑎᐤ ᐃᐢᐱ- ᒪ ᒪᑕᑯᐃᔮᐤ ᐁ ᑭ ᐃ· ᐯᑎᑌᐁᐢᑲᐃ·ᔮᐤ ᐊᓇ- ᓂ ᒪᓂᑐᐨ, ᐁ ᐊᑕ ᐁᑲ ᐃᑌᔦᑕᑯᓯᔮᐤ ᑭᑎ ᐃᓯ ᒥᔪ ᑐᑕᐃ·ᔮᐤ. ᓇᐢᑭᑲᓂ· ᑭᑕᓱᐊ·ᓱᐤ, ᐊᐤ! ᒥ ᑐᑏ ᐃ· ᑲᓇᐁ·ᔦᒥᐤ. ᑲ ᐃᓯ ᑭᐢᑌᔦᒥᑲᐃ·ᔮᐤ ᑭᓯᑯ· ᐁᑯᓯ ᓂᐢᑕ ᑕᑭ ᑭ ᐃ· ᐃᓯ ᑭᐢᑌᔦᒥᑎᐤ ᓇᒪᐃ·ᑲ- ᑭ ᑲ ᑭ ᑌᐱ ᓇᓇᐢᑯᒥᑎᐤ ᐅᓴᐨ ᐁ ᐊᑕ ᒥᐃᔮᐤ. ᑌᐱᔮ· ᐁᑫ·ᔦᑯ· ᓂ ᑲ ᑲᑫ· ᒥᔪᐊᔦᐃ·ᐤ ᓇᐊ·- ᑲᑭᔦᐸ ᑭᑎ ᒥᔪ ᑲᐢᑭᑕᒪᓱᔮᐤ.

ᐱᑕᓃ ᐁᑯᓯ ᐃᑭ·.

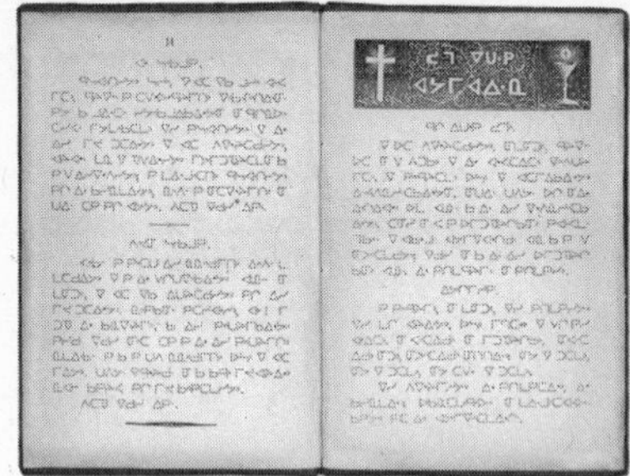

14 WHEN ONE RECEIVES COMMUNION.

You are kind Jesus. Even though I do not see You clearly, nevertheless I believe in You. I eat You when I have Communion. I am very certain, in fact, of Your kindness. You are going to do good for me, even though I am worthless. I am usually more shy in how I behaved when I had good thoughts. I pray to You; You are kind. You forgave me my sins. I very much want You in my heart all the time that You are here. So let it be.

—o—

THANKSGIVING FOR COMMUNION.

On top of Your sacrifice, in this way I thank You. You thought of me as worthy. You are going to enter into my heart today, my God, even though I am worthless. To do good for me You are in my chest, You protect me very much so that I may obtain Heaven where I, too, all the time will honour You. Never can I thank You enough because You satisfy me. Your goodness teaches me to do good for myself. So let it be.

WA SASKAMOKI.
WÂ-SASKAMÔHKI.

kesewatisiyan sesos, e ota eka mosis wapamitan,
(ê-)kisêwâtisiyan Sesos, ê-ôta êkâ mosis wâpamitân,

keyiwek ki tapwewokeyimitin e w karistiwinik kiya ka
kêyiwêk kitâpwêwakêyimitin ewkaristiwinihk kiya kâ-

mowitan siyaskamoikawiyani ni kecinaon tasipwa
môwitân siyaskamohikawîyâni nikêhcinâhon tâsipwâ

miyomaskataman esi kisewatisiyan e wi isi miyo
mîyomâskatamân ê-isi-kisêwâtisiyan ê-wî-isi-miyo-

totawiyan e ota piweyitakosiyan, ayiwak mana
itôtawiyan ê-âta-piwêyihtâkosiyan, ayiwâk mâna

e nepewisiyan miyomitoneyitamani ka ki pe isiwepisiyan;
ê-nêpêwisîyân miyo-mitonêyihtamâni kâ-kî-pê-isiwêpisîyân;

ki mawimostatin kesewatisiyan kici wi kasinamawiyan,
ki-mawimôstâtin (ê-)kisêwâtisiyân kici-wî-kâsînamâwiyan,

naspic ki nitaweyimitin ni teik taki kici kayayan. pitane
nâspic kinitawêyimitin nitêhihk tahki kici kâ-ayâyan. pitanê

ekosi ikik.
êkosi ihkik.

——o——

PIYONI SASKAMOKI.
PIYONÊ SASKAMÔHKI.

paskac ki kwitate isi nanaskomitin ispic
pâskac kikwîtatê-isi-nanâskomitin ispic

mamatakoiyan e ki wi peciteeskawiyan anoc
(ê-)mamâhtâkohiyan ê-kî-wî-pêcitêhêskawiyan anohc

ni manitom, e ata eka iteyitakosiyan kici isi miyo-
nimanitôm, ê-âta êkâ itêyihtâkosiyan kici-isi-miyo-

totawiyan. naskikanik kitasowason, aw! mitone wi
itôtawiyan. naskikanihk kitasowason, aw! mitonê wî-

kanaweyimin. ka isi kisteyimikawiyan kisikok ekosi
kanawêyimin. ka-isi-kistêyimikawiyân kîsikohk êkosi

nista taki ki wi isi kisteyimitin namawikac ki ka ki tepi
nîsta tahki kiwî-isi- kistêyimitin nama wîhkâc kika-kî-têpi-

nanaskomitin osam e ata miiyan. tepiyak ekweyikok
nanâskomitin osâm ê-âta-mihiyan. têpiyâhk êkwayikohk

ni ka kakwe miyo ayiwin nawac kakiyipa kici miyo
nika-kakwê-miyo-ayiwin nawâc kâkîpa kici-miyo-

kaskitamasoyan.
kaskîtamâsoyân.

pitane ekosi ikik.
pitanê êkosi ihkik.

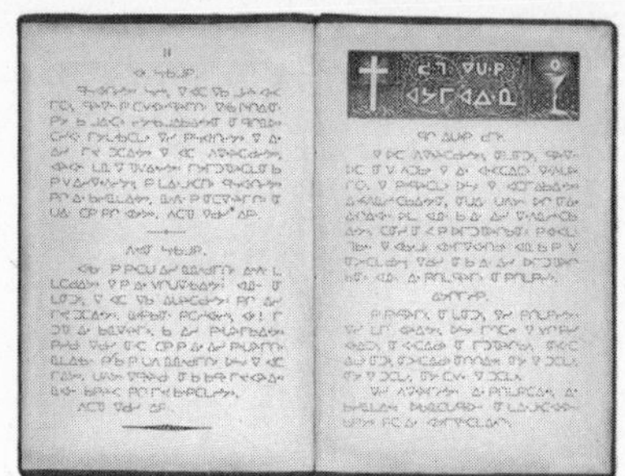

15

SAYING THE MASS PRAYERS

HOW TO PRAY THE MASS.

Here I am poor in spirit. My God, as well as I can, I enter. I am going to show You how highly I think of You. You know I am going to be satisfied. I will offer a sacrifice not in my heart only. For I am going to participate this day as the priest offers a sacred sacrifice for me. In my mind, I see Him right now, hanging on that cross, the One who died for us. In order then that I will have a good mind, have pity on me today. I am pitiful.

I CONFESS.

You know me, my God. I am being pitiful, I am evil because a lot of the time I have angered You. My mind made me sin; it caused me to sin; my mouth has caused me to sin with my sayings. Me, I did it. Me, I did it. Me truly, I did it.

I believe I am worthless. Have pity on me. Take sin from me. Let me have a clean spirit. I pray to Him, for everything. I ask the saints to pray for me.

15

LAMES ETWEKI
LAMES ITWÊKI

AYAMIAWINA
AYAMIHÂWINA

KECI ITWEKI LAMES.
KÊCI ITWÊKI LAMES.

e ota piweyitakosiyan, nimanitom, keyiwek ota ni pe
ê-ôta-pîwêyihtâkosiyân, nimanitôm, kêyiwêk ôta nipê-

pitokan e wi wapataitan espiteyimitan.
pihtokwân ê-wî-wâpahtihitân ê-ispîhtêyimitân.

e kiskeyitaman osam e atamiikawiyan
ê-kiskêyihtaman osâm ê-atamihikawiyân

weyepinasotakawiyani, niteik tepiyak oci ni-wi-
wêyêpinâsotakawiyâni, nitêhihk têpiyahk ohci niwî-

wiciiwan oma anoc ka wi isi wepinasostakawiyan. tanisi
wîcihiwân ôma anohc kâ-wî-isi-wêpinâsôstâkawîyân. tânisi

ni pa ki omitoneyicikanin kiwapamak mekwac e akwamot
nipa-ki-omitonêyihcikanin kîwâpamak mêkwâc ê-akwamot

ayamiewatikok ana ka ki pe-nipostamakoyak; ekosi
ayamihêwahtikohk ana kâ-kî-pê-nipôstamâkoyahk; êkosi

ni ka wi isi omitoneyicikanin anoc. wi kitimakeyimin ni
nika-wî-isi-omitonêyihcikanin anohc. wî-kitimâkêyimin

kitimakisin.
nikitimâkisin.

IYACIMISOKI.
IYÂCIMISÔHKI.

ki kiskeyimin, ni manitom, esi kitimakisiyan esi
kikiskêyimin, nimanitôm, (ê-)isi-kitimâkisiyân (ê-)isi

maci ayiwiyan, osam micetwaw e pecikisiwaitan.
maci-ayiwiyân, osâm mîhcêtwâw ê-pêcikisiwâhitân.

ni pastaikon ni mitoneyicikan, nipastaikon niton,
nipâstâhikon nimâmitonêyihcikan, nipâstâhikon nitôn,

nipastaikon nititiwin: niya e totaman, niya e totaman,
nipâstâhikon nititiwin: niya ê-itôtamân, niya ê-itôtamân,

niya tapwe e totaman.
niya tâpwê ê-itôtamân.

esi piweyimisoyan wi kitimakitawin, wi kasinamawin:
ê-isi-pîwêyimisoyân wî-kitimâkihtawin, wî-kâsînamawin:

okanatacakwewok ni mawimostawawo kakiyaw kita wi
okanâtahcahkwêwak nimawimôstawâwak kahkiyaw kita-wî-

ayamiestamawicik.
ayamihêstamawicik.

16

WHEN KIRIYI ELEISON IS BEING SAID.

kirie eleison
kirie eleison
kirie eleison

Christe eleison
Christe eleison
Christe eleison

kirie eleison
kirie eleison
kirie eleison

Lord have mercy. Have pity on me, Your creature, for I have been pre-occupied. You are kind. Have pity on Your children. You did a good deed for us, gave us life, You died for us. Work together with us on how to look after our life. Your good death earned our life for us. You are kind, Jesus. Do not reject us. Here we are worthless. On the contrary forgive us our sins, our evilness.

GLORY TO GOD IN HEAVEN.

Gloria in excelsis. (Et in terra pax) Hominibus bonae voluntatis Laudamus te. Bene Dicimuste. Adoramus te Glorificamus te Gratias agimus tibi Propter magnam gloriam tuam Domine Deus, Rex cae

Glory in the highest. On earth people of good heart will praise You. I recognize You as God. I truly honour You. You are almighty. Also, I thank You for Your great glory: Lord, God, King.

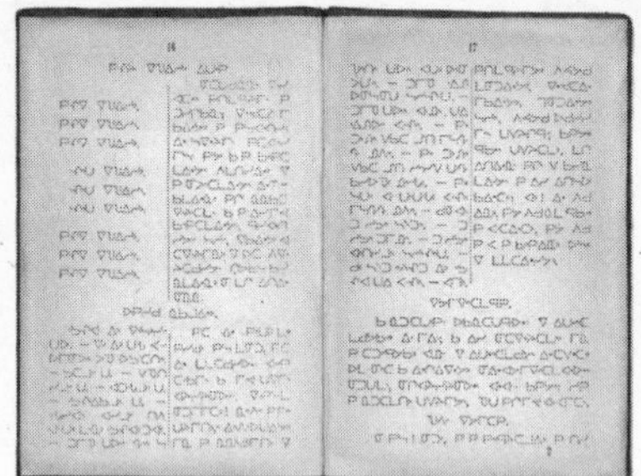

16

KIRIYI ELEISON ITWEKI.
KIRIYI ÊLÊISON ITWÊKI.

	nitacakonanak wesi *nitacâhkonânak wêsih*
	atwaw kitimakeyimik ki *atwâw kitimâkêyimik ki*
kirie eleison.	tosicikanak; weyotawimi *tôsîhcikanak; wiyôhtâwîmi*
kirie eleison.	kawiyan ki kisewatisin *kawîyân kikisêwâtisin*
kirie eleison.	wi saweyimik kitawasi *wî-sawêyimik kitawâsi*
	misak kiya ka ki kaskita *misak kiya kâ-kî-kaskîhta*
kriste eleison.	mawiyak pimatisiwin e *mawiyâhk pimâtisiwin ê-*
kriste eleison.	ki nipostamawiyak winiso *kî-nipôstamawiyâhk wî-nîsôh*
kriste eleison.	kamawinan kici nanakata *kamawinân kici-nanâkata*
	weyitamak ka ki isimiyo *wêyihtamâhk kâ-kî-isi-miyo-*
	kaskitamawiyak. kesiwati *kaskîhtamawiyâhk. (ê-)kisêwâti*
kirie eleison.	siyan sesos, ekawiya a *siyan Sesos, êkâwiya â*
kirie eleison.	taweyiminan e ota piwe *tawêyiminân ê-ôta pîwê*
	yitakosiyak tiyakwac kasi *yihtâkosiyâhk tiyakwac kâsî*
kirie eleison.	namawinan ni maci itiwi *namawinân nimacihtiwin*
	ninana. *ninâna.*

OKISIKO NAKAMOWIN.
OKÎSIKOHK NAKAMOWIN.

kloria in ekselsis
kloria in ekselsin

teo. – et in tera paks
tewo. – et in tera paks

ominipos pone poloktatin.
ominipos pone poloktatin.

– lotamos te. – peneti
– lotamos te. – peneti

simoste. – atoramos te.
simoste. – atoramos te.

– kloripikamos te. –
– kloripikamos te. –

krasias asimos tipi
krasias asimos tipi

propter maknamkloriam
propter maknamkloriam

toam.
toam.

– tomine teos reks se
– tomine teos reks se

kita wi kisteyimaw
kita-wî-kistêyimâw

kisikok kise manito, kita
kîsikohk kisê-manitow, kita-

wi mamatakosiwok waski
wî-mamâhtâkosiwak waski

taskamik ka miyo teecik
taskamik kâ-miyo-têhêcik

ayisiyiniwok. wekisema
ayisiyiniwak. wê-kisê-ma

nitomimitan! naspic kikis
nitômimitân! naspic kikis

teyimitin, ispic oteiyan
têyimitin, ispic otêhiyan

mina ki nanaskomitin e
mîna kinanâskomitin ê-

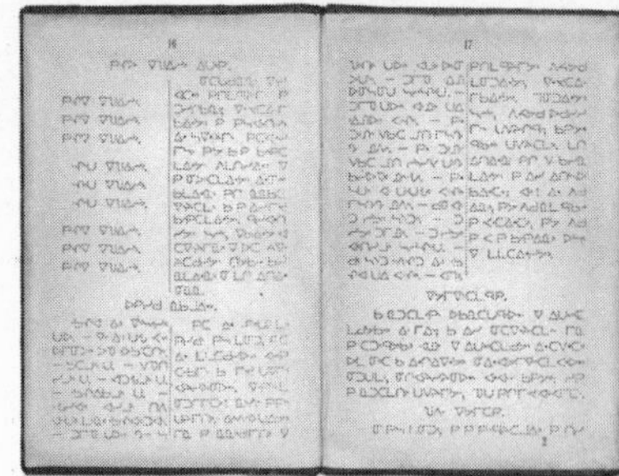

17 *Lestis, Deus Pater omni Potens, Domine Fili Unigenite, Jesu Christe Domine Deus, Agnus Dei, Filius Patris qui Tollis peccata mundi misere re nobis. Qui tollis peccata mundi suscipe depre cationem nostram qui sedes ad dexteram Patris miserere nobis. Quoniam tu solus Sanctus. Tu solus Dominus, To solus Altissimus, Jesu Christe cum sancto spiritu in gloria Dei Patris. Amen*

Have pity on us. You are the only God. You are the only Son of God. Lord Jesus, You rule everything. You came to take away our sins. Have mercy on us, Who takes away the sin of the world, accept our prayer. Free us from them. You can free some of us because You are supernatural. [in Latin:] You who sit at the right hand of the Father, have mercy on us, for You, alone are holy; You alone are Lord; You alone are the most high, Jesus Christ with the Holy Spirit, in the glory of God the Father. Amen.

WHEN ONE IS GIVING A PRAYER.

They will ask You for it. The clean spirits, speak for us. Give it to them the way they want it for you. Today they speak for us. He is going to make this true. Me too, I am part of the group. I am going to pray for them, my friends, my people, especially, for all to be strong. I listen to You. You satisfy us all, we are happy to see You well.

MY GOD, YOU MADE ME UNDERSTAND YOUR RELIGION.

You thought highly of me. There are many who do not

17 lestis teos pater omni
lestis teos pater omni

poteks. – tomine pili
poteks. – tomine pili

onisenite sesokriste. –
onisenite Sesokriste. –

tomine teos aknos tei
tomine teos aknos tei

pilios patris. – kwi
pilios patris. – kwi

tollis pekata mokti misere
tollis pekata mokti misere

re nopis. – kwi tollis
re nopis. – kwi tollis

pekata mokti sossipe tepre
pekata mokti Sossipe tepre

kasio nem nostram. – kwi
kasio nem nostram. – kwi

setes at testeram patris
setes at testeram patris

miserere naspic. – koni am
miserere naspic. – koni am

to solos saktos. – to
to solos saktos. – to

solos tomi nos. – to solos
solos tomi nos. – to solos

altisimos sesokriste. –
altisimos Sesokriste. –

kom sakto spirito in klo
kom sakto spirito in klo

ria tei patris. – amen.
ria tei patris. – Amen.

kitimakeyimiyan piyeyako
kitimâkêyimiyan piyêyako-

manitowiyan, weyotawi
manitowiyan, wiyôhtawî

mikawiyan. menitowiyan
mikawiyan. manitowiyan

sesos, piyeyako okosisi
Sesos, piyêyako okosisi

misk tepeyiciket; kakiyaw
misk (ê-)tipêyihcikêt; kahkiyaw

kekway tepeyitaman, maci
kîkwây (ê-)tipêyihtaman, maci

itiwina kici pe kasina
ihtiwina kici-pê-kâsîna

mawiyak ki isi itisao
mawiyahk ki-isi-itisahwêw

kawitay: aw! wi piko
kâwitay: aw! wî-pîkoh

inan, kiya pikonama kekway
inân, kiya pîko nama kîkwây

ki pwatawitan, kiya piko
kipwâtawihtân kiya piko

ki pa ki kaskiinan osam
kipâki-kaskihinân osâm

e mamatawisiyan.
ê-mamâtawisiyan.

EYAMIESTAMAKEKI.
AYAMIHÊSTAMÂKÊKI.

ka natotamaskik okanatacakwewok
ka-natotamâskik okanâtahcahkwêwak

e itwestamakoyakwaw wi miik; ka isi nitaweyitamask
ê-itwêstamâkoyahkwâw wî-miyik; kâ-isi-nitawêyihtamâsk

mina ki tatoskeyakan anoc e itwestamakoyak witapwetaw
mîna kitatoskêyakan anohc ê-itwêstamâkoyâhk wîtâpwêtaw

oma nista ka wiciiweyan ni wi ayamiestamawawok
ôma nîsta kâ-wîcihiwêyân niwî-ayamihêstamawâwâk

nitotemak, ni ci ayisiyiniwok wawac kakiyaw: soki
nitôtêmak, nîcayisiyiniwak wâwâc kahkiyaw: sôhki

ki natotamatin tepeyimiyak, nete kici miyo wapamitak.
kinatohtamâtin (ê-)tipêyimiyâhk, nêtê kici-miyo-wâpamitâhk.

LEPIT EYAMITAKI.
LEPIT AYAMIHTÂKI.

ni kise manitom, ki ki kiskeyitamoin ki tisi
nikisê-manitôm, kikî-kiskêyihtamôhin ki-tisih

18 know You yet. You are here. I am going to think positively of Your speech: I believe in it. It usually happens that you make it known that You are supernatural and that more is going to happen. I am glorified to love You, the Holy Spirit. I, too, wish to love You the way that clean spirits love You. The way that You were wanted a long time ago is the way I want You to have pity on me today.

READING THE GOSPEL.

You are kind, Jesus. Right now, the priest is reading Your words. In fact, I am standing that You be known, that I believe in You. On my forehead I make the sign of the cross, never to be ashamed of it. Your preachings are in my mouth, to be proud of prayers; to love it in my heart all the time. Reverently to keep Your word, especially the way that You want me to be, he is telling me: but evil is going to defeat me. Help me with this, to have a strong heart, to defeat evil. So let it be.

WHAT WE BELIEVE.

Credo in unum Deum Patrem omnipotentem,	I believe in one God, the Father almighty,

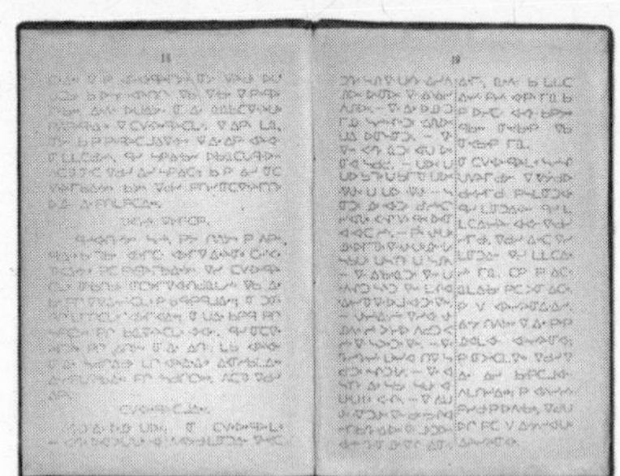

twawin e ki ayiwakeyimiyan niya eyikok ote kotakak ka
twâwin ê-kî-ayiwâkêyimiyan niya iyikohk ôtê kotakak ka

osam ayiticik eka eskwa e kiskeyimiskwaw. ispic oteiyan
osâm ayiticik êkâ cêskwa ê-kiskêyimiskwâw. ispic otêhiyan

ni wi nanakataweyiten kipikiskwein e tapwewokeyitaman.
niwî-nanâkatawêyihtên kipîkiskwêwin ê-tâpwêwâkêyihtamân.

e ikik mana, niyak ka ki kiskeyitamoiweyan e wi
ê-ihkik mâna, niyâk kâ-kî-kiskêyihtamohiwêyan ê-wî-

ikik ayiwak ni mamatakosin. kesi sakiiskwaw
ihkik ayiwâk nimamâhtâkosin. kêsi sâkihiskwâw

okanatacakwewok pitane nista ekosi isi sakiitan: ka ki isi
okanâtahcahkwêwak pitanê nîsta êkosi isi-sâkihitân: kâ-kî-isi-

nitaweyimikawiyan kayas ekosi kitisinitaeyimitin onoc
nitawêyimikawiyan kayâs êkosi kit-isi-nitawêyimitin anohc

wi kitimakitawin.
wî-kitimâkîtawin.

LEPAKSIL EYAMITAKI.
LEPAKSIL AYAMIHTÂKI.

kesiwatisiyan sesos, kiya tipiyaw ki pikiskwewin ka
(ê-)kisêwâtisiyan Sesos, kiya tipiyaw kipîkiskwêwin kâ

mekwa ayamitat ayamiewiyiniw tasipwa nepawiyan
mêkwâ ayamihtât ayamihêwiyiniw tâsipwâ (ê-)nîpawiyân

kita kiskeyimikawiyan esi tapwewokeyitaman
kita-kiskêyimikawiyan ê-isi-tâpwêwakêyihtamân

niskatikok ni tayamiewatikonamason eka wikac kici
niskâhtikohk nitayamihêwahtikonamâson êkâ wîhkâc kici

ni pe wisistaman ki kakeskikemowin; ni tonik kici
nipê-wisîstamân kikakêskihkemowin; nitônihk kici-

mamicitaman ayamiawin; ni teik kakike kici mamihcihtamân
ayamihâwin; nitêhihk kâkikê kici-

sakitayan kici kanaweyitaman wawac. kesi nitaweyimiyan
sâkihtayân kici-kanawêyihtamân wâwâc. kêsi-nitawêyimiyan

kici itiyan ni wi itik: maka ayiwak ni wi sakociikon
kici-itiyân niwî-itik: mâka ayiwâk niwî-sâkôcihikon

maci ayiiwin winisokamawin wisokiteeskawin kici
maci-âyihiwin wî-nisôhkamawin wîsôhkitêhêskawin kici-

sakocitayan. pitane ekosi ikik.
sâkôcihtâyân. pitanê êkosi ihkik.

TAPWEWOKEYITAMOWIN.
TÂPWÊWAKÊYIHTAMOWIN.

kreto in onom teom
kreto in onom teom

ni tapwewokeyimaw
nitâpwêwakêyimâw

–patrem omnipotektem pak
–patrem omnipotektempak

piyeyako manitowit weyota
piyêyako manitowit wiyôhta

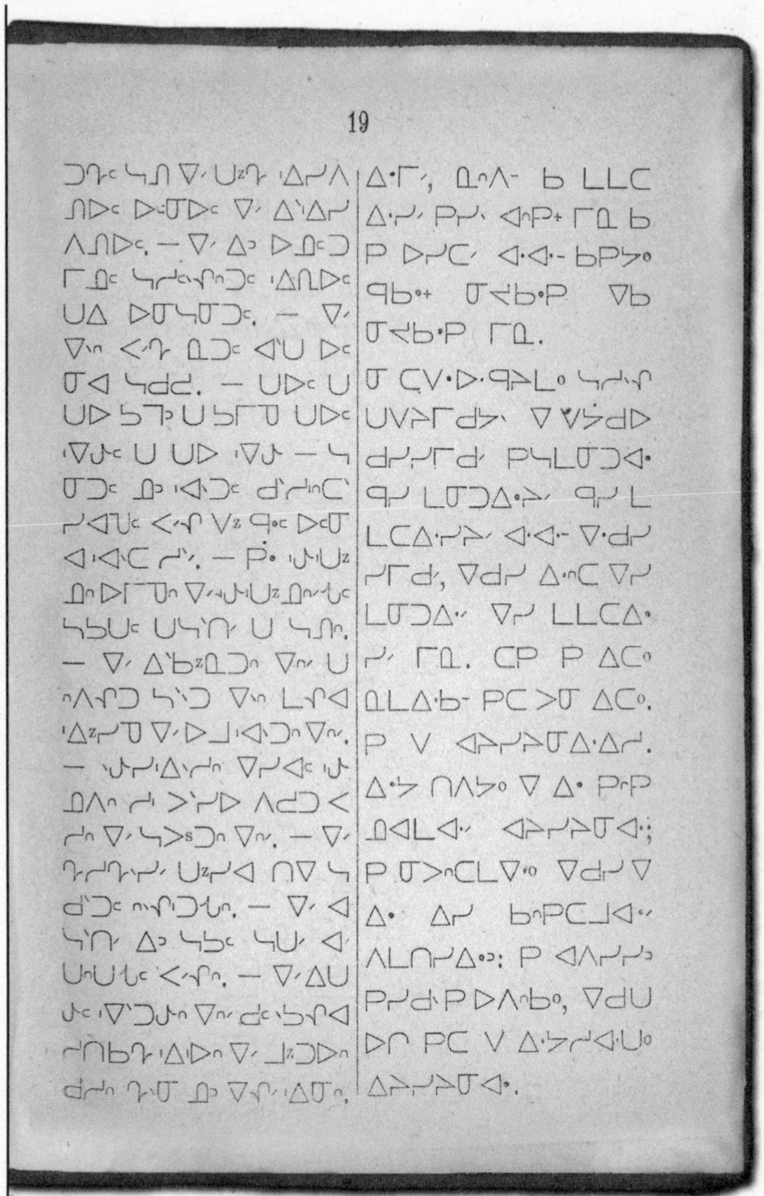

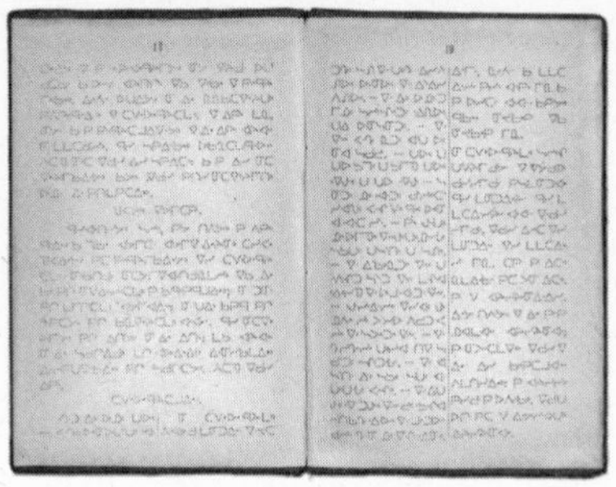

19 factorem caeli et terrae, visibilium omnium, et invisibilium. Et in unum Do minum Jesum Christum, Filium Dei unigenitum. Et ex Patre natum ante omnia saecula. Deum de deo, lumen de lumine, Deum Verum de Deo vero. Genitum non factum, consubstantialem Patri per quem omniafacta sunt. Qui propter nos homines et propter nostram salutem descendit de caelis. Et incarnatus est de Spiritu Sancto ex Maria Virgine et homo factus est. Crucifixus etiam pro nobis sub Pontio Pilato pa ssus, et sepultus est. Et resurrexit tertia die secundum scripturas. Et ascendit in caelum, sedet ad dexteram Patris. Et iterum venturus et cum Gloria judicare vivos et mortuos cujus regni non erit finis

Maker of Heaven and earth, visible and invisible, and in one Lord Jesus Christ, the only Son of the Father. God the supernatural was taken as a Son. He also is supernatural.This is what is being said about Him, and will always be said about Him. He became human. He, Himself, is going to teach the people. He died for them; He is going to obtain life for them. He rose to Heaven. He will judge the people. [in Latin:] He rose on the third day as the scriptures said and ascended to Heaven and sits at the right hand of the Father. He will come again in glory to judge the living and the dead and His kingdom will not end.

19 torem seli et tere pisipi
torem seli et terre pisipi

liom omniom et ikpisi
liom omniom et ikpisi

piliom. – et in onomto
piliom. – et in onomto

minom sesomkristom piliom
minom Sesomkristom piliom

tei onisenitom. – et
tei onisenitom. – et

eks patre natom akte om
eks patre natom akte om

nia sekola. – teom te
nia sekola. – teom te

teo lo men te lomine teom
teo lo men te lomine teom

perem te teo perem – se
perem te teo perem – se

nitom non paktom koksopstak
nitom non paktom koksopstak

sialem patri per kwem omni
sialem patri per kwem omni

apaktasokt. – kwi propter
apaktasokt. – kwi propter

nosomines et propter nostram
nosomines et propter nostrum

salotem tesektit te selis.
salotem tesektit te selis.

– et ikkarnatos est te
– et ikkarnatos est te

spirito sakto eks maria
Spirito Sakto eks Maria

wimit, naspic ka mamata
wîmit nâspic kâ-mamâhtâ

wisit kisik askiy mina ka
wisit kisik askiy mîna kâ-

ki ositat wawac kakiyaw
kî-osîhtât wâwâc kahkiyaw

kekway niyokwaki eka
kîkwây nôkwâki ekâ

niyokwaki mina.
nôkwâki mîna.

ni tapwewokeyimaw sesokri
nitâpwêwakêyimâw Sesokri

tepeyimikoyak e peyako o
(ê-)tipêyimikoyâhk ê-peyakô o

kosisimikot kise manitowa
kosisimikot kisê-manitowa

kesi manitowiyit kesi ma
kêsi-manitowiyit kêsi-ma

matawisiyit wawac wekosi
mâhtâwisiyit wâwâc wêkosi

simikot, ekosi wista esi
simikot, êkosi wîsta ê-isi-

manitowit esi mamatawi
manitowit ê-isi-mamâhtâwi

sit mina. taki ki itaw
sit mîna. tahki kî-itâw

namawikac kita poni itaw.
nama wîhkâc kita-pôni-itâw.

ki pe ayisiyiniwiiso.
kî-pê-ayisiyiniwihiso.

wiya tipiyaw e wi kiski
wiya tipîyaw ê-wî-kiski

pirsine et omopaktos est.
pirsine et omopaktos est.

– krosipiksos esiam pro
– krosipiksos esiam pro

nopis sop poksio pilato pa
nopis sop poksio Pilato pa

sos et sepoltos est. – et
sos et sepoltos est. – et

resoreksit tersia tie se
resoreksit tersia tie se

koktom skriptoros. – et a
koktom skriptoros. – et a

sektit in selom setet at
sektit in selom setet at

testeram patris. – et ite
testeram patris. – et ite

rom pektoros est kom kloria
rom pektoros est kom kloria

sotikare pipos et mortoos
sotikare pipos et mortoos

kosos rekni non erit pinis.
kosos rekni non erit pinis.

noamawat ayisiyiniwa;
nohamawât ayisiyiniwa;

ki nipostamawew êkosi e
kî-nipôstamawew ekosi ê-

wi isi kaskitamowat
wî-isi-kaskîtamawât

pimatisiwin: ki apisisin
pimâtisiwin: kî-âpisisin

kisikok ki opiskaw, ekote
kîsikohk kî-opîskaw, êkotê

oci kita pe wiyasowatew
ohci kita pê-wiyasiwâtêw

iyisiyiniwa.
ayisiyiniwa.

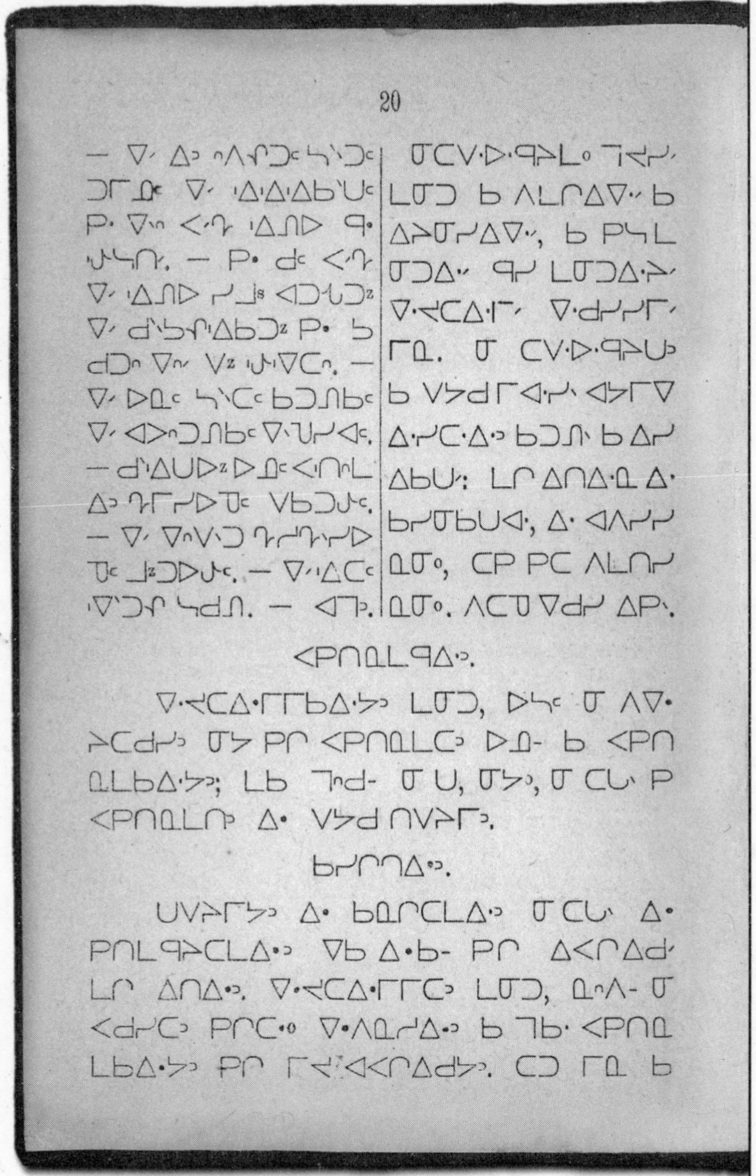

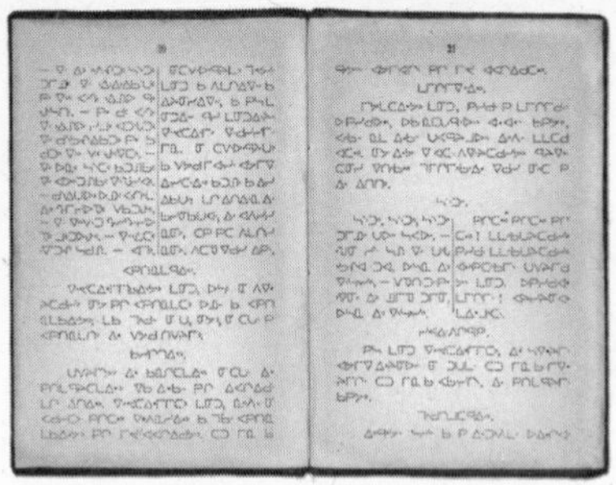

20	Et in Spiritum Sanctum Dominum, et vivificantem Qui ex Patre, Filioque Procedit. Qui cum Patre et Filio simul adoratur et conglorificatur qui locutus est per Prophetas et unam, sanctam, catholicam et apostolicam ecclesiam Confiteor unum baptisma In remissionem peccatorum Et exspecto resurrectio-Nem mortuorum, Et vitam venturi saeculi. Amen	I believe in the Holy Spirit, the Lord and giver of life, the Son who comes from the Father. I believe in one, good, holy Catholic Church. I believe in the forgiveness of sins. And I look for the resurrection of the dead. Forever there will be life. So let it be.

OFFERING.

You are my God. Because I am despised by others, I offer myself to You today. You are all-powerful, but in exchange, I give You my heart, my body, my spirit. For only You own me.

WASHING OF THE HANDS.

You satisfy me. Clean my spirit for me. Have pity on it never to be bothered by evilness. God, I greatly beg for it. It is holy to make a sacrifice right now. You are Lord.

– et in spiritom saktom
– et in spiritom saktom

tomi nom et pipipikaktem
tomi nom et pipipikaktem

kwi eks patre pilio kwe
kwi eks patre pilio kwe

prosetit. – kwi kom patre
prosetit. – kwi kom patre

et pilio simol atorator
et pilio simol atorator

et kokloripikator kwi lo
et kokloripikator kwi lo

kotos est per propetas. –
kotos est per propetas. –

et onam saktam katolikam
et onam saktam katolikam

et apostolikam ek lesiam.
et apostolikam ek lesiam.

– kok piteor onom paptisma
– kok piteor onom paptisma

in remi sionem pekatorom.
in remi sionem pekatorom.

– et espekto resoreksio
– et espekto resoreksio

nem mortoorom. – et pitom
nem mortoorom – et pitom

pektori sekoli. – amen.
pektori sekoli. – Amen.

nitapwewokeyimaw
nitâpwêwakêyimâw

meyosit manito ka
(ê-)miyosit manitow kâ-

pimaciiwet ka iyinisiiwet,
pimâcîhiwêt kâ iyinîsihiwêt,

ka kise ma nitowit kesi
ka-kisê-ma-nitowit kêsi-

manitowiyit weyotawimit
manitowiyit wiyôhtâwîmit

wekosisimit mina.
wêkosisimit mîna.

ni tapwewokeyiten ka
nitâpwêwakêyihtên kâ-

peyakomiwasik ayamie
pêyako-miywâsik ayamihê

wisitwawin katolik ka isi
wisîhtwâwin kâtolik ka-isi

ikatet: maci itiwina wi
yihkâtêk: macihtiwina

kasinikatewa, wi apisisi
kâsînikâtêwa, wî-âpisisi

naniw, taki kita pimatisi
nâniw, tahki-kita-pimâtisi

naniw. pitane ekosi ikik.
nâniw. pitanê êkosi ihkik.

PAKITINAMAKEWIN.
PAKITINAMÂKÊWIN.

weyotawimimikawiyan manito, osam
(ê-)wiyôhtâwîmimikawiyan manitow, osâm

ni piweyitakosin niya kici pakitinamatan onoc ka
nipîwêyihtâkosin niya kici-pakitinamâtân anohc kâ-

pakitinamakawiyan; maka meskoc ni te, niyaw, ni tacak ki
pakitinamâkawiyan; mâka mêskoc nitêh, niyaw, nitahcâhk

pakitinamatin wi peyako tipeyimin.
kipakitinamâtin wî-pêyako-tipêyimin.

KASICICEWIN.
KÂSÎCIHCÊWIN.

tepeyimiyan wi kanacitamawin ni tacak wi
(ê-)tipêyimiyan wî-kanâcihtamawin nitahcâhk wî-

kitimakeyitamawin eka wikac kici ipaciikot maci itiwin.
kitimâkêyihtamawin êkâ wîhkâc kici-âpacihikot macihtiwin.

weyotawimimitan manito, naspic ni pakositan
(ê-)wiyôhtâwîmimitân manitow, nâspic nipâkosîhtân

kicitwaw wepinasowin ka mekwa pakitinamakawiyan kici
kihcitwâw wêpinâsowin kâ-mêkwa-pakitinamakawiyan kici-

miyo apaciikoyan. tato tato mina ka
miyo-âpacîhikoyan. tahto mîna ka-

21 To be useful to You, many also pray properly. So may You also be useful to them.

WORDS OF PRAISE.

God in Heaven, the angels, the clean spirits, especially all of them praise You. On top of it all, never failing, these spirits are willing to praise You. I, myself, although I am despised as well, I too will say what they say to You, when they praise You.

SANCTUS.

Sanctus, sanctus, sanctus Dominus Deus Sabaoth Sanctus, sanctus Pleni sunt caeli et terra gloria tua, Hosanna in excelsis. Benedictus qui venit in nomine Domini. Hosanna in excelsis.

Holy, Holy, Holy Lord God, Amazing One, Heaven and earth are full of Your glory. He is blessed who comes in the name of the Lord! The people praise Him.

AT THE RINGING OF THE BELLS.

God, Father, my God, bless them, the priests, my friends, all the faithful, also those who hate me, have pity on them all.

THE CHANGING OF BREAD AND WINE.

At last, Jesus spoke to His friends.

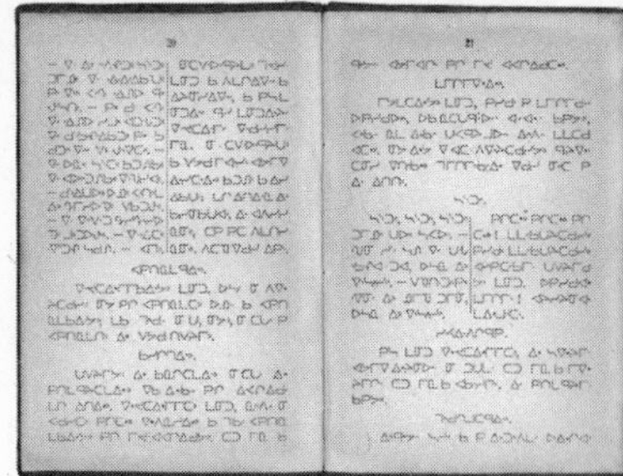

21 kweyask ayamiacik kici miyo apaciikotwaw.
kwayask-ayamihâcik kici-miyo-âpacîhikotwâw.

MAMICIMIWEWIN.

MAMIHCIMIWÊWIN.

miyomatawiyan manito, kisikok ki mamicimikwok
(ê-)miyomatawiyan manitow, kîsikohk kimamîhcimikwak

okisikowok, okanatacakwewok wawac kakiyaw, paskac
okîsikowak, okanâtahcahkwêwak wâwâc kahkiyaw, pâskac

nama wikac tepakeyimowok ispic mamatakoatwaw. niya
nama wîhkâc têpakêyimowak ispic mamâhtakohatwâw. niya

wiya e ota piweyitakosiyan keyiwek tanisi etiskwaw
wîya ê-ôta-pîwêyihtâkosiyan kêyiwêk tânisi êtiskwâw

memicimiskwawi ekosi nista ki wi ititin.
mamihcimiskwâwi êkosi nîsta kiwî-ititin.

SAKTOS.

SAKTOS.

saktos, saktos, saktos
saktos, saktos, saktos

tomi nos teos sapaot. –
tomi nos teos sapaot. –

pleni sokt seli et tera

pleni sokt seli et tera

kloria toa, osana in
kloria toa, osana in

ekselsis. – penetiktoskwi
ekselsis. – penetiktoskwi

penit in nomine tomini,
penit in nomine tomini,

osana in ekselsis.
osana in ekselsis.

kicitwaw kicitwaw kici
kihcitwâw kihcitwâw kihci

twaw! mamaskateyitakosiw
twâw! mâmaskâtêyihtâkosiw

kisikok
mamaskateyitakosiw
kîsikohk
mâmaskâtêyihtâkosiw

waskitaskamik tepeyimiko
waskitaskamik
(ê-)tipêyimiko

yak manito. okisikowa
yahk manitow. okîsikowa

mamicimik! ayisiyiniwa
mamihcimik! ayisiyiniwa

mawimostak.
mâwimôstâk.

SIYEWIPICIKEKI.

SIYÊWIPICIKÊKI.

kise manito weyotawimimitan, wi saweyimik
kisê-manitow (ê-)wiyôhtâwîmimitân, wî-sawêyimihk

ayamiewiyiniwok ni totemak tato mina ka miweyimicik
ayamihêwiyiniwak nitôtêmak tahto mîna kâ-miywêyimicik

tato mina ka pakwasicik, wi kitimakeyimik kakiyaw.
tahto mîna ka-pakwâsicik, wî-kitimâkêyimik kahkiyaw.

MESKOCEMOTAKEWIN.

MÊSKOCÊMOTÂKÊWIN.

iskweyac sesos ka ki witospimat owiciwa
iskwêyâc Sesos kâ-kî-witospimât owîciwâ

22 He took the bread. He was thankful this way. He shared it with apostles; like this He said it: "Take Me, eat Me, all of you, this is My body."

And He took wine also, He took it: it was in a Holy Cup. He was thankful. He passed it to the apostles. Also, He said, "take it, drink it, all of you, this is My blood."

PRAYERS OF OFFERING.

You are kind, Jesus. You really are God. And as I am a human, while being lifted I greet You and I respect You. And You truly show Yourself, You offer a sacrifice, here for me.

He gives Himself to you, that is in the Holy Cup; while it is being lifted I bow to it. He is God, the One, the only One who poured all His blood for me. Never will I forget His kindness.

My God, Jesus, on the altar it is right now I thank You. At this moment You are here, You have pity on me. Never will I forget that You died on the cross to save me. You are going to do a good deed for me, not to throw my spirit in the fire. I am amazed at how kind You are, because all over You are going to do good for me, even though

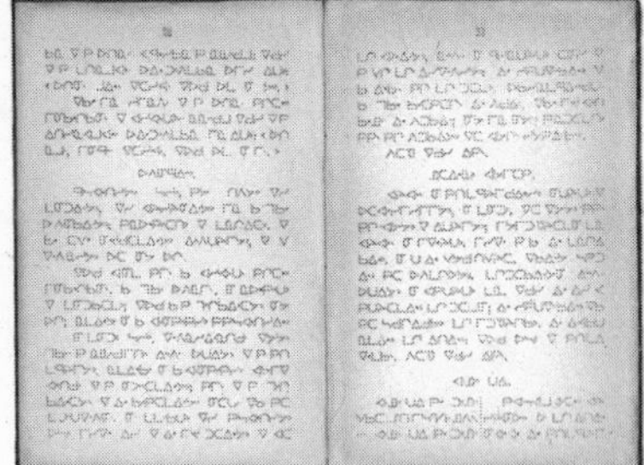

22 kana e ki otinat pakwesikana ki nanaskomo: ekosi e ki
kana ê-kî-otinât pahkwêsikana kî-nanâskomow: êkosi ê-kî-

matinamowat owitospimakana omisi itew: « otinik mowik
mâtinamawât owitospimakana omisi itêw: "otinik môwik

etasiyek eoko oma ni yaw. »
(ê-)itâsiyêk êwako ôma nîyaw."

ekwa mina sominapwi e ki otinak kicitwaw
êkwa mîna sôminâpoy ê-kî-otinahk kihcitwâw

minikwacikanik e asowateyik nanaskomo ekosi e ki
minihkwâcikanihk ê-asowatêyik nanâskomow êkosi ê-kî-

itisinaamowat owitospimakana mina itew: « otinamok,
itisinahamawât owitospimakana mîna itêw: "otinamok,

minikwek etasiyek, eoko oma ni mik. »
minihkwêk (ê-)itâsiyêk, êwako ôma nimihkok."

OPINIKEWIN.
OHPINIKÊWIN.

kesiwatisiyan sesos, kiya tipiyaw esi manitowiyan,
(ê-)kisêwâtisiyan Sesos, kiya tipiyaw ê-isi-manitowiyan,

esi ayisiyiniwiyan mina ka mekwa opinikawiyan:
ê-isi-ayisiyiniwiyân mîna kâ-mêkwa-ohpinikawiyan:

kinawokistatin e manaciitan. ekwa tapwe
kinawakîstâtin ê-manâcihitân. êkwa tâpwê

niyokotomawiyan ispiteyimiyan, e pe we pinasoyan ota
(ê-)nôkohtamawiyan (ê-)ispîhtêyimiyan, ê-pê-wêpinâsoyan ôta

niya oci.
niya ohci.

eoko anima kimik ka asowatek kicitwaw
êwako anima kimiyik kâ-asowatêk kihcitwâw

mi nikwacikanik, ka mekwa opinamik, ni nawokisten
minihkwacikanihk, kâ mêkwa ohpinamik, ninawakîstên

e manitokataman; eoko ka ki mescikawitayan niya oci;
ê-manitokâtaman; êwako ka-kî-mêscikawitayan niya ohci;

namawiya ni ka wanikiskisin ki kisewatisiwin.
namâwiya nika-wanikiskisin kikisêwâtisiwin.

ni manitom sesos, wepinasowinatikok eyayan
nimanitôm Sesos, wêpinâsowinahtikohk (ê-)ayâyan

mekwac ki nanaskomitin ispic oteiyan e ki
mêkwâc kinanâskomitin ispic otêhiyan ê-kî-

kitimakeyimiyan. namawikac ni ka wanikiskisin
kitimâkêyimiyan. namawîhkâc nika-wanikiskisin

ayamiewatikok e ki nipostamawiyan; kimik e ki
ayamihêwahtikohk ê-kî-nipôstamawiyan; kimik ê-kî-

mesci kawitayan e wi kaskitamawiyan nitacak eka kita
mêscikawitayan ê-wî-kaskîtamawiyan nitahcâhk êkâ kita-

macostewepinit. ni mamaskaten esi kisewatisiyan osam
macostêwêpinît. nimamâskâtên ê-isi-kisêwatisiyan osâm

misiwe isi e wi miyo totawiyan e ata
misiwê isi ê-wî-miyo-itôtawiyan ê-âta-

23 I am sinful. I regret that I behaved badly. Give me a strong heart, never to do any evil. You forgive our sin. Free those who suffer. I, too, I ask it of You, to take me into Your home where those ones who love You are. So let it be.

OUR FATHER, WHEN IT IS BEING READ.

I am pitied even more, I think. We are Your children. My Father, here You are in Your home. You are here, You think of me when I usually think even more that You be respected everywhere. My heart, You alone, govern it. You love to live within me. When one sins against You, You are there. I give up usually so I think You are going to give up on me. When I do evil, give me a strong heart so that it does not defeat me. The evil mind, take it, forgive me of sin because it is harmful. So let it be.

AGNUS DEI: LAMB OF GOD.

Agnus Dei, qui tollis peccata mundi, miserere nobis Agnus Dei, qui tollis

Lamb of God who takes away the sin of the people, have mercy on us. The way we obey You

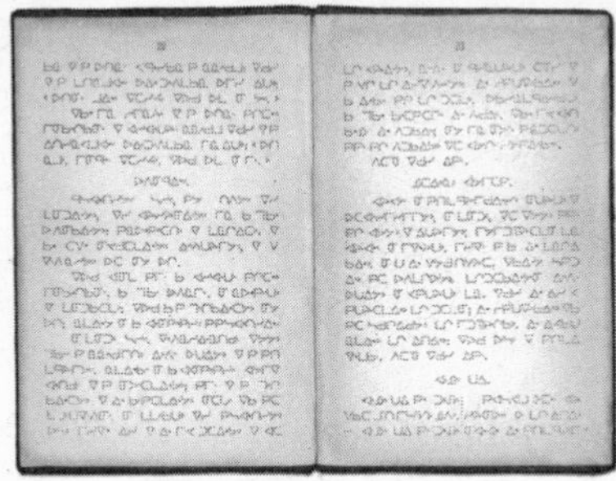

23 maci ayiwiyan, naspic ni kesinateyiten tanisi e ki peci
maci-ayiwiyan, nâspic nikêsinatêyihtên tânisi ê-kî-pêci-

maci isiwepisiyan: wi sokiteeskawin eka wikac kici maci
maci-isiwêpisiyân: wî-sôhkitêhêskawin êkâ wîhkâc kici-maci-

totaman. okasinamakewiskotek ka mekwa kwatakitacik
itôtamân. okâsînamakêw-iskotêhk kâ-mêkwa-kwâtakihtâcik

wi pikoik, ekwa miyowatikwanok wi pitokaik; niya
wî-pîkohik, êkwa miyowâtikanohk wî-pihtokwahik; niya

mina niyak kinatotamatin kikik kici pitokaiyan eta
mîna niyâk kinatohtamâtin kîkihk kici-pihtokwahiyan ê-âta-

ayacik siyakiiskwaw.
ayâcik siyâkihiskwâw.

pitane ekosi ikik.
pitanê êkosi ihkik.

NOTAWINAN AYAMITAKI.
NÔHTÂWÎNÂN AYAMIHTÂKI.

ayiwak ni kitimakeyimikowisin niteyiten e
ayiwâk nikitimâkêyimikowisin nititêyihtên ê-

otawasimisimimiyan, ni manitom, eta eyayan kikik kici
otawâsimisimimiyan, nimanitôm, âta (ê-)ayâyan kîkihk kici-

eyayan e iteyimiyan; miyomitoneyitamani mana ayiwak
ayâyan ê-itêyimiyan; miyo-mitonêyihtamani mâna ayiwâk

ni miweyiten. misiwe ki ka wi-maniciikawin. ni te
nimiywêyihtên. misiwê ki-ka wî-manâcihikawiyan. nitêh

wi peyakotipeyita, ekawiya sakitowin kita opimacioyan.
wî-pêyako-tipêyihta, êkâwiya sâkihitowin kita-opimâcihoyan.

macitotakawiyan ispic oteiyan ni pakiteyiten mana. ekosi
maci-itôtakawiyan ispic otêhiyan nipakitêyihtên mâna. êkosi

wi isi pakiteyitamawin maci totamani; wi
wî-isi-pakitêyihtamawin maci-itôtamani; wî-

sokiteeskawin eka kita sakociikoyan maci
sôhkitêhêskawin êkâ kita-sâkôcihikoyân maci-

mitoneyicikan. wi iyekatenamawin maci itiwin: eoko
mitonêyihcikan. wî-iyîkatênamawin macihtiwin: êwako

osam e kitimaiwemakak. pitane ekosi ikik.
osâm ê-kitimâhiwêmakahk. pitanê êkosi ihkik.

AKNOS TEI.
AKNOS TÊI.

aknos tei kwi tollis
aknos tei kwi tollis

pekatamoktimiserere
naspic.
pekatamoktimiserere nâspic.

– aknos tei kwi tollis
– aknos tei kwi tollis

kiaseamowatwaw, ayi
ki-âsêhamowatwâw ayi

siyiniwok o maci itiwi
siyiniwak omacihtiwi

niwawa wi kitimakeyimi
niwâwa wî-kitimâkêyimi

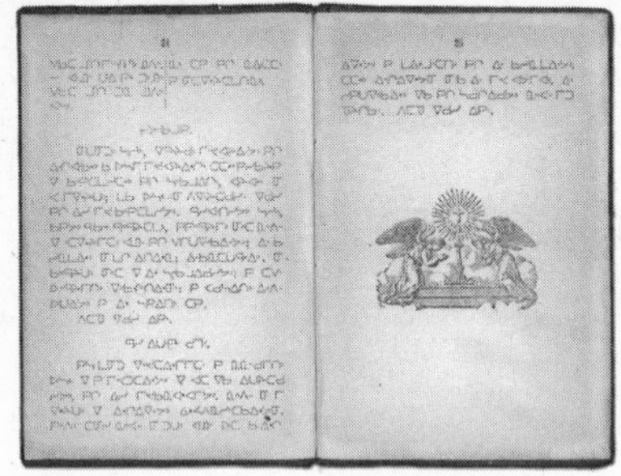

24 peccata mundi, miserere nobis Agnus Dei, qui tollis Peccata mundi, dona nobis pacem.

is the way we want others to obey You. Lamb of God who takes away the sins of the world, give us peace.

WHEN RECEIVING COMMUNION.

My God, Jesus, the holy ones earned it for themselves to receive Communion. Even more, I desire it. But, because I am despised I must earn goodness for myself. Jesus You are kind. You know everything, You know me also. I want to be with You forever. Forgive me my sins; clean my spirit. I am lonely. I am going to receive the Eucharist. I believe in You, in the Eucharist. I have hope in You. You are there, I am going to love You all the time. So let it be.

HOW TO PRAY THE MASS.

God, I thank You because You did good to me even though I am not worthy. You look kindly on me, forever; I like it that I am accompanying You when You are being offered as a sacrifice. If I have done something here today, be with me.

24 pekata moktimiserere nopis
pekata moktimiserere nopis

– aknos tei kwi tollis
– aknos tei kwi tollis

pekata mokti tona nopis
pekata mokti tona nopis

pasem.
Pasem.

nan taki kici naitatak
nân tahki kici-nahîtâtâhk

ki nitaweyitamatinan.
kinitawêyihtamâtinân.

SIYASKAMOKI.
SIYASKAMÔHKI.

ni manitom sesos, ekweyikok miyo ayiwiyan kici
nimanitôm Sesos, êkwayikohk miyo-ayiwiyan kici-

wiciwakwaw ka osami miyo ayiwicik tatwaw kisikayiki
wîcêwâhkwâw kâ-osâmi-miyo-ayiwicik tahtwâw kîsikâyiki

e kaskitamasotwaw kici saskamoicik, ayiwak
ê-kaskîtamâsotwâw kici-saskamohicik, ayiwâk

ni pamiweyiten; maka osam nipiweyitakosin ekosi kici
nipamiywêyihtên; mâka osâm nipiwêyihtâkosin êkosi kici-

isi miyo kaskitamasoyan. kesiwatisiyan sesos, kakiyaw
isi-miyo-kaskîtamâsoyan. (ê-)kisêwâtisiyan Sesos, kahkiyaw

kekway keskeyitaman, kikiskeyimin nista naspic
kîkwây (ê-)kiskêyihtaman, kikiskêyimin nîsta nâspic

e ntaweyimitan anoc kici peciteeskawiyan; we
ê-nitawêyimitân anohc kici-pêcitêhêskawiyan; wî-

kasinamawin ni maci itiwina; wikanatacakwein.
kâsînamawin nimacihtiwina; wîkanâtahcahkwêwin.

ni kaskeyiten nista e wi saskamoikosiyan:
nikaskêyihtên nîsta ê-wî-sâskamohikosiyân:

ki tapwewokeyimitin ewkaristiwinik: ki pakoseitin ispic
kitâpwêwakêyimitin ewkaristiwinihk: kipakosêhitin ispic

oteiyan ki wi sakiitin taki.
otêhiyan kiwî-sâkihitin tahki.

pitane ekosi ikik.
pitanê êkosi ihkik.

KESI ITWEKI LAMES.
KÊSI ITWÊKI LAMES.

kise manito weyotawimimitak ki nanaskomitin osam
kisê-manitow wiyôhtâwimimitâhk kinanâskomitin osâm

e ki miyototawiyan e ata eka iteyitakosiyan, kici isi
ê-kî-miyotôtawiyan ê ata êkâ itêyihtâkosiyan, (ê-)kici-isi-

miyokanawapamiyan. naspic ni mi weyiten e wiciiweyan
miyo-kanawâpamiyan. nâspic nimiywêyihtên ê-wîcihiwêyân

wiyepinasostakawiyani. kispin tanisi naspic ni toten anoc
wîyêpinâsôstâkawiyani. kîspin tânisi nâspic nititôten anohc

ota ka wici
ôta kâ-wîci-

25

ᐃᐁᐧᔭᐣ ᑭ ᒪᐃᐧᒨᐦᑕᑎᐠ ᑭᑎ ᐃᐧ ᑲᓯᓇᒪᐃᐧᔭᐣ.
ᑕᑕᐤ ᐃᐧᑎᐃᐁᐧᔭᑐ ᑐ ᑲ ᐃᐧ ᒥᔦ ᐊᔭᒥᐊᑊ. ᐃᐧ
ᓱᑭᑌᐁᐦᑲᐃᐤ ᐁᑲ ᑭᑎ ᓴᑯᑎᐃᑯᔭᐣ ᓇᐦᐸ-ᒥᑐ
ᑑᔭᑎᑲᐣ. ᐱᑕᑑ ᐁᑯᓯ ᐃᑭᐠ.

25 I will pray to You. Forgive me my sins. All the time, if You are with me, I will pray well. Give me a strong heart not to be overcome with a backsliding mind. So let it be.

[MONSTRANCE COPPERPLATE]

iweyan ki mawimostatin kici wi kasinamawiyan. tatwaw
hiwêyan kimâwimôstâtin kici-wî-kâsînamawiyan. tahtwâw

wiciiweyani ni ka wi miyo ayamian. wisokiteeskawin eka
wîcihiwêyani nika-wî-miyo-ayamihân. wîsôhkitêhiskawin êkâ

kici sakociikoyan naspic mitoneyicikan. pitane ekosi ikik.
kici-sâkôcihikoyân nâspic mitonêyihcikan. pitanê êkosi ihkik.

[MONSTRANCE COPPERPLATE]

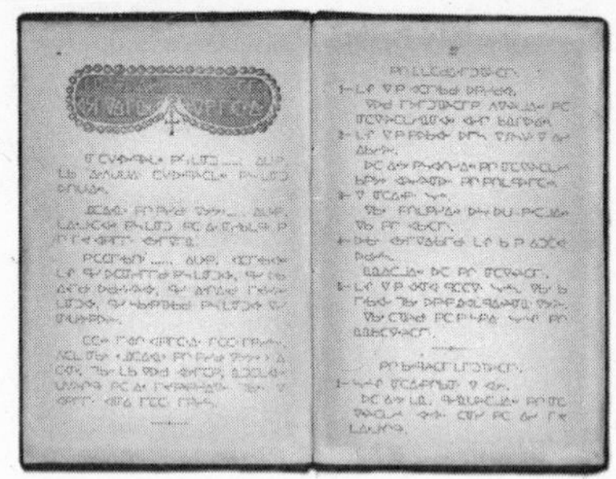

26

HOW TO LOOK AFTER AND COUNT THE PRAYERS [THE ROSARY]

I believe in God...... When this is said with all our heart we have belief in God's word.

Our Father in Heaven is where You are...... When this is being said, He is being prayed to. Go to help each other, to properly count the prayers.

I greet you...... When this is said, Mary is greeted. As a daughter, she took God as her son. She helps us. He is a good God, to fill Himself with the Holy Spirit. God is seen in three different ways—the Holy Trinity.

Each time we begin to recite the ten beads. First, before "Our Father in Heaven, You are here," is being said, ask God the One who owns us, to remind us of the fact right now, when we are reciting these ten prayer beads.

26

TANISI KICI ISI NANAKATAWEYITAMIK AYAMIEWIMINA EKIMITWAWI

TÂNISI KICI-ISI-NANÂKATAWÊYIHTAMIHK AYAMIHÊWINA AKIMIMÎTWÂWI

ni tapwewokeyimaw kise manito...... itweki, maka ispi
nitâpwêwakêyimâw kisê-manitow...... itwêki, mâka ispî

coteik tapwewokeyitaman kise manito otitwewin.
otêhihk (ê-)tâpwêwakêyihtaman kisê-manitow otitwêwin.

notawinan kici kisikok eyayan..... itweki,
nôhtâwînân kihci-kîsikohk (ê-)ayâyan..... itwêki,

mawimostawaw kise manito kita wi nisokamakek kici
mawimôstawâw kisê-manitow kita-wî-nîsôhkamâkêk kici-

miyo akimimit ayamiemina.
miyo-akimimît ayamihêwina.

kitatamiskatin...... itweki, atamiskawaw mari kesi
kitatamiskâtin...... itwêki, atamiskawâw Mari kêsi

otanisimimikot kise manitowa, kesi okawimikot
otânisimimikot kisê-manitowa, kêsi-ôkawîmikot

okosisiyiwa, kesi wiciwikot miyosiyit manitowa, kesi
okosisiyiwa, kêsi-wîciwikot (ê-)miyosiyit manitowa, kêsi-

sakaskineskakot kise manitowa esi nistweyakioyit.
sakâskinêskâkot kisê-manitowa ê-isi-nistwêyakihoyit.

tatwaw mi aci akimitawi mitatat mikisisak, pitama
tahtwâw mâci-akimimîtwâwi mitâtâht mîkisisak, pitamâ

nikan « notawinan kici kisikok eyayan » itwaniw,
nîkân "nôhtâwînân kihci-kîsikohk (ê-)ayâyan" itwâniw,

mekwac maka eoko ayamitaki, natotamawaw
mêkwâc mâka êwako ayamitâhki, natotamawâw

tepeyiciket kita wi miyokiskisoiwet mekwac e akimimit
(ê-)tipêyihcikêt kita-wî-miyo-kiskisohiwêt mêkwâc ê-akimimît

anii mitatat mikisisa.
anihi mitâtaht mîkisisa.

27

ᑭᒋ ᒪᒪᑕᑯᐃᐧᒥᑐᓂᔨᑕᒥᐠ.

1— ᒪᕆ ᐁ ᑭ ᐊᑕᒥᐢᑳᑯᐤ ᐅᑭᓯᑯᐘ.
ᐁᐅᑯ ᒥᔭᒥᑐᓂᔨᑕᒥᑭ ᐱᐁᐧᔮᒧᐃᐧᐣ ᑭᑕ
ᓂᑕᐁᐧᔨᑕᒪᓯᓇᓂᐊᐧᐣ ᐊᓯᒋ ᑳᓇᒋᐅᐃᐧᐣ.
2— ᒪᕆ ᐁ ᑭ ᑭᐅᑳᐊᐧᐤ ᐅᒥᓴ ᐁᓕᓴᐯᐟ ᐁ ᐃᓯ
ᐃᑳᓯᓯᔮᐤ.
ᐅᑕ ᐃᐧᔭ ᑭᓴᐊᐧᑎᓯᐃᐧᐣ ᑭᒋ ᓂᑕᐁᐧᔨᑕᒪᓯᐣ
ᑳᑭᔭᐤ ᐊᔮᓯᔮᓂᐅᐦ ᑭᒋ ᑭᑎᒪᑫᔮᒥᑕᐧᐤ.
3— ᐁ ᓂᑕᐃᐧᑭᐤ ᓴᓯᐣ.
ᐁᑳᐧ ᑭᑎᒪᑭᓯᐃᐧᐣ ᐅᓴᐨ ᐅᑌ ᑫᐧᑕᒧᐃᐧᐣ
ᐁᑳ ᑭᒋ ᐸᑳᐧᑕᒥᐠ.
4— ᐅᐢᑳ- ᐊᔭᒥᐁᐃᐧᑳᒥᑯᐤ ᒪᕆ ᑳ ᑭ ᐃᑐᑕᐊᐧᐤ
ᐅᑯᓯᓴ.
ᓇᓇᐃᑕᒧᐃᐧᐣ ᐅᑕ ᑭᒋ ᓂᑕᐁᐧᔨᑕᒥᐠ.
5— ᒪᕆ ᐁ ᑭ ᐊᐧᓂᐊᐤ ᑫᑕᑕᐁᐧ ᓴᓯᓴ. ᐁᑳᐧ ᑳ
ᒥᐢᑲᐊᐧᐤ ᒣᑳᐧ ᐅᑭᐢᑭᓄᐊᒪᑫᐃᐧᔨᓂᓇᐤ ᐁᔭᔮᐤ.
ᐁᑳᐧ ᑕᓂᔨᑯᐤ ᑭᑕ ᑭ ᓴᑭᐃᐤ ᓴᓯᐠᕆ ᑭᒋ
ᓇᓇᑳᑕᐁᐧᔨᑕᒥᐠ.

———o———

ᑭᒋ ᑳᐢᑫᔨᑕᒥ ᒪᒥᑐᓂᔨᑕᒥᐠ.

1— ᓴᓯᐠᕆ ᓂᑕᐃᐧᑭᒋᑳᓂᐠ ᐁ ᐊᔭᐤ.
ᐅᑕ ᐃᐧᔭ ᒪᓇ, ᑫᓯᓇᑌᔨᑕᒧᐃᐧᐣ ᑭᒋ ᓂᑕ
ᐁᐧᔨᑕᒪᓯᐠ ᐊᐧᐊᐧ- ᑕᓂᓯ ᑭᑕ ᐃᓯ ᒥᐸ
ᒪᐃᐧᒧᐢᒋᑫᐤ.

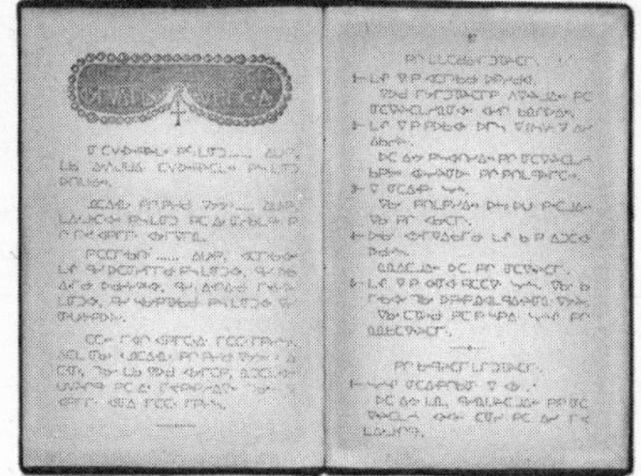

27 THINKING ABOUT THE GREAT MYSTERIES.

Annunciation	1– Mary was greeted by the angels. When we think of humility and purity, we will want to be cleansed.
Visitation	2– Mary visited her cousin Elizabeth. We want all the people to have her kindness and pity.
Nativity	3– Jesus is born; never hate poverty because of need.
Presentation	4– Mary took her Son to the temple. Listen to the way it happened.
Finding in Temple	5– Mary had suddenly lost Jesus. And when she found Him, while the teachers were there. He was in the temple teaching how much you need to love Jesus.

———o———

THINKING ABOUT THE GREAT LONELINESS.

Agony in Garden	1– Jesus is in agony. He expresses regrets. He shows us especially how to pray.

KICI MAMATAKOWIMITONEYITAMIK.
KICI MAMÂHTÂKO-WÎ-MITONÊYIHTAMIHK.

1–mari e ki atamiskakot okisikowa.
1–Mari ê-kî-atamiskâkot okîsikowa.

eoko miyamitoneyitamiki piweyimowin kita
êwako miyâ-mitonêyihtamihki piwêyimowin kita-

nitaweyitamasonaniwan asici kanaciowin.
nitawêyitamâsonâniwan asici kanâcihowin.

2–mari e ki kiokawat omisa elisapet e isi ikasoyit.
2–Mari ê-kî-kihokawât omisa Elisapet ê-isiyihkâsoyit.

ota wiya kisewatisiwin kici nitaweyitamasok
ôta wiya kisêwâtisiwin kici-nitawêyihtamâsok

kakiyaw ayisiyiniwok kici kitimakeyimitwaw.
kahkiyaw ayisiyiniwak kici-kitimâkêyimitwâw.

3–e nitawikit sesos.
3–ê-nihtâwikit Sesos.

ekwa kitimakisiwin osam ote kwitamowin eka kici
êkwa kitimâkisiwin osâm ôtê kwitamawin êkâ kici-

pakwatamik.
pakwâtamihk.

4–oskac ayamiewikamikok mari ka ki itotaat okosisa.
4–oskâc ayamihêwikâmikohk Mari ka-kî-itohtahât okosisa.

nanaitamowin ota kici nitaweyitamik.
nanahihtamowin ôta kici-nitawêyihtamihk.

5–mari e ki waniat ketatawe sesosa. ekwa ka miskawat
5–Mari ê-kî-wanihât kêtahtawê Sesosa. êkwa kâ-miskawât

mekwa okiskinoamakewiyininak eyayit.
mêkwa okiskinohamâkêwiyininak (ê-)ayâyit.

ekwa taneyikok kita ki sakiit sesokri kici
êkwa tanêyikohk kita-kî-sâkihiht Sesokri kici-

nanakataweyitamik.
nânâkatawêyihtamihk.

——o——

KICI KASKEYITAMI MAMITONEYITAMIK.
KICI-KASKÊYIHTAMI MÂMITONÊYIHTAMIHK.

1–sesokri nitawikicikanik e ayat.
1–Sesokri nihtâwikihcikanihk ê-ayât.

ota wiya mana, kesinateyitamowin kici
ôta wîya mâna, kêsinatêyihtamowin kici-

nitaweyitamasok wawac tanisi kita isi miyo mawimoscikek.
nitawêyihtamâsok wâwâc tânisi kita-isi-miyo-mawimôscikêk.

28

Scourging at Pillar	2–	Jesus is being scourged for me. I think about how the suffering will be used.
Crowning of Thorns	3–	The crown of thorns scratches Jesus's face. I look for humility.
Carrying of the Cross	4–	Jesus carried the cross on His back. I will ask God for something, how to give me encouragement.
Crucifixion	5–	Jesus was nailed to the cross. Like this He was treated poorly. Here I am completely sorrowful.

THINKING OF THE MOST HIGH.

Resurrection	1–	Jesus Christ comes back to life. I want to come back to life also.
Ascension	2–	Jesus Christ ascended to Heaven. I want to attain Heaven.
Descent of Holy Spirit	3–	The Holy Spirit entered the apostles. He wants the Holy Spirit to enter into one's body.
Assumption	4–	The angels took Mary, who was poor, into Heaven. We must be poor in a good way.

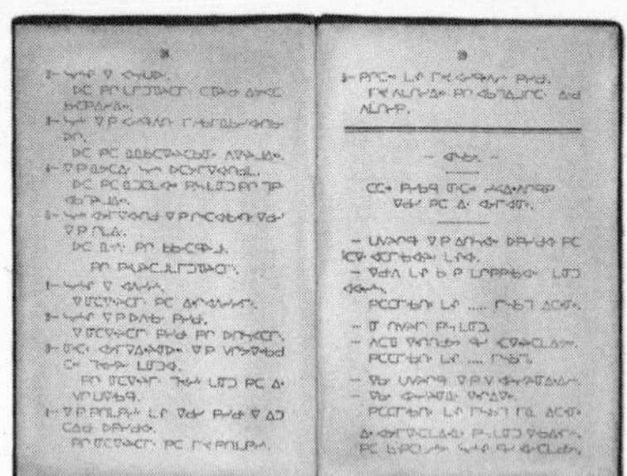

28 2–sesokri e pasasteot.
2–Sesokri ê-pasastêhôt.

ota kici mamitoneyitamik taneyikok iyapatak
ôta kici-mâmitonêyihtamihk tânêyikohk iyapatak

kwatakiisowin.
kwâtakihisowin.

3–sesos e ki pasikwepitit misokaminakasiwatikwa oci.
3–Sesos ê-kî-pasihkwêpitiht misokâminakosîwâhtikwa ôhci .

ota kita nanakataweyitakaniw piweyimowin.
ôta kita-nânâkatawêyihtakâniw pêwiyimowin.

4–e ki nayatait sesos etayamiewatikoma.
4–ê-kî-nayatahiht Sesos otayamihêwahtikoma.

ota kita natotamawaw kise manito kici mekit
ôta kita-nâtotamawâw kisê-manitow kici-mêkit

akameyimowin.
âhkamêyimowin.

5–sesos ayamiewatikok e ki cistaaskwatit ekosi e
5–Sesos ayamihêwahtikohk ê-kî-cîstahâskwâtît êkosi ê-

ki cimait.
kî-cimahît.

ota naspic kici kakwatakeyimok.
ôta nâspic kici-kakwatakêyimok.

KICI KISTEYITAMOMAMITONEYITAMIK.
KICI-KISTÊYIHTAMO-MÂMITONÊYIHTAMIHK.

1–sesoskri e apisisik.
1–Sesoskri ê-âpisisik.

e nitaweyitamik kita wiciapisisimit.
ê-nitawêyihtamihk kita-wîci-âpisisimît.

2–sesoskri e ki opiskat kisikok.
2–Sesoskri ê-kî-ohpîskât kîsikohk.

e nitaweyitamik kisikok kici otisapatamik.
ê-nitawêyihtamihk kîsikohk kici otisâpatamik.

3–nistam ayamiewiyiniwok e ki peciyaweskakotwaw
3–nistam ayamihêyiwiniwak ê-kî-pêciyâwêskakotwâw

meyosiyit manitowa.
(ê-)miyosiyit manitowa.

kici nitaweyimit meyosit manito kita wi
kici-nitawêyimit (ê-)miyosit manitow kita-wî-

peci teeskaket.
pêcitêhêskâkêt.

4–e ki kitimakisit mari ekosi kisikok e itotaikot okisikowa.
4–ê-kî-kitimâkisit Mari êkosi kîsikohk ê-itohtahikot okîsikowa.

kici nitaweyitamik kita miyo kitimakisik.
kici-nitawêyihtamihk kita-miyo-kitimâkisik.

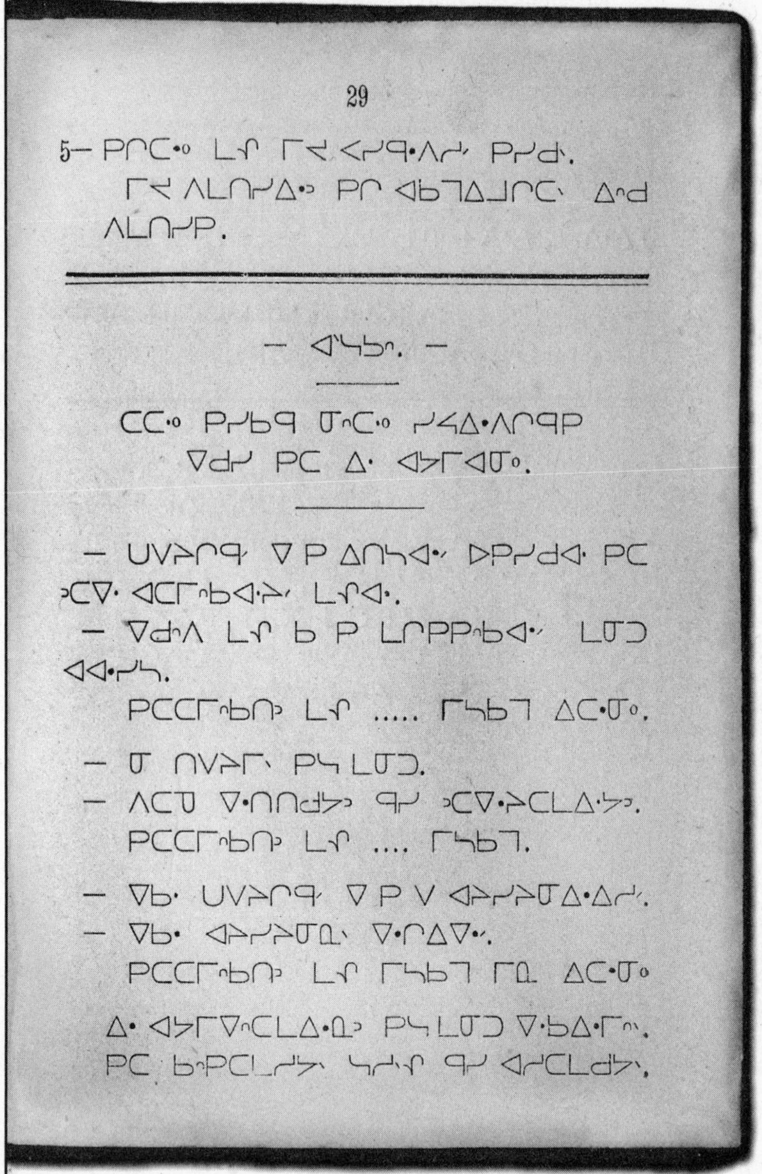

29 Coronation 5– Holy Mary is Queen in Heaven. She encourages good living as long as we live.

— ANGELUS. —

THREE TIMES, EVERY DAY, THIS IS HOW ONE WILL PRAY.

Three times, every day, this is how one will pray.	[in Latin:]
The owner of everything, He sent the angel to go and greet Mary.	The Angel of the Lord declared unto Mary.
And Mary conceived God's child.	And she conceived of the Holy Spirit.
I greet you Mary...All the time, everybody says it	Hail Mary...
God owns me.	Behold the handmaid of the Lord.
I wish His will be done the way you want it for me.	Be it done unto me according to Your word.
I greet you Mary...all the time	Hail Mary...Mother of God
And the One who owns everything became a human being.	And the word was made Flesh.
And dwelt among us. I greet you Mary. All the time, everybody says it. Pray for us Holy Mother of God that we may obtain the promises of Christ.	

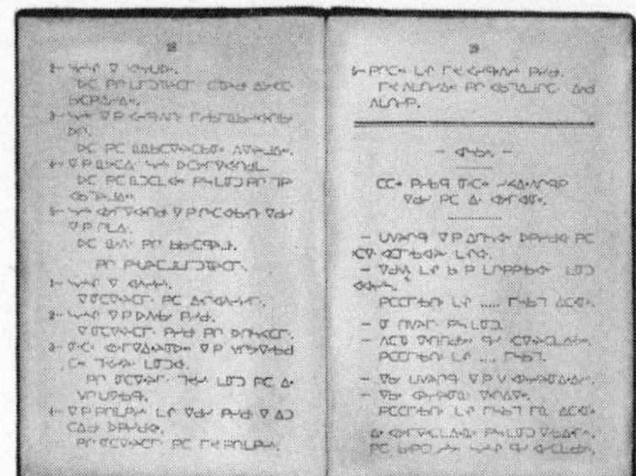

29 5–kicitwaw mari miyo pasikwepisot kisikikok.
5–kihcitwâw Mari miyo-pasihkwêpisot kîsikohk.

miyo pimatisiwin kici akameimocitak isko
miyo-pimâtisiwin kici-âhkamêhimocitahk isko

pimatisiki.
pimâtisiki.

kitatamiskatin mari misakame mina itwaniw wi
kitatamiskâtin Mari misakâmê mîna itwâniw wî-

ayamiestamawinan kise manito wekawimisk. kita
ayamihêstamawinân kisê-manitow wêkawîmisk. kita-

kaskitamasoyak sesokri kesi asotamakoyak.
kaskitamâsoyahk Sesokri kêsi-asotamakoyahk.

— AKSELOS. —
— AKSELOS. —

TATWAW KISIKAKE NISTWAW SIYEWIPICIKEKI
TAHTWÂW KÎSIKÂKI NISTWÂW SIWÊWIPICIKÊKI

EKOSI KITA WI AYAMIANIW.
ÊKOSI KITA WÎ-AYAMIHÂNIWIW.

— tepeyiciket e ki itisawat okisikowa kita ntawe
— (ê-)tipêyihcikêt ê-kî-itisahwât okîsikowa kita-nitawi-

atamiskawayit mariwa.
atamiskawâyit Mariwa.

— ekospi mari ka ki macikikiskawat manito awasisa.
— êkospî Mari ka-kî-mâci-kikiskawât manitow awâsisa.

kitatamiskatin mari..... misakame itwaniw.
kitatamiskâtin Mari..... misakâmê itwâniw.

— ni tipeyimik kise manito.
— nitipêyimik kisê-manitow.

— pitane wetitikoyan kesi ntaweyitamawiyan.
— pitanê wîtitikoyan kêsi-nitawêyihtamawiyan.

kitatamiskatin mari.... misakame.
kitatamiskâtin Mari.... misakâmê.

— ekwa tepeyiciket e ki pe ayisiyiniwiisot.
— êkwa (ê-)tipêyihcikêt ê-kî-pê-ayisiyiniwihisot.

— ekwa ayisiyininak weciiwet.
— êkwa ayisiyininak (ê-)wîcihiwêt.

30

ᐊᔭᒥᐊᑕᐠ.

ᐁᑲᐧ ᐁ ᑫᒋᓈᐅᔭᐠ ᓴᓱᐢᓯ ᐁ ᑭ ᐊᐦᐃᓱᐦ ᓂᐃᐧᐃᓯᐟ, ᐃᐢᐱ ᒪᕆ ᑳᑭᐊᑕᒥᐢᑲᑯᐟ ᐅᑭᓯᑯᐊ; ᑭ ᒪᐃᐧᔪᐢᑕᑎᓈᐤ, ᑌᐯᔨᐦᑫᔭᐤ ᑭᑕ ᐃᐧ ᓂᓯᐦᑲᒪᐃᐧᔭᐠ ᑭᑕ ᒥᒋ ᐅᑎᓴᐸᑕᒪᐠ ᐊᔭᒥᐁᐊᐧᑎᑯᐟ ᐁ ᑭ ᓂᐳᐦᑕᒪᑯᔭᐠ. ᐱᑕᓀ ᐁᑯᓯ ᐃᑭᐠ.

ᑭᑎᑕᐧᐤ ᒪᕆ ᑭᑎ ᐸᑯᓴᔨᒥᐤ.

ᓈᐢᐱᐨ ᐁ ᑳᓇᑕᐘᑫᐧᔭᐤ ᒪᕆ, ᐃᐧ ᑭᐢᑭᓯ ᐁᑲ ᐃᐧᑳᐨ ᒉᐢᑳᐧ ᐁ ᐯᑕᑳᐤ ᑭᑎ ᐁᑯ ᑭᑎᒪ ᑭᑕᐘᐤ ᐊᐃᐧᔭᐠ ᒣᐃᐧᒍᐢᑕᐢᑭ, ᐁᐅᑯ ᐅᑎ ᓂᐢᑕ ᐁᓯ ᒪᒥᓯᑐᑕᑕᐤ ᑭ ᓇᑕᒧ ᑐᑕᑎᐤ, ᐁᓯ ᑫᓯᓇ ᑌᔨᒥᓱᔭᐤ ᑫᓯ ᒪᑎ ᐊᔨᐃᐧᔭᐤ ᑭ ᐯ ᒪᐃᐧᒍᐢᑕᑎᐤ ᑭᑎ ᐃᐧ ᐊᔭᒥᐁᐢᑕᒪᐃᐧᔭᐤ. ᐁᑲᐃᐧᔭ ᐃᐧ ᐊᑕ ᐁᐧᔨᒥᐤ. ᐱᑕᓀ ᐁᑯᓯ ᐃᑭᐠ.

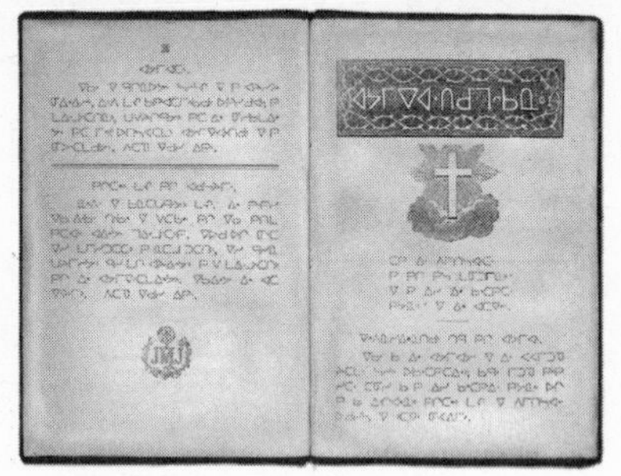

30 LET US PRAY.

We are certain that Jesus made Himself human when Mary was greeted by the angel. We pray to You, the One who owns everything, to help us together with her to attain salvation. He died for us on the cross. So let it be.

PRAYING TO HOLY MARY.

You gave me a clean spirit forever, Mary. Remember to have pity on everyone who prays to you. That is why I, too, trust in you. I ask it from you. I admit my bad ways but I am trying to change. I pray to you. Pray for me. Do not reject me. So let it be.

[JESUS MARY JOSEPH COPPERPLATE]

AYAMIATAK.
AYAMIHÂTÂHK.

ekwa e kecinaoyak sesokri e ki ayisiyiniwiisot, ispi
êkwa ê-kêhcinâhoyâhk Sesokri ê-kî-ayisiyiniwihisot, ispî

mari kaki atamiskakot okisikowa; ki mawimostatinan,
Mari ka-kî-atamiskâkot okîsikowa; kimawimôstâtinân,

tepeyicikeyan kita wi nisokamawiyak kita miyo
(ê-)tipêyihcikêyan kita-wî-nîsôhkamawiyâhk kita-miyo-

otisapatamak ayamiewatikok e ki nipostamakoyak.
otisâpatamâhk ayamihêwahtikohk ê-kî-nipôstamâkoyahk.

pitane ekosi ikik.
pitanê êkosi ihkik.

KICITWAW MARI KICI PAKOSIYEMIT.
KIHCITWÂW MARI KICI-PAKOSÊYIMÎT.

naspic e kanatacakweyan mari, wi kiskisi eka wikac
nâspic ê-kanâtahcâhkwêyan Mari, wî-kiskisi êkâ wîhkâc

ceskwa e petakwak kici eka kitimakitawat awiyak
cêskwa ê-pêtâhkwak kici êkâ kitimâkihtawat awîyak

mewimostaski, eoko ohci nista esi mamisitotatan
mêwimôstâski, êwako ohci nîsta (ê-)isi-mamisîtotatân

ki natamototatin, esi kesinateyimisoyan kesi maci
kînâtamototâtin, (ê-)isi-kêsinatêyimisoyân kêsi-maci-

ayiwiyan ki pe mawimostatin kici wi ayamiestamawiyan.
ayiwiyan kipê-mawimôstâtin kici-wî-ayamihêstamawiyan.

ekawiya wi ataweyimin. pitane ekosi ikik.
êkâwiya wî-atawêyimin. pitanê êkosi ihkik.

[JESUS MARY JOSEPH COPPERPLATE]

ᑖᑭ ᐃᐧ ᐱᒥᑎᓴᐘᑖᐠ
ᑭ ᑭᑦ ᑭᓴ ᒪᒋᑐᒥᓇᐤ
ᐁ ᑭ ᐃᔑ ᐃᐧ ᑳᐧᑕᑭᑕᐟ
ᑭᔭᓇᐤ * ᐁ ᐃᐧ ᐊᑕᐁᐧᐤ.

ᐁᐧᐱᓇᔑᐃᐧᓇᑎᔪᐠ ᑎᑫ ᑭᑦ ᐊᔭᒥᐋᐠ.

ᐁᑳᐧ ᑲ ᐃᐧ ᐊᔭᒥᐊᔮᐠ ᐁ ᐃᐧ ᐸᐸᒥᑐᑌ ᔮᑕᒪᐠ ᓴᔑᐢ ᐅᑳᐧᑕᑭᑕᐃᐧᐤ; ᑳᑫᐧ ᒥᑐᑌ ᑭᐢᑭ ᔨᑕᐠ ᑕᑌᔨ ᑳ ᑭ ᐃᔑ ᑳᐧᑕᑭᐃᐟ ᑭᔭᓇᐤ ᐅᑦ ᑭ ᑳ ᐃᐧᑎᐊᐧᓇᐤ ᑭᑦᑕᐧᐤ ᒪᕆ ᐁ ᐱᒥᑎᓴᐊᐧᐤ ᐅᑯᓯᓴ ᐁ ᐢᑕᐁᐧ ᑌᐸᐃᒥᐟ.

31

THE ROAD OF THE CROSS

[CROSS COPPERPLATE]

Follow it forever.
It shows us God,
the way He suffered
and brought us salvation.

THROUGH HIS SACRIFICE PRAYING ON THE CROSS.

And when we are going to pray we remember Jesus; His suffering. Try very hard to remember how He suffered for us. We will accompany Holy Mary as her Son was being killed.

31

AYAMIEWATIKOMESKANAW
AYAMIHÊWAHTIKO-MÊSKANAW

[CROSS COPPERPLATE]

taki wi pimitisawatak
tahki wî-pimitisahwâtâhk

ki kici kise manitominaw.
ki kihci kisê-manitôminaw.

e ki isi wi kwatakitat
ê-kî-isi-wî-kwâtakihtât

kiyanaw e wi atawet.
kîyânaw ê-wî-atâwêt.

WEPINASOWINATIKOK CEKE KICI AYAMIAK.
WÊPINÂSOWINAHTIKOHK CÎKI KICI-AYAMIHÂK.

ekwa ka wi ayamiayak e wi papamitoneyitamak
êkwa kâ-wî-ayamihâyahk ê-wî-papamitonêyihtamâhk

sesos okwatakitawin; kakwe mitone kiskisitak tanisi ka ki
Sesos okwâtakihtâwin; kakwê mitonê kiskisitâhk tânisi kâ-kî-

isi kwatakiit kiyanaw oci ki ka wiciwanaw kicitwaw mari
isi-kwâtakihît kîyânaw ohci ki-ka-wîciwânaw kihcitwâw Mari

e pimitisawa okosisa e ntawe nipaimit.
ê-pimitisahwât okosisa ê-nitawi-nipahimiht.

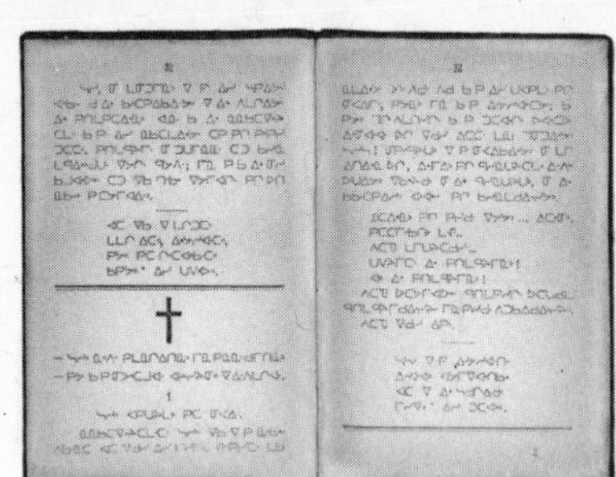

32 Jesus, our Creator, You loved us. Even as You are going to suffer, You are going to save us. You are going to have pity on us today; we must look after the way You have left us carefully. We should think greatly about You. Have pity on them, our friends, all of them, they are still suffering. Also, You will help them, every one of them who have not prayed to take Your religion.

Here He has done no evil
I cannot place judgement on Him
It doesn't matter, He will be crucified!
All of the crowd shout.

Jesus, forever we adore You. Also we thank You. You died for all the people to give them life.

I

JESUS IS CONDEMNED TO DIE.

Think about Him positively, Jesus, for He did not resist, even though like this He was betrayed. Let us remember

32 sesos, ni manitominan e ki isi sakiiyak paskac ko wi
Sesos, nimanitôminân ê-kî-isi-sâkihiyâhk pâskac ko-wî-

kwatakiikawiyan e wi pimaciiyak wi kitimakitawinan
kwâtakîhikawiyan ê-wî-pimâcihiyâhk wî-kitimâkihtawinân

anoc ka wi nanakataweyitamak ka ki isi
anohc ka-wî-nânâkatawêyihtamahk kâ-kî-isi-

nakatamawiyak taki kici kiskisitotatak. kitimakeyimik
nâkatamawiyâhk ta-kî-kihci-kiskisitohtâtâhk. kitimâkêyimik

ni toteminanak tato kasinamakewiskotek eyacik
nitôtêminânak tahto kâsînamâkêw-iskotêhk (ê-)ayâcik

keyapic; mina ki ka wi nisokamowawok tato eka ceskwa
kêyâpic; mîna kika-wî-nîsôhkamawâwak tahto êkâ cêskwa

eyamiacik kici otinakwaw ki tayamiawin.
(ê-)ayamihâcik kici otinakwâw kitayamihâwin.

---

ata eka e macitotak
âta ekâ ê-maci-itôtahk

mamaci itaw, wiyasowataw,
mamaci-itâw, wiyasiwâtâw,

kiyam kita cistaaskwataw
kîyam kita-cîstahâskwâtâw

kakiyaw isi tepwewok.
kahkiyaw isi-têpwêwak.

– sesos naspic kimanaciitinan mina kinanaskomitinan
– Sesos nâspic kimanâcihitinân mîna kinanâskomitinân

– kiya ka ki nipostamowat ayisiyiniw e wi pimaciat.
– kîyâ kâ-kî-nipôstamawat ayisiyiniw ê-wî-pimâcihat.

I

SESOS PAKITEYIMAW KITA NIPAIT.
SESOS PAKITÊYIMÂW KITA-NIPAHÎT.

nanakataweyitamwatak sesos eka e ki naskwat
nânâkatawêyihtamwâtâhk Sesos êkâ ê-kî-naskwat

pikwanata ata ekosi isi misimit. kiskisitak maka
pikwanata âta êkosi isi misimit. kiskisitâhk mâka

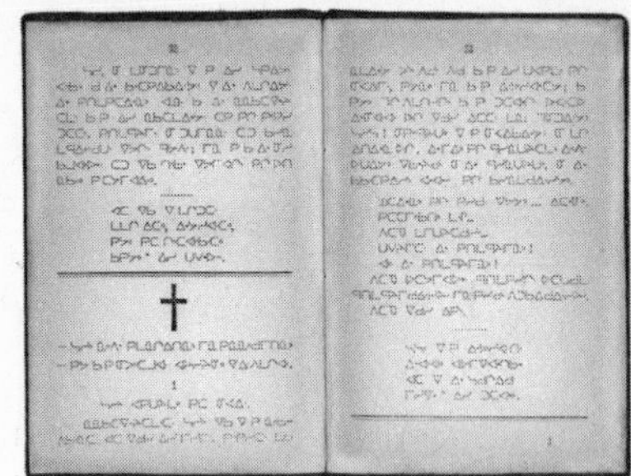

33 the words of Pontius Pilate. He counted enough of the crowd to kill Him. We also condemned Him, all of us who are living, because of our sins. You are supernatural Jesus. I know it. You were killed for my sins. Teach me how to be sorrowful. You are there, I am going to grieve greatly. I will sacrifice myself, especially to beg You to forgive me my sins.

Our Father in Heaven, You are there...
everybody says this.
I greet you Mary...
Glory be to God...
We are content with You. Have pity on us!
Oh, have pity on us!

I wish the Christians, those who are pitiful in His spirit, may have pity on Him, and also to enter into Heaven.

So let it be.

Already He is condemned
to be put on the cross.
Although it is going to conquer Him,
He accepts it.

33 namawiya poks pilat piko ka ki isi tepakimat kici
namâwiya Poks Pilat piko kâ-kî-isi-têpakimât kici-

nipaimit, kiyanaw mina ka ki wiyasowatayak; kakiyaw
nipahimiht, kîyânaw mîna ka-kî-wiyasiwâtâyâhk; kahkiyaw

meci pimatisicik ka ki totawacik opastaowiniwawa ohci
maci-pimâtisicik ka-kî-itôtawâcik opâstâhowinâwâwa ohci

ekosi itatak mana: menitowiyan sesose! nikiskeyiten
êkosi itâtâhk mâna: (ê-)manitowiyan Sesose! nikiskêyihtên

e ki nipaikawiyan ni maci itiwina oci, wimiin kici
ê-kî-nipahikawiyan nimacihtiwina ohci, wîmiyin kici

kesinateyitaman ispic oteiyan ekwayikok ni wi
(ê-)kêsinatêyihtamân ispic otêhiyan êkwayikohk niwî-

kesinateyiten, ni wi kakwatakiison wawac kici
kêsinatêyihtên, niwî-kakwâtakihison wâwâc kici

kasinamakowisiyan.
(ê-)kâsînamâkowisiyân.

notawinan kici kisikok eyayan... itwaniw.
nôhtâwînân kihci-kîsikohk (ê-)ayâyan... itwâniw.

kitatamiskatin mari...
kitatamiskâtin Mari...

pitane mamiteyitakosit...
pitanê (ê-)mâmitêyihtâkosit...

tepeyimitak wi kitimakeyiminan!
(ê-)tipêyimitahk wî-kitimâkêyiminân!

aw wi kitimakeyiminan!
aw wî-kitimâkêyiminân!

pitane otayamiawok ketimakisicik otacakoma
pitanê otayamihâwak (ê-)kitimâkisicik otahcahkoma

ketimakeyimikowisiyit mina kisikok pitokaikowisiyit.
(ê-)kitimâkêyimikowisiyit mîna kîsikohk (ê-)pihtokahikowisiyit.

pitane ekosi ikik.
pitanê êkosi ihkik.

---

sasay e ki wiyasowatit
sâsay ê-kî-wiyasiwâtiht

wiwaaw ayamiewatikwa
wîwâhâw ayamihêwahtikwa

ata e wi sakociikot
âta ê-wî-sâkôcihikot

misiwe isi totawaw.
misiwê isi tôtawâw.

34

— ᓴᓱᐢ ᓇᐢᐱ- ᑭᒪᓇᒋᐃᑎᓇᐣ ᒥᓇ ᑭᓇᓇᐢᑯᒥᑎᓇᐣ
— ᑭᔭ ᑲᑭ ᑌᐳᐢᑕᒪᐘ ᐊᐸᓯᐳᑌᐤᐁ ᐃᐧᐱᒪᒋᐘ.

2

ᓴᓱᐢ ᐃᐧᐊᐧᐊᐤ ᐊᐳᒥᐁᐊᐧᑎᑲᐧ.

ᐅᑕ ᒪᒥᑐᑌᐳᑕᑕᐠ ᑭ ᒫᑌ ᑐᒥᓇᐤ ᐁᐃᐧᐊᐧ
ᐃᐟ ᐊᐳᒥᐁᐊᐧᑎᑲᐧ ᑫᑎᓇ ᐅᓴᑦ ᒥᐢᑕᐁ ᑭ ᐃᐧ
ᓴᑫᐳᑕᑦ ᐁ ᑭ ᑲᑭᐢᑭᐃᐧᐸᐅᐟ ᐁ ᑭ ᐸᐸᓴᐢᑌᐅᐟ
ᐁᐳᐁᐤ ᑭᑌᐯᐳᒧ! ᑭᒋ ᐸᐧᐊᐧᑕᐃᐟ ᐊᐳᒥᐁᐊᑎᑲᐧ.
ᐳᔪᐢᐱᓯᔭᐣ ᓴᓱᐢ, ᓈᒪᐃᐧᔭ ᑭᔭ ᐊᑕ ᑭᒋ
ᐅᑌᑲᑕᐟ ᐊᐳᒥᐁᐊᐧᑎᐟ ᒫᑲ ᑌᔭᐣ ᐁᓯ ᐊᐳᐃᐧᔭᐠ
ᑌᐱᔭᐠ ᐃᐧ ᒥᐳᓇᐣ ᐯᔭᑎᐟ ᑭᒋ ᓇᔭᑕᒪᐠ ᑕᑐ ᑫ
ᑲᐧ ᐁᐳᒪᐠ ᐁᐧᑎᑎᑯᔭᑭ ᐊᐧᐢᑭᑕᐢᑲᒥᐠ ᐁᑯᑕ
ᐅᒋ ᑭᒋ ᑲᓯᓇᒪᓱᔭᐠ.
ᓄᑕᐃᐧᓇᐣ ᑭᒋ ᑭᓯᑯᐧ ᐁᔭᔭᐣ .....
ᑭᑕᑕᒥᐢᑲᑎᐣ ᒪᕆ...
ᐱᑕᑌ ᒪᒥᑎᐳᑕᑯᓯᐟ...
ᑌᐯᐳᒥᑕᐠ ᐃᐧ ᑭᑎᒪᑫᐳᒥᓇᐣ!
ᐊᐤ ᐃᐧ ᑭᑎᒪᑫᐳᒥᓇᐣ!
ᐱᑕᑌ ᐅᑕᓴᒥᐊᐅᐤ ᑫᑎᒪᑭᓯᒋᐠ ᐅᑕᑌᑯᒪ
ᑫᑎᒪᑫᐳᒥᑯᐃᐧᓯᐳᐟ ᒥᓇ ᑭᓯᑯᐧ ᐱᑐᑲᐃᑯᐃᐧᓯᐳᐟ
ᐱᑕᑌ ᐁᑯᓯ ᐃᑭᐠ.

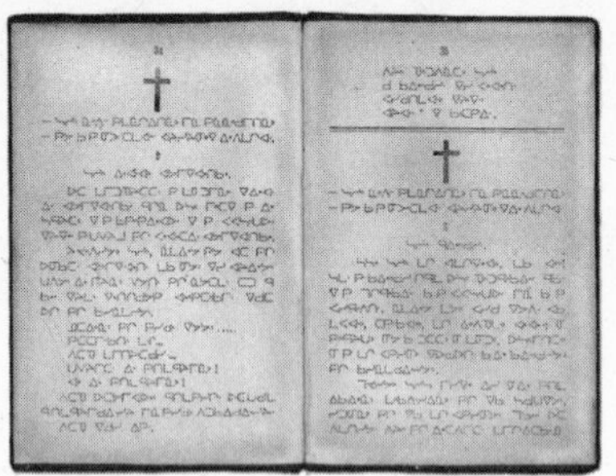

34

†

Jesus, forever we adore You. Also we thank You. You died for all the people to give them life.

2

JESUS CARRIES THE CROSS ON HIS BACK.

Here we think about You, our God. He accepted to carry the cross and He suffered terribly. He was whipped. He accepted it. He was heavily burdened with the cross.

You are gentle, Jesus, although You carry the cross on Your shoulder. Give it to us carefully, to carry it. Grant us the grace to carry our cross here on earth, for the forgiveness of our sins.

Our Father in Heaven, You are there.....
I greet you Mary...
Glory be to God...
We are content with You. Have pity on us!
Oh, have pity on us!

I wish the Christians, those who are pitiful in His spirit, may have pity on Him and enter into Heaven.

So let it be.

– sesos naspic kimanaciitinan mina kinanaskomitinan
– Sesos nâspic kimanâcihitinân mîna kinanâskomitinân

– kiya ka ki nipostamawat ayisiyiniw e wi pimaciat.
– kiya ka-kî-nipôstamawat ayisiyiniw ê-wî-pimâcihat.

2

SESOS WIWAAW AYAMIEWATIKWA.
SESOS WÎWÂHÂW AYAMIHÊWAHTIKWA.

ota mamitoneyitatak ki manitominaw e wi wait
ôta mâmitonêyihtâtâhk kimanitôminaw ê-wî-wâhît

ayamiewatikwa kecina osam mistae ki wi sakeyitam
ayamihêwahtikwa kêhcinâ osâm mistahi kî-wîsakêyihtam

e ki kakiskiwipaot e ki papasasteot eyiwek ki tepeyimo
ê-kî-kâkiskiwêpahôt ê-kî-pâpasastêhôt êyiwêk kî-têpêyimow

kici pwawatait ayamieatikwa.
kici-pwâwatahît ayamihêwahtikwa.

yiyospisiyan sesos, namawiya kiya ata kici onikatat
(ê-)yiyôspisiyan Sesos, namâwiya kiya âta kici-onikâtat

ayamiewatik maka niyan esi ayiwiyak tepiyak wi
ayamihêwahtik mâka nîyan (ê-)isi-ayiwiyahk têpiyâhk wî-

miyinan peyatik kici nayatamak tato kekway
miyinân pêyahtik kici-nayatamahk tahto kîkway

eyimak wetitikoyaki waskitaskamik ekota oci kici
(ê-)ayimak wêtitikoyâhki waskitaskamik êkota ohci kici

kasinamasoyak.
(ê-)kâsînamâsoyahk.

notawinan kici kisikok eyayan.....
nôhtâwînân kihci-kîsikohk (ê-)ayâyan.....

kitatamiskatin mari...
kitatamiskâtin Mari...

pitane mamitiyitakosit...
pitanê (ê-)mâmitêyihtâkosit...

tepeyimitak wi kitimakeyiminan!
(ê-)tipêyimitâhk wî-kitimâkêyiminân!

aw wi kitimakeyiminan!
aw wî-kitimâkêyiminân!

pitane otayamiawok ketimakisicik otacakoma
pitanê otayamihâwak (ê-)kitimâkisicik otâhcahkoma

ketimakeyimikowisiyit mina kisikok pitokaikowisiyit
(ê-)kitimâkêyimikosiyit mîna kîsikohk (ê-)pihtokahikowisiyit

pitane ekosi ikik.
pitanê êkosi ihkik.

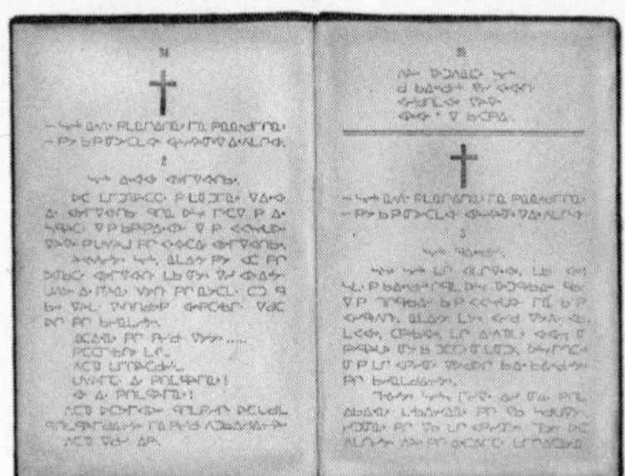

35 Eventually, Jesus falls under the blows.
He falls under the burden. He is burdened
heavily
by the weight. Nevertheless
He suffers even more greatly.

Jesus, we adore You forever. Also we thank You. You died for all the people to give them life.

3

JESUS FALLS.

Already Jesus begins climbing the hill. Immediately He fell under the burden because He is weak from loss of blood, and He lost all His blood when He was whipped and scratched on the face. As He gets up, still he strikes Him in the eye with a tool; he kicks Him; and on top of it all He is scolded. I know I did to You, my God, because many times I fell down badly. That is why You are going to fall under the burden, so that I will be forgiven.

You are good Jesus, everywhere. We are going to be treated badly. Make us strong, not to be cowardly. Strengthen us not to begin to fall right now. We long to live eternally and to be with You in Heaven.

35 piyis nestopinataw sesos
piyis nêstopinatâw Sesos

ko kawiskosot esi pwawatit
kô-kawiskôsot (ê-)isi pwâwâtiht

pasikotimawaw eyiwek
pasikotimawâw êyiwêk

ayiwak e kwatakiit.
ayiwâk ê-kwâtakihiht.

– sesos naspic kimanaciitinan mina kinanaskomitinan
– Sesos nâspic kimanâcihitinân mîna kinanâskomitinân

– kiya ka ki nipostamawat ayisiyiniw e wi pimaciat
– kiya ka-kî-nipôstamawat ayisiyiniw ê-wî-pimâcihat

3

SESOS KEWISKOSOT.
SESOS KAWISKÔSOT.

sasay sesos maci amaciweaw, maka ays! semak ki
sâsay Sesos maci-âmaciwêw, mâka ays! sêmâk kî-

kawiskoso cikema osam nestokwekawit kekac e ki
kawiskosow cikêma osâm nêstohkwêkawît kêkâc ê-kî-

mecikwekawit ka ki papasasteot mina ka ki pasikwepitit.
mêscikwêkawit ka-kî-pâpasastêhôt mîna ka-kî-pasihkwêpitiht.

namawiya mayaw pasiko eyapic pakamapawaw,
namâwiya mayaw pasikow êyâpic pakamâpahwâw,

takiskawaw, maci ispinemaw wawac; ni kiskeyiten niya ka
tahkiskawâw, maci-ispinêmâw wâwâc; nikiskêyihtên niya ka-

totatan ni manitom, osam micetwaw ni ki maci pakisinin
itôtatân nimanitôm, osâm mihcêtwâw nikî-mâci-pahkisinin

eokooci ka wi kawiskosoyan kici kasinamakowisiyan.
êwakohci kâ-wî-kawiskosiyan kici (ê-)kâsînamâkowisiyân.

meyosiyan sesose misiwe isi ni wi kitimaikawinan
(ê-)miyosiyan Sesose misiwê isi niwî-kitimahikawinân

maskawisiinan kici eka sakoteeyak, sitoninan kici eka
maskawisihinân kici- êkâ sâkôtêhêyahk, sîtoninân kici êkâ

maci pakisiniyak mekwac ota pimatisiyak piyis kici
mâci-pahkisiniyâhk mêkwâc ôta pimâtisiyâhk piyis kici-

witapimitak mamiciitakwana
wît-apimitâhk mamihcihitakwâna

36

ᑐᑕᐃᐧᑎᐣ ᑭᑎ ᑭᓯᑯᐠ ᐁᔭᔭᐣ...
ᑭᑕᑕᒥᐢᑲᑎᐣ ᒪᕆ...
ᐱᑕᕓ ᒪᒥᑌᔨᑕᑯᓯᐟ ᐁᐧᔦᑕᐃᐧᒥᐟ..
ᑌᐯᔨᒥᑕᐠ, ᐃᐧ ᑭᑎᒪᑫᔨᒥᑎᐣ!
ᐊᐤ ᐃᐧ ᑭᑎᒪᑫᔨᒥᑎᐣ!
ᐱᑕᕓ ᐅᑕᔭᒥᐊᐅᐦ ᑫᑎᒪᑭᓯᑎᐠ ᐅᑕᑌᑯᒪ ᑫᑎᒪᑫᔨᒥᑯᐃᐧᓯᔨᐟ ᒥᑎ ᑭᓯᑯᐠ ᐱᑐᑲᐃᑯᐃᐧᓯᔨᐟ
ᐱᑕᕓ ᐁᑯᓯ ᐃᑭᐠ.

ᒣᑳᐧ- ᐁ ᐃᓯ ᑭᑎᒪᐃᐟ
ᐋᐧᐋᐧ- ᐁ ᐸᐸᑲᒪᐸᐅᐟ
ᓭᓱᐢ ᐅᑲᐃᐧᔭ ᐋᐧᐸᒣᐤ
ᒪᕆᐊᐤ * ᐁ ᑎᑭᐢᑲᑯᐟ.

— ᓭᓱᐢ ᑎᐢᐱ- ᑭᒪᑎᑦᐃᑎᑎᐣ ᒥᑎ ᑭᑎᑎᐢᑯᒥᑎᑎᐣ
— ᑭᔭ ᑲ ᑭ ᑏᐳᐢᑕᒪᐋᐧ ᐊᔨᓯᔨᑏᐤ ᐁᐃᐧᐱᒪᕆᐊᐟ.

4

ᓭᓱᐢ ᐅᑲᐃᐧᔭ ᑎᑭᐢᑲᐁᐧᐤ.

ᓭᓱᐢ ᐁ ᑭ ᐸᓯᑯᐟ ᐊᑌ ᐱᒧᑌᐤ ᑲ ᑎᑭᐢᑲᐋᐧ ᐅᑲᐃᐧᔭ ᐁᑯᑕ ᑭ ᐃᐢᐸᔨᐤ ᑭᑎ ᑲᐢᑫᔨᑕᒧᐃᐧᐣ, ᓭᓱᐢ ᒪᕆ ᒥᑎ ᒧᐢᑯᐋᐧᐃᑐᐅᐦ ᐁ ᐋᐧᐸᑐᑎᐠ ᐁ

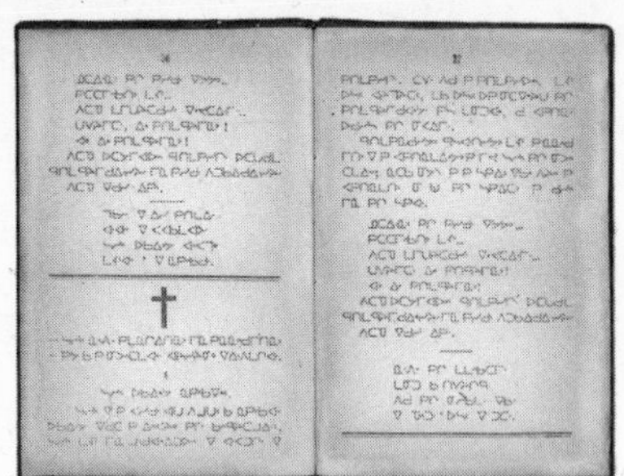

36 Our Father in Heaven, You are there...
I greet you Mary...
Glory to God the Father...
We are content with You. Have pity on us!
Oh, have pity on us!

I wish the Christians, those who are pitiful in His spirit, may have pity on Him and enter into Heaven.

So let it be.

Right now He is being treated poorly.
Especially beaten.
Jesus sees His mother
Mary. She meets Him.

Jesus forever we adore You. Also we thank You. You died for all the people to give them life.

4

JESUS MEETS HIS MOTHER.

Jesus rose, and proceeded to walk when He met her. His mother was overcome with sorrow and loneliness. Jesus and Mary cried for each other when they saw each other.

36 notawinan kici kisikok eyayan...
nôhtâwînân kihci-kîsikohk (ê-)ayâyan...

kitatamiskatin mari...
kitatamiskâtin Mari...

pitane mamiteyitakosit weyotawimit...
pitanê (ê-)mâmitêyihtâkosit wiyôhtâwîmit...

tepeyimitak, wi kitimakeyiminan!
(e-)tipêyimitâhk, wî-kitimâkêyiminân!

aw wi kitimakeyiminan!
aw! wî-kitimâkêyiminân!

pitane otayamiawok ketimakisicik
pitanê otayamihâwak (ê-)kitimakisicik

otacakoma ketimakeyimikowisiyit mina kisikok
otâhcahkoma (ê-)kitimâkêyimikowisiyit mîna kîsikohk

pitokaikowisiyit
(ê-)pihtokahikowisiyit

pitane ekosi ikik.
pitanê êkosi ihkik.

---

mekwac e isi kitimait
mêkwâc ê-isi-kitimahît

wawac e papakamapaot
wâwâc ê-pâpakamapahôt

sesos okawiya wapamew
Sesos okâwiya wâpamêw

mariwa e nakiskakot.
Mariwa ê-nakiskâkot.

– sesos naspic kimanaciitinan mina kinanaskomitinan
– Sesos nâspic kimanâcihitinân mîna kinanâskomitinân

– kiya ka ki nipostamawat ayisiyiniw e wi pimaciat.
– kiya kâ-kî-nipôstamawat ayisiyiniw ê-wî-pimâcihat.

4

SESOS OKAWIYA NAKISKAWEW.
SESOS OKÂWIYA NAKISKAWÊW.

sesos e ki pasikot ote pimotew ka nakiskawat okawiya
Sesos ê-kî-pasikôt ôtê pimohtêw kâ-nakiskawât okâwiya

ekota ki ispayiw kici kaskeyitamowin, sesos mari mina
êkota kî-ispayiw kihci kaskêyihtamowin, Sesos Mari mîna

moskowaitowok e wapatocik
môskowâhkatisowak ê-wâpahtocik

37

ᑭᑎᒪᑭᓯᒋᐠ. ᑕᐯᐧ ᐱᑯ ᑭ ᑭᑎᒪᑭᓯᐅᐧᐠ. ᒪᕆ
ᐅᓴᐦ ᐊᐳᒣᐳᑕᐦ, ᒫᑲ ᐅᓴᐦ ᐅᑭ ᓃᑕᐁᐧᔮᑌ ᑭᒋ
ᑭᑎᒪᑫᔮᒥᑯᐊᐧᓯᐠ ᑭᓴ ᒪᓃᑐᐊᐧ, ᑯ ᐸᑭᑎᓇᐤ
ᐅᑯᓯᓴ ᑭᒋ ᓂᐸᐃᒥᐤ.

ᑫᑎᒪᑭᓇᑯᓯᔾ ᑫᓴᐋᐧᑎᓯᔾ ᒪᕆ ᑭᓇᓇᐢᑯ
ᒥᑎᔾ ᐁ ᑭ ᐸᑭᑎᓇᒪᐃᐧᔾ ᑭ ᒥᔦ ᓴᓯᐢ ᑭᒋ ᓂᐳᐢ
ᑕᒪᐃᐧᐟ; ᓇᑕᑲ ᓂᔭᐠ ᑭ ᑭ ᓴᑭᐃᐧ ᐁᑲᐧ ᐱᔮᐢ ᑭ
ᐸᑭᑎᓇᒪᑎᔾ ᓂ ᐗ ᑭᒋ ᓴᑭᐃᑕᐧ ᑭ ᑯᓯᐢ
ᒥᓇ ᑭᒋ ᓴᑭᐊᐤ.

ᓄᑕᐃᐧᓇᐧ ᑭᒋ ᑭᓯᑯᐤ ᐁᔮᔭᐧ...
ᑭᑕᑕᒥᐢᑲᑎᐧ ᒪᕆ...
ᐱᑕᑌ ᒪᒥᑐᔮᑕᑯᓯᐤ ᐁᐧᔦᑕᐃᐧᒥᐤ...
ᑐᐯᔮᒥᑕᐤ ᐃᐧ ᑭᑎᑫᔮᒥᓇᐧ!
ᐊᐧ ᐃᐧ ᑭᑎᒪᑫᔮᒥᓇᐧ!

ᐱᑕᑌ ᐅᑕᔭᒥᐊᐅᐧᐠ ᑫᑎᒪᑭᓯᒋᐤ ᐅᑕᑐᑯᒪ
ᑫᑎᒪᑫᔮᒥᑯᐃᐧᓯᔮᐤ ᒥᓇ ᑭᓯᑯᐤ ᐱᒋᑲᐃᑯᐃᐧᓯᔮᐤ
ᐱᑕᑌ ᐁᑯᓯ ᐃᑭᐠ.

ᓇᐢᐱᐨ ᑭᒋ ᒪᒪᐢᑲᑕᒥᐤ
ᒪᓂᑐ ᑲ ᑎᐯᔨᒋᑫᐤ
ᐱᑯ ᑭᒋ ᓂᔦᑲᒪᐤ ᐁᑲᐧ
ᐁ ᑌᐢᑐᐤ * ᐅᓴᐦ ᐁ ᑐᑕᐤ.

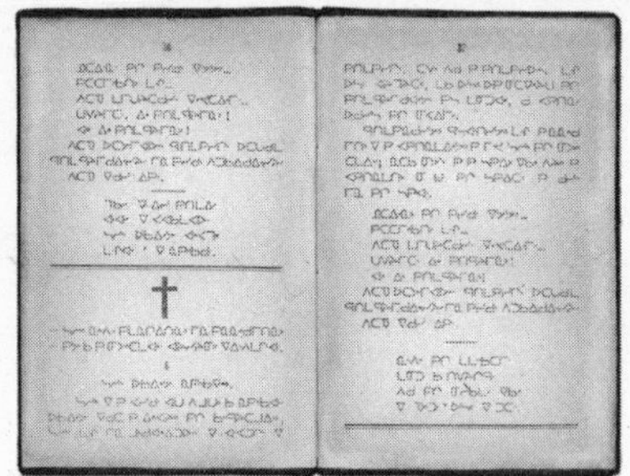

37 They are pitiful, truly they were pitiful. Mary knows it is difficult. But because she was pitied by God she can have compassion to intercede for us all.

You are beautiful. You are kind. Mary, we thank you. Your son, Holy Jesus, died for me. You did love me and finally I allowed you into my heart. Teach me how to love you and Your Son.

Our Father, You are in Heaven...
I greet you Mary...
Glory to God the Father...
We are content with You. Have pity on us!
Oh, have pity on us!

I wish the Christians, those who are pitiful in His spirit, may have pity on Him and enter into Heaven.

So let it be.

Forever, we will be amazed by it, that
Jesus, who owns everything,
Must be helped to carry the cross.
He is tired because of what is done to Him.

37 e kitimakisicik. tapwe piko ki kitimakisiwaok. mari osam
ê-kitimâkisicik. tâpwê piko kî-kitimâkisiwak. Mari osâm

ayimeyitam, maka osam okinitaweyite kici
âyimêyihtam, mâka osâm ê-kî-nitawêyihtahk kici

kitimakeyimikowayak kise manitowa, ko pakitinat okosisa
(ê-)kitimâkêyimikowâyahk kisê-manitowa, kô-pakitinât okosisa

kici nipaimit.
kici nipahimiht.

ketimakinakosiyan kesewatisiyan mari
(ê-)kitimâkinâkosiyan (ê-)kisêwâtisiyan Mari

kinanaskomitin e ki pakitinamawiyan ki miyo sesos kici
kinanâskomitin ê-kî-pakitinamawiyan ki-miyo-Sesos kici-

nipostamawit; nataka niyak ki ki sakiin ekwa piyis
nipôstamawit; nataka nîyak kikî-sâkihin êkwa piyis

ki pakitinamatin ni te kici sakiitan ki kosis mina kici
kipakitinamâtin nitêh kici-sâkihitân kikosis mîna kici

sakiak.
sâkihak.

notawinan kici kisikok eyayan...
nôhtâwînân kihci-kîsikohk (ê-)ayâyan...

kitatamiskatin mari...
kitatamiskâtin Mari...

pitane mamiteyitakosit weyotawimit...
pitanê (ê-)mâmitêyihtâkosit wiyôhtâwîmit...

tepeyimitak wi kitikeyiminan!
(ê-)tipêyimitahk wî-kitimâkêyiminân!

aw wi kitimakeyiminan!
aw wî-kitimâkêyiminân!

pitane otayamiawok ketimakisicik otacakoma
pitane otayamihâwak (ê-)kitimâkisicik otâhcahkoma

ketimakeyimikowisiyit mina kisikok pitokaikowisiyit
(ê-)kitimâkêyimikowisiyit mîna kîsikohk (ê-)pihtokahikowisiyit

pitane ekosi ikik.
pitanê êkosi ihkik.

---

naspic kici mamaskatamik
nâspic kici-mâmaskâtamihk

manito ka tipeyiciket
manitow kâ-tipêyihcikêt

piko kici nisokamat ekwa
piko kici-nîsôhkamât êkwa

e nestot osam e totat.
ê-nêstot osâm (ê-)itôtât.

38

†

Jesus, forever we adore You, and we thank You. You died for us. You saved all the people to give them life.

5

SIMON CARRIES THE CROSS WITH JESUS.

We are amazed by Jesus. He is going to be helped by the people, although He has the power to bring people back to life. Clearly He taught us how to help one another when we are suffering. Have mercy on us in Your torment.

You satisfy us Jesus. You wanted to suffer for me. Never let me doubt Your torment. I will never rejoice in what was done to You. Surely I know it, God is broken to save us. He will be rewarded. He is adored.

Our Father, in Heaven, You are there.....
I greet you Mary.....
Glory be to God the Father.....
We are content with You. Have pity on us!

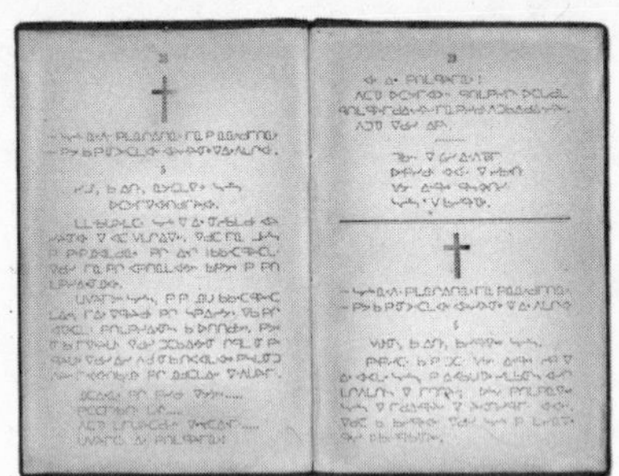

†

– sesos naspic kimanaciitinan mina kinanaskomitinan
– Sesos nâspic kimanâcihitinân mîna kinanâskomitinân

– kiya ka ki nipostamawat ayisiyiniw e wi pimaciat.
– kiya ka-kî-nipôstamawat ayisiyiniw ê-wî-pimâcihat.

5

SIMOK, KA ITIT, NAYATAMAWEW SESOSA
SIMOK, KÂ-ITÎT, NAYAHTAMAWÊW SESOSA

OTAYAMIEWATIKOMIYIWA.
OTAYAMIHÊWAHTIKOMIYIWA.

mamaskateyimatak sesos e wi nisokamakot ayisiyiniwa
mâmaskâtêyimâtâhk Sesos ê-wî-nîsôhkamâkot ayisiyiniwa

e ata pemaciiwet. ekota mina mosise ki kiskinoamakonaw
ê-âta-pimacihiwêt. êkota mîna mosis kî-kiskinohamâkonaw

kici wici kakwatakeyitamak ekosi mina kici
kici-wîci-kâkwâtakêyihtamâhk êkosi mîna kici-

pakitinamawayak kakiyaw ki kitimakisiwininowa.
pakitinamawâyahk kahkiyaw kikitimâkisiwinowa.

tepeyimiyak sesose, ki ki note kakwatakeyistamawin,
(ê-)tipêyimiyâhk Sesose, kikî-nohtê-kakwâtakêyistamawin,

miin ekweyikok kici sakiisoyan eka kici anwetaman
miyin êkwayikohk kici-sâkihisoyân êkâ kici-ânwêhtamân

kitimakisiwinisa ka otitikoyan. kiyam ni ka miweyiten
kitimâkisiwinisa kâ-otîtikoyân. kîyam nika-miywêyihtên

ekosi totakawiyani cikema ni kiskeyiten ekosi isi piko
êkosi itôtakawiyani cikêmâ nikiskêyihtên êkosi isi piko

ni ka tipaamawa kise manito piyis miyowatikwanak
nika-tipahamawâw kisê-manitow piyis miyo-wahtikwanohk

kici nokotamawit espiteyimit.
kici-nokôtamawit (ê-)ispîhtêyimit.

notawinan kici kisikok eyayan.....
nôhtâwînân kihci-kîsikohk (ê-)ayâyan.....

kitatamiskatin mari.....
kitatamiskâtin Mari.....

pitane mamiteyitakosit weyotawimit.....
pitanê (ê-)mâmitêyihtâkosit wiyôhtawîmit.....

tepeyimitak wi kitimakeyiminan!
(ê-)tipêyimitâhk wî-kitimakêyiminân!

39

ᐊᐤ ᐃᐧ ᑭᑎᒪᑫᔨᒥᓈᐤ !

ᐱᑕᑑ ᐅᑕᔭᒥᐊᐅᐧᐦ ᑫᑎᒪᑭᔨᒋᐠ ᐅᑕᑯᒪ ᑫᑎᒪᑫᔨᒥᑯᐃᐧᓯᔭᐟ ᒥᓇ ᑭᓯᑯᐠ ᐱᒍᐸᐃᑯᐃᐧᓯᔭᐟ.

ᐱᑐᑑ ᐁᑯᓯ ᐃᑭᐠ.

ᒣᑲᐧ- ᐁ ᐃᓰ ᐃᐢᐱᑑᒥᐟ
ᐅᐢᑭᓯᑯᐠ ᐊᐧᐊᐧ- ᐁ ᓯᑲᐧᑎᐟ
ᐯᔭᐠ ᐃᐢᑫᐤ ᑫᓴᐊᐧᑎᓯᐟ
ᓴᓯᓴ * ᐯ ᑲᓯᑫᐧᑑᐤ.

— ᓴᓯᐢ ᓇᐢᐱ-ᑭᒫᓇᒋᐃᑎᓈᐤ ᒥᓇ ᑭᓇᓇᐢᑯᒥᑎᓈᐤ.
— ᑭᔭ ᑳ ᑭᑑᐳᐢᑕᒪᐊᐧᐤ ᐊᔨᓯᔨᓃᐤ ᐁ ᐃᐧ ᐱᒪᒋᐊᐟ

6

ᐯᖤᓂᐠ, ᑲ ᐃᑎᐟ, ᑲᓯᑫᐧᐁᐧᐤ ᓴᓯᓴ.

ᑭᐢᑭᓯᑕᐠ ᑲ ᑭ ᑐᑕᐠ ᐯᔭᐠ ᐃᐢᑫᐤ ᓯᑭ ᐁ ᐃᐧ ᐊᐧᐸᒪᐟ ᓴᓯᓴ, ᑭ ᐃᔕᑲᐅᑑᐤ ᓯᒪᑲᓂᓴ ᐊᓯᒋ ᒪᒋᐱᒪᒋᓴ ᐁ ᒥᒉᑎᔭᐟ; ᐅᓵ ᑭᑎᒪᑭᓇᐁᐧᐤ ᓴᓯᓴ ᐁ ᒥᑯᐃᐧᑫᐧᔭᐟ ᐁ ᔮᐸᑎᓯᑫᐧᒥᐟ ᐊᐧᐊᐧ-. ᐁᑯᑕ ᑲ ᑲᓯᑫᐧᐊᐧᐟ ᐁᑯᓯ ᓴᓯᐢ ᑭ ᒪᓯᓇᐁᐧ ᑫᐧᓯ ᐅᑲᓯᑫᐧᑲᐧᑑᔭᐣ.

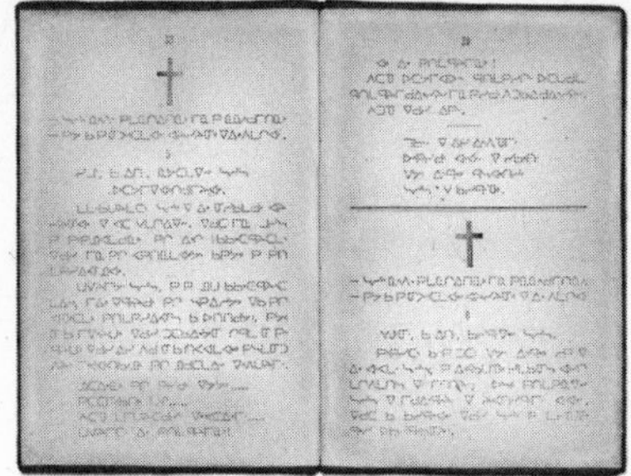

39 Oh, have pity on us!

I wish the Christians, those who are pitiful in His spirit, may have pity on Him and enter into Heaven.

So let it be.

Right now, He is insulted.
Especially in His eye, He is spit on.
One woman who is kind
Comes to Jesus and washes His face.

– Jesus, forever we adore You. Also we thank You.
– You did die for all the people to give them life.

6

VERONICA WIPES THE FACE OF JESUS.

Let us remember what this strong woman did, going to see Jesus. She pushed the soldiers aside and also the crowd; there were a lot of them. She had pity on Him because Jesus had blood and sweat on His face. When she washed His face, Jesus left his image.

39 aw wî kitimakeyiminan!
aw wî-kitimâkêyiminân!

pitane otayamiawok ketimakisicik otacakoma
pitanê otayamihâwak (ê-)kitimâkisicik otâhcahkoma

ketimakeyimikowisiyit mina kisikok pitokaikowisiyit.
(ê-)kitimâkêyimikowisiyit mîna kîsikohk (ê-)pihtokahikowisiyit.

pitane ekosi ikik.
pitanê êkosi ihkik.

---

mekwac e isi ispinemit
mêkwâc ê-isi-ispinêmiht

oskisikok wawac e sikwatit
oskîsikohk wâwâc ê-sîkwâtiht

peyak iskwew kesewatisit
pêyak iskwêw (ê-)kisêwâtisiht

sesosa pe kasikwenew.
Sesosa pê-kâsîkwênêw.

– sesos naspic kimanaciitinan mina kinanaskomitinan.
– Sesos nâspic kimanâcihitinân mîna kinanâskomitinân.

– kiya ka ki nipostamawat ayisiyiniw e wi pimaciat
– kiya ka-kî-nipôstamawat ayisiyiniw ê-wî-pimâcihat

6

PERONIK, KA ITIT, KASIKWEWEW SESOSA.
PERONIK, KÂ-ITÎT, KÂSÎKWÊNÊW SESOSA.

kiskisitak ka ki totak peyak iskwew soki e wi
kiskisitâhk kâ-kî-itôtak pêyak iskwêw sohki (ê-)wî-

wapamat sesosa, ki iyekatenew simakanisa asici
wâpamat Sesosa, kî-iyîkatênêw simâkanisa asici

macipimatisa e micetiyit; osam kitimakinawew sesosa
maci-pimâtisa ê-mihcêtiyit; osâm kitimâkinawêw Sesosa

e mikowikweyit e yipatisikwemit wawac ekota ka
ê-mihkowikwêyit ê-yipâtisihkwêmît wâwâc êkota kâ-

kasikwewat ekosi sesos ki masinawekweso
kâsîkwêhwât êkosi Sesos kî-masinawêkwêsôw

okasikwekaniyik.
okâsîkwêkaniyik.

40

ᑌ ᒪᑌᑐᑦ ᒪᒪᐃᐧᔦᐢ ᑫᑕᐊᐧᓯᓯᔮᐤ ᑭ ᓇᐅᐧ
ᑭᐢᑕᑎᐤ ᑭ ᒪᓇᒋᐃᑎᐤ ᑭ ᒪᒪᐢᑳᑎᑎᐤ ᐁ ᐃᐧ ᔩᐸ
ᑎᓯᑳᐧᑎᑳᐃᐧᔮᐤ ᒍᒋ ᑭᐢᑭᓅᐊᒪᐃᐧᔮᐤ ᐁᔩᒎ
ᐸᑳᐧᑎᒍᐃᐧᓯᔮᐤ ᐁ ᑭ ᐸᑭᑎᓇᐠ ᑌ ᑕᐡᐠ ᑭᒋᐃᐸ
ᒋᐃᒎᐟ ᒪᒋ ᐃᑎᐃᐧᐤ ᑭ ᒪᐃᐧᒍᐢᑕᑎᐤ ᑭᒋ ᑳᓇᒋ
ᑕᒪᐃᐧᔮᐤ ᐁᑳᐧ ᑲ ᐃᐧ ᑭᒋ ᒥᐁᐧᔩᒥᔮᐤ.

ᓄᑕᐃᐧᓇᐤ ᑭᒋ ᐧᑭᓯᒎ ᐁᔮᔮᐤ .....
ᑭᑕᑕᒥᐢᑳᑎᐤ ᒪᕆ .....
ᐱᑕᑌ ᒪᒥᑐᔩᑕᒎᓯᐟ .....
ᑐᐯᔩᒥᑖᐠ ᐃᐧ ᑭᑎᒪᑫᔩᒥᓇᐤ !
ᐊᐤ ᐃᐧ ᑭᑎᒪᑫᔩᒥᓇᐤ !
ᐱᑕᑌ ᐅᑕᓴᒥᐊᐅᐧᐢ ᑫᑎᒪᑭᓯᒋᐠ ᐅᑕᑐᒍᒪ
ᑫᑎᒪᑫᔩᒥᒍᐃᐧᓯᔩᐟ ᒥᓇ ᑭᓯᒎ ᐱᑐᑳᐃᒍᐃᐧᓯᔩᐟ.
ᐱᑕᑌ ᐁᒎᓯᐟ ᐃᑭᐠ.

ᓇᒣᐢᑳᐧ ᐊᐱᑕᐤ ᒣᐢᑳᓇᐧ
ᑕᒎᓯᐤ ᑲ ᑐᐯᔩᒋᑫᐟ
ᒥᓇ ᑲ ᑳᐃᐧᐢᒍᓯᐟ ᑭᑕᐧᐦ
ᒪᑳᑌ * ᓇᒪᐊᐧᐨ ᑭᑐ.

— ᓴᓯᐢ ᓇᐢᐱ- ᑭᒪᓇᒋᐃᑎᓇᐤ ᒥᓇ ᑭᓇᓇᐢᒍᒥᑎᓇᐤ
— ᑭᔮ ᑳᑭᑌᐳᐢᑕᒪᐊᐧᐟ ᐊᔩᓯᔩᑌᐤ ᐁᐃᐧ ᐱᒪᒋᐊᐧᐟ

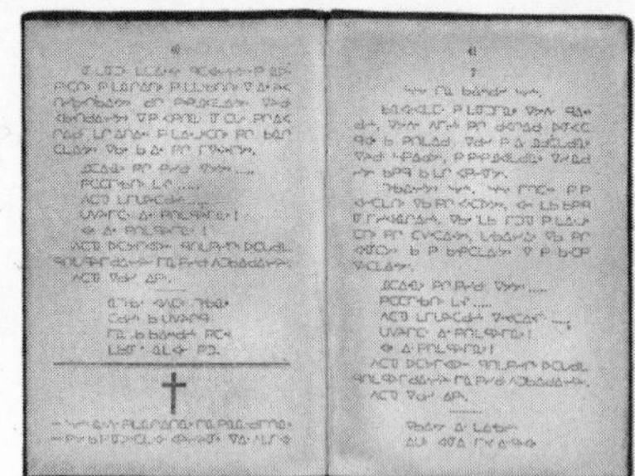

40 My Father, beyond the rest, You are beautiful. I bow to You. I adore You. I am humbled by You. Try to teach me, that when I am mocked, that I do not allow my spirit to be used by evil. I pray to You to purify my spirit and love me.

Our Father, in Heaven, You are there.....
I greet you Mary.....
Glory be to God.....
We are content with You. Have pity on us!
Oh, have pity on us!

I wish the Christians, those who are pitiful in His spirit, may have pity on Him and enter into Heaven.

So let it be.

The halfway mark
Has not yet arrived, and the One who satisfies
everything falls.
The One who falls under the burden again
Does not speak at all.

– Jesus, forever we adore You, and we thank You.
– You died for all the people to give them life.

ni manitom mamawiyes ketawasisiyan ki nawokistatin
nimanitôm mamawiyês (ê-)katawasisiyan kinawokistâtin

ki manaciitin ki mamaskatitin e wi yepatisikwatikawiyan
kimanâcihitin kimamâskâtitin ê-wî-yêpatisîkwahtikawiyan

koci kiskinoamawiyan eyikok pakwatikowisiyan e ki
koci-kiskinohamâwiyan iyikohk (ê-)pakwâtikowisiyan ê-kî-

pakitinak ni tacak kici epaciikot maci itiwin
pakitinak nitâcahk kihci ê-âpacihikot macihtiwin

ki mawimostatin kici kanacitamawiyan ekwa ka wi kici
kimawimôstâtin kici-kanâcîtamawiyan êkwa ka-wî-kici-

miweyimiyan.
miywêyimiyan.

notawinan kici kisikok eyayan.....
nôhtâwînân kihci-kîsikohk (ê-)ayâyan.....

kitatamiskatin mari.....
kitatamiskâtin Mari.....

pitane mamiteyitakosit.....
pitanê (ê-)mâmitêyihtâkosit.....

tepeyimitak wi kitimakeyiminan!
(ê-)tipêyimitâhk wî-kitimâkêyiminân!

aw wi kitimakeyiminan!
aw wî-kitimâkêyiminân!

pitane otayamiawok ketimakisicik otacakoma
pitanê otayamihâwak (ê-)kitimâkisicik otâhcahkoma

ketimakeyimikowisiyit mina kisikok pitokaikowisiyit.
(ê-)kitimâkêyimikowisiyit mîna kîsikohk (ê-)pihtokahikowisiyit.

pitane ekosi ikik.
pitanê êkosi ihkik.

---

nameskwa apitaw meskanaw
namêskwa apihtaw mêskanaw

takosin ka tepeyiciket
takosin kâ-tipêyihcikêt

mina ka kawiskosot kitwam
mîna kâ-kawiskosot kîhtwâm

makani namawac kito.
mâkani namawâc kitow.

– sesos naspic kimanaciitinan mina kinanaskomitinan
– Sesos nâspic kimanâcihitinân mîna kinanâskomitinân

– kiya ka ki nipostamawat ayisiyiniw e wi pimaciat
– kiya kâ-kî-nipôstamawat ayisiyiniw ê-wî-pimâcihat

41

7

ᓭᓭᐟ ᒥᓇ ᑳᐃᐧᐢᑯᓯᐟ ᓭᓯᐣ.

ᑲᓇᐋᐧᐸᒪᑕᐠ ᑭ ᒪᒋᑐᒥᓇᐤ ᐁᔦᐱ- ᑫᐃᐧᐢ ᑯᓯᐟ, ᐁᔦᐱ- ᐱᒥᓱᐣ ᑭᒋ ᑯᐸᒋᐃᑯᐟ ᐅᑎᐸᑕ ᑫᐊᐧ ᑲ ᑭᑎᒪᐃᑰᐟ. ᐁᑯᓯ ᑭ ᐃᐧ ᓇᑰᑕᒪᑯᓇᐤ ᐁᔦᑯᐟ ᓴᑭᐃᑯᔦᐠ, ᑭ ᑭᐢᑭᓇᐊᒪᑯᓇᐤ ᐁᓯ ᓇᑯ ᓯᔦᐠ ᑲᑭᑫ ᑲ ᒪᒋ ᐸᑭᓯᑎᔦᐠ.

ᒉᐢᑳᐃᐧᓯᔦᐣ ᓭᓯᐣ, ᓭᓭᐟ ᒥᑎᑖᐤ ᑭ ᑭ ᐊᓯᑕᒪᑎᐣ ᐁᑲ ᑭᒋ ᐸᐢᑕᐅᔦᐣ, ᐊᐟᐢ ᒪᑲ ᑳᑭᑫ ᑎ ᒥᓯᐋᐧᓇᒋᐃᓯᐣ. ᐁᑳᐧ ᒪᑲ ᒥᑐᑌ ᑭ ᒪᐃᐧᒍᐢ ᑕᑎᐣ ᑭᒋ ᑌᐯᐧᑕᐃᐧᔦᐣ, ᒪᐢᑳᐃᐧᓯᐃᐣ ᐁᑲ ᑭᒋ ᐊᐧᑎᑕᔦᐣ ᑲ ᑭ ᑳᐢᑭᑕᒪᐃᐧᔦᐣ ᐁ ᑭ ᑳᐧᑕᑭ ᐁᐢᑕᒪᐃᐧᔦᐣ.

ᓄᑕᐃᐧᓇᐣ ᑭᒋ ᑭᓯᑰᐠ ᐁᔦᔦᐣ .....
ᑭᑕᑕᒥᐢᑳᑎᐣ ᒪᕆ .....
ᐱᑕᑌ ᒪᒥᑐᔦᑕᑯᓯᐟ ᐁᐧᔭᑕᐃᐧᒥᐟ .....
ᑌᐯᔦᒥᑕᐠ ᐃᐧ ᑭᑎᒪᑫᔦᒥᓇᐣ !
ᐊᐤ ᐃᐧ ᑭᑎᒪᑫᔦᒥᓇᐣ !

ᐱᑕᑌ ᐅᑕᔭᒥᐊᐅᐧᐠ ᑫᑎᒪᑭᓯᒋᐟ ᐅᑕᐦᑯᒪ ᑫᑎᒪᑫᔦᒥᑯᐃᐧᓯᔦᐟ ᒥᓇ ᑭᓯᑰ ᐱᑐᑳᐃᑯᐃᐧᓯᔦᐟ.
ᐱᑕᑌ ᐁᑯᓯ ᐃᑭᐠ.

ᐁᑳᐃᐧᔭ ᐃᐧ ᒪᐃᐧᑳᓯᐟ
ᐃᑌᐤ ᐊᐧᑎᐃ ᒥᔦ ᐃᐢᑫᐧᐊᐧ

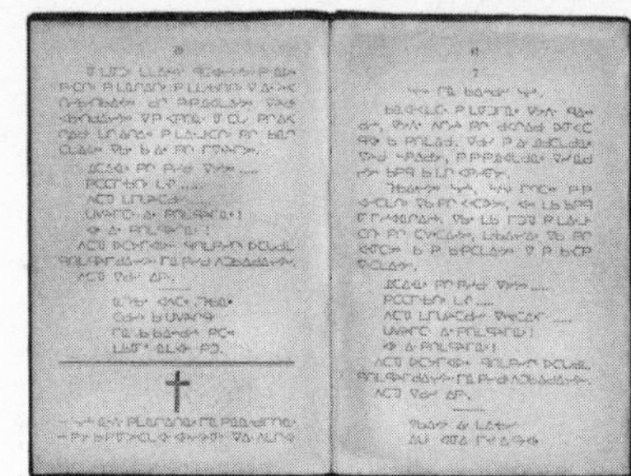

41

7

JESUS FALLS AGAIN.

Jesus falls again under the burden. Our Father, still He falls to be used by the murderers who made Him suffer, so that He is going to show us how much He loves us. He teaches us to understand. All the time when we sin, we fall down.

You are strong, Jesus. Already, many times I promised You not to sin. But all the time I spoil myself. Yet I pray to You fervently, to believe in me, make me strong, not to lose what good deed You have done for me, that You suffered for me.

Our Father in Heaven, You are there....
I greet you Mary....
Glory be to God the Father.....
We are content with You. Have pity on us!
Oh, have pity on us!

I wish the Christians, those who are pitiful in His spirit, may have pity on Him and enter into Heaven.
So let it be.

Do not cry for Me,
He says that to good women.

41

7

SASAY MINA KAWISKOSO SESOS.

SÂSAY MÎNA KAWISKOSOW SESOS.

kanawapamatak ki manitominaw eyapic kewiskosot,
kanawâpamâtâhk kimanitôminaw êyâpic (ê-)kawiskosot,

eyapic pimisin kici kopaciikot onipatakewa ka kitimaikot.
êyâpic pimisin kici-kô-âpacihikot onipâtâkêwa kâ-kitimahikot.

ekosi ki wi nokotamakonaw eyikok sakiikoyak, ki
êkosi kiwî-nokotâmâkonaw iyikohk sâkihikoyahk,

kiskinoamakonaw esi nakosiyak kakike ka maci
kikiskinohamâkonaw (ê-)isi-nâkosiyahk kâkikê kâ-maci-

pakisiniyik.
pâkisiniyâhk.

meskawisiyan sesos, sasay micetwaw ki ki asotamatin
(ê-)maskawisiyan Sesos, sâsay mihcêtwâw kikî-asotamâtin

eka kici pastaoyan, ays maka kakike ni misiwanaciison.
êkâ kici-pâstâhoyân, ays mâka kâkikê nimisi-wanâcihison.

ekwa maka mitone ki mawimostatin kici tapwetawiyan,
êkwa mâka mitonê kimawimostâtin kici-tâpwêtawiyan,

maskawisiin eka kici wanitayan ka ki kaskitamawiyan e ki
maskawisihîn êkâ kici-wanîtâyân ka-kî-kaskîtamawiyan ê-kî-

kwatakiestamawiyan.
kwâtakihêstamawiyan.

notawinan kici kisikok eyayan.....
nôhtâwînân kihci-kîsikohk (ê-)ayâyan.....

kitatamiskatin mari.....
kitatamiskâtin Mari.....

pitane mamiteyitakosit weyotawimit.....
pitanê (ê-)mâmitêyihtâkosit wiyôhtâwîmit.....

tepeyimitak wi kitimakeyiminan!
(ê-)tipêyimitâhk wî-kitimâkêyiminân!

aw wi kitimakeyiminan!
aw wî-kitimâkêyiminân!

pitane otayamiawok ketimakisicit otacakoma
pitanê otayamihâwak (ê-)kitimâkisicik otâhcahkoma

ketimakeyimikowisiyit mina kisikok pitokaikowisiyit.
(ê-)kitimâkêyimikowisiyit mîna kîsikohk (ê-)pihtokwahikowisiyit.

pitane ekosi ikik.
pitanê êkosi ihkik.

---

ekawiya wi mawikasik
êkâwiya wî-mawîkâsik

itew anii miyo iskwewa
itêw anihi miyo-iskwêwa

42

ᐊᔦᐊ·· ᑭᑎᒪᐃᓱᐅ··
ᑲ ᐃᓯ * ᑭᑎᒪᐃᑕ··.

— ᓴᓱᐢ ᓇᐢᐱ· ᑭᒪᓇᓯᐱᑎᓇᐣ ᒥᓇ ᑭᓇᓇᐢᑯᒥᑎᓇᐣ
— ᑭᔦ ᑲ ᑭ ᑌᔦᐢᑕᒪᐊ· ᐊᔨᓯᔨᑌᐤ ᐁᐃ·ᐱᒪᒋᐊ.

8

ᓴᓱᐢ ᑲᑭᒋᐁᐤ ᐊᑎᐠ ᐃᐢᑫ·ᐊ·
ᐁ ᒪᐃ·ᑲᑎᑯ.

ᐊᑎᐠ ᒥᔦ ᐃᐢᑫ·ᐅ·· ᓇᒪᐃ·ᔦ ᐃ·ᒋᐊᐁ·ᐅ·· ᓴᓱᓴ ᑲ ᑭᑎᒪᐃᒥᐟ ᑎᔦᑲ· ᐱᒥᑎᓴᐁ·ᐅ·· ᐁ ᒪᐃ·ᑲᑕᒋ. ᓴᓱᐢ ᐁ ᑭ ᐊ·ᐸᒪᐟ ᐅᒥᓯ ᐃᑌᐤ ᒪᓇ: « ᐁᑲᐃ·ᔦ ᒪᐃ·ᑲᓯ, ᓯᑕᐃ·ᐢᑫ·ᑎ, ᐃᔦᔦᐤ ᒪᐃ·ᑲᑎᓯ, ᑭᑕᐊ·ᓯᒥᓯᐊ·ᐅ·· ᒥᓇ ᒪᐃ·ᑲᓯᑯ. »

ᓯᔦᑭᐃᑯᔦᔦᐣ ᓴᓱᓴ, ᑭᔦ ᑲ ᓄᑌ ᑌᓯᑲ ᒪᐊ·ᑕ·· ᑫ·ᑕᑭᑕᒋ. ᐊᐤ ᑌᓯᑲᒪᐃ·ᐣ ᐯ·ᔦᐊ·ᑕᔦᐣ ᑲᐢᑫᔦᑕᒧᐃ·ᐣ. ᐁ ᐊᑕ ᑭᑎᒪᑭᓇᑯᓯᔦᐣ ᓇᒪᐃ·ᔦ ᑭᔦ ᑲ ᒪᐃ·ᑲᑎᑯᓯᔦᐣ. ᑌᔦᓇᐣ ᒪᑲ ᑫᑭᐢᑲᒪᐠ ᒪᒋ ᐃᑎᐃ·ᓇ ᒥᐃᓇᐣ ᑭᒋ ᒪᐃ·ᑲᑎᓯᔦᐠ ᐁ ᑭ ᐯᒋ ᐸᐢᑕᐅᔦ.

ᓄᑕᐃ·ᓇᐣ ᑭᒋ ᑭᓯᑯ ᐁᔦᔦᐣ .....
ᑭᑕᑕᒥᐢᑲᑎᐣ ᒪᔨ .....

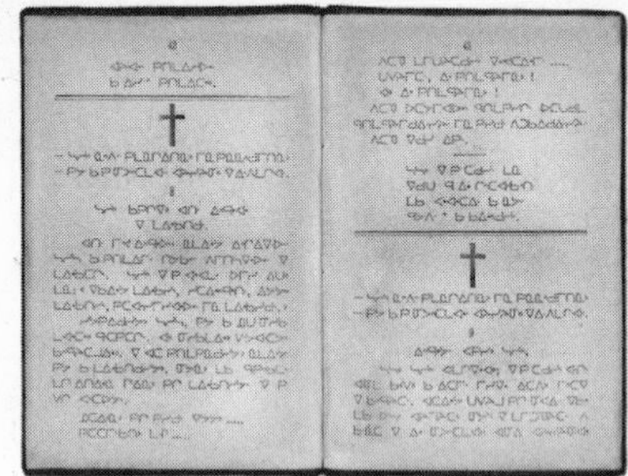

42 They are more destitute
because they oppress Me.

– Jesus, forever we adore You. Also we thank You.
– You did die for all the people to give them life.

8

JESUS COMFORTS THE CRYING WOMEN.

Some good women, who accompany Jesus, see Him being treated badly. They follow Him. They cry for Him. Jesus said to them: "Do not cry for Me, Jewish women, but cry for yourself, and for your children."

You are loved Jesus. You want to work together with those who are suffering. Oh, help me with this sinfulness. Although I am pitied, You are not. They do not cry for You. We wear evilness. Help us to cry for ourselves for we have sinned.

Our Father in Heaven, You are there....
I greet you Mary....

ayiwak kitimaisowok
ayiwâk kitimâkisowak

ka isi kitimaitwaw.
kâ-isi-kitimahîhtwâw.

– sesos naspic kimanaciitinan mina kinanaskomitinan
– Sesos nâspic kimanâcihitinân mîna kinanâskomitinân

– kiya ka ki nipostamawat ayisiyiniw e wi pimaciat.
– kiya kâ-kî-nipôstamawat ayisiyiniw ê-wî-pimâcihat.

8

SESOS KAKICIEW ATIT ISKWEWA
SESOS KÂKÎCIHÊW ÂTIHT ISKWÊWA

E MAWIKATIKOT.
Ê-MAWÎKÂTIKOT.

atit miyo iskwewok namawiya wici iwewok sesosa ka
âtiht miyo-iskwêwak namâwiya wîcêwêwak Sesosa kâ-

kitimaimit tiyakwac pimitisawewok e mawikatacik.
kitimahimiht tiyakwac pimitisahwêwak ê-mawîhkâtâcik.

sesos e ki wapamat omisi itew mana: « ekawiya
Sesos ê-kî-wâpamât omisi itêw mâna. "êkâwiya

mawikasik, sotawiskwetik, eyayaw mawikatisok,
mawîhkâsik, sotawiskwêtik, iyâyaw mawîhkâtisok,

kitawasimisiwawok mina mawikasikok. »
kitawâsimisiwâwak mîna mawîhkâsêhkok."

siyakiikosiyan sesose, kiya ka note
(ê-)siyakihikosiyan Sesose, kiya kâ-nohtê-

nisokamawatwaw kwetakitacik. aw nisokamawin
nîsôhkamawâtwâw kwâtakîtâcik. aw nîsôhkamawin

pweyawatayan kaskeyitamowin. e ata kitimakinakosiyan
(ê-)pwêyawatayan kaskêyihtamowin. ê-âta-kitimâkinakôsiyan

namawiya kiya ka mawikatikosiyan. niyanan maka
namâwiya kiya kâ-mawîhkâtikosiyan. niyanân mâka

kekiskamak maci itiwina miinan kici mawikatisoyak
kêkiskamahk macihtiwina miyinân kici-mawîhkâtisoyâhk

e ki peci pastaoyak.
ê-kî-pêci-pâstâhoyahk.

notawinan kici kisikok eyayan.....
nôhtâwînân kihci-kîsikohk (ê-)ayâyan.....

kitatamiskatin mari.....
kitatamiskâtin Mari.....

43

ᐱᑕᑑ ᒪᒥᑌᔦᑕᑯᓯᐤ ᐁᐧᕙᑕᐃᐧᒥᐤ .....
ᑌᐯᔦᒥᑕᐠ, ᐃᐧ ᑭᑎᒪᑫᔦᒥᓈᐣ !
ᐊᐤ ᐃᐧ ᑭᑎᒪᑫᔦᒥᓈᐣ !
ᐱᑕᑑ ᐅᑕᔭᒥᐊᐅᐦ ᑫᑎᒪᑭᓯᕆᐠ ᐅᑕᑌᑯᒪ
ᑫᑎᒪᑫᔦᒥᑯᐃᐧᓯᔦᐤ ᒥᓇ ᑭᓯᑯᐤ ᐱᑐᑲᐃᑯᐃᐧᓯᔦᐤ
ᐱᑕᑑ ᐁᑯᓯ ᐃᑭᐠ.

ᓴᓴ+ ᐁ ᑭ ᑕᑯᓯᐠ ᒪᓇ
ᐁᑯᑌ ᑫ ᐃᐧ ᕆᐢᑕᐊᐢᑲᐧᑎᐤ
ᒪᑲ ᐸᐧᐊᐧᑕᐃᐠ ᑲ ᓇᔭᐤ
ᑫᔭᐱ- * ᑲ ᑲᐃᐧᐢᑯᓯᐤ.

— ᓴᓯᐢ ᓇᐢᐱ- ᑭᒪᓇᕆᐃᑎᓇᐣ ᒥᓇ ᑭᓇᓇᐢᑯᒥᑎᓇᐣ
— ᑭᔭ ᑲ ᑭ ᑑᐳᐢᑕᒪᐊᐧᐤ ᐊᔦᓯᔦᑑᐤ ᐁᐃᐧᐱᒪᕆᐊᐤ.

9

ᐃᐢᑫᐧᔭ- ᐸᑭᓯᐣ ᓴᓯᐢ.

ᓴᓴ+ ᓴᓯᐢ ᐊᒪᕆᐁᐧᐊᐤ; ᐁ ᑭ ᑕᑯᓯᐠ ᐊᐧᕆᐠ ᐊᑑᒪ ᑲˢᐯᶻ ᑲ ᐃᑕᒥᐠ ᒥᓯᐁᐧ ᐃᑕᐱᐤ ᒥᐢᑕᐁ ᐁ ᑲᐢᑫᔦᑕᐠ. ᐊᑕᐃᐧᔭ ᑌᐯᔦᒧ ᑭᕆ ᑑᐸᐃᐠ ᐁᑲᐧ ᒪᑲ ᐅᓴᶜ ᐊᔦᒉᔦᑕᶜ ᑑᔭᐠ ᐁ ᒪᒥᑐᑑᔦᑕᐠ ᐱ ᑲᐧᓈᑕ ᐁ ᐃᐧ ᑑᐳᐢᑕᒪᐊᐧᐤ ᐊᑑᐃ ᐊᔦᓯᔦᑑᐊᐧ

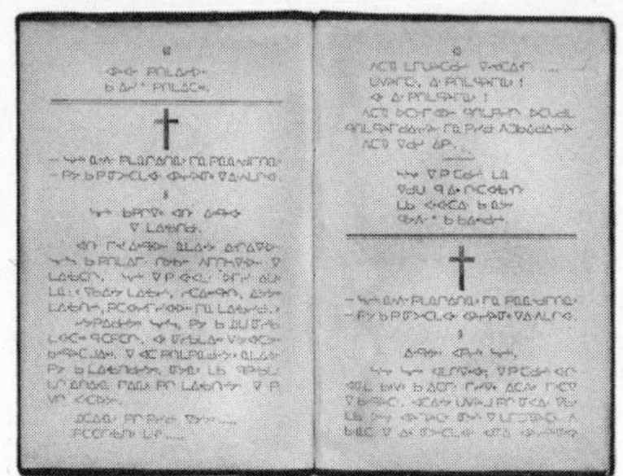

43 Glory be to God the Father.....
We are content with You. Have pity on us!
Oh, have pity on us!

I wish the Christians, those who are pitiful in His spirit, may have pity on Him and enter into Heaven.

So let it be.

When He has arrived
at the place where He is going to be crucified,
He is burdened heavily by the burden on His back.
Still, He falls under the burden.

– Jesus, forever we adore You and thank You.
– You did die for all the people to give them life.

9

JESUS FALLS THE LAST TIME.

Already Jesus started to go up the hill; He arrived on the mountain, the one that is called Calvary. He looked all over and felt alone. Anyway He knew how He would be killed. He knew it would be difficult. Is this for Me? He is thinking; He must do it. He is going to die for the people, those people.

43 pitane mamiteyitakosit weyotawimit.....
pitanê (ê-)mâmitêyihtâkosit wiyôhtâwîmit.....

tepeyimitak, wi kitimakeyiminan!
(ê-)tipêyimitâhk, wî-kitimâkêyiminân!

aw wi kitimakeyiminan!
aw wî-kitimâkêyiminân!

pitane otayamiawok ketimakisicik otacakoma
pitanê otayamihâwak (ê-)kitimâkisicik otâhcahkoma

ketimakeyimikowisiyit mina kisikok pitokaikowisiyit
(ê-)kitimâkêyimikowisiyit mîna kîsikohk (ê-)pihtokahikowisiyit

pitane ekosi ikik.
pitanê êkosi ihkik.

---

sasay e ki takosik mana
sâsay ê-kî-takosik mâna

ekote ke wi cistaaskwatit
êkotê kê-wî-cîstahâskwâtiht

maka pwawataik ka nayat
mâka pwâwatahihk kâ-nayat

keyapic ka kawiskosot.
kêyâpic kâ-kawiskôsot.

– sesos naspic kimanaciitinan mina kinanaskomitinan
– Sesos nâspic kimanâcihitinân mîna kinanâskomitinân

– kiya ka ki nipostamawat ayisiyiniw e wi pimaciat.
– kiya kâ-kî-nipôstamawat ayisiyiniw ê-wî-pimâcihat.

9

ISKWEYAC PAKISIN SESOS.
ISKWÊYAC PAHKISIN SESOS.

sasay sesos amaciweaw; e ki takosik wacik anima
sâsay Sesos âmaciwêw; ê-kî-tâkosik wâcîhk anima

kalper ka itamik misiwe itapiw mistae e kaskeyitak.
Kalper kâ-itamik misiwê itâpiw mistahi ê-kaskêyitahk.

atawiya tepeyimo kici nipait ekwa maka osam ayimeyitam
atawîya têpêyimo kici-nipahît êkwa mâka osâm âyimêyihtam

niyak e mamitoneyitak pikwanata e wi nipostamawat
niyâk ê-mâmitonêyihtahk pikwânâta ê-wî-nipôstamawât

anii ayisiyiniwa
anihi ayisiyiniwa

44

ᐁᑲ ᐁ ᓴᑭᐃᑯᐤ. ᓵᓵ+ ᐁᑯᐢᐱ ᑭᐢᑫᔨᐟᑕᑌᔨᑯᐤ
ᑫ ᐯᒋ ᒥᓯᐚᓇᒋᐃᓯᓇᓂᐃᐧᐠ.

ᓂᒪᓂᑐᐨ ᓭᓱᐢ, ᐅᓵᐨ ᒥᒋᑌᐧᔭᐠ ᑭ ᑮ ᑭᒋ ᒫᐃᒋᐤ ᒥᓯᐁᐧ ᐃᓯ ᐁ ᑭ ᐸᐢᑕᐅᔭᐤ, ᓂ ᒥᑕᑌᐤ ᐁᑳᐧ, ᑭᒋᒪᑭᓇᐃᐧᐤ, ᑲᓯᓇᒪᐃᐧᐤ ᑭᒋ ᐁᑲ ᐚᐧᓂ ᑕᔭᐤ ᑲ ᑭ ᓂᐳᐢᑕᒪᐃᐧᔭᐤ.

ᓅᑕᐃᐧᓇᐤ ᑭᒋ ᑭᓯᑰ ᐁᔭᔭᐤ .....
ᑭᑕᑕᒥᐢᑲᒋᐤ ᒪᕆ .....
ᐱᑕᑑ ᒪᒥᑌᔭᑕᑯᓯᐠ ᐁᐧᐊᑕᐃᐧᒥᐠ .....
ᑌᐯᔨᒥᑕᐠ ᐃᐧ ᑭᒋᒪᑫᔨᒥᓇᐤ!
ᐊᐤ ᐃᐧ ᑭᒋᒪᑫᔨᒥᓇᐤ!

ᐱᑕᑑ ᐅᑕᔭᒥᐊᐅᐧᐠ ᑫᒋᒪᑭᓯᒋᐠ ᐅᑕᑌᐧᑯᒪ ᑫᒋᒪᑫᔨᒥᑯᐃᐧᓯᔨᐟ ᒥᓇ ᑭᓯᑰ ᐱᑐᑲᐃᑯᐃᐧᓯᔨᐟ ᐱᑕᑑ ᐁᑯᓯ ᐃᑭᐠ.

ᐁᓯ ᑭᒋᒪᑭᓇᑯᓯᐟ
ᑕᐯᐧ ᐃᑐᑫ ᓯᑭ ᒧᓯᑕᐤ
ᒧᓯᐢ ᐁ ᑭᑕᓴᑫᐱᒋᐟ
ᒥᐢᑕᐁ * ᑭ ᓃᐯᐃᐧᓯᐤ.

— ᓭᓱᐢ ᓇᐢᐱ- ᑭᒪᓇᒋᐃᒋᓇᐤ ᒥᓇ ᑭᓇᓇᐢᑯᒥᒋᓇᐤ
— ᑭᔭ ᑲ ᑭ ᓂᐳᐢᑕᒪᐧᐤ ᐊᐱᓯᓰᓂᐤ ᐁᐃᐧᐱᒪᒋᐊᐧᐤ.

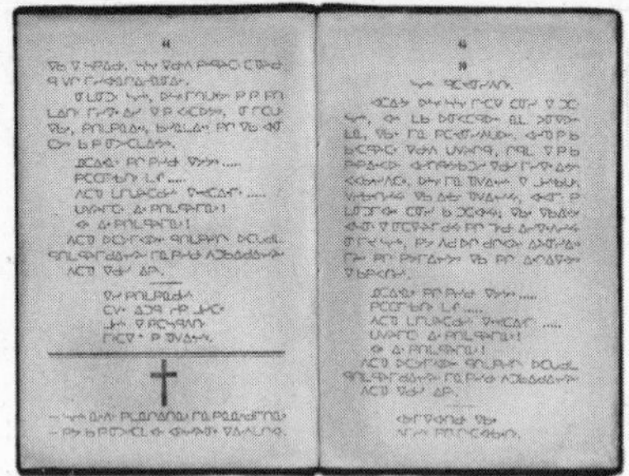

44 They do not love Him. He knows it. He knows the ones who want to kill him.

My God, Jesus, I harmed You all over like this. I sinned. I regret it now. Have pity on me. Forgive my sins. Let me not lose what You died for me to gain.

Our Father in Heaven, You are there.....
I greet you Mary.....
Glory be to God the Father.....
We are content with You. Have pity on us!
Oh, have pity on us!

I wish the Christians, those who are pitiful in His spirit, may have pity on Him and enter into Heaven.

So let it be.

Jesus looks miserable.
He feels strong ridicule.
He is stripped so all can see.
He was very much ashamed.

– Jesus, forever we adore You. And we thank You.
– You died for all the people to give them life.

44 eka e sakiikot. sasay ekospi kiskeyitam taneyikok ke peci
êkâ ê-sâkihikot. sâsay êkospî kiskêyihtam tânêyikohk kê-pêci-

misiwanaciisonaniwik.
misi-wanâcihisonâniwik.

ni manitom sesos, osam micetweyak ki ki kitimaitin
nimanitôm Sesos, osâm mihcêtwêyahk kikî-kitimâhitin

misiwe isi e ki pastaoyan, ni mitaten ekwa, kitimakinawin,
misiwê isi ê-kî-pâstâhoyan, nimihtâtên êkwa, kitimâkinawin,

kasinamawin kici eka wanitayan ka ki nipostamawiyan.
kâsînamawin kici êkâ wanîtâyan ka-kî-nipôstamawiyan.

notawinan kici kisikok eyayan.....
nôhtâwînân kihci-kîsikohk (ê-)ayâyan.....

kitatamiskatin mari.....
kitatamiskâtin Mari.....

pitane mamiteyitakosit weyotawimit.....
pitanê (ê-)mâmitêyihtâkosit wiyôhtâwîmit....

tepeyimitahk wi-kitimakeyiminan!
(ê-)tipêyimitâhk wî-kitimâkêyiminân!

aw wi kitimakeyiminan!
aw wî-kitimâkêyiminân!

pitane otayamiawok ketimakisicik otacakoma
pitanê otayamihâwak (ê-)kitimâkisicik otâhcahkoma

ketimakeyimikowisiyit mina mina kisikok
(ê-)kitimâkêyimikowisiyit mîna kîsikohk

pitokaikowisiyit
(ê-)pihtokwahikowisiyit

pitane ekosi ikik.
pitanê êkosi ihkik.

---

esi kitimakinakosit
(ê-)isi-kitimâkinâkosit

tapwe itoke soki mositaw
tâpwê êtokwê sôhki-môsihtâw

mosis e kitasakepitit
mosis ê-kêtasâkêpitiht

mistae ki nepewisiw.
mistahi kî-nêpêwisiw.

– sesos naspic kimanaciitinan mina kinanaskomitinan
– Sesos nâspic kimanâcihitinân mîna kinanâskomitinân

– kiya ka ki nipostamawat ayisiyiniw e wi pimaciat.
– kiya kâ-kî-nipôstamawat ayisiyiniw ê-wî-pimâcihat.

45

10

ᓴᓱᐣ ᑫᑕᐘᑌᓯᐱᑎᐟ.

ᐊᑕᐃᔭ ᐅᓴᑦ ᓴᓴ+ ᒥᓵᑕᐁ ᑕᑌᓯ ᐁ ᑐᑕᐟ ᓴᓱᐣ, ᐊᐦ ᒪᑲ ᐅᑌᐸᑕᑫᐅ·· ᕼᓚ ᐳᑌᐁᐅ·· ᒪᕼ, ᐁᑲ· ᒥᕼ ᑭᑕᐘᑌᓯᐱᐅᑐ··. ᐊᓱᑌ ᑭ ᑲ ᑲ·ᑕᑫᐳᑕᑦ ᐁᑯᐢᐱ ᐅᐯᐳᐢᑫ, ᑎᑫᒪ ᐁ ᑭ ᑲ ᑭᐢᑭᐃ·ᐸᐅᐟ ᐊᓱᑎᑫᔭᑲᑐᓯ ᐁᑯᓯ ᒥᓯᐁ· ᐃ·ᔭᐟ ᐸᐸᑲ·ᓯᐱᑕᐤ, ᐅᓴᑦ ᒥᕼ ᑌᐯᐃ·ᓯᐟ ᐁ ᒍᓱᐢᑲᐅᐟ. ᐯᓯᑲ·ᑎᓯᐋᐟ ᐁᑲ ᐃ·ᑲ· ᑌᐯᐃ·ᓯᐋᐟ, ᐊ·ᐸᒥᐟ ᑭ ᒪᑌᑐᒥᐊ·ᐤ ᑕᑌᓯ ᑲ ᑐᑕᐊ·ᐋᐟ; ᐁᑲ· ᐁᑲᐃ·ᔭ ᐊᓴᑌᐟ ᐁ ᑌᑕᐁ·ᔭᒥᑯᐋ ᑭᑎ ᒣᑯ· ᐃᓯᐁ·ᐱᓯᐋᐟ ᑌ ᒥᔭ ᓴᓱᐣ, ᑭᔭ ᐱᑯ ᐅᑎ ᑯᑎᐸᔭᐟ ᐃᔭᑌᓯᐃ·ᐤ ᒥᔭᐤ ᑭᑎ ᑭᔭᒥᐃ·ᓯᔭᐤ ᐁᑲ ᑭᑎ ᐃ·ᑎᐃᐁ·ᔭᐤ ᐁ ᑲᑭᐸᑎᓯᐟ.

ᓄᑕᐃ·ᓇᐤ ᑭᑎ ᑭᓯᑯᐟ ᐁᔭᔭᐤ .....
ᑭᑕᑕᒥᐢᑲᐅ ᒪᕆ .....
ᐱᑕᑌ ᒪᒥᑌᔭᑕᑯᓯᐟ ᐁ·ᐘᑕᐃ·ᒥᐟ .....
ᑌᐯᔭᒥᑕᐟ ᐃ· ᑭᑎᒪᑫᔭᒥᕼᐤ!
ᐊᐤ ᐃ· ᑭᑎᒪᑫᔭᒥᕼᐤ!

ᐱᑕᑌ ᐅᑕᔭᒥᐊᐅ·· ᑫᑎᒪᑭᓯᑎᐟ ᐅᑕᑌᑯᒪ ᑫᑎᒪᑫᔭᒥᑯᐃ·ᓯᔭᐟ ᒥᕼ ᑭᓯᑯᐟ ᐱᑐᐸᐃᑯᐃ·ᓯᔭᐟ ᐱᑕᑌ ᐁᑯᓯ ᐃᑭᐟ.

ᐊᔭᒥᐁᐊ·ᑎᑯᐟ ᐁᑲ·
ᐱᒥᓯᐤ ᑭᑎ ᑎᐢᑕᐊᐢᑲ·ᑎᐟ.

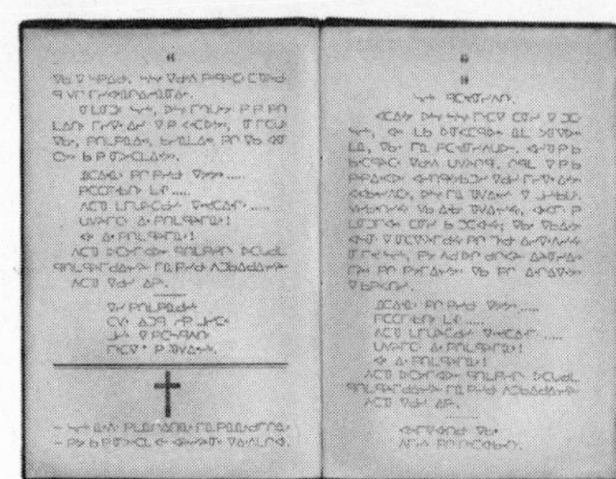

45

10

JESUS IS STRIPPED OF HIS CLOTHES.

More torment was done to Jesus. The murderers did not let Him alone. They also stripped Him of His clothes. He especially suffered because the Lord of all stood exposed. He is ashamed. He is barefoot. Those of you who commit adultery are never embarrassed. Look at your God, what you have done to Him. Do not reject Him. He wants all of you to change your behaviour. My good Jesus, You only came from Heaven to save. Give Your wisdom to me, how to be peaceful, not to be involved with the foolish ones.

Our Father in Heaven, You are there.....
I greet you Mary.....
Glory be to God the Father.....
We are content with You. Have pity on us!
Oh, have pity on us!

I wish the Christians, those who are pitiful in His spirit, may have pity on Him and enter into Heaven.

So let it be.

Now, on the cross
He hangs after He is crucified.

10

SESOS KETAYONISIPITIT.
SESOS KÊTAYIWINISÊPITIHT.

atawiya osam sasay mistae tanisi e totat sesos, ays
atawiya osâm sâsay mistahi tânisi ê-itôtât Sesos, ays

maka onipatakewok nama poniewok mana, ekwa mina
mâka onipâtâkêwak namâ ponihêwak mâna, êkwa mîna

kitayonisipitewok. asone ki ka kwatakeyitam ekospi
kitayinisipitêwak. âsônê kî-ka-kwâtakêyihtam êkospî

tepeyiciket, cikema e ki ka kiskiwipaot asitikweyakatoso
(ê-)tipêyihcikêt, cikêma ê-kî-ka-kiskiwêpahôt asitikwêyakatoso

ekosi misiwe wiyak papakwasipitaw, osam mina
êkosi misiwê wîyak papakwasipitâw, osâm mîna

nepewisit e mosiskatet. pesikwatisiyek eka wikac
nêpêwisit ê-mosiskâtêt. (ê-)pisikwâtisiyêk êkâ wîhkâc

nepewisiyek, wapamik ki manitomiwaw tanisi ka
(ê-)nêpêwisiyêk, wâpamihk kimanitômiwâw tânisi kâ-

totawayek; ekwa ekawiya asenik e nitaweyimikoyek
itôtawâyêk; êkwa êkâwiya asênihk ê-nitawêyimikoyêk

kici meskoc isiwepisiyek ni miyo sesos, kiya piko oci
kici mêskoc isiwêpisiyêk nimiyo-Sesos, kiya piko ohci

kocipayik iyinisiwin miyin kici kiyamiwisiyan eka kici
kôcipayik iyinisiwin miyin kici-kiyamiwisiyân êkâ kici-

wiciiweyan e kakipatisik.
wîcihiwêyân ê-ka-kipâtisihk.

notawinan kici kisikok eyayan.....
nôhtâwînân kihci-kîsikohk (ê-)ayâyan.....

kitatamiskatin mari.....
kitatamiskâtin Mari.....

pitane mamiteyitakosit weyotawimit.....
pitanê (ê-)mâmitêyihtâkosit wiyôhtâwîmit.....

tepeyimitak wi kitimakeyiminan!
(ê-)tipêyimitâhk wî-kitimâkêyiminân!

aw wi kitimakeyiminan!
aw wî-kitimâkêyiminân!

pitane otayamiawak ketimakisicik otacakoma
pitanê otayamihâwak (ê-)kitimâkisicik otâhcahkoma

ketimakeyimikowisiyit mina kisikok pitokaikowisiyit
(ê-)kitimâkêyimikowisiyit mîna kîsikohk (ê-)pihtokahikowisiyit

pitane ekosi ikik.
pitanê êkosi ihkik.

---

ayamiewatikok ekwa
ayamihêwahtikohk êkwa

pimisin kici cistaaskwatit.
pimisin kici-cîstahâskwâtiht.

46

ᐊᐧᐸᒥᐠ ᑭ ᒪᑎᑐᒥᐊᐧᐤ
ᑭᔮᐊᐧᐤ * ᑲ ᑐᑕᐊᐧᔦᐠ.

— ᓴᓯᐣ ᓇᐣᐱ- ᑭᒪᓇᒋᐃᑎᓇᐣ ᒥᓇ ᑭᓇᓇᐣᑯᒥᑎᓇ
— ᑭᔮ ᑲᑭᑎᔮᐣᑕᒪᐊᐦ ᐊᔦᔨᔮᑎᐤ ᐁᐃᐧᐱᒪᒋᐊ

11

ᓴᓯᐣ ᒋᐣᑕᐊᐣᑲᐧᑕᐤ.

ᐁᑲ ᒉᐣᑲᐧ ᐁ ᑭ ᐸᑭᑌᔮᒥᐟ ᓴᓯᐣ ᑭᒋ ᑎ ᐸᐃᐟ, ᓴᓴ+ ᑎᑕᐁᐧᔮᒪᐤ ᑭᒋ ᒋᐣᑕᐊᐣᑲᐧᒋᐟ, ᐁᑲ ᑕᐯᐧ ᐁᑯᓯ ᑐᑕᐊᐧᐤ. ᐯᒪᒋᐃᐁᐧᐦ ᑎᐸᐃᐟ ᐊᑎᐃ ᐊᔦᔨᔮᑎᐊᐧ ᑲ ᐃᐧ ᑎᔮᐣᑕᒪᐊᐦ ᓴᑫ ᐁᐧᐱᑎᓯ ᑕᑕᐣᑕᐁᐧᔮᑲᐣᑭᒋᓚᑎᐣᑕᐊᐧᐤ ᒥᓇ ᑕᑕᐣᑕᐁᐧᔮᑲ ᑭᓯᑌᑎᐣᑕᐊᐧᐤ ᒥᓯ ᓴᑲᐃᑲᓇ ᐅᒋ, ᐸᑲᒪᐃ ᑲᐧᑕᒪᐤ ᐊᐧᐊᐧ-, ᐱᔮᐣ ᒋᒪᐊᐤ ᐁ ᐃᐧ ᑲᑭᒋᐊ ᐁᐧᔦᑕᐃᐧᒪᐠ ᒪᑎᑐᐊᐧ.

ᐸᐣᑕᐅᐃᐤ ᑯᒋ ᑎᐸᐃᐟ ᑎ ᒥᔦ ᓴᓯᐣ, ᒪᒋ ᐸᐣᑕᐅᐃᐤ, ᐅᓴᑦ ᒥᒉᑕᐤ ᑭ ᓴᑯᒋᐃᐊᐤ. ᒥᒋ ᐅᑕᔮᒥᐊᐅᐦ ᐸᐣᑭᔮᐁᐅᐦ ᓯᑕᐃᐧᔮᑎᐊᐧ ᐁᔮ ᒪᒋ ᐯᒪᒋᓯᒋᐠ. ᑎ ᒪᑎᑐᐨ, ᑎ ᒪᑎᑐᐨ, ᑎ ᒥᑕᑌ ᐁᑯᓯ ᑎᐣᑕ ᐁ ᑭ ᐸᐣᑭᔮᑫᔮᐤ.

ᓇᑕᐃᐧᓇᐤ ᑭᒋ ᑭᓯᑯᐠ ᐁᔮᔮᐤ.....

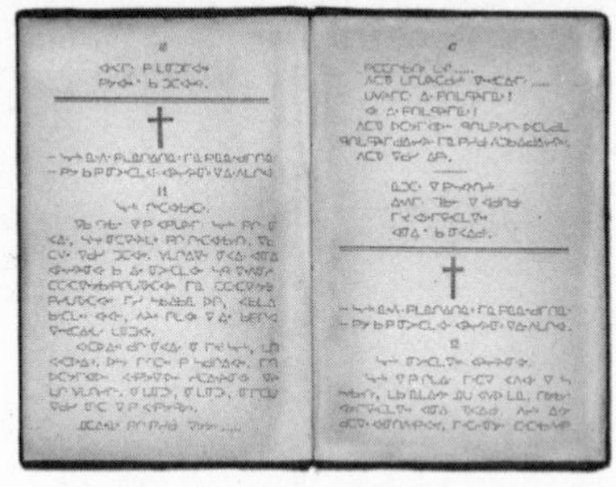

46 Watch Him, your God,
you all did this to Him.

Jesus, forever we respect You and we thank You.
You died for all the people to give them life.

II

JESUS IS NAILED TO THE CROSS.

The sacrifice was not yet over. He is nailed to a cross to save them. He saved them. He is killed. Those people He died for. Quickly the soldiers drove big nails into His hands and feet and threw gall at Him. He is going to comfort God the Father.

My good Jesus, You are killed on account of sins. A lot of time evil sins overcome the Jewish people and many who pray. Sins win us over. My God, Father God, I regret that I was overcome by sin.

Our Father in Heaven, You are there.....

wapamik ki manitomiwaw
wâpamihk kimanitômiwâw

kiyawaw ka totawayek.
kîyawâw kâ-itôtawâyêk.

– sesos naspic kimanaciitinan mina kinanaskomitinan
– Sesos nâspic kimanâcihitinân mîna kinanâskomitinân

– kiya ka ki nipostamawat ayisiyiniw e wi pimaciat.
– kiya kâ-kî-nipôstamawat ayisiyiniw ê-wî-pimâcihat.

II

SESOS CISTAASKWATAW.
SESOS CÎSTAHÂSKWÂTÂW.

eka ceskwa e ki pakiteyimit sesos kici ni pait, sasay
êkâ cêskwa ê-kî-pakitêyimiht Sesos kici-nipahiht, sâsay

nitaweyimaw kici cistaaskwatit, ekwa tapwe ekosi totawaw.
nitawêyimâw kici-cîstahâskwâtiht, êkwa tâpwê êkosi itôtawâw.

pemaciiwet nipaik anii ayisiyiniwa ka
(ê-)pimâcihiwêt nipahik anihi ayisiyiniwa kâ-

wi nipostamawat seke wepiniso, tatastaweya
wî-nipôstamawât sêhkê-wêpinisow, tâ-tastaweya-

kaskicicanestawaw mina tatastaweyakas kisitenestawaw
kaskicihcânêstawâw mîna tâ-tastaweya kaskisitânêstawâw

misi sakaikana oci, pakamais kwatamwan wawac, piyis
misi-sakahikan ohci, pakamahiskwâtamwân wâwâc, piyis

cimaaw e wi kakiciat weyotawimat manitowa.
cimâhâw ê-wî-kâkicihât wiyôhtâwîmit manitowa.

pastaowin koci nipait ni miyo sesos, maci pastaowin,
pâstâhowin koci-nipahît nimiyo-Sesos, maci-pâstâhowin,

osam micetwaw ki sakociiwan. micet otayamiawok
osâm mihcêtwâw kisâkôcihiwân. mihcêt otayamihâwak

paskiyawewok sotawiyiniwa esi maci pematisicik.
paskiyawêwak Sotawiyiniwa ê-isi-maci-pimâtisicik.

ni manitom, ni manitom, nimitaten ekosi nista e ki
nimanitôm, nimanitôm, nimihtâtên êkosi nîsta ê-kî-

paskiyakeyan.
pâskiyâkêyân.

notawinan kici kisikok eyayan.....
nôhtâwînân kihci-kîsikohk (ê-)ayâyan.....

47

ᑭᑕᑕᒥᐢᑲᑎᐣ ᒪᕆ .....
ᐱᑕᑌ ᒪᒥᑌᔨᑕᑯᔨᐟ ᐁᐧᔪᑕᐃᐧᒥᐟ .....
ᑌᐯᔨᒥᑕᐠ ᐃᐧ ᑭᑎᒪᑫᔨᒥᓇᐣ!
ᐊᐤ ᐃᐧ ᑭᑎᒪᑫᔨᒥᓇᐣ!
ᐱᑕᑌ ᐅᑕᔭᒥᐊᐅᐦ ᑫᑎᒪᑭᔨᐢ ᐅᑕᒐᑯᒪ
ᑫᑎᒪᑫᔨᒥᑯᐃᐧᔨᔭᐠ ᒥᓇ ᑭᔨᑯᐧ ᐱᑐᑲᐃᑯᐃᐧᔨᔭᐟ.
ᐱᑕᑌ ᐁᑯᔨᐟ ᐃᑭᐠ.

ᓇᑐᑕᐠ ᐁ ᑭᓴᐊᐧᑎᔨᐟ
ᐃᐢᐱᒥᐠ ᒣᑲᐧ ᐁ ᐊᑯᑎᑯᐟ
ᒥᔪ ᐊᔭᒥᐁᐢᑕᒪᐁᐧᐤ
ᐊᓂᐃ * ᑲ ᓂᐸᐃᑯᐟ.

— ᓴᔨᐢ ᓇᐢᐱ-ᑭᒪᓇᐱᓂᓇᐣ ᒥᓇ ᑭᓇᓇᐢᑯᒥᑎᓇᐣ
— ᑭᔦ ᑲᑭ ᓂᔦᐢᑕᒪᐊᐤ ᐊᔭᔨᔦᓂᐤ ᐁᐃᐧᐱᒪᑎᐊᐟ.

12

ᓴᔨᐢ ᓂᔦᐢᑕᒪᐁᐧᐤ ᐊᔭᔨᔦᓂᐊᐧ.

ᓴᔨᐢ ᐁ ᑭ ᒋᒪᐃᐟ ᒥᐢᑕᐁ ᑫᐱᐊᐤ ᐁ ᓴ ᓴᐢᑲᑎᐟ, ᒪᑲ ᓇᒪᐃᐧᔦ ᔭᑌ ᐊᐯᐅ ᒪᓇ, ᑎᔦᑲᐧ-ᐊᔦᒥᐁᐢᑕᒪᐁᐧᐤ ᐊᓂᐃ ᓂᐸᐃᑯᐟ. ᐱᔪ ᐃᐧᔦ ᑯᑕᐧ ᐊᐧᓂᑎᐱᐢᑭᐸᔨ, ᒥᐢᑕᔨᓂᔦ ᑕᐢᑕᐢᑲᐱᐢᑭ

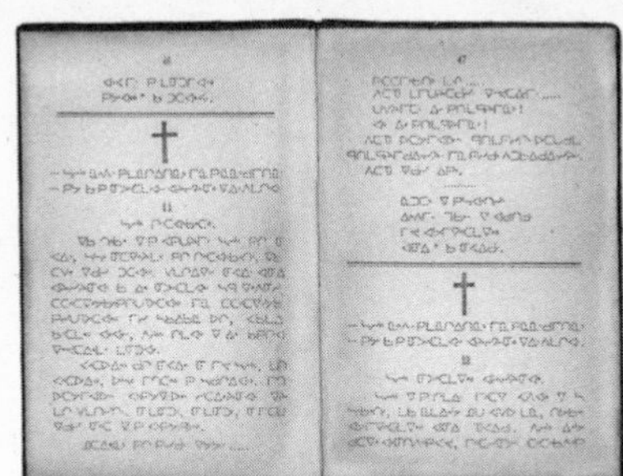

47 I greet you Mary....
Glory be to God the Father....
We are content with You. Have pity on us!
Oh, have pity on us!

I wish the Christians, those who are pitiful in His spirit, may have pity on Him and enter into Heaven.

So let it be.

I ask for it: He is kind.
Right up above, He is hung.
He prays well for them,
those who killed Him.

Jesus, forever we adore You and we thank You.
You died for all the people to give them life.

12

JESUS DIES FOR THE PEOPLE.

Jesus is made to suffer greatly. He is laughed at and continuously spat on. He is cried for, but no one wants to avenge. On the contrary He prays for those who killed Him. He is blind with pain. There is lightning. It gets dark; the stone of the temple cracks.

47 kitatamiskatin mari.....
kitatamiskâtin Mari.....

pitane mamiteyitakosit weyotawimit.....
pitanê (ê-)mâmitêyihtâkosit wiyôhtâwîmit.....

tepeyimitak wi kitimakeyiminan!
(ê-)tipêyimitâhk wî-kitimâkêyiminân!

aw wi kitimakeyiminan!
aw wî-kitimâkêyiminân!

pitane otayamiawok ketimakisicik otacakoma
pitanê otayamihâwak (ê-)kitimâkisicik otâhcahkoma

ketimakeyimikowisiyik mina kisikok pitokaikowisiyit.
(ê-)kitimâkêyimikowisiyik mîna kîsikohk (ê-)pihtokahikowisiyit.

pitane ekosi ikik.
pitanê êkosi ihkik.

---

natotak e kisewatisit
natotahk ê-kisêwâtisit

ispimik mekwac e akotikot
ispimihk mêkwâc ê-akotikot

miyo ayamiestamawew
miyo-ayamihêstamawêw

anii ka nipaikot.
anihi kâ-nipahikot.

– sesos naspic kimanaciitinan mina kinanaskomitinan
– Sesos nâspic kimanâcihitinân mîna kinanâskomitinân

– kiya ka ki nipostamawat ayisiyiniw e wi pimaciat.
– kiya kâ-kî-nipôstamawat ayisiyiniw ê-wî-pimâcihat.

12

SESOS NIPOSTAMAWAW AYISIYINIWA.
SESOS NIPÔSTAMAWÊW AYISIYINIWA.

sesos e ki cimait mistae papiaw e sasaskwatit, maka
Sesos ê-kî-cimahît mistahi pâhpihâw ê-sâsihkwâtiht, mâka

namawiya note apeo mana, tiyakwac ayamiestamawew
namâwiya nohtê-âpêho mâna, tiyakwac ayamihêstamawêw

anii nepaikot. pisin wiya kotawe wanitipiskipayo,
anihi nipahikot. pisin wiya kotawê wanitipiskipayow,

mistasiniyak tastaskpiski
mistasiniyak tastaskapiski

48 It is amazing. Everybody sees it this way, that He was the Lord. He cries aloud. "Everything is finished," He says. So there, he bowed to Him, He breathes His last.

He breathes in. Our Father, you are praying. It is impossible to be rock-like, not to be moved, to feel it in your hearts. You are remembering that He did die for you. Jesus, Lord, You died for me. That is why I am going to live for You.

Our Father in Heaven, You are there.....
I greet you Mary.....
Glory be to God the Father.....
We are content with You. Have pity on us!
Oh, have pity on us!

I wish the Christians, those who are pitiful in His spirit, may have pity on Him and enter into Heaven.

So let it be.

Jesus has breathed his last.
Already, He is very much rewarded.
He gained Heaven for us,
when we go.

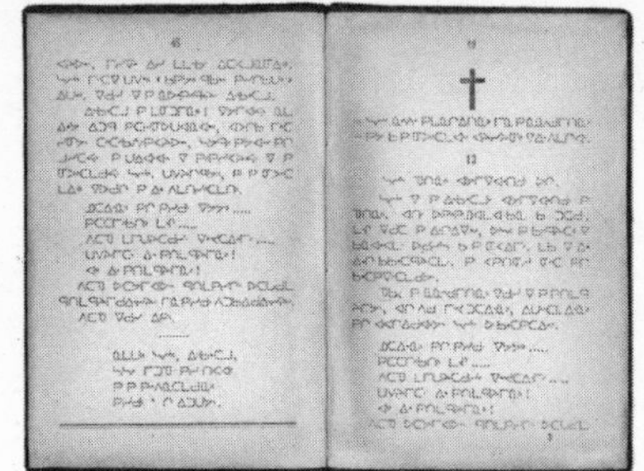

48 payiwok, misiwe isi mamaskac itapamonaniwiw. sesos
payiwak, misiwê isi mâmaskâc itâpamonâniwiw. Sesos

mistae tepwew « kakiyaw kekway kisicikatew » itwew.
mistahi têpwêw "kahkiyaw kîkway kîsihcikâtêw" itwêw.

ekosi e ki nawokiskweyit iskwatamo.
êkosi ê-kî-nawokiskwêyit iskwatâmow.

iskwatamo ki manitominaw! eyamiayek namawiya
iskwatâmow kimanitôminaw! ê-ayamihâyêk namâwiya

itoke kitasinioteanawaw, apocika mistasiniyak
êtikwê kitasinihotêhânâwâw, apocika mistasiniyâhk

tastaskapiskipayiwok, seyakes kiyawaw kici mositayek
tastaskapiskipayiwak, sêyâkês kîyawâw kici-môsîtâyêk

ki teiwawak e kiskisopayiyek e ki nipostamakoyek
kitêhiwâwak ê-kiskisopayiyek ê-kî-nipôstamakoyêk

sesos. tepeyicikeyan, ki ki nipostamawin eokoci ki wi
Sesos. (ê-)tipêyihcikêyan, kikî-nipôstamawin êwakohci kiwî-

pimatisistamatin.
pimâtisitamâtin.

notawinan kici kisikok eyayan.....
nôhtâwînân kihci-kîsikohk (ê-)ayâyan.....

kitatamiskatin mari.....
kitatamiskâtin Mari.....

pitane mamiteyitakosit weyotawimit.....
pitanê (ê-)mâmitêyihtâkosit wiyôhtâwîmit.....

tepeyimitak wi kitimakeyiminan!
(ê-)tipêyimitâhk wî-kitimâkêyiminân!

aw wi kitimakeyiminan!
aw wî-kitimâkêyiminân!

pitane otayamiawok ketimakisicik otacakoma
pitanê otayamihâwak (ê-)kitimâkisicik otâhcahkoma

ketimakeyimikowisiyit mina kisikok pitokaikowisiyit.
(ê-)kitimâkêyimikowisiyit mîna kîsikohk (ê-)pihtokwahikowisiyit.

pitane ekosi ikik.
pitanê êkosi ihkik.

---

namatew sesos, iskwatamo,
namatêw Sesos, iskwâtâmow,

sasay mitone kisi tipaam
sâsay mitonê kîsi-tipaham

ki ki kispinatamakonaw
kikî-kîspinatamâkonaw

kisikok ci itoteyak.
kîsikohk kici-itohtêyahk.

49

— ᓴᓱᐢ ᓇᐢᐱ· ᑭᒪᓇᒋᐃᑎᓇᐤ ᒥᓇ ᑭᓇᓇᐢᑯᒥᑎᓇᐤ
— ᑭᔭ ᑲ ᑭ ᒌᔭᐢᑕᓚᐞ ᐊᔭᓯᔭᒌᐤ ᐁᐃ· ᐱᒪᒋᐊ·.

13

ᓴᓱᐢ ᒍᑎᓇᐤ ᐊᔭᒥᐁᐊ·ᑎᑯᐠ ᐅᒋ.

ᓴᓱᐢ ᐁ ᑭ ᐃᐢᑲ·ᑕᒧᐠ ᐊᔭᒥᐁᐊ·ᑎᑯᐠ ᑭ ᒍᑎᓇᐤ. ᐊᒋᐠ ᐅᑭᐢᑭᐱᐊᒪᐊ ᑲᓇ ᑲ ᑐᑕᑯᐠ. ᒪᕆ ᐁᑯᑕ ᑭ ᐃ·ᒋᐃᐁ·ᐤ, ᐅᓴᐢ ᑭ ᑲᐢᕴᔭᑕᐢ ᐁ ᑲᓇᐊ·ᐸᒪᐠ ᐅᑯᓯᓴ ᑲ ᑭ ᒌᐸᐃᒥᐠ. ᒪᑲ ᐁ ᐃ· ᐃ·ᕆ ᑲᑲ·ᑕᕴᔭᑕᒪᐠ, ᑭ ᐸᑭᑎᒌᓱ ᒌᐢᑕ ᑭᒋ ᑲ·ᑕᑭᐁᐢᑕᒪᑯᔭᐠ.

ᒍᑲ, ᑭ ᓇᓇᐢᑯᒥᑎᓇᐤ ᐁᑯᓯ ᐁ ᑭ ᑭᑎᒪᕴ ᔭᒥᔭᐠ, ᐊᒋ ᐱᑯ ᒥᔦᑐᑕᐃ·ᓇᐤ, ᐃᑌ·ᐢᑕᒪ ᐃ·ᓇᐤ ᑭᒋ ᐊᐸᒋᐃᑯᐊ·ᔾ ᓴᓱᐢ ᐅ ᑲ·ᑕᑭᑕᐃ·ᐤ.

ᓄᑕᐃ·ᓇᐤ ᑭᒋ ᑭᓯᑯᐠ ᐁᔭᔭᐤ.....
ᑭᑕᑕᒥᐢᑲᑎᐤ ᒪᕆ.....
ᐱᑕᒍ ᒪᒥᑐᔭᑕᑯᓯᐟ ᐁ·ᔦᑕᐃ·ᒥᐟ.....
ᑌᐯᔭᒥᑕᐠ ᐃ· ᑭᑎᒪᕴᔭᒥᓇᐤ!
ᐊᐤ ᐃ· ᑭᑎᒪᕴᔭᒥᓇᐤ!
ᐱᑕᒍ ᐅᑕᔭᒥᐊᐅ·ᐤ ᕴᑎᒪᑭᓯᒋᐠ ᐅᑕᑐᑯᒪ

3

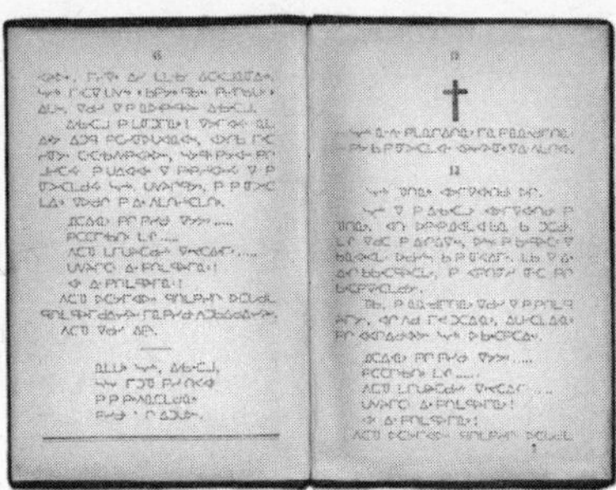

49

Jesus, forever we adore You and we thank You.
You died for all the people to give them life.

13

JESUS IS TAKEN DOWN FROM THE CROSS.

Jesus breathed His last on the cross. He was taken down. Some followers did this to Him. Mary accompanied Him there because He was lonely. She saw her Son when He was killed. But He suffered for us. He gave us life, me too. He suffers for us.

Mother, we thank you. So then, you had pity on us. Even though you do us good, say it for us so that Jesus's suffering will be useful to us.

Our Father in Heaven, You are there....
I greet you Mary....
Glory be to God the Father.....
We are content with You. Have pity on us!
Oh, have pity on us!

I wish the Christians, those who are poor in His spirit,

49 

– sesos naspic kimanaciitinan mina kinanaskomitinan
– Sesos nâspic kimanâcihitinân mîna kinanâskomitinân

– kiya ka ki nipostamawat ayisiyiniw e wi pimaciat.
– kiya ka-kî-nipôstamawat ayisiyiniw ê-wî-pimâcihat.

13

SESOS NETINAW AYAMIEWATIKOK OCI.
SESOS NÊTINÂW AYAMIHÊWAHTIKOHK OHCI.

sesos e ki iskwatamot ayamiewatikok ki netinaw. atit
Sesos ê-kî-iskwatamot ayamihêwahtikohk kî-nêtinâw. âtiht

okiskinoamawakana ka totakot. mari ekota ki wiciiwew,
okiskinohamâwakana kâ-itôtâkot. Mari êkota kî-wîcihiwêw,

osam ki kaskeyitam e kanawapamat okosisa ka ki
osâm kî-kaskêyihtam ê-kânawâpamât okosisa kâ-kî-

nipaimit. maka e wi wici kakwatakeyitamat, ki
nipahimiht. mâka ê-wî-wîci-kakwâtakêyihtamat, kî-

pakitiniso nista kici kwatakiestamakoyak.
pakitinisow nîsta kici-kwâtakihêstamâkoyahk.

neka, ki nanaskomitinan ekosi e ki kitimakeyimiyak,
nêkâ, kinanâskomitinân êkosi ê-kî-kitimâkêyimiyâhk,

aci piko miyo totawinan, itwestamawinan kici
aci piko miyo-itôtawinân, itwêstamawinân kici-

apaciikowayak sesos okwatakitawin.
âpacihikowayahk Sesos okwâtakîtawin.

notawinan kici kisikok eyayan.....
nôhtâwînân kihci-kîsikohk (ê-)ayâyan.....

kitatamiskatin mari.....
kitatamiskâtin Mari.....

pitane mamiteyitakosit weyotawimit....
pitanê (ê-)mâmitêyihtâkosit wiyôhtâwîmit....

tepeyimitak wi kitimakeyiminan!
(ê-)tipêyimitâhk wî-kitimâkêyiminân!

aw! wi kitimakeyiminan!
aw! wî-kitimâkêyiminân!

pitane otayamiawok ketimakisicik otacakoma
pitanê otayamihâwak (ê-)kitimâkisicik otâhcahkoma

50

ᑫᑎᒪᑫᔨᒥᑯᐃᐧᔨᔩᐟ ᒥᓇ ᑭᔨᑯᐧ ᐱᑐᑲᐃᑯᐃᐧᔨᔩᐟ
ᐱᑕᑌ ᐁᑯᔨ ᐃᑭᐠ.

ᓇᐢᐱ ᑭ ᓇᐅᐧᑭᐢᑖᑎᓇᐣ
ᓴᓯᐢ, ᐅᑕ ᐁ ᐱᒥᔨᓂᔭᐣ.
ᐁᑲᐧ ᐃᐧ ᓂᓯᑲᒪᐃᐧᓇᐣ
ᑲᑭᑫ * ᒋ ᓴᑭᐃᑕᐠ.

— ᓴᓯᐢ ᓇᐢᐱ ᑭᒪᓇᒋᐃᓇᐣ ᒥᓇ ᑭᓇᓇᐢᑯᒥᑎᓇᐣ
— ᑭᔭ ᑲᑭ ᓂᐳᐢᑕᒪᐊᐧ ᐊᔨᔨᔨᓂᐤ ᐁ ᐃᐧᐱᒪᒋᐊᐧ

14

ᓴᓯᐢ ᐃᐧᔭᐤ ᓇᔨᓇᒪᐤ.

ᓴᓯᐢ ᐃᐧᔭᐤ ᐁ ᑭ ᑌᑎᓇᒧᐧ ᐊᔭᒥᐁᐊᐧᑎᑯᐧ ᐅᒋ ᑭᐁᐧᐁᐧᑭᓇᒪᐤ ᑭᒋ ᓇᔨᓇᒧᐧ ᐅᐢᑭᐊᐧᑎᑲᓂᐠ ᐸᑭᑎᓇᒪᐤ. ᐁᑯᑕ ᑲ ᑭ ᐱᒥᔨᐠ ᒪᓂᑐᐊᔨᔨᔨᓂᐤ ᒉᑳ ᐅᑕᐡᑲᐧ ᐊᑕᒪᐢᑲᒥᑯᐧ ᐁ ᐃᑐᑌᔨ. ᓂ ᒥᔪᓴᓯᐢ ᐁᑯᔨ ᑭ ᑭᔨᐸᐣ ᑭ ᐱᒪᑎᓯᐃᐧᐣ ᐁ ᐃᐧ ᑭᐢᑭᓄᐊᒪᐃᐧᔭᐠ ᑭᒋ ᐃᓯᐁᐧᐱᓯᔭᐠ; ᐅᐢᑭ ᐊᐧᑎᑲᓂᐠ ᑭᑭᓇᔨᑐᑲᐃᐧᐣ ᐁᓂᑕᐁᐧᔨᒥᔭᐠ ᑭᒋ ᐅᐢᑭ ᐅᑌᐃᔭᐠ ᐁ ᐃᐧ ᐯᒋᑌᐁᐧᐢᑲᐃᐧᔭᐠ ᐊᔭᒥᐁ ᓴᑲᒧᔭᑭ. ᐃᐧ ᒥᔨᓇᐣ ᑭᒋ ᒥᐁᐧᔨᑕᒪᐠ, ᑭᒋ ᓇᓇᑲᑕ

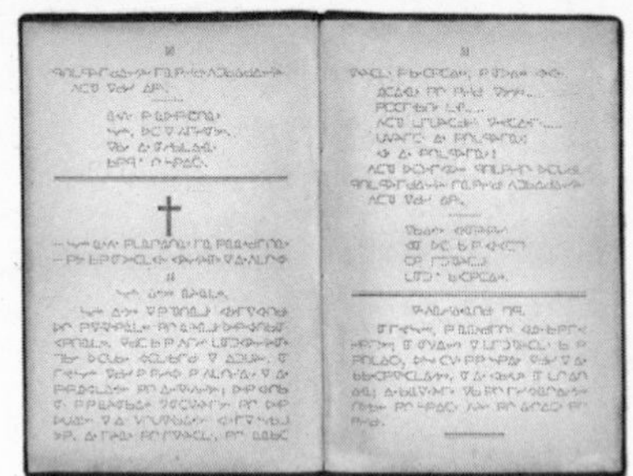

50 may have pity on Him and enter into Heaven.
So let it be.

Forever, we bow to You.
Jesus, You are lying here
and You are going to help together with this devotion
all the time that we love You.

Jesus, forever we adore You and we thank You.
You died for all the people to give them life.

14

JESUS IS LAID IN THE TOMB.

Jesus's body was taken down from the cross. His body was wrapped in linen to be buried in a new grave, to be released as the law allowed. There He lay. Right now, His spirit is going to the underworld. My good Jesus, at the end of Your life, You are going to teach us how to behave from the grave. You were buried. You are wanting us to have a good heart. You are going to enter into our heart when we receive Holy Communion. Give it to us, to like it, to treat it reverently.

50 ketimakeyimikowisiyit mina kisikok pitokaikowisiyit
(ê-)kitimâkêyimikowisiyit mîna kîsikohk (ê-)pihtokwahikowisiyit

pitane ekosi ikik
pitanê êkosi ihkik.

---

naspic ki nawokistatinan
nâspic kinawokistâtinân

sesos, ota e pimisiniyan.
Sesos, ôta ê-pimisiniyan.

ekwa wi nisokamawinan
êkwa wî-nîsôhkamawinân

kakike ci sakiitik.
kâkikê kici-sâkihitâhk.

– sesos naspic kimanaciitinan mina kinanaskomitinan
– Sesos nâspic kimanâcihitinân mîna kinanâskomitinân

– kiya ka ki nopostamawat ayisiyiniw e wi pimaciat
– kiya kâ-kî-nipôstamawat ayisiyiniw ê-wî-pimâcihat

14

SESOS WIYAW NAYINAMWAN.
SESOS WÎYAW NAYINAMWÂN.

sesos wiyaw e ki netinamot ayamiewatikok oci
Sesos wiyaw ê-kî-nîtinamôt ayamihêwahtikohk ohci

kiwewekinamwan kici nayinamot oskiwatikanik
kî-wêwêkinamwân kici-nayinamôt oski-wâtihkwânihk

pakitinamwan. ekota ka ki pimisik manitoayisiyiniw
pakitinamwân. êkota kâ-kî-pimisik manitow ayisiyiniw

mekwac otacakwa atamaskamikok e itoteyit. ni miyo
mêkwâc otâhcahkwa atamiskamikohk ê-itohtêyit. nimiyo-

sesos ekosi ki kisipan ki pimatisiwin e wi kiskinoamawiyak
Sesos êkosi kikisipan kipimâtisiwin ê-wî-kiskinohamâwiyahk

kici isiwepisiyak; oski watikanik ki ki
kici-isiwêpisiyahk; oski-wâtihkwânihk kikî-

nayinikawin enitaweyimiyak kici oski oteiyak e wi
nayinikawin ê-nitawêyimiyahk kici-oski-otêhiyâhk ê-wî-

peciteeskawiyak ayamiesaskamoyaki. wi miyinan kici
pêcitêhêskawiyahk ayamihêsaskamoyâhki. wî-miyinân kici-

miweyitamak, kici nanakata
miywêyihtamâhk, kici-nanâkata

51

ᐍᔨᑕᒪᐠ ᑭ ᑳᑕᑭᑕᐃᐧᐣ, ᑭ ᑎᐳᐃᐧᐣ ᐊᐧᐊᐧ-.

ᓈᑕᐃᐧᓇᐣ ᑭᒋ ᑭᓯᑯᐠ ᐁᔭᔭᐣ.....
ᑭᑕᑕᒥᐢᑲᑎᐣ ᒫᕆ.....
ᐱᑕᑏ ᒪᒥᑌᔨᑕᑯᓯᐠ ᐍᔦᑕᐃᐧᒥᐠ.....
ᑌᐯᔨᒥᑕᐠ ᐃᐧ ᑭᑎᒪᑫᔨᒥᓇᐣ!
ᐊᐤ ᐃᐧ ᑭᑎᒪᑫᔨᒥᓇᐣ!

ᐱᑕᑏ ᐅᑕᔭᒥᐊᐅᐧᐠ ᑫᑎᒪᑭᓯᒋᐠ ᐅᑕᒍᑯᒪ ᑫᑎᒪᑫᔨᒥᑯᐃᐧᓯᔨᐠ ᒥᓇ ᑭᓯᑯᐠ ᐱᑐᑲᐃᑯᐃᐧᓯᔨᐠ
ᐱᑕᑏ ᐁᑯᓯ ᐃᑭᐠ.

ᐁᑲᐃᐧᔭ ᐊᐧᑏᑭᐢᑭᓯᐠ
ᐊᑏ ᐅᑕ ᑲ ᑭ ᐊᐧᐸᑕᒣᐠ
ᑕᑭ ᒥᑐᑏᔨᑕᒧᐠ
ᒪᑏᑐ * ᑳᑕᑭᑕᐃᐧᐣ.

ᐍᐱᓇᓯᐃᐧᓇᑎᑯᐠ ᑎᑫ.

ᑏ ᒥᔦᓴᓯᐢ, ᑭ ᓇᓇᐢᑯᒥᑎᐣ ᐊᓈᐧ ᑲᑭᒥᔦ ᓯᑭᒥᔭᐣ; ᑏ ᑏᐯᐃᐧᓯᐣ ᐁ ᒪᒥᑐᑏᔨᑕᒪᐣ ᑲ ᑭ ᑭᑎᒪᐱᑕᐣ. ᐅᓴᐢ ᑕᐯᐧ ᑭ ᑭ ᓴᑭᐃᐣ ᐁᑯᓯ ᐁ ᐃᐧ ᑲᑳᑕᑭᐁᐢᑕᒪᐃᐧᔭᐣ, ᑏ ᐃᐧ ᐸᑳᑌᐣ ᑏ ᒪᒋ ᐃᑎ ᐃᐧᓇ; ᐃᐧ ᑲᓇᐍᔨᒥᐣ ᐁᑲ ᑭᒋ ᒥᔦᐊᐧᓇᒋᐃᑯᓯᔭᐣ ᑎᔭᑳ- ᑭᒋ ᓴᑭᐃᑕᐣ ᐱᔨᐢ ᑭᒋ ᐃᐧᒋᐃᑕᐣ ᑭᒋ ᑭᓯᑯᐠ.

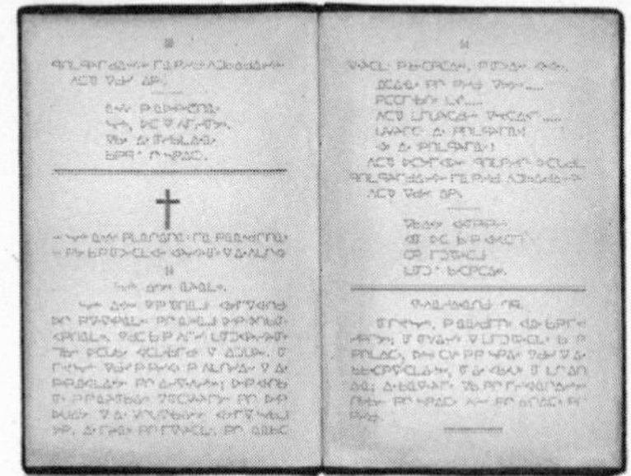

51 We consider Your suffering, Your death especially.

Our Father in Heaven, You are there.....
I greet you Mary.....
Glory to God the Father.....
We are content with You. Have pity on us!
Oh, have pity on us!

I wish the Christians, those who are pitiful in His spirit, may have pity on Him and enter into Heaven.

So let it be.

Do not forget
that here you saw it.
Always think about it,
the Lord's suffering.

NEAR THE TREE OF SACRIFICE.

My good Jesus, I thank You today. You persuaded me. I am ashamed. I am thinking about it, when I made You suffer, because You truly loved me. So there You are going to suffer for me. I will dislike my sins. You are going to take care of me, not to ruin myself. On the contrary, I promise to love You at last and hope to join You in Heaven.

---

51 weyitamak ki kwatakitawin, ki nipowin wawac.
wêyihtamâhk kikwâtakihtawin, kinipowin wâwâc.

notawinan kici kisikok eyayan.....
nôhtâwînân kihci-kîsikohk (ê-)ayâyan.....

kitatamiskatin mari.....
kitatamiskâtin Mari.....

pitane mamiteyitakosit weyotawimit.....
pitanê (ê-)mâmiteyihtâkosit wiyôhtâwîmit.....

tepeyimitak wi kitimakeyiminan!
(ê-)tipêyimitâhk wî-kitimâkêyiminân!

aw wi kitimakeyiminan!
aw wî-kitimâkêyiminân!

pitane otayamiawok ketimakisicik otacakoma
pitanê otayamihâwak (ê-)kitimâkisicik otâhcahkoma

ketimakeyimikowisiyit mina kisikok pitokaikowisiyit
(ê-)kitimâkêyimikowisiyit mîna kîsikohk ê-pihtokahikowisiyit

pitane ekosi ikik.
pitanê êkosi ihkik.

---

ekawiya wanikiskisik
êkâwiya wanikiskisik

ani ota ka ki wapatamek
ani ôta ka-kî-wâpahtamêk

taki mitoneyitamok
tahki mitonêyihtamok

manito kwatakitawin.
manitow kwâtakihtâwin.

WEPINASOWINATIKOK CEKE.
WÊPINÂSOWINÂHTIKOHK CÎKI.

ni miyo sesos, ki nanaskomitin anoc ka ki miyo
nimîyo-Sesos, kinanâskomitin anohc ka-kî-miyo-

sikimiyan; ni nipewisin e mamitoneyitaman ka ki
sîkimiyan, ninipêwisin ê-mamitonêyihtamân kâ-kî-

kitimaitan. osam tapwe ki ki sakiin ekosi e wi
kitimahitân. osâm tâpwê kikî-sâhkihin êkosi ê-wî-

kakwatakiestamawiyan, ni wi pakwaten ni maci itiwina;
kakwâtakihêstamawiyan, niwî-pakwâtên nimacihtiwina;

wi kanaweyimin eka kici misiwanaciisoyan tiyakwac kici
wî-kanawêyimin êkâ kici-misi-wanâcihisoyân tiyakwac kici-

sokiitan piyis kici wiciitan kici kisikok.
sôkihitân piyis kici-wîcihitân kihci-kisikohk.

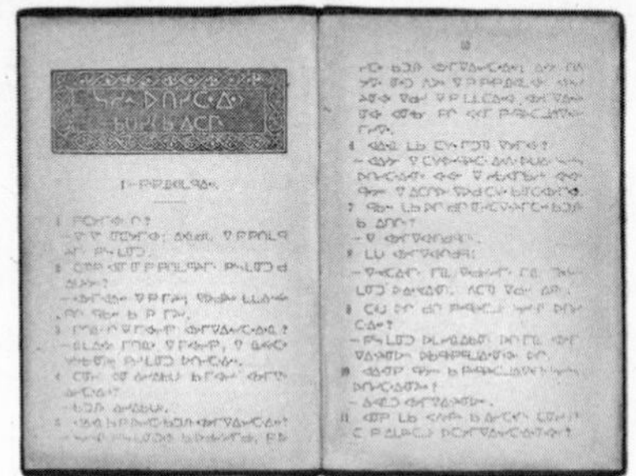

52

THE WAY OF JESUS THE ONE THAT IS CALLED CATECHISM

I – LESSON.

1 Do you pray?
– Yes I do pray. I thank You. Everybody pitied God.
2 Why is it that God pitied me?
– He gave me prayers, the greatest thing He gave me.
3 Are there many good ceremonies?
– Not many people are good, but God's rites are always good.
4 What is it called, the good praying ceremony?
– It is called Catholic.
5 Who made the praying ceremony Catholic?
– God made man, Jesus, His Son Jesus, His Son, He made

SESOS OTISITAWIN KATESIM KA ITAMIK

SESOS OTISÎHTWÂWIN KATÊSIM KÂ-ITAMIHK

I – KISKINOAMAKEWIN.
1 – KISKINOHAMÂKÊWIN.

---

1 kitayamian ci?
1 kitayamihân cî?

– ek ek nitayamian; winakoma e ki kitimakeyimit kise
– *êk êk nitayamihân; winakoma ê-kî-kitimâkêyimiht kisê-*

manito.
manitow.

2 taneki ani ni ki kitimakeyimik kise manito ko
2 tânêhki ani nikî-kitimâkêyimik kisê-manitow kô-

itweyan?
itwêyân?

– ayamiawin e ki miyit; eokoyiw mamawiyes kici
– *ayamihâwin ê-kî-miyit; êwakoyiw mâmâwiyês kihci*

kekway ka ki miyit.
kîkway ka-kî-miyit.

3 micenwa ci e miwasiki ayamiewisitwawina?
3 mihcênwa cî ê-miywâsiki ayamihêwisîhtwâwina?

– namawiya micenwa e miwasiki, e nayestaw
– *namâwiya mihcênwa ê-miywâsiki, ê-nayêstaw*

peyakwaniyik kisi manito otisitwawin.
pêyakwaniyik kisê-manitow otisîhtwâwin.

4 tanisi ani isiikatek ka miwasik
4 tânisi ani isiyihkâtêki kâ-miywâsik

ayamiew isitwawin?
ayamihewisîhtwâwin?

– katolik isiikatew.
– *kâtolik isiyihkâtêw.*

5 awina ka ki ositat katolik ayamiewisitwawin?
5 awîna ka-kî-osîhtât kâtolik ayamihêwisîhtwâwin?

– sesokri kise manitowa ka okosisimikot,
– *Sesokri kisê-manitowa kâ-okosisimikot,*

53 it the Catholic prayer ceremony. He, Himself, He taught people like this for three winters. God enabled Jesus to do miracles, to make the priests missionaries in all places, to make people aware all over the earth.

6 But who is really praying very much?

– Somebody who believes Jesus came here, especially His ceremony. He is baptized especially well in order to behave well, to truly pray well.

7 How do they remember what they are being told?

– By making the sign of the Cross.

8 Begin to make the sign of the Cross.

– In the name of the Father, God, also the Son of God, also the Holy Spirit in His name and so it shall be.

9 How do they know Jesus, His ceremony?

– From the priests, and their sermons from God's book.

10 Do they know Jesus's ceremony well?

– Yes, priests do.

11 But those who have a different ceremony, how are they going to think about their ceremony?

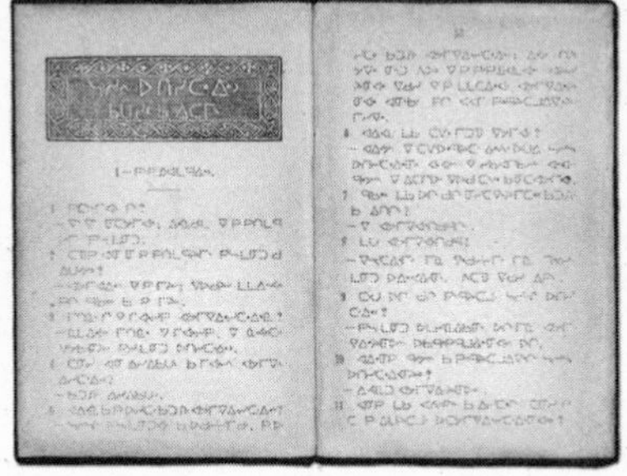

53 ki ositaw katolik ayamiewisitwawin; wiya tipiyawe
kî-osîhtâw kâtolik ayamihêwisîhtwâwin; wiya tipiyawê

nisto pipon e ki kiskinoamawat ayisiyiniwa ekosi e ki
nisto pipon ê-kî-kiskinohamâwat ayisiyiniwa êkosi ê-kî-

mamatawiat ayamiewiyiniwa aniskac kici papami
mamâhtâwihât ayamihêwiyiniwa âniskac kici-papâmi-

kiskeyitamoiweyit misiwe.
kiskêyihtamohiwêyit misiwê.

6 awina maka tapwe mitone eyamiat?
6 awîna mâka tâpwê mitonê (ê-)ayamihât?

– awiyak e tapwewokeyitak ispic oteit sesosa
– awiyak (ê-)tâpwêwakeyihtahk ispic otêhît Sesosa

otisitwawiniw wawac e sikaacikasot wawac kweyask
otisîhtwâwiniw wâwâc ê-sîkahâhcikâsot wâwâc kwayask

e itaciot eoko tapwe kanitaayamiat.
ê-itâcihot êwako tâpwê kâ-nihtâ-ayamihât.

7 kekway maka oci koci nisitaweyimitwaw katolik ka
7 kîkway mâka ohci koci-nisitawêyimitwâw kâtolik kâ-

iticik?
itîcik?

– e ayamiewatikokecik.
– ê-ayamihêwahtikokêcik.

8 mate ayamiewatikoke!
8 mâci-ayamihêwahtikokê!

– weyotawimit mina wekosisimit mina meyosit
– wiyôhtâwîmit mîna wêkosisimit mîna (ê-)miyosit

manito owiyowinik. pitane ekosi ikik.
manitow owîhowinihk. pitanê êkosi ihkik.

9 tante oci koci kiskeyitamot sesokri otisitwawin?
9 tânitê ohci koci-kiskêyihtamôt Sesokri otisîhtwâwin?

– kise manito omasinaikanik oci mina
– kisê-manitow omasinahikanihk ohci mîna

ayamiewiyiniwok okakeskikemowiniwak oci.
ayamihêwiyiniwak okâkêskikêmowiniwak ohci.

10 awiniki kweyask ka kiskeyitamoiwecik sesosa
10 awîniki kwayask kâ-kiskêyihtamohiwêcik Sesosa

otisitwawiniyiw?
otisîhtâwiniyiw?

– iyenato ayamiewiyiniwok.
– iyênato ayamihêwiyiniwak.

11 aniki maka papiskis ka isitwacik tanisi ki ta ki
11 aniki mâka papiskis kâ-isîhtwâcik tânisi kita-kî-

iteyitamot otayamiewisitwawiniwaw?
itêyihtamot otayamihêwisîhtwâwiniwâw?

54

– Nobody, anywhere, should think that this ceremony of belief is worthless. They made their ceremony with conviction.

2 – LESSON.

1 From where is the way of belief in God known?

– The priest's prayer teaches to believe in Jesus's ceremony in this way. I believe in God, the One who is holy.

2 Who is it, who made the faith?

– In the beginning the priests, they taught us to pray

§ 1 "I believe in God, God the Father." This way I believe in Him, God the Father, the One who made everything including the earth.

3 Who is God?

– God is natural. He is divine. He is a spirit who creates and owns everything.

4 How many winters now since God made everything?

– Just about six thousand winters since God made

– namawiya nantaw kita ki iteyitamot eka nantaw
– *namâwiya nânitaw kita-kî-itêyihtamot êkâ nânitaw*

e itapataniyik wiyawaw seke e ki isitwasocik.
ê-itapataniyik wîyawâw sêhkê ê-kî-isîhtwâsocik.

---

2 – KISKINOAMAKEWIN.
2 – KISKINOHAMÂKÊWIN.

1 tante ka oci kiskeyitakaniwik eyikok osam kita
1 tânitê kâ ohci kiskêyihtakaniwak iyikohk osâm kita-

tapwewakeyitamik sesos otisitwawinik?
tâpwêwakêyihtamihk Sesos otisîhtwâwinihk?

– ayamiewiyiniwok o tayamietapwewo
– *ayamihêwiyiniwak otayamihêtâpwêwa*

keyitamowiniwak « ni tapwewokeyimaw kise
kêyihtamowiniwak "nitâpwêwakeyimâwkisê-

manitow weyotawimit » ka isi kicitiniyik.
manitow wiyôhtâwîmit" kâ-isi-kihcitiniyik.

2 aweniki ka ki ositacik ayamietapwewokeyitamowin?
2 awîniki ka-kî-osîhtâcik ayamihêtâpwêwakêyihtamowin?

– nistam ayamiewiyiniwok ki mamawi ositawik.
– *nistam ayamihêwiyiniwak kî-mamawi-osîhtâwak.*

∫ 1 « ni tapwewokeyimaw kise manito weyotawimit
∫ 1 "nitâpwêwakêyimâw kisê-manitow wiyôhtâwîmit

kakiyaw kekway netawitat kisik ka ki ositat askiy
kahkiyaw kîkway nêtawîtât kisik kâ-kî-osîhtât askiy

kiki. »
kiki."

3 awina ana kise manito?
3 awîna ana kisê-manitow?

– kesi manito iyenataw manitowiw e pisisik acakowit,
– *kêsi-manitow iyênataw manitowiw ê-pisîsik âhcahkowit,*

wiya ka ki ositat wawac ka tipeyitak kakiyaw kekway.
wiya kâ-kî-osîhtât wâwâc kâ-tipêyitahk kahkiyaw kîkway.

4 tantato pipon ekwa aspin kise manito kakiyaw
4 tânitahto pipon êkwa aspin kisê-manitow kahkiyaw

kekway ka ki ositat.
kîkway kâ-kî-osîhtât.

– kekac ekwa nikotowasikwaw kici mitatatomitanaw
– *kêkâc êkwa nikôtowâsikwâw kihci-mitâtahtomitanaw*

tato pipon aspin ka ositat kise manito
tahto pipon aspin kâ-osîhtât kisê-manitow

55 Heaven and earth.

6 Was God busy for a long time as He made everything?

– Six days He was busy, so then on the seventh day He rested.

7 Did He make it in parts or all at once?

– In parts, He did it. Yes, He performs wonders.

8 Why did God decide to be busy for six days making everything He was going to make?

– He determined to do it for the people. He was going to give this work of six days to them. So then, to honour each time it was the seventh day.

It was called Sunday, God's day.

9 Is He continually called God?

– He always was and always will be God.

10 Where is God?

– God is all over. In Heaven and on earth.

11 Does he know everything – God?

– He knows everything; He sees everything; He can do everything; there is nothing He cannot do.

12 Can God be seen?

– Nobody sees Him because He has no body.

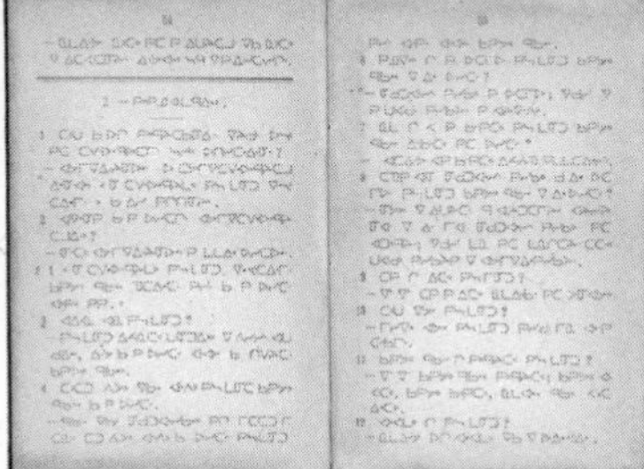

55 kisik askiy wawac kakiyaw kekway.
kîsik askiy wâwâc kahkiyaw kîkway.

6 kinowes ci ki otamio kise manito kakiyaw kekway
6 kinowês cî kî-otamihow kisê-manitow kahkiyaw kîkway

e wi ositat?
ê-wî-osîhtât?

– ni kotowasik kisikaw ki otamio; ekosi e ki tepakop
– nikotwâsik kîsikâw kî-otamihow; êkosi ê-kî-têpakohp

kisikayik ke ayiwepiw.
kîsikâyik kî-ayiwêpiw.

7 nama ci pa ki kaskitaw kise manito kakiyaw kekway
7 nama cî pahkî-kaskihtâw kisê-manitow kahkiyaw kîkway

iskwatam kita ositat?
iskwatam kita osîhtât?

– atawiya paki kaskitaw iyepine emamatawisit.
– âtawiya pahkî-kaskihtâw iyêpinê ê-mamâhtâwisit.

8 taneki ani nikotowasik kisikaw ko wi ota miot kise
8 tânêhki ani nikotwâsik kîsikâw kô-wî-otamihot kisê-

manito kakiyaw kekway e wi ositat?
manitow kahkiyaw kîkway ê-wi-osîhtât?

– niyank e iteyitak ke ayitotamiyit ayisiyiniwa e wi
– niyâk ê-itêyihtahk kê-ay-itôtamiyit ayisiyiniwa ê-wî-

miat nikotowasik kisikaw kita atoskeyit; ekosi mana
miyât nikotwâsik kîsikâw kita-atoskêyit; êkosi mâna

kita manacitayit tatwaw tepakop kisikayiki
kita-manâcihtâyit tahtwâw têpakohp kîsikâyiki

e ayamiewikisikayik.
ê-ayamihêwi-kîsikâyik.

9 taki ci itaw kise manito?
9 tahki cî itâw kisê-manitow?

– ek ek taki ki itaw namawikac kita poni ayaw
– êk êk tahki-kî-itâw nama wîhkâc kita-poni-ayâw

10 tante eyat kise manito?
10 tânitê (ê-)ayât kisê-manitow?

– misiwe ayaw kise manito kisikok mina waskitaskamik.
– misiwê ayâw kisê-manitow kîsikohk mîna waskitaskamik.

11 kakiyaw kekway ci kiskeyitam kise manitow?
11 kahkiyaw kîkway cî kiskêyihtam kisê-manitow?

– ek ek kakiyaw kekway kiskeyitam; kakiyaw
– êk êk kahkiyaw kîkway kiskêyihtam; kahkiyaw

wapatam, kakiyaw kaskitaw, namawac kekwa
wâpahtam, kahkiyaw kaskîtâw, namawac kîkway

pwatawitaw.
pwâtawihtâw.

12 wapamaw ci kise manito?
12 wâpamâw cî kise-manitow?

– namawiya oci wapamaw eka e owiyowit.
– namâwiya ohci wâpamâw êkâ ê-owîhowit.

56

13 What does it say when we see in God's book about His eyes and His hands?

– God sees everything. That is why God's eyes, it is said, see everything. Because He could make everything, that is why God's hands, it is said, not really His eyes, see everything.

---

3 – LESSON.

1 How is God known?

– He is seen in His creation. It is good. Especially, He was being heard in His Son's prayer. He made Him to be known. That is why He is known, God.

2 Why is it that I say that I believe in God, God the Father?

– He had a Son. The Father was first, but there were three in the divine unity.

3 Are there many gods?

– There are not many. There is one God, but in three ways: God, the Father; and the Son of God; and the Holy Spirit.

13 tanisi ani e wi itwek anima ka wapatamik kise
13 tânisi ani ê-wî-itwêhk anima kâ-wâpahtamihk kisê-

manito o masinaikanik: kise manito oskisikwa
manitow omasinahikanihk: kisê-manitow oskîsikwa

mina kise manito ociciya?
mîna kisê-manitow ocihciya?

– kise manito kakiyaw kekway e wapatak eoko oci
– *kisê-manitow kahkiyaw kîkway ê-wâpahtahk êwako ohci*

kise manito oskisikwa ko itwek; kakiyaw kekway
kisê-manitow oskîsikwa kô-itwêhk; kahkiyaw kîkway

mina e nita ositat eoko oci kise manito ociciya
mîna ê-nihtâ-osîhtât êwako ohci kisê-manitow ocihciya

ko itwek; namawiya tapwe e oskisikot mina e ocicit.
kô-itwêhk; namâwiya tâpwê ê-oskîsikot mîna ê-ocihciyit.

---

3 – KISKINOAMAKEWIN.
3 – KISKINOHAMÂKÊWIN.

1 kekway oci koci kiskeyimit kise manito?
1 kîkway ohci kôci-kiskêyimit kisê-manitow?

– e wapatamot o tosicikana esi mamiwasiniyiki wawac
– *ê-wâpahtamôt otosîhcikana ê-isi-mamiwâsiniyiki wâwâc*

e ki petawimit okosisa, ayamiawin ka ki pe
ê-kî-pêtawimiht okosisa, ayamihâwin kâ-kî-pê-

kiskeyitamoiweyit; eokoyiw oci koci kiskeyimit
kiskêyihtamohiwêyit; êwakoyiw ohci koci-kiskêyimiht

kise manito.
kisê-manitow.

2 taneki ani ko itweyan « ni tapwewokeyimaw kise
2 tânêhki ani kô-itwêyân "nitâpwêwakêyimâw kisê-

manito weyotawimit. »
manitow wiyôhtâwîmit?"

– e ki okosisit ana ka nistamisit esi nistweyakisitwaw
– *ê-kî-okosisit ana kâ-nistamisit ê-isi nistwêyakîsitwâw*

kise manitowinik.
kisê-manitowinik.

3 miscetiwok ci kise manitowok?
3 mihcêtiwak cî kisê-manitowak?

– namawiya miscetiwok; peyako kise manito. maka
– *namâwiya mihcêtiwak; pêyakow kisê-manitow. mâka*

nistweyakio, weyotawimit, mina wekosisimit, mina
nistwêyakihow, wiyôhtâwîmit, mîna wêkosisimit, mîna

meyosit manito.
(ê-)miyosit manitow.

57

4 ᑕᐱᐢᑯ- ᑎ ᐃᓯ ᑭᓴ ᒪᓂᑐᐃᐧᐅᐧᐦ ᐁᓯ
ᓂᐢᑎᑕᐧᐤ ?
— ᐁᐠ ᐁᐠ, ᑕᐱᐢᑯ- ᐃᓯ ᒪᓂᑐᐃᐧᐅᐧᐦ.
5 ᓇᐢᐱ- ᑎ ᒥᓇ ᑕᐱᐢᑯ- ᑭᑎᑕᐧᐁᐧᐳᑕᑯᓯᐅᐧᐦ ?
— ᐁᐠ ᐁᐠ, ᒥᑐᓃ ᑕᐱᐢᑯ- ᑭᑎᑕᐧᐁᐧᐳᑕᑯᓯᐅᐧᐦ.
6 ᑕᑐ ᑲ ᐃᑕᑎᓂᐳᑭ ᑭᓴ ᒪᓂᑐ ᐅᑐᓯᒋᑲᓇ
ᑕᓂᒪᐳᐤ ᐊᐳᐊᐧᐦ ᒥᐊᐧᓯᓂᐳᐤ ?
— ᐅᑭᓯᑯᐅᐧᐦ ᐊᐳᓯᐳᓂᐅᐧᐦ ᐊᐧᐊᐧ-.
7 ᑫᑲᐧᔭᐠ ᐊᓂᑭ ᐅᑭᓯᑯᐅᐧᐦ ?
— ᐃᐳᓇᑕᐤ ᐊᒍᑯᐃᐧᐅᐧᐦ ᓇᒪᐊᐧᐊᐧ- ᐅᐃᐧᐸᐃᐧᐅᐧᐦ.
8 ᓇᒪ ᑎ ᓇᐢᐸ- ᑭ ᑐᑕᒧᐧᐦ ᐊᑎᐠ ?
— ᑕᐯᐧ ᒥᐢᑕᐁ ᑭ ᒪᒋ ᑐᑕᒧᐧᐦ ᐊᑎᐠ ᐁ ᐅᓴᐨ
ᐊᐳᐊᐧᑫᐳᒧᑕᐧᐤ, ᑕᓯᐸᐧ ᑲ ᑭ ᒪᒍᐢᑌᐧᐱᓂᒋᐠ.
9 ᑕᓂᓯ ᐊᓂ ᐃᓯᐃᑲᓯᐅᐧᐦ ᐅᑭᓯᑯᐅᐧᐦ ᑲ ᑭ
ᒪᒍᐢᑌᐧᐱᓂᑕᐧᐤ ?
— ᒪᒋ ᒪᓂᑐᐅᐧᐦ ᐃᑕᐅᐧᐦ.
10 ᑕᓂᓯ ᑲ ᑭ ᐃᓯᐃᑲᓱᐠ ᓂᐢᑕᐨ ᐃᐳᓂ ᐤ ?
— ᐊᑕᐠ ᑭ ᐃᓯᐃᑲᓱ.
11 ᑕᓂᓯ ᑲ ᑭ ᐃᓯᐃᑲᓱᐠ ᓂᐢᑕᐨ ᐃᐢᑫᐧᐤ ?
— ᐁᐧ ᑭ ᐃᓯᐃᑲᓱ.
12 ᐁᐅᑯᓂᐠ ᑎ ᓂᓱ ᐊᐳᓯᐳᓂᐅᐧᐦ ᐊᓂᐢᑲ-
ᑯᑎᑕᐧᐤ ᐊᐳᓯᐳᓂᐅᐧᐦ ᑲᑭᔭᐤ ?
— ᐁᐠ ᐁᐠ, ᐁᐅᑯᓂᐠ ᐅᑎ.
13 ᑕᓂᓯ ᑲ ᑐᑕᐠ ᑭᓴ ᒪᓂᑐ ᓂᐢᑕᐨ ᓇᐯᐊᐧ ᐁ
ᐃᐧ ᐅᓯᐊᐧ ?

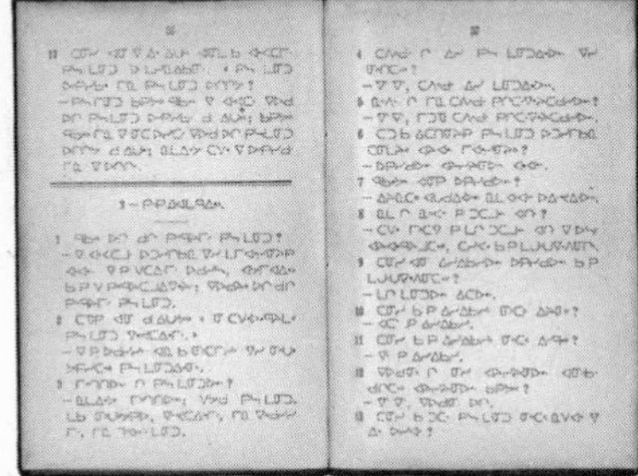

57

4 Are they like gods? The three of them?
– Yes, they are all Gods.
5 Are they forever to be thought sacred?
– Very much to be thought sacred.
6 Who among God's creations are much better?
– The angels, next the people.
7 What kind are they, those angels?
– Natural, pure spirits. They do not especially have names.
8 Didn't some of them do the opposite?
– Truly many of them did evil. Some because they thought highly of themselves. For that reason they were cast into the fire.
9 What are their names, the angels, that were cast into the fire?
– They are called devils.
10 What was he called, the first human?
– Adam was his name.
11 What was her name, the first woman?
– Eve was her name.
12 Are these two creatures the models for the people, all of them?
– Yes, for all human beings.
13 What did God do when man first was going to be made?

57

4 tapiskoc ci isi kise manitowiwok esi nistitwaw?
4 tâpiskôc cî isi kisê-manitowiwak ê-isi nistitwâw?

– ek ek, tapiskoc isi manitowiwok.
– *êk êk, tâpiskôc isi manitowiwak.*

5 naspic ci mina tapiskoc kicitwaweyitakosiwok?
5 nâspic cî mîna tâpiskôc kihcitwâwêyihtâkosiwak?

– ek ek, mitone tapiskoc kicitwaweyitakosiwok.
– *êk êk, mitonê tâpiskôc kihcitwâwêyihtâkosiwak.*

6 tato ka itatiniyiki kise manito o tosicikanatanimayiw
6 tahto kâ-itatiniyiki kisê-manitow otosîhcikana tânimayiw

ayiwak miwasiniyiw?
ayiwâk miywâsiniyiw?

– okisikowok ayisiyiniwak wawac.
– *okîsikowak ayisiyiniwak wâwâc.*

7 kekwayak aniki okisikowok?
7 kîkwayak aniki okîsikowak?

– iyinataw acakowiwok nama wawac owiyowiwok.
– *iyinataw ahcâhkowiwak nama wâwâc owîhowiniwak.*

8 nama ci naspac ki totamwok atit?
8 nama cî naspâc kî-itôtamwak âtiht?

– tapwe mistae ki maci totamwok atit e osam
– *tâpwê mistahi kî-maci-itôtamwak âtiht ê-osâm*

ayiwakeyimotwaw, tasipwa ka ki macostewepinicik.
ayiwâkêyimotwâw, tâsipwa kâ-kî-macostêwêpinîcik.

9 tanisi ani isiikasiwok okisikowok ka ki
9 tânisi ani isiyihkâsowak okîsikowak kâ-kî-

macostewepinitwaw?
macostêwêpinitwâw?

– maci manitowok itawok.
– *maci-manitowak itâwak.*

10 tanisi ka ki isi ikasot nistam iyiniw?
10 tânisi kâ-kî-isiyihkâsot nistam iyiniw?

– atak ki isi kikaso.
– *Atak kî-isiyihkasow.*

11 tanisi ka ki isi ikasot nistam iskwew?
11 tânisi kâ-kî-isiyihkâsot nistam iskwêw?

– ep ki isi ikaso.
– *Ep kî-isiyihkâsow.*

12 eokonik ci niso ayisiyiniwok aniskac kocitwaw
12 êwakonik cî nîso ayisiyiniwak aniskâc kocîhtwâw

ayisiyiniwok kakiyaw?
ayisiyiniwak kahkiyaw?

– ek ek, eokonik oci.
– *êk êk, êwakonik ohci.*

13 tanisi ka totak kise manito nistam napewa
13 tânisi kâ-itôtahk kisê-manitow nistam nâpêwa

e wi osiat?
ê-wî-osîhât?

58

— ᐊᓯᐢᑭ+ ᐅᑕᐃᐧᐃᐧᒋᐤ ᐁ ᐃᐧ ᐃᑎᐢᑭᐅᐧᑭᓇᐟ ᐁᓯ
ᐅᐃᐧᐹᐃᐧᐣᐟ ᐁ ᓇᐯᐃᐧᐣᐟ, ᐁᑯᓯ ᐅᑕᒐᑯᐁᐤ.
14 ᑕᒋᓯ ᐃᓯ ᓇᑯᓯᐣᐟ ᐊᐣᓯᐣᒋᐤ ᐅᑕᒐᑲᐨ ?
— ᑭᓭ ᒪᒋᑐ ᑲ ᐃᓯ ᓇᑯᓯᐟ ᐃᓯ ᓇᑯᓯᐣᐊᐧ,
ᐁ ᑭ ᐃᓯ ᒥᐣᒥᐟ ᑭᑎ ᐁᑲ ᑭᓯᐸᒋᐣᐠ ᐅᐱᒪ
ᑎᓯᐃᐧᒋᐣᐤ.
15 ᒋᐢᑕᐨ ᐃᐢᑫᐧᐊᐧ ᑭᑕ ᐅᓯᐊᐟ ᑕᒋᓯ ᐊᒋ ᑲᑭ
ᑐᑕᐠ ᑭᓭ ᒪᒋᑐ ?
— ᓇᐯᐊᐧ ᐅᐢᐱᑫᑲᒋᐣᐤ ᐁ ᑭ ᐅᑎᓇᒪᐧᐟ ᐅᑕ
ᐃᐧᐃᐧᒋᐤ ᐃᐢᑫᐧᐊᐧ ᑭᑕ ᐅᒋ ᐅᓯᐊᐟ.
16 ᑕᒍᑭ ᐊᒋ ᑯᒋ ᐸᑭᑎᒋᑯᔭᐠ ᑭᓭ ᒪᒋᑐ
ᐊᐧᐢᑭᑕᐢᑲᒥᐠ ?
— ᑭᑕ ᑭᐢᑫᐣᒥᐟ, ᑭᑕ ᓴᑭᐃᐟ, ᑭᑕ ᓇᓇᐃᑕᐟ,
ᐊᐧᐊᐧ- ᑭᑕ ᓇᑎᐟ ᑕᑭ ᑭᒋ ᐃᐧᑕᐱᒥᐟ.

4 — ᑭᐢᑭᓄᐊᒪᑫᐃᐧᐣ.

1 ᒋᐢᑕᐨ ᐊᐣᓯᐣᒋᐅᐧᐠ ᐁ ᑭ ᑭᓯᐃᑕᐧᐤ ᑕᐣᑕ
ᑲ ᑭ ᐊᐣᑕᐧᐤ ?
— ᒋᑕᐃᐧᑭᒋᑲᒋᐠ ᐃᓴᐱᒍ ᐁ ᒥᐊᐧᓯᒋᐣᐠ, ᓇ
ᓇᐠᑐᐠ ᒥᐢᑎᑲᐧ ᐁ ᒪᒥᒋᓯᐃᐧᐣᐟ ᑭ ᐊᔭᐅᐧᐠ.
2 ᑕᒋᓯ ᐊᒋ ᑲ ᑭ ᐃᑕᐟ ᑭᓭ ᒪᒋᑐ ᒋᐢᑕᐨ
ᐊᐣᓯᐣᒋᐊᐧ ᒋᑕᐃᐧᑭᒋᑲᒋᐠ ᐁ ᑭ ᐊᔭᐟ ?
— ᓇᓇᑐᐠ ᒥᒋᓭ ᒥᒋᑫᐠ ᑭ ᐃᑌᐤ, ᐁᑯᓯ ᐁ

58 – He made man in His image.

14 What did the people's spirit look like?

– How God looks is what they look like. He made me in His eternal image.

15 At the beginning when He was to make woman, what did God do?

– He took man's rib, and here made woman from it.

16 What did God allow us, to be on earth?

– To know Him, to love Him, to listen to Him well. Especially to be present with Him.

4 – LESSON.

1 Where did He put the first people that He made?

– In the beginning, after the people were created they were placed where everything was very good and abundant.

2 What is it that God said to the first people when he placed them in the garden?

– He said there were all kinds of berries.

– asiskiy otawiwiniw e wi itiskiwokinat esi owiyowiyit
– *asiskiy otawiwiniw ê-wî-itiskiwakinât (ê-)isi-owîhowiyit*

e napewiyit, ekosi otacakoew.
ê-nâpewiyit, êkosi otâhcahkohew.

14 tanisi isi nakosiyit ayisiyiniw otacakwa?
14 *tânisi (ê-)isi-nâkosiyit ayisiyiniw otâhcahkwa?*

– kise manito ka isi nakosit isi nakosiyiwa, e ki isi
– *kisê-manitow kâ-isi-nâkosit isi-nâkosiyiwa, ê-kî-isi-*

miyimit kici eka kisipaniyik opimatisiwiniyiw.
miyimit kici êkâ kisipaniyik opimâtisiwiyiniw.

15 nistam iskwewa kita osiat tanisi ani ka ki totak kise
15 *nistam iskwêwa kita-osîhât tânisi ani kâ-kî-itôtâhk kisê-*

manito?
manitow?

– napewa ospikekaniyiw e ki otinamwat otawiwiniw
– *nâpêwa ospikêkaniyiw ê-kî-otinamwât ôtawîyiwîniw*

iskwewa kita oci osiat.
iskwêwa kita-ohci-osîhât.

16 taneki ani koci pakitinikoyak kise manito
16 *tânêhki ani koci-pakitinikoyahk kisê-manitow*

waskitaskamik?
waskitaskamik?

– kita kiskeyimit, kita sakiit, kita nanaitat, wawac
– *kita-kiskêyimiht, kita-sâkihiht, kita-nanahihtâht, wâwâc*

kita natit taki kici witapimit.
kita-nâtiht tahki kici-wîtapimiht.

4 – KISKINOAMAKEWIN.
4 – KISKINOHAMÂKÊWIN.

1 nistam ayisiyiniwok e ki kisiitwaw tanta ka ki
1 *nistam ayisiyiniwak ê-kî-kîsihîtwâw tânita ka-kî-*

ayitwaw?
ayîtwâw?

– nitawikicikanik iyepine e miwasiniyik, nanaktok
– *nihtâwikihcikanihk iyêpinê ê-miywâsiniyik, nanâtohk*

mistikwa e maminisiwiyik ki ayawok.
mistikwa ê-maminisiwiyik kî-ayâwak.

2 tanisi ani ka ki itat kise manito nistam ayisiyiniwa
2 *tânisi ani ka-kî-itât kisê-manitow nistam ayisiyiniwa*

nitawikicikanik e ki ayat?
nihtâwikihcikanihk ê-kî-ayât?

– nanatok minisa micikek ki itew, ekosi e
– *nanâtohk mînisa mîcîkêk kî-itêw, êkosi ê-*

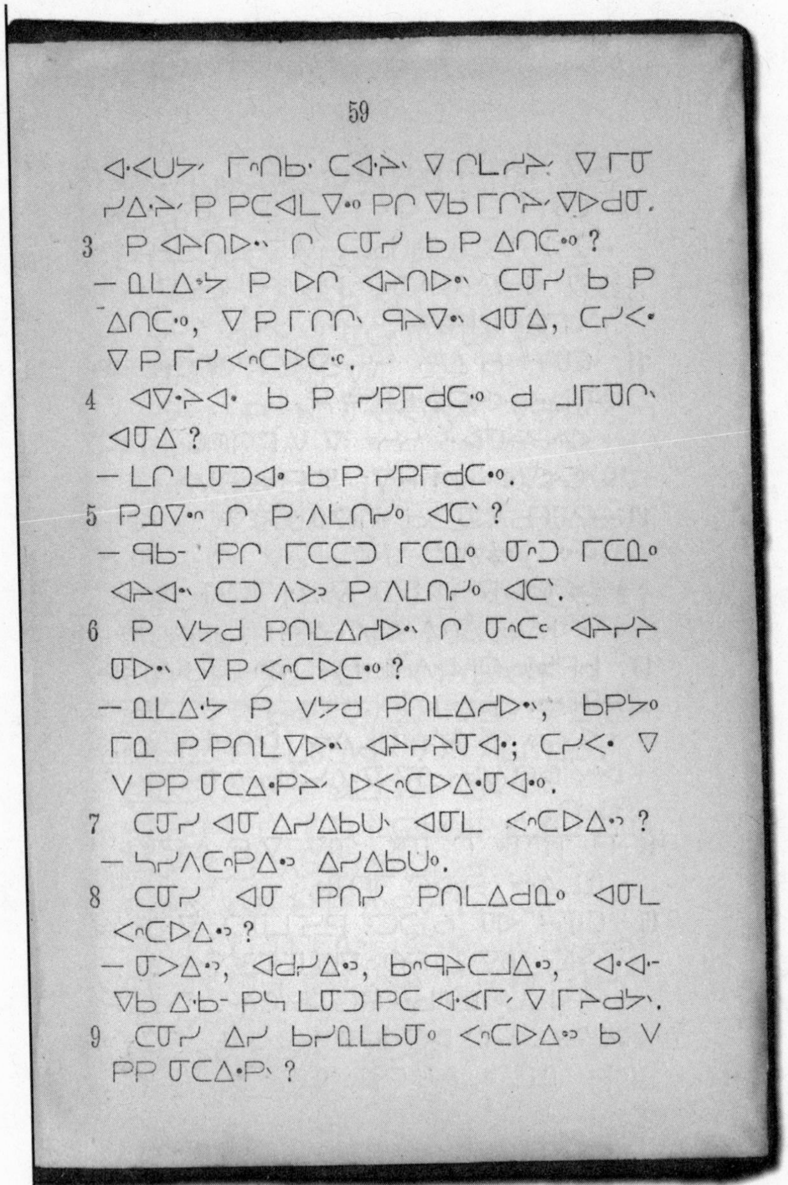

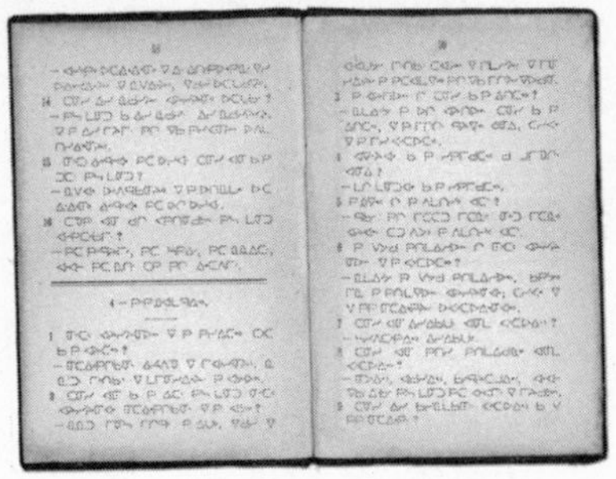

59

– Then He showed them the tree in the centre. It was planted with lots of berries. He told them not to eat it, this one.

3 Did they do what they were told?

– They did not do as they were told. They ate from this tree; for that reason their sin was great.

4 Who was it that urged them to eat from this tree?

– The devil urged them to do this.

5 Did Adam live for long?

– Three hundred winters. He was alive for more winters than that.

6 Did they repent, the first people, when they had sinned?

– No, they did not repent. They disrespected each other. For that reason, one is born with it: their sins.

7 What is it called, that sin?

– Disobedience, it is called.

8 How is it that it harms us, that sin?

– Death, sickness, loneliness, especially not ever seeing God, they are all part of this sin.

9 How is one forgiven of his sin when one is born with it?

59 wapateyat mistikwa tawayik e cimasoyit e minisiwiyit
wâpahtihât mistikwa tawayik ê-cimasoyît ê-minisiwiyit

ki kita amawew kici eka miciyit eokoni.
kî-itahamawêw kici êkâ mîcîyit êwakoni.

3 ki ayitiwok ci tanisi ka ki ititwaw?
3 *kî-ayihtiwak cî tânisi ka-ki-itîtwâw?*

– namawiya ki ohci ayitiwok tanisi ka ki ititwaw, e ki
– *namâwiya kî ohci ayitiwak tânisi kâ-kî-itîtwâw, ê-kî-*

micicik keyiwek anii, tasipwa e ki misipastaotwaw.
mîcicik kêyiwêk anihi, tâsipwâ ê-kî-misi-pâstâhotwâw.

4 aweyiwa ka ki sikimikotwaw ko mominecik anii?
4 *awêyiwa kâ-kî-sîkimikotwâw kô-môminêcik anihi?*

– maci manitowa ka ki sikimikotwaw.
– *maci-manitowa kâ-kî-sîkimikotwâw.*

5 kinowes ci ki pimatisiw atak?
5 *kinowês cî kî-pimâtisiw Atak?*

– kekac kici mitatato mitanaw nisto mitanaw ayiwak
– *kêkâc kihci-mitâtahtomitanaw nistomitanaw ayiwâk*

tato pipon ki pimatisiw atak.
tahto pipon kî-pimâtisiw Atak.

6 ki peyako kitimaisowok ci nistam ayisiyiniwok e ki
6 *kî-pêyako-kitimahisowak cî nistam ayisiyiniwak ê-kî-*

pastaotwaw?
pâstâhotwâw?

– namawiya ki peyako kitimaisowok, kakiyaw mina
– *namâwiya kî-pêyako-kitimahisowak, kahkiyaw mîna*

ki kitimaewok ayisiyiniwa; tasipwa e-pe ki ki
kî-kitimahêwak ayisiyiniwa; tâsipwâ ê-pe-kiki-

nitawikiyit opastaowiniwaw.
nihtâwikiyit opâstâhowiniwâw.

7 tanisi ani isi ikatek anima pastaowin?
7 *tânisi ani isi isiyihkâtêk anima pâstâhowin?*

– sasipitaskiwin isi ikatew.
– *sasîpihtaskiwin isiyihkâtêw.*

8 tanisi ani kitisi kitimaikonaw anima pastaowin?
8 *tânisi ani kitisi kitimahikonaw anima pâstâhowin?*

– nipowin, akosiwin, kaskeyitamowin, wawac eka
– *nipowin, ahkosiwin, kaskêyihtamowin, wâwâc êkâ*

wikac kise manito kita wapamit e-miyikoyak.
wîhkâc kisê-manitow kita-wâpamiht ê-miyikoyahk.

9 tanisi isi kasinamakaniw pastaowin ka pe ki ki
9 *tânisi isi kâsînamâkaniw pâstâhowin kâ-pê-kiki-*

nitawikik?
nihtâwikiht?

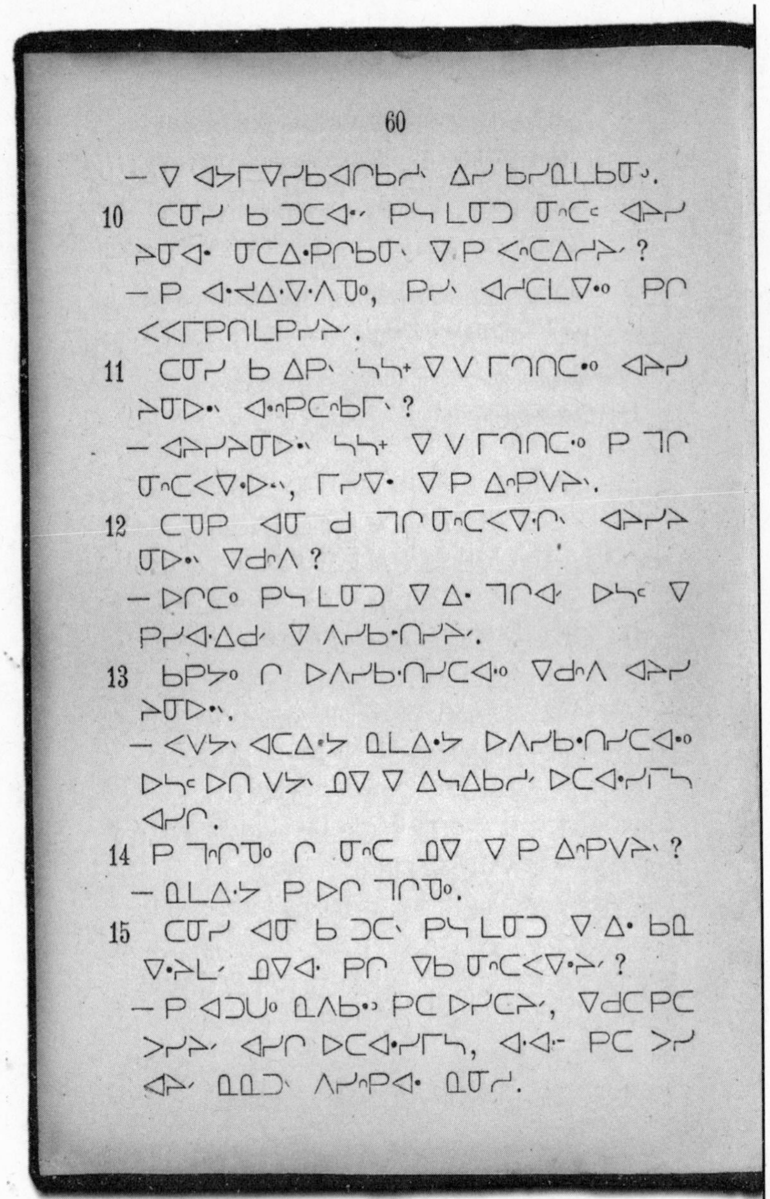

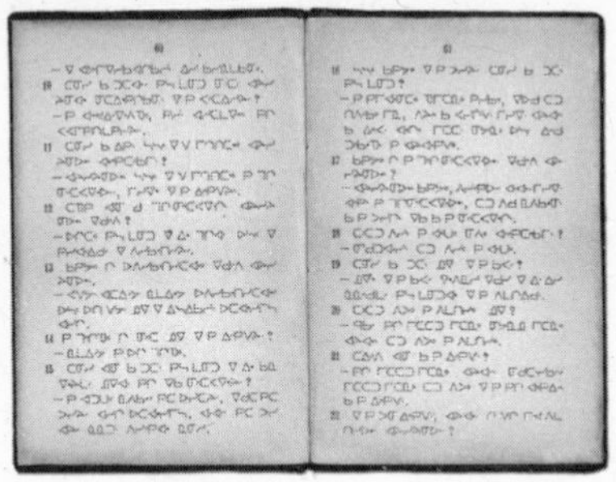

60

– Being baptized is how one is forgiven the sin.

10 What did God do to the first people when they had sinned in the garden?

– He threw them out of paradise. He promised them that they would always be needy.

11 What happened when there were already lots of people on earth?

– When there were lots of people already, they all drowned when the earth flooded.

12 Why was it that all of them drowned, the people back then?

– By all means, God was going to destroy them because they angered Him. They committed adultery or other similar crimes.

13 Did all of them commit adultery then, the people?

– Almost everyone. Not all committed adultery since there was Noah, and his children also.

14 Was Noah also destroyed when it was flooded?

– No, he was not destroyed.

15 What is it that God did to keep Noah from drowning?

– He asked Noah to make an ark, to ride in it, with his children. And to put in their different animals two by two.

60

– e ayamiesikaacikasok isi kasinamakaniw.
– *ê-ayamihêsîkahâhcikâsok isi kâsînamâkaniw.*

10 tanisi ka totawat kise manito nistam ayisiyiniwa
10 *tânisi kâ-itôtawât kisê-manitow nistam ayisiyiniwa*

nitawikicikanik e ki pastaisoyit?
nihtâwikihcikanihk ê-kî-pâstâhisoyit?

– ki wayowiwepinew, kisik asotamawew kici
– *kî-wayiwiwêpinêw, kîsik asotamawêw kici-*

papamikitimakisiyit.
papâmikitimâkisiyit.

11 tanisi ka ikik sasay e pe micetitwaw ayisiyiniwok
11 *tânisi kâ ihkik sâsay ê-pê-mihcêtitwâw ayisiyiniwak*

waskitaskamik?
waskitaskamik?

– ayisiyiniwok sasay e pe micetitwaw ki
– *ayisiyiniwak sâsay ê-pê-mihcêtitwâw kî-*

mecinistapawewok, misiwe e ki iskipeyik.
mêscinistâpâwêwak, misiwê ê-kî-iskipêyik.

12 taneke ani ko mecinistapawecik ayisiyiniwok ekospi?
12 *tânêhki ani kô-mêscinistâpâwêcik ayisiyiniwak êkospî?*

– ocitaw kise manito e wi meciat osam e kisiwaikot
– *ohcitaw kisê-manito ê-wî-mêscihât osâm ê-kisiwâhikot*

e pisikwatisiyit.
ê-pisikwâtisiyit.

13 kakiyaw ci opisikwatisitawaw ekospi ayisiyiniwok.
13 *kahkiyaw cî opisikwâtisitawâw êkospî ayisiyiniwak.*

– papeyak atawiya namawiya opisikwatisitawaw osam
– *pâpêyak atawiya namâwiya opisikwâtisitawâw osâm*

oti peyak noe e isiikasot otawasimisa asici.
oti-pêyak Noe ê-isiyihkâsot otawâsimisa asici.

14 ki mescinew ci nista noe e ki iskipeyik?
14 *kî-mêscinêw cî wîsta Noe ê-kî-iskipêyik?*

– namawiya ki oci mecinew.
– *namâwiya kî ohci mêscinêw.*

15 tanisi ani ka totak kise manito e wi kanaweyimat
15 *tânisi ani kâ-itôtahk kisê-manitow ê-wî-kanawêyimât*

noewa kici eka nistapaweyit?
Noewa kici êkâ nistâpâwêyit?

– ki atotew napikwan kita ositayit, ekota kita posiyit
– *kî-atotêw napikwan kita-osîhtâyit, êkota kita-pôsiyit*

asici otawasimisa, wawac kita posiayit nanatok
asici otawâsimisa, wâwâc kita-pôsi-ayit nanâtohk

pisiskiwa naniso.
pisikiwa nânîso.

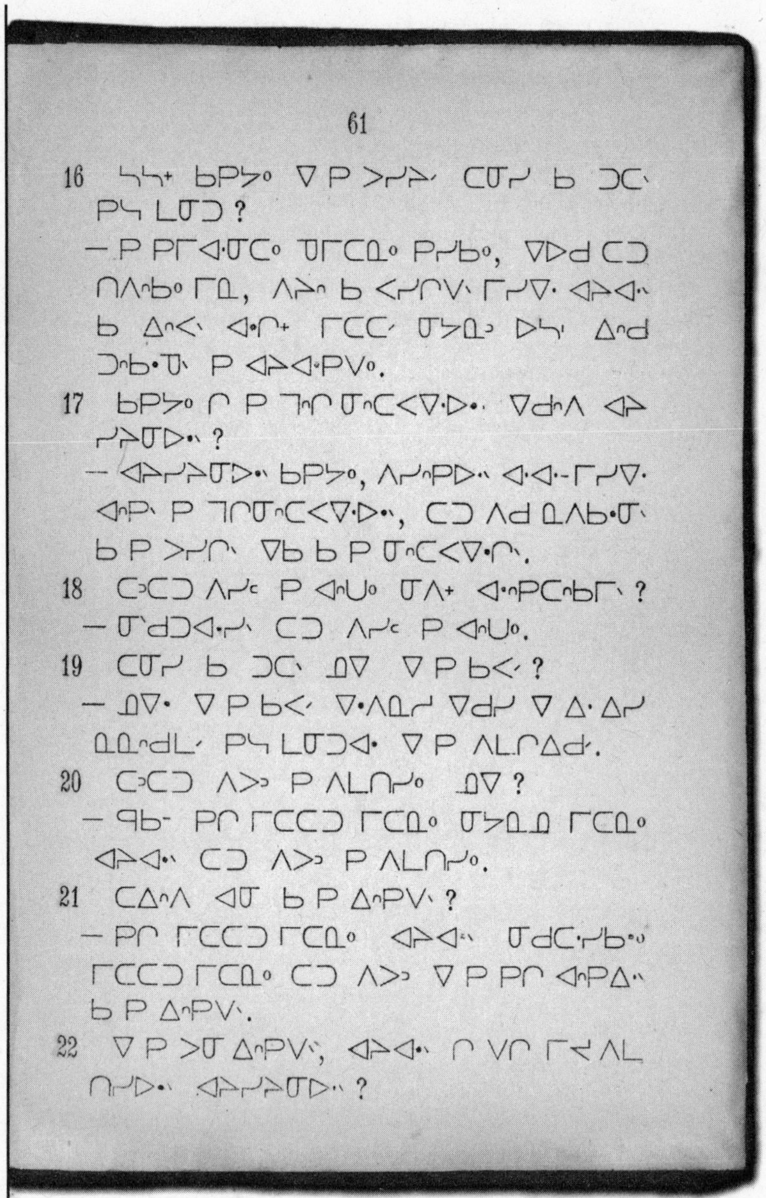

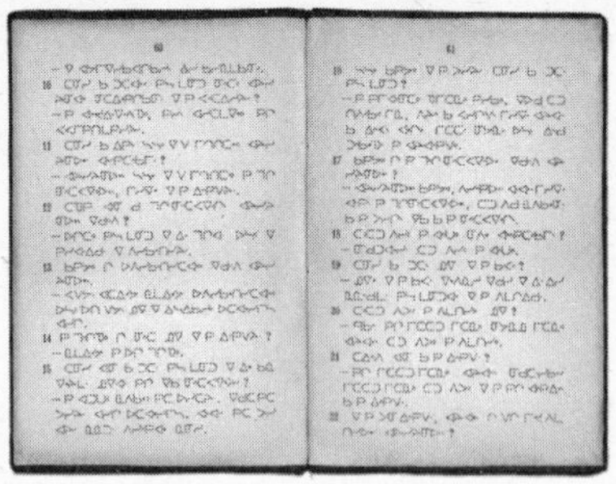

61

16 When all of them were in, what did God do?

– He made it rain for forty days, that many nights also. Eventually it flooded all over, even the mountains. For another fifteen days it rained over the earth.

17 Did all the people drown then?

– All of the people, animals especially all over the land, they all drowned. Only those who rode with the captain, they did not drown.

18 How many months did the water stay on top of the earth?

– Six months it stayed.

19 What did Noah do when he was ashore?

– When Noah was ashore he offered a sacrifice to God; Noah sacrificed to Him.

20 How many months did Noah live?

– He lived more than one hundred fifty winters.

21 When did it flood?

– More than six thousand years ago.

22 When it had finished flooding, did they have a good life, the people, more than before?

61

16 sasay kakiyaw e ki posiyit tanisi ka totak kise
16 sâsay kahkiyaw ê-kî-pôsiyit tânisi kâ-itôtâhk kisê-

manito?
manitow?

– ki kimiwanitaw nemitanaw kisikaw, eoko tato
– kî-kimiwanîtâw nêmitanaw kîsikâw, êwako tahto

tipiskaw mina, piyis ka pasicipek misiwe ayiwak
tipiskâw mîna, piyis kâ-pasicipêk misiwê ayiwâk

ka ispak waciy mitatat niyanan osap isko toskwanik
kâ-ispâk waciy mitâtaht nîyânanosâp isko-toskwanik

ki ayiwakipew.
kî-ayiwâkipêw.

17 kakiyaw ci ki mesci nistapawewok ekospi
17 kahkiyaw cî kî-mêsci-nistâpâwêwak êkospî

ayisiyiniwok?
ayisiyiniwak?

– ayisiyiniwok kakiyaw, pisiskiwok wawac misiwe
– ayisiyiniwak kahkiyaw, pisiskiwak wâwâc misiwê

askik ki mecinistapawewok, tato piko napikwanik
askîhk kî-mêscinistâpâwêwak, tahto piko napikwanik

ka ki posicik eka ka ki nistapawecik.
kâ-kî-posicik êkâ kâ-kî-nistâpâwêcik.

18 tantato pisim ki astew nipiy waskitaskamik?
18 tânitahto pîsim kî-astêw nipiy waskitaskamik?

– nikołowasik tato pisim ki astew.
– nikotwâsik tahto pîsim kî-astêw.

19 tanisi ka totak noe e ki kapat?
19 tânisi kâ-itôtahk Noe ê-kî-kapât?

– nowe e ki kapat wepinaso ekosi e wi isi nanaskomat
– Nowe ê-kî-kapât wêpinâsow êkosî ê-wî-isi-nanâskomât

kise manitowa e ki pimaciikot.
kisê-manitowa ê-kî-pimâcihikot.

20 tantato pipon ki pimatisiw noe?
20 tânitahto pipon kî-pimâtisiw Noe?

– kekac kici mitatato mitanaw niyanano mitanaw
– kêkâc kihci-mitâtahtomitanaw niyânanomitanaw

ayiwak tato pipon ki pimatisiw.
ayiwâk tahto pipon kî-pimâtisiw.

21 taispi ani ka ki iskipek?
21 tânispî ani kâ-kî-iskipêk?

– kici mitatato mitanaw ayiwak nikotwasikwaw
– kihci-mitâtahtomitanaw ayiwâk nikotwâsikwâw

mitatato mitanaw tato pipon e ki kici askiwik ka ki
mitâtahtomitanaw tahto pipon ê-kî-kihci-askîwik kâ-kî-

iskipek.
iskipêk.

22 e ki poni iskipek, ayiwak ci peci miyo pimatisiwok
22 ê-kî-pôni-iskipêk, ayiwâk cî pêci-miyo-pimâtisiwak

ayisiyiniwok?
ayisiyiniwak?

62

— ᐊᔨᐊᐧ ᑭ ᐯᒋ ᒥᔪ ᐱᒪᑎᓯᐅᐧ ᑭᓭ ᒪᓂᑐᐊᐧ
ᐁ ᐊᐢᑕᐃᑯᑕᐤ; ᒪᑲ ᐁ ᐯᒋ ᒥᒣᑎᒋᐠ ᑫᑕᑕᐍ
ᒪᒋ ᐱᒪᑎᓯᐅᐧ.

23 ᓇᒪᒋ ᑭ ᑯᐢᑕᒧᐧ ᒥᓇ ᑭᑕᐟ ᑭᑕ ᐃᐢᑭᐯᔨᐠ ?

— ᐁᐦ ᐁᐦ ᐁᑯᓯ ᑭ ᐃᓯ ᑯᐢᑕᒧᐧ; ᑕᓯᐸᐧ ᑲ ᑭ
ᐃᐧ ᐅᓯᑕᒋᐠ ᐊᓯᓂ ᐊᐧᐢᑲᐃᑲᐣ ᓇᐢᐱ- ᐁᐢᐸᔨᐠ
ᐁᑯᑕ ᐁ ᐃᐧ ᐱᑐᑫᔭᒧᑕᐤ ᑭᒋ ᐁᑲ ᓂᐢᑕᐸ
ᐍᒋᐠ ᑭᑕᐟ ᐃᐢᑭᐯᔨᑭ.

24 ᐅᒥᐍᔨᑌᑕᐩ ᒋ ᑭᓭ ᒪᓂᑐ ᐁ ᐅᓯᑕᐃᐧᐟ ᐁ
ᐊᑯᔨᐤ ᐊᐧᐢᑲᐃᑲᐣ ?

— ᓇᒪᐃᐧᔭ ᑭ ᐅᒋ ᒥᐍᔨᑕᐟ ᐁᓭ; ᑯ ᒪᔭ
ᑯᐊᐧ ᑲᑭᔭᐤ.

25 ᑭ ᑭᓯᑕᓂᐤ ᒋ ᐁᐅᑯ ᐊᓯᓂ ᐊᐧᐢᑲᐃᑲᐣ ?

— ᓇᒪᐃᐧᔭ ᐅᒋ ᑭᓯᑕᓂᐤ, ᐃᔨᓂᐅᐧ ᑫᑕᑕᐍ
ᐸᐯᑐᐢ ᐁ ᐃᑕᑕᒧᒋᐠ· ᐁᑲ ᐁ ᓂᓯᑐᑕᑐᒋᐠ,
ᐅᒋᑕᐤ ᐁ ᐃᑌᔨᒥᑯᐃᐧᓯᒋᐠ, ᐣᑕᐊᐧ- ᓇᐣᑕᐤ ᑭ
ᐳᔦᐅᐧ.

26 ᐊᔨᐊᐧ ᒋ ᑭ ᐯᒋ ᒥᔪ ᐱᒪᑎᓯᐅᐧ ᐁ ᑭ
ᒪᔭᑯᓯᒋᐠ ?

— ᓇᒪᐃᐧᔭ ᐊᔨᐊᐧ ᑭ ᒥᔪ ᐱᒪᑎᓯᐅᐧ; ᑫᑲ-
ᑲᑭᔭᐤ ᐁ ᐯᒋ ᐊᐧᓂᔨᒪᑕᐤ ᑭᓭ ᒪᓂᑐᐊᐧ, ᐱ
ᑲᐧᓇᑕ ᑫᑲᐧᐩ ᓇᓇᐦᑐᐠ ᐁ ᒪᓂᑐᑲᑕᑲᐧᐤ.

27 ᑲᑭᔭᐤ ᒋ ᐊᔨᓯᔨᓂᐅᐧ ᐊᐧᐢᑭᑕᐢᑲᒥᐠ ᑲ ᑭ
ᐊᔭᒋᐠ ᐁᑯᐢᐱ ᐊᐧᓂᔨᒣᐅᐧ ᑭᓭ ᒪᓂᑐᐊᐧ ?

— ᓇᒪᐃᐧᔭ ᐊᑕᐃᐧᔭ ᑲᑭᔭᐤ: ᑭ ᓇᐊᐧᓯᐊᐧᐸᒣᐤ

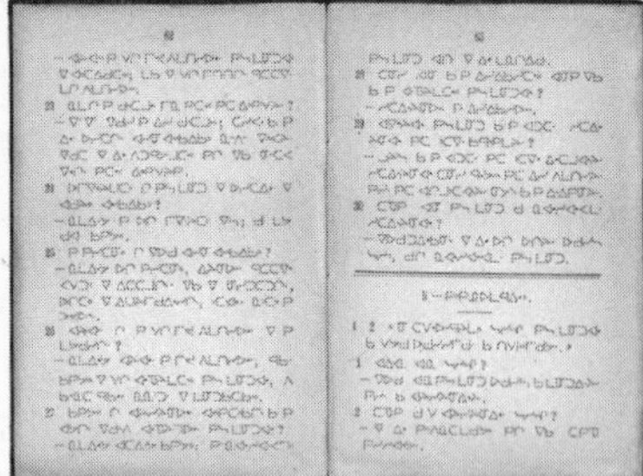

62

– They had a better life when God made them more conscious, but there came more people and eventually they had evil lives.

23 Were they not scared that it would flood again?

– Yes, they were scared for that reason. They were going to make a strong stone house if it happened, to help them in case it floods.

24 Did God like it that that house was being made?

– Nobody liked it, they say; He made them all unlucky.

25 Was it finished that stone house?

– Nobody finished it; the people eventually spoke differently, they did not understand each other. Deliberately, the higher powers quit building the house.

26 Did they have a better life when they had the misfortune?

– They did not have a better life. Just about all of them, they doubted God, even though they spoke different languages.

27 Did all the people on earth, that were here then, did they doubt God?

– Not all of them anyway. God chose those

62

– ayiwak ki peci miyo pimatisiwok kise manitowa
– *ayiwâk kî-pêci-miyo-pimâtisiwak kisê-manitowa*

e astaikotwaw; maka e peci miceticik ketatawe maci
ê-astahikotwâw; mâka ê-pêci-mihcêticik kêtahtawê maci-

pimatisiwok.
pimâtisiwak.

23 namaci ki kostamwok mina kitwam kita iskipeyik?
23 *namacî kî-kostamwak mîna kîhtwâm kita-iskipêyik?*

– ek ek ekosi ki isi kostamwok; tasipwa ka ki wi
– *êk êk êkosi kî-isi-kostamwak; tâsipwa kâ-kî-wî-*

ositacik asini waskaikan naspic espayik ekota
osîhtâcik asinîwâskahikan nâspic (ê-)ispayik êkota

e wi pitokeyamotwaw kici eka nistapawecik kitwam
ê-wî-pihtokêyamotwâw kici êkâ nistâpâwêcik kîhtwâm

iskipeyiki.
iskipêyiki.

24 omiweyitetay cî kise manito e ositawit e akoyiw
24 *omiywêyihtêtay cî kisê-manitow ê-osîhtâwît êwakoyiw*

waskaikan?
wâskahikan?

– namawiya ki ohci miweyitam esa; ko mayakoat
– *namâwiya kî-ohci-miywêyihtam êsa; kô-mayakohât*

kakiyaw.
kahkiyaw.

25 ki kisitaniw ci eoko asini waskaikan?
25 *kî-kîsitâniw cî êwako asinîwâskahikan?*

– namawiya ohci kisitaniw, iyiniwok ketatawe papetos
– *namâwiya ohci kîsitâniw, iyiniwak kêtahtawê pâpîtos*

e itatamocik. eka e nisitotatocik, ocitaw
ê-itatâmocik. êkâ ê-nisitohtâtocik, ohcitaw

e iteyimikowisicik, ntawac nantaw ki poyowok.
ê-itêyimikowisicik, nitawac nânitaw kî-poyowak.

26 ayiwak ci ki peci miyo pimatisiwok e ki mayakosicik?
26 *ayiwâk cî kî-pêci-miyo-pimâtisiwak ê-kî-mayakosicik?*

– namawiya ayiwak ki miyo pimatisiwok, kekac
– *namâwiya ayiwâk kî-miyo-pimâtisiwak, kêkâc*

kakiyaw e peci waneyimatwaw kise-manitowa,
kahkiyaw ê-pêci-wanêyimatwâw kisê-manitowa,

pikwanata kekway nanaktok e manitokatakwaw.
pikwanata kîkway nanâtohk ê-manitokâtâkwâw.

27 kakiyaw ci ayisiyiniwok waskitaskamik ka ki ayacik
27 *kahkiyaw cî ayisiyiniwak waskitaskamik kâ-kî-ayâcik*

ekospi waneyimewok kise manitowa?
êkospî wanêyimêwak kisê-manitowa?

– namawiya atawiya kakiyaw: ki nawasowapamew
– *namâwiya atawiya kahkiyaw: kî-nawasowâpamêw*

63

ᑭᓭ ᒪᓂᑐ ᐊᑎᐟ ᐁ ᐃᐧ ᒪᓇᒋᐃᑯᐟ.
28 ᑕᓂᓯ ᐊᓂ ᑲ ᑭ ᐃᓯᐃᑲᓱᑖᐤ ᐊᓂᑭ ᐁᑲ
ᑲ ᑭ ᐋᓃᐸᐦᑖᐤ ᑭᓭᒪᓂᑐᐊ?
— ᓱᑖᐃᐧᔫᓂᐤ ᑭ ᐃᓯᐃᑲᓱᐅᐤ.
29 ᐊᐍᔭᐊ ᑭᓭᒪᓂᑐ ᑲ ᑭ ᐊᑐᑕᐟ ᓱᑖᐃᐧ
ᔫᓂᐊ ᑭᑕ ᐟᑌᐧ ᑲᑫᑭᒪᔭᐟ?
— ᒨᓭᓴ ᑲ ᑭ ᐊᑐᑕᐟ ᑭᑕ ᐟᑌᐧ ᐃᐧᑕᒧᐊᔭᐟ
ᓱᑖᐃᐧᔫᓂᐊ ᑕᓂᓯ ᑫᐧᔦᐦ ᑭᑕ ᐃᓯ ᐱᒪᑎᓯᔭᐟ
ᑭᓯᐢ ᑭᑕ ᐊᑎᒧᐦᑕᐊᔭᐟ ᓂᔭᐠ ᑲ ᑭ ᐃᐧᑭᓂᔭᐟ.
30 ᑕᓂᑭ ᐊᓂ ᑭᓭᒪᓂᑐ ᑯ ᓇᐊᐧᓯᐊᐧᐸᒪᐟ
ᓱᑖᐃᐧᔫᓂᐊᐧ?
— ᐁᐅᑯᑐᐃᐧᑲᓂᐧ ᐁ ᐃᐧ ᐅᑎᐦ ᐅᑎᔭᐟ ᐅᑯᓯᓴ
ᓴᓯᐦ, ᑯᑎᐦ ᓇᐊᐧᓯᐊᐧᐸᒪᐟ ᑭᓭᒪᓂᑐ.

5 — ᑭᐢᑭᓄᐅᒪᑫᐃᐧᐣ.

§ 2 «ᓂ ᑕᐻᐅᐧᑫᔭᒪᐤ ᓴᓱᓯ ᑭᓭᒪᓂᑐᐊ
ᑲ ᐯᔭᑯ ᐅᑯᓯᓯᒥᑯᐟ ᑲ ᑎᐯᔭᒥᑯᔭᐠ.»
1 ᐊᐃᐧᓇ ᐊᓇ ᓴᓱᓯ?
— ᐁᐅᑯ ᐊᓇ ᑭᓭᒪᓂᑐ ᐅᑯᓯᓴ ᑲ ᒪᓂᑐᐃᐧᔭᐟ
ᑭᓯᐢ ᑲ ᐊᔭᓯᔫᓂᐃᐧᔭᐟ.
2 ᑕᓂᑭ ᑯ ᐯ ᐊᔭᓯᔫᓂᐃᐧᐟ ᓴᓱᓯ?
— ᐁ ᐃᐧ ᑭᐢᐸᓇᑕᒪᑯᔭᐠ ᑭᐢ ᐁᑲ ᑕᑭᓂ
ᑭᓯᓯᐊᐧᔭᐠ.

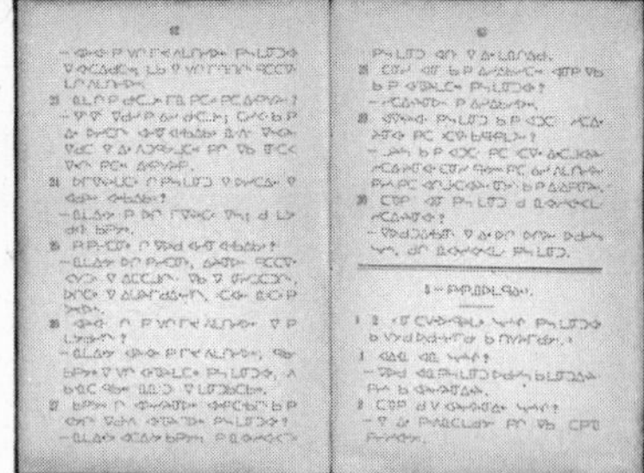

63 who were going to respect Him.
28 What were their names those that did not doubt God?
– The Jewish people was their name.
29 Who is it that God asked to do this mission to go and counsel them?
– He asked Moses to go and tell the Jewish people to live a proper life, also to tell them about God.
30 Why was it that God chose the Jewish people?
– He chose them so that His Son could come from them.

5 – LESSON.

§ 2 "I believe in him, Jesus Christ. God takes Him as His son to redeem us all."
1 Who is Jesus Christ?
– That is God's Son who is supernatural and also human.
2 Why is it that He was a human being, Jesus Christ?
– He is going to gain life for us so that we not perish.

63 kise manito atit e wi manaciikot.
kisê-manitow atiht ê-wî-manâcihikot.

28 tanisi ani ka ki isi ikasotwaw aniki eka ka ki
28 tânisi ani kâ-kî-isiyihkâsotwâw aniki êkâ kâ-kî-

waneyimatwaw kise manitowa?
wanêyimatwâw kisê-manitowa?

– sotawiyiniwok ki isi ikasowok.
– *Sotawiyiniwak kî-isiyihkâsowak.*

29 aweyiwa kise-manito ka ki atotat sotawiyiniwa kita
29 awêyiwa kisê-manitow kâ-kî-atotât Sotawiniyiwa kita-

ntawe kakeskimayit?
nitawi-kakêskimâyit?

– moyisa ka ki-atotat kita ntawe witamowayit
– *Moyisa kâ-kî-atotât kita-nitawi-wîhtamawâyit*

sotawiyiniwa tanisi kweyask kita isi pimatisiyit kisik
Sotawiyiniwa tânisi kwayask kita-isi-pimâtisiyit kisik

kita acimostawayit niyak ka ki wiikiniyik.
kita-âcimostawâyit niyâk kâ-kî-wihikiniyik.

30 taneki ani kise manito ko nawasowapamat
30 tânêhki ani kisê-manitow kô-nawasô-wâpamât

sotawiyiniwa?
Sotawiyiniwa?

– eokotowikanik e wi oci ociyit okosisa sesos, koci
– *êwakotowikanik ê-wî-ohci-ohcîyit okosisa Sesos, koci-*

nawasowapamat kise manitow.
nawasô-wâpamât kisê-manitow.

---

5 – KISKINOOMAKEWIN.
5 – KISKINOHAMÂKÊWIN.

§ 2 « ni tapwewokeyimaw sesokri kise manitowa ka
§ 2 "nitâpwêwakêyimâw Sesokri kisê-manitowa kâ-

peyako okosisimikot ka tipeyimikoyak. »
pêyako-okosisimikot kâ-tipêyimikoyahk."

1 awina ana sesokri?
1 awîna ana Sesokri?

– eoko ana kise manito okosisa ka manitowiyit kisik
– *êwako ana kisê-manitow okosisa kâ-manitowiyit kisik*

ka ayisiyiniwiyi.
kâ-ayisiyiniwiyi.

2 taneki ko pe ayisiyiniwit sesokri?
2 tânêhki kô-pê-ayisiyiniwît Sesokri?

– e wi kispinatamakoyak kici eka takine kisisowayak.
– *ê-wî-kîspinatamâkoyahk kici êkâ tahkinê kisisowayâhk.*

64

3 How is it that He saved us from burning?

– In exchange He gave His life on the cross. He was crucified.

§ 3 "The Holy Spirit lent her to Him. The Virgin Mary gave Him birth."

4 Who is it that is a Father to Him, Jesus Christ that is supernatural?

– God was a Father to him.

5 Who gave birth to Jesus?

– Holy Mary gave Him birth.

6 Who is Mary, who is called holy?

– That is the woman who was very holy, sacred, pure. This is why God chose her to give birth to Him.

7 How is it that Holy Mary gave birth?

– The Holy Spirit gave her a Son.

8 Did Jesus not have a man as a father?

– He did not have a human being as a father, but Saint Joseph kept Him.

9 Who is Saint Joseph?

– That is who Holy Mary lives with.

10 Where was Jesus born?

– Mary gave birth to Him in a stable in the city of Bethlehem.

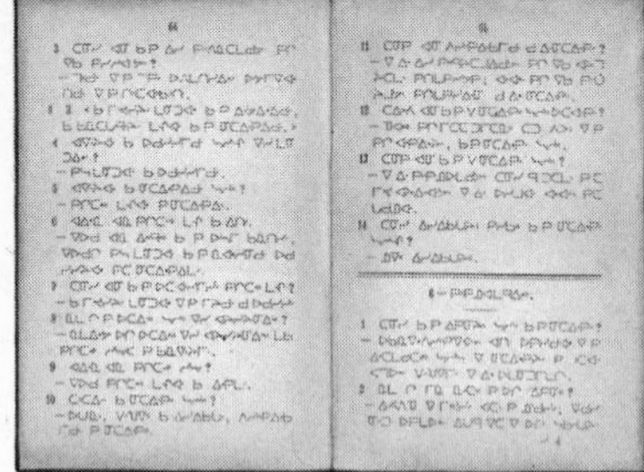

64

3 tanisi ani ka ki isi kispinatamakoyak kici eka
3 *tânisi ani kâ-kî-isi-kîspinatamâkoyahk kici êkâ*

kisisoayak?
kîsisoyahk?

– meskoc e ki mekit opimatisiwin oyamiewatikok e ki
– *mêskôc ê-kî-mêkit opimâtisiwin ayamihêwahtikohk ê-kî-*

cistaaskwatit.
cîstahâskwâtiht.

§ 3 « ka miyosiyit manitowa ka ki wiyawiikot, ka
§ 3 *"kâ-miyosiyit manitowa kâ-kî-wiyawihikot, kâ-*

kanatacakweyit mariwa ka ki nitawikiikot. »
kanâhcahkwêyit Mariwa ka-kî-nihtâwikihikot."

4 aweyiwa ka okosisimikot sesokri esi manitowit?
4 *awêyiwa kâ-okosisimikot Sesokri êsi manitowit?*

– kise manitowa ka okosisimikot.
– *kisê-manitowa kâ-okosisimikot.*

5 aweyiwa ka nitawikiikot sesos?
5 *awêyiwa kâ-nihtâwikihikot Sesos?*

– kicitwaw mariwa ki nitawikiik.
– *kihcitwâw Mariwa kî-nihtâwikihik.*

6 awina ana kicitwaw mari ka itit.
6 *awîna ana kihcitwâw Mari kâ-itiht?*

– eoko ana iskwew ka ki osami kanatisit, eokoci kise
– *êwako ana iskwêw kâ-kî-osâmi-kanâtisit, êwakôci kisê-*

manitowa ka ki nawasonikot okosisiyiwa kita
manitowa kâ-kî-nawasonikot okosisiyiwa kita-

nitawikiimat.
nihtâwikihimât.

7 tanisi ana ka ki otawasimisit kicitwaw mari?
7 *tânisi ana kâ-kî-otawâsimisit kihcitwâw Mari?*

– ka miyosiyit manitowa e ki miyikot ko okosisit
– *kâ-miyosiyit manitowa ê-kî-miyikot kô-okosisit*

8 nama ci ki otawiw sesos esi ayisiyiniwit?
8 *nama cî kî-ohtâwîw Sesos (ê-)isi-ayisiyiniwît?*

– namawiya oci otawiw esi ayisiyiniwit maka
– *namâwiya ohci ohtâwîw (ê-)isi-ayisiyinîwît mâka*

kicitwaw sosepa ki kanaweyimik.
kihcitwâw Sosepa kî-kanawêyimik.

9 awina ana kicitwaw sosep?
9 *awîna ana kihcitwâw Sosep?*

– eoko kicitwaw mariwa ka wikimat.
– *êwako kihcitwâw Mariwa kâ-wîkimât.*

10 tantawik ka nitawikit sesos?
10 *tânitawik kî-nihtâwikit Sesos?*

– otenak, petleem ka isiikatek, pisiskiwikamikok ki
– *otênâhk, Petlehem kâ-isiyihkâtêk, pisiskiwikamikohk kî-*

nitawikiw.
nihtâwikiw.

65

11 ᑕᑌᑭ ᐊᑌ ᐱᓯᐢᑭᐃᐧᑲᒥᑯᐧ ᑯ ᐃᐧᑌᑕᐃᐧᑭᐟ ?
— ᐁ ᐃᐧ ᐃᓯ ᑭᐢᑫᐯᑕᒧᐃᑯᔦᐧ ᑭᑎ ᐁᑲ ᐊᐯᒣ
ᐯᑕᒪᐧ ᑭᑎᒪᑭᓯᔦᑭ; ᐊᐧᐊᐧ- ᑭᑎ ᐁᑲ ᑭᐢᑌ
ᐯᒧᔦᐧ ᑭᑎᒪᑭᓯᐃᐧᑌᐧ ᑯ ᐃᐧ ᑌᑕᐃᐧᑭᐟ.
12 ᑕᐃᐢᐱ ᐊᑌ ᑲ ᑭ ᐯ ᑌᑕᐃᐧᑭᐟ ᓴᓯᐢ ᐅᑕᐊᐢᑭᐧ ?
— ᑍᐊᐧᐤ ᑭᑎ ᒥᑕᑕᑐᒥᑕᓇᐤ ᑕᑐ ᐱᐳᐣ ᐁ ᑭ
ᑭᑎ ᐊᐢᑭᐃᐧᐯᐧ, ᑲᑭᑌᑕᐃᐧᑭᐟ ᓴᓯᐢ.
13 ᑕᑌᑭ ᐊᑌ ᑲ ᑭ ᐯ ᑌᑕᐃᐧᑭᐟ ᓴᓯᐢ ?
— ᐁ ᐃᐧ ᑭᐢᑭᓄᐅᒪᑯᔦᐧ ᑕᑌᓯ ᑫ ᑐᑕᒪᐧ ᑭᑕ
ᒥᔪ ᐊᐯᐃᐧᐊᐧᔦᐧ ᐁ ᐃᐧ ᐅᓯᒧᐊᐟ ᐊᐧᐊᐧ- ᑭᑕ
ᑲᑯᓄᐊᐧ.
14 ᑕᑌᓯ ᐃᓯᐃᑲᑌᔦᐤ ᑭᓯᑲᐤ ᑲ ᑭ ᑌᑕᐃᐧᑭᐟ
ᓴᓯᐢᐦ ?
— ᓄᐁᐢ ᐃᓯᐃᑲᑌᔦᐤ.

6 — ᑭᐢᑭᓄᐊᒪᑫᐃᐧᐤ.

1 ᑕᑌᓯ ᑲ ᑭ ᐃᑭᑍᔦᐧ ᓴᓯᐢ ᑲᑭᑌᑕᐃᐧᑭᐟ ?
— ᐅᑲᓇᐁᐧᐱᓯᐢᑭᐁᐧᐅᐧᐦ ᐊᑎᐟ ᐅᑭᓯᑯᐊᐧ ᐁ ᑭ
ᐃᐧᑕᒪᑯᑕᐧᐦ ᓴᓯᓴ ᐁ ᑌᑕᐃᐧᑭᔦᐟ ᑭ ᐤᑕᐊᐧ
ᐸᒣᐅᐧᐦ ᐯᐟᑍᐁᒥᐧ ᐁ ᐃᐧ ᐅᒪᑌᑐᒥᒪᑎᐧ.
2 ᓇᒪ ᑎ ᒥᓇ ᓇᐧᑕᐤ ᑭ ᐅᑎ ᐃᑭᑌᐤ ?
— ᐃᔦᐱᑍ ᐁ ᒥᔭᓯᐟ ᐊᑕᐧ ᑭ ᓄᐦᑯᓯᐤ; ᐁᑯᓯ
ᑌᐢᑐ ᐅᑭᒪᐅᐧᐦ ᐃᑌᑫ ᐁᑕ ᐁ ᐅᑎ ᓴᑲᐢᑌᔦᐧ

4

65 11 Why did she give birth in a stable?
– She is going to show us not to complain when we are poor, especially not to be conceited. In poverty she gave Him birth.
12 When is it that Jesus was born here on earth?
– Four thousand winters past on the great earth was Jesus born.
13 Why was it that Jesus was born?
– He is going to teach us how to live well. He is going renew our spirit.
14 What is it called the day that Jesus Christ was born?
– It is called Noel.

6 – LESSON.

1 What happened when Jesus was born?
– The shepherds that kept animals were told by some angels that Jesus was being born. They went to see Him in Bethlehem. They were going to take Him as their God.
2 Did something else not also happen?
– A very bright star appeared and then three kings followed where it shone.

65 11 taniki ani pisiskiwikamikok ko winitawikit?
11 *tânêhki ani pisiskiwikamikohk kô-wî-nihtâwikît?*

– e wi isi kiskeyitamoikoyak kici eka ayimeyitamak
– *ê-wî-isi-kiskêyihtamohikoyahk kici êkâ âyimêyihtamahk*

kitimakisiyaki; wawac kici eka kisteyimoyak
kitimâkisiyâhki; wâwâc kici êkâ kistêyimoyahk

kitimakisiwinik ko wi nitawikit.
kitimâkisiwinihk kô-wî-nihtâwikiht.

12 taispi ani ka ki pe nitawikit sesos ota askik?
12 *tânispî ani kâ-kî-pê-nihtâwikiht Sesos ôta askîhk?*

– newaw kici mitatato mitanaw tota pipon e ki kici
– *nêwâw kihci-mitâtahtomitanaw tahto pipon ê-kî-kihci-*

askiwiyik, ka ki nitawikit sesos.
askiwiyik, ka-kî-nihtâwikît Sesos.

13 taniki ani ka ki pe nitawikit sesos?
13 *tânêhki ani ka-kî-pê-nihtâwikit Sesos?*

– e wi kiskinoomakoyak tanisi ke totamak kita miyo
– *ê-wî-kiskinohamâkoyahk tânisi kê-itôtamahk kita-miyo-*

ayiwiwayak e wi osimoat wawac kitacakonowa.
ayiwiwayahk ê-wî-osimohât wâwâc kitâhcahkonowa.

14 tanisi isi ikateyiw kisikaw ka ki nitawikit sesokri?
14 *tânisi isiyihkâtêyiw kîsikâw ka-kî-nihtâwikiht Sesokri?*

– Noel isi ikateyiw.
– *Noel isiyihkâtêw.*

6 – KISKINOAMAKEWIN.
6—KISKINOHAMÂKÊWIN.

1 tanisi ka ki ikiniyik sesos ka ki nitawikit?
1 *tânisi kâ-kî-ikiniyik Sesos kâ-kî-nihtâwikît?*

– okanawepisiskiwewok atit okisikowa e ki
– *okanawêpisikiwêwak âtiht okîsikowa ê-kî-*

witamakotwaw sesosa e nitawikiyit ki nta-
wihtamâkotwâw Sesosa ê-nihtâwikiyit kî-nitawi-

wapamewok petleemik e wi omanitomimacik.
wâpamêwak Petlehemihk ê-wî-omanitômimâcik.

2 nama ci mina nantaw ki oci ikiniw?
2 *nama cî mîna nânitaw kî ohci ikinîw?*

– iyepine e miyosit atak ki nokkosiw; ekosi nisto
– *iyêpinê ê-miyosit ahcâhk kî-nôkosiw; êkosi nisto*

okimawok iteke eta e oci sakasteyik
okimâwak itêkê êta ê-ohci-sâkâstêyik

66

From their land they saw it. Also they were told God's Son was born.

3 What did they do when they saw the star?

– In Jerusalem they went to go and see Jesus, but they could not find Him in Bethlehem. They went to go and find Him.

4 What did they do to Jesus when they found Him?

– They knelt down before Him. They were going to make Him their God. Also they gave Him gold, and incense that smelled good.

5 What did they also do when they took Him as their God?

– They went home back to their land. They were going to go and tell about God's Son, that He was born.

6 In Jerusalem, when they had arrived, did something not happen?

– Yes Herod heard them talk of this noble birth. Then he heard another King was born, Jesus was His name. Herod was very scared.

7 What is it that Herod did, when he was very scared?

– He ordered Jesus to be killed, because he was also scared that Jesus would take his rule away from him.

66

e otaskitwaw, ki wapamewok kisik witamakowisiwok
ê-otaskîtwâw, kî-wâpamewak kîsik wihtamâkowisiwak

kise manito okosisa e ki nitawikiyit.
kisê-manitow okosisa ê-kî-nihtâwikiyit.

3 tanisi ani ki totamwok atakwa e ki wapamacik?
3 *tânisi ani kî-itôtamwak ahcâhkwa ê-kî-wâpamâcik?*

– serosalemik ki itotewok sesosa e ntawapamacik;
– *Serosalemihk kî-itohtêwak Sesosa ê-nitawi-wâpamâcik;*

maka eka e ki miskawacik petleemik ki ntawe
mâka êkâ ê-kî-miskawâcik Petlehemihk kî-nitawi-

miskawewok.
miskawêwak.

4 tanisi ani ki totawewok sesosa e ki miskawacik?
4 *tânisi ani kî-itôtawêwak Sesosa ê-kî-miskawâcik?*

– ki ocicikwanapistawewok e wi omanitomimacik kisik
– *kî-ocihcihkwanapîstawêwak ê-wî-omanitômimâcik kîsik*

mamiyewok osawasoniyawa asici pikiwa
mamiyêwak osâwasoniyawa asici pikiwa

e miyomakosiyit.
ê-miyomâkosiyit.

5 tanisi mina ki totamwok e ki omanitomimacik sesosa?
5 *tânisi mîna kî-itôtamwak ê-kî-omanitômimâci Sesosa?*

– kawi ki kiwewok otaskiwak e wi ntawe acimimatwaw
– *kâwi-kî-kîwêwak otaskiwâhk ê-wî-nitawi-âcimimatwâw*

kise manitowa okosisiyiwa e ki nitawikiyit.
kisê-manitowa okosisiyiwa ê-kî-nihtâwikiyit.

6 serosalemik e ki takosikwaw nama ci nantaw ki ohci
6 *Serosalemihk ê-kî-takosikwâw nama cî nânitaw kî-ohci-*

ikiniw?
îkiniw?

– tapwe, erot ka itit, ana mamawiyes ka ki kici ayiwit
– *tâpwê, Erot kâ-itît, ana mamawiyês kâ-kî-kihci-ayiwit*

ekote ekospi, e ki petak kotaka e nitawikiyit okimawa,
êkotê êkospî, ê-kî-pêtak kotaka ê-nihtâwikiyit okimâwa,

sesosa e siikasoyit, mistae sekisiw esa.
Sesosa ê-isiyihkâsoyit, mistahi sêkisiw êsa.

7 tanisi ani ka totak erot e osami sekisit?
7 *tânisi ani kâ-itohtâhk Erot ê-osâmi-sêkisit?*

– o wi nipaatay sesosa osam e kostak ki kik
– *o-wî-nipahatay Sesosa osâm ê-kostak kikik*

otipeyicikewin kita maskamikot.
otipêyihcikêwin kita-maskamikot.

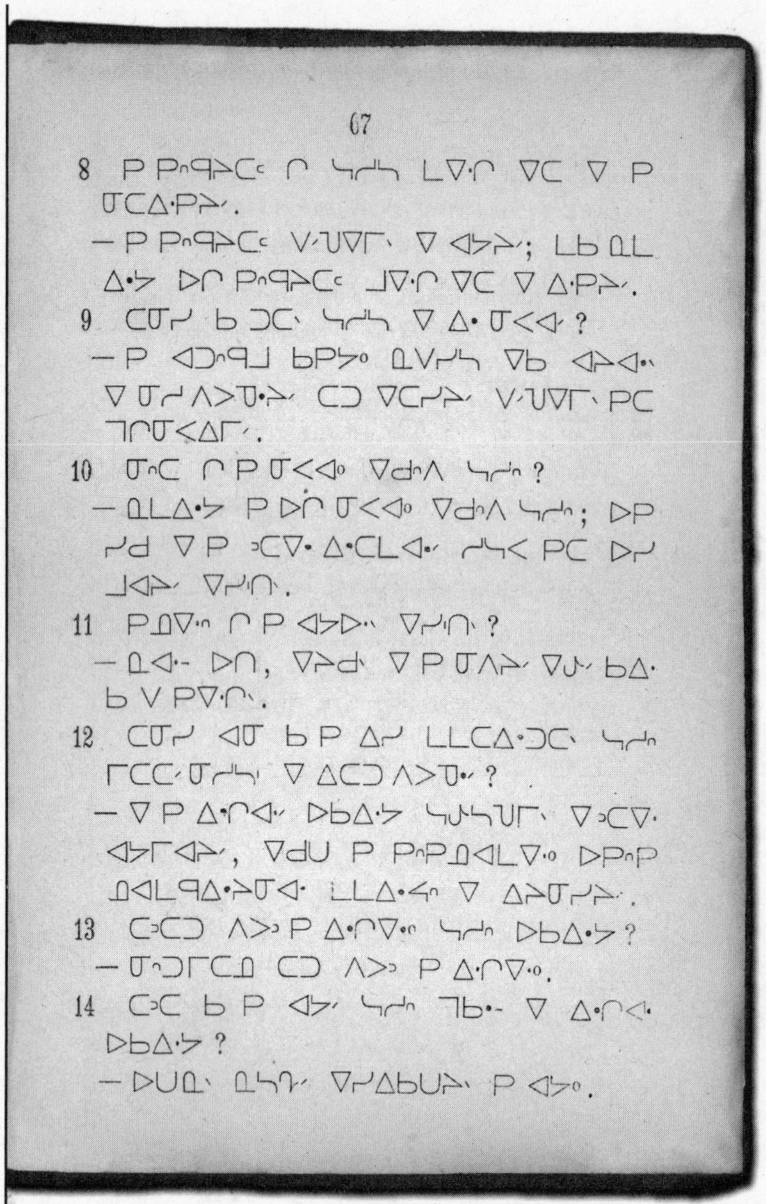

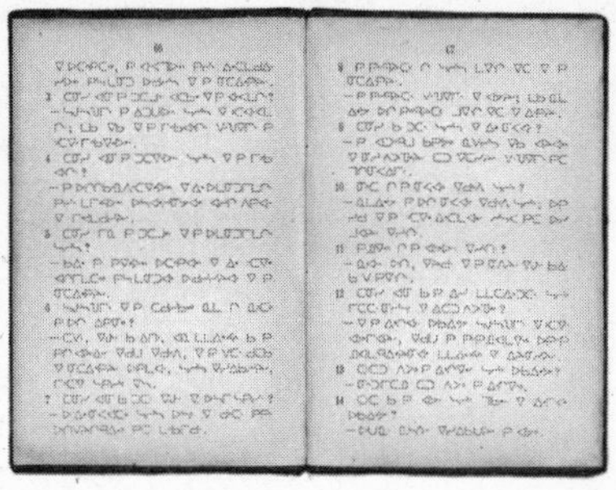

67

8 Did he know where exactly Jesus was born?

– He knew He was in Bethlehem, but nobody knew exactly where He was living.

9 How did he try to kill Him?

– He had asked that all boys not more than two years old in Bethlehem be killed.

10 Was Jesus then killed?

– Jesus was not killed then. An angel went to tell Joseph how to escape from Egypt.

11 Were they there long in Egypt?

– Jesus did not die, as Herod had wished, and they came home again.

12 What was it that was supernatural that Jesus did when He was twelve years old?

– He went with His mother to Jerusalem to go to the temple. He taught the teachers, mostly the wise ones.

13 How many winters did Jesus go with His mother?

– For thirty winters He helped her.

14 Where was Jesus while He was with His mother?

– The town of Nazareth is where He was.

67

8 ki kiskeyitam ci sesosa maweci eta e ki nitawikiyit.
8 *kî-kiskêyihtam cî Sesosa mawêci êta ê-kî-nihtâwikiyit.*

– ki kiskeyitam petleemik e ayayit; maka nama wiya
– *kî-kiskêyihtam Petlehemihk ê-ayâyit; mâka nama wiya*

oci kiskeyitam moweci eta e wikiyit.
ohci kiskêyihtam mowêci êta ê-wîkiyit.

9 tanisi ka totak sesosa e wi nipaat?
9 *tânisi kâ-itôtahk Sesosa ê-wî-nipahât?*

– ki atoskemo kakiyaw napesisa eka ayiwak e niso
– *kî-atoskêmow kahkiyaw nâpêsisa êkâ ayiwâk ê-nîso-*

piponweyit tato etasiyit petleemik kita
piponwêyit tahto (ê-)itâsiyit Petlehemihk kita-

mecinipaimit.
mêscinipahimiht.

10 nista ci ki nipaaw ekospi sesos?
10 *wîsta cî kî-nipahâw êkospî Sesos?*

– namawiya ki oci nipaaw ekospi sesos; okisiko e ki
– *namâwiya kî-ohci-nipahâw êkospî Sesos; okîsiko ê-kî-*

ntawe witamawat sosepa kita osimoayit esiptik.
nitawi-wîhtamawât Sosepa kita-osimohôyit Esiptihk.

11 kinowes ci ki ayawok esiptik?
11 *kinowês cî kî-ayâwak Esiptihk?*

– nawac oti, eyikok e ki nipiyit erot kawi ka pe kiwecik.
– *nawâc ôti, iyikohk ê-kî-nipîyit Erot kawî-kâ-pê-kîwêcik.*

12 tanisi ani ka ki isi mamatawitotak sesos mitatat
12 *tânisi ani kâ-kî-isi-mamatawitohtahk Sesos mitâtaht*

nisosap e itato piponwet?
nîsosâp ê-itahto-piponwêt?

– e ki wiciwat okawiya serosalemik e ntawe ayamiayit,
– *ê-kî-wîcêwât okâwiya Serosalemihk ê-nitawi-ayamihâyit,*

ekote ki kiskinoamawew okiskinoamakewiyiniwa
êkotê kî-kiskinohamâwêw okiskinohamâkêwiyiniwa

mamawiyes e iyinisiyit.
mamawiyês ê-iyinisiyit.

13 tantato pipon ki wiciwew sesos okawiya?
13 *tânitahto pipon kî-wîcêwêw Sesos okâwiya?*

– nistomitano tato pipon ki wiciwew.
– *nistomitanaw tahto pipon kî-wîcêwêw.*

14 tanta ka ki ayat sesos mekwac e wiciwaw okawiya?
14 *tânita kâ-kî-ayât Sesos mêkwâc ê-wîcêwât okâwiya?*

– otenak nasaret esiikateyik ki ayaw.
– *ôtênâhk Nasaret (ê-)isiyihkâtêyik kî-ayâw.*

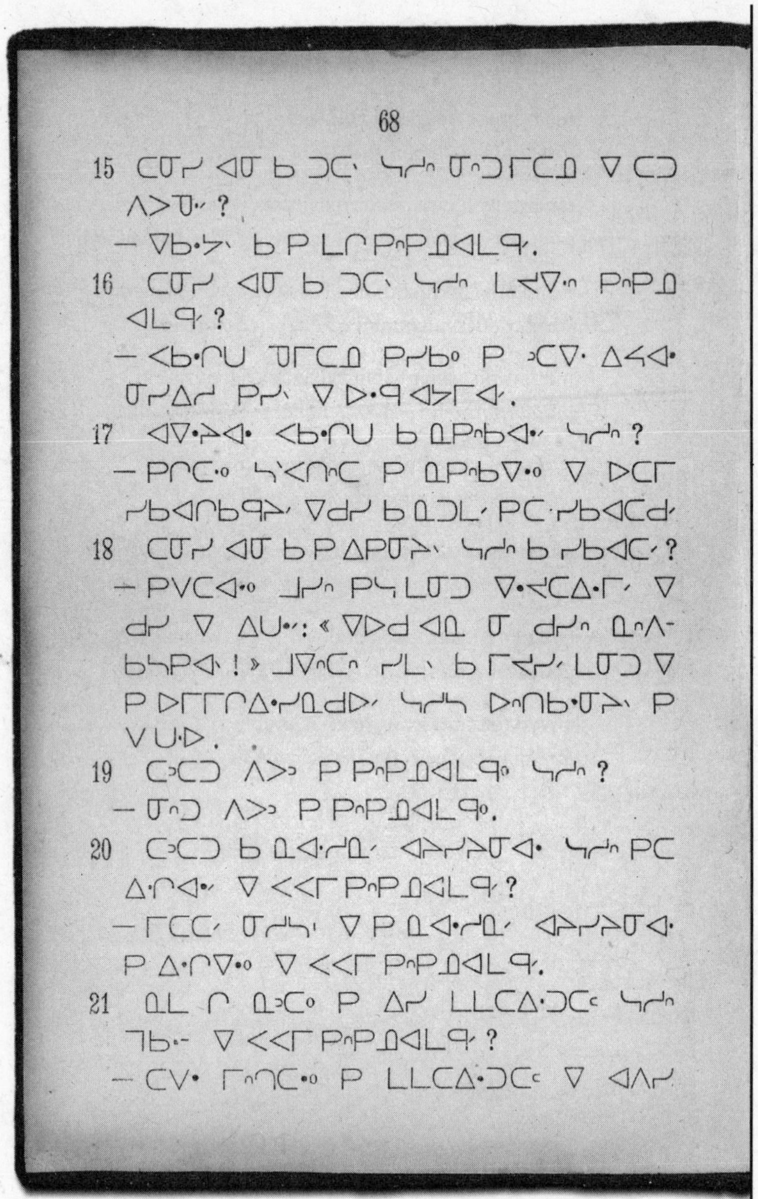

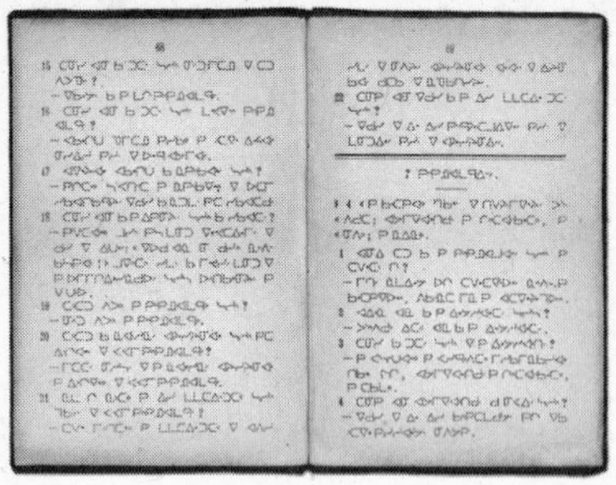

68

15 What is it that Jesus did when He was 30 years old?
– That was when He began to teach.

16 What is it that Jesus did before He taught?
– For forty days He went and He fasted and also prayed.

17 Who did Jesus meet?
– Saint John the Baptist He met while he was baptizing, so then He asked him to baptize Him.

18 What is it that happened when Jesus was baptized?
– God was heard clearly. God the Father said: "This is my One, my Son, forever. He will be loved." Right away the Holy Spirit descended on Jesus's head.

19 How many years did Jesus teach?
– Three years He taught.

20 How many people did He choose, Jesus, to go with Him and teach?
– He chose twelve people to go with Him to teach all over.

21 Did He not do something supernatural, Jesus, at the time He was teaching all over?
– That's true. Many times He was supernatural. He brought dead people back

68

15 tanisi ani ka totak sesos nistomitano e tato
15 *tânisi ani kâ-itôtahk Sesos nistomitanaw ê-tahto-*

piponwet?
piponwêt?

– ekwayak ka ki maci kiskinoamaket.
– *êkwayâk kâ-kî-mâci-kiskinohamâkêt.*

16 tanisi ani ka totak sesos mayowes kiskinoamaket?
16 *tânisi ani kâ-itôtahk Sesos mayowês kiskinohamâkêt?*

– pakwacite nemitano kisikaw ki ntawe iyewanisiiso
– *pakwacitê nêmitanaw kîsikâw kî-nitawi-iyêwanisihisow*

kisik e woke ayamiat.
kisik ê-wokê-ayamihât.

17 aweyiwa pakwacite ka nakiskawat sesos?
17 *awêyiwa pakwacitê kâ-nakiskawât Sesos?*

– kicitwaw sakpatista ki nakiskawew
– *kihcitwâw Sakpatista kî-nakiskawew*

e otamisikaacikakeyit ekosi ka natomat kita
ê-otamisîkahâcikâkêyit êkosi kâ-natomât kita-

sikaatakot.
sîkahâhtâkot.

18 tanisi ani ka ki ikiniyik sesos ka sikaatat?
18 *tânisi ani kâ-kî-ikiniyik Sesos kâ-sikahatât?*

– kipetawaw mosis kise manito weyotawimit ekosi
– *kî-pêtawâw mosis kisê-manitow wiyôhtâwîmit êkosi*

e itwet: « eoko ana ni kosis naspic kasakiak! »
ê-itwêt: "êwako ana nikosis nâspic kâsâhkihak!"

moestas simak ka miyosit manito e ki
mwêstas sêmak kâ-miyosit manitow ê-kî-

omimiciwisinakoot sesosa ostikwaniyik ki petweo.
omimiciwêsinakohot Sesosa ostikwâniyik kî-pêtwêhow.

19 tantato pipon ki kiskinoamakew sesos?
19 *tânitahto pipon kî-kiskinohamâkew Sesos?*

– nisto pipon ki kiskinoamakew.
– *nisto pipon kî-kiskinohamâkêw.*

20 tantato ka nawasonat ayisiyiniwa sesos kita wiciwat
20 *tânitahto kâ-nawasônât ayisiyiniwa Sesos kita-wîcêwât*

e papami kiskinoamaket?
ê-papâmi-kiskinohamâkêt?

– mitatat nisosap e ki nawasonat ayisiyiniwa ki
– *mitâtaht nîsosâp ê-kî-nawasônât ayisiyiniwa kî-*

wiciwew e papami kiskinoamaket?
wîcêwêw ê-papâmi-kiskinohamâkêt?

21 nama ci nantaw ki isi mamatawitotam sesos mekwac
21 *nama cî nânitaw kî-isi-mamatawitôtam Sesos mêkwâc*

e papami kiskinoamaket?
ê-papâmi-kiskinohamâkêt?

– tapwe miscetwaw ki mamatawitotam e apisi
– *tâpwê miscêtwaw kî-mamâtawitôtam ê-apisi-*

69

ᓯᒪᐟ ᐁ ᓂᐱᔨᐟ ᐊᔨᓯᔨᓂᐚ ᐚᐚ- ᐁ ᐃᔨᓂ
ᑲᐚ ᑯᑕᑲ ᐁ ᓇᓃᑲᑎᓯᔨᐟ.

22 ᑕᓂᑭ ᐊᓂ ᐁᑯᓯ ᑲ ᑭ ᐃᓯ ᒪᒪᑕᐃᐧ ᑐᑕᐠ ᓭᓱᐢ?

— ᐁᑯᓯ ᐁ ᐃᐧ ᐃᓯ ᑭᐢᑫᔨᑕᒧᐃᐁᐧᐤ ᑭᓯᐠ ᐁ ᒪᓂᑐᐃᐧᐤ ᑭᓯᐠ ᐁ ᐊᔨᓯᔨᓂᐃᐧᐤ.

7 ᑭᐢᑭᓄᐊᒪᑫᐃᐧᐣ.

§ 4 « ᑭ ᑲᐧᑕᑭᐊᐤ ᐅᑲᐧ- ᐁ ᑎᐯᔨᒥᐁᐧᔨᐟ ᐳᐢ « ᐱᓚᑦ; ᐊᔭᒥᐁᐊᐧᑎᑯᐠ ᑭ ᒋᐢᑕᐦᐊᐦᑲᐧᑕᐤ, ᑭ « ᓂᐱᐤ; ᑭ ᓇᐃᓇᐤ.

1 ᐊᓂᐃ ᑕᑐ ᑲ ᑭ ᑭᐢᑭᓄᐊᒪᐊᐧᐟ ᓭᓱᐢ ᑭ ᑕᐯᐧᑕᐠ ᒋ?

— ᒥᒐᐟ ᓇᒪᐃᐧᔭ ᐅᒋ ᑕᐯᐧᑕᐁᐧᐅᐧ ᓇᐢᐱ- ᑭ ᑲᐧᑕᑭᐁᐅᐧ, ᐱᑲᐧᓇᑕ ᒥᓇ ᑭ ᐊᑕᐁᐧᔨᒣᐅᐧ.

2 ᐊᐃᐧᓇ ᐊᓇ ᑲ ᑭ ᐃᐧᔭᓯᐊᐧᑕᐟ ᓭᓱᓴ?

— ᐳᐢᐱᓚᐟ ᐃᑕᐤ ᐊᓇ ᑲ ᑭ ᐃᐧᔭᓯᐊᐧᑕᐟ.

3 ᑕᓂᓯ ᑲ ᑐᑕᐟ ᓭᓱᐢ ᐁ ᑭ ᐃᐧᔭᓯᐊᐧᑎᐟ?

— ᑭ ᐸᓴᐢᑌᐊᐧᐤ ᑭ ᐸᓯᑫᐧᐱᑕᐤ ᒥᓯᑲᒥᓇᑲᓯᐊᐧ ᑎᑲᐧ ᒥᒋ, ᐊᔭᒥᐁᐊᐧᑎᑯᐠ ᑭ ᒋᐢᑕᐦᐊᐦᑲᐧᑕᐤ, ᑭ ᑕᑲᒪᐤ.

4 ᑕᓂᑭ ᐊᓂ ᐊᔭᒥᐁᐊᐧᑎᑯᐠ ᑯ ᓂᐸᐃᐟ ᓭᓱᐢ?

— ᐁᑯᓯ ᐁ ᐃᐧ ᐃᓯ ᑲᐦᑭᑕᒪᑯᔭᐠ ᑭᒋ ᐁᑲ ᐟᑕᐁᐧ ᑭᓯᓯᐊᐧᔭᐠ ᓂᐱᔭᑭ.

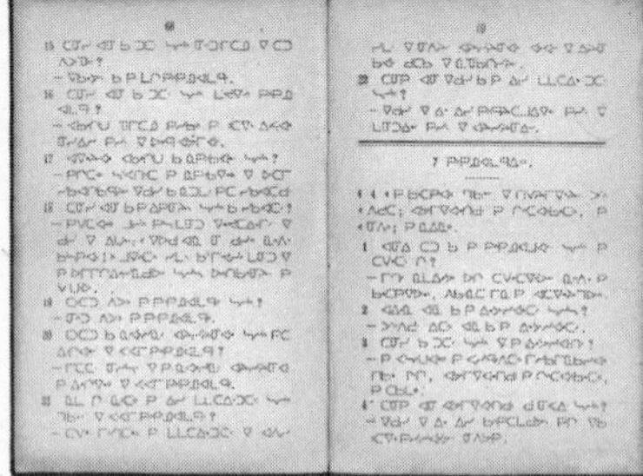

69 to life. He healed others who were in pain.

22 Why did Jesus do these things?

– So, in this way He is going to make known His supernaturalness in making man.

7 – LESSON.

§ 4 "He was made to suffer while he was on earth."
On the cross He was crucified. He Died. He was buried.

1 Did those that Jesus taught believe in Him?

– Many did not believe in Him forever. They made Him suffer without reason; also they disliked Him.

2 Who was it that was going to place judgement on Jesus?

– Pontius Pilate is his name that was going to place judgement on Him.

3 What was done to Jesus when He was being judged?

– He was whipped, He was blindfolded, He was crucified on the cross, He was crucified, He was pierced.

4 Why was Jesus killed on the cross?

– He was obtaining life for us not to be burned when we die.

69 simat e nipiyit ayisiyiniwa wawac e iyinikaat kotaka
simât ê-nipiyit ayisiyiniwa wâwâc ê-iyinikahât kotaka

e nanekatisiyit.
ê-nanêkatisiyit.

22 taniki ani ekosi ka ki isi mamatawi totak sesos?
22 *tânêhki ani êkosi kâ-kî-isi-mamâtawitohtahk Sesos?*

– ekosi e wi isi kiskeyitamoiwet kisik e manitowit kisik
– *êkosi ê-wî-isi-kiskêyihtamohiwêt kisik ê-manitôwit kisik*

e ayisiyiniwit.
ê-ayisiyiniwit.

---

7 KISKINOAMAKEWIN.
7 KISKINOHAMÂKÊWIN.

§ 4 « ki kwatakiaw mekwac e tipeyimiweyit poks « pilata;
§ 4 *"kî-kwâtakihâw mêkwâc ê-tipêyimiwêyit Poks "Pilata;*

ayamiewatikok ki citaaskwataw, ki nipiw; ki
ayamihêwahtikohk kî-cîstahâskwâtâw, kî nipiw; kî-

nainaw?
nahinâw?

1 anii tato ka ki kiskinoamawat sesos ki tapwetak ci?
1 *anihi tahto kâ-kî-kiskinohamawât Sesos kî-tâpwêtahk cî?*

– micet namawiya oci tapwetawewok naspic ki
– *mihcêt namâwiya ohci tâpwêtawêwak nâspic kî-*

kwatakiewok, pikwanata mina ki ataweyimewok.
kwâtakihêwak, pikwânâta mîna kî-atawêyimêwak.

2 awina ana ka ki wiyasowatat sesosa?
2 *awîna ana kâ-kî-wiyasiwâtât Sesosa?*

– pokspilat itaw ana ka ki wiyasowatat.
– *Pokspilat itâw ana kâ-kî-wiyasiwâtât.*

3 tanisi ka totat sesos e ki wiyasowatit?
3 *tânisi kâ-itôtât Sesos ê-kî-wiyasiwâtiht?*

– ki pasastewaw ki pasikwepitaw mi
– *kî-pasastêhwâw kî-pasihkwêpitâw mi-*

sokaminakasiwatikwa oci, ayamiewatikok ki
sokaminakasiwatikwa ohci, ayamihêwahtikohk kî-

cistaaskwataw, ki takamaw.
cîstahâskwâtâw, kî-tâkamâw.

4 taniki ani ayamiewatikok ko nipait sesos?
4 *tânêhki ani ayamihêwahtikohk kô-nipahiht Sesos?*

– ekosi e wi isi kaskitamakoyak kici eka ntawe
– *êkosi ê-wî-isi-kaskîtamâkoyâhk kici êkâ nitawi-*

kisisowayak nipiyaki.
kîsisowayâhk nipiyâhki.

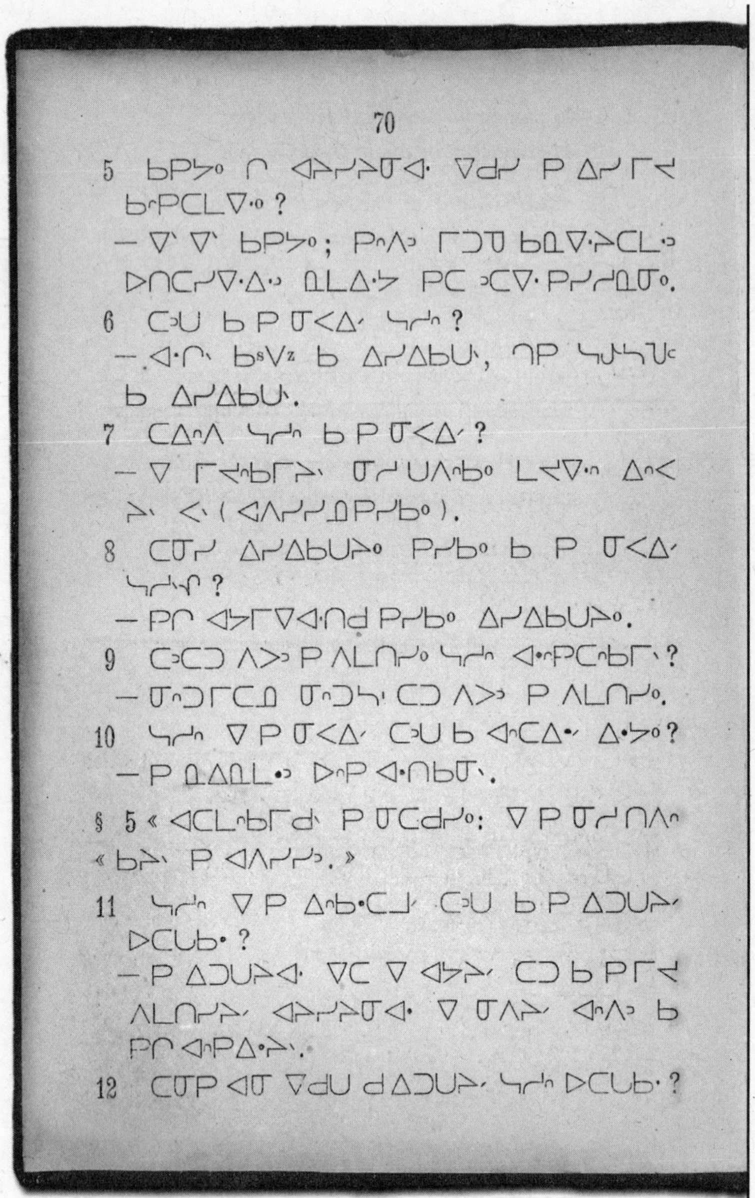

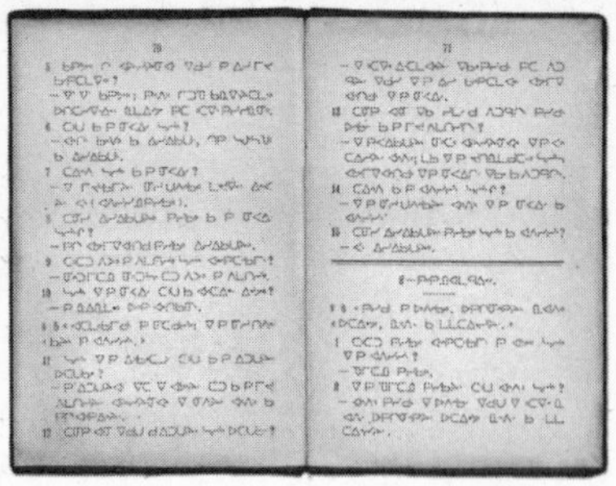

70

5 Did He gain this way for all people?
– Yes, everybody; if people completely follow His rule, nobody will be getting burned.
6 Where was Jesus killed?
– It is called Mount Calvary, near Jerusalem.
7 When was Jesus killed?
– It happened in the spring, two nights before Easter.
8 What is it called that day that Jesus Christ was killed?
– Good Friday is what it is called.
9 How many winters was He alive, Jesus, on earth?
– Thirty-three winters He lived.
10 When Jesus was killed where was His body placed?
– It was buried in a new grave.
§ 5 "He descended to the underworld; in two nights He came back to life."
11 When Jesus breathed His last, where did His spirit go?
– It went to the place where good living people go when they die.
12 Why is it that Jesus's spirit went there?

70

5 kakiyaw ci ayisiyiniwa ekosi ki isi miyo
5 *kahkiyaw cî ayisiyiniwa êkosi kî-isi-miyo-*

kaskitamawew?
kaskîtamawêw?

– ek ek kakiyaw; kispin mitone kanaweyitamwan
– *êk êk kahkiyaw, kîspin mitonê kanawêyihtamwan*

otitasiwewin namawiya kita ntawe kisisonaniw.
otitasiwêwin namâwiya kita nitawi-kîsisonâniw.

6 tante ka ki nipait sesos?
6 *tânitê kâ-kî-nipahiht Sesos?*

– wacik kalper ka isiikatek, ceki serosalem ka
– *wacîhk Kalper kâ-isiyihkâtêk, cîki Serosalem kâ-*

isiikatek.
isiyihkâtêk.

7 taispi sesos ka ki nipait?
7 *tânispî Sesos kâ-kî-nipahiht?*

– e miyoskamiyik niso tepiskaw mayowes ispayik pak
– *ê-miyoskamiyik nîso tipiskâw mayowês ispayik pak*

(apisisinokisikaw).
(apisisinowi-kîsikâw).

8 tanisi isiikateyiw kisikaw ka ki nipait sesokri?
8 *tânisi isiyihkâtêyiw kîsikâw kâ-kî-nipahiht Sesokri?*

– kici ayamiewatiko kisikaw isiikateyiw.
– *kihci-ayamihêwahtiko-kîsikâw isiyihkâtêyiw.*

9 tantato pipon ki pimatisiw sesos waskitaskamik?
9 *tânitahto pipon kî-pimâtisiw Sesos waskitaskamik?*

– nisto mitano nistosap tato pipon ki pimatisiw.
– *nistomitanaw nistosâp tahto pipon kî-pimâtisiw.*

10 sesos e ki nipait tante ka astawit wiya?
10 *Sesos ê-kî-nipahiht tânitê kâ-astâwiht wîyâw?*

– ki nainamwan oski watikanik.
– *kî-nahinamwân oski-wâtîkânihk.*

§ 5 « atamaskamikok ki nitakosiw: e ki niso tipis
§ 5 *"atamaskamikohk kî-nihtakosîw: ê-kî-nîso-tipiskâyik*

kayik ki apisisin. »
kî-apisisin."

11 sesos e ki iskwatamot tante ka ki itoteyit otacakwa?
11 *Sesos ê-kî-iskwatâmot tânitê kâ-kî-itohtêyit otâhcahkwa?*

– ki itoteyiwa eta e ayayit tato ka ki miyo pimatisiyit
– *kî-itohtêyiwa êta ê-ayâyit tahto kâ-kî-miyo-pimâtisiyit*

ayisiyiniwa e nipiyit aspin ka kici askiwiyik.
ayisiyiniwa ê-nipiyit aspin kâ-kihci-askiwiyik.

12 taniki ani ekote ko itoteyit sesos otacakwa?
12 *tânêhki ani êkotê kô-itohtêyit Sesos otâhcahkwa?*

71 – He went to tell them how to enter Heaven. He obtained this life for them, on the cross when He died.

13 Why is it that they did not enter Heaven immediately since they had a good life?

– At first they were allowed. Jesus died on the cross to allow sinners to enter.

14 When did Jesus come back to life?

– It was the second night since He was killed that He came back to life.

15 What is the day called when Jesus came back to life?

– Easter it is called.

---

8 – LESSON.

§ 6 "He rose to Heaven. He sits at the right hand of God, His Father who is supernatural."

1 How many days was it before Jesus returned to earth?

– Forty days.

2 When it was forty days where was Jesus?

– Since He rose to Heaven He is going to see clearly. He sits at the right hand of His Father. Forever He will be supernatural.

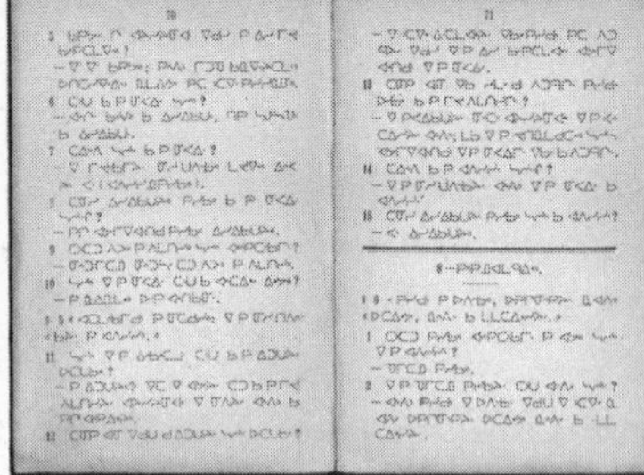

71 – e ntawe witamawayit ekwa kisikok kita pitokeyit
– *ê-nitawi-wîhtamawâyit êkwa kîsikohk kita-pîhtokwêyit*

ekosi e ki isi kaskitamawat ayamiewatikok e ki
êkosi ê-kî-isi-kaskîtamawât ayamihêwahtikohk ê-kî-

nipait.
nipahiht.

13 taniki ani eka simat ko pitokecik kisikok oskac ka
13 tânêhki ani êkâ sêmâk kô-pîhtokwêcik kîsikohk oskâc kâ-

ki miyo pimatisicik?
kî-miyo-pimâtisicik?

– e ki paikateyik nistam ayisiyiniwa e ki pastaisoyit
– *ê-kî-pahikâtêyik nistam ayisiyiniwa ê-kî-pâstâhisoyit*

aspin; maka e ki yotinamakotwaw sesosa
aspin; mâka ê-kî-yotinamâkotwâw Sesosa

ayamiewatikok e ki nipaimit ekwa ka pitokecik.
ayamihêwahtikohk ê-kî-nipahimît êkwa ka-pîhtokwêcik.

14 taispi ka ki apisisik sesokri?
14 tânispî kâ-kî-âpisisik Sesokri?

– e ki niso tepiskayik aspin e ki nipait ka apisisik
– *ê-kî-nîso-tipiskâyik aspin ê-kî-nipahiht kâ-âpisisik*

15 tanisi isiikateyik kisikaw sesos ka apisisik?
15 tânisi ê-isiyihkâtêyik kîsikâw Sesos kâ-âpisisik?

– pak isiikateyiw.
– *Pak isiyihkâtêyiw.*

---

8 – KISKINOAMAKEWIN.
8 – KISKINOHAMÂKÊWIN.

§ 6 « kisikok ki opiskaw, okiciniskiyik naapiw otawiya,
§ 6 "kîsikohk kî-ohpîskaw, okihciniskiyik, nahapiw ohtâwiya,

naspic ka mamatawisiyit. »
nâspic kâ-mamâhtâwisiyit."

1 tantato kisikaw waskitaskamik ki ayaw sesos e ki
1 tânitahto kîsikâw waskitaskamik kî-ayâw Sesos ê-kî-

apisisik?
apisisik?

– nemitano kisikaw.
– *nêmitanaw kîsikâw.*

2 e ki nemitano kisikayik tante aspin sesos?
2 ê-kî-nêmitanaw kîsikâyik tânitê aspin Sesos?

– aspin kisikok e opiskat ekote e ntawe naapit
– *aspin kîsikohk ê-ohpiskât êkotê ê-nitawi-nahapit*

okiciniskiyik otawiya naspic ka mamatawisiyit.
okihciniskiyik ohtâwîya nâspic kâ-mamâhtâwisiyit.

72

3 Is God at the right hand?

– Nobody else will be at the right hand. There will be nobody else.

4 What does it mean that Jesus sits at the right of His Father, the One who is supernatural?

– He is supernatural in the way His Father is. He is God in the way His Father is God.

5 Where is Jesus today?

– God is everywhere and He is in the Eucharist.

6 Does Jesus ever leave Heaven to be in the Eucharist?

– No, He never leaves. He is in Heaven as well as the Eucharist.

§7 "Over there He will command and place judgement on those who are living and also those who are dying."

7 When also will Jesus be seen on earth?

– At the end of the world, He will be seen. He is going to place judgement on those who are living and those who are dead.

8 How is that going to be said: "He is going to place judgement on those who are living, also those who are dead."?

– He will place judgement on all people, everyone

72

3 okiciniskiw ci kise manito?
3 okihciniskiw cî kisê-manitow?

– namawiya okiciniskiw eka e owiyowit.
– *namâwiya okihciniskiw êkâ ê-owîhowiht.*

4 tanisi e wi itwek anima « sesos naapiw okiciniskiyik
4 tânisi ê-wî-itwêk anima "Sesos nahapiw okihciniskiyik

otawiya ka mamatawisiyit »?
ohtâwîya kâ-mamâhtâwisiyit"?

– kesi mamatawisiyit otawiya ekosi e mamatawisit,
– *kêsi mamâhtâwisiyit ohtâwîya êkosi ê-mamâhtâwisît,*

kesi manitowiyit ekosi isi e manitowit nista wi
kêsi manitowiyit êkosi isi ê-manitowit nîsta wî-

itwaniw.
itwâniw.

5 tante eyat anoc sesos?
5 tânitê (ê-)ayât anohc Sesos?

– misiwe ayaw esi manitowit; maka esi ayisiyiniwit
– *misiwê ayâw (ê-)isi-manitowit; mâka (ê-)isi-ayisiyiniwit*

kisikok mina kicitwaw ekaristiwinik ayaw.
kîsikohk mîna kihcitwâw ekaristiwinihk ayâw.

6 nakatam ci kisik sesos ekaristiwinik kici pe ayat?
6 nakatam cî kîsik Sesos ekaristiwinihk kici pê-ayât?

– namawiya oci nakatam; kisikok kisik ekaristiwinik
– *namâwiya ohci nakatam; kîsikohk kîsik ekaristiwinihk*

ayaw.
ayâw.

§7 « ekote kita ototew e wi pe wiyasowatat tato e
§7 "êkotê kita ôtôtêw ê-wî-pê-wiyasiwâtât tahto

pimatisiyit tato mina e nipiyit. »
ê-pimâtisiyit tahto mîna ê-nipiyit."

7 taneyikok mina sesos mosis ke wapamit
7 tânêyikohk mîna Sesos mosis kê-wâpamiht

waskitaskamik?
waskitaskamik?

– eyikok poni askiwiki mina kita wapamaw, e wi pe
– *iyikohk pôni askîwiki mîna kita wâpamâw, ê-wî-pê-*

wiyasowatat tato e pimatisiyit tato mina e nipiyit.
wiyasiwâtât tahto ê-pimâtisiyit tahto mîna ê-nipiyit.

8 tanisi e wi itwek anima: « e wi pe wiyasowatat tato
8 tânisi ê-wî-itwêk anima: "ê-wî-pê-wiyasiwâtât tahto

e pimatisiyit tato mina e nipiyit »?
ê-pimâtisiyit tahto mîna ê-nipiyit"?

– kakiyaw kita wiyasowatew ayisiyiniwa tato
– *kahkiyaw kita-wiyasiwâtêw ayisiyiniwa tahto*

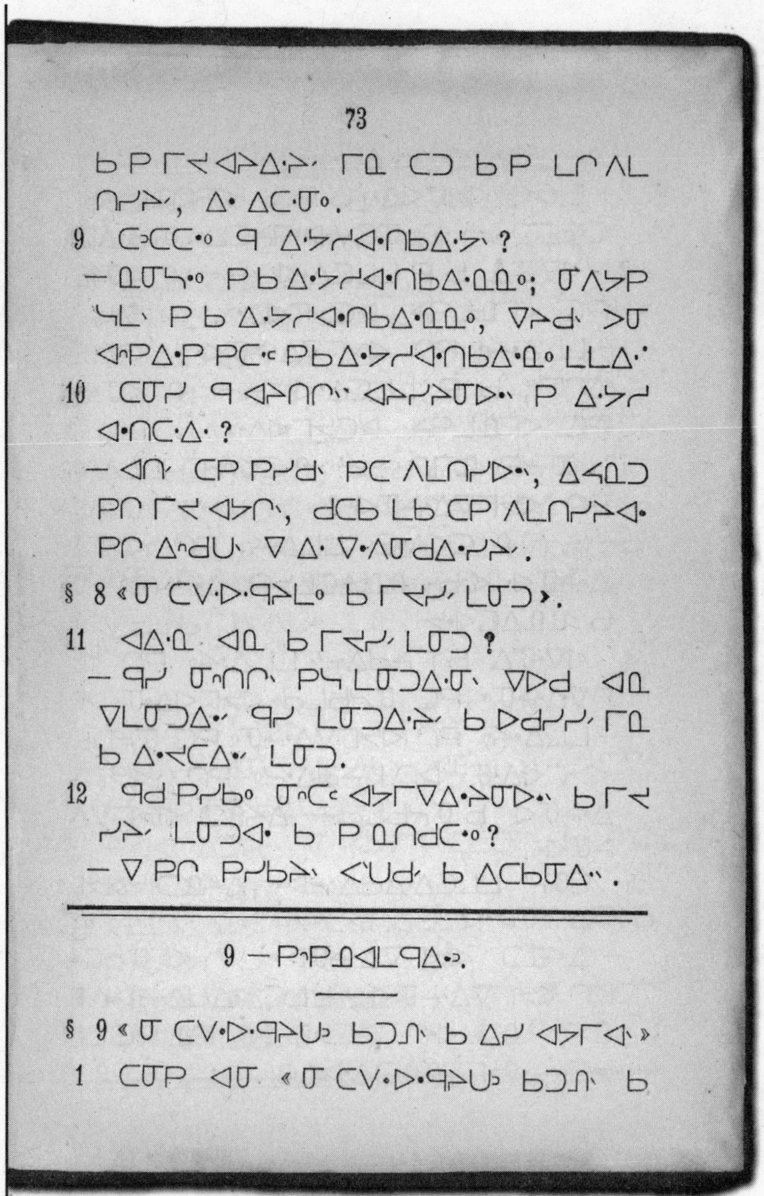

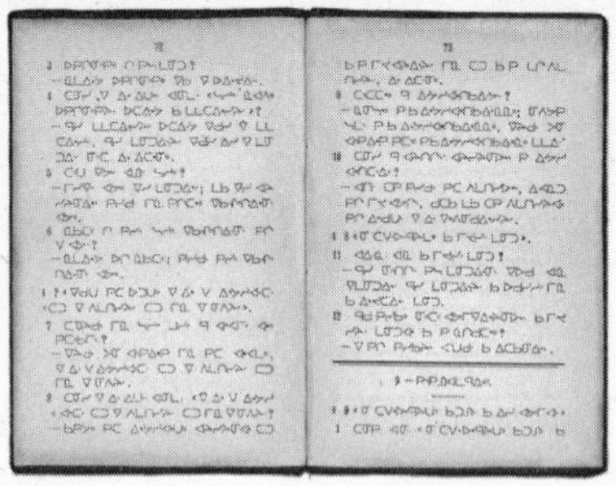

73 who was good and also everyone who lived badly, it was said.

9 How many times will judgement be passed?

– Twice we will be passed judgement on; when we die right away we will be judged and then at the end of the world again we will be judged altogether.

10 What will be said to the people after they are passed judgement on?

– Some will live in Heaven with Him and have a good life, but others will be living in the fire; they are going to be rejected by God.

§ 8 "I believe in the Holy Spirit."

11 Who is the Holy Spirit?

– The three of them in the Trinity are all supernatural as His son and also as God, the Father.

12 On which day at first, did the priests receive the Holy Spirit?

– On the feast of Pentecost.

---

9 – LESSON.

§ 9 "I believe in Catholic praying."

1 Why is it that I believe in the Catholic prayer

73 ka ki miyo ayiwiyit mina tato ka ki maci pimatisiyit,
kâ-kî-miyo-ayiwiyit mîna tâhto kâ-kî-maci-pimâtisiyit,

wi itwaniw.
wî-itwâniw.

9 tantatwaw ke wiyasowatikawiyak?
9 tânitahtwâw kê-wiyasiwâtikawiyahk?

– naniswaw ki ka wiyasowatikawinanaw; nipiyakisemat
– nânîswâw ki-ka-wiyasiwâtikâwinânâw; nipiyâkisêmât

ka ki wiyasowatikawinanaw, eyikok poni askiwiki
kâ-kî-wiyasiwâtikâwinânâw, iyikohk pôni-askîwiki

kitwam ka ki wiyasowatikawinaw mamawi.
kîhtwâm ka-kî-wiyasiwâtikâwinâw mâmâwi.

10 tanisi ke ayiticik ayisiyiniwok ki wiyasowatitwawi?
10 tânisi kê-ayiticik ayisiyiniwak kî-wiyasiwâtitwâwi?

– atit taki kisikok kita pimatisiwok, iyenato kici miyo
– âtiht tahki kîsikohk kita-pimâtisiwak, iyênato kici miyo-

ayacik, kotaka maka taki pimatisiyiwa kici iskotek
ayâcik, kotaka mâka tahki pimâtisiyiwa kihci-iskotêhk

e wi wepinikowisiyit.
ê-wî-wêpinikowisiyit.

§ 8 « ni tapwewokeyimaw ka miyosit manito. »
§ 8 "nitâpwêwakêyimâw kâ-miyosit manitow."

11 awina ana ka miyosit manito?
11 awîna ana kâ-miyosit manitow?

– kesi nisticik kesi manitowinik eoko ana emanitowit
– kêsi nisticik kêsi manitowinik êwako ana ê-manitowit

kesi manitowiyit ka okosisit mina ka wiyotawit manito.
kêsi manitowiyit kâ-okosisit mîna kâ-wiyotawit manitow.

12 keko kisikaw nistam ayamiewiyiniwok ka miyosiyit
12 kêko kîsikâw nistam ayamihêwiyiniwak kâ-miyosiyit

manitowa ka ki natikotwaw?
manitowa kâ-kî-natikotwâw?

– e kici kisikayik paktekot ka itakaniwik.
– ê-kihci-kîsikâyik Paktekot kâ-itakaniwik.

---

9 – KISKINOAMAKEWIN.

9 – KISKINOHAMÂKÊWIN.

§ 9 « ni tapwewokeyiten katolik ka isi ayamiak. »
§ 9 "nitâpwêwakêyihtên kâtolik kâ-isi-ayamihâk."

1 taniki ani « ni tapwewokeyiten katolik ka
1 tanêhki ani "nitâpwêwakêyihtên kâtolik kâ-

74

ᐃᓯ ᐊᔭᒥᐊᐧ» ᑯ ᐃᑌᐧᔭᐣ?
— ᑲᐧᔭᐣ ᐊᔭᒥᐊᐃᐧᐣ ᑲ ᑭ ᐯ ᐸᑭᑎᓇᐠ ᐊᐧᐣᑭ
ᑕᐣᑲᒥᐠ ᓴᓯᐣ ᐧᓱ ᑎᑕᐯᐧᐅᐧᑫᐳᑕᒪᐧᐣ ᑎ ᐃᐧᐃᑕᐧᐣ
2 ᐊᐁᐧᑎᐃ ᑲ ᑭ ᒪᒪᑕᐃᐧᐊᐟ ᓴᓯᐣᐧᓱ ᐊᑎᐣᑲ-
ᑭᑕ ᐸᒥᓇᒪᑫᐳᐟ ᐅᑕᔭᒥᐊᐃᐧᐣ.
— ᒪᒪᐃᐧᕂᐣ ᑭᑎ ᐊᔭᒥᐁᐃᐧᐳᑎᐊᐧ, ᐸᐸ ᑲ
ᐃᑎᒥᐟ, ᑲ ᑭ ᒪᒪᑕᐃᐧᐊᐟ ᓴᓯᐣ ᐧᓱ ᐊᑎᐣᑲ-
ᑭᑕ ᐸᒥᓇᒪᑫᐳᐟ ᐅᑕᔭᒥᐊᐃᐧᐣ.
3 ᐊᑎᓯᑭᐣ ᓇᒣᑎ ᓴᓯᐣᐧᓱ ᑕᐸᐱᐣᑕᐠ ᒪᒪᐃᐧᕂᐣ
ᑭᑎ ᐊᔭᒥᐁᐃᐧᐳᑎᐊᐧ?
— ᓴᓯᐣᐧᓱ ᑕᐸᐱᐣᑕᐠ ᒪᒪᐃᐧᕂᐣ ᑭᑎ ᐊᔭᒥᐁ
ᐃᐧᐳᑎᐊᐧ ᐸᐣᑲ- ᓇᓇᐃᑕᒪᔭᑭ ᐃᐧᔭ ᑎᐱᔭᐁᐧ
ᑲ ᓇᓇᐃᑕᐊᐧᔭᐠ.
4 ᐊᐁᐧᑎᐃ ᑲ ᒥᐳᑯᐃᐧᓯᐟ ᒪᒪᐃᐧᕂᐣ ᑭᑎ ᐊᔭ
ᒥᐁᐃᐧᐳᑎᐤ ᑭᑕ ᑎᓯᑲᒪᑯᐟ ᐊᔭᒥᐊᐃᐧᑎᐠ ᐅᑎ
— ᒪᒪᐃᐧᕂᐣ ᑭᑎ ᐊᔭᒥᐁᐃᐧᐳᑎᐤ ᑭᑕ ᑎᓯᑲᒪᐟ
ᐊᔭᒥᐊᐃᐧᑎᐠ ᐅᑎ ᒥᐳᑯᐃᐧᓯᐤ ᑭᑎ ᐊᔭᒥᐁ
ᐃᐧᐳᑎᐊᐧ ᑲ ᑎᓯᑲᒪᑯᐳᐟ ᐃᕂᓇᑐ ᐊᔭᒥᐁᐃᐧ
ᐳᑎᐊᐧ.
5 ᑕᑎᓯ ᒪᒪᑕᐃᐧᐃᑯᐃᐧᓯᐅᐧᐠ ᐃᕂᓇᑐ ᐊᔭᒥ
ᐁᐃᐧᐳᑎᐅᐧᐠ?
— ᐃᕂᓇᑐ ᐊᔭᒥᐁᐃᐧᐳᑎᐅᐧᐠ ᐁ ᐸᒥᑎᑯᑕᐧᐤ
ᑭᑎ ᐊᔭᒥᐁᐃᐧᐳᑎᐊᐧ, ᒪᒪᑕᐃᐧᐃᑯᐃᐧᓯᐅᐧᐠ ᑭ
ᑕ ᑭᐣᑭᓃᐊᒪᐊᐧᑎᐠ ᐅᑕᔭᒥᐊᐊᐧ ᒥᓇ ᑭᑕᒪᒥ
ᔭᑕᐧᐤ ᐊᔭᒥᐁᓇᓇᑐᐃᐧᐅᐃᐧᓇ.

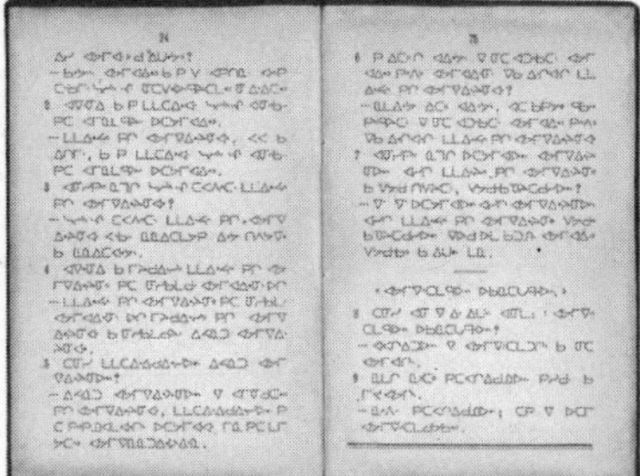

74

I am saying?

– Jesus explained proper praying for us on earth. We believe in His ways, I am going to say.

2 Who is it that Jesus Christ made to minister His prayer.

– Mainly the noble priest is the one that Jesus Christ appointed to minister His prayer.

3 Is Jesus Christ replaced by him, the noble priest?

– The priest replaces Jesus Christ. As far as we listen to him, himself, we are listening to Him.

4 With whom does the noble priest work?

– Mostly the noble priest works together with the religion he receives from other noble priests to help him pray and teach.

5 How did they receive power of judgement from Heaven, only the priests?

– Only the priest ministers to the people. The noble priests, they receive power from Heaven to teach those who pray and also to give them the sacraments.

74

isi ayamiak » ko itweyan?
isi-ayamihâk" ko-itwêyân?

– kwayask ayamiawin ka ki pe pakitinak
– *kwayask ayamihâwin kâ-kî-pê-pakitinak*

waskitaskamik sesoskri ni tapwewokeyitamwan
waskitaskamik Sesoskri nitâpwêwakêyihtamwan

ni wiitwan.
niwî-itwân.

2 awinii ka ki mamatawiat sesoskri aniskac kita
2 *awîniki kâ-kî-mamâhtâwihât Sesoskri âniskac kita-*

paminamakeyit otayamiawin?
paminamakêyit otayamihâwin?

– mamawiyes kici ayamiewiyiniwa, papa ka itimit, ka
– *mamawiyês kihci-ayamihêwiyiniwa, papa-ka-itimît, ka-*

ki mamatawiat sesos kri aniskac kita
kî-mamâhtâwihât Sesos Kri âniskac kita-

paminamakeyit otayamiawin.
paminamâkêyit otayamihâwin.

3 anisikis nameci sesos kri tapapistak mamawiyes kici
3 *anisikis namêci Sesos Kri tapapîstahk mamawiyês kihci-*

ayamiewiyiniwa?
ayamihêwiyiniwa?

– sesos kri tapapistak mamawiyes kici
– *Sesos Kri tapapîstahk mamawiyês kihci-*

ayamiewiyiniwa paskac nanaitamayaki wiya
ayamihêwiyiniwa paskac nanahîtamayahki wîya

tipiyawe ka nanaitawayak.
tipiyawê kâ-nanahihtâwâyahk.

4 awenii ka miyokowisit mamawiyes kici
4 *awînihi kâ-miyokowisit mamawiyês kihci-*

ayamiewiyiniw kita nisokamakot ayamiawinik oci
ayamihêwiyiniw kita-nîsôhkamâkot ayamihâwinihk ohci

– mamawiyes kici ayamiewiyiniw kita nisokamat
– *mamawiyês kihci-ayamihêwiyiniw kita-nîsôhkamât*

ayamiawinik oci miyikowisiw kici
ayamihawinihk ohci miyikowisiw kihci-

ayamiewiyiniwa ka ni sokamakoyit iyenato
ayamihêwiyiniwa kâ-nîsôhkamâkoyit iyênato

ayamiewiyiniwa.
ayamihêwiyiniwa.

5 tanisi mamatawiikowisiwok iyenato
5 *tânisi mamâhtâwihikowisiwak iyênato*

ayamiewiyiniwok?
ayamihêwiyiniwak?

– iyenato ayamiewiyiniwok e paminikotwaw kici
– *iyênato ayamihêwiyiniwak ê-paminikotwâw kihci-*

ayamiewiyiniwa, mamatawiikowisiwok
ayamihêwiyiniwa, mamâhtâwihikowisiwak

kita kiskinoamawacik otayamiawa mina kita
kita-kiskinohamâwacik otayamihâwa mîna kita-

mamiyatwaw ayamienanatowiowina.
mamiyatwâw ayamihênanatowihowina.

75

6 ᑭ ᐃᑕᐤᒋ ᐊᐃᐧᔭᐠ ᐁ ᑘᑕ ᐊᑐᐢᑲᑕᐠ ᐊᔭᒥ
ᐊᐃᐧᐣ ᑭᐢᐱᐣ ᐊᔭᒥᐊᐃᐧᑘᐠ ᐁᑲ ᐃᐧᒋᐊᐧᒋ ᒪᒪ
ᐃᐧᓭᐢ ᑭᒋ ᐊᔭᒥᐁᐃᐧᔩᑘᐊᐧ?
— ᓇᒪᐃᐧᔭ ᐃᑕᐤ ᐊᐃᐧᔭᐠ, ᐊᑕ ᑲᑭᔭᐤ ᑫᑲᐧ
ᑭᐢᑫᔦᑕᐠ ᐁ ᑘᑕ ᐊᑐᐢᑲᑕᐠ ᐊᔭᒥᐊᐃᐧᐣ ᑭᐢᐱᐣ
ᐁᑲ ᐃᐧᒋᐊᐧᒋ ᒪᒪᐃᐧᓭᐢ ᑭᒋ ᐊᔭᒥᐁᐃᐧᔩᑘᐊᐧ
7 ᐊᑘᓯᑭᐢ ᓇᒣᒋ ᐅᑕᔭᒥᐊᐅᐧ ᐊᔭᒥᐁᐃᐧᔩ
ᑘᐅᐧ ᐊᓯᒋ ᒪᒪᐃᐧᔩᐢ, ᑭᒋ ᐊᔭᒥᐁᐃᐧᔩᑘᐤ
ᑲ ᐯᔭᑯ ᑎᐯᔦᑕᐠ, ᐯᔭᑯᐢᑲᑗᔦᑕᑯᓯᐅᐧ?
— ᐁᐠ ᐁᐠ ᐅᑕᔭᒥᐊᐅᐧ ᐊᓯᒋ ᐊᔭᒥᐁᐃᐧᔩᑘᐅᐧ
ᐊᓯᒋ ᒪᒪᐃᐧᓭᐢ ᑭᒋ ᐊᔭᒥᐁᐃᐧᔩᑘᐤ ᐯᔭᑯᐢ
ᑲᑗᔦᑕᑯᓯᐅᐧ ᐁᐅᑯ ᐅᒪ ᑲᑐᔑᐠ ᐊᔭᒥᐊᐃᐧᐣ
ᐯᔭᑯᐢᑲᐣ ᑲ ᐃᑌᐧ ᒪᓇ.

« ᐊᔭᒥᐁᐢᑕᒪᑫᐅᐧ ᐅᑲᓇᑕᓫᑫᐅᐧ. »

8 ᑕᑘᓯ ᐊᑘ ᐁ ᐃᐧ ᐃᑌᐧ ᐊᑘᒪ: ᐊᔭᒥᐁᐢ
ᑕᒪᑫᐅᐧ ᐅᑲᓇᑕᓫᑫᐅᐧ?
— ᐊᐸᒋᐃᑐᐅᐧ ᐁ ᐊᔭᒥᐁᐢᑕᒪᑐᒋᐠ ᑲ ᑘᑕ
ᐊᔭᒥᐊᒋᐠ.
9 ᓇᒪᒋ ᓇᐣᑕᐤ ᑭᑕᐸᒋᐃᑯᓇᐅᐧ ᑭᓯᑯᐠ ᑲ
ᒥᔦ ᐊᔭᒋᐠ.
— ᓇᐢᐱ ᑭᑕᐸᒋᐃᑯᓇᐅᐧ; ᑕᑭ ᐁ ᐅᑕᒥ
ᐊᔭᒥᐁᐢᑕᒪᑯᔭᑲᐤ.

75

6 Can somebody say he works well with the religion if he does not follow the principal priest?
– Although he knows everything, he cannot work well with the religion if he does not follow the principal priest.
7 Is that why those who pray, the priests also the principal priest, are they thought of as one holy family?
– Yes, the worshippers and the priests, also the principal priest are one family. That is in the Catholic religion why they usually say one family.

"Intercessors' souls are pure."

8 What does it mean that the intercessors' souls are pure?
– They pray for each other to know how to pray.
9 Do they not intercede for us for Heaven to be there?
– They intercede for us all the time. They are busy praying for us.

75

6 ki itaw ci awiyak e nita atoskatak ayamiawin kispin
6 kî-itâw cî awiyak ê-nihtâ-atoskâtahk ayamihâwin kîspin

ayamiawinik eka wici waci mamawiyes kici
ayamihâwinik êkâ wîciwâci mamawiyês kihci-

ayamiewiyiniwa?
ayamihêwiyiniwa?

– namawiya itaw awiyak, ata kakiyaw kekway
– namâwiya itâw awiyak, âta kahkiyaw kîkway

kiskeyitak e ni ta atoskatak ayamiawin kispin eka
(ê-)kiskêyihtahk ê-nihtâ-atoskâtahk ayamihâwin kîspin êkâ

wiciwaci mamawiyes kici ayamiewiyiniwa.
wîciwâci mamawiyês kihci-ayamihêwiyiniwa.

7 anisikis nameci otayamiawok ayamiewiyiniwok asici
7 anisikis namêcî otayamihâwak ayamihêwiyiniwak asici

mamawiyes kici ayamiewiyiniw ka peyakotipeyitak,
mamawiyês kihci-ayamihêwiyiniw kâ-peyako-tipêyitahk,

peyakoskan eyitakosiwok?
pêyakôskân iyihtâkosiwak?

– ek ek otayamiawok asici ayamiewiyiniwok asici
– êk êk otayamihâwak asici ayamihêwiyiniwak asici

mamawiyes kici ayamiewiyiniw
mamawiyês kihci-ayamihêwiyiniw

peyakoskaneyitakosiwok eoko oma katolik
pêyakôskânêyihtâkosiwak êwako ôma kâtolik

ayamiawin peyakoskan ka itwek mana.
ayamihâwin pêyakôskân kâ-itwêk mâna.

« ayamiestamakewok okanatacakwewok. »
"ayamihêstamâkêwak okanâtahcahkwêwak."

8 tanisi ani e wi itwek anima: ayamiestamakewok
8 tânisi ani ê-wî-itwêk anima: ayamihêstamâkêwak

okanatacakwewok?
okanâtahcahkwêwak?

– apaciitowok e ayamiestamatocik ka nita ayamiacik.
– âpacihitowak ê-ayamihêstamâtocik kâ-nihtâ-ayamihâcik.

9 namaci nantaw kitapaciikonowok kisikok ka miyo
9 namacî nânitaw kitâpacihikonowak kîsikohk kâ-miyo-

ayacik.
ayâcik.

– naspic kitapaciikonowok; taki e
– nâspic kitâpacihikonawak; tahki ê-

otamiayamiestamakoyakwaw.
otami-ayamihêstamâkoyahkwâw.

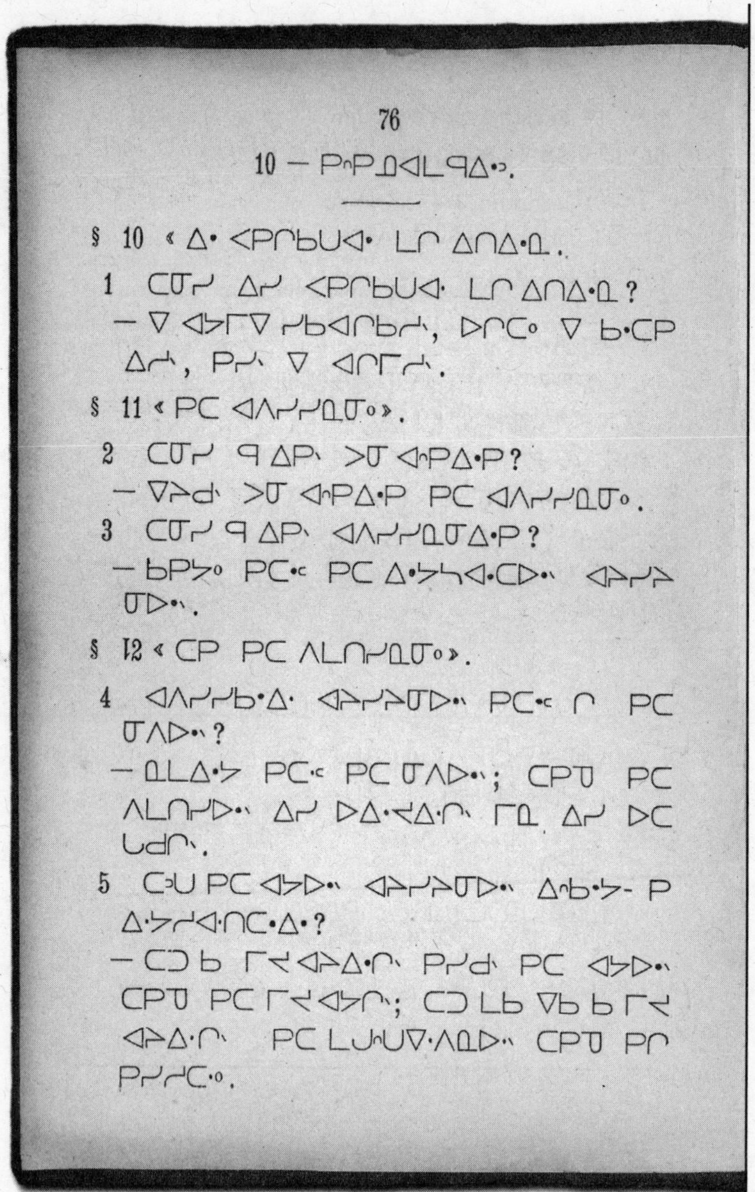

76

10 — ᑭᐢᑭᓄᐊᒪᑫᐃᐧᐣ.

§ 10 « ᐃᐧ ᐸᑭᒋᑲᑌᐊᐧ ᒪᒋ ᐃᑎᐃᐧᓇ.

1 ᑕᑌᓯ ᐃᓯ ᐸᑭᒋᑲᑌᐊᐧ ᒪᒋ ᐃᑎᐃᐧᓇ ?

— ᐁ ᐊᔦᒥᐁ ᓯᑲᐊᒋᑲᓯ, ᐅᒋᑕᐤ ᐁ ᑲᐧᑕᑭ ᐃᓯ, ᑭᓯ ᐁ ᐊᑎᒥᓯ.

§ 11 « ᑭᑕ ᐊᐱᓯᓯᓇᑌᐤ ».

2 ᑕᑌᓯ ᑫ ᐃᑭ ᐳᑌ ᐊᐢᑭᐃᐧᑭ ?

— ᐁᐳᑯ ᐳᑌ ᐊᐢᑭᐃᐧᑭ ᑭᑕ ᐊᐱᓯᓯᓇᑌᐤ.

3 ᑕᑌᓯ ᑫ ᐃᑭ ᐊᐱᓯᓯᓇᑌᐃᐧᑭ ?

— ᑲᑭᔅᐤ ᑭᑕ ᑭᑕ ᐃᐧᔅᓴᐊᐧᑕᐅ ᐊᐳᓯᐳ ᑌᐅ.

§ 12 « ᑕᑭ ᑭᑕ ᐱᒪᑎᓯᓇᑌᐤ ».

4 ᐊᐱᓯᓯᑲᐧᐃᐧ ᐊᐳᓯᐳᑌᐅ ᑭᑕ ᒋ ᑭᑕ ᑌᐱᐅ ?

— ᓇᒪᐃᐧᔅ ᑭᑕ ᑭᑕ ᑌᐱᐅ; ᑕᑭᑌ ᑭᑕ ᐱᒪᑎᓯᐅ ᐃᓯ ᐅᐃᐧᔦᐃᐧᒋ ᒥᓇ ᐃᓯ ᐅᑕ ᑲᑯᒋ.

5 ᑕᑐᑌ ᑭᑕ ᐊᔦᐅ ᐊᐳᓯᐳᑌᐅ ᐃᐢᑲᐧᔅ- ᑭ ᐃᐧᔅᓯᐊᐧᑎᑕᐃᐧ ?

— ᑕᑐ ᑲ ᒥᔦᐊᐳᐃᐧᒋ ᑭᓯᑯ ᑭᑕ ᐊᔦᐅ ᑕᑭᑌ ᑭᑕ ᒥᔦᐊᔦᒋ; ᑕᑐ ᒪᑲ ᐁᑲ ᑲ ᒥᔦ ᐊᐳᐃᐧᒋ ᑭᑕ ᒪᒍᐢᑌᐁᐧᐱᓇᐅ ᑕᑭᑌ ᑭᒋ ᑭᓯᓯᑕᐤ.

76 10 – LESSON.

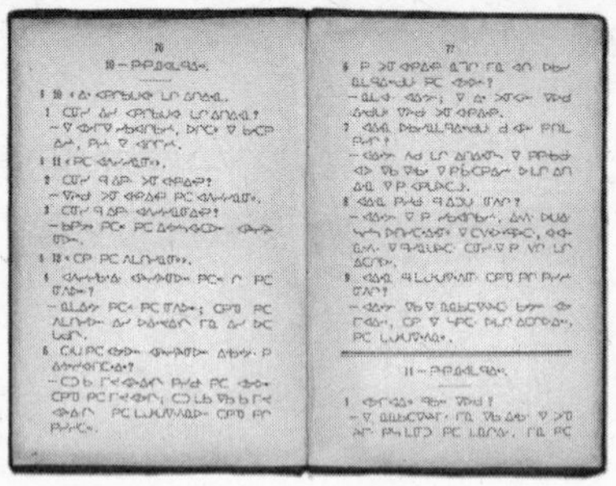

§ 10 "The sins are being released."

1 How are the sins being released?

– We are baptized since we must suffer; also we make confession.

§ 11 "Everybody will come back to life."

2 What is going to happen at the ending of the world?

– At the end of the world everyone will come back to life.

3 What will happen when one is brought back to life?

– All of the people will be judged.

§ 12 "Everybody will live forever."

4 When they are brought to life will the people die again?

– They will not die again; always they will be alive in their name. Also He is in their spirit.

5 Where will the people be the last time, when they are being judged?

– Everyone who has good behaviour will be in Heaven to be well always. But those who do not have good behaviour will be burned, always in hell.

IO – KISKINOAMAKEWIN.

10 – KISKINOHAMÂKÊWIN.

§ 10 « wi pakicikatewa maci itiwina. »
§ 10 "wî-pakicikâtêwa macihtiwina."

1 tanisi isi pakicikatewa maci itiwina?
1 tânisi isi pakicikâtêwa macihtiwina?

– e ayamie sikaacikasok, ocitaw e kwatakiisok, kisik
– ê-ayamihe-sîkahâhcikâsok, ohcitaw ê-kwâtakîhisok, kisik

e acimisok.
ê-âcimisok.

§ 11 « kita apisisinaniw. »
§ 11 "kita-âpisisinâniw."

2 tanisi ke ikik poni askiwiki?
2 tânisi kê ihkik pôni-askîwiki?

– eyikok poni askiwiki kita apisisinaniw.
– iyikohk pôni askîwiki kita-âpisisinâniw.

3 tanisi ke ikik apisisinaniwiki?
3 tânisi kê ihkik âpisisinâniwiki?

– kakiyaw kitwam kita wiyasawatawok ayisiyiniwok.
– kahkiyaw kîhtwâm kita wiyasiwâtâwak ayisiyiniwak.

§ 12 « taki kita pimatisinaniw »
§ 12 "tahki kita-pimâtisinâniw."

4 apisisikwawi ayisiyiniwok kitwam ci kita nipiwok?
4 âpisisikwâwi ayisiyiniwak kîhtwâm cî kita-nipiwak?

– namawiya kitwam kita nipiwok; takine kita
– namâwiya kîhtwâm kita-nipiwak; tahkinê kita-

pimatisiwok isi owiyowicik mina isi otakakocik.
pimâtisiwak isi owihowicik mîna isi otahcâhkocik.

5 tante kita ayawok ayisiyiniwok iskwayac
5 tânitê kita-ayâwak ayisiyiniwak iskwêyâc

kiwiyasowatitwawi?
kî-wiyasiwâtîtwâwi?

– tato ka miyo ayiwicik kisikok kita ayiwok takine
– tahto kâ-miyo-ayiwicik kîsikohk kita ayâwak tahkinê

kita miyo ayacik; tato maka eka ka miyo ayiwicik kita
kita-miyo-ayâcik; tahto mâka ekâ kâ-miyo-ayiwicik kita-

macostewepinawok takine kici kisisotwaw.
macostêwêpinâwak tahkinê kici kisisotwâw.

77

6 When the world is over will some not also be in purgatory?

– Nobody. Purgatory will last until the world has ended.

7 Who is going to be placed in purgatory when he is poor in spirit?

– Somebody who bears sin or even has not yet suffered for the sin for which he was forgiven.

8 Who is going to Heaven when he dies?

– Someone who has been baptized and believes in Jesus's ceremony especially someone who is forever sorrowful for his sins and bad upbringing.

9 Who will be cast into the fire always when he dies?

– Someone who does not heed religion carefully. He loves his bad behaviour all the time; he will be cast into the fire.

II – LESSON.

1 What is religion?

– God looks after me carefully. I must never forget about God. I must respect Him, also.

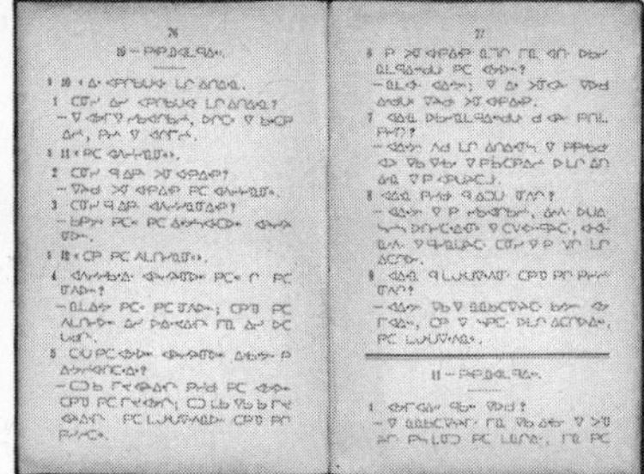

77 6 ki poni askiwiki nameci mina atit
6 kî-pôni-askîwiki namêcî mîna âtiht

ekasinamakewiskotek kita ayawok?
ê-kâsînamâkêwiskotêhk kita-ayâwak?

– namawac awiyak; e wi poni payik eoko iskotew
– *namawâc awiyak; ê-wî-pôni-payik êwako iskotêw*

eyikok poni askiwiki.
iyikohk pôni-askîwiki.

7 awina okasinamakewiskotek ko ayit kitimakisici?
7 awîna okâsînamâkêw-iskotêhk kô-ayit kitimâkisici?

– awiyak piko maci itiwinisa e kikiskakot apo eka
– *awiyak piko macihtiwinisa ê-kikiskâkot ahpô êkâ*

eskwa e kikwatakiisot o maci itiwina e ki
cêskwa ê-kî-kwâtakihisot omacihtiwina ê-kî-

pakiteyitamot.
pakitêyihtamôt.

8 awina kisikok ke itotet nipici?
8 awîna kîsikohk kê-itohtêt nipici?

– awiyak e ki sikaacikasot, ispic oteit sesosa
– *awiyak ê-kî-sîkahâhcikâsot, ispic otêhit Sesosa*

otisitwawiniw e tapwewokeyitak, wawac naspic
otisîhtwâwiniw ê-tâpwêwâkêyihtahk wâwâc nâspic

e kesinateyitak tanisi e ki peci maci itaciot.
ê-kêsinatêyihtahk tânisi ê-kî-pêci-macihtâcihot.

9 awina ke macostewepinit takine kici kisisot nipici?
9 awîna kê-macostêwipinît tahkinê kihci-kîsisohk nipici?

– awiyak eka e nanakataweyitak kwayask ayamiawin,
– *awiyak êkâ ê-nânâkatawêyihtahk kwayask ayamihâwin,*

taki e sakitat omaci itaciowin; kita macostewepinaw.
tahki ê-sâkihtât omacihtâcihowin, kita-macostêwêpinâw.

II – KISKINOAMAKEWIN.
11 – KISKINOHAMÂKÊWIN.

1 ayamiawin kekway eoko?
1 ayamihâwin kîkway êwako?

– e nanakataweyimit mina eka wikac e poni payit kise
– *ê-nânâkatawêyimiht mîna êkâ wîhkâc ê-pôni-payit kisê-*

manito kita manaciit, mina kita
manitow kita-manâcihiht, mîna kita-

78

ᐸᑯᓴᔨᒥᐟ, ᐁᐅᑯ ᐅᒪ ᐊᔭᒥᐊᐃᐣ ᑲ ᐃᑌᐦ.
2 ᑕᑐᔨ ᑭᑕ ᑭ ᐃᔨ ᐊᔭᒥᐊᐤ ᐊᐃᐧᔭᐠ ᑭᑕ
ᒥᐊᐧᔨᑐᔨᐠ ᐅᑕᔭᒥᐊᐃᐣ ?
— ᐃᐣᐱᐨ ᐅᑌᐃᐟ ᑭᑕ ᓇᓇᑲᑕᐁᐧᔨᑕᐦ ᑫᔨ ᐊ
ᔭᒥᐊᐧ ᑭᓴ ᒪᑐᑐᐊᐧ ᐁ ᐸᑯᓴᔨᒪᐟ.
3 ᑕᓇ ᐊᔨᐊᐦ ᑲ ᑭᒋᑕᐧᐁᐧᔨᑕᑲᐦ ᐊᔭᒥᐊᐃᐣ ?
— ᐊᔭᒥᐊᐃᐣ ᑲ ᐃᔨ ᑭᒋᑎᐠ : « ᓄᑕᐃᐧᓇᐣ ᑭᒋ
ᑭᔨᑯᐠ ᐁᔭᔭᐣ. » ᐁᐅᑯ ᐅᒪ ᐊᔨᐊᐦ ᑲ ᑭ
ᒋᑕᐧᐁᐧᔨᑕᑲᐦ.
4 ᑕᑐᑭ ᐊᑐ ᓄᑕᐃᐧᓇᐣ ᑯ ᐃᑕᔭᐠ ᑭᓴᒪᑐᑐ ?
— ᐁ ᑭ ᐅᔨᐃᑯᔭᐠ ᐊᐧᐊᐧᐨ ᑲᑭᔭᐤ ᐁ ᒪᒥᔨ
ᑯᔭᐠ ᓄᑕᐃᐧᓇᐣ ᑯ ᐃᑕᔭᐠ.
5 ᑫᑲᐧ+ ᑐᑐᑕᒍᐊᐧᔭᐠ ᑭᓴ ᒪᑐᑐ : « ᐱᑕᑐ
ᒥᐁᐧᔨᒋᑲᑌᐠ ᑭ ᐃᐧᔨᐃᐣ » ᐁᑕᔭᑭ ?
— ᑭ ᓇᑐᑕᒍᐊᐧᓇᐤ ᑭᑕ ᑭᐣᑫᔨᒥᐟ ᑭᑕ ᓴᑭᐃᐟ
ᑭᑕ ᓇᓇᐃᑕᐟ, ᑭᑕ ᒪᓇᒋᐃᐟ ᒥᔨᐁᐧ.
6 « ᐱᑕᑐ ᐅᒋᒋᐸᔨᐠ ᑭ ᑎᐯᔨᒋᑫᐃᐣ » ᑕᑐᔨ
ᐊᑐ ᐁ ᐃᐧ ᐃᑌᐦ ᐁᐅᑯ ?
— ᐁᑯᔨ ᐁᑌᐧᔭᑭ ᑭ ᓇᑐᑕᒍᐊᐧᓇᐤ ᑭᔨ ᒪᑐᑐ
ᑭ ᑌᐃᓄᐊᐧᐦ ᑭᑕ ᐃᐧ ᐊᐣᑕᐟ ᐅ ᓴᑭᐃᑐᐃᐧᐣ,
ᐁᔨᑯᐠ ᒥᓇ ᑐᐱᔭᑭ ᑭᔨᑯᐠ ᑭᑕ ᐃᐧ ᐅᑎᑐᑯᔭᐠ.
7 ᑫᑲᐧ+ ᑲ ᓇᑐᑕᒪᐟ ᑭᓴ ᒪᑐᑐ « ᑲ ᐃᔨ ᓇᑐ
ᑕᑲᐃᐧᔭᐣ ᑭᔨᑯᐠ ᐱᑕᑐ ᐁᑯᔨ ᐃᔨ ᐊᐧᐣᑭᑕᐣ
ᑲᒥᐠ » ᐁᑌᐧᑭ ?
— ᐁᑯᔨ ᐃᔨ ᓇᑐᑕᒍᐊᐧᐤ ᑭᑕ ᐃᐧ ᑭᑎᒪᑭᓇᐊᐧᐟ

78 This is what religion expects.

2 How will one pray so that his prayer is good?

– From his heart. He will consider it carefully, how to pray. God hopes for it.

3 How is religion more than ever to be thought holy?

– Religion declares: "Our Father you are in Heaven." This is greater than to be thought of as holy.

4 Why is it that we call God our Father?

– Because He made us, especially everybody was given much by God, our Father. This is why we call Him Father.

5 What do we ask from God when we say: "I wish Your name to be holy."?

– We ask to be able to recognize Him, to love Him, to listen to Him, and to respect Him always.

6 "May Your name be honoured." How is that going to happen?

– When we say this, we ask it from God, to place mutual love there, in our hearts and also when we die, to take us into Heaven.

7 What do we ask God for when we say this: "Let us listen to You on earth as in Heaven."?

– We the people on earth are meant to listen well to

78

pakoseyimit, eoko oma ayimiawin ka itwek.
pakosêyimiht, êwako ôma ayamihâwin kâ-itwêk.

2 tanisi kita ki isi ayamiaw awiyak kita miwasiniyik
2 *tânisi kita kî-isi-ayamihâw awiyak kita-miywâsiniyik*

otayamiawin?
otayamihâwin?

– ispic oteit kita nanakataweyitam kesi ayamiat kise
– *ispic otêhit kita-nânâkatawêyihtam kêsi-ayamihât kisê-*

manitowa e pakoseyimat.
manitowa ê-pakosêyimât.

3 tana ayiwak ka kicitaweyitakwak ayamiawin?
3 *tâna ayiwâk kâ-kihcitwâwêyihtakwak ayamihâwin?*

– ayamiawin ka isi kicitik: « notawinan kici kisikok
– *ayamihâwin kâ-isi-kihcitik: "nôhtâwînân kihci-kîsikohk*

eyayan. » eoko oma ayiwak ka
(ê-)ayâyan." êwako ôma ayiwâk kâ-

ki citwaweyitakwak.
kîhcitwâwêyihtakwak.

4 taniki ani notawinan ko itayak kisemanito?
4 *tânêhki ani nôhtâwînân kô-itâyahk kisê-manitow?*

– e ki osiikoyak wawac kakiyaw e mamiyikoyak
– *ê-kî-osihikoyahk wâwâc kahkiyaw ê-mâmîyikoyahk*

notawinan ko itayak.
nôhtâwînân kô-itâyahk.

5 kekway netotamowayak kise manito: « pitane
5 *kîkway nêtotamowayahk kisê-manitow: "pitanê*

miweyicikatek ki wiyowin » etayaki?
miywêyihcikâtêk ki-wîhowin" êtayâki?

– ki natotamowanaw kita kiskeyimit kita sakiit kita
– *kinatôtamowânaw kita-kiskêyimiht kita-sâkihiht kita-*

nanaitat, kita manaciit misiwe.
nanahihtâht, kita-manâcihiht misiwê.

6 « pitane ocicipayik ki tipeyicikewin » tanisi ani e wi
6 *"pitanê ocihcipayik kitipêyihcikêwin" tânisi ani ê-wî-*

itwek eoko?
itwêk êwako?

– ekosi etweyaki ki natotamowanaw kisi manito
– *êkosi itwêyahki kinatotamawânaw kisê-manitow*

ki teinowak kita wi astat o sakiitowin, eyikok mina
kitêhinawak kita wî-astât osâkihitowin, iyikohk mîna

ni piyaki kisikok kita wi otinikoyak.
nipiyâhki kîsikohk kita wî-otinikoyahk.

7 kekway ka natotamat kise manito « ka isi
7 *kîkway kâ-natotamât kisê-manitow "kâ-isi-*

natotakawiyan kisikok pitane ekosi isi
natotakawiyan kîsikohk pitanê êkosi isi

waskitaskamik » etweki?
waskitaskamik" itwêki?

– ekosi isi natotamowaw kita wi kitimakinawat
– *êkosi isi-natotamawâw kita-wî-kitimâkinawât*

79 Him; His soul is pure in Heaven. This is how we will listen to Him.

8 What do I ask God for when I say this: "Give us our daily bread."?

– I ask Him, God, to give it to me every day to maintain myself in His name also in my spirit.

9 "The way in which You forgive their sins, those who did us evil, like this forgive us our sins, the evil that we did." What does this mean?

– When we say this we are praying to God to forgive us our sins when we do evil the way that You forgive those who did evil to us.

10 If someone is angry at his own people, will a bit of his sins be forgiven when he does evil?

– Someone who does not forgive his own people who do him evil, too, he will not be forgiven his sins. When he is angry at his own people, he is not pitied.

11 What do we ask for when we say this: "Look after us so that we do nothing evil."?

– We ask God to give us strong hearts to escape from evil thoughts,

79

kita wi miyat ayisiyiniwa ota askik kici nanaitakot,
kita-wî-miyât ayisiyiniwa ôta askîhk kici-nanahihtâkot,

okanatacakwewa kisikok kesi nanaitakot.
okanâtahcâhkwêwa kîsikohk kêsi nanahihtâkot.

8 kekway natotamowat kise manito: « anoc ka kisikak
8 kîkway natotamawât kisê-mantiow: "anohc kâ-kîsikâk

miyinan ni pakwesikaniminan » etweyani?
miyinân nipahkwêsikaniminân" itwêyâni?

– ni natotamowaw kise manito kita wi miyit tatwaw
– ninatotamawâw kisê-manitow kita-wî-miyit tahtwâw

kisikake kita opimacioyan isi owiyowiyan mina isi
kîsikâki kita-opimâcihoyân isi owihowiyan mîna isi

otacakoyan.
otahcâhkoyân.

9 « ka isi kasinamawakitwaw ka ki maci totakoyakwaw,
9 "ka-isi-kâsînamawakihtwâw kâ-kî maci-itôtakoyâhkwâw,

ekosi wi isi kasinamawinan ka ki maci totamak »
êkosi wî-isi-kâsînamawinân kâ-kî maci-itôtamahk"

tanisi e wi itwek eoko?
tânisi ê-wî-itwêk êwako?

– ekosi etweyaki ki mawimostawanaw kise manito kita
– êkosi itwêyahki kimawimôstawânaw kisê-manitow kita-

wi kasinamakoyak maci totamaki, kesi
wî-kâsînamakoyahk maci-itôtamahki, kêsi

kasinamawakitwaw ka ki maci totakoyakwaw.
kâsînamawakihtwâw kâ-kî maci-itôtahkoyahkwâw.

10 awiyak kisistawaci wici ayisiyiniwa maci totakoci
10 awiyak kisîstawâci wîci-ayisiyiniwa maci-itôtakoci

keyiwek ci kita kasinamakowisi maci totaki?
kêyiwêk kici kita kâsînamakowisiw maci-itôtahki?

– awiyak eka ka nitakasinamawat wici ayisiyiniwa
– awiyak êkâ ka-nihtâ-kâsînamawât wîci-ayisiyiniwa

mecitotakoci nista namawiya kita kasinamakowisiw;
maci-itôtâkoci nisto namâwiya kita-kâsînamâkowisiw;

eyikok ke kisistawat wici ayisiyiniwa namawiya
iyikohk kê-kisîsitawât wîci-ayisiyiniwa namâwiya

kitimakeyimikowisiw.
kitimâkêyimikowisiw.

11 kekway netotamak: « pisiskeyiminan kici eka maci
11 kîkway nêtotamâhk: "pisiskêyiminân kici êkâ maci-

mamitoneyitamak » etweyaki?
mâmitonêyihtamahk" itwêyahki?

– kita wi sokiteeskakoyak kise manito kici
– kita-wî-sôhkitêhêskâkoyahk kisê-manitow kici-

tapasitayak maci mitoneyicikana wetitikoyaki,
tapasîtayahk maci-mitonêyihcikana wêtitikoyahki,

80

ᒪᒋ ᐱᒪᑎᓯᐃᐤ ᑭᒋ ᓴᑯᒋᑕᔾ, ᑭᑎᓯ ᓇᑐ
ᐅᓇᓇᐤ.
12 ᕋᑲᐩ ᑌᑕᐁᐧᔨᑕᒪᐤ: « ᐃᐊᑲᐅᓇᓇᒪᐃᐧᓇᐤ ᑲ
ᒪᔨᑕᐧ » ᐁᐅᐧᔭᑌ ?
— ᑌ ᐸᑯᓴᔨᒪᐤ ᑭᓴ ᒪᓂᑐ ᑭᒋ ᑲᑭᕋ ᑲᓇ
ᐁᐧᔨᒥᐟ ᑭᒋ ᐁᑲ ᒪᒋ ᑐᑕᒪᐤ, ᑭᒋ ᐁᑲ
ᑲᐢᑭᐃᐟ ᒪᒋ ᒪᓂᑐ.

12 — ᑭᐢᑭᓄᐊᒪᕋᐃᐧᐣ.

1 ᐊᐃᐧᓇ ᐊᓇ ᑲ ᐊᔭᒥᐊᐟ: ᑮᑕᑕᒥᐢᑲᑎᐤ ᒪᕒ
ᐁᐅᐧᑭ ?
— ᑭᒋᑕᐤ ᒪᕒ, ᓇᐢᐱ- ᑲ ᑭ ᑲᓇᑕᑯᕋᐤ ᓴᒋᓴ
ᑲ ᑭ ᐅᑲᐃᐧᒥᑯ ᑲ ᐊᔭᒥᐃᐟ.
2 ᐊᐸᑕᐤ ᒋ ᑭᒋᑕᐤ ᒪᕒ ᐁ ᐊᔭᒥᐃᐟ ?
— ᐁᐦ ᐁᐦ ᐊᐸᑕᐤ ;ᐊᔨᐊᐤ ᐁ ᓇᓇᐃᑕᑯᓯᐟ, ᑭᓯᑯᐟ
ᕋᑲᐩ ᐸᑯᓴᐢᑕᒪᑯᔭᑭ.
3 ᑲ ᐃᐢᐱᑌᔨᒥᐟ ᑭᓴ ᒪᓂᑐ ᐁᑯᓯ ᐃᓯ ᐃᐧᐢᐱ
ᑌᔨᒪᐤ ᒋ ᑭᒋᑕᐤ ᒪᕒ ?
— ᓇᒪᐃᐧᔭ ᐁᑯᓯ ᐃᓯ ᐃᐢᐱᑌᔨᒪᐤ, ᐱᑯ ᐁ
ᐸᑯᓴᔨᒥᐟ ᑭᑕ ᐊᔭᒥᐁᐧᐢᑕᒪᕋ.
4 ᑭᐢᑫᔨᑕᐠ ᒋ ᑭᒋᑕᐤ ᒪᕒ, ᑭᐢᑫᔨᑕᒧᐤ ᒋ
ᒥᓇ ᐅᑲᓇᑕᐧᑫᐅᐧ ᑯᐃᐧᔪᐢᑕᑕᐃᐧ ?
— ᐁᐦ ᐁᐦ ᑭᐢᑫᔨᑕᒧᐤ ᒋᑫᒪ ᑭᓴ ᒪᓂᑐᐊᐧ ᐁ
ᑭᐢᑫᔨᑕᒧᐃᑯᒋᐟ.

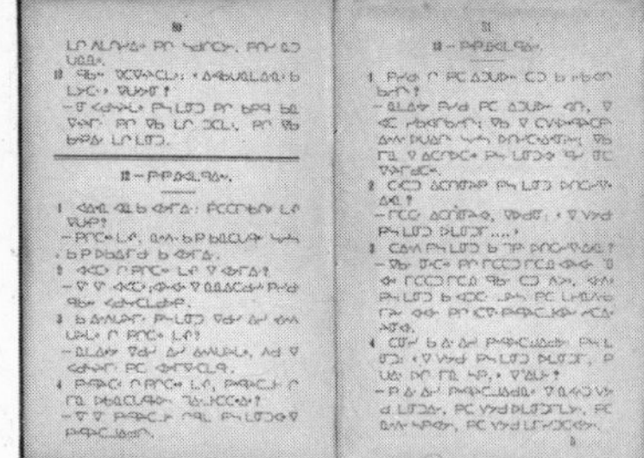

80 to not let evil life overpower us.

12 What do I want when I say this: "Remove evil from us."?

– I hope God will watch over me. For me not to do evil. For the devil not to be able to convince me.

---

12 – LESSON.

1 Who are you praying to when you say: "I greet you Mary."?

– Holy Mary forever, her soul is forever pure. Jesus, He has her as His mother.

2 Is it useful to pray to Holy Mary?

– Yes, it is useful. She is listened to more in Heaven when we are hoping for something.

3 When one thinks highly of God, is that how highly Holy Mary is also thought of?

– Nobody else is thought of highly like this. Only she is expected to pray for them.

4 Do the saints know Holy Mary when they pray to her?

– Yes, they know because God makes them aware of this.

maci pimatisiwin kici sakocitayak, kitisi natotenanaw.
maci-pimâtisiwin kici-sâkocitâyahk, kitisi-natotênânâw.

12 kekway netaweyitaman: « iyekatenamawinan ka
12 kîkway nitawêyihtamân: "iyîkatênâmawinân kâ-

mayatak » etweyani?
mayatahk" itwêyâni?

– ni pakoseyimaw kise manito kici kakike kanaweyimit
– nipakosêyimâw kisê-manitow kici kâkikê kanawêyimit

kici eka maci totaman, kici eka kaskiit maci manito.
kici êkâ maci-itôtamân, kici-êkâ kaskihit maci-manitow.

---

12 – KISKINOAMAKEWIN.
12 – KISKINOHAMÂKÊWIN.

1 awina ana ka ayamiit: kitatamiskatin mari etweki?
1 awîna ana kâ-ayamihiht: kitatamiskâtin Mari itwêki?

– kicitwaw mari, naspic ka ki kanatacakwet sesosa
– kihcitwâw Mari, nâspic kâ-kî-kanâtahcâhkwêt Sesosa

ka ki okawimikot ka ayamiit.
kâ-kî okawîmikot kâ-ayamihit.

2 apatan ci kicitwaw mari e ayamiit?
2 âpatan cî kihcitwâw Mari ê-ayamihit?

– ek ek apatan; ayiwak e nanaitakosit kisikok kekway
– êk êk âpatan; ayiwâk ê-nanahihtâkosit kîsikohk kîkway

pakosestamakoyaki.
pakosêstamâkoyâhki.

3 ka ispiteyimit kise manito ekosi isi ispiteyimaw
3 kâ-ispîhtêyimit kisê-manitow êkosi isi-ispîhtêyimâw

ci kicitwaw mari?
kihcitwâw Mari?

– namawiya ekosi isi ispiteyimaw, piko e pakoseyimit
– namâwiya êkosi isi-ispîhtêyimâw, piko ê-pakosêyimît

kita ayamiestamaket.
kita-ayamihêstamâkêt.

4 kiskeyitam ci kicitwaw mari, kiskeyitamwok ci mina
4 kiskêyihtam cî kihcitwâw Mari, kiskêyihtamwak cî mîna

okanatacakwewok mewimostatwawi?
okanâtahcâhkwêwak mêwimôstâtwâwi?

– ek ek kiskeyitamwok cikema kise manitowa
– êk êk kiskêyihtamwak cikêma kisê-manitowa

e kiskeyitamowikocik.
ê-kiskêyihtamohikocik.

81

13 — ᑭⁿᑭᓇᐊᒪᑫᐃᐧᐣ.

1 ᑭᓯᑯᐧ ᑎ ᑭᑕ ᐃᑐᑌᐅᐧᐦ ᑕᑐ ᑲ ᓯᑲᐊᑎ
ᑲᓯᑎᐠ ?
— ᓇᒪᐃᐧᔦ ᑭᓯᑯᐧ ᑭᑕ ᐃᑐᑌᐅᐧᐦ ᐊᑎᐠ, ᐁ
ᐊᑕ ᓯᑲᐊᑎᑲᓯᑎᐢ; ᐁᑲ ᐁ ᑕᐯᐧᐅᐧᑫᔦᑕᑭᐠ
ᐃⁿᐱ- ᐅᑌᐃᑎᐠ ᓴᓯᓴ ᐅᑎᓯᑕᐧᐃᐧᑎᔦᐤ; ᐁᑲ
ᒥᓇ ᐁ ᐃᑕᑎᐅᑕᐤ ᑭᓴ ᒪᑎᑐᐊᐧ ᑫᓯ ᑎᑕ
ᐁᐧᔦᒥᑯᑕᐧᐤ.
2 ᑕᐣᑕᑐ ᐃᑕᑎᑎᔦᑭ ᑭᓴ ᒪᑎᑐ ᐅᑎᑕᓯᐁᐧ
ᐃᐧᓇ ?
— ᒥᑕᑕᐠ ᐃᑕᑎᑎᔦᐊᐧ, ᐁᐅᑯᑎ: « ᐁ ᐯᔦᑯᐧ
ᑭᓴ ᒪᑎᑐ ᐅᒪᑎᑐᒥ.... »
3 ᑕᐃⁿᐱ ᑭᓴ ᒪᑎᑐ ᑲ ᒣᑭᐠ ᐅᑎᑕᓯᐁᐧᐃᐧᓇ ?
— ᐁᑲᐧ ᑎⁿᑕᐧᐤ ᑭᑎ ᒥᑕᑕᑐ ᒥᑕᓇ ᐊᔦᐊᐧᐦ ᑎ
ᐊᐧᐤ ᒥᑕᑕᑐ ᒥᑕᓇ ᑫᑲ- ᑕᑐ ᐱᔦᐣ, ᐊⁿᐱᐣ
ᑭᓴ ᒪᑎᑐ ᑲ ᐊᑐᑕᐠ ᒧᔦᓴ ᑭᑕ ᒪᓯᓇᐱⁿᑲ
ᒥᔦᐠ ᐊᐧᐊᐧ- ᑭᑎ ᐣᑕᐁᐧ ᑭⁿᑫᔦᑕᒧᐊᔦᐠ ᓯᑕᐃᐧ
ᔦᑎᐊᐧ.
4 ᑕᑎᓯ ᑲ ᐃᐧ ᐃᓯ ᑭⁿᑫᔦᑕᒧᐊᑯᔦᐠ ᑭᓴ ᒪ
ᑎᑐ: « ᐁ ᐯᔦᑯᐧ ᑭᓴ ᒪᑎᑐ ᐅᒪᑎᑐᒥ, ᑭ
ᑌᐃᐠ ᐅᑎ ᒥᓇ ᓴᑭ, » ᐁ ᐃᑌᐦ ?
— ᑭ ᐃᐧ ᐃᓯ ᑭⁿᑫᔦᑕᒧᐊᑯᓇᐤ ᐁ ᓇᓴⁿᑐ ᐯᔦ
ᑯ ᒪᑎᑐᐃᐦ, ᑭᑕ ᐯᔦᑯ ᐅᒪᑎᑐᒥᒪᔦᐠ, ᑭᑕ
ᓇⁿᐱ- ᓴᑭᐊᔦᐠ, ᑭᑕ ᐯᔦᑯ ᒪᒥᓯᑐᑕᐊᐧᔦᐠ.

5

81

13 – LESSON.

1 Will they go to Heaven, those that have been baptized?

– Some of them will not go to Heaven even though they are baptized because they do not believe in Jesus's commandments from their hearts; they also do not live this way, the way that He wants them to live.

2 How many of God's commandments are there?

– There are ten of them: "There is only one God, that we have as a God...."

3 When did God give His commandments?

– More than three thousand winters since God had asked Moses to write down His commandments and make the Jews aware of them.

4 How is He going to make them aware of God: "He is one God that we have as God to love from our heart."

– He is going to make us aware that we have one God to love us forever, to have faith in Him only.

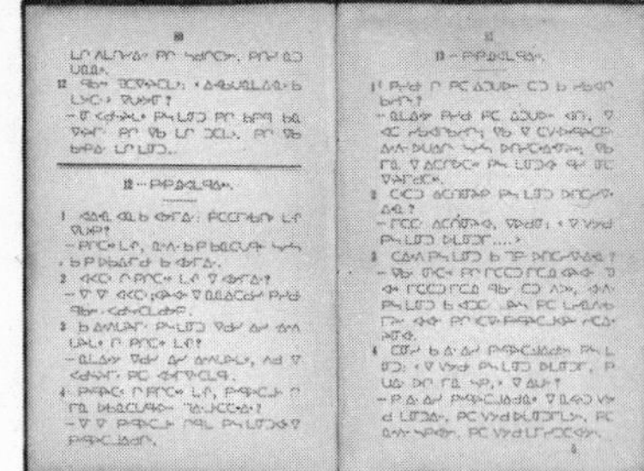

13 – KISKINOAMAKEWIN.
13 – KISKINOHAMÂKÊWIN.

1 kisikok ci kita itotewok tato ka sikaacikasocik?
1 kîsikohk cî kita-itohtêwak tahto kâ-sîkahâhcikâsocik?

– namawiya kisikok kita itotewok atit, e ata
– namâwiya kîsikohk kita-itohtêwak âtiht, ê-âta-

sikaacikasocik; eka e tapwewokeyitakik ispic
sîkahâhcikâsocik; êkâ ê-tâpwêwakêyihtahkik ispic

oteicik sesosa otisitwawiniyiw; eka mina
otêhicik Sesosa otisîhtwâwiniyiw; êkâ mîna

e itaciotwaw kise manitowa kesi nitaweyimikotwaw.
ê-itâcihotwâw kisê-manitowa kêsi-nitawêyimikotwâw.

2 tantato itatiniyiki kise manito otitasiwewina?
2 tânitahto itâtiniyiki kisê-manitow otitasiwêwin?

– mitatat itatiniyiwa, eokoni: « e peyakot kise manito
– mitâtaht itâtiniyiwa, êwakoni: "ê-pêyakôt kisê-manitow

omanitomi.... »
omanitômi...."

3 taispi kise manito ka mekit otitasiwewina?
3 tânispî kisê-manitow kâ-mêkit otitasiwêwina?

– ekwa nistwaw kici mitatato mitano ayiwak ne waw
– êkwa nîstwâw kihci-mitâtahtomitanaw ayiwâk nêwâw

mitatato mitano kekac tato pipon, aspin kise
mitâtahtomitanaw kêkâc tahto pipon, aspin kisê-

manito ka atotat moyisa kita masinapiskamiyit
manitow kâ-atotât Moyisa kita-masinâpiskamiyit

wawac kici ntawe kiskeyitamoayit sotawiyiniwa.
wâwâc kici-nitawi-kiskêyihtamohâyit Sotawiyiniwak.

4 taǹisi ka wi isi kiskeyitamoikoyak kise manito:
4 tânisi kâ-wî-isi-kiskêyihtamohikoyahk kisê-manitow:

« e peyakot kise manito omanitomi, ki teik oci mina
"ê-pêyakot kisê-manitow omanitômi, kitêhik ohci mîna

saki, » e itwet?
sâkih," ê-itwêt?

– ki wi isi kiskeyitamoikonaw e nayesto peyako
– ki-wî-isi-kiskêyihtamohikonaw ê-nayêsto-pêyako-

manitowit, kita peyako omanitomimayak, kita naspic
manitowit, kita-pêyako-omanitômimâyâhk, kita nâspic

sakiayak, kita peyako mami sitotawayak.
sâkihâyahk, kita-pêyako-mamisîtotawâyahk.

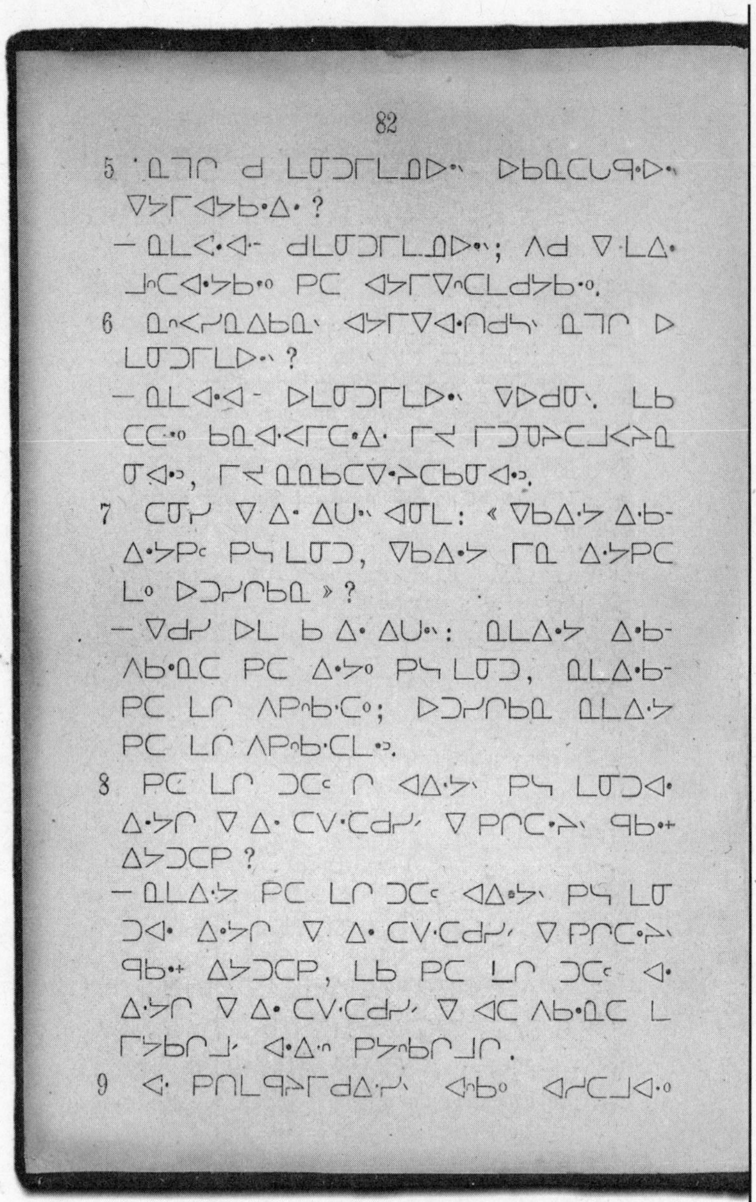

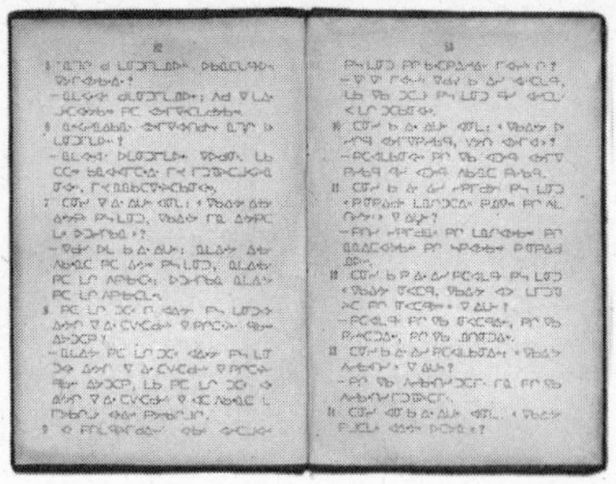

82

5 Do we speak to the saints when we pray?

– We should not think of them as God: we must pray to them to pray for us.

6 Can we think of God in images on a small cross?

– We believe in one God. But each time we look at these images we begin to imagine God.

7 What is being said by this: "Do not ever degrade God; do not also degrade His creations."?

– This is what is being said: Nobody for any reason should ever speak badly about God's creations.

8 Will somebody be believed as holy, if he does it?

– Nobody will do evil to God. No one will be believed as holy if he does evil. If he brags for no reason, especially if he tells false tales, he will not be believed.

9 Is it good to promise to have pity on people sometimes

82

5 nameci ko manitomimanowok okanatacakwewok
5 *namêcî kô-manitômimanowak okanâtahcâhkwêwak*

eyamiayakwawi?
ayamihayahkwâwi?

– namawawac ko manitomimanowok; piko
– *namawâwâc kô-manitômimanowak; piko*

e mawimostawayakwaw kita
ê-mawimostawayahkwâw kita-

ayamiestamakoyakwaw.
ayamihêstamâkoyahkwâw.

6 naspasiniikanak ayamiewatikosak nameci
6 *naspasinâhikanak ayamihêwahtikosâhk namêcî*

omanitomimawok?
omanitômimâwak?

– namawawac omanitomimawok eokonik. maka
– *namawâwâc omanitômimawak êwakonik. mâka*

tatwaw kanawapamitwawi miyo
tâhtwâw kânawâpamitwâwi miyo-

mitoneyitamopayinaniwan, miyo
mitonêyihtamopayinâniwan, miyo-

nanakataweyitakaniwan.
nânâkatawêyihtakâniwan.

7 tanisi e wi itwek anima: « ekawiya wikac wiyakim
7 *tânisi ê-wî-itwêk anima: "êkâwiya wîhkâc wiyakim*

kise manito, ekawiya mina wiyakitamaw
kisê-manitow, êkâwiya mîna wiyakihtamâw

otosicikana »?
otosîhcikana"?

– ekosi oma ka wi itwek: namawiya wikac pikwanata
– *êkosi ôma kâ-wî-itwêk: namâwiya wîhkâc pikwânata*

kita wiyaw kise manito, namawikac kita maci
kita-wiyâw kisê-manitow, namâwîhkâc kita-maci-

pikiskwataw; otosicikana namawiya kita maci
pîkiswâtâw; otosîhcikana namâwiya kita-maci-

pikiskwatamwan.
pîkiswâtamwân.

8 kita maci totam ci awiyak kise manitowa wiyaci e wi
8 *kita-maci-itôtam cî awiyak kisê-manitowa wiyacî ê-wî-*

tapwetakosit e kicitwayik kekway iyatotaki?
tâpwêtâkosit ê-kihcitwâyik kîkway iyatôtâki?

– namawiya kita maci totam awiyak kise manitowa
– *namâwiya kita-maci-itôtam awiyak kisê-manitowa*

wiyaci e wi tapwetakosit e kicitwayik kekway iyatotaki,
wiyacî ê-wî-tâpwêtâkosit ê-kihcitwâyik kîkway itotâhki,

maka kita maci totam wawiyaci e wi tapwetakosit e
mâka kita-maci-itôtam wâwiyaci ê-wî-tâpwêtâkosit ê-

ota pikwanata mamiyakacimot wawis kiyaskaci moci.
ôta-pikwanata mâmiyakacimot wâwîs kiyâskacimoci.

9 wa kitimakeyimikowisik askaw asotamowaw
9 *wâ kitimâkêyimikowisik askâw asotamawâw*

83

ᑭᓭ ᒪᓂᑐ ᑭᑎ ᑿᑕᑭᐃᓯᐃᐦ ᒥᐋᓯᐣ ᑎ ?
— ᐁᐠ ᐁᐠ ᒥᐋᓯᐣ ᐁᑯᓯ ᑲ ᐃᓯ ᐊᓯᑕᒪᑫᐟ,
ᒪᑲ ᐁᑲ ᑐᑕᒧᐟ ᑭᓭ ᒪᓂᑐ ᑫᓯ ᐊᓯᑕᒪᐟ
ᐸ ᒪᑎ ᑐᑕᑲᓂᐋᐧᐤ.
10 ᑕᓂᓯ ᑲ ᐃᐧ ᐃᑌᐦ ᐊᓂᒪ : « ᐁᑲᐃᐧᔭ ᐅ
ᓯᑎᑫ ᐊᔭᒥᐁᑭᓯᑲᑫ, ᐯᔭᑎᐠ ᐊᔭᒥᐊ » ?
— ᑭᑕᐊᒪᑲᓂᐋᐧᐤ ᑭᑎ ᐁᑲ ᐊᑐᐣᑫᐠ ᐊᔭᒥᐁ
ᑭᓯᑲᑫ ᑫᓯ ᐊᑐᐣᑫᐠ ᐱᑳᓈᑕ ᑭᓯᑲᑫ.
11 ᑕᓂᓯ ᑲ ᐃᐧ ᐃᓯ ᓯᑭᒥᑯᔭᐠ ᑭᓭ ᒪᓂᑐ
« ᑭᓂᑭᐃᑯᐦ ᒪᓇᑎᑐᑕᐃᐦ ᑭᓄᐁᐦ ᑭᑎ ᐱᒪ
ᑎᓯᔪ » ᐁ ᐃᑌᐦ ?
— ᑭᑎᓯ ᓯᑭᒥᑯᓇᐤ ᑭᑎ ᒪᓇᑎᐊᔭᑲᐤ ᑭᑎ
ᓇᓇᐃᑕᐋᐧᔭᑲᐤ ᑭᑎ ᓴᑭᐊᔭᑲᐤ ᑭᓂᑭᐃᑯ
ᓄᐅᐦ.
12 ᑕᓂᓯ ᑲ ᑭ ᐃᐧ ᐃᓯ ᑭᑕᐊᒪᑫᐟ ᑭᓭ ᒪᓂᑐ
« ᐁᑲᐃᐧᔭ ᓂᐸᑕᑫ, ᐁᑲᐃᐧᔭ ᐊᐳ ᒪᒥᑐᓂ
ᔦᑕ ᑭᑎ ᓂᐸᑕᑫᔭᐣ » ᐁ ᐃᑌᐦ ?
— ᑭᑕᐊᒪᑫᐤ ᑭᑎ ᐁᑲ ᓂᐸᑕᑫᐃᐦ, ᑭᑎ ᐁᑲ
ᑭᓯᐣᑕᑐᐃᐦ, ᑭᑎ ᐁᑲ ᓄᑎᓂᑐᐃᐦ.
13 ᑕᓂᓯ ᑲ ᐃᐧ ᐃᓯ ᑭᑕᐊᒪᑲᓂᐃᐦ: « ᐁᑲᐃᐧᔭ
ᐱᓯᑳᐧᑎᓯ » ᐁ ᐃᑌᐦ ?
— ᑭᑎ ᐁᑲ ᐱᓯᑳᐧᑎᓯ ᑐᑕᒥᐠ ᒥᓇ ᑭᑎ ᐁᑲ
ᐱᓯᑳᐧᑎᓯ ᒥᑐᓂᔦᑕᒥᐠ.
14 ᑕᓂᓯ ᐊᓂ ᑲ ᐃᐧ ᐃᑌᐦ ᐊᓂᒪ: « ᐁᑲᐃᐧᔭ
ᑭᒧᑕᒪᐤ ᐊᐃᐧᔭᐠ ᐅᑕᔭᓇ » ?

83 in the way that God has suffered?

– Yes, it is good to promise that way but it is not done the way that God promises it.

10 What is meant when it is said: "Do not make anything on Sunday, and pray carefully."?

– It is forbidden to work on Sunday the way that you work on any other day.

11 How is it that God is going to guide us? God says: "If you respect your parents, you will have a long life."

– He orders us to respect our parents, to listen to them obediently, and to love them.

12 How does God discipline us? He says: "Do not kill, do not even think about how to kill."

– He warns us not to kill for Him. Do not be angry with each other; do not fight.

13 How does one discipline oneself when this is said: "Do not commit adultery."?

– It means not to commit adultery and also not even to think about committing adultery.

14 How is it that this is going to be said: "Do not steal anyone's belongings."?

83 kise manito kici kwatakiisowit miwasin ci?
kisê-manitow kici-kwâtakihisowit miywâsin cî?

– ek ek miwasin ekosi ka isi asotamakek, maka eka
– *êk êk miywâsin êkosi ka-isi-asotamâkêk, mâka êkâ*

totamot kise manito kesi asotamat pa maci
itôtamôt kisê-manitow kêsi-asotamât pa-maci-

totakaniwan.
itôtakâniwan.

10 tanisi ka wi itwek anima: « ekawiya osicike
10 *tânisi ka wî-itwêk anima: "êkâwiya osîhcikê*

ayamiekisikake, peyatik ayamia »?
ayamihewi-kîsikâki pêyâhtik ayamihâ"?

– kita amakaniwan kici eka atoskek ayamiekisikake
– *kita-amâkâniwan kici êkâ atoskêhk ayamihewi-kîsikâki*

kesi atoskek pikwanata kisikake.
kêsi atoskêhk pikwânata kîsikâki.

11 tanisi ka wi isi sikimikoyak kise manito
11 *tânisi ka-wî-isi-sîkimikoyahk kisê-manitow*

« kinikiikwok manacitotawik kinowes kici
"kinîkihikwak manâcihtôtawik kinowês kici-

pimatisiyan » e itwet?
pimâtisiyan" ê-itwêt?

– kitisi sikimikonaw kici manaciayakwaw kici
– *kitisi sihkimikonâw kici-manâcihayahkwâw kici-*

nanaitawayakwaw kici sakiayakwaw
nanahihtawayahkwâw kici-sâkihayahkwâw

kinikiikonowok.
kinîkihikonawak.

12 tanisi ka ki wi isi kitaamaket kise manito « ekawiya
12 *tânisi ka-kî-wî-isi-kitahamâkêt kisê-manito "êkâwiya*

nipatake, ekawiya apo mamitoneyita kici
nipahtakê, êkâwiya ahpô mâmitonêyihta kici-

nipatakeyan » e itwet?
nipâtâkêyan" ê-itwêt?

– kitaamakew kici eka nipatakewit, kici eka
– *kitahamâkêw kici êkâ nipahtâkêwiht, kici êkâ*

kisistatowit, kici eka notinitowit.
kisîstâtowiht, kici êkâ notinitôwiht.

13 tanisi ka wi isi kitaamakaniwik: « ekawiya
13 *tânisi ka-wî-isi kitahamâkaniwik: "êkâwiya*

pisikwatisi » e itwek?
pisikwâtisi" ê-itwêk?

– kici eka pisikwatisitotamik mina kici eka
– *kici êkâ pisikwâtisitôtamihk mîna kici êkâ*

pisikwatisimitoneyitamik.
pisikwâtisimitonêyihtamihk.

14 tanisi ani ka wi itwek anima: « ekawiya kimotamaw
14 *tânisi ani kâ wî-itwêk anima: "êkâwiya kimotamâw*

awiyak otayana »?
awiyak otayâna"?

84

— ᑎᒪᐃᐧᔦ ᑭᑕ ᑭᒧᑎᑎᑎᐊᐧᐤ, ᑎᒪᐃᐧᔦ ᑭᑕ
ᑎᓯᑳᒪᑳᑎᐊᐧᐤ ᑭᒋ ᑭᒧᑎᐠ; ᑎᒪᐃᐧᔦ ᑭᑕ
ᑳᑎᐁᐧᔨᑕᑳᑎᐊᐧᐤ ᑫᑳᐦ ᑳ ᑭ ᑭᒧᑎᐠ; ᐊᐧᐊᐧ-
ᑎᒪᐃᐧᔦ ᑭᑕ ᑳᑎᐁᐧᔨᑕᑳᑎᐊᐧᐤ ᐁ ᑭ ᒥᐢᑳᒥᐠ.
15 ᑕᑎᓯ ᑭᑕ ᑐᑕᑳᑎᐊᐧᐤ ᐁ ᑭ ᒥᐢᑳᒥᑭ ?
— ᑭᑕ ᑳᑫᐧᒋᑫᒧᑎᑎᐊᐧᐤ ᐊᐃᐧᑎ ᐁᐧᑕᔦᑎᑫᐧ;
ᑎᒪᐃᐧᔦ ᐁᑯᓯ ᐃᓯ ᓱᐢᑳ ᑭᑕ ᐃᐧ ᐅᑕᔦᑎᐊᐧᐤ.
16 ᑕᑎᓯ ᑳ ᐃᐧ ᐃᓯ ᑭᑕᐊᒪᑯᔦᐠ ᑭᓭ ᒪᑎᑐ
« ᐁᑳᐃᐧᔦ ᑭᔦᐢᑭ » ᐁ ᐃᑌᐧ ?
— ᑭᑎᓯ ᑭᑕᐊᒪᑯᑎᐤ ᐁᑳ ᑭᑕ ᑭᔦᐢᑭᔦᐠ
ᒥᑎ ᑭᒋ ᐁᑳ ᒪᒋ ᐊᐦᒉᐧᔦᐠ.
17 ᑕᑎᓯ ᑳ ᐃᐧ ᐃᑌᐦ ᐊᑎᒪ: « ᐯᔦᑯᐃᑐᐠ ᐃᐧᓴ
ᑭᑐᓴᐠ » ?
— ᐁᑯᓯ ᐅᒪ ᑳ ᐃᐧ ᐃᑌᐦ: ᑕᑐ ᑳ ᐃᐧᑭᑐᑕᐤ
ᑭᑕ ᐯᔦᑯᐃᑐᐅᐦ; ᑎᒪᐃᐧᔦ ᐯᑐᐢ ᐊᐃᐧᔦ
ᑭᑕ ᐃᐧ ᒧᓯᑕᐃᐧᑎᐁᐧᐅᐦ.
18 « ᐁᑳᐃᐧᔦ ᑳᑳᓭᓯᑎᐃᑫ » ᑕᑎᓯ ᑳ ᐃᐧ
ᐃᑌᐦ ᐁᐅᑯ ?
— ᑎᒪᐃᐧᔦ ᑭᑕ ᑳᑳᓭᓯᐃᑐᑎᑎᐤ ᑫᑳᐦ ᐁᑐ
ᑕᑭ, ᒥᓭᐢᑯᑐᑎᒪᑐᑭ, ᐁᓯᑕᒪᑐᑭ.
19 ᐊᐁᐧᑎᑭ ᑳ ᑎᑕ ᑳᑳᓭᓯᑎᐃᑫᒋᐠ ?
— ᑎᑕ ᑳᑳᓭᓯᑎᐃᑫᐅᐦ ᑳ ᐅᓭᒥ ᓴᓴᑭᓯᒋ.

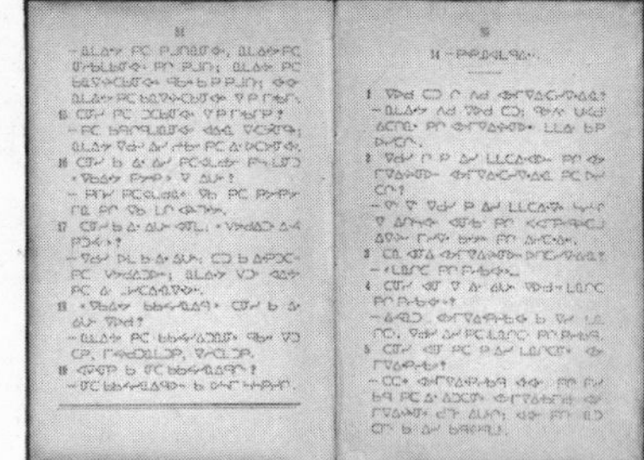

84 – There will be no stealing. There will be no helping each other to steal; there will be no keeping of something that has been stolen: especially it will not be kept if it has been found.

15 What will we do to something that has been found?

– It will be asked who it belongs to; one cannot just go ahead and claim it.

16 How is it that God counsels us when He says: "Do not lie."?

– He warns us not to lie, also not to speak badly about anyone.

17 What does it mean to say: "Remain unified when you are married."?

– This is how it is going to be said: Those who are married, they will be unified; they should not be with anyone different or have feelings for someone else.

18 "Do not be a hypocrite." What does this mean?

– No one should be deceitful when he is doing something, when trading with one another, when promising one another.

19 Who is it that is good at being deceitful?

– Those that are greedy are good at being deceitful.

84

- namawiya kita kimotinaniwan, namawiya kita
- *namâwiya kita-kimotinâniwan, namâwiya kita-*

nisokamakaniwan kici kimotik; namawiya kita
nîsôhkamâkâniwân kici-kimotik; namâwiya kita-

kanaweyitakaniwan kekway ka ki kimotik; wawac
kanawêyihtakâniwan kîkway kâ-kî-kimotik; wâwâc

namawiya kita kanaweyitakaniwan e ki miskamik.
namâwiya kita-kanawêyihtakâniwan ê-kî-miskamihk.

15 tanisi kita totakaniwan e ki miskamiki?
15 *tânisi kita-itôtakâniwân ê-kî-miskamihki?*

- kita kakwecikemonaniwan awina wetayanikwe;
- *kita-kâkwêcîkêmonâniwan awîna wêtayanikwê;*

namawiya ekosi isi soskwac kita wi otayaniwan.
namâwiya êkosi isi soskwâc kita-wî-otayâniwan.

16 tanisi ka wi isi kitaamakoyak kise manito « ekawiya
16 *tânisi ka-wî-isi kitahamâkoyahk kisê-manitow "êkâwiya*

kiyaski » e itwet?
kiyâski" ê-itwêt?

- kitisi kitaamakonaw eka kita kiyaskiyak mina kici
- *kitisi-kitahamâkonâw êkâ kita-kîyâskiyahk mîna kici*

eka maci ayimweyak.
êkâ maci-âyimwêyahk.

17 tanisi ka wi itwek anima: « peyakoitok wiyekitoyek »?
17 *tânisi kâ-wî-itwêk anima: "pêyakohitok wîyêkitoyêk"?*

- ekosi oma ka wi itwek: tato ka wikitotwaw kita
- *êkosi ôma kâ-wî-itwêk: tahto kâ-wî-kîtotwâw kita-*

peyakoitowok; namawiya petos awiya kita wi
pêyakohitowak; namâwiya pîtos awiya kita-wî-

mositawinawewok.
mositawinawêwak.

18 « ekawiya kakayesinaike » tanisi ka wi itwek eoko?
18 *"êkâwiya kakayêsinahikê" tânisi kâ-wî-itwêk êwako?*

- namawiya kita kakayesiitonaniw kekway eto taki,
- *namâwiya kita-kakayêsihitonâniw kîkway itôtâki,*

miyeskotonamatoki, esotamatoki.
miyêskotônâmâtohki, asotamâtohki.

19 aweniki ka nita kakayesinaikecik?
19 *awîniki kâ-nihtâ-kakayêsinahikocik?*

- nita kakayesinaikewok ka osami sasakisicik.
- *nihtâ-kakayêsinahikêwak kâ-osâmi-sasâkisîcik.*

85

14 — ᑭᐣᑭᓄᐊᒪᑫᐃᐧᐡ.

---

1 ᐁᐅᑯ ᑕᑐ ᒋ ᐱᑯ ᐊᔭᒥᐁᐃᐧᑕᓯᐁᐧᐃᐧᓇ?
— ᓇᒪᐃᐧᔦ ᐱᑯ ᐁᐅᑯ ᑕᑐ; ᑫᔦᐱ- ᑌᐸᑯ'
ᐃᑕᑎᓇᐧ ᑭᒋ ᐊᔭᒥᐁᐃᐧᔩᑎᐅᐧᐟ ᒪᒪᐃᐧ ᑲᑭ
ᐅᓯᑕᒋᐠ.
2 ᐁᑯᓯ ᒋ ᑭ ᐃᓯ ᒪᒪᑕᐃᐧᐊᐅᐦ ᑭᒋ ᐊᔭ
ᒥᐁᐃᐧᔩᑎᐅᐦ ᐊᔭᒥᐁᐃᐧᑕᓯᐁᐧᐃᐧᓇ ᑭᑕ ᐅᓯ
ᑕᒋᐠ?
— ᐁᐠ ᐁᐠ ᐁᑯᓯ ᑭ ᐃᓯ ᒪᒪᑕᐃᐧᐁᐤ ᓴᓵᔑ
ᐁ ᐃᑎᓴᐊᐧᐤ ᐊᑎᐢᑲ- ᑭᒋ ᐸᐸᒥᑭᐢᑫᔩᑕᒧ
ᐃᐁᐧᔩᐤ ᒥᓯᐁᐧ ᑲᐧᔦᐦ ᑭᒋ ᐃᓯᑕᐧᐃᐧᐤ.
3 ᑕᓇ ᐊᑎᐃ ᐊᔭᒥᐁᐃᐧᔩᑎᐅᐦ ᐅᑎᑕᓯᐁᐧᐃᐧᓇ?
— «ᒪᓇᒋᑕ ᑭᒋ ᑭᓯᑲᐊᐧ»....
4 ᑕᑎᓯ ᐊᑎ ᐁ ᐃᐧ ᐃᑌᐦ ᐁᐅᑯ «ᒪᓇᒋᑕ
ᑭᒋ ᑭᓯᑲᐊᐧ»?
— ᐃᓵᓇᑐ ᐊᔭᒥᐁᐃᐧᑭᓯᑲᐊᐧ ᑲ ᐁᓯ ᒪᓇ
ᒋᑖᐠ, ᐁᑯᓯ ᐃᓯ ᑭᑕ ᒪᓇᒋᑖᐠ ᑭᒋ ᑭᓯᑲᑫ.
5 ᑕᑎᓯ ᐊᑎ ᑭᑕ ᑭ ᐃᓯ ᒪᓇᒋᑕᑎᐤ ᐊᔭ
ᒥᐁᐃᐧᑭᓯᑲᐤ?
— ᑕᑖᐧᐤ ᐊᔭᒥᐁᐃᐧᑭᓯᑲᑫ ᐋᐊᐧ- ᑭᒋ ᑭᓯ
ᑲᑫ ᑭᑕ ᐃᐧ ᐃᑐᑕᑎᐤ ᐊᔭᒥᐁᐃᐧᑲᒥᑯᐠ ᐊᔭ
ᒥᐁᐃᐧᔩᑎᐤ ᒐᒣᐦ ᐃᑌᐧᒋ; ᐊᐋᐧ- ᑮᒋ ᓇᑐ
ᑕᒥᐠ ᑲ ᐃᓯ ᑲᑫᑮᐅᑫᒧᐣ.

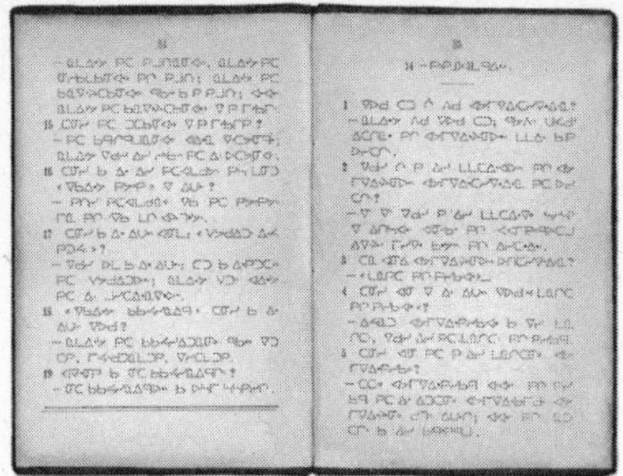

85

14 – LESSON.

---

1 Are there only this many religious commandments?
– There is not only that many; there are still seven more for the ordained priest to proclaim.
2 So were the noble priests given powers to proclaim them?
– Yes, in that way Jesus Christ had given them power. He sent them successively to go around to make it known all over to follow these ceremonies.
3 Which one of those priests' commands?
– "Respect the holy days."....
4 How is that going to be done "Respect the holy days."?
– Naturally, the prayer days [Sundays] are to be respected; in this way Sunday will be respected.
5 How is it that everyone can respect Sunday?
– Every Sunday, as a holy day, everybody should go to church. When the priest says the Mass, he asks to make the day holy.

85

14 – KISKINOAMAKEWIN.
14 – KISKINOHAMÂKÊWIN.

---

1 eoko tato ci piko ayamiewitasiwewina?
1 êwako tahto cî piko ayamihêwitasiwêwina?

– namawiya piko eoko tato; keyapic tepakop itatinwa
– *namâwiya piko êwako tahto; kêyâpic têpakohp itâtinwa*

kici ayamiewiyiniwot mamawi ka ki ositacik.
kihci-ayamihêwiyiniwot mâmâwi kâ-kî-osîhtâcik.

2 ekosi ci ki isi mamatawiawok kici ayamiewiyiniwok
2 êkosi cî kî-isi-mamâhtâwihâwak kihci-ayamihêwiyiniwak

ayamiewitasiwewina kita ositacik?
ayamihêwitasiwêwina kita-osîhtâcik?

– ek ek ekosi ki isi mamatawiew sesokri e itisawat
– *êk êk êkosi kî-isi-mamâhtâwihêw Sesokri ê-itisahwât*

aniskac kici papamikiskeyitamoiweyit misiwe
aniskâc kita-papami-kiskêyihtamohiwêyit misiwê

kwayask kici isitwawit.
kwayask kihci-isîhtwâwiht.

3 tana anii ayamiewiyiniwok otitasiwewina?
3 tâna anihi ayamihêwiyiniwak otitasiwêwina?

– « manacita kici kisikawa ».....
– *"manâcihtâ kihci-kîsikâwa".....*

4 tanisi ani e wi itwek eokwo « manacita kici kisikawa »?
4 tânisi ani ê-wî-itwêk êwako "manâcihtâ kihci-kîsikâwa"?

– iyenato ayamiewikisikawa ka esi manacitak, ekosi
– *iyênato ayamihewi-kîsikâwa ka-êsi-manâcihtâhk, êkosi*

isi kita manacitak kici kisikake.
isi-kita-manâcihtahk kihci-kîsikâki.

5 tanisi ani kita ki isi manacitaniw ayamiewikisikaw?
5 tânisi ani kita-kî-isi-manâcihtâniw ayamihêwi-kîsikâw?

– tatwaw ayamiewikisikake wawac kici kisikake kita
– *tahtwâw ayamihêwi-kîsikâki wâwâc kihci-kîsikâki kita-*

wi itotaniw ayamiewikamikot ayamiewiyiniw
wî-itôhtâniw ayamihêwikamik otayamihêwiyiniw

lames itweci; awac kici natotamik ka isi
Lames itwêci; wâwâc kici-natotamik ka-isi-

kakeskikemok.
kaskêskîkêmok.

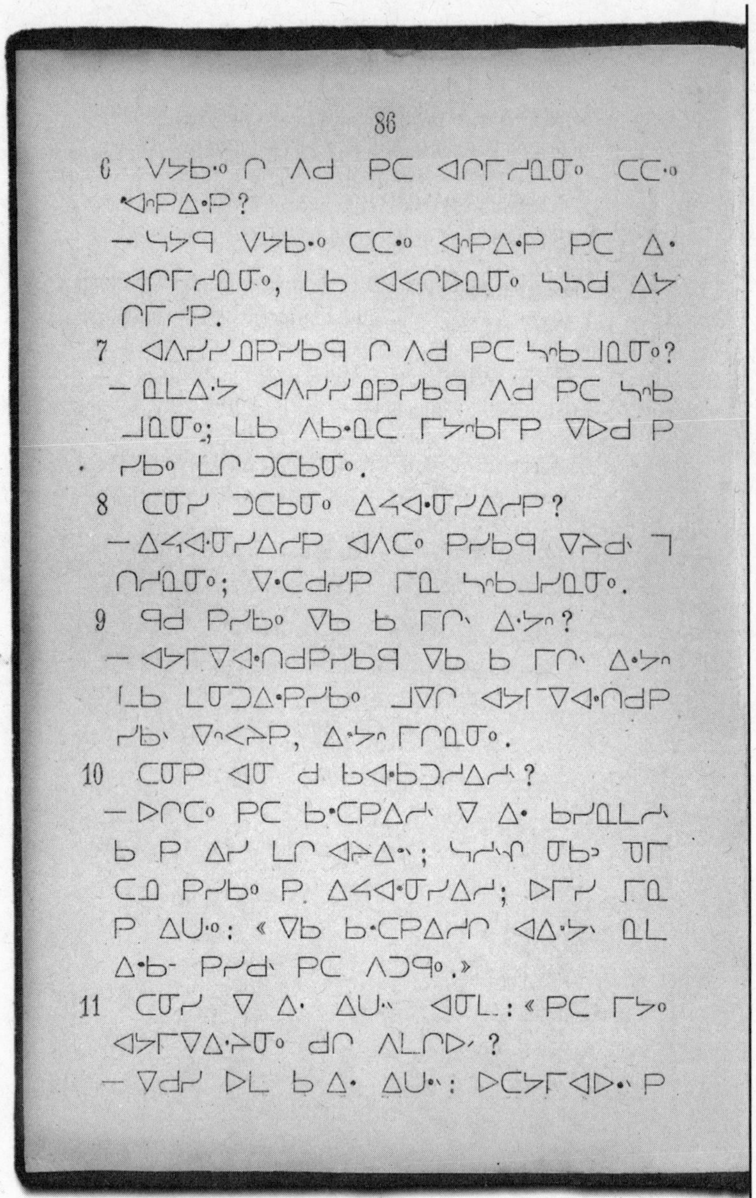

86

6 Is it only once that one will confess every year?

– At least once every year everyone should go to confession, but it is useful to confess more often.

7 When does one receive Communion?

– Not on Easter only is everyone to receive Communion but even on Good Friday, that day when one recalls evil deeds.

8 How should one fast?

– One should fast from noon until everyone eats in the evening and also before receiving Communion.

9 On which day does one not eat meat?

– On Good Friday one does not eat meat, but on Christmas, on that day, meat is eaten.

10 Why is it that one fasts?

– By all means one will deprive himself. He is going to be forgiven for bad behaviour. Jesus Christ made His fast for forty days. This way also He said: "Those who do not fast will never enter Heaven."

11 What does this mean: "he will support the living of the priest."?

– This is what it means: The worshippers

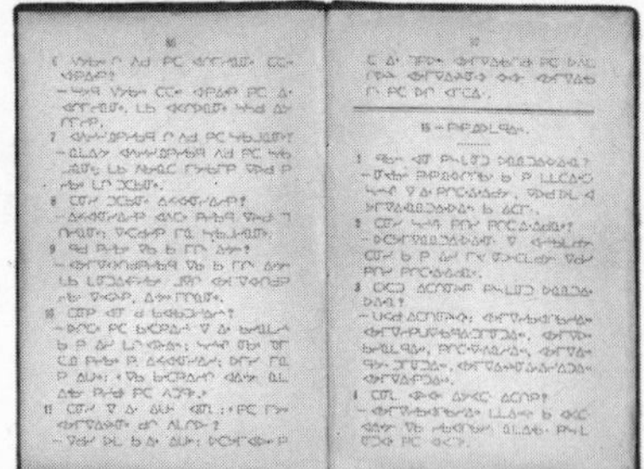

86

6 peyakwaw ci piko kita acimisonaniw tatwaw askiwiki?
6 pêyakwâw cî piko kita-âcimisonâniw tahtwâw askîwiki?

– seyake peyakwaw tatwaw askiwiki kita wi
– *sêyakê pêyakwâw tahtwâw askîwiki kita-wî-*

acimisonaniw, maka apacionaniw sasako iyacimisoki.
acimisonâniw, mâka âpacihonâniw sasakoh iyacimisôki.

7 apisisinokisikake ci piko kita saskamonaniw?
7 apisisino-kîsikâki cî piko kita-saskamonâniw?

– namawiya apisisinokisikake piko kita saskamonaiw;
– *namâwiya apisisino-kîsikâki piko kita-saskamonâniw;*

maka pikwanata miyaskamiki eoko kisikaw maci
mâka pikwanata miyoskamiki êwako kîsikâw maci-

totakaniw.
itôtahkaniw.

8 tanisi totakaniw iyewanisiisoki?
8 tânisi itôtahkaniw iyêwanisihisohki?

– iyewanisiisoki apitaw kisikake eyikok metisonaniw;
– *iyêwanisihisohki âpihtaw-kîsikâki iyikohk mîcisonâniw;*

wetakosiki mina saskamosinaniw.
wêtâkosîki mîna saskamosinâniw.

9 keko kisikaw eka ka micik wiyas?
9 kîko kîsikâw êkâ kâ-mîcihk wîyâs?

– ayamiewatikokisikake eka ka micik wiyas maka
– *ayamihewahtiko-kîsikâki êkâ kâ-mîcihk wîyâs mâka*

manitowikisikaw moeci ayamiewatikokisikak
manitowi-kîsikâw mwêhci ayamihêwahtiko-kîsikâk

espayiki, wiyas micinaniw.
ispayiki, wîyâs mîcinâniw.

10 taniki ani ko kawakatosoisok?
10 tânêhki ani kô-kawakatosohisok?

– ocitaw kita kwatakiisok e wi kasinamasok ka ki isi
– *ohcitâw kita-kwatakihisok ê-wî-kâsînamâsok kâ-kî-isi-*

maci ayiwik; sesokri nikan nemitano kisikaw ki
maci-ayiwik; Sesokri nîkân nêmitanaw kîsikâw kî-

iyewanisiiso; omisi mina ki itwew: « eka kwatakiisoci
iyêwanisihisow; omisi mîna kî-itwêw: "êkâ kwâtakihisoci

awiyak namawikac kisikok kita pitokew »
awiyak namâwîhkâc kîsikohk kita-pîhtokwêw"

11 tanisi e wi itwek anima: « kita miyaw ayamiewiyiniw
11 tânisi ê-wî-itwêk anima: "kita-miyâw ayamihêwiyiniw

koci pimaciot »?
koci-pimâcihot"?

– ekosi oma ka wi itwek: otayamiawok ki
– *êkosi ôma kâ-wî-itwêk: otayamihâwâk ki*

87

ᑕ ᐃᐧ ᒣᑭᐅᐧᐦ ᐊᔭᒥᐁᐃᐧᑲᒥᑯᐧ ᑭᑕ ᐅᐱᒪ
ᑎᐅᔾ ᐊᔭᒥᐁᐃᐧᔾᑐᐊᐧ ᐊᐧᐊᐧᐨ ᐊᔭᒥᐁᐃᐧᑲ
ᒥᐠ ᑭᑕ ᐅᑎ ᐸᒥᑕᐃᐧᐦ.

15 — ᑭᐢᑭᓄᐅᒪᑫᐃᐧᐤ.

1 ᑫᑲᐧ+ ᐊᑐ ᑭᓴᒪᑐᑐ ᐅᓇᓇᑐᐃᐧᐅᐃᐧᓇ ?
— ᑐᕙᑲᐧᐦ ᑭᐢᑭᓄᐊᐧᑎᑎᑲᐤ ᑲ ᑭ ᒪᒪᑕᐃᐧᑕᐟ
ᓴᔾᔅ ᐁ ᐃᐧ ᑭᑎᑕᐧᐃᐧᐃᑯᔭᐠ, ᐁᐅᑯ ᐅᒪ ᐊ
ᔭᒥᐁᐃᐧᓇᓇᑐᐃᐧᐅᐃᐧᐤ ᑲ ᐃᑕᒥᐠ.
2 ᑕᑐᔾ ᓴᔾᑫ ᑭᑎᔾ ᑭᑎᑕᐧᐃᐧᐃᑯᓇᐤ?
— ᐅᑕᔭᒥᐁᓇᓇᑐᐃᐧᐅᐃᐧᑐᐠ ᐁ ᐊᔾᐢᑲᒪᑯᔭᐠ
ᑕᑐᔾ ᑲ ᑭ ᐃᔾ ᒥᕙ ᑐᔭᐢᑕᒪᑯᔭᐠ ᐁᑯᔾ
ᑭᑎᔾ ᑭᑎᑕᐧᐃᐧᐃᑯᓇᐤ.
3 ᑕᑕᑐ ᐃᑕᑎᑐᔭᑭ ᑭᓴᒪᑐᑐ ᐅᓇᓇᑐᐃᐧ
ᐅᐃᐧᓇ ?
— ᐅᕙᑯ ᐃᑕᑎᑐᔭᐊᐧ: ᐊᔭᒥᐁᔾᑲᐊᑎᑲᔾᐃᐧᐤ
ᐊᔭᒥᐁᔾᑭᐅᐁᐢᑲᑫᐃᐧᑐᒥᑐᑐᐃᐧᐤ, ᐊᔭᒥᐁᐅᐧ
ᑲᔾᓇᒪᑫᐃᐧᐤ, ᑭᑎᑕᐧᐁᐧᐱᓇᔾᐃᐧᐤ, ᐊᔭᒥᐁᐃᐧᐣ
ᑫᐧᔭ- ᑐᒥᑐᑐᐃᐧᐤ, ᐊᔭᒥᐁᐃᐧᔾᑐᐃᐧᐃᐧᔾᐃᑐᐃᐧᐤ
ᐊᔭᒥᐁᐃᐧᑭᑐᐃᐧᐤ.
4 ᑕᑐᒪ ᐊᐃᐧᐊᐧᐦ ᐃᔭᐸᑕᐠ ᐃᑕᑎᑭ?
— ᐊᔭᒥᐁᔾᑲᐊᑎᑲᔾᐃᐧᐤ ᒪᒪᐃᐧᔪᐣ ᑲ ᐊᐸᑕᐠ
ᐊᐃᐧᔭᐠ ᐁᑲ ᔾᑲᐊᑎᑲᔾᐟ ᓇᒪᐃᐧᑲ- ᑭᓴ ᒪ
ᑐᑐᐊᐧ ᑭᑕ ᐊᐧᐸᒣᐤ.

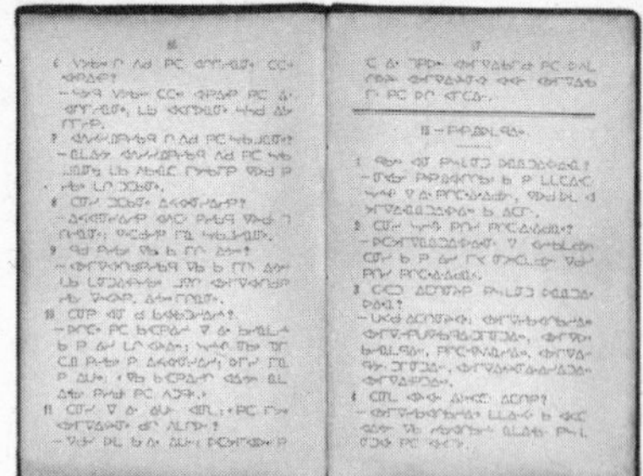

make an offering in church; the priest takes care of the church. He takes care of it.

15 – LESSON.

1 What are God's sacraments?
– A sacrament is a sign from glorious Jesus Christ to make us holy. This is what is called a sacrament.
2 How is Jesus Christ to make us holy?
– In His sacrament, He shows us how to have a good life; this is how to make us holy.
3 How many of God's sacraments are there?
– There are seven: Baptism, Confirmation, Confession, Holy Communion, the Act of Anointing the Sick, Holy Orders, and Marriage.
4 Which one is used more out of all of them?
– Baptism mostly is used. Those who are not baptized will never see God.

87 ta wi mekiwok ayamiewikamikok kita opimacioyit
ta-wî-mêkiwak ayamihêwikamikohk kita-opimâcihoyit

ayamiewiyiniwa wawac ayamiewikamik kita oci
ayamihêwiyiniwa wâwâc ayamihêwikamik kita-ohci-

pamitawit.
pamitawît.

---

15 – KISKINOOMAKEWIN.
15 – KISKINOHAMÂKÊWIN

---

1 kekway ani kise manito onanatowiowina?
1 kîkwây ani kisê-manitow onanâtawihowina?

– niyokwat kiskinowacicikan ka ki mamatawitat
– niyokwat kiskinowacîcikan kâ-kî-mamâhtawîtât

sesokri e wi kicitwawiikoyak, eoko oma
Sesokri ê-wî-kihcitwâwihikoyahk, êwako ôma

ayamiewinanatowiowin ka itamik.
ayamihêwinanâtawihowin kâ-itamik.

2 tanisi sesokri kitisi kicitwawiikonaw?
2 tânisi Sesokri kitisi kihcitwâwihikonaw?

– otayamienanatowiowinik e asoskamakoyak tanisi
– otayamihênanâtawihowinihk ê-asoskamâkoyahk tânisi

ka ki isi miyo nipostamakoyak ekosi kitisi
kâ-kî-isi- miyo-nipôstamâkoyahk êkosi kitisi

kicitwawiikonaw.
kihcitwâwihikonaw.

3 tantato itatiniyiki kise manito onanatowiowina?
3 tânitahto itâtiniyiki kisê-manitow onanâtawihowina?

– tepakop itatiniyiwa: ayamiesikaacikasowin
– têpakohp itâtiniyiwa: ayamihêsîkahacikâsowin

ayamiesokiteeskakewitominitowin,
ayamihêsôhkitêhêskakêwitominitowin,

ayamiewokasinamakewin, kicitwawepinasowin,
ayamihewikâsînamâkewin, kihcitwâwêpinâsowin,

ayamiewin kweyac tominitowin,
ayamihêwin kwêyac tominitowin,

ayamiewiyiniwiisoitowin ayamiewikitowin.
ayamihêwiyiniwihisihitowin ayamihêwîkitowin.

4 tanima ayiwak iyapatak itatiki?
4 tânima ayiwâk iyapatâhk itâtiki?

– ayamiesikaacikasowin mamawiyes ka apata awiyak
– ayamihêsîkahâhcikâsowin mamawiyês kâ âpata awiyak

eka sikaacikasot namawikac kise manitowa kita
êkâ sîkahâhcikâsot namâwîhkâc kisê-manitowa kita-

wapamew.
wâpamêw.

88

5 What happens when one is baptized?

– When one is baptized all sins are forgiven: sin that one is born with, along with sins we have done before we are baptized.

6 Why also is it useful to be baptized?

– It is useful to us so that we are God's children, that we go with Him, and obey His commands.

7 Who performs the baptism?

– Only priests. If the people are not near and if someone is going to pass on, their own people partly baptize them.

8 What happens to one when one is baptized?

– Water is poured on the forehead. Also this way is how everyone talks: "I baptize you in the name of God, the Father, the Son of God, and the Holy Spirit."

9 How many times will one be baptized?

– Only once.

10 Why is it only once that someone is baptized?

– He is going to forgive his sins once when he has been anointed by His spirit.

11 When the priest baptizes someone, why

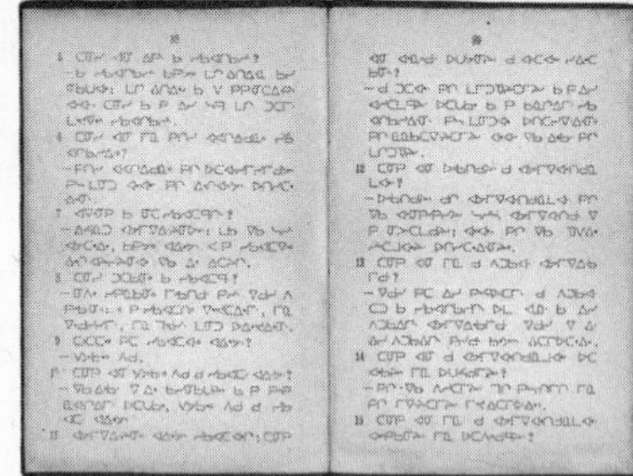

88

5 tanisi ani ikik ka sikaocikasok?
5 tânisi ani ihkik kâ-sîkahâhcikâsok?

– ka sikaacikasok kakiyaw maci itiwina kasinikatewa:
– kâ-sîkahâhcikâsok kahkiyaw macihtiwina kasînikâtêwa:

maci itiwin ka pe kikinitawikik wawac tanisi ka ki isi
macihtiwin kâ-pê-kikî-nihtawikik wâwâc tânisi kâ-kî-isi-

seke maci totamik mayowes sikaacikasok.
sêhkê-maci-itôtamik mayowes sîkahâhcikâsok.

6 tanisi ani mina kitisi apaciikonaw sikaacikasowin?
6 tânisi ani mîna kitisi âpacihikonaw sîkahâhcikâsowin?

– kitisi apaciikonaw kici otawasimisimikoyak kise
– kitisi âpacihikonaw kici-otawâsimisimikoyahk kisê-

manito wawac kici wiciwayak otisitwawinik.
manitow wâwâc kici-wîciwâyahk otisîhtwâwinihk.

7 aweniki ka nita sikaatakecik?
7 awîniki ka-nihtâ-sîkahâtakêcik?

– iyenato ayamiewiyiniwok: maka eka sesik ayatwawi,
– iyênato ayamihêwiyiniwak: mâka êkâ sêsik ayâtwâwi,

kakiyaw awiyak pa ki sikaatawew wici ayisiyiniwa
kahkiyaw awiyak pahki sîkahâhtawêw wîci ayisiyiniwa

eka wi itayici.
êkâ wî-itâyici.

8 tanisi totakaniw ka sikaatakek?
8 tânisi tôtakâniw kâ-sîkahâhtâkek?

– nipiy sikinakaniw miskatikok kisik ekosi
– nipiy sîkinakâniw miskâtikohk kisik êkosi

pikiskwaniw: « ki sikaatatin weyotawimik, mina
pîkiskwâniw: "ki-sîkahâtâtin wiyôhtâwîmihk, mîna

wekosisimit, mina meyosit manito owiyowinik. »
wêkosisimit, mîna (ê-)miyosit-manito owihowinihk."

9 tantatwaw kita sikaatawew awiyak?
9 tânitahtwâw kita-sîkahâhtâwêw awiyak?

– peyakwaw piko.
– peyakwâw piko.

10 taneki ani peyakwaw piko ko sikaatat awiyak?
10 tânêhki ani pêyakwâw piko kô-sîkahâtât awiyak?

– eka wikac e wi kasinikateyik ka ki kiskinowaciimit
– êkâ wîhkâc ê-wî-kâsînikâtêyik kâ-kî-kiskinowacihimiht

otacakwa, peyakwaw piko ko sikaatat awiyak.
otahcâhkwa, pêyakwâw piko kô-sîkahâhtât awiyak.

11 ayamiewiyiniw awiyak sikaatawaci; taniki
11 ayamihêwiyiniw awiyak sîkahâhtâwaci; tânêhki

89

ᐊᑌ ᐊᐧᑎᐢᑯ ᐅᑌᔭᑌᔭᐠ ᑯ ᐊᐢᑕᐊᐧᐟ ᓯᐃᐧᑕ ᑲᑌᐢ ?

— ᑯ ᑐᑕᐊᐧᐟ ᑭᑦ ᒫᒥᑐᑌᔭᑕᒥᔭ ᑲ ᑭ ᐃᓯ ᐊᓯᑕᒪᑫᔭᐠ ᐅᑕᒐᑲ· ᑲ ᑭ ᑲᑎᑭᐃᒥᐠ ᓯᑲ ᐊᑦᑲᓯᐃᐧᑌᐠ ᑭᓴ ᒪᑌᑐᐊᐧ ᐅᑎᑕᓯᐁᐧᐃᐧᑌᐤ ᑭᑦ ᑎᑎᑲᑕᐁᐧᔭᑕᒥᔭ ᐊᐧᐊᐧ- ᐁᑲ ᐃᐧᑲ- ᑭᑦ ᒪᑦᑐᑌᔭᐠ.

12 ᑕᑌᑭ ᐊᑌ ᐅᐢᑲᑎᑯᔭᐠ ᑯ ᐊᔭᒥᐁᐊᐧᑎᑯᑎ ᒪᐊᐧ ?

— ᐅᐢᑲᑎᑯᔭᐠ ᑯᑦ ᐊᔭᒥᐁᐊᐧᑎᑯᑎᒪᐊᐧ ᑭᑦ ᐁᑲ ᐊᐧᑌᑭᐢᑭᓯᔭᐠ ᓴᓯᓴ ᐊᔭᒥᐁᐊᐧᑎᑯᐠ ᐁ ᑭ ᑌᔭᐢᑕᒪᑯᔭᐠ; ᐊᐧᐊᐧ- ᑭᑦ ᐁᑲ ᑌᐯᐃᐧ ᓯᐢᑕᒪᐊᐧᔭᐠ ᐅᑎᓯᑕᐁᐧᑌᔭᐤ.

13 ᑕᑌᑭ ᐊᑌ ᒥᑎ ᑯ ᐱᑐᑲᐊᐧ ᐊᔭᒥᐁᐃᐧᑲ ᒥᑯᐠ ?

— ᐁᑯᓯ ᑭᑕ ᐃᓯ ᑭᐢᑫᔭᑕᒥᐠ ᑯ ᐱᑐᑲᐊᐧ ᑕᑐ ᑲ ᓯᑲᐊᑎᑲᓯᑎᐠ ᐅᒪ ᐊᑎ- ᑲ ᐃᓯ ᐱᑐᑲᐃᑎᐠ ᐊᔭᒥᐁᐃᐧᑲᒥᑯᐠ ᐁᑯᓯ ᐁ ᐃᐧ ᐃᓯ ᐱᑐᑲᐃᑎᐠ ᑭᓯᑯᐠ ᑲᐧᔭᐢ ᐃᑕᑎᐅᑕᐃᐧ.

14 ᑕᑌᑭ ᐊᑌ ᑯ ᐊᔭᒥᐁᐊᐧᑎᑯᑎᒧᐊᐧ ᐅᑕ ᐊᐧᑲᔭᐠ ᒥᑎ ᐅᑌᐢᑯᒥᔭᐠ ?

— ᑭᑦ ᐁᑲ ᐱᓯᑕᒥᔭ ᒉᑦ ᑭᓴᐠᑎᒥᑦ ᒥᑎ ᑭᑦ ᒥᐁᐧᔭᑕᒥᔭ ᒥᔪ ᐃᑕᑎᐅᐃᐤ.

15 ᑕᑌᑭ ᐊᑌ ᒥᑎ ᑯ ᐊᔭᒥᐁᐊᐧᑎᑯᑎᒪᐊᐧ ᐊᐧᐢᑭᑲᑌᔭᐠ ᒥᑎ ᐅᑕᐱᐢᑯᑫᔭᐠ ?

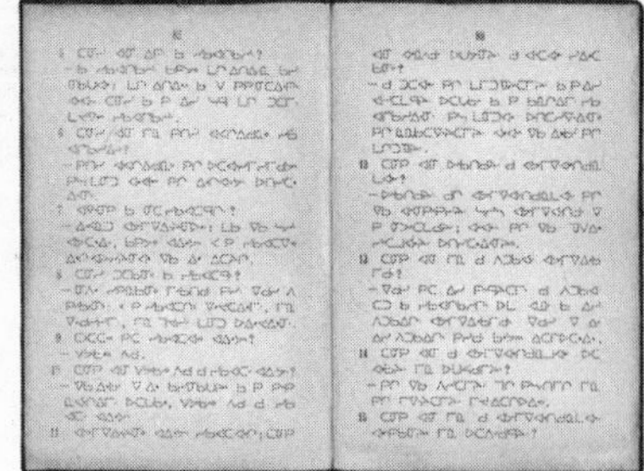

89 does he place some salt on the tip of his tongue?

– He does it for him to think about what he was promised; his spirit was cleaned by being baptized. He should honour God's commandments to look after them carefully.

12 Why is it that the priest makes the sign of the cross on his forehead?

– On his forehead he makes the sign of the cross for him not to forget about Jesus on the cross. He died for him, especially for him not to be ashamed of His sacrament.

13 Why is it also that he brings him into the church?

– He brings them to the church so that it will be known. Those who are baptized this day as they enter the church, they are going to enter Heaven, if they behave properly.

14 Why is it that he makes the sign of the cross in his ear and in his nostril?

– Not to overhear speaking about him with anger, and for him to lead a good life.

15 Why is it also that he makes the sign of the cross on his chest, and on his jaw?

89 ani wanaskoc oteyaniyik ko astawat siwitakanis?
ani wânaskoc otêyiniyik kô-astâwât sîwîtâkanis?

– ko totawat kici mamitoneyitamiyit ka ki isi
– *kô-itôtawât kici-mâmitonêyihtamiyit kâ-kî-isi-*

asotamakeyit otacakwa ka ki kanaciimit
asotamâkêyit otahcâhkwa kâ-kî-kanâcihimiht

sikaacikasowinik kise manitowa otitasiwewiniw
sîkahâhcikâsowinihk kisê-manitow otitasiwêwinîw

kici nanakataweyitamiyit wawac eka wikac kici
kici-nânâkatawêyihtamiyit wâwâc êkâ wîhkâc kici-

macitoneyit.
macitônêyit.

12 taniki ani oskatikoyik ko ayamiewatikonamawat?
12 *tânêhki ani oskâtikoyik kô-ayamihêwahtikonamawât?*

– oskatikoyik koci ayamiewatikonamawat kici eka
– *oskâtikoyik koci-ayamihêwahtikonamawât kici êkâ*

wanikiskisiyit sesosa ayamiewatikok e ki
wanikiskisiyit Sesosa ayamihêwahtikohk ê-kî-

nipostamakoyit; wawac kici eka nepewisistamowayit
nipôstamâkoyit; wâwâc kici êkâ nêpêwisîstamôwâyit

otisitwawiniyiw.
otisîhtwâwiniyiw.

13 taniki ani mina ko pitokaat ayamiewikamikok?
13 *tânêhki ani mîna kô-pîhtokahât ayamihêwikamikohk?*

– ekosi kita isi kiskeyitamik ko pitokaat tato ka
– *êkosi kita-isi-kiskêyihtamihk kô-pîhtokahât tahto kâ-*

sikaacikasocik oma anoc ka isi pitokaicik
sîkahâhcikâsocik ôma anohc kâ-isi- pîhtokahîcik

ayamiewikamikok ekosi e wi isi pitokaicik kisikok
ayamihêwikamikohk êkosi ê-wî-isi-pîhtokahîcik kîsikohk

kwayask itaciotwawi.
kwayask itâcihotwâwi.

14 taniki ani ko ayamiewatikonamowat ota wakayik
14 *tânêhki ani kô-ayamihêwahtikonamowât ôta wâkayihk*

mina oteyekomiyik?
mîna otêyêkomiyihk?

– kici eka pisotamiyit meci kiswatimici mina kici
– *kici êkâ pisôtamiyit mêci kiswâtimici mîna kici-*

miweyitamiyit miyoitaciowin.
miywêyihtamiyit miyo-itâcihowin.

15 taniki ani mina ko ayamiewatikonamawat
15 *tânêhki ani mîna kô-ayamihêwahtikonamawât*

waskikaniyik mina otapiskokeyik?
wâskikaniyik mîna otâpiskokêyik?

90 – He knows in his heart that God loves him. That is why he makes the sign of the cross so that he will not be angry when something is said to him, but will carefully endure suffering; Jesus Christ did not reject His cross but suffered.

16 Why is it that he puts a white cap on his head?

– So that it be known that this white cap will show how clean our spirit is when we have been baptized.

17 Why is it that he is made to hold a candle when one has been baptized?

– The candle makes it known at first to quit being in the dark, but to live by seeing the light. He is to follow Jesus's teaching well.

---

16 – LESSON.

1 What is Holy Confirmation?

– It is one of God's medicines.

2 What is it used for, this Holy Confirmation?

90

– eta e itateyitamawat oteyiw ka
– *(ê-)âta ê-itatêyihtamawât otêyiw kâ-*

ayomiewatikonamowat ispic oteiyit kise manitowa
ayamihêwahtikonamawât ispic otêhiyit kisê-manitowa

kita sakiayit ko ayomiewatikonamowat kici eka
kita-sâkihâyit kô-ayamihêwahtikonamawât kici êkâ

kisiwasiyit nanto itiyici; peyatik kici nayatamiyit
kisiwâsiyit nanitaw itiyici; pêyâhtik kici-nayâtamiyit

kwatakitawin; sesokri eka e ki ataweyitak
kwâtakîtâwin; Sesokri êkâ ê-kî-atawêyihtâhk

otayamiewatikoma kita nayat.
otayamihêwahtikoma kita-nayat.

16 taniki ani wapiskastotinis ostikwaniyik ko astawat?
16 tânêhki ani wâpiskascocinis ostikwâniyik kô-astâwât?

– kici kiskeyitamik oma ka isi waspiskak astotinis
– *kici-kiskêyihtamihk ôma kâ-isi-wâpiskâk ascocinis*

ekosi kita isi kanatisiwok kitacakonowok ki
êkosi kita-isi-kanâtisiwak kitahcâhkonawak kî-

sikaaocikasoyaki.
sîkahâhcikâsoyahki.

17 taniki wasaskotenikan ko miciminamoit ana ka
17 tânêhki wâsaskotênikan kî-miciminamôhît ana kâ-

sikaotat?
sîkahâhtât?

– e wi kiskeyitamoit ekwayak e ponitepiskinak isko
– *ê-wî-kiskêyihtamohit êkwayahk ê-pôni-tipiskinâhk isko*

pimatisit kita wi wasekwenak e
pimâtisit kita-wî-wâsêkwênahk ê-

miyonakataweyitamwot sesosa otisitwawiniyiw.
miyo-nâkatawêyihtamwât Sesosa otisîhtwâwiniyiw.

16 – KISKINOAMAKEWIN.
16 – KISKINOHAMÂKÊWIN.

1 kekway ani eoko
1 kîkwây ani êwako

kicitwawisokiteeskakewitominitowin?
kihcitwâwisôhkitêhêskâkêwitôminitowin?

– eoko oma kise manito onanatawiowin peyak.
– *êwako ôma kisê-manitow onanâtawihowin pêyak.*

2 tanisi etapaciikoyak
2 tânisi êtâpacihikoyahk

kicitwawisokiteeskakewitominitowin?
kihcitwâwisôhkitêhêskâkêwitôminitowin?

91

— ᑭ ᒥᔑᑯᓇᐤ ᑭᒋ ᐯᒋᑌᐁᐢᑲᑯᔕᐠ ᒣᕑᔨᐟ ᒪ
ᑐᑐ ᐅᑭᓴᐚᒋᓯᐄᓇ ᑭᑭ.
3 ᓇᒣᒋ ᑭ ᑭ ᐯᒋᑌᐁᐢᑲᑯᓇᐤ ᒣᕑᔨᐟ ᒪᑐᑐ
ᑲ ᑭ ᓯᑲᐊᒋᑲᓯᔕᐠ ?
— ᐊᑕᐄᔕ, ᒪᑲ ᑭᒋᑖᐄᓯᑭᑌᐁᐢᑲᑫᐄᑐᒥ
ᑐᑐᐄᐤ ᒥᔑᑲᐄᔕᑭ ᐊᔑᐋᐠ ᑭ ᐯᒋ ᓴᑲᐢᑭ
ᑑᐢᑯᓇᐤ ᒣᕑᔨᐟ ᒪᑐᑐ ᐅᓴᑭᐃᑐᐃᐤ.
4 ᐊᐄᓇ ᑲ ᒣᑭᐟ ᐁᐅᑯ ᓇᓇᑕᐄᐅᐃᐤ ?
— ᑭᒋ ᐊᔑᒥᐁᐄᔑᑐᐤ.
5 ᑕᑕᑕᐤ ᒥᔑᑐᐠ ᑭᒋᑖᐄᓯᑭᑌᐁᐢᑲᑫᐄᑐᒥ
ᑐᑐᐃᐤ ?
— ᐯᔑᑳᐤ ᐱᑯ.
6 ᑕᑐᑭ ᐊᑐ ᐯᔑᑳᐤ ᐱᑯ ᑯᒥᔑᑐᐠ ᐁᐅᑯ ?
— ᐁᑲ ᐃᑳ ᐁ ᐄ ᑲᓯᐃᑲᑌᔑᐟ ᑲ ᐃᓯ ᑭᐢᑭ
ᔪᐚᒋᐃᑖᐤ ᑕᑐ ᑲ ᒥᔑᒋᐟ ᑭᒋᑖᐄᓯᑭᑌ
ᐁᐢᑲᑫᐄᑐᒥᑐᑐᐃᐤ.
7 ᑕᑐᑭ ᐊᑐ ᐅᓴ ᑯ ᒪᒋ ᐱᒪᑎᓯᒋᐟ ᐊᑎᐟ
ᐊᑕ ᐁ ᑭ ᒥᔑᑖᐤ ᑭᒋᑖᐄᓯᑭᑌᐁᐢᑲᑫᐄᑐ
ᒥᑐᑐᐃᐤ ?
— ᐊᐦ! ᓇᒪᐄᔕ ᓇᓇᐃᑕᐁᐅᐠ ᒣᕑᔨᔑᐟ ᒪᑐ
ᑐᐋ ᑲ ᐃᓯ ᒥᕑ ᓯᑭᒥᑯᒋᐟ.
8 ᑕᑐᓯ ᐊᑐ ᑫ ᑐᑖᐠ ᐊᐄᔕᐠ ᐋ ᒥᔑᒋ ᑭᒋ
ᑖᐄᓯᑭᑌᐁᐢᑲᑫᐄᑐᒥᑐᑐᐃᐤ ?
— ᐱᑕᒪ ᑭᑕ ᐄ ᑳᔑᐢᑫᐋᔑᑕᒣᐤ ᓴᓴ ᐅᑎ
ᓯᑖᐄᑐᐤ; ᑭᑕ ᑲᓇᑕᑯᑫᐄᓯ; ᓯᑭ ᑭᑕ

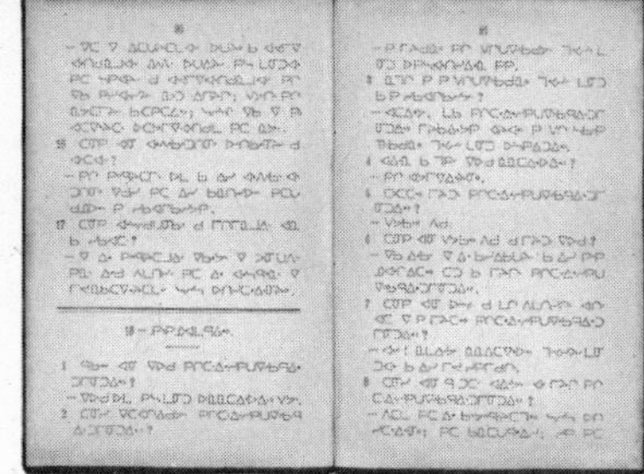

91 – He gave it to us so that the Holy Spirit and His Kindness would enter into our heart.

3 Did the Holy Spirit not also enter into our heart when we were baptized?

– Yes but when we are given the Holy Confirmation we have more of the love of the Holy Spirit in us.

4 Who is it that gives that remedy?

– The noble priest.

5 How many times is it given, the Confirmation?

– Only once.

6 Why is it given only once?

– That is always the way he anoints those who receive Confirmation.

7 Why is it that some live as sinners although they received the Confirmation?

– Because they do not obey the Holy Spirit that gives them good guidance.

8 What is someone to do when he receives Confirmation?

– At first he will be made to understand Jesus's teaching to clean his spirit, and strengthen it,

91 – ki miyikonaw kici peciteeskakoyak meyosit
– *ki-miyikonaw kihci-pêcitêhêskâkoyahk (ê-)miyosit*

manito okisewatisiwina kiki.
manitow okisêwâtisiwina kiki.

3 nameci ki ki peciteeşkakonaw meyosit manito ka ki
3 namêcî kikî-pêcitêhêskâkonaw (ê-)miyosit manitow kâ-kî-

sikaacikasoyak?
sîkahâhcikâsoyahk?

– atawiya, maka kicitwawisokiteeskakewitominitowin
– *atawiya, mâka kihcitwâwisôhkitêhêskâkêwitôminitowin*

miyikawiyaki ayiwak ki peci sakaskineskakonaw
miyikawiyahki ayiwâk kî-pêci sâkaskinêskâkonaw

meyosit manito osakiitowin.
(ê-)miyosit manitow osâkihitowin.

4 awina ka mekit eoko nanatawiowin?
4 awîna kâ-mêkit êwako nanâtawihowin?

– kici ayamiewiyiniw.
– *kihci-ayamihêwiyiniw.*

5 tantatwaw miyitok
5 tânitahtwâw miyitok

kicitwawisokiteeskakewitominitowin?
kihcitwâwisôhkitêhêskâkêwitôminitowin?

– peyakwaw piko.
– *pêyakwâw piko.*

6 taniki ani peyakwaw piko ko miyitok eoko?
6 tânêhki ani pêyakwâw piko kô-miyitok êwako?

– eka wikac e wi kasiikateyik ka isi kiskinowaciitwaw
– *êkâ wîhkâc ê-wî-kasihikâtêyik kâ-isi-kiskinowâcîhtwâw*

tato ka miyicik kicitwawisokiteeskakewitominitowin.
tahto kâ-miyicik kihcitwâwisôhkitêhêskâkêwitôminitowin.

7 taniki ani osam ko maci pimatisicik atit ata e ki
7 tânêhki ani osâm kô-maci-pimâtisicik âtiht âta ê-kî-

miyitwaw kicitwawisokiteeskakewitominitowin?
miyitwâw kihcitwâwisôhkitêhêskâkêwitôminitowin?

– ays! namawiya nanaitawewok meyosiyit manitowa
– *ays! namâwiya nanahîtawêwak (ê-)miyosiyit manitow*

ka isi miyosikimikocik.
kâ-isi-miyo-sîhkimikocik.

8 tanisi ani ke totak awiyak wa miyici
8 tânisi ani kê-itôtahk awiyak wâ-miyici

kicitwawisokiteeskakewitominitowin?
kihcitwâwisôhkitêhêskâkêwitôminitowin?

– pitama kita wi kwayaskweyitamwew sesosa
– *pitamâ kita wî-kwayaskwêyihtamwêw Sesosa*

otisiwawiniw; kita kanatacakweiso; soki kita
otisîhtwâwinîw; kita-kanâtahcâhkwêhisow; sôhki-kita-

92 to follow it carefully so that he is treated well in his heart. This is how he will pray:

"God, my Father I believe in You. I believe also in everything that You taught me. I greet You, Holy Spirit, I want You with me. Your love enters and fills my heart. It is surprising for You to have pity on me. You are very kind. You grieved for me when I sinned. In my heart I love You. I wish You would guard me all the time! I wish to reach the salvation Jesus obtained for me!"

9 What does the noble priest do when he gives the Confirmation?

– He stretches his hands on his head. He also prays for them, then he makes the sign of the cross for them. Also he anoints them on the forehead with holy oil.

10 What happens while the noble priest stretches his hands on him?

– Just then the Holy Spirit enters the heart.

11 Why is it that he makes the sign of the cross on the forehead?

– He indicates not being ashamed of Jesus's teaching.

92

nanakataweyitam ka isi miyo totat; ispic ote it ekosi
nânâkatawêyihtam ka-isi-miyo-itôtât; ispic otêhit êkosi

kita isi ayamiaw:
kita-isi-ayamihâw:

« kise manito nota, ki tapwetatin
"kisê-manitow nohtâ, kitâpwêtâtin

ni tapwewokeyiten mina kakiyaw ka ki isi
nitâpwêwâkêyihtên mîna kahkiyaw kâ-kî-isi-

kiskinoamakawiyan. kitatamiskatin meyosiyan
kiskinohamâkawiyân. kitatamiskâtin (ê-)miyosiyan

manito, ki ntaweyimitin kici peciteeskawiyan
manitow, kinitawêyimitin kici-pêcitêhêskawiyan

kici sakaskineskakoyan ki sokiitowin. ayiwak
kici-sâskaskinêskâkêyan kisâkihitowin. ayiwâk

e piweyitakosiyan, ka wikitimakinawiyan esi
ê-piwêyihtâkosiyan, ka-wîkitimâkinawiyan ê-isi-

kisiwatisiyan mitoni e kesinateyitaman ka ki isi
kisêwâtisiyan mitoni ê-kêsinatêyihtaman kâ-kî-isi-

maci pimatisiyan. ispic oteiyan ki sakiitin pitane
maci-pimâtisiyan. ispic otêhiyân kisâkihitin pitanê

taki kanoskawiyan! pitane otitaman eta ka ki
tahki kanoskawiyan! pitanê otîtaman êta kâ-kî-

kispinatamawit sesos! »
kîspinâtamawit Sesos!"

9 tanisi ani totam kici ayamiewiyiniw
9 *tânisi ani itôtam kihci-ayamihêwiyiniw*

kicitwawisokiteeskakewitominitowin mekici?
kihcitwâwisôhkitêhêskâkêwitôminitowin mêkici?

– sowiciciestawew ostikwaniyik anii ka miyat kisik
– *sowicicihêstawêw ostikwâniyik anihi kâ-miyât kisik*

ayamiestamawew, ekosi ayamiewatikototawew kisik
ayamihêstamawêw, êkosi ayamihêwahtikotôtawêw kisik

e tominat oskatikoyik ekwa pasanawewesiw.
ê-tominât oskâtikoyik êkwa pasanawêwêsiw.

10 tanisi ani ekiniyik mekwac sowiciciestaket kici
10 *tânisi ani êkiniyik mêkwâc sowicicihêstaket kihci-*

ayamiewiyiniw?
ayamihêwiyiniw?

– ekwayak peciteeskakeyiwa ka miyosiyit manitowa.
– *êkwayak pêcitêhêskâkêyiwa kâ-miyosiyit manitowa.*

11 taniki ani ko ayamiewatikototaket miskatikok?
11 *tânêhki ani kô-ayamihêwahtikotôtâkêt miskâtikohk?*

– kici eka nipewisistamot sesosa otisitwawiniw.
– *kici êkâ nipêwisîstamot Sesosa otisîhtwâwinîw.*

93

12 ᑕᑌᑭ ᐊᑌ ᑯ ᐸᓱᓇᐁᐧᐊᐧ ᐊᑌᐃ ᑲ ᒥᔦ
ᐁᐅᑯ ᐊᔦᒥᐁᓇᓇᑕᐃᐧᐅᐃᐅ ?
— ᑭᑕ ᐃᐧ ᓱᐯᔦᑕᒥᔦ ᑭᑎ ᐁᑲ ᑭᓱᐊᐧᓱᔦ
ᒣᔦᑐᑕᒥᑎ, ᐁᑯᓱ ᐁ ᑭ ᐃᓱ ᑭᐢᑭᓈᐊᐧᑎ
ᓱᑭᐢᑲᒥᑯᔦ ᓴᓱᐢᐧᔑ.
13 ᑕᑌᓱ ᐊᑌ ᕴ ᑐᑕ ᐊᐃᐧᔦ ᑭᑎᑕᐧᐃᐧᓱᑭᑫ
ᐁᐢᑲᕴᐃᐧᑐᒥᑌᑐᐃᐅ ᑭ ᒥᔦᑎ ?
— ᑭᑕ ᐃᐋᑲᑫᑫᐤ ᑭᑕ ᓇᓇᐢᑯᒪ ᑭᓴ ᒪᑌ
ᑐᐊᐧ ᐁ ᑭ ᑭᑎᒪᑭᓇᑯ, ᒥᑐᑌ ᑭᑕ ᐃᐧ
ᐊᔦᑎᓇ ᑲ ᑭ ᐃᓱ ᒥᕓ ᑐᑕ:
« ᑭᑕᑕᒥᐢᑲᑎ ᒣᕓᓱᔦ ᒪᑌᑐ, ᑭᒪᒧᔦᐁᐧ
ᑕᑎ ᐁ ᑭ ᑭᑎᒪᑭᓇᐃᐧᔦ, ᑭᑎᑕᐧᐃᐧᓱᑭᑫᐁᐢᑲ
ᕴᐃᐧᑐᒥᑌᑐᐃᐅ ᐁ ᑭ ᒥᔦᑲᐃᐧᔦ; ᑭ ᒪᐃᐧᒨᐢᑕ
ᑎ ᑭᑕ ᐃᐧ ᒥᕓ ᑲᓇᐁᐧᔦᒥᔦ ᑭᑎ ᐁᑲ ᓴᑯ
ᒋᐃᑯᔦ ᕴᑲ ᐁ ᒪᔦᑕ. ᐱᑕᑌ ᐃᑕᑎᐅᔦ
ᑭᓱᑯ ᑭᑎ ᐅᑎᑎᑕ ᑌᐱᔦᑌ !»

17 — ᑭᐢᑭᓈᐊᒪᕴᐃ.

1 ᕴᑲ ᐁᐅᑯ ᐊᔦᒥᐁᐅᐧᑲᓱᓇᒪᕴᐃ ?
— ᑭᓴ ᒪᑌᑐ ᐅᓇᓇᑕᐃᐧᐅᐃ ᑯᑎ ᑲᓱᓇᒪᑯᔦ
ᐁ ᑭ ᓱᑲᐊᑎᑲᓱᔦ ᒧᐁᐢᑕ ᒣᑎ ᑐᑕᒪᑭ.
2 ᐊᐃᐧᓇ ᐊᓇ ᑲ ᑭ ᐅᓱᑕ ᐊᔦᒥᐁᐅᐧᑲᓱᓇ
ᒫᕴᐃ ?
— ᓴᓱᐢᐧᔑ ᑭ ᐅᓱᑕ ᐃᐢᐱ ᑲ ᒪᒪᑕᐃᐧᐊ ᐊᔦ

93

12 What benefit does Confirmation have?
– He is going to be patient, will not be angry, will do a good deed willingly so that he will be a follower of Jesus Christ.
13 What is someone to do after receiving Holy Confirmation?
– He will leave, he will thank God. God has pitied him very much. He will offer thanks, for this is a good deed:

"I greet You Holy Spirit. You had pity on me. You gave me Holy Confirmation, I pray to You. You are going to guard me well, very well, not to be overcome by anything evil. I wish to behave to gain Heaven and to greet You when I die!"

17 – LESSON.

1 What is religious forgiveness?
– God's healing is where we get forgiveness. We were baptized because mankind had sinned.
2 Who is it that had made religious forgiveness?
– Jesus Christ had made it when He gave supernatural power to

93

12 taniki ani ko pasanawewat anii ka miyat eoko
12 tânêhki ani kô-pasanawêwât anihi kâ-miyât êwako

ayamienanatawiowin?
ayamihênanâtawihowin?

– kita wi sipeyitamiyit kici eka kisiwasiyit meyitotamici,
– kita-wî-sîpêyihtamiyit kici êkâ kisiwâsiyit miyitôtamîci,

ekosi e ki isi kiskinowacisikiskamikoyak sesoskri.
êkosi ê-kî-isi-kiskinowâcisikiskamikoyahk Sesoskri.

13 tanisi ani ke totak awiyak
13 tânisi ani ka-itôtâhk awiyak

kicitwawisokiteeskakewitominitowin ki miyici?
kihcitwâwisôhkitêhêskâkêwitôminitowin kî-miyici?

– kita iyekatetew kita nanaskomat kise manitowa e ki
– kita-iyîkatêtêw kita-nanâskomât kisê-manitowa ê-kî-

kitimakinakot, mitone kita wi ayatinan ka ki isi
kitimâkinâkot, mitonê kita-wî-ayâtinân kâ-kî-isi-

miyototat:
miyo-itôtât:

« kitatamiskatin meyosiyan manito,
"kitatamiskâtin (ê-)miyosiyan manitow,

kimamoyawestatin e ki kitimakinawiyan,
kimamoyawêstâtin ê-kî-kitimâkinawiyan,

kicitwawisokiteeskakewitominitowin e
kihcitwâwisôhkitêhêskâkêwitôminitowin ê-

ki miyikawiyan; ki mawimostatin kita wi
kî-miyikawiyan; kimawimostâtin kita-wî-

miyokanaweyimiyan kici eka sakociikoyan kekway
miyo-kanawêyimiyan kici êkâ sakôcihikoyan kîkway

e mayatak. pitane otacioyan kisikok kici otititan
ê-mayatahk. pitanê (ê-)itâcihoyan kîsikohk kici-otititân

nipiyani! »
nipiyâni!"

17 – KISKINOAMAKEWIN.
17 – KISKINOHAMÂKÊWIN.

1 kekway eoko ayamiewokasinamakewin?
1 kîkwây êwako ayamihêwikâsînamâkêwin?

– kesi manito onanatawiowin koci kasinamakoyak
– kisê-manitow onanâtawihowin koci-kâsînamâkoyahk

e ki sikaacikasoyak moestan meci totamaki.
ê-kî-sîkahâhcikâsoyahk mwêstas maci-itôtamâhki.

2 awina ana ka ki ositat ayamiewokasinamakewin?
2 awîna ana kâ-kî-osîhtât ayamihêwikâsînamâkêwin?

– sesoskri ki ositaw ispi ka mamatawiat
– Sesoskri kî-osîhtâw ispî kâ-mamâtawihât

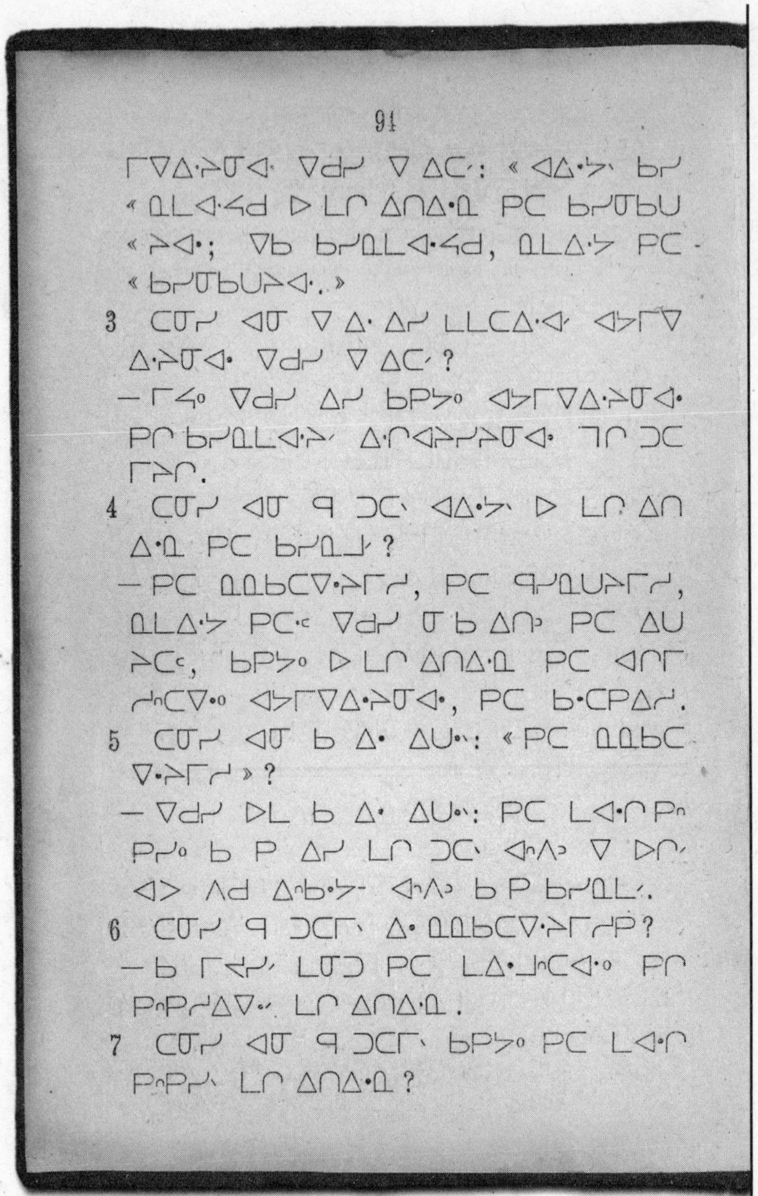

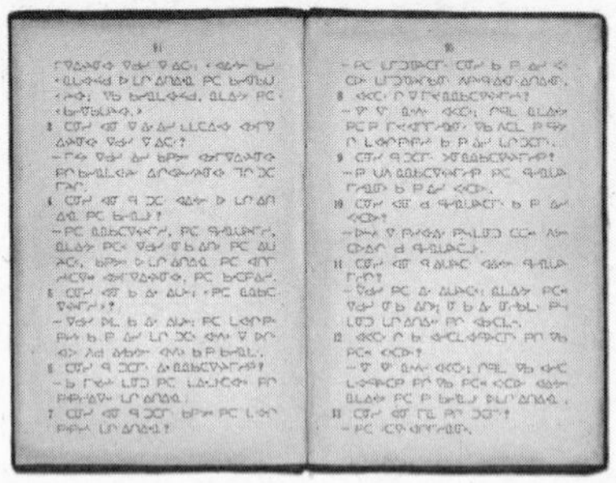

94 the priest. So then Jesus told the people when you "forgive them their sins they will be forgiven." "If you are not forgiven, no one will be forgiven."

3 How is it that He is going to give the priests this power, as He is saying to them?

– He gave them all this power, all the priests, to forgive His people if they do evil.

4 What is somebody supposed to do for his sins to be forgiven?

– He will examine himself, he will grieve for himself, not ever again like this will he sin. He will think of all his sins; he will tell all of them to the priest; he will do penance.

5 What does it mean to say: "He will examine his conscience."?

– This is what is meant: He will remember all that he did badly since the beginning, even if the last time he confessed, he was forgiven his sins.

6 What is to be done when you are going to examine yourself?

– You will pray to the Holy Spirit, to make you remember your sins.

7 What is to be done to remember all sins?

94 ayamiewiyiniwa ekosi e itat: « awiyak
ayamihêwiyiniwa êkosi ê-itât: "awiyak

kasinamawayeko o maci itiwina kita kasinikateyiwa;
kâsînamawayêko omacihtiwina kita-kâsînikâtêyiwa;

eka kasinamawayeko, namawiya kita
êkâ kâsînamawâyêko, namâwiya kita-

kasinikateyiwa. »
kâsînikâtêyiwa."

3 tanisi ani e wi isi mamatawiat ayamiewiyiniwa ekosi
3 tânisi ani ê-wî-isi-mamâhtâwihât ayamihêwiyiniwa êkosi

e itat?
ê-itât?

– miyew ekosi isi kakiyaw ayamiewiyiniwa kici
– miyêw êkosi isi kahkiyaw ayamihêwiyiniwa kici-

kasinamawayit wiciayisiyiniwa meci totamiyici.
kâsînamawâyât wîci-ayisiyiniwa maci-itôtamiyici.

4 tanisi ani ke totak awiyak o maci itiwina kita
4 tânisi ani kê-tôtahk awiyak omacihtiwina kita-

kasinamot?
kâsînamôt?

– kita nanakataweyimiso, kita kesinateyimiso,
– kita-nânâkatawêyimisow, kita-kêsinâtêyimisow,

namawiya kitwam ekosi ni ka itin kita iteyitam,
namâwiya kîhtwâm êkosi nika-itin kita-itêyihtam,

kakiyaw o maci itiwina kita acimisostawew
kahkiyaw omacihtiwina kita-âcimisôstawêw

ayamiewiyiniwa, kita kwatakiiso.
ayamihêwiyiniwa, kita-kwâtakihisow.

5 tanisi ani ka wi itwek: « kita nanakataweyimiso »?
5 tânisi ani kâ wî-itwêk: "kita-nânâkatawêyimisow"?

– ekosi oma ka wi itwek: kita mawacikiskisiw ka ki isi
– êkosi ôma kâ-wî-itwêk: kita mawâcikiskisiw kâ-kî-isi-

maci totak aspin e ocit apo piko iskwayac aspin ka
maci-itôtahk aspin ê-ohcît ahpô piko iskwayâc aspin kâ-

ki kasinamat.
kî-kâsînamât.

6 tanisi ke totamik wi nanakataweyimisoki?
6 tânisi kê-itôtamik wî-nânâkatawêyimisohki?

– ka miyosit manito kita mawimostawew kici
– kâ-miyosit manitow kita-mawimôstawâw kici-

kiskisoiwet maci itiwina.
kiskisohiwêt macihtiwina.

7 tanisi ani ke totamik kakiyaw kita mawacikiskisik
7 tânisi ani kê-itôtamihk kahkiyaw kita-mawacîkiskisik

maci itiwina?
macihtiwina?

95
— ᑭᑕ ᒪᒥᑐᓀᔨᑕᒥᕽ ᑖᓂᓯ ᑲ ᑭ ᐃᓯ ᐸᐢ
ᑕᐅᐠ ᒪᒥᑐᓀᔨᒋᑲᓂᕽ ᐱᑭᐢᑵᐃᐧᓂᕽ ᐃᑎᐃᐧᓂᕽ.
8 ᐊᐸᑖᐤ ᒋ ᐁ ᒥᔪ ᓇᓇᑲᑕᐍᔨᒥᓯᐠ?
— ᐁᐦ ᐁᐦ ᓇᐢᐱᐨ ᐊᐸᑖᐤ; ᒋᑫᒪ ᓇᒪᐃᐧᔭ
ᑭᑕ ᑭ ᒥᔪᐊᒋᒥᓱᓇᓂᐤ ᐁᑲ ᐱᑕᒪ ᑭ ᑫᐧᔭ
ᒋ ᒪᐚᒋᑭᐢᑭᓯᐠ ᑲ ᑭ ᐃᓯ ᒪᒋᑐᑕᒥᕽ.
9 ᑖᓂᓯ ᑫ ᑐᑕᒥᕽ ᐳᓂ ᓇᓇᑲᑕᐍᔨᒥᓯᑭ?
— ᑭ ᑌᐱ ᓇᓇᑲᑕᐍᔨᒥᓯᑭ ᑭᑕ ᑫᓯᓇᑌᔨ
ᒥᓯᓇᓂᐤ ᑲ ᑭ ᐃᓯ ᐸᐢᑕᐅᐠ.
10 ᑖᓂᓯ ᐊᓂ ᑯ ᑫᓯᓇᑌᔨᑕᒥᕽ ᑲ ᑭ ᐃᓯ
ᐸᐢᑕᐅᐠ?
— ᐅᓵᐨ ᐁ ᑭᓯᐚᐏᐟ ᑭᓭᒪᓂᑐ ᑕᑕᐤ ᐱᔭᐢ
ᑕᐅᐃᐧᒋ ᑯ ᑫᓯᓇᑌᔨᑕᒧᐟ.
11 ᑖᓂᓯ ᐊᓂ ᑫ ᐃᑌᔨᑕᐠ ᐊᐃᐧᔭᐠ ᑫᓯᓇᑌᔨ
ᒥᓯᒋ?
— ᐁᑯᓯ ᑭᑕ ᐃᐧ ᐃᑌᔨᑕᐟ: ᓇᒪᐃᐧᔭ ᑭᑖᐟ
ᐁᑯᓯ ᓂ ᑲ ᐃᑎᐤ; ᓂ ᑲ ᐃᐧ ᓂᓯᑲᒪᐠ ᑭᓴ
ᒪᓂᑐ ᒪᒋ ᐃᑎᐏᐤ ᑭᒋ ᐸᑳᑕᒪᐠ.
12 ᐊᐸᑖᐤ ᒋ ᑲ ᐊᓯᑕᒪᐚᑫᔨᑕᒥᕽ ᑭᒋ ᐁᑲ
ᑭᑖᐟ ᐸᐢᑕᐅᐠ?
— ᐁᐦ ᐁᐦ ᓇᐢᐱᐨ ᐊᐸᑖᐤ; ᒋᑫᒪ ᐁᑲ ᐊᓯᑕ
ᒪᐚᑫᔨᑕᑭ ᑭᒋ ᐁᑲ ᑭᑖᐟ ᐸᐢᑕᐅᐟ ᐊᐃᐧᔭᐠ
ᓇᒪᐃᐧᔭ ᑭᑕ ᑭ ᑲᓯᓇᒧᐟ ᐅᒪᒋ ᐃᑎᐃᐧᓇ.
13 ᑖᓂᓯ ᐊᓂ ᒥᓇ ᑭᒋ ᑐᑕᒥᕽ?
— ᑭᑕ ᐤᑕᐍ ᐊᒋᒥᓱᓇᓂᐤ.

95

– To think about how you had sinned in your thoughts, your conversation, your actions.

8 Is it good to examine one's conscience?

– Yes, it is always good, because no one would talk about their wrongdoings if he does not gather his thoughts about his bad behaviour.

9 What is to be done when one quits examining oneself?

– When one has sufficiently examined oneself, everyone will grieve on this account for the way that she or he has sinned.

10 How is one to be sorrowful for the way one has sinned?

– Because sin angers God; each time one has sinned, one will be sorrowful on this account.

11 How is it that one is to think when someone is sorrowful?

– Like this is how he is going to think: Never again will I sin like this; God will work together with me to hate sin.

12 Is it useful to think about promising not to sin again?

– Yes, forever it is useful, surely to promise not to sin again. Without this, he will not be forgiven his sins.

13 How is this also to be done?

– They will go and confess.

95

– kita mamitoneyitamik tanisi ka ki isi pastaok
– *kita-mâmitonêyihtamihk tânisi kâ-kî-isi-pâstâhok*

mamitoneyicikanik pikiskwewinik itiwinik.
mâmitonêyihcikanihk pîkiskwêwinihk ihtiwinihk.

8 apatan ci e miyonanakataweyimisok?
8 âpatan cî ê-miyo-nânâkatawêyimisok?

– ek ek naspic apatan; cikema namawiya kita ki miyo
– *êk êk nâspic âpatan; cikêma namâwiya kita-kî-miyo-*

acimisonaniw eka pitama kikweya ci mawacikiskisik
âcimisonâniw êkâ pitamâ kîkwaya cî mawacîkiskisik

ka ki isi maci totamik.
kâ-kî-isi-maci-itôtamihk.

9 tanisi ke totamik poni nanakataweyimisoki?
9 tânisi kê-tôtamik pôni-nânâkatawêyimisohki?

– ki tepi nanakataweyimisoki kita kesinateyimisonaniw
– *kî-têpi-nânâkatawêyimisohki kita-kêsinatêyimisonâniw*

ka ki isi pastaok.
kâ-kî-isi-pâstâhok.

10 tanisi ani ko kesinateyitamik ka ki isi pastaok?
10 tânisi ani kô-kêsinâtêyihtamihk kâ-kî-isi-pâstâhok?

– osam e kisiwait kise manito tatwaw piyastaowici
– *osâm ê-kisiwâhiht kisê-manitow tahtwâw pîyâstâhowici*

ko kesinateyitamot.
kô-kêsinatêyihtamôt.

11 tanisi ani ke iteyitak awiyak kesinateyimisoci?
11 tânisi ani kê-itêyihtak awiyak kêsinatêyimisôci?

– ekosi kita wi iteyitam: namawiya kitwam eḳosi ni ka
– *êkosi kita-wî-itêyihtam: namâwiya kîhtwâm êkosi nika-*

itin; ni ka wi nisokamak kise manito maci itiwin kici
itin; nika-wî-nîsôhkamâk kisê-manitow macihtiwin kici-

pakwatamwak.
pakwâtamwak.

12 apatan ci ka asotamawakeyitamik kici eka kitwam
12 âpatan cî ka-asotamawâkêyihtamihk kici êkâ kîhtwâm

pastaok?
pâstâhok?

– ek ek naspic apatan; cikema eka asotamawakeyitaki
– *êk êk nâspic âpatan; cikêma êkâ asotamawâkêyihtahki*

kici eka kitwam pastaot awiyak namawiya kita ki
kici êkâ kîhtwâm pâstâhot awiyak namâwiya kita-kî-

kasinamot omaci itiwina,
kâsînâmôt omacihtiwina,

13 tanisi ani mina kici totamik?
13 tânisi ani mîna kici-itôtamihk?

– kita ntawe acimisonaniw.
– *kita-nitawi-âcimisonâniw.*

96

14 ᑕᒋᓯ ᐊᒋ ᑐᑕᑲᒋᐤ ᐊᐧ ᐊᑎᒥᓱᕽ?
— ᐣᑕᐁᐧ ᐅᑎᑳᐧᓇᐱᐣᑕᐊᐧᐣ ᐊᔦᒥᐁᐃᐧᔨᒋᐤ ᐊ
ᔦᒥᐁᐊᐧᑎᑯᑲᒋᐤ, ᐁᑲᐧ ᒥᓇ ᐊᔦᒥᑕᒋᐤ ᐊ
ᔦᒥᐊᐃᐧᐣ ᑲ ᑭᑎᑎᐧ: « ᒋᑕᑎᒥᓱᐣᑕᐊᐧᐤ » ...ᐁᐧ
ᑯᓯ ᐁᑲᐧ ᒪᑎ ᐊᑎᒥᓱᓇᒋᐤ.
15 ᑲᑭᔭᐤ ᑎ ᑭᑕ ᐊᑐᑕᑲᒋᐃᐧᐊᐧ ᒪᑎ ᐃᑎ
ᐃᐧᓇ?
— ᐁᐠ ᐁᐠ ᒥᑐᒋ ᑲᑭᔭᐤ ᑭᑕ ᐊᑐᑕᑲᒋᐃᐧᐊᐧ.
16 ᐸᒥᓯᐸᐣᑕᐅᓇᒋᐤ ᑎ ᐅᑎᑕᐤ ᑲᑕᐠ ᒪᑎ ᐃ
ᑎᐃᐧᐣ?
— ᓇᐣᐱ- ᒥᓯᐸᐣᑕᐅᓇᒋᐤ ᒪᑎ ᐃᑎᐃᐧᐣ ᑲᑕᐠ.
17 ᑕᒋᓯ ᐊᒋ ᑫ ᐃᑕᑐᑕᐠ ᐊᐃᐧᔦᐠ ᐅᒪᑎ
ᐃᑎᐃᐧᓇ?
— ᒣᒧ- ᑭᑕ ᐊᑐᑕᐨ ᑕᑕᐧᐤ ᑲ ᑭ ᐃᓯ ᒪᑎ
ᑐᑕᐠ.
18 ᐁᑲ ᑭ ᑲᓯᓇᒪᐠ ᐃᐣᑳᐧᔦ- ᑲ ᑭ ᐊᑎᒥᓱᐠ
ᑕᒋᓯ ᑭᑕ ᑐᑕᐨ ᑭᑕᐧᐨ ᐣᑕᐁᐧᐊᑎᒥᓱᑎ?
— ᑲᐃᐧ ᑭᑕ ᑌᐸᑐᑕᐨ ᐃᐣᑳᐧᔦ- ᑲ ᑭ ᐊᑐᑕᐠ
ᑭᐣᐱᐣ ᑯᑕᑲ ᐊᔦᒥᐁᐃᐧᔨᒋᐊᐧ ᐊᑎᒥᓱᐣᑕᐊᐧᑎ
ᐁᑲ ᐁ ᑭ ᐅᑎ ᑲᓯᓇᒪᐠ.
19 ᑕᒋᓯ ᐊᒋ ᑫᑐᑕᐠ ᐸᒋ ᐊᑎᒥᓱᑎ?
— ᐸᒋ ᐊᑎᒥᓱᑎ ᒥᑐᒋ ᑭᑕ ᐃᐧ ᓇᓇᑲᑐᐁᐧᔨ
ᑕᐨ ᐊᐧᐊᐧ- ᑭᑕ ᐃᐧ ᑐᑕᐨ ᐊᔦᒥᐁᐃᐧᔨᒋᐊᐧ ᑕ
ᒋᓯ ᐃᑎᑯᑎ, ᐁᑲᐧ ᑭᑕ ᑫᔭᓇᑎ ᐊᔦᒥᐊᐧᐤ:
« ᓇᐣᐱ- ᒋ ᑲᑳᐧᑕᑫᔨᒧᐣ » ᑭᑕ ᑳᐧᑕᑭᐃᓯ.

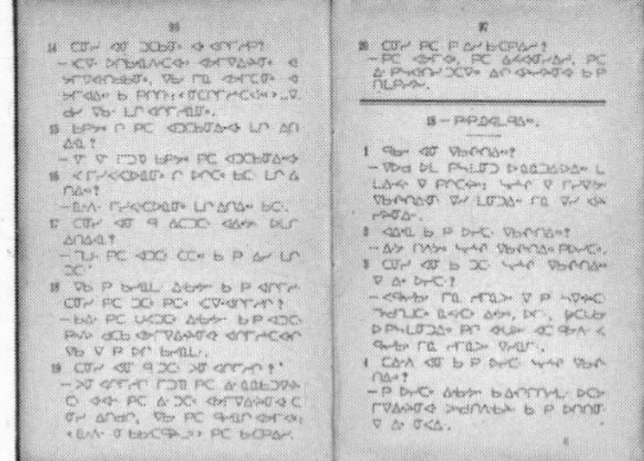

96

14 What happens when one confesses?
– He goes and kneels to the priest, the sign of the cross is made and also he reads the prayer that is holy: "He goes and confesses."… He confesses everything.

15 Will all the bad sins be confessed?
– Yes, all of them will be confessed.

16 If we hide one sin, are we sinning in a big way?
– If we hide sin, we are committing a big sin forever.

17 How is it that someone confesses his sins?
– Clearly he will confess how many times he did evil.

18 If he is not forgiven in the end after he confesses, what will he do when he goes to confess again?
– He will speak about it in the end. He should confess, if it is another priest that he confesses to, if he could not be forgiven.

19 What is he to do after he is done confessing?
– When he is finished confessing he will follow the penance. Especially he will do what the priest tells him to do and he will surely pray: "forever I am sorrowful; I will suffer."

96

14 tanisi ani totakaniw wa acimisoki?
14 *tânisi ani itôtâkaniw wâ-âcimisihki?*

– ntawe ocikwanapistawaw ayamiewiyiniw
– *nitawi-ocihkwanapîstawâw ayamihêwiyiniw*

ayamiewatikokaniw, ekwa mina ayamitaniw
ayamihêwahtikokâniw, êkwa mîna ayamîtâniw

ayamiawin ka kicitik: « nitacimisostawew »...ekosi
ayamihâwin kâ-kihcihitik: "nitâcimisôstawêw"...êkosi

ekwa maci acimisonaiw.
êkwa maci-âcimisôsaniw.

15 kakiyaw ci kita atotakaniwiwa maci itiwina?
15 *kahkiyaw cî kita-atôtakâniwiwa macihtiwina?*

– ek ek mitone kakiyaw kita atotakaniwiwa
– *êk êk mitonê kahkiyaw kita-atôtakâniwiwa*

16 pa misipastaonaniw ci ocitaw katak maci itiwin?
16 *pâ-misi-pâstâhonâniw cî ohcitaw kâtâk macihtiwin?*

– naspic misipastaonaniw maci itiwin katak.
– *nâspic misi-pâstâhonâniw macihtiwin kâtâk.*

17 tanisi ani ke itatotak awiyak omaci itiwina?
17 *tânisi ani kê-itatotak awiyak omacihtiwina?*

– memoc kita atotam tatwaw ka ki isi maci totak.
– *mêmôc kita-âtotam tahtwâw kâ-kî-isi-maci-itôtahk.*

18 eka ki kasinamat iskwayac ka ki acimisot tanisi kita
18 *êkâ kî-kâsînamât iskwayac kâ-kî-âcimisot tânisi kita-*

totam kitwam ntaweacimisoci?
itôtam kîhtwâm nitawi-âcimisoci?

– kawi kita tepatotam iskwayac ka ki atotak kispin
– *kawi-kita-têpâtôtam iskwayâc kâ-kî-âtotahk kîspin*

kotaka ayamiewiyiniwa acimisostawaci eka e ki oci
kotaka ayamihêwiyiniwa âcimisôstawâci êkâ ê-kî-ohci-

kasinamat.
kâsînamât.

19 tanisi ani ke totak poni acimisoci?
19 *tânisi ani kê-itôtahk pôni-âcimisoci?*

– poni acimisoci mitone kita wi nanakataweyitam
– *pôni-âcimisoci mitonê kita-wî-nânâkatawêyihtam*

wawac kita wi totam ayamiewiyiniwa tanisi itikoci,
wâwâc kita-wî-itôtam ayamihêwiyiniwa tânisi itikoci,

ekwa kita kesinaci ayamiaw: « naspic
êkwa kita-kêsinâci ayamihâw: "nâspic

ni kakwatakeyimon » kita kwatakiiso.
nikakwâtakêyimon" kita-kwâtakihisow.

97

20 ᑕᑌᓯ ᑭᑕ ᑭ ᐃᓯ ᑳᑕᑭᐃᓱ ?

— ᑭᑕ ᐊᔭᒥᐊᐤ, ᑭᑕ ᐃᕙᐋᑌᓯᐃᓱ, ᑭᑕ ᐃᐧ ᑭᓴᐋᑎᓯ ᑐᑕᐁᐤ ᐃᐧᒋ ᐊᔮᓯᔮᑌᐋ ᑲ ᑭ ᑎᒪᑭᓯᔮᐟ.

---

18 — ᑭᐢᑭᓅᐊᒪᑫᐃᐤ.

1 ᑫᑲᐤ ᐊᑌ ᐁᑲᕆᐢᑎᐃᐤ ?

— ᐁᐅᑯ ᐅᒪ ᑭᓴᒪᑌᑐ ᐅᓇᓇᑐᐃᐅᐃᐤ ᒪ ᒪᐃᐧᕙᐢ ᐁ ᑭᒋᑕᐧᔮᐠ: ᓴᓱᕁ ᐁ ᒥᓯᐁᐧᔭᐟ ᐁᑲᕆᐢᑎᐃᐧᑌᐠ ᐁᓯ ᒪᑌᑐᐃᐧ ᒥᓇ ᐁᓯ ᐊᔮ ᓯᔮᑌᐃᐧ.

2 ᐊᐃᐧᓇ ᑲ ᑭ ᐅᓯᑕᐟ ᐁᑲᕆᐢᑎᐃᐤ ?

— ᐃᐧᔭ ᑎᐱᔭᐤ ᓴᓱᕁ ᐁᑲᕆᐢᑎᐃᐤ ᑭᐅᓯᑕᐤ.

3 ᑕᑌᓯ ᐊᑌ ᑲ ᑐᑕᐠ ᓴᓱᕁ ᐁᑲᕆᐢᑎᐃᐤ ᐁ ᐃᐧ ᐅᓯᑕᐟ ?

— ᐸᑫᐧᓰᑲᐤ ᒥᓇ ᓯᒥᓇᐳᐦ ᐁ ᑭ ᓴᐁᐧᔮᑕᐠ ᒉᐢᑯᒐᒍᑕᐤ ᓇᕙᐢᑕᐤ ᐃᐧᔭᐤ, ᐅᒥᐠ, ᐅᑕᐅᑲᐧ ᐅᑭᓴᒪᑌᑐᐃᐤ ᑭᒋ ᐊᐢᑐᔮᐠ ᐊᑕ ᑫᔭᐱ ᐸ ᑫᐧᓯᑲᐤ ᒥᓇ ᓯᒥᓇᐳᐦ ᐁᓯᓇᒥᐠ.

4 ᑕᐃᐢᐱ ᐊᑌ ᑲ ᑭ ᐅᓯᑕᐟ ᓴᓱᕁ ᐁᑲᕆᐢ ᑎᐃᐤ ?

— ᑭ ᐅᓯᑕᐤ ᐃᐢᑳᐧᔭ ᑲ ᐃᐧᒋᒥᑎᓱᒪᐟ ᐅᑕᔭ ᒥᐁᐃᐧᔮᑌᐋ ᐳᐢᑯᑎᐱᐢᑲᔮᐠ ᑲ ᑭ ᐅᑎᑎᑌᐟ ᐁ ᐃᐧ ᑌᐸᐃᐟ.

6

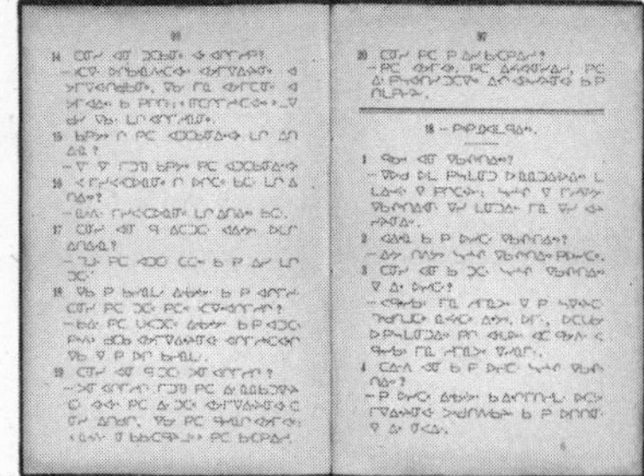

97

20 How can one make himself contrite?

– He will pray. He will change what he is doing to be kind to his people who are poor in spirit.

---

18 – LESSON.

1 What is the Eucharist?

– It is the experience of God's healing holiness. Jesus Christ is the first communicant; He is both God and a human being.

2 Who made the Eucharist?

– He Himself, Jesus Christ. He made the Eucharist.

3 What did Jesus Christ do when He was making the Eucharist?

– He blessed bread and wine and changed them spiritually at that moment. He placed His spirit, His body and blood, in the bread and wine as He elevated them.

4 When was it that Jesus Christ made the Eucharist?

– He made it in the end when He ate with the apostles. In the middle of the night He was arrested when He was going to be killed.

97

20 tanisi kita ki isi kwatakiiso?
20 tânisi kita-kî-isi-kwâtakihisow?

– kita ayamiaw, kita iyewanisiiso, kita wi kisewatisi
– *kita-ayamihâw, kita-iyêwânisihisow, kita-wî-kisêwâtisi-*

totawew wici ayisiyiniwa ka-kitimakisiyit.
itôtawêw wîci-ayisiyiniwa kâ-kitimâkisiyit.

---

18 – KISKINOAMAKEWIN.
18 – KISKINOHAMÂKÊWIN.

1 kekway ani ekaristiwin?
1 kîkwây ani êkaristiwin?

– eoko oma kise manito o nanatawiowin mamawiyes
– *ewako ôma kisê-manitow onanâtawihowin mamawiyês*

e kicitwayik: sesokri e misiweyat ekaristiwinik esi
ê-kihcitwâyik: Sesokri ê-misiwêhayât êkaristiwinihk êsi

manitowit mina esi ayisiyiniwit.
manitowit mîna (ê-)isi ayisiyiniwit.

2 awina ka ki ositat ekaristiwin?
2 awîna kâ-kî-osîhtât êkaristiwin?

– wiya tipiyaw sesokri ekaristiwin kiositaw.
– *wîya tipiyaw Sesokri êkaristiwin kî-osîhtâw.*

3 tanisi ani ka totak sesokri ekaristiwin e wi ositat?
3 tânisi ani kâ-itôtahk Sesokri êkaristiwin ê-wî-osîhtât?

– pakwesikan mina sominapoy e ki saweyitak
– *pahkwêsikan mîna sôminâpoy ê-kî-sawêyihtâhk*

meskocemotaw nayestaw wiyaw, omik, otacakwa
mêskocîmôtaw nayêstaw wîyaw, omihko, otahcâhkwa

kise manitowin kici asteyik ata keyapic pakwesikan
kisê-manitowin kici astêyik âta kêyâpic pahkwêsikan

mina sominapoy esinamik.
mîna sôminâpoy ê-(it)isinamihk.

4 taispi ani ka ki ositat sesokri ekaristiwin?
4 tânispî ani kâ-kî-osîhtât Sesokri êkaristiwin?

– ki ositaw iskwayac ka wicimitisomat
– *kî-osîhtâw iskwayac kâ-wîci-mîcisômât*

otayamiewiyiniwa poskotipiskayik ka ki otitinit e wi
otayamihêwiyiniwa poskotipiskâyik kâ-kî otîtinît ê-wî-

nipait.
nipahiht.

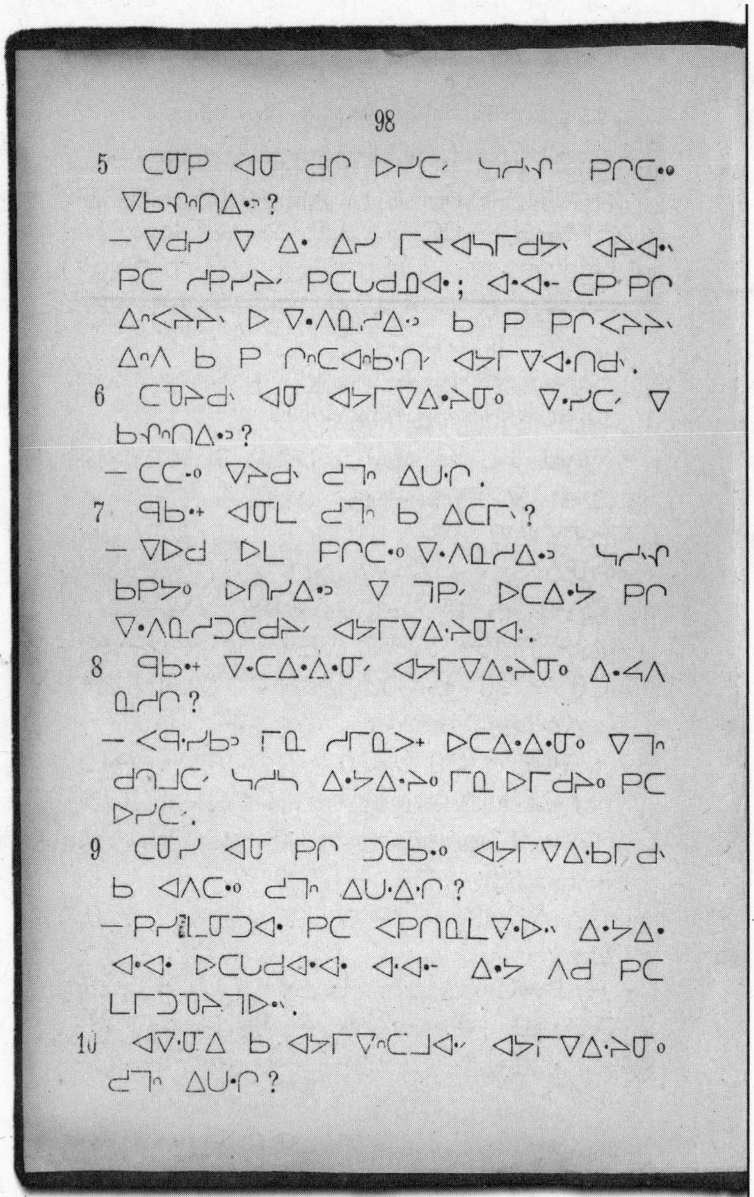

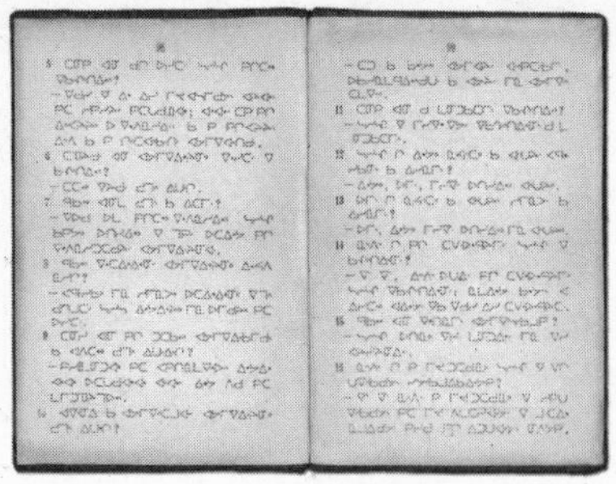

98

5 Why was it that Jesus Christ made the Holy Eucharist?

– This is how He is going to feed us well and satisfy our spirit; when we pray at the Mass, He offers Himself as a sacrifice in the same way He was sacrificed on the cross.

6 When does the priest offer Holy Eucharist?

– Each time he says Mass.

7 What is the Mass called?

– It is the holy offering of the sacrifice of Jesus Christ, of all of the gains He gave to His Father. The priest offers this sacrifice.

8 What does the priest offer when he makes the sacrifice?

– He offers bread and wine: the bread becomes Jesus's body; the wine becomes His blood.

9 How does the Mass affect those who are in the church?

– They will allow God into their body; their spirit especially thinks about Him.

10 Who does the priest pray for when he celebrates the Mass?

5 taniki ani koci ositat sesokri kicitwaw ekaristiwin?
5 tânêhki ani kôci-osîhtât Sesokri kihcitwâw êkaristiwin?

– ekosi e wi isi miyo asamikoyak ayiwak kita sokisiyit
– êkosi ê-wî-isi miyo-asamikoyahk ayiwâk kita-sôkisiyit

kitacakonowa; wawac taki kici ispayiyik
kitahcâkonowa; wâwâc tahki kici-ispayiyik

o wepinasowin ka ki kici payiyik ispi ka ki
owêpinâsowin kâ-kî-kici-payiyik ispî kâ-kî-

cistaaskwatit ayamiewatikok.
cîstahâskwâtiht ayamihêwahtikohk.

6 taneyikok ani ayamiewiyiniw wesitat e karistiwin?
6 tânêyikohk ani ayamihêwiyiniw wêsîtât êkaristiwin?

– tatwaw eyikok lames itweci.
– tahtwâw iyikohk Lames itwêci.

7 kekway anima lames ka itamik?
7 kîkway anima Lames kâ-itamihk?

– eoko oma kicitwaw wepinasowin sesokri kakiyaw
– êwako ôma kihcitwâw wêpinâsowin Sesokri kahkiyaw

otisiwin e mekit otawiya kici wepinasototakoyit
otisiwin ê-mêkit ohtâwiya kici-wêpinâsotôtâkoyit

ayamiewiyiniwa.
ayamihêwiyiniwa.

8 kekway wetawiwinit ayamiewiyiniw wiyepinasoci?
8 kîkway wêtawîwinit ayamihêwiyiniw wêpinâsoci?

– pakwesikan mina sominapoy otawiwiniw
– pahkwêsikan mîna sôminâpoy otâwiwiniw

emeskocemotat sesosa wiyawiyiw mina omikoyiw
ê-mêskocimôtât Sesosa wiyâwîyiw mîna omîhkoyîw

kita ositat.
kita-osîhtât.

9 tanisi ani kici totakwaw ayamiewikamikok ka
9 tânisi ani kici-itôtâkwâw ayamihêwikamikohk kâ-

apitwaw lames itwewici?
âpihtwâw Lames itwêwici?

– kisi manitowa kita pakitinamawewok wiyawi wawa
– kisê-manitowa kita-pakitinamawêwak wiyawi wâwa

otacakowawa wawac wiya piko kita
otahcâhkowâwa wâwâc wiya piko kita-

mamitoneyimewok.
mâmitonêyimêwak.

10 awenii ka ayamiestamowat ayamiewiyiniw lames
10 awînihi kâ-ayamihêstamowât ayamihêwiyiniw Lames

itweci?
itwêci?

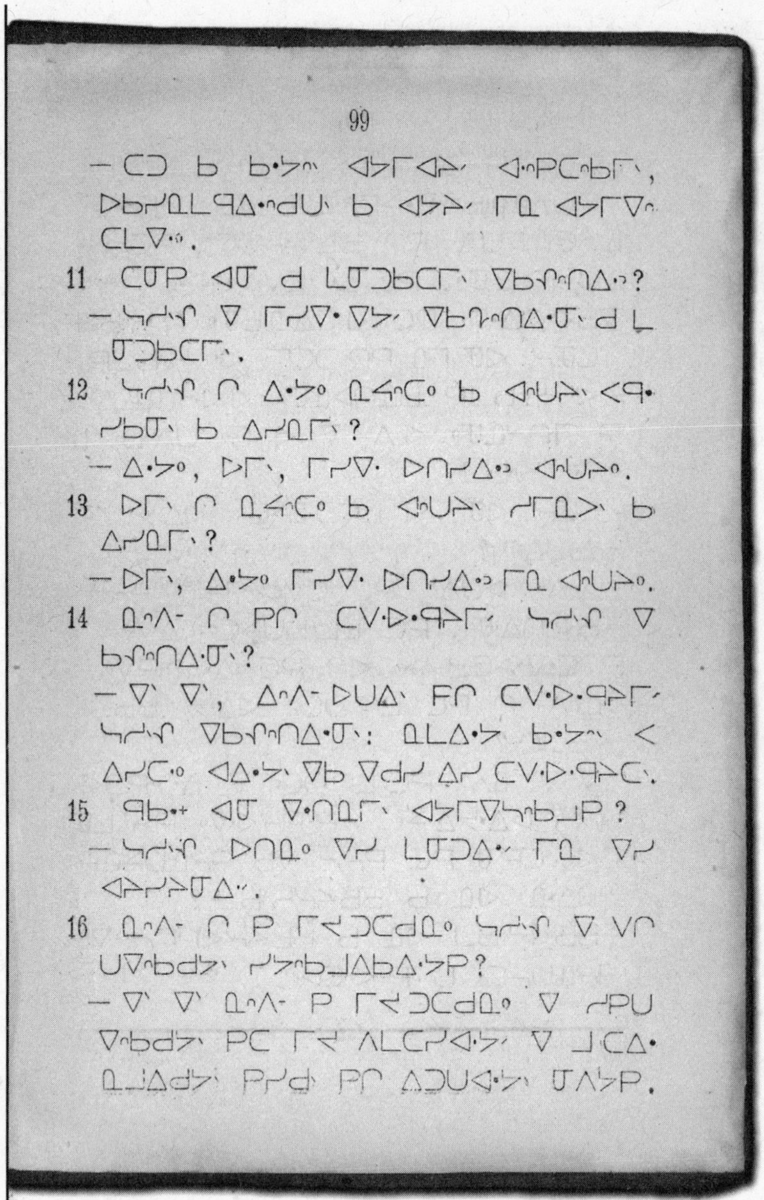

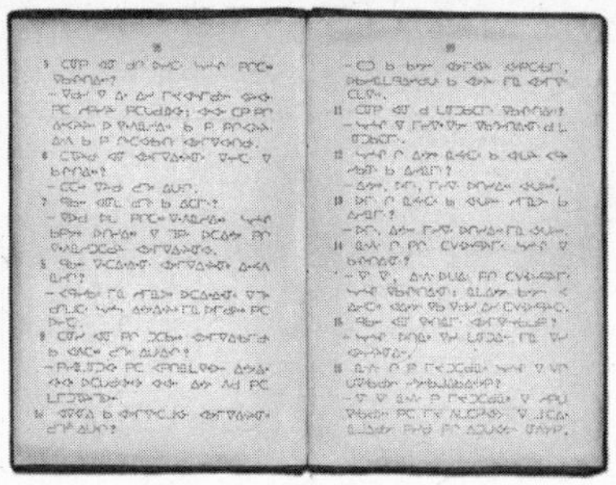

99

– He prays for those who are on earth. Also he prays for those who are in purgatory.

11 Why does one worship the Holy Eucharist?

– Jesus Christ is the Eucharist; that is why it is being worshipped.

12 Is Jesus Christ's body always in the bread when it is being presented?

– Yes, His body is there.

13 Is His blood all the time there, when the wine is being presented?

– Just as His body is there, so is His blood.

14 Will Jesus Christ forever be remembered in the Eucharist?

– Yes, in our heart we always believe in Him. Let us always believe in Jesus Christ.

15 What is being received when one receives Holy Eucharist?

– Jesus Christ is received as He is supernatural and human.

16 Does Jesus Christ help us forever, when He enters our heart when we receive Communion?

– Yes, forever He makes us well, makes us strong-hearted to have a good life. To wish that we might recognize it, and go to Heaven when we die.

99

- tato ka kwayask ayamiayit waskitaskamik,
- *tahto kâ-kwayask-ayamihâyit waskitaskamik,*

okasinamakewiskotek ka ayayit mina
okâsînamâkew-iskotêhk kâ-ayâyit mîna

ayamiestamawew.
ayamihêstamawêw.

11 taniki ani ko manitokatamik ekaristiwin?
11 tânêhki ani kô-manitôkâtamihk êkaristiwin?

- sesokri e misiwe eyat ekarestiwinik ko
- *Sesokri misiwê-ayât êkaristiwinihk kô-*

manitokatamik.
manitôkâtamihk.

12 sesokri ci wiyaw nayestaw ka asteyik pakwesikanik
12 Sesokri cî wîyaw nayêstaw kâ-astêyik pahkwêsikanihk

ka isinamik?
kâ-(it)isinamihk?

- wiyaw, omik, misiwe otisiwin asteyiw.
- *wiyaw, omihko, misiwê otisiwin astêyiw.*

13 omik ci nayestaw ka asteyik sominapok ka
13 omihko cî nayêstaw kâ-astêyik sôminâpôk kâ-

isinamik?
(it)isinamihk?

- omik, wiyaw misiwe otisiwin mina asteyiw.
- *omihko, wîyâw misiwê otisiwin mîna astêyiw.*

14 naspic ci kici tapwewokeyimit sesokri e karistiwinik?
14 nâspic cî kici-tâpwêwakêyimît Sesokri êkaristiwinihk?

- ek ek, ispic oteik kici tapwewokeyimit sesokri
- *êk êk, ispic otehihk kici-tâpwewakêyimît Sesokri*

ekaristiwinik: namawiya kwayask pa isitwaw awiyak
êkaristiwinihk: namâwiya kwayask pâ-isitwâw awiyak

eka ekosi isi tapwewokeyitak.
êkâ êkosi isi tâpwêwakêyihtahk.

15 kekway ani wetinamik ayamiesaskamoki?
15 kîkway ani wêtinamik ayamihêsaskamohki?

- sesokri otinaw esi manitowit mina esi
- *Sesokri otinâw (ê-)isi-manitowit mîna (ê-)isi-*

ayisiyiniwit.
ayisiyinîwit.

16 naspic ci ki miyo totakonaw sesokri e peci
16 nâspic cî kî-miyo-itôtâkonâw Sesokri ê-pêci-

teeskakoyak siyaskamoikawiyaki?
têhêskâkoyahk sîyaskamohikawiyâhki?

- ek ek naspic ki miyototakonaw e sokiteeskakoyak
- *êk êk nâspic kî-miyo-tôtâkonâw ê-sôhkitêhêskâkoyahk*

kita miyo pimatasiwayat e mostawinamoikoyak
kita-miyo-pimâtisiwayat ê-mostawinamohikoyahk

kisikok kici itotewayak nipiyaki.
kîsikohk kici-itohtêwâyahk nipiyâhki.

100

17 ᑕᒋᓱ ᑫ ᑐᑕᒥᐠ ᑭᑎ ᒥᔪᓴᐢᑲᒧᐠ?
— ᑭᑕ ᓇᓇᑲᑕᐌᔨᒥᓱᓇᒋᐤ ᐁᑲ ᑫᑳᐧ ᐁ
ᒪᔭᑕᐠ ᒥᑐᐃᐠ ᑭᑎ ᑲᓇᐌᔨᑕᒥᐠ, ᑭᑕ ᑫᓱ
ᓇᑐᔨᒥᓱᓇᒋᐤ, ᑭᑕ ᐃᐧ ᑕᐯᐧᐅᐧᑫᔨᒪᐤ ᓴᓱᐢ
ᐁᑲᔑᐢᑎᓀᐃᐧᒋᐠ ᑭᑕ ᒍᐢᑕᐃᐧᓇᑲᒋᐤ ᑎ ᓴᐢᑲᒧᐠ
18 ᑕᒋᓱ ᐊᒋ ᒥᓇ ᑭᑎ ᑐᑕᒥᐠ ᐊᐧ ᓴᐢᑲᒧᑭ?
— ᐊᐧ ᓴᐢᑲᒧᑭ ᑲᓇᑎᐅᓇᒋᐤ ᐊᐧᐊᐧ- ᓇᒪᐃᐧᔭ
ᑭ ᒣᑎᓱᓇᒋᐤ ᐊᐢᐱᐣ ᐁ ᐊᐱᑕᐤ ᑌᐱᐢᑲᐠ ᒪ
ᔦᐌᐢ ᓴᐢᑲᒧᐠ.
19 ᑕᒋᓱ ᐊᒋ ᑫ ᒪᒥᑐᒍᔨᑕᐠ ᐊᐃᐧᔭᐠ ᐊᐧ
ᓴᐢᑲᒧᐃᐧᑎ?
— ᐃᐢᐱ- ᐅᑌᐃᐤ ᑭᑕ ᑕᐯᐧᐅᐧᑫᔨᒣᐤ ᓴᓱᓴ
ᐁᑲᔑᐢᑎᓀᐃᐧᒋᐠ, ᑭᑕ ᒪᒪᐢᑲᑌᔨᑕᐨ ᐃᐢᐱ- ᐁ
ᑭᑎᑕᐧᐁᐧᔨᑕᑯᓯᔨᐤ ᐊᑎ ᑭᑕ ᐃᐧ ᓴᑭᐁᐤ.
20 ᓇᐢᐱ- ᑎ ᑭᑕ ᒪᑎ ᑐᑕᐨ ᐊᐃᐧᔭᐠ ᑲᑲᔦᓱ
ᓴᐢᑲᒧᒋ?
— ᐁᐠ ᐁᐠ ᓇᐢᐱ- ᑭᑕ ᒪᑎ ᑐᑕᐨ ᐁ ᐃᐧᔭᑭᑐᐊᐧᐟ
ᓴᓱᓴ ᐅᐃᐧᔭᐃᐧᔨᐤ, ᓱᑭ ᑭᓱᐊᐧᐁᐤ ᑭᓴ ᒪᒋ
ᑐᐊᐧ ᑕᑭᑌ ᑭᑕ ᑭᓱᓱ ᐁᑲ ᑫᓱᓇᑌᔨᑕᑭ.
21 ᐊᐃᐧᓇ ᐊᓇ ᑲ ᑲᑲᔦᓱᓴᐢᑲᒧᐟ?
— ᑲᑲᔦᓱᐢᑲᒧ ᐊᓇ ᑲ ᑲᑲᔦᓱᐊᐦᑎᒥᓱᐟ ᐁᑲ
ᑫᓱᓇᑌᔨᑕᐠ ᑲ ᑭ ᐸᐢᑕᐅᐟ.

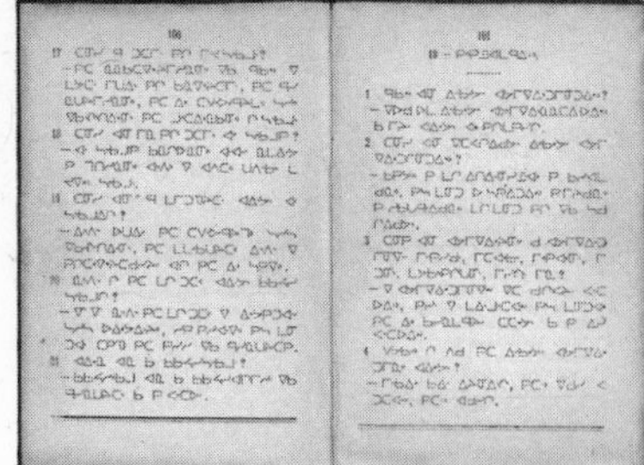

100

17 What is to be done to have a good Communion?
– Everybody will examine themselves carefully, not to do something evil and keep it in the heart but to be sorrowful for oneself, to believe in Jesus. Everybody will wish for Communion.

18 What is also to be done when one receives Communion?
– When one receives Communion, he is purified especially when he has not eaten since midnight before he receives Communion.

19 What is someone to think about when he receives Communion?
– From his heart he will believe in Jesus; he will be amazed by grace. He is becoming more and more holy, he is going to love Jesus.

10 Will someone sin forever if he makes a false Communion?
– Yes, forever he will do evil because he spoils it. This makes God very angry. He always will burn if he is not sorrowful.

21 Who is it that makes a bad Communion?
– He makes a bad Communion if he is not sincere in his prayer. He does not repent for his sins.

100

17 tanisi ke totamik kici miyo saskamok?
17 tânisi kê-tôtamik kici-miyo-saskamôk?

– kita nanakataweyimisonaniw eka kekway e mayatak
– *kita-nânâkatawêyimisonâniw êkâ kîkway ê-mâyâtahk*

miteik kici kanaweyitamik, kita
mitêhihk kici-kanawêyihtamihk, kita-

kesinateyimisonaniw, kita wi tapwewokeyimaw sesos
kêsinâtêyimisonâniw, kita-wî-tâpwêwakêyimâw Sesos

ekaristiwinik kita mostawinakaniw ci saskamok.
êkaristiwinihk kita-mostawinakâniw kici-saskamok.

18 tanisi ani mina kici totamik wa saskamoki?
18 tânisi ani mîna kici-tôtamik wâ-saskamohki?

– wa saskamoki kanacionaniw wawac namawiya ki
– *wâ-saskamôki kanâcohonâniw wâwâc namâwiya kî-*

metisonaniw aspin e apitaw tepiskak mayowes
mîcisonâniw aspin ê-âpihtaw-tipiskâk mayowês

saskamok.
saskamok.

19 tanisi ani ke mamitoneyitak awiyak wa saskamoici?
19 tânisi ani kê-mâmitonêyihtahk awiyak wâ-saskamôhîci?

– ispic oteit kita tapwewokeyimew sesosa ekaristiwinik,
– *ispic otêhit kita-tâpwêwakêyimêw Sesosa êkaristiwinik,*

kita mamaskateyitam ispic e kicitwaweyitakosiyit
kita-mâmaskatêyihtam ispic ê-kihcitwâwêyihtâkosiyit

aci kita wi sakiew.
âci kita-wî-sâkihêw.

20 naspic ci kita maci totam awiyak kakayesisaskamoci?
20 nâspic cî kita-maci-itôtam awiyak kâkayêsisaskamôci?

– ek ek naspic kita maci totam e wiyakitowat sesosa
– *êk êk nâspic kita-maci-itôtam ê-wîyakitowât Sesosa*

owiyawiyiw, soki kisiwaew kise manitowa takine
owîyâwiyiw, sôhki-kisiwahêw kisê-manitowa tahkinê

kita kisiso eka kesinateyitaki.
kita-kîsisow êkâ kêsinatêyihtâki.

21 awina ana ka kakayesisaskamot?
21 awîna ana kâ-kakayêsisaskamot?

– kakayesaskamo ana ka kakayesiacimisot eka
– *kâkayêsaskâmo ana kâ-kakayêsihâcimisot êkâ*

kesinateyitak ka ki pastaot.
kêsinatêyihtahk kâ-kî-pâstâhot.

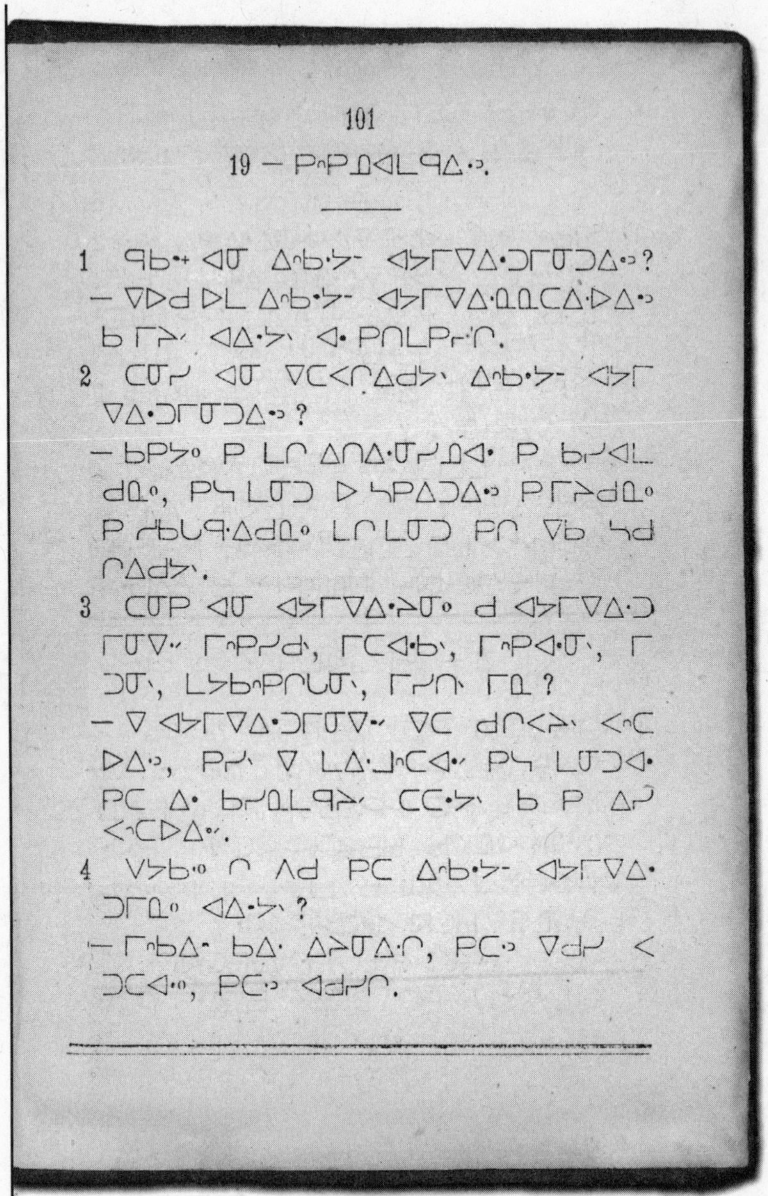

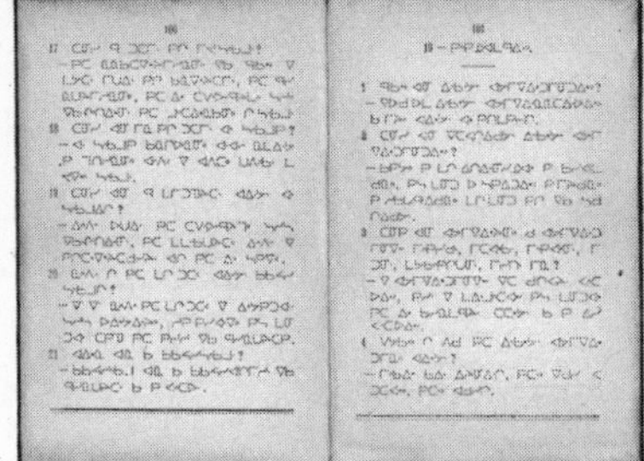

101 19 – LESSON.

1 What is the final and holy anointment?
– At the very end of someone's life, the sacrament is given to someone who is dying.
2 How is that useful to us in the end, the holy anointment?
– God forgives all of our bad sins through His mutual love. He gives to us a strong spirit for the devil not to overpower us.
3 Why does the priest administer holy oil in the eye, in the ear, in the nose, in the mouth, the sole of the foot, and on the leg also?
– He gives Holy Communion and also prays to God to forgive the sins committed from these parts of his body.
4 Can this sacrament happen more than once?
– By chance if he survives, it will be done to him again when he is sick.

19 – KISKINOHAMAKEWIN.
19 – KISKINOHAMÂKÊWIN.

1 kekway ani iskwayac ayamiewitominitowin?
1 kîkwây ani iskwayâc ayamihêwitôminitowin?

– eoko oma iskwayac ayamiewinanatawiowin ka
– êwako ôma iskwayâc ayamihêwinanâtawihowin kâ-

miyit awiyak wa kitimakisici.
miyit awiyak wâ-kitimâkisici.

2 tanisi ani etapaciikoyak iskwayac
2 tânisi ani ê-tâpacihikoyahk iskwayâc

ayamiewitominitowin?
ayamihêwitôminitowin?

– kakiyaw ki maci itiwinisinowa ki kasiamakonaw, kise
– kahkiyaw kimacihtiwinisinawa kikâsîhamâkonaw, kisê-

manito o sakiitowin kimiyikonaw
manitow osâkihitowin kimiyikonaw

ki sokacakweikonaw maci manito kici eka
kisôkahcâhkwêhikonaw maci-manito kici êkâ

sakociikoyak.
sâkocihikoyahk.

3 taniki ani ayamiewiyiniw ko ayamiewitominiwet
3 tânêhki ani ayamihêwiyiniw kô-ayamihêwitôminiwêt

miskisikok, mitawakak, miskiwanik, mitonik,
miskîsikohk, mihtawâkâhk, miskiwanihk, mitônihk,

mayakaskicicanik, misitik mina?
mayakaskicicanihk, misitihk mîna?

– e ayamiewitominiwet eta kocipayik pastaowin,
– ê-ayamihêwitôminiwêt (ê-)ita-kôcipayik pâstâhowin,

kisik e mawimostawat kise manitowa kita wi
kisik ê-mawimôstawât kisê-manitowa kita-wî-

kasinamakeyit tatwayak ka ki isi pastaowit.
kâsînamâkêyit tahtwâyak kâ-kî-isi-pâstâhowît.

4 peyakwaw ci piko kita iskwayac ayamiewitominaw
4 pêyakwâw cî piko kita-iskwayâc ayamihêwitôminâw

awiyak?
awiyak?

– miskawi kawi iyiniwici, kitwam ekosi patotawaw,
– miskawi kâwi-iyiniwici, kîhtwâm êkosi patôtawâw,

kitwam akosici.
kîhtwâm âkosici.

102

20 — ᑭᐢᑭᓄᐊᒪᑫᐃᐧᐣ.

1 ᑫᑳᐧ ᐊᓂ ᐊᔭᒥᐁᐃᐧᔨᓂᐃᐧᐃᓯᐃᑐᐃᐧᐣ ?
— ᐁᐅᑯ ᐅᒪ ᐊᔭᒥᐁᐃᐧᓇᓇᑕᐃᐧᐅᐃᐧᐣ ᑳ ᒥᔨᐟ
ᐊᓇ ᑳ ᐃᐧ ᐊᔭᒥᐁᐃᐧᔨᓂᐃᐧᐃᐧᐟ, ᑭᓭ ᒪᓂᑐᐊᐧ
ᐊᓂᐢᑳ ᑭᒋ ᐊᑐᐢᑳᐊᐧᐤ.
2 ᑖᓂᓯ ᑳ ᑭ ᐃᓯ ᒪᒪᑕᐃᐧᐊᐧ ᑭᓭ ᒪᓂᑐ
ᐊᔭᒥᐁᐃᐧᔨᓂᐊᐧ ?
— ᑭ ᐃᓯ ᒪᒪᑕᐃᐧᐁᐤ ᒦᓯᐍ ᑭᒋ ᐸᐸᒥᑭᐢ
ᑫᔮᑕᒨᐃᐧᐁᐧᔮᐟ, ᑭᒋ ᑳᓯᓇᒪᐊᐧᔮᐟ ᐃᐧᒋ ᐊᔮ
ᓯᔨᓂᐊᐧ ᐅ ᒪᒋ ᐃᑎᐃᐧᓂᔨᐊᐧᐊᐧ, ᒦᓯᐍ ᑭᒋ
ᐃᓯ ᒥᔪ ᑐᑕᐊᐧᔮᐟ ᒥᓇ ᑭᒋ ᓱᓂᔮᐤ ᐃᑌᐧᔮᐟ.

21 — ᑭᐢᑭᓄᐊᒪᑫᐃᐧᐣ.

1 ᑫᑳᐧ ᐊᓂ ᐊᔭᒥᐁᐃᐧᑭᑐᐃᐧᐣ ?
— ᐁᐅᑯ ᐅᒪ ᐊᔭᒥᐁᐃᐧᓇᓇᑕᐃᐧᐅᐃᐧᐣ ᐯᔭᐠ
ᑳ ᒥᔨᒋᐠ ᑳ ᑭᒋ ᐃᐧᑭᑕᐃᑕᐤ ᑭᒋ ᓴᑭᐃᑐᒋᐠ
ᒥᓇ ᑭᒋ ᓂᑕ ᐅᐱᑭᐊᑕᐤ ᐅᑕᐊᐧᓯᒥᓯᐊᐧᐊᐧ
ᐁᔭᐊᐧᑕᐃᐧ.
2 ᐊᐃᐧᓇ ᐍᑭᑕᐊᐧ ᐅᑕᔭᒥᐊᐊᐧ ?
— ᐊᔭᒥᐁᐃᐧᔨᓂᐅᐦ ᑳ ᑭᒋ ᐃᐧᑭᑕᐊᒋᐠ.
3 ᑖᓂᓯ ᐊᓂ ᑭᒋ ᑐᑲᐤ ᑳ ᐃᐧ ᑭᒋ ᐃᐧᑭ
ᑕᐃᑕᐤ ?
— ᑭᑕ ᐃᐧ ᑫᓯᓇᑌᔨᒥᓱᐦ, ᒥᑐᓂ ᑭᑕ ᐊᒋ

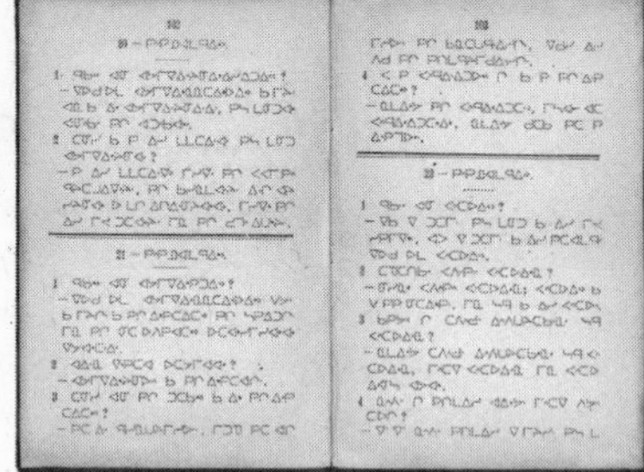

20 – LESSON.

1 What is this Holy Order?
– This is the sacrament that is given to the person who is going to be a priest, in which God works with him.
2 What spiritual gifts does God give the priest?
– He is made holy, to go all over the world and spread the gospel, to forgive his people of their sins, to worship God, and to say Mass.

21 – LESSON.

1 What is marriage?
– This is a sacred union of two people to love each other and to be good at raising their children when they have them.
2 Who conducts the marriage for the worshippers?
– The priest conducts the marriage.
3 What is done with them when they are going to get married?
– They are going to be very thoughtful. They will

20 – KISKINOAMAKEWIN.
20 – KISKINOHAMÂKÊWIN.

1 kekway ani ayamiewiyiniwiisiitowin?
1 kîkwây ani ayamihêwiyiniwihisihitowin?

– eoko oma ayamiewinanatawiowin ka miyit ana ka
– êwako ôma ayamihêwinanâtawihowin kâ-miyit ana kâ-

wi ayamiewiyiniwiit, kise manitowa aniskac kici
wî-ayamihêwiyiniwihiht, kisê-manitowa âniskac kici-

atoskawat.
atoskawât.

2 tanisi ka ki isi mamatawiat kise manito
2 tânisi kâ-kî-isi-mamâhtâwihât kisê-manitow

ayamiewiyiniwa?
ayamihêwiyiniwa?

– ki isi mamatawiew misiwe kici
– kî-isi-mamâhtâwihew misiwê kici-

papamikiskeyitamoiweyit, kici kasinamawayit wici
papâmi-kiskêyihtamohiwêyit, kici-kâsînamawâyit wîci-

ayisiyiniwa o maci itiwiniyiwawa, misiwe kici isi
ayisiyiniwa omacihtiwiniyiwâwa, misiwê kici-isi-

miyo totawayit mina kici lames itweyit.
miyo-itôtawâyit mîna kici-Lames itwêyit.

21 – KISKINOAMAKEWIN.
21 – KISKINOHAMÂKÊWIN.

1 kekway ani ayamiewikitowin?
1 kîkwây ani ayamihêwîkîtôwin?

– eoko oma ayamiewinanatawiowin peyak ka miyicik
– êwako ôma ayamihêwinanâtawihowin pêyak kâ-miyicik

ka kici wikitaitwaw kici sakiitocik mina kici nita
kâ-kihci-wîkihtahitwâw kici-sâkihitocik mîna kici-nihtâ-

opikiatwaw otawasimisiwawa eyawatwawi.
ohpikihâtwâw otawâsimisiwâwa ayâwâtwâwi.

2 awina wekitaat otayamiawa?
2 awîna wêkîtahât otayamihâwa?

– ayamiewiyiniwok ka kici wikitaacik.
– ayamihêwiyiniwak kâ-kihci-wîkihtahâcik.

3 tanisi ani kici totakwaw ka wi kici wikitaitwaw?
3 tânisi ani kici-itôtakwâw kâ-wî-kihci-wîkihtahitwâw?

– kita wi kesinateyimisowok, mitone kita aci
– kita-wî-kêsinâtêyimisowak, mitonê kita-âci

103

ᒥᓯᐅ" ᑭᑎ ᑲᓇᑕᑌᑫᐃᓯᑎᐠ, ᐁᑯᓯ ᐃᓯ
ᐱᑯ ᑭᑎ ᑭᑎᒪᑫᔨᒥᑯᐃᓯᑎᐠ.

4 ᐸ ᑭ ᐸᐢᑫᐃᐃᑐᐅ" ᑎ ᑲ ᑭ ᑭᑎ ᐃᑭ ᑕᐃᑕᐤ?

— ᓇᒪᐃᔭ ᑭᑎ ᐸᐢᑫᐃᐃᑐᑕᐠ, ᒥᓴᐧ ᐊᑕ ᐸᐢᑫᐃᐃᑐᑕᐃ, ᓇᒪᐃᔭ ᑯᑕᑲ ᑭᑕ ᑭ ᐃᑭᒣᑐ".

22 — ᑭᐢᑭᓄᐊᒪᑫᐃᐤ.

1 ᑫᑳ ᐊᑐ ᐸᐢᑕᐅᐃᐤ?

— ᐁᑲ ᐁ ᑐᑕᒥᐠ ᑭᓭ ᒪᓂᑐ ᑲ ᐃᓯ ᒥᓭ ᓯᑭᒥᐁᐤ, ᐊᐳ ᐁ ᑐᑕᒥᐠ ᑲ ᐃᓯ ᑭᑕᐊᒪᑫ ᐁᐅᑯ ᐅᒪ ᐸᐢᑕᐅᐃᐤ.

2 ᑕᓂᑕᑎᑲᐧ ᐸᐱᑭᐣ ᐸᐢᑕᐅᐃᓇ?

— ᓂᓱᓇᐧ ᐸᐱᑭᐣ ᐸᐢᑕᐅᐃᓇ; ᐸᐢᑕᐅᐃᐤ ᑲ ᐯ ᑭᑭ ᓂᑕᐃᑭᐠ, ᒥᓇ ᓴᑫ ᑲ ᐃᓯ ᐸᐢᑕᐅᐠ.

3 ᑲᑭᔭᐤ ᑎ ᑕᐱᐢᑯᐟ ᐃᐢᐱᑎᔨᑕᑲᐧᓇᐧ ᓴᑫ ᐸᐢᑕᐅᐃᓇ?

— ᓇᒪᐃᔭ ᑕᐱᐢᑯᐟ ᐃᐢᐱᑎᔨᑕᑲᐧᓇᐧ ᓴᑫ ᐸᐢᑕᐅᐃᓇ, ᒥᐢᑕᐁ ᐸᐢᑕᐅᐃᓇ ᒥᓇ ᐸᐢᑕᐅ ᐃᐧᓂᓴ ᐊᔭᐊᐧ.

4 ᓇᐢᐱᐨ ᑎ ᑭᑎᒪᐃᓱ ᐊᐃᐧᔭᐠ ᒥᐢᑕᐁ ᐱᔭᐣ ᑕᐅᑎ?

— ᐁᐠ ᐁᐠ ᓇᐢᐱᐨ ᑭᑎᒪᐃᓱ ᐁᒥᔨᓱᐠ ᑭᓭ ᒪ

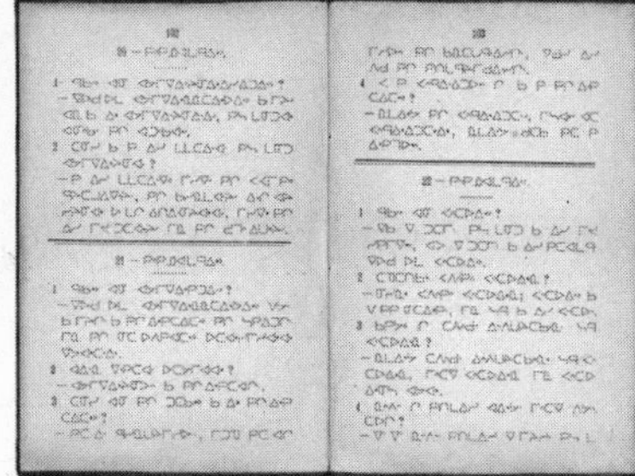

103 confess to prepare themselves to be holy. This is how they will have a good spirit.

4 Do some of them separate when they have been married?

– They will not separate; if they separate no other will marry them.

22 – LESSON.

1 What is sin?

– Sin is not doing what God encourages or else doing what He forbids.

2 How many separate sins are there?

– There are two separate sins: sin that one is born with, also sin that one commits.

3 Is it considered a good thing when one sins willingly?

– Willingly doing sin is not highly regarded. There are many kinds of sin; there are small sins also.

4 Does someone oppress himself when he has sinned many times?

– Yes, forever he oppresses himself. He refuses the Holy

103 misowok kici kanatacakweisocik, ekosi isi piko kici
misowak kici-kanatahcâhkwêhisocik, êkosi isi piko kici-

kitimakeyimikowisicik.
kitimâkêyimikowisicik.

4 pa ki paskewiitowok ci ka ki kici wikitaitwaw?
4 pahki paskêwihitowak cî kâ-kî-kihci wîkihtahitwâw?

– namawiya kici paskewiitotwaw, misawac ata
– namâwiya kici-paskêwihitôtwâw, misawâc âta

paskewiitotwawi, namawiya kotaka kita ki
paskêwihitôtwâwi, namâwiya kotaka kita kî-

wikimewok.
wîkimêwak.

---

22 – KISKINOAMAKEWIN.

22 – KISKINOHAMÂKÊWIN.

1 kekway ani pastaowin?
1 kîkwây ani pâstâhowin?

– eka e totamik kise manito ka isi miyosikimiwet,
– êkâ ê-itôtamihk kisê-manitow kâ-isi-miyo-sîhkimiwêt,

apo e totamik ka isi kitaamaket eoko oma
ahpô e-itôtamihk kâ-isi-kitahâmâkêt êwako ôma

pastaowin.
pâstâhowin.

2 tanetatikwa papiskis pastaowina?
2 tânêtâtikwa papiskis pâstâhowina?

– nisinwa papiskis pastaowina; pastaowin ka pe kiki
– nîsinwa pâpiskis pâstâhowina; pâstâhowin kâ pê-kiki-

nitawikik, mina seke ka isi pastaok.
nihtâwikihk, mîna sêhkê kâ-isi-pâstâhok.

3 kakiyaw ci tapiskoc ispiteyitakwanwa seke
3 kahkiyaw cî tâpiskôc ispîhtêyihtâkwanwa sêhkê

pastaowina?
pâstâhowin?

– namawiy tapiskoc ispiteyitakwanwa seke
– namâwiya tâpiskôc ispîhtêyihtâkwanwa sêhkê

pastaowina, mistae pastaowina mina pastaowinisa
pâstâhowina, mistahi pâstâhowina mîna pâstâhowinisa

ayawa.
ayâwa.

4 naspic ci kitimaiso awiyak mistae piyastaoci?
4 nâspic cî kitimâhisow awiyak mistahi piyâstahoci?

– ek ek naspic kitimaiso e miyisot kise ma
– êk êk nâspic kitimâhisow ê-miyisot kisê-ma

104

ᒉᑕᐊᐧ ᑕᑭᑌ ᑭᒋ ᐸᑳᐧᑎᑯᐟ, ᐊᐧᐊᐧ- ᑭᒋ
ᑭᓯᓯᐃᑯᐟ ᒪᒋ ᒪᒉᑐᐊᐧ.
5 ᐱᑯ ᐁ ᐸᐣᑕᑐᓯᐠ ᒥᓯᐁᐧ ᒋ ᐊᐧᒉᑕᒉᐊᐧᐤ
ᑭᓴ ᒪᒉᑐ ᐅ ᓴᑭᐃᑐᐃᐧᐤ?
— ᐱᑯ ᐁ ᐸᐣᑕᑐᓯᐠ ᘛᒪᐃᐧᔭ ᐊᑕᐃᐧᔭ ᒥᓯᐁᐧ
ᐊᐧᒉᑕᒉᐊᐧᐤ ᑭᓴ ᒪᒉᑐ ᐅ ᓴᑭᐃᑐᐃᐧᐤ, ᒪᑲ
ᑫᔮᐁᐧᐦ ᑭᑕ ᘛᘛᑲᑕᐁᐧᔮᑕᑲᒉᐊᐧᐤ ᑭᒋ ᐁᑲ
ᐊᐳ ᐸᐣᑕᑐᓯᐠ, ᒋᑫᒪ ᑭᓴ ᒪᒉᑐ ᐃᓭᐱᑌ
ᐁ ᐸᑳᐧᑕᐠ ᘛᘛᑐᐠ ᑲ ᐃᓯ ᐸᐣᑕᑐᐃᐧᐠ.
6 ᐸ ᑭ ᑐᑕᑲᒉᐊᐧᐤ ᒋ ᑭᒋ ᐁᑲ ᐸᐣᑕᑐᐠ
ᑭᓴ ᒪᒉᑐ ᐁᑲ ᒉᓯᑲᒪᑫᒋ?
— ᘛᒪᐃᐧᔭ ᑭᒋ ᑭ ᑐᑕᒥᐠ, ᑕᓯᐸᐧ ᑭᓴ ᒪᒉᑐ
ᑕᑭ ᐁ ᒪᐃᐧᒧᐣᑕᐟ ᑭᑕ ᐃᐧ ᒉᓯᑲᒪᑫᐟ ᑭᒋ
ᐁᑲ ᐸᐣᑕᑐᐃᐧᐠ.
7 ᑕᑌᑕᑎᑲᐧ ᒥᐣᑕᐁ ᐸᐣᑕᑐᐃᐧᘛ?
— ᑌᐸᑯᑊ ᐃᑕᑎᘛᐧ: ᒪᒥᑎᓯᐃᐧᐤ, ᓴᓴᑭᓯᐃᐧᐤ,
ᐱᓯᑳᐧᑎᓯᐃᐧᐤ, ᓴᐊᐧᘛᑫᔮᒧᐃᐧᐤ, ᑳᓴᑫᐃᐧᐤ,
ᑭᓯᐊᐧᓯᐃᐧᐤ, ᑭᑎᒥᐃᐧᐤ.
8 ᑕᒉᑭ ᐊᔮᐊᐧᐦ ᒥᐣᑕᐁ ᐸᐣᑕᑐᐃᐧᘛ ᑯ ᐃᓯ
ᐃᑳᑌᑭ ᐊᒉᐃ?
— ᐊᔮᐊᐧᐦ ᒥᐣᑕᐁ ᐸᐣᑕᑐᐃᐧᘛ ᑯ ᐃᓯᐃᑳᑌᑭ
ᐁᐅᑯᒉ ᑯᒋᐸᔮᑳᐧᐤ ᘛᘛᑐᐠ ᐸᐣᑕᑐᐃᐧᘛ.

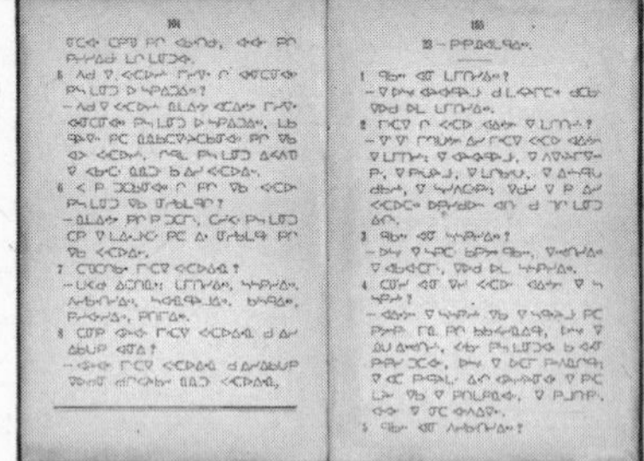

104 Spirit all the time and risks being burned by the devil.

5 Have sinners lost God's love forever?

– Sinning is the loss of God's love. They must examine their lives even if they think they do not sin. God hates most the different ways that they sin.

6 When one does not sin, is God working together with that person?

– God is always being prayed to, to work together with Him who does not sin.

7 How many serious sins are there?

– There are seven: pride, stinginess, adultery, envy, greed, anger, and laziness.

8 Why are those ones called serious sins?

– They are called serious sins because of where the different sins come from.

104

nitowa takine kici pakwatikot, wawac kici kisisoikot
nitowa tahkinê kici-pakwâtikot, wâwâc kici-kîsisohikot

maci manitowa.
maci-manitowa.

5 piko e pastaosik misiwe ci wanitoniwan kise manito
5 piko ê-pâstâhocik misiwê kici wanîtâniwan kisê-manitow

o sakiitowin?
osâkihitowin?

– piko e pastaosik namawiya atawiya misiwe
– piko ê-pâstâhocik namâwiya atawiya misiwê

wanitaniwan kise manito o sakiitowin, maka keyiwek
wanîtâniwan kisê-manitow osâkihitowin, mâka kêyiwêk

kita nanakataweyitakaniwan kici eka apo pastaosik,
kita-nânâkatawêyihtâkâniwan kici êkâ ahpô pâstâhocik,

cikema kise manito iyepine e pakwatak nanatok ka
cikêma kisê-manitow iyêpinê ê-pâkwatahk nanâtohk kâ-

isi pastaowit.
isi-pâstâhowît.

6 pa ki totakaniwan ci kici eka pastaok kise manito eka
6 pa-ki-tôtâkâniwan cî kici êkâ pâstâhok kisê-manitow êkâ

nisokamakeci?
nîsôhkamâkêci?

– namawiya kici ki totamik, tasipwa kise manito taki
– namâwiya kici kî-tôtamik, tâsipwâ kisê-manitow tahki

e mawimostat kita wi nisokamaket kici eka
ê-mawimôstât kita wî-nîsôhkamâkêt kici êkâ

pastaowit.
pâstâhowiht.

7 tanetatikwa mistae pastaowina?
7 tânêtâtikwa mistahi ê-pâstâhowina?

– tepakop itatinwa: mamitisiwin, sasakisiwin,
– têpahkohp itâtinwa: mamihcisiwin, sasâkisîwin,

pisikwatisiwin, sawanakeyimowin, kasakewin,
pisikwâtisiwin, sâwanakêyimowin, kâsakêwin,

kisiwasiwin, kitimiwin.
kisiwâsiwin, kîtimiwin.

8 taniki ayiwak mistae pastaowina ko isi ikateki
8 tânêhki ayiwâk mistahi pâstâhowina kô-isiyihkâtêki

anii?
anihi?

– ayiwak mistae pastaowina ko isi ikateki eokoni
– ayiwâk mistahi pâstâhowina kô-isiyihkâtêki êwakoni

koci payikwaw nanatok pastaowina.
koci-payikwâw nanâtohk pâstâhowina.

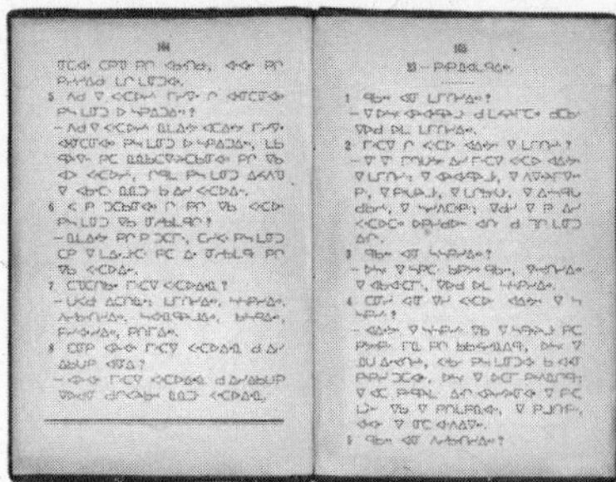

105

23 – LESSON.

1 What is pride?

– When someone has too much pride they despise others. This is pride.

2 Does someone sin seriously who is conceited?

– Yes, in many ways someone has sinned seriously who is conceited: being proud, being rude, being haughty; he brags; he is a crook; a cheat, one who does not listen. This is how the angels had sinned and why some are devils.

3 What is greed?

– Today, everything is desired, wealth is being wished for; this is greed.

4 How is it that someone sins who is greedy?

– Someone who is selfish does not hesitate to lie and is a big cheater, because he wants to acquire wealth, and on top of it all does this to God by losing sight of Him because he is busy acquiring wealth. Although he knows his people, he is bad to them and does not respect them; he is a thief and on top of it all he is especially good at mistreating his people.

5 What is adultery?

23 – KISKINOAMAKEWIN.
23 – KISKINOHAMÂKÊWIN.

---

1 kekway ani mamitisiwin?
1 kîkwây ani mamihcisiwin?

– e osam ayiwakeyimok ko mayeyimitwaw kotakak
– ê-osâm-ayiwakêyimok kô-mayêyimitwâw kotakak

eoko oma mamitisiwin.
êwako ôma mamihcisiwin.

2 mistae ci pastao awiyak e mamitisit?
2 mistahi cî pâstâhow awiyak ê-mamihcisit?

– ek ek micetweyak isi mistae pastao awiyak
– êk êk mihcêtwêyahk isi mistahi pâstâhow awiyak

e mamitisit: e ayiwakeyimot, e piweyimiweskit,
ê-mamihcisit: ê-ayiwakêyimot, ê-pîwêyimiwêskit,

e kisteyimot, e macikastet, e wisakecakokasot,
ê-kistêyimot, ê-macikâstêt, ê-wîsâkêcâkôkâsot,

e sasipitaski; ekosi e ki isi pastaotwaw okisikowok atit
ê-sasîpîtâski; êkosi ê-kî-isi pâstâhotwâw okîsikowak âtiht

ko meci manito wicik.
ko-maci-manitowicik.

3 kekway ani sasakisiwin?
3 kîkwây ani sasâkisiwin?

– osam e sakitak kakiyaw kekway, weyotisiwin
– osâm ê-sâkihtâk kahkiyaw kîkway, wiyotisiwiin

e akawatamik, eoko oma sasakisiwin.
ê-akâwâhtamihk, êwako ôma sasâkisiwin.

4 tanisi ani esi pastaot awiyak e sasakisit?
4 tânisi ani (ê-)isi pâstâhot awiyak ê-sasâkisît?

– awiyak e sasakisit eka e sakweyimot kita kiyaskit
– awiyak ê-sasâkisît êkâ ê-sâkwêyimot kita-kiyâskit

mina kici kakayesinaiket, osam e note wiyotisit,
mîna kici-kakayêsinâhikêt, osâm ê-nohtê-wiyôtisit,

paskac kise manitowa ka wani kiskisi totawat, osam
pâskac kisê-manitow kâ wanikiskisitôtawât, osâm

e otami kispinaciket; e ata kiskeyimat wici ayisiyiniwa
ê-otami-kîspinacikêt; ê-âta-kiskêyimât wîci-ayisiyiniwa

e kita mayit eka e kitimakinawat, e kimotiskit, wawac
ê-kita-mayît êkâ ê-kitimâkinawât, ê-kimotiskît, wâwâc

e nita aspiiwet.
ê-nihtâ-aspihiwêt.

5 kekway ani pisikwatisiwin?
5 kîkwây ani pisikwâtisiwin?

106

– When they make fools out of themselves even today, and when they make a fool of some people, this is adultery.

6 Is adultery always a serious sin?

– Yes, adultery is a serious sin. For that reason at one time God had drowned all people that committed adultery; also in the beginning he burned five cities because the young people committed adultery there.

7 What is jealousy?

– When one is lonely or else angry that someone else is being more seen or is more highly regarded or sympathized with, this is jealousy.

8 Is there only one form of jealousy?

– It is not just one, there are many forms: the one who sins through jealousy, he is good at speaking badly. He despises his own people; especially he likes to speak badly when he is despised because he is happy when he does evil. He despises the way he lives although it is not bad.

9 What is greediness?

– If one eats a lot also and drinks lots, this is greediness.

106

– e metawakatisok maci anok, apo ekotawik
– *ê-mêtawâkâtisok mâci anohc, ahpô êkotawik*

e metawakatit awiyak eoko oma pisikwatisiwin.
ê-mêtawâkâtiht awiyak êwako ôma pisikwâtisiwin.

6 naspic ci mistae pastaowin pisikwatisiwin?
6 nâspic cî mistahi pâstâhowin pisikwâtisiwin?

– ek ek mistae pastaowin pisikwatisiwin tasipwa
– *êk êk mistahi pâstâhowin pisikwâtisiwin tâsipwâ*

peyakwaw kise manito e ki mecinistapaweyat
pêyakwâw kisê-manitow ê-kî-mêscinistapawêyât

ayisiyiniwa e pisikwatisiyit, mina astamispi e ki
ayisiyiniwa ê-pisikwâtisiyit, mîna astamîspî ê-kî-

mecikasak niyanan otenawa, osam e pisikwatisiyit
mêscîkasâhk niyânan ôtênawa, osâm ê-pisikwâtisiyit

ekote ka otaskiyit.
êkotê kâ-otaskiyit.

7 kekway ani sawanakeyimowin?
7 kîkwây ani sawânakêyimowin?

– e kaskeyitamik apo e kisiwasik weyapamici awiyak
– *ê-kaskêyihtamihk ahpô ê-kisiwâsik wêyâpamîci awiyak*

ayiwak e kisteyimit e kitimakeyimikowisit apo, eoko
ayiwâk ê-kistêyimiht ê-kitimâkêyimikowisit ahpô, êwako

oma sawanakeyimowin.
ôma sawânêkêyimowin.

8 peyakwaniyiw ci ka sawanakeyimoskit o maci itiwin?
8 pêyakwaniyiw cî kâ-sawânakêyimoskit omacihtiwin?

– namawiya peyakwaniyiw, ayiwak misceniyiwa ka
– *namâwiya pêyakwaniyiw, ayiwâk miscêniyiwa kâ-*

sawanakeyimoskit o maci itiwina, e nita maci
sawânakêyimoskit omacihtiwina, ê-nihtâ-maci-

ayimomat e piweyimat wici ayisiyiniwa, wawac
âyimômât ê-pîwêyimât wîci-ayisiyiniwa, wâwâc

e miweyitak meci ayimomici peweyimici, osam
ê-miywêyihtahk maci-âyimômîci pîwêyimîci, osâm

e ataminat meci nakiskamasoyici; e piweyitamwat
ê-âtaminât maci-nakiskamâsoyici; ê-pîwêyitamwât

otitaciowiniyiw, ata eka e mayataniyik.
otitacihowinîyiw, âta êkâ ê-mâyâtaniyik.

9 kekway ani kasakewin?
9 kîkwây ani kâsakêwin?

– osam e mistae mitisok mina osam mistae
– *osâm ê-mistahi mîcisohk mîna osâm mistahi*

e minikwek, eoko oma kasakewin.
ê-minihkwêk, êwako ôma kâsakêwin.

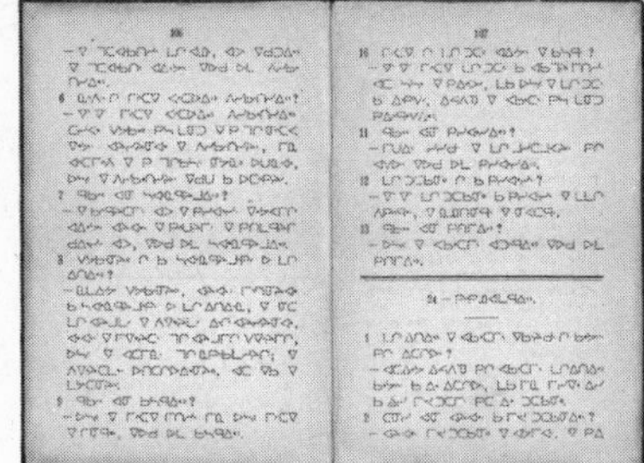

107

10 Does someone do much evil when he is greedy?

– Yes, he does lots of evil because he keeps eating although he is full already, and because he did evil, he likes to drink a lot. God hates drunkenness.

11 What is anger?

– All of a sudden in the heart there is a bad feeling for him; he seeks revenge. This is anger.

12 Does one do evil when one is angry?

– Yes, everyone does evil when he is angry: there is evil talk, there is fighting; there is killing.

13 What is laziness?

– When work is hated, this is laziness.

---

24 – LESSON.

1 If they hate sin very much, do they live life properly?

– They must hate sin to live life properly and behave well. Everyone will be greedy.

2 How do we do a good deed?

– More good is done for one who is praying

10 mistae ci maci totam awiyak e kasaket?
10 mistahi cî maci-itôtam awiyak ê-kâskakêt?

– ek ek mistae maci totam ka akameyimitisot ata sasay
– êk êk mistahi maci-itôtam kâ-âhkamêyimîcisot âta sâsay

e kiispot, maka osam e maci totak ka wikipet, iyepine
ê-kîspot, mâka osâm ê-maci-itôtahk kâ-wîkipêt, iyêpinê

e pakwatak kise manito kiiskwepewin.
ê-pakwâtahk kisê-manitow kîskwêpêwin.

11 kekway ani kisiwasiwin?
11 kîkwây ani kisiwâsiwin?

– miteik sisikoc e maci mositamopayik kici apeok
– mitêhihk sisikôc ê-maci-môsîtamopayik kici-apêhok

eoko oma kisiwasiwin.
êwako ôma kisiwâsiwin.

12 maci totakaniw ci ka kisiwasik?
12 maci-itôtakâniw cî kâ-kisiwâsihk?

– ek ek maci totakaniw ka kisiwasik e
– êk êk maci-itôtakâniw kâ-kisiwâsik ê-

mamacipikiskwek, e nanotinikek e nipatakek.
mâmaci-pîkiskwêhk, ê-nânotinikêhk ê-nipâtâhkêk.

13 kekway ani kitimiwin?
13 kîkwây ani kîtimiwin?

– osam e pakwatamik atoskewin eoko oma kitimiwin.
– osâm ê-pâkwâtamik atoskêwin êwako ôma kîtimiwin.

---

24 – KISKINOAMAKEWIN.
24 – KISKINOHAMÂKÊWIN.

1 maci itiwin e pakwatamik ekwa yikok ci kwayask kici
1 macihtiwin ê-pakwâtamihk êkwayikohk cî kwayask kici-

itaciok?
itâcihok?

– atawiya iyepine kici pakwatamik maciitiwin kwayask
– atawiya iyêpinê kici-pakwâtamihk macihtiwin kwayask

ka wi itaciok, maka mina misiwe isi ka isi miyo
kâ-wî-itâcihok mâka mîna misiwê isi kâ-isi-miyo-

totamik kita wi totakaniw.
itôtamihk kita-wî-tôtakâniw.

2 tanisi ani ayiwak ka miyo totakaniwik?
2 tânisi ani ayiwâk kâ-miyo-tôtakâniwik?

– ayiwak miyo totakaniw e ayamiak,
– ayiwâk miyo-itôtakâniw ê-ayamihâhk,

108

ᑯᓯᒧᐃᓯᐠ, ᐁ ᑭᓭᐚᑎᓯᐠ, ᐁᑯᓯ ᐁ ᐃᑌᐧ
ᓭᓯᐣ:
1 ᒥᔪ ᓴᐌᔮᑕᑯᓯᐤ ᐊᐃᐧᔾ ᐁ ᐊᑕ ᑮᑕᒪᐟ
ᑫᔦᐌᐦ ᐁ ᒥᐌᔮᑕᐠ ᐁᑯᓯ ᐁ ᐃᑌᔨᒥᑯᐃᐧᓯᐟ.
2 ᒥᔪᓴᐌᔮᑕᑯᓯᐤ ᐊᐃᐧᔾ ᐁ ᒥᔪᑌᐃᐟ ᐁᑲ
ᑳ ᐃᐧ ᑭᓯᐚᓯᐟ ᐁ ᐊᑕ ᒪᔮᑐᑕᐟ.
3 ᒥᔪ ᓴᐌᔮᑕᑯᓯᐤ ᐊᐃᐧᔾ ᐁ ᑫᓯᓇᑌᔮᑕᐠ
ᐁ ᑭ ᒫᒋ ᑐᑕᐠ ᑭᓭ ᒪᓂᑐᐘ ᐁ ᑭ ᑭᓯᐘᐚᐟ.
4 ᒥᔪ ᓴᐌᔮᑕᑯᓯᐤ ᐊᐃᐧᔾ ᐁᑲ ᐃᐧᑳ ᐁ
ᑳᑫᐧᒋᓯᐘᐟ ᐃᐧᒋ ᐊᔮᓯᔮᓂᐘ ᐋᐚ ᐁ ᒥᔪ
ᓇᓇᑲᑕᐌᔮᑕᐠ ᑭᓯ ᒪᓂᑐᐘ ᑳ ᐃᓯ ᒥᔪ
ᓯᑭᒥᑯᐟ.
5 ᒥᔪ ᓴᐌᔮᒥᑯᓯᐤ ᐊᐃᐧᔾ ᐁ ᓂᑕ ᑭᑎᒪᑭ
ᓇᐚᐧ ᐃᐧᒋ ᐊᔮᓯᔮᓂᐘ ᑫᑎᒪᑭᓯᔮᒋ.
6 ᒥᔪ ᓴᐌᔮᑕᑯᓯᐤ ᐊᐃᐧᔾ ᐁ ᑳᓇᒋ ᐱᒪᑎᓯᐟ
ᐁ ᐸᑳᐧᑕᐠ ᐱᓯᑳᐧᑎᓯᐃᐧᐣ ᐱᓯᑳᐧᒋᒥᑐᓃᔮᒋᑳᐣ
ᐱᓯᑳᐧᒋᑭᓭᐃᐧᐣ.
7 ᒥᔪᓴᐌᔮᑕᑯᓯᐤ ᐊᐃᐧᔾ ᐁᑲ ᐁ ᑭᓯᐘᓯᐢᑭᐟ.
8 ᒥᔪ ᓴᐌᔮᑕᑯᓯᐤ ᐊᐃᐧᔾ ᐸᑳᐧᓇᑕ ᑫᐧᑕᑭ
ᒥᒋ ᐯᐌᔮᒥᒋ.

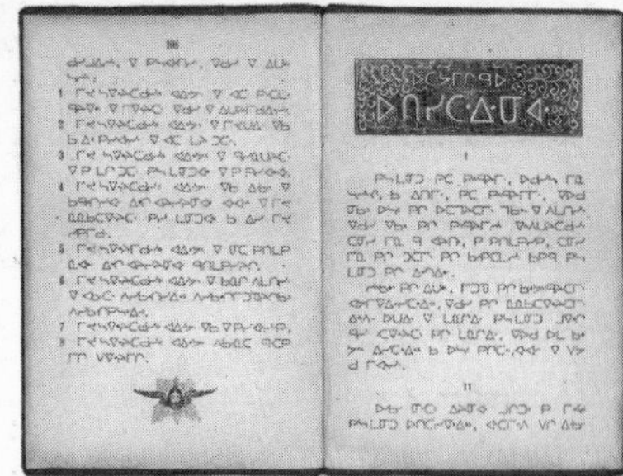

108

sincerely and kindly speaking to Jesus:
1 Blessed are those who fulfil in this way.
2 Blessed are the people here who like nothing more than to
be holy.
3 He receives good blessing if he has a good heart, one that is
not going to get angry although some do evil.
4 He receives good blessing who regrets that he has done
evil, and angered God. He receives good blessing who
never cheats his own people especially one who looks
carefully; and follows God's good orders.
5 He receives good blessing who pities his own people if they
are poor.
6 He receives good blessing who has a clean life that dislikes
adultery. One who thinks of adultery speaks of adultery.
7 He receives good blessing if he does not get angry.
8 He receives good blessing if he suffers through a hard time
when he is being despised.

[ANGEL COPPERPLATE]

108

e ki i kosimoisok, e kisewatisik, ekosi e itwet sesos:
ê-kî-i kosimohisok, ê-kisêwâtisik, êkosi ê-itwêt Sesos:

1 miyo saweyitakosiw awiyak e ata kwitamat keyiwek
1 miyo-sawêyihtâkosiw awiyak ê-âta-kwitamât kêyiwêk

e miweyitak ekosi e iteyimikowisit.
ê-miywêyihtahk êkosi ê-itêyimikowisit.

2 miyo saweyitakosiw awiyak e miyoteit eka ka wi
2 miyo-sawêyihtâkosiw awiyak ê-miyotêhit êkâ kâ-wî-

kisiwasit e ata mayi totat.
kisiwâsit ê-âta-mâyi-tôtât.

3 miyo saweyitakosiw awiyak e kesinateyitak e ki maci
3 miyo-sawêyihtâkosiw awiyak ê-kêsinâteyihtahk ê-kî-maci-

totak kise manitowa e ki kisiwaat.
itôtahk kisê-manitowa ê-kî-kisiwâhât.

4 miyo saweyitakosiw awiyak eka wikac e kakwecisiat
4 miyo-sawêyihtâkosiw awiyak êkâ wîhkâc ê-kâkwêcîsihât

wici ayisiyiniwa wawac e miyo nanakataweyitak kisi
wîci-ayisiyiniwa wâwâc ê-miyo-nânâkatawêyihtahk kisê-

manitowa ka isi miyo sikimikot.
manitowa kâ-isi-miyo-sîhkimikot.

5 miyo saweyimikosiw awiyak e nita kitimakinawat
5 miyo-sawêyimikosiw awiyak ê-nihtâ-kitimâkinawât

wici ayisiyiniwa ketimakisiyici.
wîci-ayisiyiniwa kêtimâkisiyici.

6 miyo saweyitakosiw awiyak e kanaci pimatisit
6 miyo-sawêyihtâkosiw awiyak ê-kanâci-pimâtisit

e pakwatak pisikwatisiwin pisikwacimitoneyicikan
ê-pakwâtahk pisikwâtisiwin pisikwâcimitonêyihcikan

pisikwacikiswewin.
pisikwâcikîswêwin.

7 miyo saweyitakosiw awiyak eka e kisiwasiskit.
7 miyo-sawêyihtâkosiw awiyak êkâ ê-kisiwâsiskit.

8 miyo saweyitakosiw awiyak pikwanata kwetaki mici
8 miyo-sawêyihtâkosiw awiyak pikwânata kwâtakimîci-

peweyimici.
pîwêyimihci.

[ANGEL COPPERPLATE]

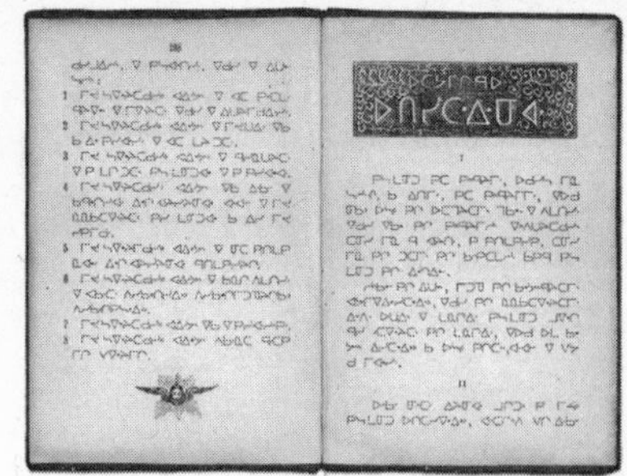

THEIR READINGS THEIR CUSTOMS FOR WORSHIP

I

We must know God and His son, Jesus Christ. This is the first duty while one is alive and then to love one's neighbour as oneself. Also how to behave when one is poor of spirit, and how to act so that God will be with us all the time.

We must understand clearly the word of God, to follow it properly. In the heart God is to be respected. This is the word of God because it is very holy and it alone is good.

II

At the very beginning God gave the people His commandments directly.

109

OTAYAMICIKEWOK OTISITWAWINIWA

OTAYAMIHÊCIKÊWAK OTISÎHTWÂWINIWA

I

kise manito kita kiskeyimit, okosisa mina sesokri, ka
kisê-manitow kita-kiskêyimît, okosisa mîna Sesokri, kâ-

itimit, kita kiskeyimimit, eoko nikan osam kici
itimît, kita-kiskêyimimît, êwako nîkan osâm kici-

otameyitamik mekwac e pimatisik ekosi ekwa kici
otamêyihtamihk mêkwâc ê-pimâtisik êkosi êkwa kici-

kiskeyimisok espiteyitakosik tanisi mina ke ayitik, ki
kiskêyimisok ê-ispîhtêyihtâkosik tânisi mîna kê-ayîtik, kî-

kitimakisiki, tanisi mina kici totamik kici kaskitamasok
kitimâkisiki, tânisi mîna kici-itôtamihk kici-kâskîtamâsok

kakike kise manito kici wicewit.
kâkikê kisê-manitow kici-wîcêwiht.

soskwac kici itwek, mitone kici kwayaskeyitamik
sôskwâc kici-itwêk, mitonê kici-kwayaskêyihtamihk

ayamiewisitwawin, ekosi kici nanakataweyitamik ispic
ayamihêwisîhtwâwin, êkosi kici-nânâkatawêyihtamihk ispic

oteik e manaciit kise manito moweci kesi
otêhihk ê-manâcihiht kisê-manitow môwêci kêsi

ntaweyitwak kici manaciit, eoko oma kwayask
nitawêyihtahk kici-manâcihiht êwako ôma kwayask

isitwawin ka osam kicitwak, wawac e peyako miwasik.
isîhtwâwin kâ osâm kihcitwâk, wâwâc ê-pêyako-miywâsik.

II

oskac nistam iyiniwa mociton ki miyew kise manito
soskwâc nistam iyiniwa moscitôn kî-miyêw kisê-manitow

otitasiwewin, astamispi peci wikac
otitasiwêwin, astamispî pêci wîhkâc

110 He Himself, He wrote it, so then He clarified it for his priests to go all over and teach it until the end of the world.

Those ones for sure are to keep God's words; they only were made extraordinary to understand Him clearly.

III

There is one God made in three different ways; He is tri-une. God, the Father also the Son of God, and the Holy Spirit, this is called the Trinity. This is God's tradition, although it is not well understood usually for Him to be believed in. He Himself twice, He had made it known like this. He is made in three different ways. He is in all ways supernatural God and glorious spirit all the time. He has been spoken of, but not ever to be spoken of being owned. He made all kinds of rules Himself long before He came to earth. Still today it is like that. He is here; so then also all the time He remains here. He sees everything, He can do everything; there is nothing that He cannot do.

——o——

110 eyikok wiya tipiyaw ki masinapiskaam; piyis ka itisawat
iyikohk wîya tipiyâw kî-masinâpiskaham; piyis kâ-itisahwât

okosisa kici pe kisikwayaskweyitamoat otayamiewiyinima
okosisa kici-pê-kîsikwayaskwêyihtamôhât otayamihêwiyinîma

aniskac misiwe kici papamikiskinoamakeyit isko poni
âniskac misiwê kici-papâmi-kiskinohamâkêyit isko pôni-

askiwiyiki.
askîwiyiki.

eokonik kecina ka kanaweyitakwaw ka
êwakonik kêhcinâ kâ-kanawêyihtakwâw kâ-

masinaikateyiki kise manitowa otitweiniyiwa; wiyawaw
masinahikâtêyiki kisê-manitowa otitwêwiniyiwa; wîyawâw

piko e ki isi mamatawiicik kici kwayaskweyitamoiwecik.
piko ê-kî-isi-mamâhtâwihicik kici-kwayaskwêyihtamohiwêcik.

111

peyako kise manito e nistweyakiot maka: weyotawimit,
pêyako kisê-manitow ê-nistwêyakihot mâka: wiyôhtâwîmit,

mina wekosisimit, mina meyosit manito. eoko oma
mîna wêkosisimit, mîna (ê-)miyosit manitow. êwako ôma

nistapeyakowin ka itamik.
nistapêyakowin kâ-itamihk.

eokoyiw oma kise manito otisiowin e ata eka ki
êwakoyiw ôma kisê-manitow otisihowin ê-âta êkâ kî-

kwayaskweyitamik, keyiwek mana ekosi kici isi
kwayaskêyihtamihk, kêyiwêk mâna êkosi kici-isi-

tapwewokeyitamot, wiya tipiyaw niswaw osam e ki
tâpwêwakêyihtamôt, wîya tipiyâw nîswâw osâm ê-kî-

kiskeyitamoiwet, ekosi e isi nistweyakiot. iyenato
kiskêyihtamohiwêt, êkosi ê-isi-nistwêyahkihôt. iyênato

manitowiw kise manito e pisisikacakowit. kakike ki
manitowiw kisê-manitow ê-pisisikahcâhkowît. kâkikê kî-

peci itaw; namawikac ki itayiwa kita tipeyimikot, e iyenato
pêci-itâw; namâwîhkâc kî-itayiwa kita-tipêyimikot, ê-iyênato

tipeyimisot; kayate ka ki isi ayat keyapic anoc moeci ekosi
tipêyimisot; kayâtê kâ-kî-isi-ayât kêyâpic anohc mowêci êkosi

isi ayaw; ekosi mina taki ke isi ayat. kakiyaw wapatam,
isi-ayâw; êkosi mîna tahki kê-isi-ayât. kahkiyaw wâpahtam,

kakiyaw kaskitaw nama kekway pwatawitaw.
kahkiyaw kaskîtwâw nama kîkway pwâtawîtâw.

———o———

III

IV

Although nothing existed, nevertheless God brought everything into being wonderfully. He thought and made the world. He also made the angels and the people.

Only by God's thought was everything made good. Through His wisdom everything was correct. For six days God was going to be busy. He made His creatures, people, like Him. He completed creation.

In the beginning there was a man, Adam he was called. In the beginning there was a woman, Eve. From these two successively we have become everyone that God had made. God gave people honour; beyond them were the angels. Because like this He has made them, He is going to own them forever. He gave them the earth to know Him.

Some always followed God's idea. They saw Him clearly; they sat with Him, forever they listened to Him and they looked after His way. But others listened to the devil. They are said to have separated from God through their pride.

III IV

e ata eka ki kici itat kise manito, wiya atawiya ka
ê-âta êkâ kî-kihci-ihtât kisê-manitow, wîya atawîya kâ-

kicitat kakiyaw kekway. eyikok e ki iteyitak kisik
kihci-ihtât kahkiyaw kîkway. iyikohk ê-kî-itêyihtahk kisik

mina askiy ki ositaw; okisikowa mina ayisiyiniwa ki
mîna askiy kî-osîhtâw; okîsikowa mîna ayisiyiniwa kî-

kisiew.
kisihêw.

piko e ki iteyitak kise manito ekosi kakiyaw kekway
piko ê-kî-itêyihtahk kisê-manitow êkosi kahkiyaw kîkway

ki maci itakoniyiw; kita isi mamataikot e isitatat: ekosi
kî-mâci-ihtakoniyiw; kita-isi-mamâhtâhikot ê-isitatât: êkosi

e peyakomaminoak kakiyaw espic iyinisit. nikkotowasik
ê-pêyakomâmînohahk kahkiyaw ispic iyinîsît. nikotwâsik

kisikaw ki wi otamio kise manito kici maminototak
kîsikâw kî-wî-otamihow kisê-manitow ê-kici-maminotôtahk

otosicikewin. ayisiyiiniwa e ki kisiat ekosi ani e ki poni
otosîhcikêwin. ayisiyiniwa ê-kî-kîsihât êkosi ani ê-kî-pôni-

osiciket.
osîhcikêt.

nistam napew atak ki isiikaso, nistam iskwew wiya ep.
nistam nâpêw Atak kî-isiyîhkâsow, nistam iskwêw wîya Ep.

eokonik niso aniskac kociyak kakiyaw. tato ka ki osiat
êwakonik nîso âniskac kôciyahk kahkiyaw. tahto kâ-kî-osîhât

kise manito kici opimatisiwiniyit mamawiyes okisikowa
kisê-manitow kici-opimâtisiwiniyit mamawiyês okîsikowa

mina ayisiyiniwa ki osami kisteyitakosiyiwa, ocitaw ekosi
mîna ayisiyiniwa kî-osâmi-kistêyihtâkosiyiwa, ohcitaw êkosi

e ki isiat e wi naspic tepiyaweat e miyat kita kiskeyimikot.
ê-kî-isîhât ê-wî nâspic têpiyawêhât ê-miyât kita-kiskêyimikot.

okisikonak atit taki e ki micikeyimacik kisi manitowa
okîsikônahk âtiht tahki ê-kî-micimêyimâcik kisê-manitowa

mosis wapamewok, e witapimacik. naspic naitawewok
mosis wâpamêwak, ê-wîtapimâcik. nâspic nahîtawêwak

mana tanisi isi nataweyitamakotwawi. kotakak maka
mâna tânisi isi-nâtawêyihtamâkotwâwi kotakak mâka

maci manitowok ka iticik ki paskewiewok kise manitowa
maci-manitowak kâ-itîcik kî-paskêwihêwak kisê-manitowa

otayiwakeyimowi
otayiwâkêyimowi

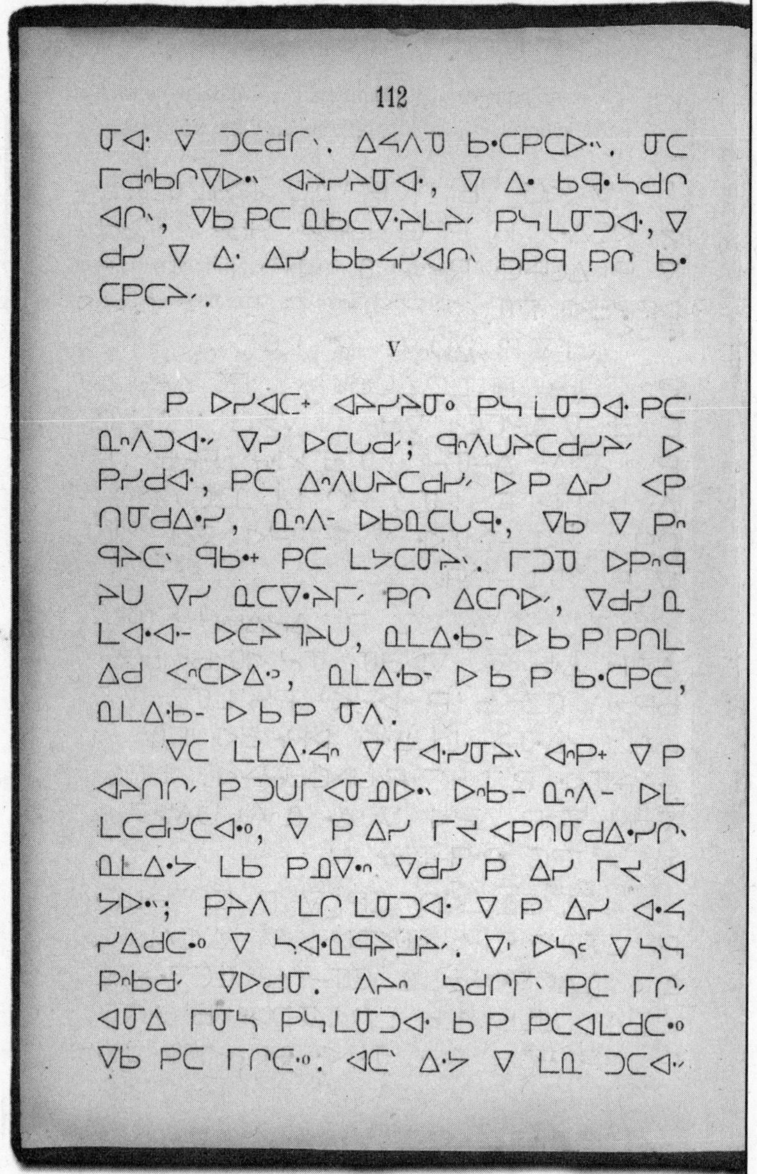

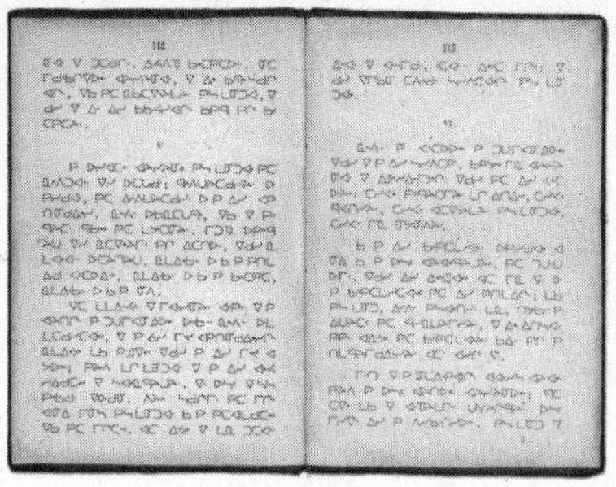

112 Because of what they did, they suffered. They were trying to overpower and trouble the people not to look after God. So then they are trying to cheat God all the time so that He suffers.

v

God made people to copy Him. His spirit is to be considered highly. His angels are to be considered more highly. He entrusts the Holy Spirit; if someone doesn't know something that is evil, the Holy Spirit will know how to look after him to behave well. So then he will never find it tiresome, never suffer from sin, never be suffering, never die.

Although in the beginning the land was exceptionally good, our late friends were told that everything was holy. They were set down by the powers, but they did not remain like this for a long time. Quickly the devil cheated them, because he is jealous, yes, because he made them afraid. The devil finally persuaded them to eat those berries that God had forbidden them to eat, even though he is sly with them.

112 niwa e totakocik. iyepine kwatakitawok.
niwa ê-tôtâkocik. iyêpinê kwâtakîtâwak.

nitamikoskaciewok ayisiyinwa, e wi kakwesakociacik, eka
nitamikôskacihêwak ayisiyiniwa, ê-wî-kakwêsâkôcihâcik, êkâ

kita nakataweyimayit kise manitowak, ekosi e wi isi
kita-nâkataweyimâyit kisê-manitowak, êkosi ê-wî-isi-

kakayesiacik kakike kici kwatakitayit.
kakayêsihâcik kâkikê kici-kwâtakihtâyit.

v

ki osiatay ayisiyiniw kise manitowa kita naspitowat
kî-osîhatay ayisiyiniw kisê-manitowa kita-naspitawât

esi otacakot; kespiteyitakosiyit okisikowa, kita
(ê-)isi-otahcâhkot; (ê-)kî-ispîhtêyihtâkosiyit okîsikowa, kita-

ispiteyitakosit o ki isi pakitinikowisi, naspic
ispîhtêyihtâkosit okî-isi-pakitinikowisi, nâspic

okanatacakwe, eka e kiskeyitak kekway kita
okanâhtahcâhkwa, êkâ ê-kiskêyihtahk kîkway kita-

mayataniyik. mitone okiskeyite esi nataweyimit kici
mayâtaniyik. mitonê okiskêyihtê (ê-)isi nâtawêyimît kici-

itaciot, ekosi namawawac otayimeyite, namawikac
itâcihot, êkosi namawâwâc otayimêyihta, namawîhkâc

o ka ki kitimaiko pastaowin, namawikac o ka ki
o-kâ-kî-kitimâhikow pâstâhowin, namawîhkâc o-kâ-kî-

kwatakita, namawikac o ka ki nipi.
kwâtakihtâw, namawîhkâc o-kâ-kî-nipiw.

eta mamawiyes e miwasiniyik askiy e ki ayiticit
(ê-)âta mamawiyês ê-miywâsiniyik askiy ê-kî-ayitîcit

ki totemipaninowok oskac naspic oma matakositawaw, e
kitôtêmipaninawak oskâc nâspic ôma mâhtakosîtâwâw, ê-

ki isi miyo pakitinikowisicik namawiya maka kinowes
kî-isi-miyo-pakitinikowisicik namâwiya mâka kinowês

ekosi ki isi miyo ayawok; kiyipi maci manitowa e ki isi
êkosi kî-isi miyo-ayâwak; kiyipa maci-manitowa ê-kî-isi-

wayesiikotwaw e sawanakeyimoyit. ep osam e sasekiskakot
wayêsihikotwâw ê-sawânakêyimoyît. Ep osâm ê-sasêkiskâkot

eokoni. piyes sakocimik kita micit anii minisa kise
êwakoni. piyisk sâkôcimik kita-mîcît anihi mînisa kisê-

manitowa ka ki kitaamakotwaw eka kita micitwaw. atak
manitowa kâ-kî-kitahamâkotwâw êkâ kita-mîcitwâw. Atak

wiya e mana totawat
wiya ê-manâtôtawât

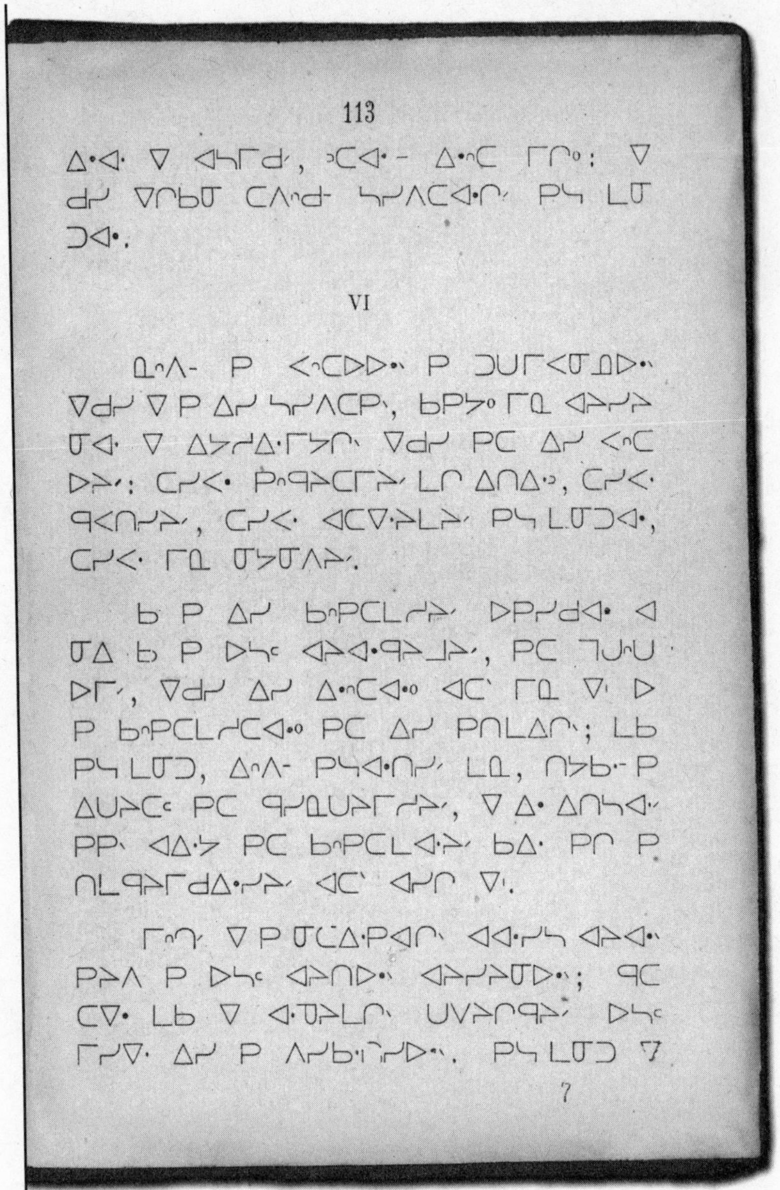

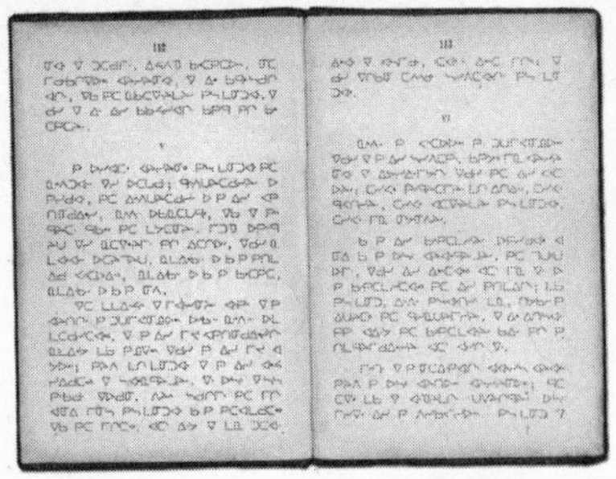

113 His wife fed Adam instead. He too ate it; so then indeed they disobeyed God.

VI

Forever they sinned, our late friends. So then all the people also disobeyed, all of them. They passed it to them. Like this they will sin. For that reason it is known as original sin; for that reason man is foolish; for that reason God is disappointed in mankind. For that reason also they will die.

When the angels sinned, they thought highly of themselves and deserved to be burned. So then Adam and Eve too disobeyed the Spirit. He caused them to be put through misery. But God is kind. On the contrary He took pity on them. He considered someone to achieve forgiveness and redemption for His people.

They had given birth to children very quickly. The world was overpopulated, to be true. But they had abandoned the Lord because all over they committed adultery. God

113 wiwa e asamikot, ntawac wista miciw: ekosi ecikani
wîwa ê-asamikot, nitawâc wîsta mîciw: êkosi êcikâni

tapiskoc sasipitawacit kise manitowa.
tâpiskôc sasîpîtawacit kisê-manitowa.

VI

naspic ki pastaowok ki totemi paninowok ekosi e ki isi
nâspic kî-pâstâhowak kitôtêmipaninowak êkosi ê-kî-isi-

sasipitakik, kakiyaw mina ayisiyiniwa e iyasowimiyacik
sasîpîtâhkik, kahkiyaw mîna ayisiyiniwa ê-iyasowimiyâcik

ekosi kita isi pastaoyit: tasipwa kiskeyitamiyit maci itiwin,
êkosi kita-isi-pâstâhoyit: tâsipwâ kiskêyihtamiyit macihtiwin,

tasipwa kepatisiyit, tasipwa ataweyimayit kise manitowa,
tâsipwâ kêpâtisiyit, tâsipwâ âtawêyimâyit kisê-manitowa,

tasipwa mina niyanipiyit.
tâsipwâ mîna nîyanipiyit.

ka ki isi kaskitamasoyit okisikowa anii ka ki osam
kâ-kî-isi-kaskîtamâsoyit okîsikowa anihi kâ-kî-osâm-

ayiwakeyimoyit, kita mecosteomit, ekosi isi wistawaw atak
ayiwakêyimoyit, kita-macostêhomît, êkosi isi-wîstawâw Atak

mina ep o ki kaskitamasotawaw kita isi kitimaicik; maka
mîna Ep ô-ki-kaskîtamâsotawâw kita-isi-kitimahîcîk; mâka

kise manito, ispic kisewatisit mana, tiyakwac ki iteyitam
kisê-manitow, ispic kisêwâtisit mâna, tiyakwâc kî-itêyihtam

kita kesinateyimisoyit, e wi itisawat kikik awiya kita
kita-kêsinâtêyimisoyit, ê-wî-itisawât kikik awîya kita-

kaskitamawayit kawi kici kitimakeyimikowisiyit atak
kâskîtamawâyit kâwi-kici-kitimâkêyimikowisiyit Atak

asici ep.
asici Ep.

miscet e ki nitawikiocik awasisa ayiwak kiyipi ki osam
mihcêt ê-kî-nihtâwikihocik awâsisa ayiwâk kiyipi kî osâm

ayitiwok ayisiyiniwok; ketatawe maka e waneyimacik
ayitiwak ayisiyiniwak; kêtahtawê mâka ê-wanêyimâcik

tepeyicikeyit osam misiwe isi ki pisikwatisiwok. kise
(ê-)tipêyihcikêyit osâm misiwe isi-kî-pisikwâtisiwak. kisê-

manito e
manitow ê-

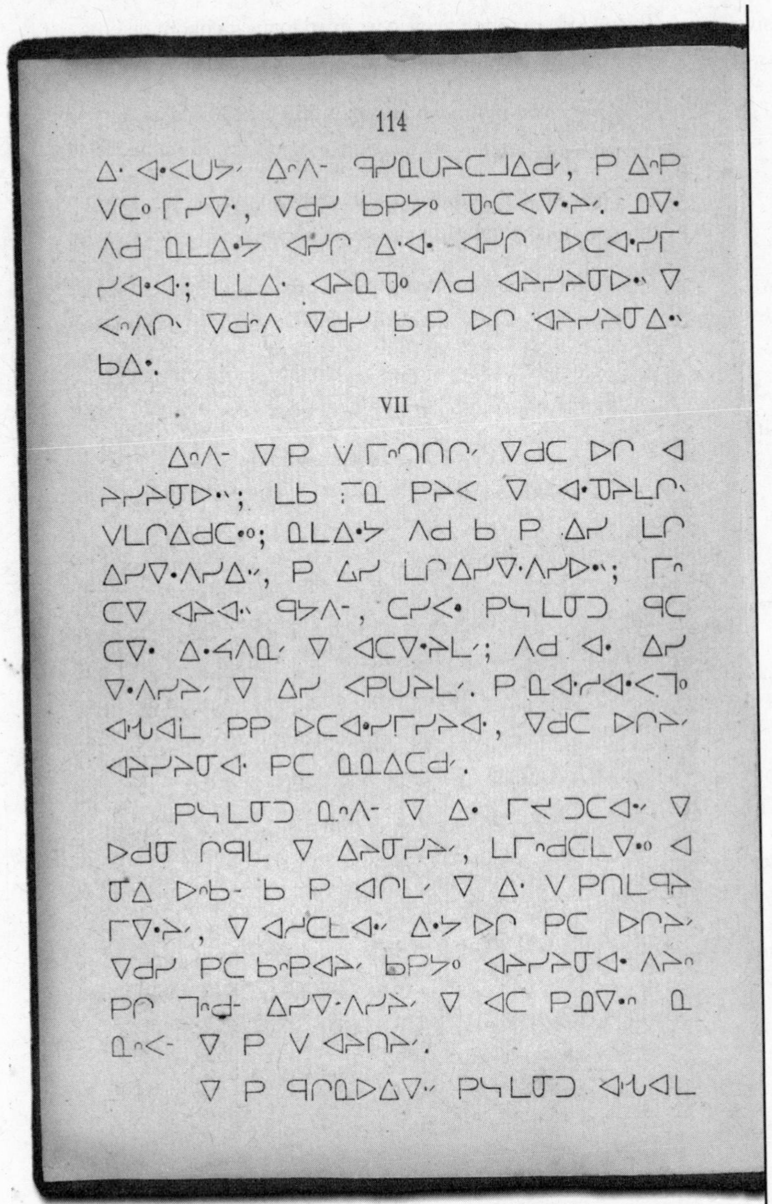

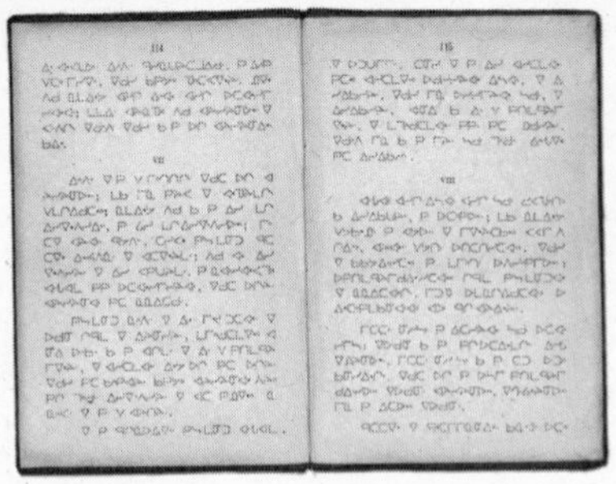

114 was going to make them realize their sin. He was sorrowful. He flooded the world all over so then all of them drowned. Only Noah and his wife and their children, all together only eight people, survived. So then they became people once again.

VII

Then there were many people in the Near East; but also soon they were restless. He helped them survive, including those who showed bad behaviour. Because their bad behaviour persisted, they abandoned God. He rejected them. But to Abraham and his children and the people who came from there that listened to him, His attitude was different.

God forever was going to reward them well, because they were wise. He mentioned it to them in the beginning. He told them He would pity them. He promised them that they would increase so then all the people would be from there, in exchange for their covenant, even though for a long time they held tightly to their old ways.

God had made it certain that He was Abraham's

114 wi wapateyit ispic kesinateyitamoikot, ki iskipetaw misiwe,
wî-wâpahtêyit ispic kêsinâtêyihtâmohikot, kî-iskipêtâw misiwe,

ekosi kakiyaw nestapaweyit. nowe piko namawiya asici
êkosi kahkiyaw nêstâpâwêyit. Nowe piko namâwiya asici

wiwa asici otawasimisiwawa; mamawi ayinanew piko
wîwa asici otawâsimisîwâwa; mâmawi ayinânêw piko

ayisiyiniwok e paspicik ekospi ekosi ka ki oci ayisiyiniwik
ayisiyiniwak ê-paspîcik êkospî êkosi kâ-kî ohci ayisiyiniwak

kawi.
kâwi.

VII

ispic e ki pe misceticit ekota oci ayisiyiniwok; maka
ispic ê-kî-pê-mihcêticik êkota ohci ayisiyiniwak; mâka

mina kiyipa e waneyimacik pemaciikotwaw; namawiya
mîna kiyipa ê-wanêyimâcik pêmacihikotwâw; namâwiya

piko ka ki isi maci isiwepisiwit, ki isi maci isiwepisiwok;
piko kâ-kî-isi-maci-isiwêpisiwît, kî-isi-maci-isiwêpisiwak;

mistae ayiwak keyapic, tasipwa kise manito ketatawe
mistahi ayiwâk kêyâpic, tâsipwâ kisê-manitow kêtahtawê

wiyepinat e ataweyimat; piko wa isi wepisiyit e isi
wiyêpinât (ê-)âtawêyimât; piko wâ-isi-wêpisiyit ê-isi

pakiteyimat. ki nawasowapamew apraoma kiki
pakitêyimât. kî-nawâsôwâpamêw Aprahoma kiki

otawasimisiyiwa, ekota ociyit ayisiyiniwa kita nanaitakot.
otawâsimisiyiwa, êkota ohcîyit ayisiyiniwa kita-nanahihtâkot.

kise manito naspic e wi miyo totawat eokoni cikema
kisê-manitow nâspic ê-wî-miyo-itôtawât êwakoni cikêma

e iyinisiyit, mamiskotamawew anii oskac ka ki acimat e wi
ê-iyinîsiyit, mamiskotamawêw anihi oskâc kâ-kî âcimât ê-wî-

pe kitimakeyimiweyit, e asotamawat wiya oci kita ociyit
pê-kitimâkêyimiwêyit, ê-asotamâwât wîya ohci kita-ohcîyit

ekosi kita kaskiayit kakiyaw ayisiyiniwa piyis kici meskoc
êkosi kita-kaskihâyit kahkiyaw ayisiyiniwa piyis kici meskoc

isiwepisiyit e ata kinowes na naspic e ki pe ayitiyit.
isîwêwipisiyit ê-âta-kinowês na nâspic ê-kî-pê-ayîtiyît.

e ki kecinaoiwet kise manito apraoma
ê-kî-kêhcinâhohiwêt kisê-manitow Aprahoma

115 protector. He had promised him again. He promised his son Isaac in his name like this, also his grandchild Jacob in his name, that they were going to have favour, that they were going to be noticed. He changed Jacob's name to Israel.

VIII

Abraham and Isaac and Jacob were in Palestine. That is the name of their land but no one can stay in one area. They liked to travel all over, and observe God's ways in their behaviour. They were hard workers; they had lots of animals to tend to because God had shown them favour. He was very careful with them, and with those who helped them who listened to God.

There were twelve of Jacob's children, those who had accepted him as a father of Israel, twelve of them that were to be a family. These people, Abraham's people, those ones were known.

Eventually it happened that

e ototemimit, tanisi e ki isi asotamawat kitwam
ê-otôtemimît, tânisi ê-kî isi asotamawât kîhtwâm

asotamawew okosisiyiwa isaak, e i siikasoyit, ekosi mina
asotamawêw okosisiyiwa Isaak, ê-isiyihkâsoyit, êkosi mîna

osisimiyiwa sakop, e isiikasoyit. anii ka wi pe
osisimiyiwa Sakop, ê-isiyihkâsoyit. anihi kâ-wî-pê-

kitimakeyimiweyit, e mameskotamawat kikik kita
kitimâkêyimiwêyit, ê-mamêskotamawât kikik kita-

nokosiyit. ekospi mina ka ki miyit sakop meskoc israel
nôkosiyit. êkospî mîna kâ-kî miyît Sakop mêskôc Israel

kita isiikasot.
kita-isiyihkâsot.

VIII

apraam asici isaak asici sakop lapalestin ka
Apraham asici Isaak asici Sakop Lapalestine kâ-

isiikateyik, ki otaskiwok; maka namawiya peyakwanak ki
isiyihkâtêyik, kî-otaskîwak; mâka namâwiya pêyakwanak kî-

ayawok e miweyitakwaw papami piciwin. ayiwak
ayâwak ê-miywêyihtahkwâw papâmi-piciwin. ayiwâk

peyatik otitatisitawaw. ekosi e kakayawisitwaw ki
pêyâhtik otitâtisîtawâw. êkosi ê-kakâyawisitwâw kî-

mamiscet opisiskimiwok: okitimakeyimikowisitawaw
mâmihcêt opisiskimiwak: okitimâkêyimikowisîtawâw

cikema kise manitowa e nanaitawacik. mitone
cikêma kisê-manitowa ê-nanahihtawâcik. mitonê

omanaciikotawaw o witaskimakaniwawa apo keci
omanâcihikotwâwâw owîtaskimâkaniwâwa ahpô kêci

ayiwiyit.
ayiwiyit.

mitatat ni sosap ki itasiyiwa sakop otawasimisa: eokoni
mitâtaht nîsosâp kî-itâsiyiwa Sakop otawâsimisa: êwakoni

ka ki kici otawimacik israeliyiniwok, mitatat nisosap ka ki
kâ-kî kici-otâwîmâcik Israeliyiniwak, mitâtaht nîsosâp kâ-kî

tato otoskanisiwicik. ekota oci ki osami
tahto otoskanisiwicik. êkota ohci kî-osâmi-

kitimakeyimikowisiwok eokonik ayisiyiniwok.
kitimâkêyimikowisiwak êwakonik ayisiyiniwak.

eprewiyiniwok mina ka itawok eokonik.
Eprewiyiniwak mîna kâ-itâwak êwakonik.

ketatawe e kwetamicinaniwik kanaan otas
kêtahtawê ê-kwêtamîcinâniwik Kanaan otas

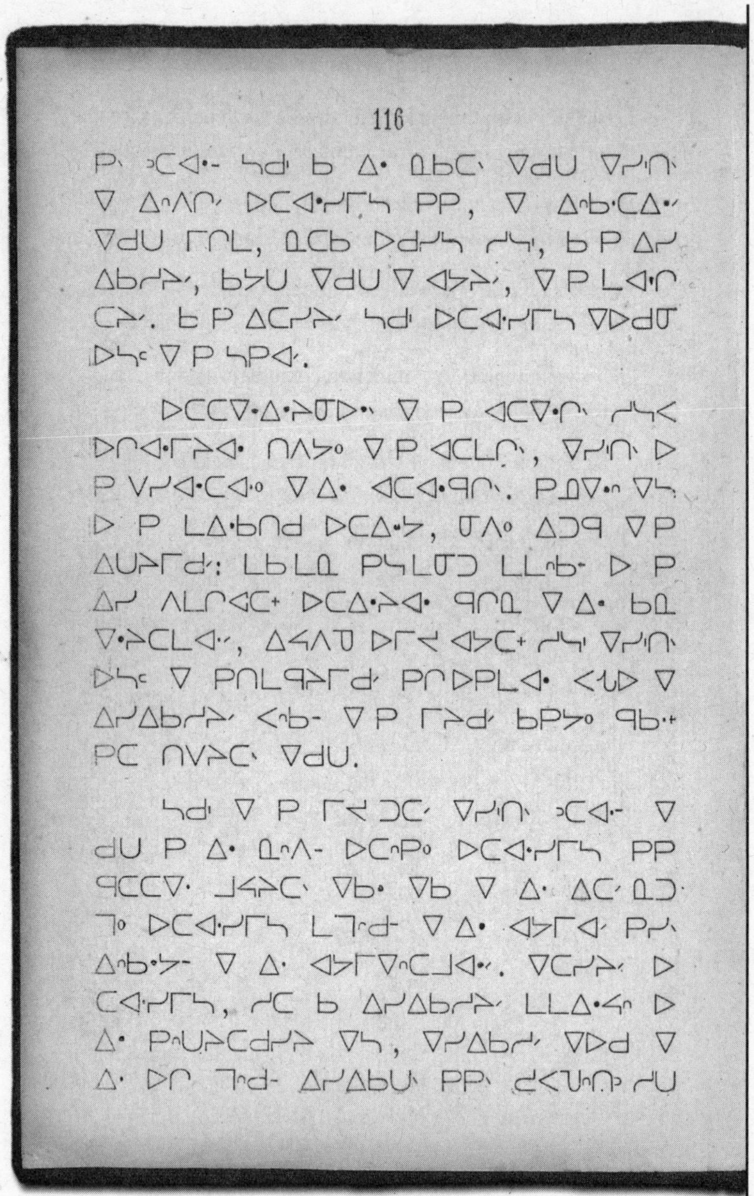

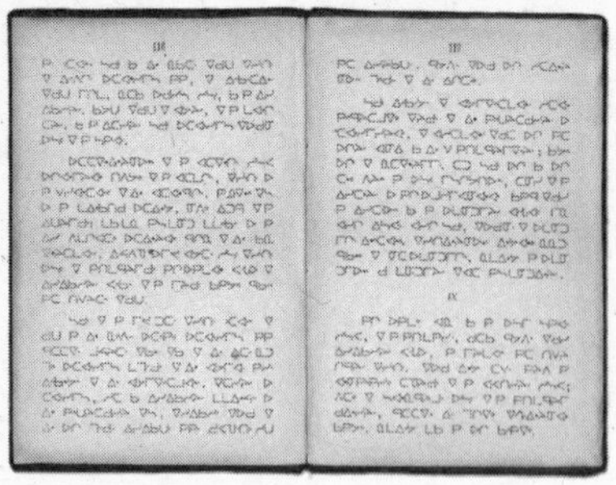

116 Jacob was going to leave his land. He moved his children and he journeyed towards the shore. His son's name was Joseph. There they gathered, Jacob's children, because he loved them.

The city people bought Joseph, his son, himself; they bought him as a slave. His brothers were going to sell him. For a long time Joseph cried for his father. His father was probably dead he thought. But God amazingly brought him to life. His father for sure, he was going to keep the inheritance for him in a good state. When Joseph was in Egypt, the king, great Pharaoh was his name, felt sorry for him and had given him everything to own over there.

Joseph was treated well in Egypt. Finally it is going to be forever his land, and his children's also. Eventually he felt it and he was not going to say it. He invited his children in turns. He is going to pray as well. Anyway he is going to pray for them, all of his children. They are called Jews. They are going to be honourable descendants. The land of the Jews is going to be named Palestine.

116 kik ntawac sakop ka wi nakatak ekote esiptik e ispicit
kîhk nitawâc Sakop kâ-wî-nakatahk êkotê Esiptihk ê-ispicit

otawasimisa kiki, e iskwatawit ekote micima, nataka
otawâsimisa kiki, ê-iskwâtawit êkotê mîcima, nataka

okosisa sosep, ka ki isi ikasoyit, kayate ekote e ayayit, e ki
okosisa Sosep, kâ-kî-isiyihkâsoyit, kayâte êkotê ê-ayâyit, ê-kî-

mawacitayit. ka ki itasiyit sakop otawasimisa eokoni osam
mawâcitâyit. kâ-kî-itâsiyit Sakop otawâsimisa êwakoni osâm

e ki sakiat.
ê-kî-sâkihât.

otatawewiyiniwok e ki atawecik sosepa ociwamiyiwa
otatâwêwiyiniwak ê-kî-atâwêcik Sosepa ociwâmiyiwa

tipiyaw e ki atamacik, esiptik o ki pesiwatawaw e wi
tipiyaw ê-kî-atamâcik, Esiptihk o-kî-pesiwâtâwâw ê-wî-

atawakecik. kinowes esa o ki mawikatiko otawiya, nipiw
atâwâkêcik. kinowês êsa oki-mawîkâtiko ohtâwiya, nipiw

itoke e ki iteyimikot: maka mana kise manito
itokê ê-kî-itêyimikot: mâka mâna kisê-manitow

mamaskac o ki isi pimaciatay otawiyiwa kecina e wi
mâmâskâc o-kî-isi-pimâcihatay ohtâwiya kêhcinâ ê-wî-

kanaweyitamawat, iyepine omiyo ayatay sosep esiptik
kanawêyihtamâwât, iyêpinê omiyo-ayâtay Sosep Esiptihk

osam e kitimakeyimikot kici okimawa parao e isiikasoyit
osâm ê-kitimâkêyimikot kihci-okimâwa Paroa ê-isiyihkâsoyit

paskac e ki miyikot kakiyaw kekway kita tipeyitak ekote.
paskâc ê-kî-miyikot kahkiyaw kîkway kita-tipêyihtahk êkotê.

sakop e ki miyo totat esiptik ntawac ekote ki wi naspic
Sakop ê-kî-miyo-itôtât Esiptihk nitawâc êkotê kî-wî-nâspic

otaskiw otawasimisa kiki ketatawe moyeyitak ekwa eka
otaskîw otawâsimisa kiki kêtahtawê moyêyitahk êkwa êkâ

e wi itat natomew otawasimisa mameskoc e wi ayamiat
ê-wî-itât nâtomêw otawâsimisa mâmêskoc ê-wî-ayamihât

kisik iskwayac e wi ayamiestamowat. etasiyit otawasimisa,
kisik iskwayâc ê-wî-ayamihêstamawât. ê-itâsiyit otawâsimisa,

sota ka isiikasoyit mamawiyes o wi kisteyitakosiyi
Sota kâ-isiyihkâsoyit mamawiyês o-wî-kistêyihtâkosiyit

esa, esi kikasot eoko e wi oci meskoc isiikatek kikik
êsa, ê-isiyihkâsot êwako ê-wî ohci mêskoc isiyihkâtêk kikik

lapalestin sote
Lapalestine Sote

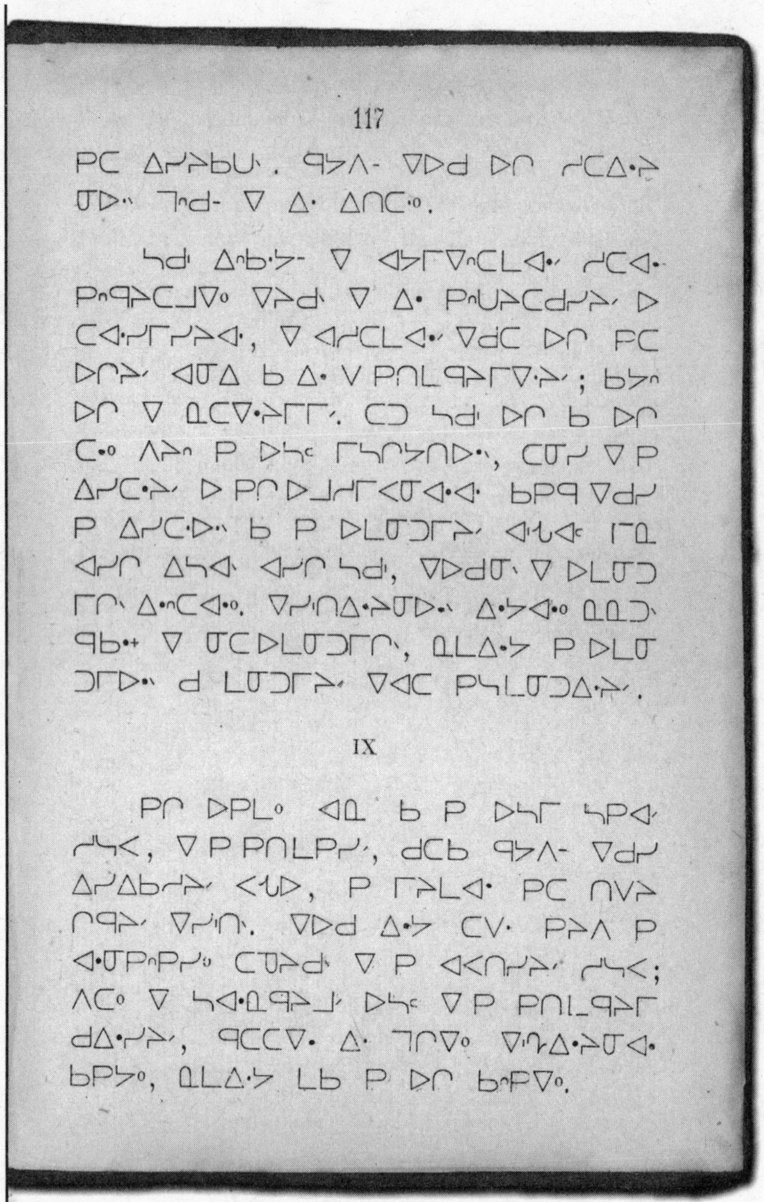

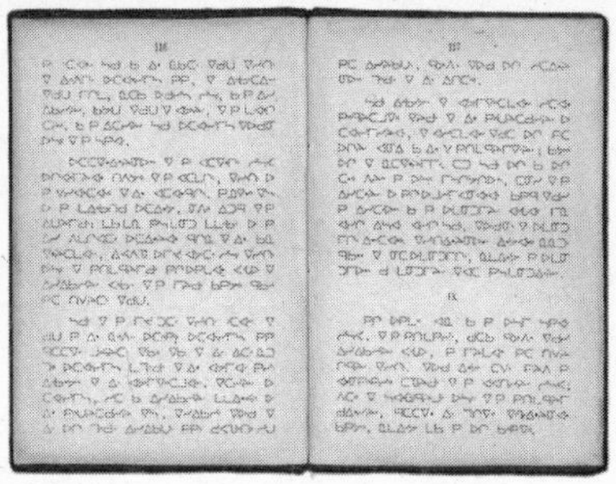

117 It is still called so. This is what is said of the Jews.

Jacob in the end prays for the Jews. He makes them know that they are going to be honourable. He promises their children, those who are from there and those who are going to come, that they will have favour. A long time ago those who came from Jacob were looked after. Finally there were too many of them. They behaved like their great grandfathers all the time. Like this they behaved when they had Abraham, Isaac and Jacob as their leaders. Those ones they accepted as their God. They also behaved like their grandfathers all the time; like this they behaved when they had as their god Abraham and also Isaac, also Jacob, those ones they accepted as their god. They also accepted the Egyptians' gods. They behaved as though they did not have a God, although there is a God here.

IX

The king loved poor Joseph too much. His other name was Pharaoh; he owned everything in Egypt. Truly he abandoned Joseph, because he was jealous. Because he was poor in spirit, eventually he was going to destroy all of Abraham's people, but he was not able to do it.

117 kita isiyikatek. keyapic eoko oci sotawiyiniwok meskoc
kita-isiyihkâtêk kêyâpic êwako ohci Sotawiyiniwak mêskoc

e wi ititwaw.
ê-wî-itîtwâw.

sakop iskwayac e ayamiestamawat sotawa
Sakop iskwayâc ê-ayamihêstamawât Sotawa

kiskeyitamoew eyikok e wi kisteyitakosiyit
kiskêyihtamohêw iyikohk ê-wî-kistêyihtâkosiyit

o tawasimisiyiwa, e asotamawat ekota oci kita ociyit anii
otawâsimisiyiwa, ê-asotamawât êkota ohci kita-ohcîyit anihi

ka wi pe kitimakeyimiweyit; kayas oci e nataweyimimit.
kâ-wî pê-kitimâkêyimiwêyit; kayâs ohci ê-nâtawêyimimiht.

tato sakop oci ka ocitwaw piyis ki osam misaciyatiwok,
tahto Sakop ohci kâ ohcîtwâw piyis kî-osâmi-misâciyâtiwak,

tanisi e ki isitwayit o kici omosomipaniwawa kakike
tânisi ê-kî-isîtwâyît okihci-omosômipaniwâwa kâkikê

ekosi ki isitwawok ka ki omanitomiyit apraam mina
êkosi kî-isîtwâwak kâ-kî omanitômiyit Apraham mîna

asici isaak asici sakop, eokonik e omanitomicik
asici Isaak asici Sakop, êwakonik ê-omanitômicik

wistawaw. esiptiwiyiniwok wiyawaw nanatok kekway
wîstawâw. Esiptiwiyiniwak wîyawâw nanâtohk kîkway

e nita omanitomicik, namawiya ki omanitomiwok ka
ê-nihtâ-omanitômicik, namâwiya kî-omanitômiwak kâ-

manitomiyit ekota kise manitowiyit.
manitômiyit êkota kisê-manitowiyit.

IX

kici okimaw ana ka ki osami sakiat sosepa, e ki
kihci-okimâw ana kâ-kî-osâmi-sâkihât Sosepa, ê-kî-

kitimakisit, kotaka keyapic ekosi isiikasoyit parao, ki
kitimâkisît, kotaka kêyâpic êkosi ê-isiyihkâsoyit Parao, ki-

miyimawa kita tipeyicikeyit esiptik. eoko wiya tapwe
miyimâwa kita-tipêyihcikêyit Esiptihk. êwako wîya tâpwê

kiyipi ki wanikiskisiw taneyikok e ki apatisiyit sosepa;
kiyipi kî-wânikiskisiw tânêyihkohk ê-kî-âpatisiyit Sosepa;

pitaw e sawanakeyimat osam e ki kitimakeyimikowisiyit,
pihtâw ê-sawânakêyimât osâm ê-kî-kitimâkêyimikowisiyit,

ketatawe wi meciew eprewiyiniwa kakiyaw, namawiya
kêtahtawê wî-mêscihêw Eprewiyiniwa kahkiyaw, namâwiya

maka ki oci kaskiew.
mâka kî ohci kaskihêw.

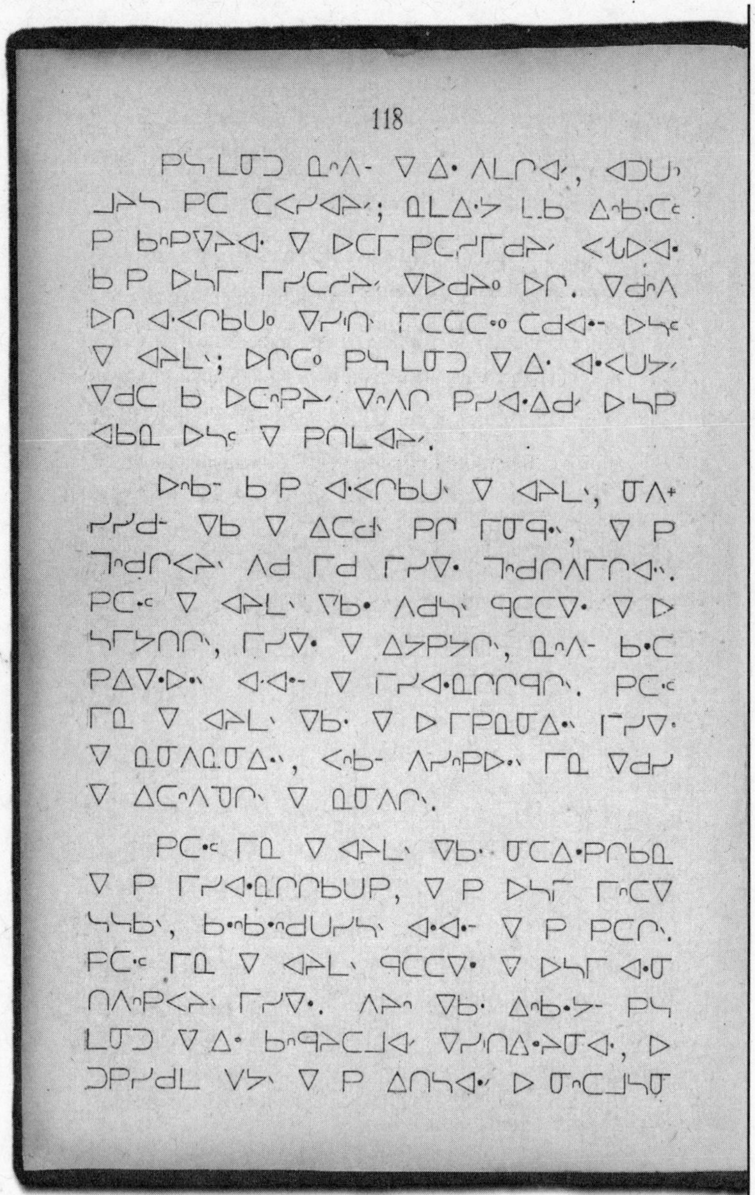

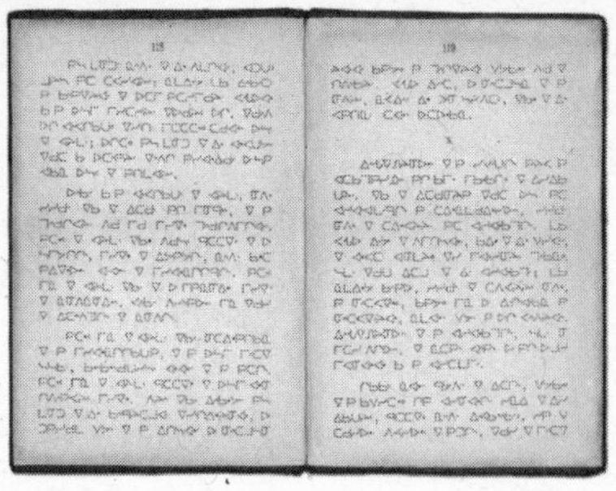

118 Eternal God is going to save His people. He asks them to be good. But no one soon was able to do so. They were busy doing the work of the Pharaoh. They were over burdened. They worked in Egypt ten times harder because it is difficult. By all means God is going to show that this is His land. He is angered because His loved ones are being treated unfairly.

It happened that Pharaoh had a difficult time. All of a sudden there was no water to drink. It was changed; blood flowed all over. Once again it was difficult and all of a sudden there were many insects all over. Forever they make one suffer. They destroyed everything. Again it was difficult and the people had sores. All over everybody was dying. Animals also were diseased; they were dying.

Once again it was difficult and the garden was destroyed. There was lots of hail. Even the grasshoppers devoured everything. Once again it was difficult. All of a sudden it became very dark all over. God was going to conquer the Egyptians, to destroy

118 kise manito naspic e wi pimaciat, atotew moyiṣa kita
kisê-manitow nâspic ê-wî-pimâcihât, atotêw Moyisa kita-

tapasiayit; namawiya maka iskwatam ki kaskieyiwa
tapasîhâyit; namâwiya mâka iskwatam kî-kaskihêyiwa

e otami kitasomikoyit paraowa ka ki osami misitasoyit
ê-otami-kitâsômîkoyit Paraowa kâ-kî-osâmi-misitasoyit

eokoyiw oci. ekospi oci wapacikatew esiptik
êwakoyiw ohci. êkospî ohci wâpahcikâtêw Esiptihk

mitatatwaw takowac osam e ayimak; ocitaw kise manito
mitâtahtwâw tâkowâc osâm ê-âyimak; ohcitaw kisê-manitow

e wi wapateyit ekota ka otaskiyit espici kisiwaikot
ê-wî-wâpahtâyit êkota kâ-ostaskiyit êspici kisiwâhikot

o sakiakana osam e kitimaayit. oskac ka ki wapacikatek
osâkihâkana osâm ê-kitimâhâyit. oskâc kâ-kî-wâpahcikâtêk

e ayimak, nipiy sisikoc eka e itakok kici minikwek, e ki
ê-âyimak, nipiy sisikoc êkâ ê-ihtakok kici-minihkwêk, ê-kî-

meskocipayik piko miko misiwe meskocipimiciwak.
mêskocipayik piko mihko misiwê mêskocipimiciwak.

kitwam e ayimak ekwa pikosak ketatawe e o samiyaticik,
kîhtwâm ê-âyimak êkwa pîkosak kêtahtawê ê-osamiyaticik,

misiwe e iyakiyacik, naspic kwatakiiwewok wawac
misiwê ê-iyakiyâcik, nâspic kwâtakihiwêwak wâwâc

e misiwanacicikecik. kitwam mina e ayimak ekwa e o
ê-misiwanâcihcikêcik. kîhtwâm mîna ê-âyimak êkwa ê-o-

mikinaniwik misiwe e nanipinaniwik, paskac pisiskiwok
mikînâniwik misiwê ê-nânipinâniwik, pâskac pisikiwak

mina ekosi e itaspinecik e nanipicik.
mîna êkosi ê-itâspinêcik ê-nânipicik.

kihtwam mina e ayimak ekwa nitawikicikana e ki
kîhtwâm mîna ê-âyimak êkwa nihtâwikihcikanâ ê-kî-

misiwanacicikateki, e ki osami mistae sesekak,
misiwanâcihcikâtêki, ê-kî osâmi mistahi sîsîkâhk,

kwaskwaskotesisak wawac e ki kitacik. kitwam mina
kwâskwâskotêsisak wâwâc ê-kî-kitâcik. kîhtwâm mîna

e ayimak ketatawe e osami wanitipiskipayik misiwe.
ê-âyimak kêtahtawê ê-osâmi-wanitipiskipâyik misiwê.

piyis ekwa iskwayac kise manito e wi kaskeyitamoat
piyis êkwa iskwayâc kisê-manitow ê-wî-kaskêyihtamôhât

esiptiwiyiniwa, otokisikoma peyak e ki itisawat
Esiptiwiyiniwa, otokisikôma pêyak ê-kî-itîsawât

o nistamosani
onistamosâni

119 all of them. Pharaoh himself and his family died in their sleep.

X

The Israelites had left quickly in the ocean; the Red Sea is what it is called. There was no boat for them to cross the water. All of a sudden there was an opening in the water for them to get across, but Pharaoh who followed was going to bring them back. He saw how open this road was. He followed quickly; he was going to go across but he was not able to. All of a sudden the path in the water closed. He drowned with all his army; they drowned; not one survived. After the Israelites crossed the sea, they moved to claim land their grandfather had promised them, close to the shore, as they had been told.

They had spent the night near Mount Sinai. All of a sudden it was very cloudy; they heard a loud trumpet blast. There was thunder and lightning.

119 yiwawa kakiyaw ki mescieyiwa peyakwaw piko e
yiwâwa kahkiyaw kî-mêscihêyiwa pêyakwâw piko ê-

tipiskayik. parao wista, o-nistamosana e ki nipiyit,
tipiskâyik. Paraoh wîsta, onistamosana ê-kî-nipiyit,

napawis wi poni sasipitam, ekwa e wi pakitinat ntawac
nipâwis wî-pôni-sasîpîtam, êkwa ê-wî-pakitinât nitawâc

otawokana.
otawâkana.

x

israeliyiniwok e ki sipwetecik kiyipa ki
Israeliyiniwak ê-kî-sipwêhtêcik kiyipa kî-

atakamekisinwak kici kamiy mikwakamiy e isiikateyik.
atakamêkisinwak kihcikamiy mihkwâkamiy ê-isiyihkâtêyik.

eka e itakoniyiki ekota osa kita asowaamwakecik
êkâ ê-ihtakoniyiki êkota ôsa kita-asowahamwakêcik

ki tawinamakowisiwok, sisikoc nipiy e tawipayiyik kita
kî-tawinamâkowisiwak, sisikoc nipiy ê-tawipayiyik kita-

asowakamecik. maka parao wiya e pimitisawat, kawi e wi
asowakâmêcik. mâka Paroa wîya ê-pimitisahwât, kâwî ê-wî-

pesiwat, e wapatak animayiw esi miwasiniyik meskanaw,
pêsiwât, ê-wâpahtahk animayiw ê-isi miywâsiniyik mêskanaw,

semak ekote itamo e wi asowakamet; maka namawiya
sêmâk êkote itamo ê-wî-asôwâkâmêt; mâka namâwiya

kaskio, sisikoc e tapipayiyik nipiy, ki nistapawew,
kaskihow, sisikoc ê-tapipâyiyik nipiy, kî-nistâpâwêw,

kakiyaw mina o wiciwakana ki nistapaweyiwa, namawac
kahkiyaw mîna owîciwâkana kî-nistâpâwêyiwa, namawâc

peyak ki oci paspiyiwa. israeliyiniwok e ki asowakamecik,
pêyak kî ohci paspiyiwa. Israeliyiniwak ê-kî-asowâkâmêcik,

semak ni mitasi piciwok, e natakik askiy o kici
sêmâk nimitâsipiciwak, ê-nâtâhkik askiy okihci-

omosomipaniwawa ka ki asotamamit.
omosômipaniwâwa kâ-kî-asotamâmît.

cikakam nawac keyapic e itacik, peyakwaw e ki
cikâkam nawâc kêyâpic ê-itâcik, pêyakwâw ê-kî-

kapesitwaw ciki asiniwacik sinai e isi ikateyik, ketatawe
kapêsitwâw cîki asinîwacîhk Sinai ê-isiyihkâtêyik, kêtahtawê

naspic iyekwaskwan, soki pe takosiwok piyesiwok e
nâspic iyêkwaskwan, sôhki-pê-tâkosiwak piyêsiwak ê-

kitocik, ekosi e mistae
kitocik, êkosi ê-mistahi

120 Indeed God showed this kindness to those He had pitied. There He wrote his commandments on two stones that were flat tablets.

Thereby He instructed them how to know Him, how to behave until He appeared. He was going to come and have pity on them. But the people were still undecided about the way they should act, even though usually they chose bad behaviour. Eventually they adored an idol as their god.

XI

For forty winters they had wandered. It was decreed for them because they had sinned a great deal. But God never abandoned them. As well, every morning He allowed them to make a living from the desert. He gave them food called manna. Every morning before sunrise they went to gather it up to feed themselves, except only on the Sabbath.

They had a hard time to find water to drink.

waseskotepayik. ecikani kise manito eokotowik e wi
wasêskotêpayik. êcikâni kisê-manitow êwakotowik ê-wî-

nokoot, o kitimakeyimakana e wi ayamiat, wiya tepiyawe
nôkohot, okitimâkêyimâkana ê-wî-ayamihât, wîya tipiyawê

ekota ki masinapiskaan otitasiwewina, niso asiniya
êkota kî-masinâpiskahân otitasiwêwina, nîso asiniya

e napakapiskisiyit e apaciat eokoni oci.
ê-napakâpiskisiyit ê-âpacihât êwakoni ohci.

ekota ka ki kiskeyitamoat tanisi esi nitaweyimat
êkota kâ-kî-kiskêyihtamohât tânisi (ê-)isi-nitawêyimât

kici isitwayit isko kici nokosiyit anihi ka ki wi pe
kici-isîhtwâyit isko kici-nôkosiyit anihi kâ-kî-wî-pê-

kitimakeyimiweyit. kiyipa maka e ki waniyitakik esi
kitimâkêyimiwêyit. kiyipa mâka ê-kî-wanêyihtahkik (ê-)isi-

ntaweyimikowisicik kita isitwacik, pikwanata mana
nitawêyimikowisicik kita-isîtwâcik, pikwânâta mâna

misiwe isi ki kepatisi ayitiwok, paskac manitokana
misiwê isi kî-kêpâtisiw ayitiwak, pâskac manitokana

weyomanito micit piyis.
wêyomanitow micit piyis.

XI

nemitanaw tato pipon ki itasi papami piciwok ekosi
nêmitanaw tahto pipon kî-itâsi-pâpâmi-piciwak êkosi

e iteyimikowisicik, e ki misi pastaotwaw; namawiya
ê-itêyimikowisicik, ê-kî-misi-pâstâhotwâw; namâwiya

otawiya ki oci wepinew kise manito, keyiwek tatwaw
ohtâwiya kî-ohci-wêpinêw kisê-manitow, kêyiwêk tahtwâw

kekisepayiki e pakitinamawat kita opimacioyit. mano
kîkisêpâyiki ê-pakitinamawât kita-opimâcihoyit. mâna

ki isiikatamwok animayiw miciwin. tatwaw kesikayiki
kî-isiyihkâtamwak animâyiw mîciwin. tahtwâw kîsikâyiki

mayowes sakasteyik o nitawe moksakinetawaw kici
mayowês sâkâstêyik o-nitawi-môsâhkinêtawâw kici-

tepikiispocik, namawikac otastowatawaw, piko wa
têpikîhispocik, namâwîhkâc otastowatâwâw, piko wâ-

ayamiekisikayiki.
ayamihêwi-kîsikâyiki.

peyakwaw e kwataminikweyit, asinik ki oci
pêyakwaw ê-kwâtaminihkwêyit, asinîk kî-ohci-

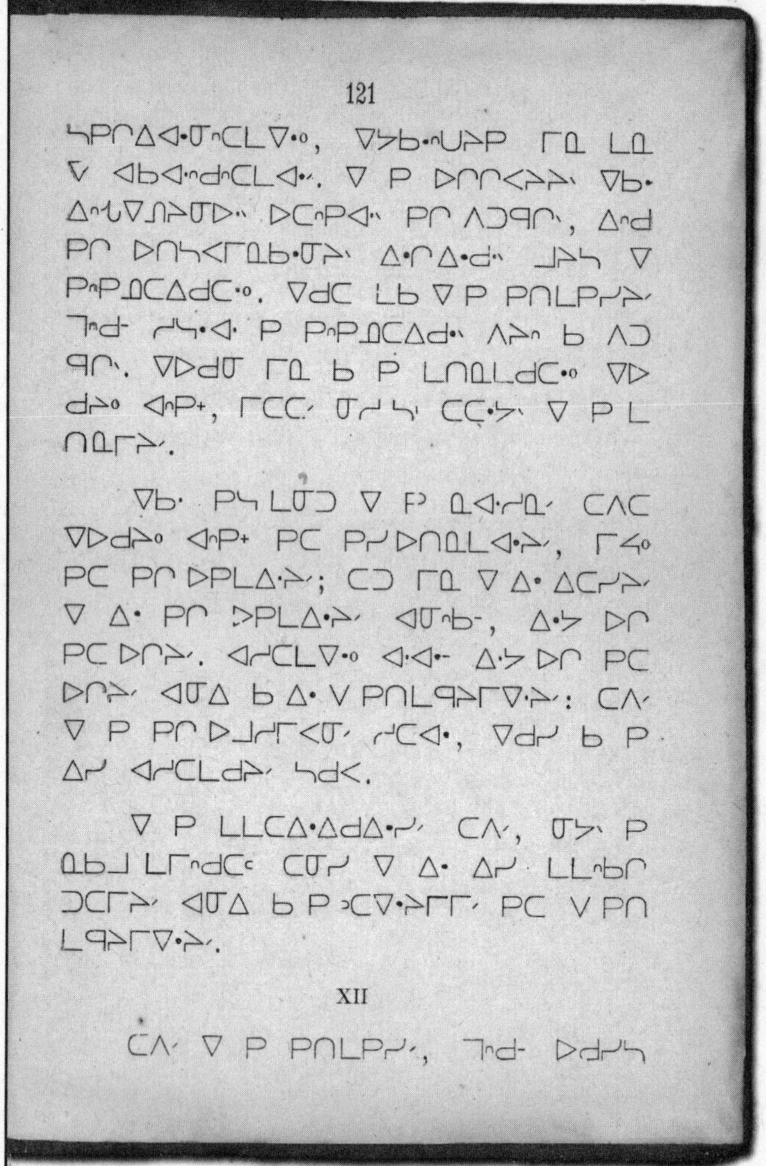

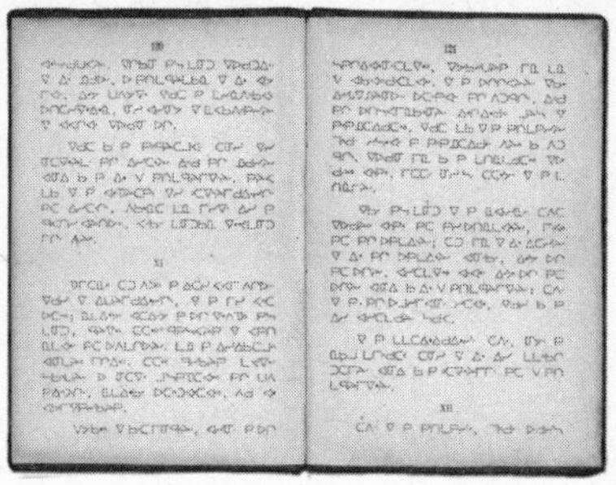

121 He made water flow from a rock. The Israelites relied on Moses to guide them. They lived in the desert. Moses was leading them there, but they were poor. When the Jews were led to this land, they agreed to share it among the twelve tribes.

And God chose David to rule this land for them. He made David the king, and arranged successive kings from David's line. He promised that future compassionate kings would come from him. David had a great grandfather who had been promised by Jacob.

David was exceptional. He sang and promised that someone would come to perform miracles for those in need and to have pity on them.

XII

David sinned. After him his son,

121 sakiciiwanistamawew, eyakwasteyiki mina mana
sakicihiwanistamawêw, êyakwâstêyiki mîna mâna

e akawaskostamawat. e ki ocicipayiyik ekwa israeliyiniwok
ê-akawaskostamâwât. ê-kî-ocihcipayiyik êkwa Israeliyiniwak

otaskiwak kici pitokecik, isko kici otisapaminakwaniyik
otaskîwak kici-pîhtokwêcik, isko kici-otisâpaminakwaniyik

wiciwikwok moyisa e kiskinotaikotwaw. ekota maka e ki
wîciwîkwak Moses ê-kiskinohtahikotwâw. êkota mâka ê-kî-

kitimakisiyit meskoc soswewa ki kiskinotaikwok piyis
kitimâkisiyit mêskoc Soswewa kî-kiskinohtahikwak piyis

ka pitokecik. eokoni mina ka ki matinamakotwaw
kâ-pîhtokwêcik. êwakoni mîna kâ-kî-mâtinamâkotwâw

eokoyiw askiy, mitatat nisosap tatwayik e ki matinamiyit.
êwakoyiw askiy, mitâtaht nîsosâp tahtwâyik ê-kî-mâtinâmiyit.

ekwa kise manito e ki nawasonat tapita eokoyiw askiy
êkwa kisê-manitow ê-kî-nawasônât Tapita êwakoyiw askiy

kita kisi otinamawayit, miyew kita kici okimawiyit; tato
kita kisi-otinamawâyit, miyêw kita-kihci-okimâwiyit; tahto

mina e wi itasiyit e wi kici okimawiyit aniskac, wiya oci
mîna ê-wî-itâsiyit ê-wî-kihci-okimâwiyit âniskac, wîya ohci

kita ociyit. asotamawew wawac wiya oci kita ociyit anii
kita-ohcîyit asotamawêw wâwâc wîya ohci kita-ohcîyit anihi

ka wi pe kitimakeyimiweyit: tapit e ki kici omosomipanit
kâ-wî pê-kitimâkêyimiwêyit: Tapit ê-kî-kihci-omosômipanît

sotawa, ekosi ka ki isi asotamakoyit sakopa.
Sotawa, êkosi kâ-kî-isi-asotamâkoyit Sakopa.

e ki mamatawiikowisit tapit, niyak ki nakamo
ê-kî-mamâhtâwihikowisit Tapit, niyâk kî-nakamow

mamiskotam tanisi e wi isi mamaskacitotamiyit anii ka ki
mâmiskôtam tânisi ê-wî-isi-mamâskâcitôtamiyit anihi kâ-kî

ntaweyimimit kita pe kitimakeyimiweyit.
nitawêyimimiht kita-pê-kitimâkêyimiwêyit.

XII

tapit e ki kitimakisit, meskoc okosisa
Tapit ê-kî-kitimâkisit, mêskoc okosisa

122

ᓴᓗᒧ ᐁ ᐃᓯᐃᑲᓯᔨ, ᑭ ᑭᒋ ᐅᑭᒪᐃᐧᔨᐊᐧ.
ᐁ ᒣᑲ– ᑎᐯᔨᑕ ᓴᓗᒧ, ᓴᓗᓴᒉᒥᐠ ᑭ ᑭᓯ
ᑕᑐᐊᐤ ᐊᔭᒥᐁᐃᐧᑲᒥᐠ ᐅᓴᐢ ᐁ ᒥᐊᐧᓯᐠ ᐁᑲᐧᔭ.
ᐅᐢᑲ– ᓴᓗᒧ ᐁ ᐃᔨᑐᓯ, ᓇᐢᐱ– ᑭ ᑭᑎᒪᑫ
ᔨᒥᑯᐃᐧᓯᐤ. ᒪᑲ ᑫᑕᑕᐁᐧ ᐁ ᐊᐧᑌᔨᒪ, ᑭᓴ
ᒪᑐᒍᐊᐧ ᑭ ᒪᒥᓯ ᐸᐢᑕᐅ. ᑭ ᒪᑎᓇᒧᑕᐊᐤ ᐅ
ᑎᐯᔨᒋᑫᐃᐤ ᒣᑲ– ᐅᑯᓯᓴ ᒍᐳᐊᐟ ᐁ ᐃᓯᐃ
ᑲᓯᔨ ᐁ ᑎᐯᔨᑕᒥᔨ. ᐁᐢᒋᐃᐧᔨᑐᐅᐧ ᐊᑎ ᐁ
ᐊᑕᐁᐧᔨᒪᒋᐠ ᒍᐳᐊᒪ, ᑭ ᓇᐊᐧᓯᑌᐅᐧ ᓴᒍᐳ
ᐊᐧᒪ ᐁ ᐃᐧ ᐅᑐᑭᒪᒥᒋᐠ.

ᓯᑕᐃᐧᔨᑐᐅᐧ ᐃᐧᔭᐊᐤ, ᐊᑕ ᐁᑲ ᐁ ᑭ
ᐸᐢᑫᐃᐧᔭᒋᐠ ᑲᔭᑌ ᐅ ᑭᒋ ᐅᑭᒪᒥᐊᐧᐊᐧ, ᑫᔨᐁᐧ
ᒥᐢᒣᑕᐤ ᑭ ᑭᑎᒪᐃᓯᐅᐧ ᑭᓴ ᒪᑐᒍᐊᐧ ᐁ ᐊᐧᑌ
ᔨᒪᒋᐠ.

ᓇᐳᑯᑐᓇᒋᓯz ᐁ ᑭ ᒥᓯᐊᐧᓇᒋᑕ ᓴᓗᓴᒉᐠ
ᐅᑌᓇᐤ, ᑭ ᒣᒋᑲᓴᐠ ᐊᔭᒥᐁᐃᐧᑲᒥᐠ, ᐁᑯᓯ
ᑲᑭᔭᐤ ᐁᑯᑌ ᐁ ᐅᑕᐢᑭᔨ ᑭ ᓯᐯᐧᑕᐁᐤ ᐸᐱ
ᔭᑐᐠ ᐁ ᐃᐧ ᐅᑕᐅᐧᑲᑐ. ᒪᑲ ᑭᓴ ᒪᑐᒍ ᑲᑭᑫ
ᐁ ᑭᐢᑭᓯ ᑕᑌᔨᑯ ᐁ ᑭᑎᒪᑫᔨᒪ ᐁᐅᑯᑐ,
ᑕᑐᓯ ᒥᓇ ᐁ ᑭ ᐃᓯ ᐊᓯᑕᒪᐊᐧ ᑲᔭᐣ ᐅᒋ
ᑕᐊᐧ– ᐯᓯᐁᐤ ᑲᐃᐧ ᐅᑕᐢᑭᐊᐧ, ᑌᐸᑯᐳᒥᑕᓇ
ᑕᑯ ᐱᐳ ᐊᐢᐱ ᐁ ᐊᐅᐧᑲᑎᒥ ᐁᑯᑌ.

ᐅᑌᓇᐤ ᓴᓗᓴᒉᐠ ᑭ ᐊᒋᑕᑐᐤ, ᐊᔭᒥᐁ
ᐃᐧᑲᒥᐠ ᒥᓇ ᒧᐁᐧᒋ ᐁᑕ ᑭ ᐊᐢᑌ ᐅᐢᑲ–.

122 Solomon, was the king. While Solomon was ruler, the temple in Jerusalem was finished. At first Solomon was wise; forever he was respected but suddenly he was in doubt about God. He sinned seriously and his reign suffered. His son Rehoboam was the ruler of Abraham's people. Some disliked Rehoboam; they chose Jeroboam to become their king.

The Jews, then, oppressed themselves. They could not depose him who was their king. They were confused about God.

Nebuchadnezzar destroyed the city of Jerusalem. He burnt the temple; he took them into exile to Babylon, which became their city. But God all the time remembered and felt pity for the chosen to whom He had promised a long time ago. So then He brought them to reclaim their city after seventy years of exile.

The temple in the city of Jerusalem was rebuilt just as it had been at the beginning.

122 salomo e isiikasoyit, ki kici okimawiyiwa. e mekwac
Salomo ê-isiyihkâsoyit, kî-kihci-okimâwiyiwa. ê mêkwâc

tipeyitak salomo, serosalemik ki kisitaniwan
tipêyihtahk Salomo, Serosalemihk kî-kîsîtâniwan

ayamiewikamik osam e miwasik ekwayak. oskac salomo
ayamihêwikamik osâm ê-miywâsik êkwayâhk. oskâc Salomo

e iyinisit, naspic ki kitimakeyimikowisiw. maka ketatawe
ê-iyinîsit, nâspic kî-kitimâkêyimikowisiw. mâka kêtahtawê

e waniyimat kise manitowa ki mamisi pastao. ki
ê-wânêyimât kisê-manitowa kî-mâmisi-pâstâhow. kî-

matinamotawan o tipeyicikewin mekwac okosisa
mâtinamotawan otipêyihcikêwin mêkwâc okosisa

ropoam e isiikasoyit e tipeyitamiyit. eprewiyiniwok atit
Ropoham ê-isiyihkâsoyit ê-tipêyihtamiyit. Eprewiyiniwak âtiht

e ataweyimacik ropaama, ki nawasonewok seropawama
ê-âtawêyimâcik Ropohama, kî-nawasônêwak Jeroboama

e wi otokimamicik.
ê-wî-otokimâmicik.

sotawiyiniwok wiyawaw, ata eka e ki paskewiyacik
Sotawiyiniwak wîyawâw, âta êkâ ê-kî-paskwêyâcik

kayate o kici okimamiwawa, keyiwek miscetwaw ki
kayâtê okihci-okimâmiwâwa, kêyiwêk mihcêtwâw kî-

kitimaisowok kise manitowa e waneyimacik.
kitimâhisowak kisê-manitowa ê-wânêyimâcik.

napokotonosor e ki misiwanacitat serosalem otenaw, ki
Napokotonosor ê-kî-misiwanâcihtât Serosalem ôtênaw, kî-

mecikasam ayamiewikamik, ekosi kakiyaw ekote
mêstihkasam ayamihêwikamik, êkosi kahkiyaw êkotê

e otaskiyit ki sipwetaew papilanik e wi otawokanit. maka
ê-otaskiyit kî-sipwêhtahêw Papilonihk ê-wî-otawokanît. mâka

kise manito kakiyaw e kiskisit taneyikok e kitimakeyimat
kisê-manitow kahkiyaw ê-kiskisit tânêyikohk ê-kitimâkêyimât

eokoni, tanisi mina e ki isi asotamawat kayas oci ntawac
êwakoni, tânisi mîna ê-kî-isi-asotamawât kayâs ohci nitawâc

pesiwew kawi otaskiwak, tepakopomitano tato pipon
pêsiwêw kâwî-otaskîwak, têpakohpomitanaw itâhtopiponê

aspin e awokatimit ekote.
aspin ê-awokatimit êkotê.

otenaw serosalem ki acitaniw, ayamiewikamik mina
ôtênaw Serosalem kî-acitâniw, ayamihêwikamik mîna

moweci eta ki astek oskac.
mowêci êta kî-astêk oskâc.

123

ᐯᐢᓭᐃᐧᐳᓂᐅᐦ ᐅᑐᑭᒪᒥᐊᐧᐊᐧ ᓱᒍᐣ ᑲ ᑭ ᐃᓱ
ᐃᑲᓱᐳᐟ ᑲ ᑭ ᐅᓱᑕᐳᐟ. ᐁᐣᐟᒍᐣ ᐊᓱᒋ ᓀᐁᒥᔭᐣ
ᑭ ᐊᔭᑐᐣᑫᐅᐦ ᐁᑯᑕ, ᐁᐅᑯᓂ ᐅᑭᒪᐊᐧ ᐁ
ᐊᑐᑎᑯᑕᐤ.

ᐁᑯᐣᐱ ᒧᑲᐦ, ᐊᐣᑕᒥᐣᐱ ᒥᓇ ᐯᒋ ᒥᐣᒉ
ᑕᐤ ᑭᓭ ᒪᓂᑐ ᑭ ᐊᐳᑎᓭᐁᐧᐤ ᐊᐳᓱᐳᓂᐊᐧ
ᐊᑎᐟ ᐅ ᑭᑎᒪᑫᐳᒪᑲᓇ ᑭᑕ ᒥᓇᒪᐳᐟ ᑭᓱᐠ
ᑭᑕ ᐊᒋᒧᐣᑕᐊᐧᐳᐟ ᓂᔭᐠ ᑕᓂᓱ ᐁ ᐃᐧ ᐃᑭ
ᓂᐳᐠ, ᑕᓀᐳᑯᐟ ᐁ ᐃᐧ ᑲᐧᑕᑭᑕᐳᐟ ᐊᓂᐃ ᑲ
ᑭ ᐃᐧ ᐯ ᑭᑎᒪᑫᐳᒥᐁᐧᐳᐟ.

ᑕᓂᓱ ᐁ ᑭ ᐃᑭᐠ ᐊᐧᐣᑭᑕᐣᑲᒥᐠ, ᒪᐸᐁᐧᐣ
ᓂᑕᐃᐧᑭᐟ ᓴᓱᕐ, ᐁᐅᑯ ᐅᒪ ᑲ ᒋᒪᑐᑕᒥᐠ
ᐅᑕ ᐃᐣᑯ.

XIII

ᓭᓭ+ ᓀᐊᐧᐤ ᑭᒋ ᒥᑕᑕᑐ ᒥᑕᓇ ᑕᑐ ᐱᐳᐣ
ᐊᐢᐱᐣ ᐁ ᑭ ᑭᒋ ᐊᐢᑭᐃᐧᐳᐠ, ᑭᓭ ᒪᓂᑐ ᑲ ᐯ
ᐃᑎᓭᐊᐧᐟ ᐊᓂᐃ ᑲ ᑭ ᐃᐧ ᐯ ᑭᑎᒪᑫᐳᒥᐁᐧᐳᐟ
ᒥᒋᒪᐧᒋ ᐁ ᐯᐃᒥᐟ, ᒥᐢᑐᑕᐤ ᓇᐊᐊᐧᐠ ᐁ ᐯᒋ
ᐊᒋᒥᒥᐟ. ᑲ ᑭ ᐊᒋᒪᒋᐠ ᐅᒋᑕᐤ ᐁ ᑭ ᑭᐢᑫ
ᐳᑕᒧᐃᑯᐃᐧᓱᒋᐠ, ᒥᑐᓀ ᑭ ᐃᐧᑕᒧᐤ ᐁᐳᑯᐠ ᐁ
ᐃᐧ ᓂᑕᐃᐧᑭᐳᐟ. ᑲ ᑭ ᐃᐧ ᐯ ᑭᑎᒪᑫᐳᒥᐁᐧᐤ,
ᐁᐅᑯ ᐊᓇ ᑭᓭ ᒪᓂᑐ ᐅᑯᓯᓭ ᑲ ᑭ ᓂᑕᐃᐧ
ᑭᐃᑯᐳᐟ ᐅ ᑲᓇᑎᐢᑫᐧᐊᐧ ᒪᕒ ᑲ ᐃᓱᐃᑲᓱᐳᐟ.
ᐁ ᐃᐧ ᑲᐢᑭᑕᒪᐊᐧᐤ ᐊᐳᓱᐳᓂᐊᐧ ᐁᑲ ᑭᑕ ᐤᑕᐁᐧ

123 Cyrus, the Persian king, asked Ezra and Nehemiah working in Babylon to build a temple as the story is told.

Since then many times God has sent prophets to His people to correct them and also to tell them about Him: to disclose what is going to happen, who is going to suffer, which ones are going to have pity shown them.

What happened on earth before Jesus Christ was born here? This is the story up to here.

XIII

Over four thousand years ago God sent those prophets who came and taught the people while they waited for His coming. They told of Him. They told of Him for a reason. They were commissioned; they foretold how He was going to be born. He was going to come and show pity to them. God's Son born of the holy woman Mary was going to counsel the people not to sin and

123 persewiyiniwot otokimamiwawa siros ka ki isi ikasoyit
Persewiyiniwot otokimâwiwâwa Siros kâ-kî-isi-isiyihkâsoyit

ka ki ositayit. estras asici neemiyas ki ayatoskewok ekote,
kâ-kî-osîhtâyit. Estras asici Nehemiyas kî-ayatoskêwak êkotê,

eokoni okimawa e atotikotwaw.
êwakoni okimâwa ê-atotikotwâw.

ekospi mekwac, astamispi mina peci miscetwaw kise
êkospî mêkwâc, astamispî mîna pêci-mihcêtwâw kisê-

manito ki ayitisawew ayisiyiniwa atit
manitow kî-ayitisahwêw ayisiyiniwa âtiht

o kitimakeyimakana kita minomayit kisik kita
okitimâkêyimâkana kita-mînomayit kisik kita-

acimostawayit niyak tanisi e wi ikiniyik, taneyikok e wi
âcimostawâyit niyâk tânisi ê-wî-ikiniyik, tânêyikohk ê-wî-

kwatakitayit anii ka ki wi pe kitimakeyimiweyit.
kwâtakitâyit anihi kâ-kî wî-pê-kitimâkêyimiwêyit.

tanisi e ki ikik waskitaskamik, mayowes nitawikit
tânisi ê-kî-ikihk waskitaskamik, mayowês nihtâwikit

sesokri, eoko oma ka cimatotamik ota isko.
Sesokri, êwako ôma kâ-cimâtotamihk ôta isko.

XIII

sasay newaw kici mitatato mitana tato pipon aspin
sâsay nêwâw kihci-mitâtahtomitanaw tahto pipon aspin

e ki kici askiwiyik, kise manito ka pe itisawat anii ka ki
ê-kî-kici-askîwiyik, kisê-manitow kâ-pê-itisahwât anihi kâ-kî

wi pe kitimakeyimiweyit micimwaci e peimit, miscetwaw
wî-pê-kitimâkêyimiwêyit micimwâci ê-pêhimît, mihcêtwâw

naaway e peci acimimit. ka ki acimacik ocitaw e ki
nâway ê-pêci-âcimimît. kâ-kî âcimâcik ohcitaw ê-kî-

kiskeyitamoikowisicik, mitone ki witamwok eyikok
kiskêyihtamohikowisicik, mitonê kî-wîhtamwak iyikohk

e wi nitawikiyit. ka ki wi pe kitimakeyimiwet, eoko ana
ê-wî-nihtâwikiyit. kâ-kî-wî-pê-kitimâkêyimiwêt, êwako ana

kise manito okosisa ka ki nitawikiikoyit o kanatiskwewa
kisê-manitow okosisa kâ-kî-nihtâwikihikoyit okanâtiskwêwa,

mari ka isiikasoyit. e wi kaskitamawat ayisiyiniwa eka
Mari kâ-isiyihkâsoyit. ê-wî-kaskîtamawât ayisiyinwa êkâ

kita ntawe
kita-nitawi-

124

124 suffer in the underworld. He came to obtain the forgiveness of their sins; this is why He became a human being.

Jesus Christ was His name; He is our God and a member of the human race. When He was thirty years old He began to teach them; He told the people how to behave, to be compassionate. He chose companions while He was teaching, but only twelve. They were His apostles, those ones He sent successively all over to make people aware of His teaching.

Jesus Christ showed that He was divine. Many times He performed miracles: He brought the dead back to life; from all kinds of sicknesses also He suddenly brought people back to health. He did well for all the people. He obtained the forgiveness of their sins; He even died for them on the cross, allowing Himself to be crucified. As a human, Jesus Christ suffered, He was killed; but He was also divine because He made it possible for His suffering to be useful to us.

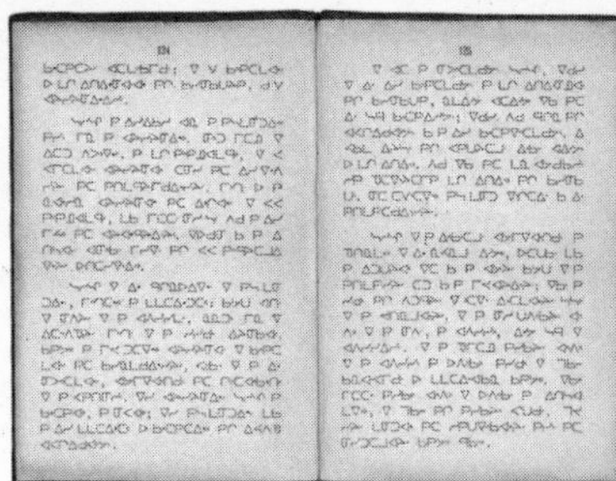

124 kwatakitayit atamaskamikok; e pe kaskitamawat
kwâtakihtâyit atamaskamikohk, ê-pê-kaskîtamawât

o maci itiwiniwawa kici kasinikateyiki, ko pe
omacihtiwiniwâwa kici-kâsînikâtêyiki, kô-pê-

ayisiyiniwiisot.
ayisiyiniwihisot.

sesokri ki isiikaso ana ki kisemanitowiw kisik mina
Sesokri kî-isiyihkâsow ana kî kisê-manitowiw kisik mîna

ka ayisiyiniwiw. nisto mitano e itato piponwet, ki maci
kî-ayisiyiniwiw. nistomitanaw ê-itahtopiponwêt, kî-mâci-

kiskinoamakew, e papamitamawat ayisiyiniwa
kiskinohamâkêw, ê-papamitamawât ayisiyiniwa

tanisi kita isi wepisiyit kita kitimakeyimikowisiyit. miscet
tânisi kita-isi-wêpisiyit kita-kitimâkêyimikowisiyit. mihcêt

o kinawasona ayisiyiniwa kita wiciwat e papa
ê-kînawâsônât ayisiyiniwa kita-wîcêwât ê-papa-

kiskinoamaket, maka mitatat nisosap piko ki isi miyew
kiskinohamâkêt, mâka mitâtaht nîsosâp piko kî-isi-miyêw

kita ayiwakeyiwiyit. eokoni ka ki itisawat aniskac misiwe
kita-ayiwâkêyiwiyit. êwakoni kâ-kî itisahwât âniskac misiwê

kici papa kiskeyitamoiweyit otitasiwewin.
kici-papa-kiskêyihtamohiwêyit otitasiwêwin.

sesokri e wi kecinaoiwet e kise manitowit, miscetwaw
Sesokri ê-wî-kêhcinâhohiwêt ê-kisê-manitowit, mihcêtwâw

ki mamatawitotam: kayate atit e nipiyit e ki apisisimat,
kî-mamâhtâwitôtam: kayâtê âtiht ê-nipiyit ê-kî-apisisimât,

nanatok mina e itaspineyit miscet e ki sisikoc iyinikaat.
nanâtohk mîna ê-itâspinêyit mihcêt ê-kî-sisikoc-iyinikâhât.

kakiyaw ki miyo totawew ayisiyiniwa e kaskitamawat
kahkiyaw kî-miyo-itôtawêw ayisiyiniwa ê-kaskîtamawât

kita kasinamakowisiyit, paskac e ki wi nipostamawat,
kita- kâsînamâkowisiyit, pâskac ê-kî-wî-nipôstamawât,

ayamiewatikok kita cistaaskwatit e ki pakitinisot.
ayamihewahtikohk kita-cîstahâskwâtît ê-kî-pakitinisot.

esi ayisiyiniwit sesokri ki kwatakiaw, ki nipaaw; esi
(ê-)isi-ayisiyiniwit Sesokri kî-kwâtakihâw, kî-nipahâw; (ê-)isi

kise manitowit maka ki isi mamatawitam okwatakitawin
kisê-manitowit mâka kî-isi-mamâhtâwîtam okwâtakihtawin

kici iyepine apaciikowayak.
kici-iyêpinê âpacihikowâyahk.

125

125 Because He died for us, Jesus Christ obtained the forgiveness of our sins. He did not avoid hard suffering to be useful to us. He suffered for us without regret to let it take its course. When anyone wants his sins forgiven, he must repent. He believes in God's help when he shows remorse.

Jesus Christ was hung on the cross. His body was taken down, to be buried, but His spirit had gone where He had been before. He went to tell those who were compassionate and who had good behaviour how to enter Heaven. Already He had opened the door for them. On the second night after He died, He came back to life. All of a sudden He brought Himself to life. Forty days later He came back to earth. He rose to Heaven while He was being watched by those who believed in Him, all of them. And after ten days on a holy day He sent the Holy Spirit on Pentecost to give them a strong heart and to make them understand everything.

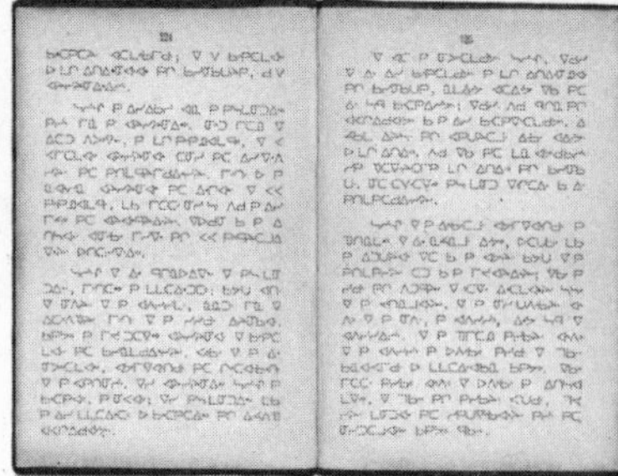

125 e ata ki nipostamakoyak sesokri, ekosi e wi isi
ê-âta kî-nipôstamâkoyahk Sesokri, êkosi ê-wî-isi-

kaskitamakoyak ki maci itiwininowa kici kasinikateki,
kaskihtamâkoyahk kimacihtiwininowa kici-kâsînikâtêki,

namawiya atawiya eka kita wi seke kwatakiisoyak; ekosi
namâwiya âtawiya êkâ kita-wî-sêhkê-kwâtakihisoyahk; êkosi

piko kecina kici apaciikowayak ka ki isi
piko kêhcinâ kici-âpacihikowâyahk kâ-kî-isi-

kwatakiestamakoyak. i yekama iyisac kici pakiteyitamot
kwâtakihêstamâkoyahk. iyêkamâ iyisâc kici-pakitêyihtamôt

wikac awiyak o maci itiwin. piko eka kita mana
wîhkâc awiyak omacihtiwin. piko êkâ kita mâna

ayakokasok soki netaweyitamiki maci itiwin kici
ayakôkâsok sôhki-nêtawêyihtamihki macihtiwin kici-

kasinikatek. nita tapwetawew kise manito wecitawi ka
kâsînikatêk. nihtâ-tâpwêtawêw kisê-manitow wîcihitowin kâ-

wi kitimakitakowisiyit.
wî-kitimâkitakowisiyit.

sesokri e ki iskwatamot ayamiewatikok ki netinamwan
Sesokri ê-kî-iskwâtamot ayamihêwahtikohk kî-nîtinamwân

e wi nayenamot wiyaw, otacakwa maka ki itoteyiwa eta
ê-wî-nayênamot wiyaw, otahcâhkwa mâka kî-itohtêyiwa âta

ka ki ayayit kayate e ki kitimakisiyit tato ka ki miyo
kâ-kî-ayâyit kayâtê ê-kî-kitimâkisiyit tahto kâ-kî-miyo-

ayiwiyit; ekwa kisikok kici pitokeyit e ntawe witamawayit
ayiwiyit; êkwa kîsikohk kici-pihtokwêyit ê-nitawi-wîtamawâyit

sasay e ki yotinamowayit. e ki niso tepiskayik aspin e
sâsay ê-kî-yôtinamowâyit. ê-kî-nîso-tipiskâyik aspin ê-

ki nipit, ki apisisin, wiya seke e apisisiisot. e ki nemitano
kî-nipit, kî-apisisin, wîya sêhkê ê-apisisihîsot. ê-kî-nêmitanaw

kisikayik aspin e ki apisisik ke opiskaw kisikok e mekwac
kîsikâyik aspin ê-kî-apisisik kî-opiskâw kîsikohk ê-mêkwâc-

kanawapamikot o mamatawiakana kakiyaw. ekwa
kanawâpamikot omamâhtâwihâkana kahkiyaw. êkwa

mitatat kisikaw aspin e opiskat ki itisaamawew,
mitâtaht kîsikâw aspin ê-ohpiskât kî-itisahamawêw,

e mekwac kici kisikayik paktekot, meyosiyit manitowa
ê-mêkwâc-kihci-kîsikâyik Paktekot,(ê-)miyosiyit manitowa

kita sokiteeskawayit kisik kita nisitotamoayit kakiyaw
kita-sôhkitêhêskawâyit kisik kita-nisitohtamohâyit kahkiyaw

kekway.
kîkway.

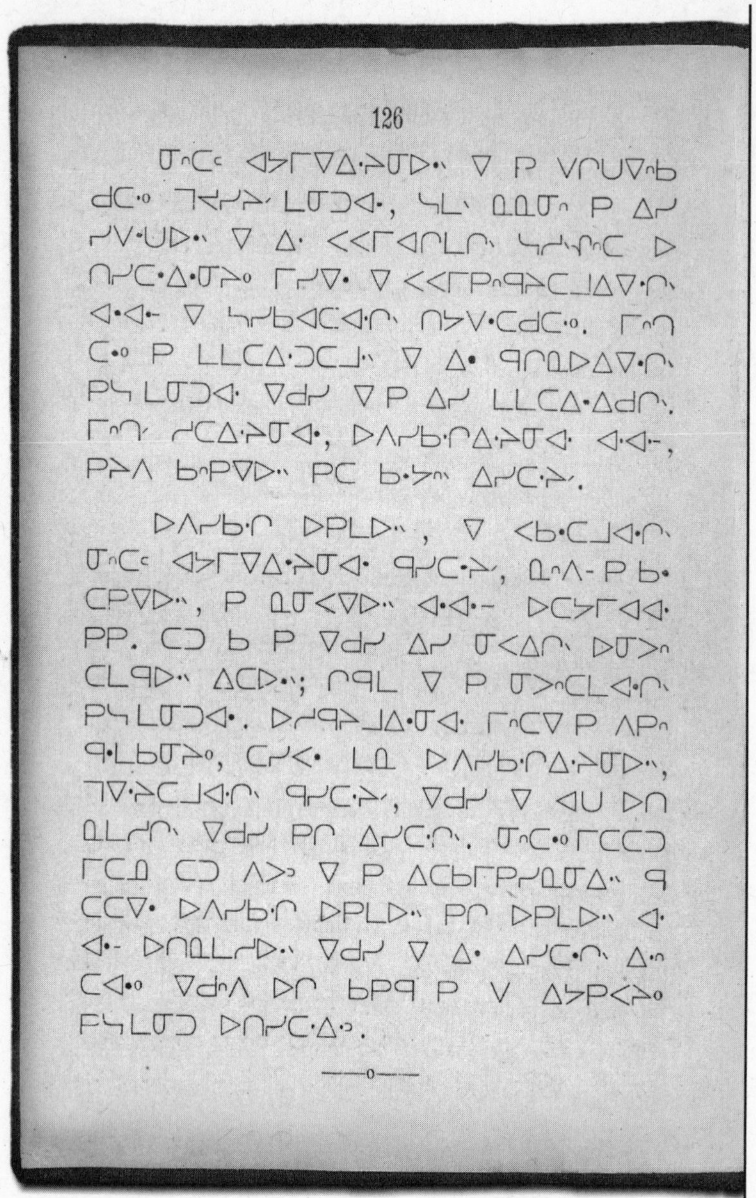

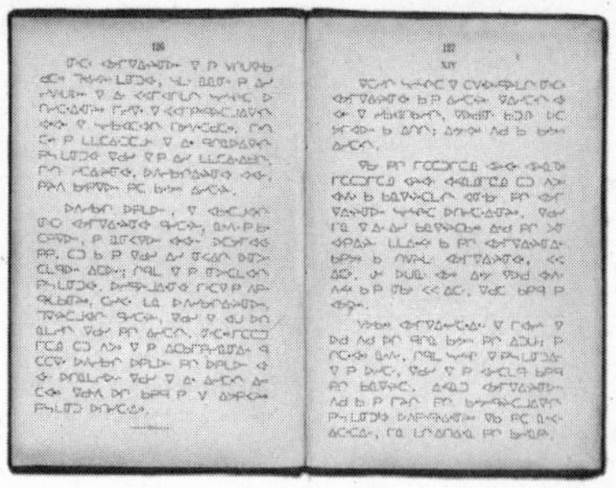

126 In the beginning the Holy Spirit entered the hearts of the disciples. Right away in all directions they set out. They travelled to spread Jesus Christ's teaching. All over they travelled to let others know of Him. They blessed those who believed.

Since God had performed miracles, they were going to make sure to make Him known. They directed sinners to reform and behave well. In the beginning the disciples were despised. Their behaviour forever made them suffer. Many early disciples and believers were martyred. Those that died for others died for Jesus. Their bravery speaks clearly. Over three thousand winters ago a ceremony occurred. The bishops chose a leader. They selected one among them; this ceremony is followed today.

——o——

nistam ayamiewiyiniwok e ki peciteeskakotwaw
nistam ayamihêwiyiniwak ê-kî-pêcitêhêskâkotwâw

meyosiyit manitowa, semak nananiw ki isi sipwetewok e
(ê-)miyosiyit manitowa, sêmâk nanânisk kî-isi-sipwêhtêwak ê-

wi papami acimacik sesokrista o tisitwawiniyiw misiwe
wî-papâmi-âcimâcik Sesokrista otisîhtwâwiniyiw misiwê

e papamikiskeyitamoiwecik wawac e sasikaatawacik
ê-papâmi-kiskêyihtamohiwêcik wâwâc ê-sâsîkahatawâcik

tiyapwetakotwaw. miscetwaw ki mamatawitotamwok
tâpwêtâkotwâw. mihcêtwâw kî-mamâhtâwitôtamwak

e wi kecinaoiwecik kise manitowa ekosi e
ê-wî-kêhcinâhohiwêcik kisê-manitowa êkosi ê-

ki isi mamatawiikocik. miscet sotawiyiniwa,
kî-isi-mamâhtâwihikocik. mihcêt Sotawiyiniwa,

opisikwaciwiyiniwa wawac, kiyipi kaskiewok kita kwayask
opisikwâciwiyiniwa wâwâc, kiyipi kaskihêwak kita-kwayask-

isitwayit.
isîhtwâyit.

opisikwaci okimawok, e pakwatamowacik nistam
opisikwâci okimâwak, ê-pakwâtamowâcik nistam

ayamiewiyiniwa kesitwayit, naspic ki kwatakiewok, ki
ayamihêwiyiniwa kê-isîhtwâyit, nâspic kî-kwâtakihêwak, kî-

nanipaewok wawac otayamiawa ki ki. tato ka ki
nânipahêwak wâwâc otayamihâwa kiki. tahto kâ-kî

ekosi isi nipaicik onipostamakewok itawok; cikema e
êkosi isi-nipahîcik onipôstamâkêwak itâwak; cikêma ê-

ki nipostamawacik kise manitowa. osokeyimowiniwa
kî-nipôstamawâcik kisê-manitowa. osokêyimowiniwa

mistae ki pikiskwemakaniyiw, tasipwa mana
mistahi kî-pîkiskwêmâkaniyîw, tâsipwâ mâna

o pisikwaciwiyiniwok, meweyitamowacik kesitwayit,
opisikwâciwiyiniwak, (ê-)miywêyihtamowâcik kê-isîhtwâyit,

ekosi e ate otinamasocik ekosi kici isitwacik. nistwaw
êkosi ê-ati-otinamâsocik êkosi kici-isîhtwâcik. nistwâw

mitatatomitano tato pipon e ki itakamikisinaniwik
mitâtahtomitanaw tahto pipon ê-kî-itâkamikisinâniwak

ketatawe opisikwaci okimawok kici okimawok wawac
kêtahtawê opisikwâci okimâwak kihci-okimâwak wâwâc

otinamasowok ekosi e wi isitwacik wistawaw ekospi oci
otinamâsowak êkosi ê-wî-isîhtwâcik wîstawâw êkospî ohci

kakike ki pe iyakipayiw kise manito otisitwawin.
kâkikê kî-pê-iyâkipayiw kisê-manitow otisîhtwâwin.

——o——

127

XIV

ᐁᑕᓱᕆᐠ ᓴᓱᐧᓂᑕ ᐁ ᑕᐯᐧᐅᐧᑫᔭᒪᕆᐠ ᑎᓇᑕᑦ
ᐊᔭᒥᐁᐃᐧᔭᑎᐊᐧ ᑲ ᑭ ᐃᓱᑕᐧᔭ ᐁᐃᓱᑕᐧᕆᐠ ᐊᐧ
ᐊᐧ ᐁ ᓱᑲᐊᕆᑲᓱᕆᐠ, ᐁᐅᑯᑎᐠ ᑲᑐᕈᐠ ᐅᑕ
ᔭᒥᐊᐅᐦ ᑲ ᐃᑎᕆᐠ; ᐃᐧᔭᐊᐧᐤ ᐱᑯ ᑲ ᑲᐧᔭᐦ
ᐃᓱᑕᐧᕆᐠ.

ᐁᑲᐧ ᑭᕆ ᒥᑕᑕᑐᒥᑕᓇ ᐊᐳᐊᐧᐦ ᐊᐳᓇᑎᐤ
ᒥᑕᑕᑐᒥᑕᓇ ᐊᐳᐊᐧᐦ ᐊᔦᓇᓇᒥᑕᓇ ᑕᑐ ᐱᔮ
ᐊᐦᐱᔮ ᑲ ᑲᓇᐁᐧᔭᑕᒪᕆᐠ ᐊᑎᐦᑲ ᑭᕆ ᐊᔭᒥ
ᐁᐃᐧᔭᑎᐅᐦ ᓴᓱᐧᓂᑕ ᐅᑎᓱᑕᐧᐃᐧᑎᔭᐤ, ᐁᑯᓱ
ᒥᓇ ᐁ ᐃᐧ ᐃᓱ ᑲᓇᐁᐧᔭᑕᑲᐧᐤ ᐃᐦᑯ ᑭᕆ ᐳᑎ
ᐊᐦᑭᐃᐧᔭᐠ ᒪᒪᐃᐧᔦᐦ ᑲ ᑭᕆ ᐊᔭᒥᐁᐃᐧᔭᑎᐃᐧᐦ
ᑲᑭᔭᐤ ᑲ ᑎᐯᔭᒪᐟ ᐊᔭᒥᐁᐃᐧᔭᑎᐊᐧ, ᐸᐸ
ᐃᑕᐤ, ᔪᑦ ᐅᐣᑌᐠ ᐊᔭᐤ ᐃᐧᔭ ᐁᐅᑯ ᐊᐦᐱᔮ
ᐱᔦᙆ ᑲ ᑭ ᑎᑲᔮ ᐸᐸ ᐃᑕᐟ, ᐁᑯᑕ ᑲᑭᑫ ᑭ
ᐊᔭᐅᐦ.

ᐯᔭᑲᐤ ᐊᔭᒥᐁᐃᐧᓱᑕᐧᐃᐧᔮ ᐁ ᒥᐊᐧᓱᐠ ᐁ
ᐅᑯ ᐱᑯ ᐅᕆ ᑫᕆᓇ ᑲᐧᔭᐦ ᑭᕆ ᐃᑐᐡ: ᑭ
ᕆᑕᐧᐊᐧᐤ ᓇᐦᐱ, ᕆᑫᒪ ᓴᓱᐧᕆ ᐁ ᑭᓴᒪᑎᑐᐃᐧᐦ
ᐁ ᑭ ᐅᓱᑕ, ᐁᑯᓱ ᐁ ᑭ ᐊᓱᑕᒪᑫ ᑲᑭᑫ
ᑭᕆ ᑲᓇᐁᐧᔭᑕᐠ. ᐃᔦᓇᑐ ᐊᔭᒥᐁᐃᐧᔭᑎᐅᐦ
ᐱᑯ ᑲ ᑭ ᒥᔭᕆᐠ ᑭᕆ ᑲᐧᔭᐦᑫᐧᔭᑕᒧᐃᐧᕆᐠ
ᑭᓴᒪᑎᑐᐊᐧ ᐅᐱᑭᐦᑫᐧᐃᐧᑎᔭᐤ ᐁᑲ ᑭᑕ ᓇᐦᐸᐦ
ᐃᑕᐦᑕᐃᐧᐦ, ᒥᓇ ᒪᕆᐃᑎᐃᐧᓇ ᑭᕆ ᑲᓯᓇᑭᐠ,

127 XIV

All of the first priests believed in Jesus Christ. They behaved according to His teaching. So did those who were baptized, those Catholic worshippers, those who behaved properly.

For over one thousand and eight hundred and eighty more winters the bishops and priests have been keeping the ceremony of Jesus Christ and they are going to keep it until the world has ended. The bishop of Rome, since the time of Saint Pierre, is their leader.

They keep the same religion according to the teaching of Jesus Christ who is supernatural. He did make it so. He had promised forever to care for it dearly. The priests were charged to clarify God's word, not to contradict it, and to remove evil sins.

etasicik sesokrista e tapwewokeyimacik nistam
ê-itasicik Sesokrista ê-tâpwêwakêyimâcik nistam

ayamiewiyiniwa ka ki isitwayit e isitwacik wawac
ayamihêwiyiniwa kâ-kî-isîhtwâyit ê-isîhtwâcik wâwâc

e sikaacikasocik, eokonik katolik otayamiawok ka
ê-sîkahâhcikâsocik, êwakonik kâtolik ôtayamihâwak kâ-

iticik; wiyawaw piko ka kwayask isitwacik.
itîcik; wîyawâw piko kâ-kwayask-isîhtwâcik.

ekwa kici mitatatomitano ayiwak ayinanew
êkwa kihci-mitâtahtomitanaw ayiwâk ayinânêw

mitatatomitano ayiwak ayenanomitano tato pipon
mitâtahtomitanaw ayiwâk ayênânomitanaw tahto pipon

aspin ka kanaweyitamwacik aniskac kici
aspin kâ-kanawêyihtamwâcik âniskac kihci-

ayamiewiyiniwok sesokrista otisitwawiniyiw, ekosi
ayamihêwiyiniwak Sesokrista otisîhtwâwiniyiw, êkosi

mina e wi isi kanaweyitakwaw isko kici poni askiwiyik
mîna ê-wî-isi-kanawêyihtâhkwâw isko kici-pôni-askîwiyik

mamawiyes ka kici ayamiewiyiniwit kakiyaw ka
mamawiyês kâ-kihci-ayamihêwiyiniwît kahkiyaw kâ-

tipeyimat ayamiewiyiniwa, papaitaw, rom otenak ayaw
tipêyimât ayamihêwiyiniwa, papâ itâw Rom ôtênâhk ayâw

wiya eoko aspin piyer ka ki nikan papa itat, ekota kakike
wîya êwako aspin Piyer kâ-kî nîkan papâ-itât êkota kâkikê

ki ayawok.
kî ayâwak.

peyakwan ayamiewisitwawin e miwasik eoko piko
pêyakwan ayamihêwisîhtwâwin ê-miywâsik êwako piko

oci kecina kwayask kici itotek: kicitwawin naspic, cikema
ohci kêhcinâ kwayask kici-itohtek: kihcitwâwin nâspic, cikêma

sesokri e kise manitowit e ki ositat, ekosi e ki asotamaket
Sesokri ê-kisê-manitowit ê-kî-osîhtât, êkosi ê-kî-asotamâkêt

kakike kici kanaweyitak. iyenato ayamiewiyiniwok piko
kâkikê kici-kanawêyihtahk. iyênato ayamihêwiyiniwak piko

ka ki miyicik kici kwayaskweyitamoiwecik kise manitowa
kâ-kî mîyicik kici-kwayaskwêyihtamohiwêcik kisê-manitowa

opikiskwewiniyiw eka kita naspic itastawit, mina
opîkiskwêwiniyiw êkâ kita-nâspic itastâwît, mîna

maci itiwina kici kasinakik.
macihtiwina kici-kâsînâhkik.

128 The priests instruct believers with all their hearts so they listen to the priests. God took them as His children to be with Him forever and to live well. While they are living they encourage them to follow His commandments.

As soon as someone is sinful, right away his spirit leaves him. God returns his spirit to him by passing judgement. If he is pure, He will renew him. It he is not pure, he will go to the underworld to get rid of it, to suffer continuously. If he bears sin only in purgatory, he will partly renew him until he is forgiven.

When the world ends, all of them will rise. Never again will anyone die. Jesus will come and place judgement on them all. When for the last time He places judgement, no one will be in purgatory. Up until the time they are going to Heaven, those who must partly atone are going to enter purgatory. If they behave badly in the underworld, they will be placed in hell. They will lose their spirit and

128 tato ka tapwewokeyitakik ispicoteicik iyenato
tahto kâ-tâpwêwâkêyihtahkik ispicotêhicik iyênato

ayamiewiyiniwa kesi kiskinoamakotwaw, ekosi
ayamihêwiyiniwa kêsi kiskinohamâkotwâw, êkosi

e nanaitawacik; eokonik kise manitowa ka
ê-nanahihtawâcik; ewakonik kisê-manitowa kâ

otawasimimikotwaw; eokonik ke wiciwacik
otawâsimimikotwâw; êwakonik ka-wîcêwâcik

kakike kici miyo ayacik kispin isko pimatisicik
kâkikê kici-miyo-ayâcik kîspin isko pimâtisicik

akameyinakataweyitamwewok otitasiwewiniyiw.
âhkamêyinâkatawêyihtamwewak otitâsiwêwinîyiw.

mayaw ketimakisici awiyak semak otacakwanakatik
mayaw kêtimâkisici awiyak sêmâk otahcâhkwanakatihk

kise manitowa e natayit kici wiyasowatikoyit, kispin
kisê-manitowa ê-nâtâyit kici-wiyasiwâtikoyit, kîspin

kanatisiyici kita miyo pakitinimawa kispin eka
kanâtisiyici kita-miyo-pakitinimawâwa kîspin êkâ

kanatisiyici, atamaskamikok kita wepinimawa, taki
kanâtisiyici, atâmiskamikohk kita-wêpinimawa, tahki

kita kwatakitayit; kispin kikiskakoyici pastaowinisa piko,
kita-kwatakihtâyit; kîspin kikiskakoyici pâstâhowinisa piko,

okasinamakewiskotek kita nomi pakitinimawa isko kici
okâsînamâkêwiskotêhk kita-nômi-pakitinimawa isko kici-

kisi kasinamasoyit.
kîsi-kâsînamâsoyit.

poni askiwiki kakiyaw kita apisisinwok eka kitwam kici
pôni-askîwiki kahkiyaw kita-apisisinwak êkâ kîhtwâm kici-

nipitwaw. ekwa sesokri kita pe wiyasowatew kakiyaw
nipitwâw. êkwa Sesokri kita-pê-wiyasiwâtêw kahkiyaw

mamawi. iskwayac ki wiyasowatitwawi, namawiya awiyak
mâmawi. iskwayâc kî-wiyasiwâtitwâwi, namâwiya awiyak

o kasinamakewiskotek kitwam kita ayaw, ekwayikok
okâsînamâkewiskotehk kîhtwâm kita-ayâw, ekwayikohk

e wi poni payik eoko; kisikok e wi pitokaicik tato ekota
e-wî-pôni-payik êwako; kîsikohk ê-wî-pihtokahîcik tahto êkota

ka ki ntawe nomi kwatakitacik.
kâ-kî-nitawi-nômi-kwâtakihtâcik.

meci isiwepesicik atamaskamikok kita
mwêhci isiwêpisicik atâmiskamikohk kita-

macostewepinawok esi owiyawicik mina isi otaca
macostêwêpinâwak ê-isi-owiyawicik mîna isi-otahcâ

129 experience much suffering all the time. Everyone will burn with the devils and suffer with them; they will be hateful to one another.

They have good behaviour on earth, it is said of them, if they follow carefully the commandments of Jesus Christ. They have bad behaviour, it is said of them, if they do not follow carefully Jesus's commandments. In this way they will live poorly.

In the beginning the great priests were going to separate in all directions, to go and teach. They wrote their belief so that faith remains the same. We read the way in which they followed faith. Exactly like this is the way in which we believe. All the time, until the end of the world, we are going to have faith.

Even though I follow Him properly and behave, no one earns Heaven for himself. No one will go there if he does not live well and humbly.

——o——

129 kocik, iyepine kwatakitaniw ekote kakike e kisisok, maci
hkocik, iyêpinê kwâtakîhtâniw êkotê kâkikê ê-kîsisohk, maci-

manitowok e wici kitimakisimicik e wici
manitowak ê-wîci-kitimâkisimicik ê-wîci-

pakwatikowisimicik.
pakwâtikowisimicik.

o miyoisiwepisiwok itawok waskitaskamik, aniki ka
omiyo-isiwêpisiwak itâwak waskitaskamik, aniki kâ

mitone nanakataweyitamwacik sesokrista
mitonê nânâkatawêyihtamwâcik Sesokrista

o titasiwewiniyiw. o maci isiwepisiwok itawok maka aniki
otitâsiwêwiniyiw. omaci-isiwêpisiwak itâwak mâka aniki

eka ka nanakataweyitamwacik sesosa o titasiwewiniyiw,
êkâ kâ-nânâkatawêyihtamwâcik Sesosa otitâsiwêwiniyiw,

piyis ekosi ka isi kitimakisicik.
piyis êkosi ka-isi-kitimâkisicik.

nistam kici ayamiewiyiniwok ispi e wi paskewiitocik
nistam kihci-ayamihêwiyiniwak ispî ê-wî-paskêwîhitôcik

nananis e wi ntawe kiskinoamakecik, pitama ki
nanânis ê-wî-nitawi-kiskinohamâkêcik, pitamâ kî-

masinaamwok tanisi isi tapwewokeyitakwaw, mitone kici
masinahamwak tânisi isi-tâpwêwakêyihtakwâw, mitonê kici-

peyakwaniyik otisitapwewokeyitamowiniwa. eokoyiw oma
pêyakwaniyik otisi-tâpwêwakêyihtamowiniwa. êwakoyiw ôma

ka ayamitayak. ka isi tapwewokeyitakik moweci ekosi
kâ-ayamihtâyahk. kâ-isi-tâpwêwakêyihtâhkik mowêci êkosi

isi e tapwewokeyitamak; mina kakike piyis isko kici
isi ê-tâpwêwakeyihtamâhk; mîna kâkikê piyis isko kici-

ponaskiwiki, ekosi e wi isi tapwewokeyitamik.
pôni-askîwiki, êkosi ê-wî-isi-tâpwêwakêyihtamihk.

e ata wiciiwek kwayask kesitwak namawiya pa ki
ê-âta-wîcihiwêk kwayask kêsîtwâk namâwiya pahki

kaskitamasonaniw kisikok kici itotek eka mitone
kaskitamasonâniw kîsikohk kici-itohtêk êkâ mitonê

nanakataweyitamiki, eka miyo kitimakisiki.
nânâkatawêyihtamihki, êkâ miyo-kitimâkisiki.

——o——

Two things are wanted on earth. First is to have good behaviour and love God forever. Then a sinful life must be avoided. We must continuously flee sin and think of the future. God must be loved. It is also necessary to behave well always.

Every time one breaks the teaching of God, through bad behaviour, one sins. Sin happens in two ways: at first he will come born with it. To act badly to another is its own sin. It is made in two ways: one big sin is called mortal and the other, a small sin, is called venial. Sins grow big if everyone is satisfied so to make it great. Sometimes one commits a small sin when it is not purely bad what one does.

There are seven serious sins: pride, stinginess, adultery, envy, greed, anger and laziness. There are still lots of sins.

XV

niso kekway ntaweyicikatewa waskitaskamik mekwac
nîso kîkway nitawêyihcikâtêwa waskitaskamik mêkwâc

e ayak kici miyo isiwepisik: nikan kise manito naspic kita
ê-ayâk kici-miyo-isiwêpisik: nîkân kisê-manitow nâspic kita-

sakiit, ekosi ekwa maci itiwin kici pakwatamik, piko
sâkihiht, êkosi êkwa macihtiwin kici-pakwâtamihk, piko

taki kici akameyitapasitak. kise manito kita sakiit,
tahki kici-âhkamêyitapasîhtâhk. kisê-manitow kita-sâkihiht,

piko iyepine miyo itatisiwin kici nocitak.
piko iyêpinê miyo-itâtisiwin kici-nôcitâhk.

tato pekwatak kise manito, eoko oma maci itiwin
tahto pakwâtahk kisê-manitow, êwako ôma macihtiwin

ka itamik. niswayakanwa maci itiwina nikan micimwaci
kâ-itamihk. nîswayakanwa macihtiwina nîkan micimwâci

maci itiwin ka pe kikinitawikik eoko ôma maci itiwin
macihtiwin ka-pê-pikînihtâwikik êwako ôma macihtiwin

ka oci kitimaiwet atak ekwa mina seke maci itiwin
ka-ohci-kitimâhiwêt âtak êkwa mîna sêhkê macihtiwin

ka itamik. niswayakanwa seke maci itiwina: peyak kici
kâ-itamihk. nîswayakanwa sêhkê macihtiwina: pêyak kihci-

maci itiwin isiikatew, kotak maka apisci maci itiwinis.
macihtiwin isiyihkâtêw, kotak mâka apisci macihtiwinis.

kici maci totakaniw mana kispin naspic tepeyimonaniw
kihci-maci-tôtakâniwiw mâna kîspin nâspic têpêyimonâniw

aci piko kici totamik kekway e ata mitone kiskeyitamik
aci piko kici-itôtamihk kîkway ê-âta-mitonê-kiskêyihtamihk

naspic e mayatak. apisci maci totakaniw maka kispin eka
nâspic ê-mâyâtahk. apisci maci-itôtakâniw mâka kîspin êkâ

iyenato mayataki ka totamik.
iyênato mâyâtahki kâ-itôtamihk.

tepakop itatinwa mamawiyes kici maci itiwina
têpakohp itâtinwa mamawiyês kici-macihtiwina

mamitisiwin, sasakisiwin, pisikwatisiwin,
mamihcisiwin, sasâkisiwin, pisikwâtisiwin,

sawanakeyimowin, kasakewin, kisiwasiwin, kitimiwin.
sawânakêyimowin, kâsakêwin, kisiwâsiwin, kîtimiwin.

eokoni maci itiwina oci kocipayiki keyapic miscet
êwakoni macihtiwina ohci kôcipayiki kêyâpic mihcêt

maci itiwina.
macihtiwina.

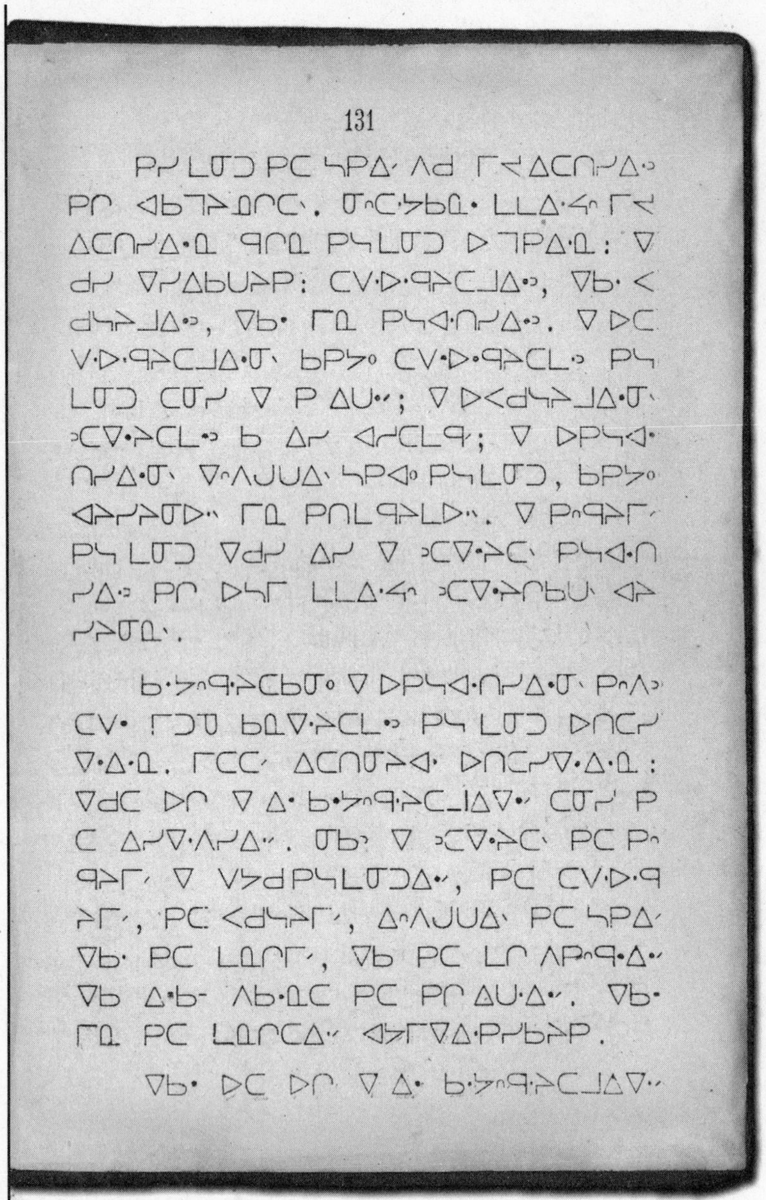

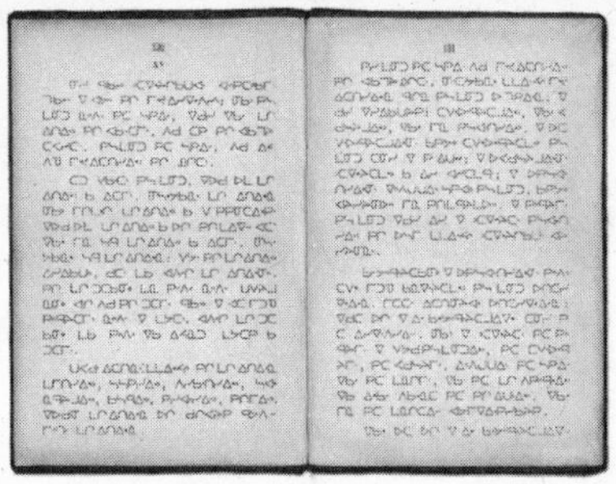

131 To love God one must have good behaviour and always be courageous. There are three important gifts from God: they are called gifts. To have faith and hope and also kindness from his faith, all are gifts. God had said and promised His hope from His kindness. From his heart, God is love. All of the people are loving. God is known to want His people to be kind. This is very necessary.

To be kind it is necessary to keep God's commandments. There are ten commandments. They make clear how to behave. First He is one God. We have faith in Him, have hope in Him, and we love Him through His heart. We respect Him and do not speak His name badly. We respect Sunday.

From His teachings we change our ways.

131 kisi manito kita sakiit piko miyo itatisiwin kici
kisê-manitow kita-sâkihiht piko miyo-itâtisiwin kici-

akameyi nocitak. nistwayakanwa mamawiyes miyo
âhkamêyi-nôcihtâhk. nîstwayakanwa mamawiyês miyo-

itatisiwina kecina kise manito o mekiwina: ekosi
itâtisiwina kêhcinâ kisê-manitow omêkiwina: êkosi

esiikateyiki: tapwewokeyitamowin, ekwa pakoseyimowin,
ê-isiyihkâtêyiki: tâpwêwakêyihtamowin, êkwa pakosêyimowin,

ekwa mina kisewatisiwin. e otapwewokeyitamowinik
êkwa mîna kisêwâtisiwin. ê-otâpwêwakêyihtamowinihk

kakiyaw tapwewokeyitamwan kise manito tanisi
kahkiyaw tâpwêwakêyihtamwan kisê-manitow tânisi

e ki itwet; e opakoseyimowinik ntaweyitamwan ka isi
ê-kî-itwêt; ê-opakosêyimowinihk nitawêyihtamwân kâ-isi-

asotamoket; e okisewatisiwinik espicoteik sakiaw kise
asotamâkêt; ê-okisêwâtisiwinik ê-ispicotêhik sâkihâw kisê-

manitow, kakiyaw ayisiyiniwok mina kitimakeyimawok.
manitow, kahkiyaw ayisiyiniwak mîna kitimâkêyimâwak.

e kiskeyimit kise manito ekosi isi e ntaweyitak
ê-kiskêyimiht kisê-manitow êkosi isi ê-nitawêyihtahk

kisewatisiwin kici osami mamawiyes ntaweyicikatek
kisêwâtisiwin kici osâmi mamawiyês nitawêyihcikâtêk

ayisiyininak.
ayisiyinînâhk.

kwayaskweyitakaniw e okisewatisiwinik kispin tapwe
kwayaskwêyihtâkâniw ê-okisêwâtisiwinihk kîspin tâpwê

mitone kanaweyitamwan kise manito otitasiwewina.
mitonê kanawêyihtamwân kisê-manitow otitâsiwêwina.

mitatat itatiniyiwa otitasiwewina: ekota oci e wi
mitâtaht itâtiniyiwa otitâsiwêwina: êkota ohci ê-wî-

kwayaskweyitamoiwet tanisi ki ta isiwepisiwit. nikan
kwayaskwêyihtamôhiwêt tânisi kita-isiwêpisiwit. nîkân

e ntaweyitak kita kiskeyimit e peyako kise manitowit,
ê-nitawêyihtahk kita- kiskêyimiht ê-pêyako-kisê-manitowit,

kita tapwewokeyimit, kita pakoseyimit, ispicoteik kita
kita-tâpwêwakêyimiht, kita-pâkosêyimiht, ê-ispicotêhik kita-

sakiit ekwa kita manacimit, eka kita maci pikiskwewit
sâhkihht êkwa kita-manâcimht, êkâ kita-maci-pîkiskwêwht

eka wikac pikwanata kita kici itwewit. ekwa mina kita
êkâ wîhkâc pikwânâta kita- kici-itwêwiht. êkwa mîna kita-

manacitawit ayamiewikisikayiki.
manâcihtwâwit ayamihêwi-kîsikâyiki.

ekwa ota oci e wi kwayaskweyitamoiwet
êkwa ôta ohci ê-wî-kwayaskwêyihtamohiwêt

132

ᑕᑌᓯ ᐃᓯ ᐣᑕᐁᐧᔨᒪᐟ ᐊᔨᓯᔨᑌᐊᐧ ᑭᑕ ᐃᓯ
ᒪᑎᑎᐃᑐᔨᐟ; ᑕᓯᐸᐧ ᐁᑌᐧᐦ: ᐁᐧᔭᑌᑭᐃᑯᔦᐠ ᑭᐣ
ᑌᔨᒥᓛᐠ, ᒪᑎᑎᐃᑯᐠ, ᓴᑭᐃᑯᐠ, ᑎᑎᐃᑕᐃᐧᑯᐠ,
ᐊᔭᑎᑎᒪᒪᐃᐧᑯᐠ ᑭᑎ ᐅᐱᒪᑎᐅᑕᐧ°.

ᐁᑲᐃᐧᔭ ᐃᐧᑲ- ᑭᑕ ᐃᐧ ᑌᐸᑕᑲᑌ° ᐊᐅ
ᑭᑕ ᐃᐧ ᑌᐸᐃᓕᐠ ᐊᐧᐃᐧᐣ. ᐁᑲᐧ ᒥᑎ ᑭᑕᐊᒪᑫᐟ
ᐁᑲ ᑎ ᐊᔨᒣᐧᐃᐧᐦ, ᐁᑲ ᑭᑕ ᐱᔨᑲᐧᑎᒥᑐᑌᔨᑕᒧᐟ
ᐁᑲ ᑭᑕ ᑌᑕᐊᑕᒥᒥᐁᐧᐃᐧᐦ, ᐁᑲ ᑭᑕ ᑲᑲᔦ
ᔨᐃᐧᐦ ᑭᑎ ᐃᐧᔭᑎᔨᐠ.

ᑭᑎ ᐊᔭᒥᐁᐃᐧᔨᑌᐅᐦ ᒪᒪᐃᐧ ᐁ ᐣᑕᐁᐧᔨ
ᑕᒪᐊᐧᑎᐠ ᐅᑭᐣᑭᑏᐊᒪᑲᑌᐊᐧᐊᐧ, ᑌᐸᑯᐠ ᕿᑲᐧ+
ᐊᔨᐊᐧᐦ ᑭᑎ ᑎᑎᑲᑕᐁᐧᔨᑕᒥᔨᐟ ᑲᐧᔭᐦ ᑭᑎᐃᓯ
ᑕᐧᔨᐟ ᐁᑯᓯ ᑲ ᐃᑕᐣᑌᔨᑭ ᐅᑎᑕᓯᐁᐧᐃᐧᑌᐊᐧᐊᐧ
ᑭᑎ ᑭᓯᑲᐊᐧ ᑭᑕ ᒪᑎᑎᑕᑌᐃᐧᐊᐧ. ᐊᔭᒥᐁᐃᐧ
ᑭᓯᑲᕿ ᒥᐧᑎ ᑭᑎ ᑭᓯᑲᕿ. ᐊᔭᒥᐁᐃᐧᑲᒥᑯᐠ ᑭᑕ
ᐣᑕᐁᐧ ᐊᔭᒥᐊᑌ° ᑯᒣᐣ ᐁᑌᐧᑭ. ᐅᑕᔭᒥᐊᐅᐧᐠ
ᑲᑭᔭ° ᑭᑕ ᐃᐧ ᐊᑎᒥᓱᐅᐦ ᓴᔭᕿ ᐯᔭᑲᐧ° ᑕᑕᐧ°
ᐊᐣᑭᐃᐧᔨᑭ. ᑭᑕ ᑲᐣᑭᑕᒪᓱᐅᐦ ᑭᑎ ᓴᐣᑲᒧᐃ
ᑎᐠ ᓴᔭᕿ ᑕᑕᐧ° ᐃᐣᐸᔨᑭ ᐸᐠ ᑭᑕ ᐃᐧ ᐃᔦᐊᐧ
ᑌᓯᐃᓱᑎᑌ° ᑌᒥᑕᑎ ᑭᓯᑲ° ᒪᔦᐁᐧᐣ ᐸᐠ ᐃᐣᐸᔨᐠ.

ᐊᔭᒥᐁᐊᐧᑎᑯᑭᓯᑲᕿ ᐁᑲᐃᐧᔭ ᐃᐧᔭᐣ ᑭᑕ
ᒥᑎᑎᑌ°. ᐅᑕᔭᒥᐊᐅᐧᐦ ᑭᑕ ᐃᐧ ᐅᑎᑎᒪᐁᐧᐅᐧᐦ
ᑭᑕ ᐅᐱᒪᑎᐅᔨ ᐊᔭᒥᐁᐃᐧᔨᑌᐊᐧ.

——o——

132 He wants the people to have respect for one another. For that reason be proud of your parents, respect them, love them, listen to them, hold firmly to how they live.

Never kill someone or kill oneself, and never be cruel and talk about someone. Do not think about committing adultery; do not steal and do not cheat in order to be rich.

Priests and bishops want all people, all of them, to follow these beliefs. There are seven precepts. Look after properly how to behave as they are written. Respect the holy days and Sunday; on holy days, go to church and attend Mass. All worshippers will confess at least once a year to be worthy to receive Communion. Each Lent one should make a sacrifice for forty days before Easter arrives.

On Good Friday do not eat meat. Worshippers will follow how to live their life from the priests.

——o——

132 tanisi isi ntaweyimat ayisiyiniwa kita isi manaciitoyit;
tânisi isi-nitawêyimât ayisiyiniwa kita-isi-manâcihitoyit;

tasipwa etwek: weyonikiikoyek kisteyimikok, manaciikok,
tâsipwâ itwêk: wêyonikihikoyêk kistêyimihkok, manâcihihkok,

sakiikok, nanaitawikok, ayatinamawikok
sâkihihkok, nanahihtâwihkok, ayatinamawihkok

kici opimaciotwaw.
kici-opimâcihotwâw.

ekawiya wikac kita wi nipatakaniw apo kita wi
êkâwiya wîhkâc kita-wî-nipâtâkâniw ahpô kita-wî-

nipaisok wawis. ekwa mina kitaamaket eka ci ayimwewit,
nipâhisok wâwîs. êkwa mîna kitahamâkêt êkâ kici-âyimwêwit,

eka kita pisikwacimitoneyitamot eka kita nita
êkâ kita-pisikwâcimitonêyihtamôt êkâ kita-nihtâ-

atamimiwewit, eka kita kakayesiwit kici wiyatisik.
atamimiwêwiht, êkâ kita-kakayêsiwit kici-wiyatisik.

kici ayamiewiyiniwok mamawi e ntaweyitamawacik
kihci-ayamihewiyiniwak mâmawi ê-nitawêyihtamawâcik

o kiskinoamakaniwawa, tepakop kekway ayiwak kici
okiskinohamâkaniwâwa, têpakohp kîkway ayiwâk kici-

nanakataweyitamiyit kwayask kici isitwayit ekosi ka
nânâkatawêyihtamiyit kwayask kici-isîhtwâyit êkosi kâ-

itasteyiki otitasiwewiniwawa kici kisikawa kita
itastêyiki otitâsiwêwiniwâwa kihci-kîsikâwa kita-

manacitaniwiwa. ayamiewikisikake mina kici kisikake.
manâcihtâniwiwa. ayamihêwi-kîsikâki mîna kihci-kîsikâki.

ayamiewiwikamikok kita ntawe ayamianiw lames
ayamihêwikamikohk kita-nitawi-ayamihâniw Lames

etweki. otayamiawok kakiyaw kita wi acimisowok seyake
itwêki. otayamihâwak kahkiyaw kita-wî-âcimisowak sêyakê

peyakwaw tatwaw askiwiyiki. kita kaskitamasowok
pêyakwâw tahtwâw askîwiyiki. kità-kaskîtamâsowak

kici saskamoicik seyake tatwaw ispayiki pak kita wi
kici-saskamohicik sêyakê tahtwâw ispayiki pak kita-wî-

iyewanisiisonaniw nemitano kisikaw mayowes pak ispayik.
iyêwanisihisonâniw nêmitano-kîsikâw mayowês pak ispayik.

ayamiewatikokisikake ekawiya wiyas kita micinaniw.
ayamihêwahtiko-kîsikâki êkâwiya wîyâs kita-mîcinâniw.

otayamiawok kita wi otinamawewok kita opimacioyit
otayamihâwak kita-wî-otinamawêwak kita-opimâcihoyit

ayamiewiyiniwa.
ayamihêwiyiniwa.

——o——

If God's commandments and those of the priests are followed very carefully, so then for certain, we will live properly. God wants us to be able to achieve His work here. He has never denied someone what He wants for them. Jesus died for us. He achieved salvation for us, so then we are able to work together for Heaven. He aids us in two ways, as the best way to achieve salvation for ourselves: with a prayer and the healing gifts of the Spirit.

There are seven sacraments. Jesus made everything. Jesus cleans us of the original sin we are born with. To be cleaned in that way first happens in baptism.

Confirmation later affirms our belief in the power of prayer.

When Communion is taken, it is the eating of Jesus as God, and also as a human Being.

kispin mitone nanakataweyitamwan kisemanito
kîspin mitonê nânâkatawêyihtamwan kisê-manitow

otitasiwewina, mina kici ayamewiyiniwok
otitâsiwêwina, mîna kihci-ayamihêwiyiniwak

otitasiwewiniwawa, ekosi kecina kwayask kita ki
otitasiwêwiniwâwa, êkosi kêhcinâ kwayask kita-kî-

itotaniwan; maka ekosi kici isi kaskitak ntaweyitamwan
itôtâniwân; mâka êkosi kici-isi-kaskîtâhk nitawêyihtamwan

kise manito o nisokamakewin. ata wiya namawikac
kisê-manitow onîsôhkamâkêwin. âta wîya namâwîhkâc

eokoyiw kici sakitowat awiya nitaweyitamakoci, sesokri
êwakoyiw kici-sâkîtowat awiya nitawêyihtamâkoci, Sesokri

e ki nipostamakoyak ki ki kaskitamakonaw ekosi kici
ê-kî-nipôstamâkoyahk ki-kî-kaskîtamâkonaw êkosi kici-

isi nisokamakowisiyak. ki ki isi miyikonaw niswayak
isi-nîsôhkamâkowisiyahk. ki-kî-isi-miyikonaw nîswayak

kici isi kaskitamasowayak kita nisokamakoyak:
kici-isi-kaskîtamâsowâyahk kita-nîsôhkamâkoyahk:

mawimescikewin, ekwa micacak onanatawiowina.
mawimôscikêwin, êkwa micahcâhk onânâtawihowina.

tepakop itatinwa micacak o nanatawiowina sesokri
têpakohp itâtinwa micahcâhk onanâtawihowina Sesokri

ka ki ositat kakiyaw, kitacakonowa e wi kanaciat
kâ-kî-osîhtât kahkiyaw, kitahcâhkonowa ê-wî-kanâcîhât

eokoni oci. ayamiewisikaacikasowin nikan ka
êwakoni ohci. ayamihêwi-sikahacikâsowin nîkân kâ-

mekinaniwik, maci itiwin ka pe kiki nitawikik kici
mêkinâniwik, macihtiwin kâ-pê kiki nihtâwikihk kici-

kasinikatek; micacak ekwa e kanaciit eokoyiw oci,
kâsînikâtêk; micahcâhk êkwa ê-kanâcihiht êwakoyiw ohci,

ekwayak iteyitakosiw kici sakiikowisit.
êkwayak itêyihtâkosiw kici-sâkihikowisit.

kicitwawisokiteeskakewitominitowin moestas ka
kihcitwâwisôhkitêhêskâkêwitôminitowin mwêstas kâ-

mekinaniwik ayiwak keyapic mistae kici iteyitakosik,
mêkinâniwik ayiwâk kêyâpic mistahi kici-itêyihtâkosik,

ayiwak kici sokeyitamik ayamiawin.
ayiwâk kici-sôhkêyihtamihk ayamihâwin.

ewkaristiwin wetinamiki, sesokri kesi manitowit mina
ewkaristiwin wî-otinamihki, Sesokri kêsi manitowit mîna

kesi ayisiyiniwit e mowit.
kêsi-ayisiyiniwit ê-mowiht.

134 Confession is the way in which the sins of the baptized are forgiven. This is the only way in which to have a clean spirit again.

A religious act of anointing is given to someone when he is near death.

Holy Orders give the religious powers to those who work for God.

Holy Matrimony is the formal marriage of a man and woman for the rest of their life, as noble beings.

Prayer also is very useful. For that reason we are asked all the time to pray often so that when we pray we please Him, the One who made us, and who gained salvation for us. One should make good use of everything when one prays, if one is going to be pitied. From his heart he will ask for help from God. He does not want to be in a position of honour, which is only praying from his mouth.

Jesus teaches us how to pray well. Only He made the prayer: "Our Father who art in Heaven." It is for that reason that it is called the Lord's Prayer.

134 ayamiewikasiamakewin ka oci kasinikateki seke
ayamihêwikâsîhamâkêwin kâ ohci kâsînikâtêki sêhkê

maci itewina. sasay e ki sikaacikasok, meci totamiki, eoko
macihtiwina. sâsay ê-kî-sîkahâhcikâsok, mêci-tôtamîki, êwako

piko kici pakoseyitamik kita kanatacakweisok kawi.
piko kici-pakosêyihtamihk kita-kanâtahcâhkwêhisok kâwi.

iskwayac ayamiewitominitowin ka miyit awiyak wa
iskwayâc ayamihêwitôminitowin kâ-mîyit awiyak wâ

kitimakisici.
kitimâkisici.

ayamiewiyiniwiisiitowin, koci mamatawiicik atit,
ayamihêwiyiniw-isîhtwâwin, koci-mamâhtâwihicik âtiht,

kise manitowa kita atoskawacik.
kisê-manitowa kita-atoskawâcik.

kici wikitowin, koci wikitaicik napew asici iskwew
kihci-wîkihtowin, koci-wîkihtahîcik nâpêw asici iskwêw

isko pimatisitwawi tapiskoc kici ayacik.
isko pimâtisitwâwi tâpiskôc kici-ayâcik.

mawimoscikewin mina ayiwak e apaciikoyak, tasipwa
mawimoscikêwin mîna ayiwâk ê-âpacihikoyahk, tâsipwa

netaweyimikowisiyak kakike kici mawimoscikeyak;
(ê-)nitawêyimikowisiyahk kâkike kici-mawimôscikeyahk;

mewimoscikeyaki maka e atami ayak ka tipeyimikoyak,
mawimôscikeyâhki mâka ê-atamihayahk kâ-tipêyimikoyâhk,

ekosi isi e kaskitamasoyak kita otinamakoyak kakiyaw
êkosi isi ê-kâskîtamâsoyahk kita-otinamâkoyahk kahkiyaw

kekway kici miyo apacitawayak. mewimoscikeki, kispin
kikway kici-miyo-âpacîhâwâyahk. mawimôscikêki, kîspin

wi kitimakitakosinaniw, espicoteik kita natotamawaw
wî- kitimâkihtâkosinâniwiw, ê-ispicotêhik kita-natotamawâw

kise manito ka isi ntaweyitamat, namawiya kici ki
kisê-manitow ka-isi-nitawêyihtamât, namâwiya kici-ki-

cikeyitakowisit awiyak tepiyak otonik oci mawimosciket.
cikêyihtâkowisît awiyak têpiyak otônihk ohci mawimoscikêt.

mitone ki kiskinoamakonaw sesokri tanisi kita miyo
mitonê kikiskinohamâkonaw Sesokri tânisi kita-miyo-

mawimoscikewayak, wiya tepiyaw e ki ositat ayamiawin:
mawimôscikêwayahk, wîya tipiyaw ê-kî-osîhtât ayamihâwin:

« notawinan kici kisikok eyayan, » ka isi kicitiniyik,
"nohtâwinân kihci-kîsikohk ê-ayâyân," ka-isi- kihcitiniyik,

tasipwa manito mawimoscikewin esiikateyik.
tâsipwâw manitôw mawimôscikêwin ê-isiyihkâtêyik.

135 God is offered in a sacrifice, when the Mass is said. There mostly God is pleased.

For a long time, God wanted animals to be sacrificed. He recalls those sacrifices when He is given as a sacrifice. He alone is the ultimate, atoning sacrifice.

A great sacrifice that God wanted, had happened when His Son was crucified. It happened on Mount Calvary that Jesus was sacrificed to comfort His Father. He is going to be able to have His people show pity on one another. Each day this sacrifice is repeated. When sacrifice is offered at Mass, when Jesus is being offered, no one will be killed again. But He will be eaten, for sure in a great offering of a special kind, because the people are using it to live and to be compassionate.

It is good and useful to have a clean spirit. It helps to understand others. Those without pride are disbelieved. Mary, the mother of God, had a clean spirit. She gave birth to Jesus Christ.

135 wiyeciiweki wiyepinasoki (lames etweki) ekota
wiyêcihiwêki wêpinâsôki (Lames itwêki) êkota

mamawiyes ka atamiit kise manito.
mamawiyês kâ-atamihiht kisê-manitow.

e ki ntaweyite kayas kise manito pisiskiwa kita
ê-kî-nitawêyihtahk kayâs kisê-manitow pisiskiwa kita-

wepinasostakewit, maka ko miweyitak eokoni
wêpinâsôstakewiht, mâka kâ-miywêyihtahk êwakoni

wepinasowina, nataka niyak e kiskisit kikik e wi kici
wêpinâsowina, nataka nîyak ê-kiskisit kikik ê-wî kici-

wepinasostat okosisa e wi wepinasostakeyit, wiya tepiyaw
wêpinâsôstât okosisa ê-wî-wêpinâsôstâkêyit, wîya tipiyaw

e wi wepinisoyit.
ê-wî-wêpinâsôyît.

sasay ki ispayiw kici wepinasowin ka ki ntaweyitak
sâsay kî-ispayiw kici-wêpinâsowin kâ-kî-nitawêyihtahk

kise manito, ekospi ka ki nipaimit okosisa osetinak
kisê-manitow, êkospî kâ-kî-nipahimôt okosisa osêtinâhk

anima kalper ka itamik. ekota ka ki wepinisot sesokri,
anima Kalper kâ-itamihk. êkota kâ-kî-wêpinâsot Sesokri,

ekosi e wi isikakiciat otawiya, e wi kaskiat kawi kita
êkosi ê-wî-isi-kâkîcihât ohtâwiya, ê-wî-kaskihât kâ-wî kita-

kitimakeyimayit ayisiyiniwa. taki peci sakamopayiw
kitimâkêyimâyit ayisiyiniwa. tahki pêci sakamopayiw

eoko wepinasowin, tatwaw kisikaki wiyepinasoki (lames
êwako wêpinâsowin, tahtwâw kîsikâki wêpinâsoki (Lames

etweki) kawi wiyepinisot sesokri. namawiya atawiya
itwêki) kâwî-wêpinâsot Sesokri. namâwiya atawiya

kitwam kita nipait maka kitamowit. eoko mamawiyes
kîhtwâm kita-nipahît mâka kitamôwiht. êwako mamawiyes

kici mawimoscikewin. eokoyiw osam e apaciikotwaw
kici-mawimoscikewin. êwakoyiw osâm ê-âpacihikotwâw

pematisicik mina ketimakisicik.
pimâtisicik mîna kitimâkisicik.

miwasin ekosi mina apatan okanatacakwewok
miywâsin êkosi mîna âpatan okanâtahcahkwêwak

e pakosiitwaw kita itwestamakecik, e kisteyitakositwaw,
ê-pakosihitwâw kita-itwêstamâkecik, ê-kistêyihtâkositwâw,

eka wikac e anwetakowisitwaw, osam oti kenatacakwet
êkâ wîhkâc ê-anwêhtâkowisitwâw, osâm ati kênâtahcahkwêt

mari, kise manitowa ka okawimikot, sesokrista
Mari, kisê-manitowa kâ-okâwîmikot, Sesokrista

e kisemanitowiyit e ki nita
ê-kisê-manitowiyit ê-kî-nihtâ-

135

ᐃᐧᑭᐊᐟ. ᑕᓂᓯ ᐁ ᑭ ᐃᑎᑯᐟ ᐃᐢᐱ ᐁ ᑭ ᐯ ᐊᑕᒥᐢᑲᑯᐟ ᐅᑭᓯᑯᐊᐧ, ᐁᑯᓯ ᐃᓯ ᑲᑭᑫ ᐱ ᑭᐢᑳᐧᑕᐤ ᑫᓇᑕᐅᑫᐟ ᒪᕆ ᒣᐃᐧᒧᐢᑕᑎ ᒪᓇ ᑭᑕ ᐃᑌᐧᐢᑕᒪᑫᐟ.

ᐊᔭᒥᐁᐃᐧᑲᒥᑯᐠ ᒪᐃᐧᒧᐢᑎᑲᓂᐤ, ᑭᑎ ᐁᐧᐱ ᓇᓯᓇᓂᐤ ᑯᒣᐢ ᐁ ᐃᑌᐧᐠ, ᐊᔭᒥᐁᐢᑕᒪᑐᓇᓂᐤ, ᑲᑭᑫ ᒪᒥᐢᑯᑕᒪᐧᐤ ᑭᓭ ᒪᓂᑐ ᐅᐱᑭᐢᑫᐧᐃᐧᐤ ᑫ ᑫᐢᑭᑫᒨᑭ, ᑫᐢᑭᓅᐊᐦᑫᑭ, ᐅᓵᐣ ᐁᑯᑕ ᒥᓯᐁᐧ ᐃᓯ ᐁ ᐃᐧ ᒥᔪ ᐊᐸᑎᐃᑲᐃᐧᔭᐠ ᐤᑐᑌᒥᑎᐠ, ᐁ ᐃᐧ ᑲᐢᑭᐃᑲᐃᐧᔭᐠ ᑲᑭᑫ ᑭᑎ ᒥᔪ ᐃᐧᑎ ᐊᐧᔭᐠ ᑭ ᑭᓭ ᒪᓂᑐᒥᓈᐤ.

ᑲᓇᐊᐧᐸᑕᒧᐠ, ᐤᑐᑌᒥᑎᐠ, ᐅᒪ ᑲ ᐃᑎᓴᐊ ᒪᑲᐃᐧᔭᐠ ᒪᓯᓇᐃᑲᓂᐢ ᒥᑐᓃ ᑭᑎ ᑳᐧᔥᑫᐧᔨ ᑖᒣᐠ ᑭᓭ ᒪᓂᑐ ᑫᓯ ᐤᑕᐁᐧᔨᒥᑯᔭᐠ ᑭᑎ ᐃᓯ ᑕᐊᐧᔭᐠ.

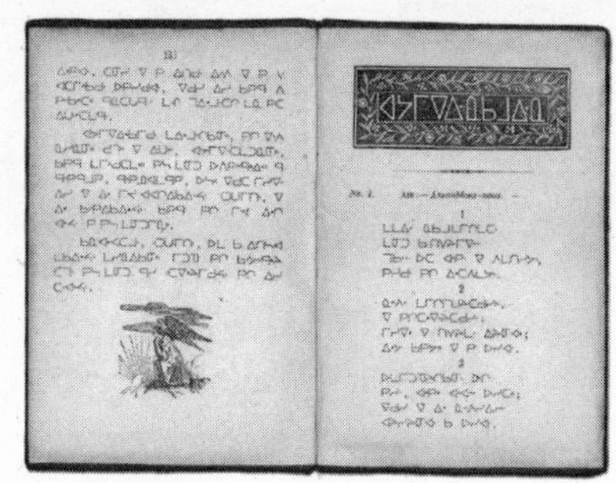

136 The angel greeted her when He came. If we pray like this to Mary, she will intercede for us.

In the church everyone makes an offering when Mass is being said. Everyone prays for one another. All the time the priest mentions God's word when he preaches, when he teaches. In this way you are going to be directed on the good earth, my friends. You people are going be with our Father.

Look at this small book my friends, this one that we follow closely to change our minds. This is the way God wants you to behave.

[ANGEL COPPERPLATE]

136 wikiat. tanisi e ki itikot ispi e ki pe atamiskakot okisikowa,
wikihât. tânisi ê-kî-itikot ispî ê-kî-pê-atamiskâkot okîsikowa,

ekosi isi kakike pi kiskwataw kenatacaket mari
êkosi isi kâkikê pîkiskwâtâw kanâtahcahkêt Mari

mewimostaci mana kita itwestamaket.
mawimostâci mâna kita-itwêstamâkêt.

ayamiewikamikok mawimoscikaniw, kici
ayamihêwikamikohk mawimoscikâniw, kici-

wepinasonaniw lames e itwek, ayamiestamatonaniw,
wêpinâsonâniw Lames ê-itwêk, ayamihêstamâtonâniw,

kakike mamiskotamwan kise manito opikiskwewin ke
kâkikê mâmiskotamwân kisê-manitow opîkiskwêwin kî-

keskikemoki, keskinoamakeki, osam ekota misiwe isi e wi
kêskîkêmôhki, kiskinohamâkêki, osâm êkota misiwê isi ê-wî-

miyo apaciikowiyek ntotemitik, e wi kaskiikawiyek kakike
miyo-âpacihikâwiyêk nitôtêmitik, ê-wî-kaskihikawiyêk kâkikê

kici miyo wiciwayek ki kise manitominaw.
kici-miyo-wîciwâyêk kikisê-manitôminaw.

kanawapatamok, ntotemitik, oma ka itisaamakawiyek
kanawâpahtamok, nitôtêmitik, ôma kâ-itisahamâkawiyêk

masinaikanis mitone kici kwayaskweyitamek kise manito
masinahikanis mitonê kici-kwayaskwêyihtamêk kisê-manitow

kesi ntaweyimikoyek kici isi twawayek.
kêsi nitawêyimikoyêk kici-isîhtwâwayêk.

[ANGEL COPPERPLATE]

No. 1. Air: — *Assemblons-nous.* —

1

2

3

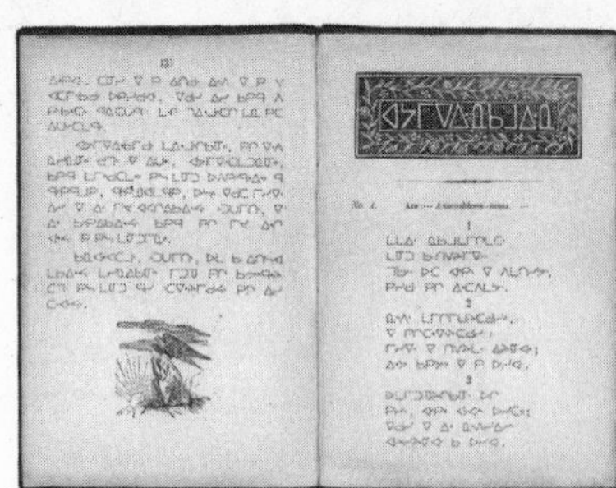

137 PRAYER SONGS

No. 1. Air: – *Assemblons-nous. (Let us come together.)*

1

All praise Him in our song,
God who satisfied us all.
He is here on this land where we are living.
In the Heavens He wishes us to sit with Him.

2

Forever He is adored.
He is holy.
He created the inhabitants of the earth.
He made all of them.

3

Through His word, at the beginning,
He also made earth.
In His image He made
people, when He fashioned them.

137 **AYAMIEWINAKAMOWINA**

AYAMIHEWI-NIKAMOWINA

No. 1. Air: – Assemblons-nous.
No. 1. Air: – Assemblons-nous.

1

mamawi nakamomamicimatak
mâmawi-nakamomamihcimâtâhk

manito ka tipeyimiwet
manitow kâ-tipêyimiwêt

mekwac ota askik e pimatisiyik,
mêkwâc ôta askîhk ê-pimâtisiyik,

kisikok kici witapimayak.
kîsikohk kici-wîtapimâyahk.

2

naspic mamicimiteyitakosiw,
nâspic mamihcimitêyihtâkosiw,

e kicitwaweyitakosit;
ê-kihcitwâwêyihtâkosit;

misiwe e tipeyimat iyiniwa;
misiwê ê-tipêyimât iyiniwa;

wiya kakiyaw e ki osiat.
wîya kahkiyaw ê-kî-osîhât.

3

omamitoneyicikanik oci
omâmitonêyihcikanihk ohci

kisik, askiy wawac ositaw;
kisik, askiy wâwâc osîhtâw;

ekosi e wi naspisiisot
êkosi ê-wî-nâspisihisot

ayisiyiniwa ka osiat.
ayisiyiniwa kâ-osîhât.

138

4

ᒪᔮᐤ ᐁ ᑭ ᐅᓯᐃᐟ ᐊᔨᓯᔨᓂᐤ
ᓂᑕᐃᐧᑭᒋᑲᓂᕽ ᐊᔮᐤ,
ᑲᑭᔮᐤ ᐁᑯᑕ ᐁ ᐃᑕᑯᓂᐠ
ᑕᑭ ᓇᐢᐱᐨ ᑭᒋ ᒥᔪᐊᔮᐠ.

5

ᓴᐧᓇᑫᔨᒧ ᒪᒋᒪᓂᑐ
ᐃᔨᓂᐊᐧ ᐃᓯ ᐊᔮᔨᐟ;
ᐁᑯᓯ ᑭᑎᒪᐁᐤ ᐁ ᓯᑭᐢᑭᒪᐟ
ᒥᓯᒥᓂᓴ ᑭᑕ ᒥᒋᔮᐟ.

No. 2. AIR:—*A servir le Seigneur.*

1

ᓂᑐᑲᒪᐃᐧᓇᐣ,
ᑭᓴᒪᓂᑐ ᓅᑕ,
ᑭᒋ ᑭᐢᑫᔨᑕᒪᐠ
ᑭ ᑭᒋ ᐃᑌᐃᐧᐃᐧᓇᐣ,
ᓂᑐᑲᒪᐃᐧᓇᐣ.

2

ᐊᑲᓭᔨᒥᓇᐣ
ᑕᓂᓯ ᑫ ᐃᔑᔭᐠ
ᑭᒋ ᐃᐧ ᑕᐯᐧᑕᒪᐠ
ᐃᐢᐱᐦ ᐅᑌᐦᐃᔭᐠ
ᐊᑲᓭᔨᒥᓇᐣ.

3

ᐊᐦ ᐊᐦ ᐃᐧᓇᑯᒪ
ᐁ ᐃᐧ ᐅᑎᑎᑯᔭᐠ
ᐊᓄᐦ ᐁ ᓇᑎᑯᔭᐠ
ᑲ ᑎᐯᔨᒋᑫ
ᐊᐦ ᐊᐦ ᐃᐧᓇᑯᒪ.

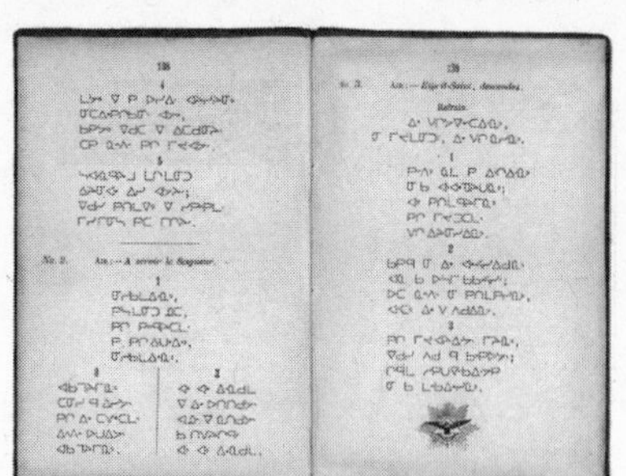

138

4

The very moment that man was made,
He was in a garden,
where everything that existed,
was forever good.

5

The devil was jealous.
The people in the garden
he makes them suffer; he entices them
to eat the big berries.

No. 2. AIR: – *A servir le Seigneur (To serve the Lord.)*

1

Work together with us
God, our Father,
to be able to know
Your holy word.
Work together with us.

2

Encourage us
how to be,
to believe in Him
from our heart.
Encourage us.

3

Thank you.
He is going to reach us.
Today He receives us,
The One who satisfies us.
Thank you.

4

mayaw e ki osiit ayisiyiniw
mayaw ê-kî-osîhît ayisiyiniw

nitawikicikanik ayaw,
nihtâwikihcikanihk ayâw,

kakiyaw ekota e itakoniyik
kahkiyaw êkota ê-ihtakoniyik

taki naspic kici miyo ayat.
tahki nâspic kici-miyo-ayât.

5

sawanakeyimo maci manito
sawânakêyimow maci-manitow

iyiniwa isi ayayit;
iyiniwa isi (ê-)ayâyit;

ekosi kitimaew e sikiskimat
êkosi kitimâhêw ê-sikisimât

misiminisa kita miciyit.
misimînisa kita-mîciyit.

No. 2. Air: – A servir le Seigneur.
No. 2. Air: – A servir le Seigneur.

1

nisokamawinan,
nîsôhkamawinân,

kise manito nota,
kisê-manitow nohtâ,

kici kiskeyitamak
kici-kiskêyihtamahk

ki kici itwewin,
kikihci-itwêwin,

nisokamawinan.
nîsôhkamawinân.

2

akameyiminan
âhkamêyiminân
tanisi ke isiyak
tânisi kê isîyak
kici wi tapwetamak
kici-wî-tâpwêtamahk
ispic oteiyak
ispic otêhiyahk
akameyiminan.
âhkamêyiminân.

3

ay ay winakoma
ay ay wînakoma
e wi otitikoyak
ê-wî-otîtikoyahk
anoc e natikoyak
anohc ê-nâtikoyahk
ka tipeyiciket
kâ-tipêyihcikêt
ay ay winakoma.
ay ay wînakoma.

139

No. 3. Air : — *Esprit-Saint, descendez.*

Refrain.

ᐃᐧ ᐯᑎᔭᐍᐢᑕᐃᐧᓇᐤ,
ᓂ ᒥᔦᒪᓂᑐᐨ, ᐃᐧ ᐯᑎ ᓇᓯᓇᐤ.

1

ᑭᐢᐱᐤ ᓇᒪ ᑭ ᐃᐧᑎᐃᐧᓇᐤ
ᓂ ᑲ ᐊᐧᐊᐧᓃᐸᑌᓇᐤ;
ᐊᐤ ᑭᑎᒪᑫᐸᒥᓇᐤ
ᑭᑎ ᒥᐧᔦᑐᑕᒪᐠ
ᐯᑎ ᐃᐸᓂᓯᐃᓇᐤ.

2

ᑲᑭᑫ ᓂ ᐃᐧ ᐊᐧᓴᓯᐃᑯᓇᐤ
ᐊᓇ ᑲ ᐅᓴᒥ ᑲᑲᓴᓯᐟ;
ᐅᑕ ᓇᐢᐱ- ᓂ ᑭᑎᒪᑭᓯᓇᐤ,
ᐊᐢᑕᐨ ᐃᐧ ᐯ ᐱᑯᐃᓇᐤ.

3

ᑭᑎ ᒥᔦᐊᐸᐃᐧᔭᐠ ᒥᐸᓇᐤ,
ᐁᑯᓯ ᐱᑯ ᑫ ᑲᐢᑭᐅᔭᐠ;
ᑎᑫᒪ ᓯᑭᑌᐍᐦᑲᐃᐧᔭᑭ
ᓂ ᑲ ᒪᐢᑲᐃᐧᓯᓇᐤ.

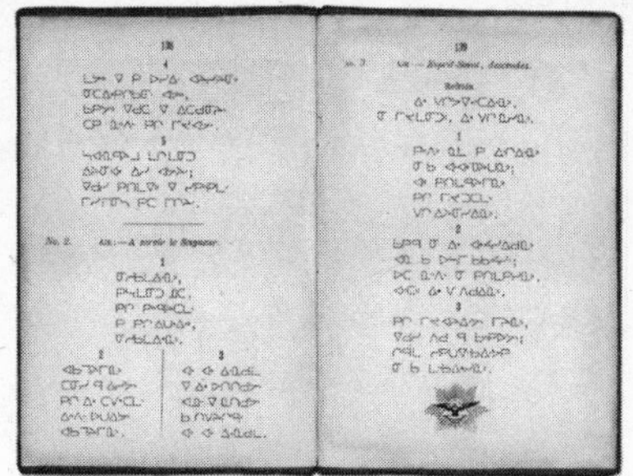

139 *No. 3.* Air: – *Esprit-Saint, descendez.*
(Come down, Holy Spirit.)

Refrain.
Enter into our bodies.
Our good God come and save us.

1
If you are not with us,
we will be confused.
Ah, have pity on us,
for we have sinned.
Make us wise.

2
All the time the devil is going to deceive us,
that one who is very deceitful.
Here forever we are poor in spirit.
Come, you are going to free us

3
To behave well; give us Your help.
That is the only way we can overcome it.
Surely with Your help,
we will be strong.

[HOLY SPIRIT COPPERPLATE]

139 No. 3. Air: – Esprit-Saint, descendez.
No. 3. Air: – Esprit-Saint, descendez.

Refrain.
wi peciyawestawinan,
wî-pêciyawêstawinân,

ni miyomanitom, wi pecinasinan.
nimiyo-manitôm, wî-pêcinâsinân.

1

kispin nama ki wiciwinan
kîspin namâ kiwîciwinân

ni ka wawa neyitenan;
nika-wawanêyihtênân;

aw kitimakeyiminan
âw kitimâkêyiminân

kici miyototamak
kici-miyotôtamâhk

peci iyinisiinan.
pêci-iyinisihinân.

2

kakike ni wi wayesiikonan
kâkikê niwî-wayêsihikonân

ana ka osami kakayesit;
ana kâ-osâmi-kakayêsit;

ota naspic ni kitimakisinan,
ôta nâspic nikitimâkisinân,

astam wi pe pikoinan.
âstam wî-pê-pîkohinân.

3

kici miyo ayiwiyak miyinan,
kici-miyo-ayiwiyahk miyinân,

ekosi piko ke kaskioyak;
êkosi piko kê-kaskihoyâhk;

cikema sokiteeskawiyaki
cikêma sôhkitêhêskawiyâhki

ni ka maskawisinan.
nika-maskawisînân.

[HOLY SPIRIT COPPERPLATE]

140

No. 4. Air: — *Travaillez à votre salut.*

Refrain.

ᒥᓯ ᑫᑳᐧᐩ ᐁ ᒪᔭᑕᐠ
ᓇᐢᐱᐨ ᐃᐧᔭᑲᑌᓂᒧᕽ.

1	4
ᓇᓇᑲᑕᐁᐧᐸᑕᒧᕽ ᒪᓂᑐ ᐅᑎᑕᓯᐁᐧᐃᐧᐣ, ᑭᔭᐋᐧᐤ ᐁᔭᒥᐊᔦᐠ ᐯᔭᑎᐠ ᐃᐧᐃᓯᐁᐧᐱᓯᐠ.	ᑭᔭ ᐁᐧᓴᒥᑐᒋᔭᐣ ᐃᐧᒥᒋᒥᓇ ᑭ ᑌᔭᒋᐩ ᑭᒋ ᐊᐸᓯᐸᒋᐅᐧᐠ ᑭᒋ ᐁᑲ ᑳᐧᑕᑭᒪᑕᐤ.
2	5
ᑲ ᐃᐧ ᒪᓂᑐᑲᓯᔦᐠ ᓇᐢᐱᐨ ᑭ ᒪᒋᑐᑌᓇᐋᐧᐤ ᐯᔭᑯ ᑭᓭ ᒪᓂᑐ ᐃᐧᔭ ᐱᑯ ᐅᒪᓂᑐᒥᐠ.	ᐊᐸᒪᐣ ᒪᒋ ᒪᓂᑐ ᑳᑭᑫ ᑭᒥ ᐃᐧᑕᐱᒥᐟ; ᐁ ᑳᑳᐧᑕᑫᐸᑕᒥᐠ ᑳᑭᑫ ᐃᐢᑯᑌᐠ ᐁᐊᔭᐠ.
3	6
ᐅᓭᐨ ᐁ ᑭᑎᒪᐃᓯᐟ ᐊᐃᐧᔭᐠ ᐁᑭᐃᐢᑫᐧᐯᐢᑭᐟ ᐊᐧᐊᐧᐨ ᐁ ᐱᓯᑳᐧᑎᓯᐟ ᒥᓇ ᐁ ᒋᑕᑭᓯᐊᐧᓯᐟ.	ᑭᑎᒪᑫᐸᒥᐣ ᓅᑕ ᐊᓅᐨ ᐁ ᐸᑯᓭᐸᒥᑕᐣ ᑭᒋ ᑳᓯᓇᒪᐃᐧᔭᐣ ᑲ ᑭᐃᓯ ᑭᓯᐊᐧᐃᑕᐣ.

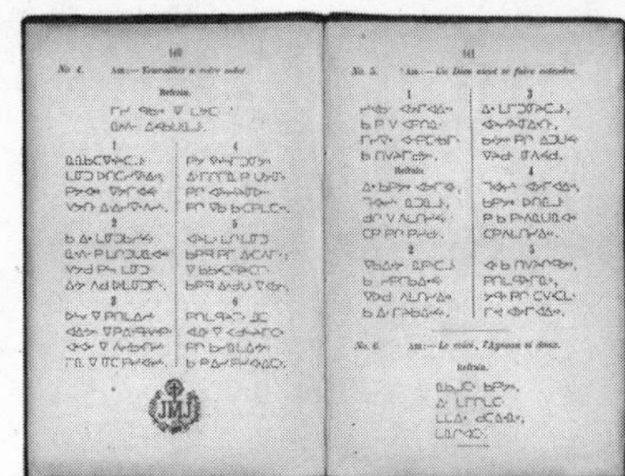

140 *No. 4.* Air: – *Travaillez à votre salut.*
(Work for your salvation.)

Refrain.

A lot of things are evil.
Forever remove them from us.

1	4
Look after God's commandment. You are praying to behave carefully.	If you gossip too much, hold onto your tongue. For important people do not torment them.
2	5
Do not be proud. Forever you all sin. There is only one God. Have only Him as God.	It is difficult to sit with the devil always, everyone is suffering and always in the fire.
3	6
Because he does not listen someone who has foolish behaviour is committing adultery and is good at being angry.	Have pity on me, Father. Today, I am hoping that You will remove from me the way in which I angered You.

[JESUS MARY JOSEPH COPPERPLATE]

140 No. 4. Air: – Travaillez à votre salut.
No. 4. Air: – Travaillez à votre salut.

Refrain.
misi kekway e mayatak
misi kîkway ê-mâyâtahk

naspic iyekatenamok.
nâspic iyîkâtênamok.

1
nanakataweyitamok
nânâkatawêyihtamok

manito otitasiwewin,
manitow otitâsiwêwin,

kiyawaw eyamiayek
kîyawâw (ê-)ayamihâyek

peyatik wiisiwepisik.
pêyâhtik wî-isiwêpisik.

2
ka wi manitokasoyek
ka-wî-manitokâsoyêk

naspic ki macitotenawaw
nâspic kimacitôtênâwâw

peyako kise manito
peyako kisê-manitow

wiya piko omanitomik.
wîya piko omanitômik.

3
osam e kitimaisot
osâm ê-kitimahisot

awiyak e ki iskwepeskit
awiyak ê-kî-iskwêpêskît

wawac e pisikwatisit
wâwâc ê-pisikwâtisit

mina e nitakisiwasit.
mîna ê-nihtâ-kisiwâsit.

4
kiya wesamitoniyan
kiya wêsâmitonêyan

wi micimina ki teyaniy
wî-mîcimina ki-têyaniy

kici ayisiyiniwok
kihci-ayisiyiniwak

kici eka kwatakimatwaw.
kici êkâ kwâtakimatwâw.

5
ayiman maci manito
ayiman maci-manitow

kakike kici witapimit;
kâkikê kici-wîtapimiht;

e kakwatakeyitamik
ê-kakwâtakêyihtamihk

kakike iskotek e ayak.
kâkikê iskotêhk ê-ayâk.

6
kitimakeyimin nota
kitimâkêyimin nohtâ

anoc e pakoseyimitan
anohc ê-pakosêyimitân

kici kasinamawiyan
kici-kâsînamawiyan

ka ki isikisiwaitan.
kâ-kî-isi-kisiwahitân.

[JESUS MARY JOSEPH COPPERPLATE]

141

No. 5. Air: — *Un Dieu vient se faire entendre.*

1

ᓯᐸᑳᐠ ᐊᔭᒥᐊᐃᐧᐣ
ᑳ ᑭ ᐯ ᐸᑭᑎᓇᐠ
ᒥᓯᐍ ᐊᐢᑭᑕᐢᑳᒥᐠ
ᑳ ᑎᐯᔨᒥᑯᔭᐠ.

Refrain.

ᐃᐧ ᑲᑭᔭᐤ ᐊᔭᒥᐊᐠ,
ᒣᐊᐧᓯᐠ ᓇᑐᓇᒧᐠ,
ᑯᑎ ᐯ ᐱᒪᑎᓯᔪᐠ
ᑕᑭ ᑭᑎ ᑭᓯᑰᐠ.

2

ᐁᑳᐃᐧᔭ ᓇᑭᐢᑕᒧᐠ
ᑳ ᓯᑭᒥᑳᐃᐧᔪᐠ
ᐁᐅᑯ ᐱᒪᑎᓯᐃᐧᐣ
ᑳ ᐃᐧ ᒥᔨᑳᐃᐧᔪᐠ.

3

ᐃᐧ ᒪᒥᑐᓀᔨᑕᒧᐠ,
ᐊᔨᓯᔨᓃᐃᐧᑎᐠ,
ᑳᐧᔭᐢ ᑭᓯ ᐃᑐᑌᔪᐠ
ᐁᔨᑯᐠ ᓃᐱᔪᑯ.

4

ᒣᐊᐧᓯᐠ ᐊᔭᒥᐊᐃᐧᐣ,
ᑲᑭᔭᐤ ᐅᑎᓇᒧᐠ
ᑭ ᑲ ᑭᐢᐱᓇᑌᓇᐊᐤ
ᑕᑭᐱᒪᑎᓯᐃᐧᐣ.

5

ᐊᐤ ᑳ ᑎᐯᔨᒋᑫᔭᐣ,
ᑭᑎᒪᑫᔨᒥᓇᐣ,
ᔭᑫᐢ ᑭᑎ ᑕᐯᐧᑕᒪᐠ
ᒥᔪ ᐊᔭᒥᐊᐃᐧᐣ.

No. 6. Air: — *Le voici, l'Agneau si doux.*

Refrain.

ᓇᑲᒧᑕᐠ ᑲᑭᔭᐤ,
ᐃᐧ ᒪᒥᒋᒪᑕᐠ
ᒪᒪᐃᐧ ᑯᑕᐃᐧᓇᐤ,
ᒪᓇᒋᐊᑕᐠ.

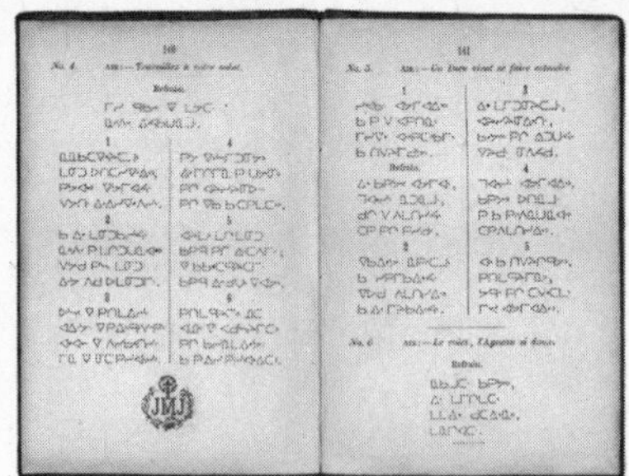

141 No. 5. Air: – *Un Dieu vient se faire entendre.*
(The Lord comes to be heard.)

1

It is a strong prayer
that He delivered here,
all over on earth,
the One who made us,

Refrain.

All of you pray.
Search for the good.
For everyone to
live by it
and be forever
in Heaven.

2

Do not stop there.

When you are being
encouraged
to a new kind of life,
you are going to
be given it.

3

Think about it,
my people,
to walk properly
until you die.

4

Prayer is good.
If we pray,
we will earn

eternal life.

5

Ah, the One who
made us all,
have pity on us.

Help us to believe in You
by good prayer.

No. 6. Air: – *Le voici, L'Agneau si doux.*
(Behold the gentle Lamb.)

Refrain.

Let us sing all of us.
Let us praise Him.
Our Father,
let us respect Him.

---

141 No. 5. Air: – Un Dieu vient se faire entendre.
No. 5. Air: – Un Dieu vient se faire entendre.

1

siyokak ayamiawin
siyokak ayamihâwin

ka ki pe pakitinak
kâ-kî-pê-pakitinahk

misiwe waskitaskamik
misiwê waskitaskamik

ka tipeyimikoyak.
kâ-tipêyimikoyahk.

Refrain.

wi kakiyaw ayamiak,
wî kahkiyaw ayamihâk,

mewasik natonamok,
miywâsik natonamok,

koci pe pimatisiyek
koci-pê-pimâtisiyek

taki kici kisikok.
tahki kihci-kîsikohk.

2

ekawiya nakistamok
êkâwiya nakîstamok

ka sikimikawiyek
kâ-sîhkimikawiyêk

eoko pimatisiwin
êwako pimâtisiwin

ka wi miyikawiyek.
kâ-wî-miyikawiyêk.

3

wi mamitoniyitamok,
wî-mâmitonêyihtamok,

ayisiyiniwitik,
ayisiyiniwitik,

kwayask kici itoteyek
kwayask kici-itohtêyêk

eyikok nipiyeko.
iyikohk nipiyêko.

4

mewasik ayamiawin,
miywâsik ayamihâwin,

kakiyaw otinamok
kahkiyaw otinamok

ki ka kispinatenawaw
ki-ka-kîspinatênâwâw

taki pimatisiwin.
tahki pimâtiswin.

5

aw ka tipeyicikeyan,
âw kâ-tipêyihcikêyan,

kitimakeyiminan,
kitimâkêyiminân,

yakes kici tapwetamak
yakês kici-tâpwêtamâhk

miyo ayamiawin.
miyo-ayamihâwin.

No. 6. Air: – Le voici, l'Agneau si doux.
No. 6. Air: – Le voici, l'Agneau si doux.

Refrain.

nakamotak kakiyaw,
nakamotâhk kahkiyaw,

wi mamicimatak
wî-mamihcimâtâhk

mamawi kotawinaw,
mâmawi-kôhtawînaw,

manaciatak.
manâcihâtâhk.

142

1

ᑭ ᑭ ᒥᔨᑯᓇᐤ
ᐱᒪᑎᓯᐃᐧᐣ
ᐃᐧ ᓇᓇᐢᑯᒪᑕᐠ
ᐃᐧ ᓴᑭᐊᑕᐟ

2

ᑭ ᒪᓂᑐᒥᓇᐤ
ᑕᐯᐧᑕᐊᐧᑕᐠ
ᒍᓴᐠ ᑭᐢᑭᓯᑕᐠ
ᑭᓴ ᒪᓂᑐ.

3

ᓂ ᓴᑭᐊᐤ ᓴᓯᐣ
ᑫᓯᐊᐧᑎᓯᐟ
ᓂ ᓴᑭᐊᐤ ᓴᓯᐣ
ᑲ ᐱᒪᑎᐃᐟ

4

ᐊᐩ ᐊᐩ ᐃᐧᓇᑯᒪ,
ᒫᓂᑐ ᓅᑕ,
ᐊᓄ- ᑲ ᑌᐱᐢᑳᐠ
ᑳᓇᐌᔨᒥᐤ.

No. 7. Air: — *Tout n'est que vanité.*

1

ᑳᑭᑫ ᑭ ᐃᑕᐤ
ᑭᑎ ᑭᓴᒪᓂᑐ
ᑕᑭ ᐁ ᑭ ᐯᔭᑯᐟ
ᐊᑕ ᐁ ᓂᐢᑌᐧᔭᑭᐅᐟ
ᐁ ᐁᐧᔦᑕᐃᐧᒥᐟ
ᐁᐧᑯᓯᓯᒥᐟ
ᒣᔭᓯᐟ ᒪᓂᑐ; ᑯ ᐅᑎ
ᑫᓯᐃᑲᑌᐠ
ᑭᑎ ᓂᐢᑐᐯᔭᑯᐃᐧᐣ.

2

ᑭᑎ ᑭ ᐯᔭᑯᐟ
ᐊᑕ ᐁ ᓂᐢᑌᐧᔭᑭᐅᐟ
ᐁᑲ ᓂᓯᑐᑕᒥᐠ
ᓇᒪ ᓇᐤᑐ ᐊᑕ ᒪᓇ
ᑎ ᐃᑌᔨᑕᒥᐠ
ᐃᐧᔭ ᐱᑯ
ᑭᓴᒪᓂᑐ ᑭᐢᑫᔨᑕᐦ
ᐁ ᐃᐢᐸᔨᔨᐠ
ᐅ ᐯᔭᑯᐊᔨᐃᐧᐃᐧᐣ.

142

1

He gave us
life.
Let us give
Him thanks.
Let us love Him.

2

Our Father,
let us believe in Him.
Let us remember
God's promise
to Moses.

3

I love Jesus.
He is kind.
I love Jesus.

He gave me life.

4

Thank you.
God, my Father,
today and this night

take care of me.

No. 7. Air: – *Tout n'est que vanité. (All is but vanity.)*

1

Forever it was said
the Great spirit
always was alone
although He is of three:
the Father,
the Son,
the Holy Spirit.
Here, it is called
the great Trinity

2

Great God was singular:
all three were in Him.
No one understands
although usually
it is thought that
He alone,
God, knows
what happens.
His being is one.

142

1

ki ki miyikonaw
kikî-miyikonaw

pimatisiwin
pimâtisiwin

wi nanaskomatak
wî-nanâskomâtâhk

wi sakiatat
wî-sâkihâtâhk

2

ki manitominaw
kimanitôminaw

tapetawatak
tâpwêtawâtâhk

mosak kiskisitak
mosak kiskisitâhk

kise manito.
kisê-manitow.

3

ni sakiaw sesos
nisâkihâw Sesos

kesiwatisit
kêsiwâtisit

ni sakiaw sesos
nisâkihâw Sesos

ka pimaciit
kâ-pimâcihit

4

ay ay winakoma,
ay ay winakoma,

manito nota,
manitow nohtâ,

anoc ka tepiskak
anohc kâ-tipiskâk

kanaweyimin.
kanawêyimin.

No. 7. Air: – Tout n'est que vanité.
No. 7. Air: – Tout n'est que vanité.

1

kakike ki itaw
kâkikê kî-itâw

kici kise manito
kihci-kisê-manitow

taki e ki peyakot
tahki ê-kî-pêyakot

ata e nistweyakiot
âta ê-nistwêyakihot

e weyotawimit
ê-wiyôhtâwîmit

wekosisimit
wêkosisimit

meyosit manito; ko oci
(ê-)miyosit manitow;
kô ohci

kesi ikatek
ke-isiyîhkâtêk

kici nistopeyakowin.
kihci-nistopêyakowin.

2

kici ki peyakot
kihci-kî-pêyakot

ata e nistweyakiot
âta ê-nistwêyakihot

eka nisitotamik
êkâ nisitohtamihk

nama nanto ata mana
namâ nanitaw âta mâna

ci iteyitamik
kici-itêyihtamihk

wiya piko
wîya piko

kise manito kiskeyitam
kisê-manitow kiskêyihtam

e ispayiyik
ê-ispayiyik

o peyakoayiwiwin.
opêyakohayiwiwin.

143

3

He is beyond body.
He is an eternal Spirit.

But He is everywhere
in Heaven, on earth...
everywhere.

He looks at everything;
He knows all things.
No one
will ever be able to hide
from Him.

4

He can do anything;
He is supernatural.
He directs
things all over.
He shapes correctly

this land
He also controls
the stars
to shine.

5

This great place,
these high mountains,
the different things
that exist
these trees, all of them.

When you see it,
when you hear it,
especially what is
happening,
wind and rain,
remember the One
who governs.

6

He also made them
all the animals
that fly up above,
also those that walk on
the ground.
Even fish
in the water
that swim
He controls truly, strongly,
The One who governs
forever.

7

He made
all of these.
No one can do
what He has done.
He has to think this way
as He said.
And when the world
began,
all sorts of events
happened.
The One who governs
forever.

143

3

nama owiyawiw
namâ owîyawiw

pisisik acakowiw
pisisik ahcâhkowiw

maka misiwe ayaw
mâka misiwê ayâw

kisikok waskitaskamik
kîsikohk waskitaskamik

kahkiyaw kekwaya
kahkiyaw kîkwaya

kitapatam
kitâpâtam

mitone tapwe kiskeyitam
mitonê tâpwê kiskêyihtam

nama awiya
namâ awiya

wikac kita ki kasostak
wîhkâc kita-kî-kâsôstâk

4

kakiyaw kaskitaw
kahkiyaw kaskîtâw

esi mamatawisit
ê-isi-mamâhtâwisit

namawac pwatawitaw
namawâc pwâtawihtâw

misiwe isi kekwaya
misiwê isi kîkwaya

wiya ka minoak
wîya kâ-minohahk

oma askiy
ôma askiy

wapamayekwawi
wâpamayêkwâwi

petameko
pêtamêko

wawac tanisi ka ispeyik
wâwâc tânisi kâ-ispayik

yotin, kimiwan
yôtin, kimowan

kiskisik tepeciket.
kiskisik (ê-)tipêyicikêt.

6

ki osiew mina
kî-osîhêw mîna

kakiyaw pisiskiwa
kahkiyaw pisikiwa

ispimik pemiyoyit
ispimihk pêmiyoyit

mocit mina pemoteyit
môcit mîna pimohtêyit

kinosewa wawac
kinosêwa wâwâc

atamipek
atâmipêk

ka pimiskayit; tapwe soki
kâ-pimiskâyit; tâpwê sôhki-

mamatakosiw
mamâhtâkosiw

naspic katipeyiciket.
nâspic kâ-tipêyihcikêt.

7

e ki wi osiat
ê-kî-wî-osîhât

pisimwa mina acakosa
pîsimwa mîna ahcâhkosa

niyokwaniyit,
niyokwaniyit,

eka niyokwaniyiki.
êkâ niyokwaniyiki.

5

oma kicikami
ôma kihcikamiy

e- ispakwaw waciya
ê-ispâkwâw wacîya

nanatok ka ayakwaw
nanâtohk kâ-ayâkwâw

oki mistikwok kakiyaw
ôki mistikwak kahkiyaw

eokoni kakiyaw
êwakoni kahkiyaw

namawiya otawiya
namâwiya ohtâwiya

kekway e otawiwinit
kîkway ê-ohtâwiwinit

piko eteyitak
piko ê-itêyihtahk

mina etwet
mîna ê-itwêt

ekwa atiniyokwaniyik
êkwa atiniyokwâniyik

nanatok kekway
nanâtohk kîkway

naspic ka tipeyiciket.
nâspic kâ-tipêyihcikêt.

144

8

No. 8. Air ;—*Assemblons-nous.*

1

2

3

144

8

My Father,
You can do anything.
If they ask it from You,
The angels will give it to them.
Your helpers are
Here on this earth.
Ah, come and have pity on me.
Up there in Heaven
forever to sit with You.

No. 8. Air: – *Assemblons-nous. (Let us come together.)*

1

When the Heavens and earth and
everything in them
God completed,
He made people.
Surely He made them in His own image.

2

God is the Holy Trinity.
"Let us make people," He said.
And then man came into being.
He was very wise.

3

He used dirt all the time.

8

ni kise manitom
nikisê-manitôm

kakiyaw kaskitayan,
kahkiyaw kaskîtâyan,

kesi natotamaskik
kê-isi natotamâskik

okisikowok, wi miyik
okîsikowak, wî-miyik

kitosicikanak
kitosîhcikanak

ota askik:
ôta askîhk:

aw wi pe kitimakinawik,
âw wî-pê-kitimâkinawik,

ekote kisikok
êkotê kîsikohk

taki ci witapimiskwaw.
tahki kici-wîtapimiskwâw.

No. 8. AIR: – Assemblons-nous.
No. 8. AIR: – Assemblons-nous.

I

kisik askiy wawac kakiyaw kekway
kisik askiy wâwâc kahkiyaw kîkway

e ki kisitat kise manito,
ê-kî-kîsihtât kisê-manitow,

ayisiniwa ekwa ka osiat
ayisiyiniwa êkwa kâ-osîhât

cikema e wi naspisiisot.
cikêma ê-wî-nâspisihisot.

2

e nisto peyakot kise manito
ê-nisto-pêyakot kisê-manitow

osiatak ayisiyiniw etwet
osîhâtâhk ayisiyiniw (ê-)itwêt

ekwa ka nokosiyit napewa
êkwa kâ-nôkosiyit napêwa

mistae ani eyinisiyit.
mistahi ani (ê-)iyinîsiyit.

3

asaskiy pisisik ki apacitaw
asaskiy pisisik kî-apacîhtâw

145

ᓇᐯᐚ ᐅᐄᔮᐄᔫᐤ ᐍᓯᑕᐦ;
ᐁᑳ· ᑎ ᐅᐱᒪᑎᓯᐏᓂᔫᐠ
ᑭ ᒥᓴᐤ ᑭᑕ ᐅᑕᑯᑯᔫᐠ.

4

ᐁᑳ ᑭᑎ ᐯᔮᑯᔫᐠ ᓇᐯᐚ
ᐅᐢᐱᑫᑳᓂᔪ ᐍᑎᓇᒪᐧ
ᐃᐢᑵᐚ ᑮᑕ ᐅᑎ ᑭᓱᐊᐠ:
ᐁᑳᐧ ᑲ ᑭ ᑭᑎ ᐄᑭᑕᐋᐠ.

5

ᓂᐢᑕᐣ ᓇᐯᐤ ᐊᑕᐠ ᐁᓯᐃᑳᓱᐠ,
ᓂᐢᑕᐣ ᐃᐢᑵᐤ ᐁᐤ ᐁᓯᐃᑳᓱᐠ:
ᐁᐅᑯᓂᐠ ᓂᓱ ᐊᔨᓰᔨᓂᐅᐧᐠ
ᐊᓂᐢᑲ- ᑲ ᑭ ᐅᑎᓭᐠ ᑳᑭᓭᐤ

6

ᐁ ᑭ ᐅᓱᐃᐠ ᓂᐢᑕᐣ ᐊᔨᓰᔨᓂᐤ
ᓂᑕᐄᑭᑎᑳᓂᐠ ᑭ ᐊᔮᐤ;
ᑳᑭᓭᐤ ᐁᑯᑕ ᐁ ᐃᑕᑯᓂᔫᐠ,
ᑕᑭ ᓇᐢᐱ- ᑭᑎ ᒥᓂ ᐊᔮᐠ.

7

ᒪᑎ ᒪᓂᑐᐋ ᐁ ᑯᑎᒥᑯᐠ
ᐅᓴᐣ ᑕᐯᐧ ᑭ ᒥᓱ ᐸᐢᑕᐅ
ᑳᓂᑕᐯᐧ ᐁ ᑭ ᒥᑎᐠ ᒥᓂᓴ
ᑲ ᑭᑕᐊᒪᑯᐠ ᐍᓱᐃᑯᐠ.

8

ᑳᑭᓭᐤ ᐁ ᐯ ᐊᓱᐢᑲᒪᑯᔮᐠ

9

145

He made a man's body.
and then He did give him life;
He gave him a spirit.

4

So that the man was not alone,
He takes his rib from him.
He creates woman from the rib.
and He gave them formal marriage.

5

The first man, Adam, was his name.
The first woman, Eve, was her name.
From these two people
successively all of us have come to be.

6

At first when man was made
he was in a garden.
At that time everything existed
great and good, there forever.

7

The devil tempted him
because he was a great sinner.
It was true Adam did eat berries
when he was forbidden to do so by Him who made him.

8

He passed this sin onto all of us,

145

napewa owiyawiyiw wesitwat;
nâpêwa owîyâwiyiw wî-osîhtât;

ekwa ci opimatisiwiniyit
êkwa kici-opimâtisiwiniyit

ki miyew kita otacakoyit.
kî-miyêw kita-otahcâhkoyit.

4

eka kici peyakoyit napewa
êkâ kici-pêyakoyit nâpêwa

ospikekaniyo wetinamwat
ospikêkaniyiw wêtinamwât

iskwewa kita oci kisiat:
iskwêwa kita-ohci-kisihât:

ekwa ka ki kici wikitaat.
êkwa kâ-kî-kihci-wîkihtahât.

5

nistam napew atak esiikasot,
nistam nâpew Atak (ê-)isiyihkâsot,

nistam iskwew ep esiikasot:
nistam iskwêw Ep (ê-)isiyihkâsot:

eokonik niso ayisiyiniwok
êwakonik nîso ayisiniyiwak

aniskac ka ki ociyak kakiyaw
âniskac kâ-kî-ohcîyahk kahkiyaw

6

e ki osiit nistam ayisiyiniw
ê-kî-osîhât nistam ayisiyiniw

nitawikicikanik ki ayaw;
nihtâwikihcikanihk kî-ayâw;

kakiyaw ekota e itakoniyik,
kahkiyaw êkota ê-ihtakoniyik,

taki naspic kici miyo ayat.
tahki nâspic kihci-miyo-ayât.

7

maci manitowa e kocimikot
maci-manitowa ê-kocimikot

osam tapwe ki misipastao
osâm tâpwê kî-misi-pâstâhow

kanitapwe e ki micit minisa
kani-tâpwê ê-kî-mîcit mînisa

ka kita amakot wesiikot.
kâ-kitahâmâkot wêsihikot.

8

kakiyaw e pe asoskamakoyak
kahkiyaw ê-pê-asôskamâkoyahk

146

His offspring, His sons.
We are all born with this sin,
to live with it in neediness.

No. 9. Air: – *Je te salue, ô Pain de l'Ange.*
(I greet You, O Bread of the Angels.)

1

The angels are said
all the time to be spirits.
He made them for a reason:
to be in Heaven.

2

Slyly sin enters.
They think highly of
themselves.
They are going to
disobey
their God.

3

But they fail.

They do not overpower.

They are ruined.

They are expelled.

4

They are thrown to
the fire.
There they must
remain,
and the devil
leads the evil ones.

5

Those who remained
believed and adored.

They did much for
themselves
so then they are protected.

6

They who are continually
in Heaven,
are there to be good
forever.
Forever they take pride
in Him,
their God.

7

Those here on earth,

alone or together,

all the people
encourage one another.

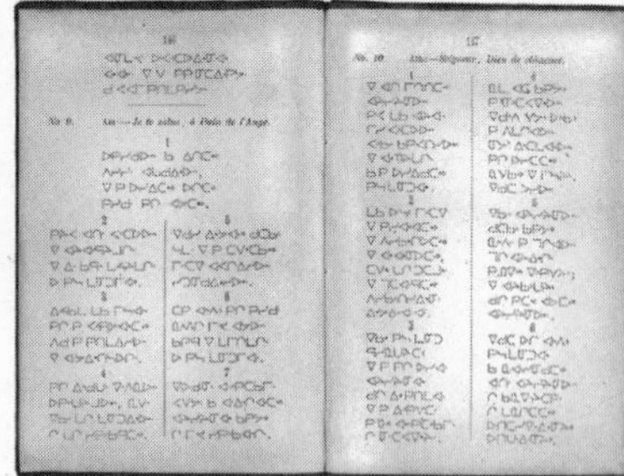

animayo opastaowiniwa
animayo opâstâhowiniwa

wawac e pe kikinitawikyak
wâwâc ê-pê-kiki-nihtâwikiyahk

ko papami kitimakisiyak.
kô-papâmi-kitimâkisiyahk.

No. 9. AIR: – Je te salue, ô Pain de l'Ange.
No. 9. AIR: – Je te salue, ô Pain le l'Ange.

1

okisikowok ka ititwaw
okîsikowak kâ-ititwâw

pisisik acakowiwok,
pisisik ahcâhkowiwak,

e ki osiitwaw ocitaw
ê-kî-osîhtwâw ohcitaw

kisikok kici ayatwaw.
kîsikohk kici-ayâtwâw.

2

kiyipa atit pastaowok
kiyipa atiht pâstâhowak

e ayiwakeyimocik
ê-ayiwâkêyimocik

e wi kakwe mayeyimacik
ê-wî-kâkwê-mayêyimâcik

o kise manitomiwa.
okisê-manitômiwa.

3

iyekama maka misawac
iyêkama mâka misawâc

kici ki paskiyawatwaw
kihci-kî-paskiyawâtwâw

piko ki kitimaisowok
piko kî-kitimahisowak

e wayawitisaocik.
Ê-wayawîtisahôcik.

4

kici iskotek wepinawok
kici-iskotêhk wêpinâwak

okisteyimowok, napec

okistêyimowak, nâspic

ekwa maci manitowiwok
êkwa maci-manitowiwak

ci maci sikiskaketwaw.
kici-maci-sîkiskâkêtwâw.

5

ekosi wiyawaw kotakak
êkosi wîyawâw kotakak

semak e ki tapwetakwaw
sêmâk ê-kî-tâpwêtakwâw

mistae apaciisowok
mistahi âpacihisowak

sitoni kowisiwok.
sihtonikôwisiwak.

6

taki aspin kici kisikok
tahki aspin kihci-kîsikohk

naspici miyo ayawok
nâspici miyo-ayâwak

kakike e mamicimacik
kâkikê ê-mamihcimâcik

o kise manitomiwa.
okisê-manitômiwa.

7

eokonik waskitakamik
êwakonik waskitaskamik

papeyak ka
wawiciwatwaw
pâpêyahk kâ-
wawîciwâtwâw

ayisiyiniwa kakiyaw
ayisiyiniwa kahkiyaw

ci miyo sikiskawacik.
kici-miyo-sîkiskawâcik.

147

No. 10. Air: —*Seigneur, Dieu de clémence.*

147 *No. 10.* Air: – *Seigneur, Dieu de clémence.*
(Lord, God of Mercy.)

1

There were great numbers
of people.
But very quickly many of them
sinned a great deal.
Worst of all, they were foolish
and confused about Him,
the One who made them,
God.

2

But very many
angered Him.
They committed adultery.
They were lost.
Truly they did evil.
They played with sin,
committing adultery,
with their own bodies.

3

And God
remembered it well.
He had created
wonderful people,
but made them suffer.
He had made it rain
for a long time on earth.
They drowned.

4

Not all of them
drowned.
One family
were survivors.
God told Noah
how to make
a big ship,
In which they journeyed.

5

And the people,
all the others,
they had drowned,
the evil ones.
For a long time
the earth flooded.
Only a few people
were spared.

6

Since that time.
God
chose some people
as His
chosen ones,
to look after it,
to respect it,
His way and His word.

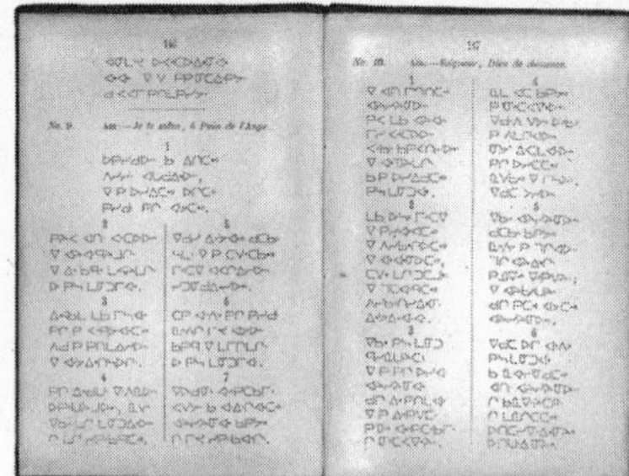

147 No. 10. Air: – Seigneur, dieu de clémence.
No. 10. Air: – Seigneur, dieu de clémence.

1

e ati micetitwaw
ê-ati-mihcêtitwâw

ayisiyiniwok
ayisiyiniwak

kipa maka ayiwak
kîpa mâka ayiwâk

misi pastaowok
misi-pâstâhowak

paskac kakipatisiwok
pâskac kâkîpâtisiwak

e waneyimacik
ê-wanêyimâcik

ka ki osiikotwaw
kâ-kî-osîhikotwâw

kise manitowa.
kisê-manitowa.

2

maka osam mistae
mâka osâm mistahi

e kisiwaatwaw
ê-kisiwâhâtwâw

e pisikwaciotwaw
ê-pisikwâcihâtwâw

e wawaniotaw,
ê-wâwanihotwâw,

tapwe maci totamwok
tâpwê maci-itôtamwak

e metawaketwaw
ê-mêtawâkêtwâw

pisikwatisiwinik
pisikwâtisiwinihk

wiyawiwawa.
wîyawiwâwa.

4

nama ata kakiyaw
namâ âta kahkiyaw

ki nistapawewok
kî-nistâpâwêwak

ekospi peyak oskan
êkospî pêyak oskân

ki pimaciawok
kî-pimâcihâwak

niyak witamawawok
niyâk wihtamawâwâk

kici ositatwaw
kici-osîhtâtwâw

napekwan e misayik
napêkwan ê-misâyik

ekota posiwok
êkota pôsiwak

5

ekwa ayisiyiniwok
êkwa ayisiyiniwak

kotakak kakiyaw
kotakak kahkiyaw

naspic ki meciawok
nâspic kî-mêscihâwak

meci ayiwicik
mêsci-ayiwicik

kinowes eskipeyik;
kinowês ê-iskipêyik;

e ayikasteyik
ê-ayikastêyik

koci kitwam ayatwaw
koci kîhtwâm ayâtwâw

ayisiyiniwok.
ayisiyiniwak.

3

ekwa kise manito
êkwa kisê-manitow

kesinateyitam
kêsinâteyihtam

e ki kici osiat
ê-kî-kihci-osîhât

ayisiyiniwa
ayisiyiniwa

koci wi kitimaat
koci-wî-kitimahât

e ki iskipetat
ê-kî-iskipêtât

kinwes waskitaskamik
kinwês waskitaskamik

ci nistapaweyit.
kici-nistâpâwêyit.

6

ekota oci aspin
êkota ohci aspin

kise manitowa
kisê-manitowa

ka nawasoni kotwaw
kâ-nawâsônikotwâw

atit ayisiyiniwok
âtiht ayisiyiniwak

ci kanaweyitakik
kici-kanawêyihtâhkik

ci manacitatwaw
kici-manâcihtâtwâw

otitasiwewiniyiw
otitâsiwêwiniyiw

otitwewiniyiw.
otitwêwiniyiw.

148

No. 11. Air: — *Ut queant laxis.*

1

ᒥᕙ ᒪᓂᑐ
ᐊᐩ ᐊᐩ ᐃᐧ ᓇᑯᒪ
ᑭ ᐱᒪᑎᐃᐣ
ᐁᔪᐱ ᐯᔪᑳᐤ,
ᓂ ᓇᓇᐢᑯᒧᐣ
ᐃᐢᐱ ᐅᑌᐃᔪᐣ,
ᒥᕙ ᒪᓂᑐ.

2

ᓂᓯᑲᒪᐃᐤ
ᐊᓇ ᑲ ᑭᓯᑳᐠ
ᒋ ᒥᓂᒉᔪᐣ
ᑭᑕᔪᒥᐊᐃᐤ
ᑲ ᑭ ᒥᔦᔪᐣ.
ᐊᓇ ᑲ ᑭᓯᑳᐠ
ᑲᓇᐁᐧᔦᒥᐣ.

3

ᒥᕙ ᑭᐢᑭᓯᐠ
ᑕᑕᐤ ᑭᑭᓭᐸ
ᐅᐯᔦᒥᐁᐧᐦ
ᑲᑭᔪᐤ ᐊᐃᐧᔪ
ᑲ ᐱᒪᑎᐊ
ᐁ ᑭᓭᐊᐧᑎᓯᐠ
ᒥᕙ ᑭᐢᑭᓯᐠ.

4

ᑯᑕᐠ ᑭᓯᑳᐤ
ᐁ ᐃᐧ ᒥᔦᑯᔪᐠ
ᒥᕙᐅ ᑌᐦᑎ
ᐃᐧ ᐊᑕᒥᐊᑕᐠ
ᓇᓇᐢᑯᒪᑕᐠ
ᓯᔪᑭᐃᑯᓯᐠ
ᒥᕙ ᒪᓂᑐ.

5

ᐅᐯᔦᒥᐁᐧᐦ
ᓇᑲᒧᐢᑕᐊᐧᑕᐠ.
ᑭᓭ ᒪᓂᑐ
ᐃᐧ ᓇᓇᐢᑯᒪᑕᐣ
ᑕᐯᐧᑕᐊᐧᑕᐠ
ᐁᓇ ᑲ ᑭᓯᑳᐠ
ᑲ ᒥᔦᑯᔪᐠ.

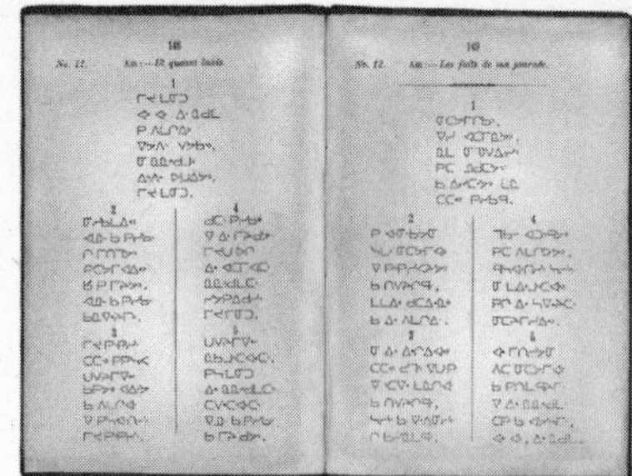

148 No. 11. Air: – *Ut queant laxis. (So that Your servants may sing at the top of their voices.)*

1

Good God
Thank You.
You give me life.
Still one more time
I give thanks
that You are here,
good God.

2

Work together with me
this day
to follow
Your prayer
that You have written.
Today
look after me.

3

Remember well
every morning
the Lord.
Everyone
He gave them life.
He is compassionate.
Remember Him well.

4

Another day
He is going to give to us
from a good heart.
Let us be grateful.
Let us give Him thanks.
He is loved,
God.

5

He is Lord
let us sing to Him.
God,
let us give Him thanks.
Let us believe in Him.
Today, this day,
He gave to us.

148 No. 11. Air: – Ut queant laxis.

No. 11. Air: – Ut queant laxis.

1

miyo manito
miyo-manitow

ay ay wi nakoma
ay ay wî-nakoma

ki pimaciin
kipimâcihin

eyapic peyakwaw,
êyâpic pêyakwâw,

ni nanaskomon
ninanâskomon

ispic oteiyan,
ispic otêhiyan,

miyo manito.
miyo-manitow.

2

nisokamawin
nîsôhkamawin

anoc ka kisikak
anohc kâ-kîsikâk

ci mitimeyan
kici-mitimêyan

kitayamiowin
kitayamihâwin

ka ki miyiyan.
kâ-kî-miyiyan.

anoc ka kisikak
anohc kâ-kîsikâk

kanaweyimin.
kanawêyimin.

3

miyo kiskisik
miyo-kiskisik

tatwaw kikisepa
tahtwâw kîkisêpa

tepeyimiwet
(ê-)tipêyimiwêt

kakiyaw awiya
kahkiyaw awiya

ka pimaciat
kâ-pimâcihât

e kisewatisit
ê-kisêwâtisit

miyo kiskisik.
miyo-kiskisik.

4

kotak kisikaw
kotak kîsikâw

e wi miyikoyak
ê-wî-miyikoyahk

miyote oci
miyotêh ohci

wi atamiatak
wî-atamihâtâhk

nanaskomatak
nanâskomâtâhk

siyakiikosit
siyakihikosit

miyo minito.
miyo-manitow.

5

tepeyimiwet
(ê-)tipêyimiwêt

nakamostawatak.
nakamôstawâtâhk.

kise manito
kisê-manitow

wi nanaskomatan
wî-nanâskomâtân

tapwetawatak
tâpwêtawâtâhk

anoc ka kisikak
anohc kâ-kîsikâk

ka miyikoyak.
kâ-miyikoyahk.

149

No. 12. AIR:—*Les faits de ma journée.*

1

ᓂᑕᔭᒥᒋᑲᐣ,
ᐁᓯ ᐊᑕᒥᓇᔭᐣ,
ᓇᒪ ᓂ ᓀᐯᐏᓯᐣ
ᑭᑕ ᓈᑯᑕᔭᐣ
ᑲ ᐃᓯᑖᔭᐣ ᒪᓇ
ᑕᑖᐤ ᑭᓯᑲᑫ.

2

ᑭ ᐋᓂᐢᑲᔭᓂ
ᓴᒪᐠ ᓂᑕᔭᒥᐊᐤ
ᐁ ᑭᐢᑭᓯᐸᔮᔭᐣ
ᑲ ᑎᐯᔮᒋᑫᐟ,
ᒪᒪᐏ ᐅᑕᐏᓈᐤ
ᑲ ᐏ ᐱᒪᒋᐃᐟ.

3

ᓂ ᐃ ᐏᒋᐃᐊᐤ
ᑕᑖᐤ ᐅᒉᐢ ᐁᑌᐧᑭ
ᐁ ᐅᑕᐍ ᒪᓇᒋᐊ
ᑲ ᑎᐯᔮᒋᑫᐟ,
ᓴᓰᐢ ᑲ ᐍᐱᓂᓯᐟ
ᒋ ᑲᓯᓈᒪᑫᐟ.

4

ᒉᑳ- ᐊᑐᐢᑫᔭᐣ
ᑭᑕ ᐱᒪᒋᐅᔭᐣ,
ᑫᓴᐚᑎᓯᐟ ᓴᓰᐢ
ᓂ ᒪᐏᒧᐢᑕᐚᐤ
ᑭᒋ ᐃ ᓴᐍᔮᑕᐠ
ᓂᑕᔮᒥᓯᐏᐤ.

5

ᐚ ᒥᑎᓱᔭᓂ
ᐱᑕ ᓂᑕᔭᒥᐊᐤ
ᑲ ᑭᑎᒪᑫᔮᒥᐟ
ᐁ ᐃ ᓇᓇᐢᑯᒪᐠ
ᑕᑭ ᑲ ᐊᔭᓴᒥᐟ,
ᐋ ᐋ, ᐃ ᓇᑯᒪ.

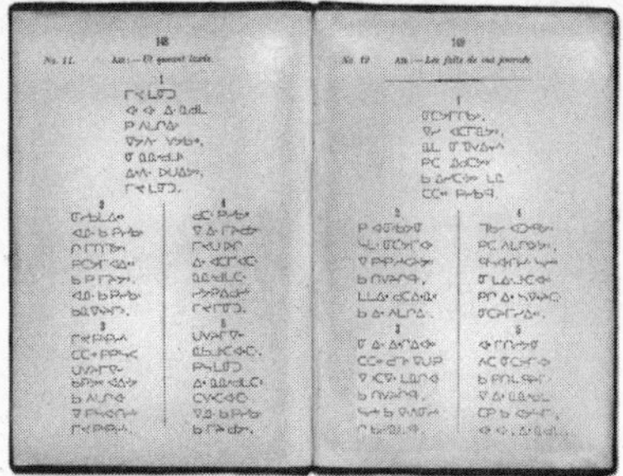

149 No. 12. AIR: – *Les faits de ma journée.*
(The events of my day.)

1

I read
to be happy this way.
Also I am not shy
to show it.
This is the way I usually behave
every day.

2

When I wake up
I pray right away.
I remember
the One who is Lord
our Father,
who gives us life.

3

I am going to attend
each time Mass is said.
I will follow

the One who is Lord,
the One who
continuously
feeds me,
for removing my sins.

4

While I am working
to make a living,
I will pray to kind Jesus;
I will pray to Him
to bless my work,
to relieve my trouble.

5

When I eat,
first, I pray
to the One who has pity
on me.
I am going to thank Him
all the time He feeds me.

Thank You.

149 No. 12. AIR: – Les faits de ma journée.
No. 12. AIR: – Les faits de ma journée.

1

nitayamicikan,
nitayâmihcikân,

esi ataminayan,
ê-isi-ataminâyan,

nama ni nepewisin
namâ ninêpêwisin

kita nokotayan
kita-nôkôtâyân

ka isitwayan mana
kâ-isîhtwâyân mâna

tatwaw kisikake.
tahtwâw kîsikâki.

2

ki waniskayani
kî-waniskâyâni

semak nitayamian
sêmâk nitayamihân

e kiskisopayiyan
ê-kiskisopayiyân

ka tipeyiciket,
kâ-tipêyihcikêt,

mamawi kotawinaw
mâmawi-kôhtâwînaw

ka wi pimaciit.
kâ-wî-pimâcihit.

3

ni wi wiciiwan
niwî-wicihiwân

tatwaw lames etweki
tahtwâw Lames itwêki

e ntawe manaciak
ê-nitawi-manâcihak

ka tipeyiciket,
kâ-tipêyihcikêt,

sesos ka wepinisot
Sesos kâ-wêpinisot

ci kasinamaket.
kici-kasînamâkêt.

4

mekwac atoskeyan
mêkwâc atoskêyan

kita pimacioyan,
kita-pimâcihoyan,

kesewatisit sesos
(ê-)kisêwâtisit Sesos

ni mawimostawaw
nimawimôstâwâw

kici wi saweyitak
kici-wî-sawêyihtahk

nitayimisiwin.
nitayimisiwin.

5

wa mitisoyani
wâ-micisoyâni

pita nitayamian
pita nitayamihân

ka kitimakeyimit
kâ-kitimâkêyimit

e wi nanaskomak
ê-wî-nanâskomahk

taki ka ayasamit,
tahki kâ-ayasamit,

ay ay, wi nakoma.
ay ay, wî-nakoma.

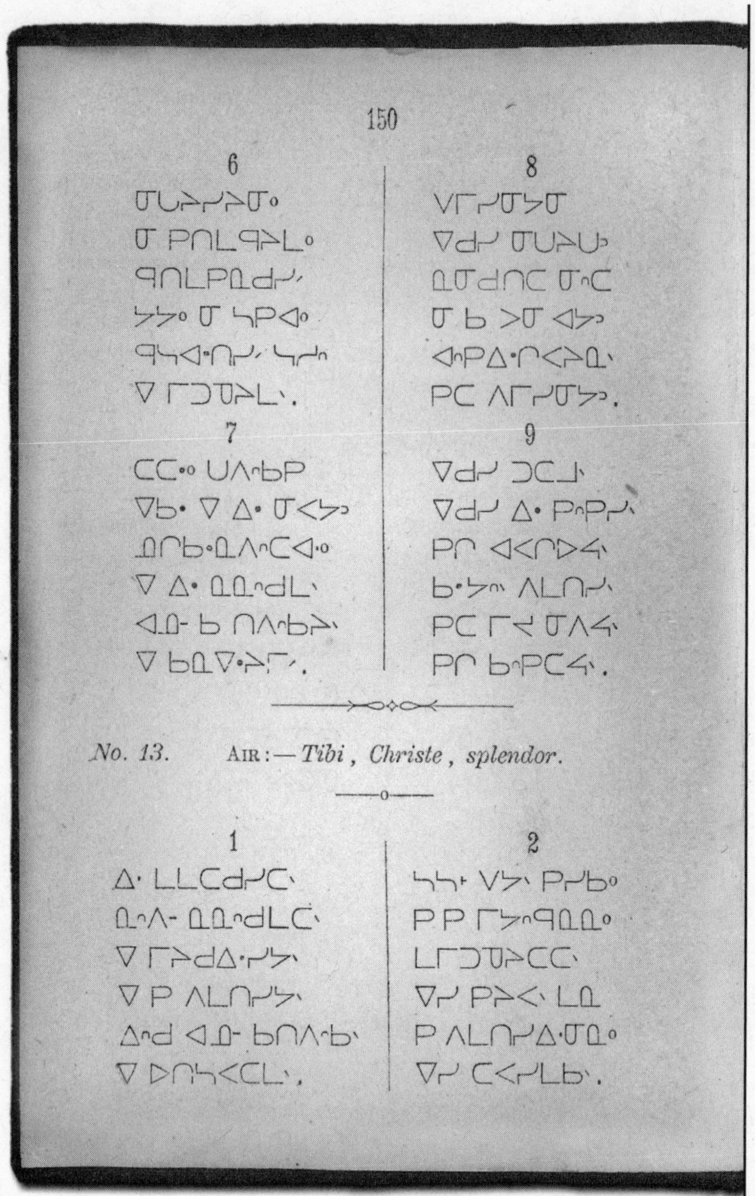

150

6

[syllabic text]

7

[syllabic text]

8

[syllabic text]

9

[syllabic text]

No. 13. Air:—*Tibi, Christe, splendor.*

1

[syllabic text]

2

[syllabic text]

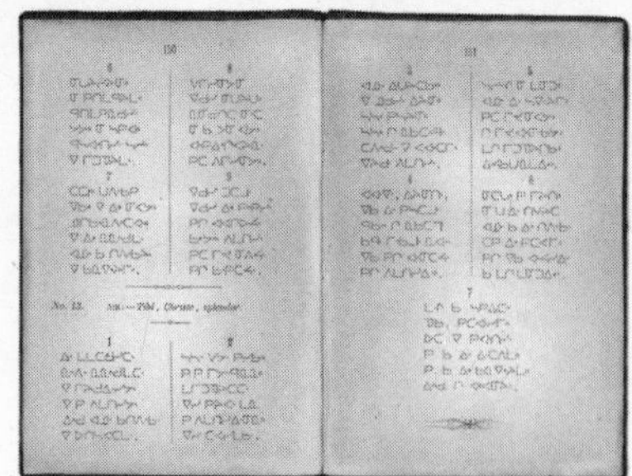

150

6

My people
He feels sorrow for us.
He looks pitiful
and I love Him.
He is kind, Jesus.
I think of Him.

7

Every night
when I am going
to sleep,
I kneel down to Him.
I am going to thank
Him.
This night,
He is looking after
me.

8

When I lie down,
so then I think
a day will come, when
I will not be alive
on earth.
I will be lying under
the earth.

9

Do it like this.
Then remember Him.

So that you help yourselves
to live properly,

to die well,
to achieve it for yourselves.

No. 13. Air: – *Tibi, Christe, splendor.*
(Brilliance to You, O Christ.)

1

We are gifted.
Let us thank Him
forever.
Life is given to us.
We have life.
On this night
we are seeing it.

2

Already in one day
our life can pass.

Let us think about it
how quickly usually
Our life passes;
how it flies from us.

6

nicayisiyiniw
nîcayisiyiniw

ni kitimakeyimaw
nikitimâkêyimâw

ketimakinakosit
kitimâkinâkosit

yayaw ni sakiaw
yâyaw nisâkihâw

kesewatisit sesos
ê-kisêwâtisit Sesos

e mitoneyimak.
ê-mâmitonêyimahk.

7

tatwaw tepiskaki
tahtwâw tipiskâki

ekwa e wi nipayan
êkwa ê-wî-nipâyan

nocikwanapistawaw
nôcihkwanapîstawâw

e wi nanaskomak
ê-wî-nanâskomahk

anoc ka tipiskayik
anohc kâ-tipiskâyik

e kanaweyimit.
ê-kanawêyimit.

8

pemi siniyani
pimisiniyâni

ekosi niteyiten
êkosi nitêyihtên

nani kotita nista
nani-kôtîta nîsta

ni ka poni ayan
nika-pôni-ayân

askiwicipayinak
askîwicipayinak

kita pimisiniyan.
kita-pimisiniyân.

9

ekosi totamok
êkosi tôtamok

ekosi wi kiskisik
êkosi wî-kiskisik

kici apacioyek
kici-âpacihoyêk

kwayask pimatisik
kwayask pimâtisik

kita miyo nipiyek
kita-miyo-nipiyêk

kici kaskitayek.
kici-kaskîtâyêk.

No. 13. AIR: – Tibi, Christe, splendor.
No. 13. AIR: – Tibi, Christe, splendor.

1

wi mamatakositak
wî-mamâhtâkosîtâhk

naspic nanaskomatak
nâspic nanâskomâtâhk

e miyikowisiyak
ê-miyikowisiyahk

e ki pimatisiyak
ê-kî-pimâtisiyahk

isko anoc katipiskak
isko anohc kâtipiskâk

e otisapatamak.
ê-otisapâtamahk.

2

sasay peyak kisikaw
sâsay pêyak kîsikâw

ki ki miyoskenanaw
ki-kî-miyoskênânaw

mamitoneyitatak
mâmitonêyihtâtâhk

esi kiyipak mana
ê-isi-kiyipak mâna

ki pimatisiwininaw
ki-pimâtisiwininaw

esi tapasimakak.
ê-isi-tapasîmakahk.

151

3

Today it seems
a person is born.
already the old man
dies
already he leaves
the earth,
just as in a dream
life passes.

4

Strive for wisdom.
Do not stay
if you leave something,
rather try to find it.

Do not lose

the good life.

5

Jesus Christ, my God,
today have pity on me
to have a good sleep,

to wake up well,

to remove from me
the bad thoughts.

6

I offer to You my spirit.
You own my heart.
Today this night
watch over me
continuously.
Help me not to be
deceived by
the devil.

7

Mary, I love you,
as a child does his mother.
Here, as with an orphan,
You will sit with us.
You will look after us
Until it is dawn.

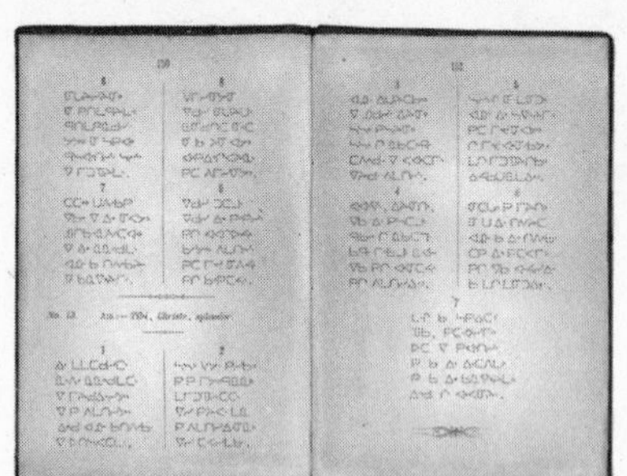

151

3

anoc iteyitakwan
anohc itêyihtakwan

e nokosit iyiniw
ê-nôkosit-iyiniw

sasay kiseyiniw
sâsay kisêyiniw

sasay ci nakatasket
sâsay kici-nakataskêt

tapiskoc e pawatamik
tâpiskôc ê-pawâtamihk

eyikok pimatisik.
iyikohk pimâtisik.

4

awaek, iyinitik,
awiyak, iyinîtik,

eka wi kisatamok
êkâ wî-kisâtamok

kekway ci nakatamek
kîkway kici-nakatamêk

kakwe miskamok nawac
kâkwê miskamok nâwâc

eka kici wanitayek
êkâ kici-wanîhtâyek

kihci pimatisiwin.
kihci-pimâtisiwin.

5

sesokri ni manitom
Sesokri nimanitôm

anoc wi saweyimin
anohc wî-sawêyimin

kita miyonipayan
kita-miyonipâyân

ci miyowaniskayan
kici-miyo-waniskâyân

maci mitoneyicikan
maci-mitonêyihcikan

iyekatenamawin.
iyêkâtênamawin.

6

nitacak ki miyitin
nitahcâhk kimiyitin

ni te wi tipeyita
nitêhk wî-tipêyihtahk

anoc ka wi tipiskak
anohc kâ-wî-tipiskâk

taki wi kitapamin
tahki-wî-kitâpamin

kihci eka wayesiit
kici êkâ wayêsihit

ka maci manitowit.
kâ-maci-manitowit.

7

mari ka sakiitan
Mari kâ-sâkihitân

neka, kitawasimis
nêkâ, kitawâsimis

ota e kiwatisit
ôta ê-kiwâtisit

ki ka wi witapimaw
kika-wî-wîtapimâw

ki ka wi kanaweyimaw
kika-wî-kanawêyimâw

isko ci wapaniyik.
isko kici-wâpaniyik.

152

No. 14. AIR;—*Au Dieu de l'univers.*

1

ᑌᐯᐳᒥᑯᔭᐠ
ᑕᑭ ᒪᒥᕆᒪᑕᐠ
ᑲ ᐸᑭᑎᑏᑯᔭᐠ
ᑭᑕ ᒥᔪ ᐊᐳᐃᐧᔭᐠ
ᐃᐧ ᑕᐯᐧᑕᐊᐧᑕᐠ
ᒪᒪᐃᐧᔦᐣ
ᐁ ᑭᕆ ᐊᐳᐃᐧᐟ;
ᐃᐧᔭ ᐱᑯ ᒪᒪᑕᐃᐧᓯᐤ
ᓇᐢᐱᐦ ᑲ ᑎᐯᐳᕆᑫᐟ.

2

ᐁ ᑭᓴᐊᐧᑎᓯᐟ
ᒥᓯᐁᐧ ᓈᑳᐧᑏᐳᐤ
ᐁ ᑭ ᒪᒥᐳᑯᔭᐠ
ᑭᕆ ᐃᐧᐱᒪᑎᓯᔭᐠ
ᐅᑕᔭᒥᐊᐃᐤ
ᐁᑳᐧ ᐊᐧᐋ
ᐁ ᑭᐣᑫᐳᑕᒪᐠ
ᑕᐯᐧ ᓯᑭ ᑭᓴᐊᐧᑎᓯᐤ
ᓇᐢᐱᐦ ᑲ ᑎᐯᐳᕆᑫᐟ.

3

ᐁ ᑭ ᕆᐣᑕᐊᐣᑳᐧᑎᐟ
ᐊᔭᐦᒣᐁᐊ ᑎᑯᐠ
ᐁ ᐃᓯ ᑳᐧᑕᑭᐃᐟ
ᐁ ᐃᐧᑏᐳᐣᑕᒪᑯᔭᐠ
ᐁᓯ ᓴᑭᐃᑕᐠ
ᓴᑭᐊᑕᐠ
ᐃᐧ ᓇᓇᐣᑯᒪᑕᐠ
ᐊᕆᐱᑯ ᑕᐯᐧᑕᐊᐧᑕᐠ
ᓇᐢᐱᐦ ᑲ ᑎᐯᐳᕆᑫᐟ.

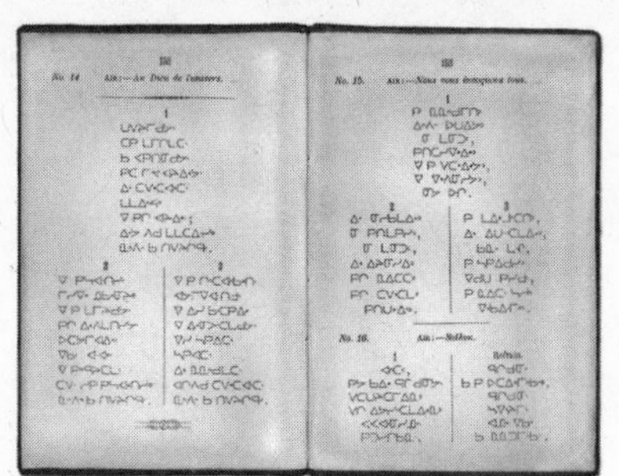

152 *No. 14.* AIR: – *Au Dieu de l'univers.*
(To the Lord of the universe.)

I

The Lord governs us.
Forever, let us praise Him,
The One who allows us
to have a good life.
Let us believe in Him.
Above the rest,
He is the greatest.
He alone is divine,
the One who is Lord forever.

2

He is kind,
compassionate.
All over His grace
shows.
He has given to us
the way that we live
through His prayer.
And even now
we know this prayer.
Truly He is very kind,

The One who is
Lord forever.

3

He was nailed

to the cross.

He suffered this way.
He died for us.
This way He loves us.
Let us love Him.
Let us thank Him.
Further let us believe
in Him,
The One who is Lord
forever.

152 No. 14. Air: – Au Dieu de l'univers.

No. 14. Air: – Au Dieu de l'univers.

1

tepeyimikoyak
(ê-)tipêyimikoyahk

taki mamicimatak
tahki mamihcimâtâhk

ka pakitinikoyak
kâ-pakitinikoyahk

kita miyo ayiwiyak
kita-miyo-ayiwiyak

wi tapwetawatak
wî-tâpwêtawâtâhk

mamawiyes
mamawiyês

e kici ayiwit;
ê-kihci-ayiwit;

wiya piko mamatawisiw
wîya piko mamâhtâwisiw

naspic ka tipeyiciket.
nâspic kâ-tipêyihcikêt.

2

e kisewatisit
ê-kisêwâtisit

misiwe nokwaniyiw
misiwê nôkwaniyiw

e ki mamiyikoyak
ê-kî-mâmiyikoyahk

kici wipimatisiyak
kici-wîpimâtisiyahk

otayamiawin
otayamihâwin

ekwa wawac
êkwa wâwâc

e kiskeyitamak
ê-kiskêyihtamahk

tapwe soki kisewatisiw
tâpwê sôhki-kisêwâtisiw

naspic ka tipeyiciket.
nâspic kâ-tipêyihcikêt.

3

e ki cistaaskwatit
ê-kî-cîstahâskwâtît

ayamiewatikok
ayamihêwâhtikohk

e isi kwatakiit
ê-isi-kwâtakihît

e winipostamakoyak
ê-wînipôstamâkoyahk

esi sakiitak
ê-isi-sâkihitahk

sakiatak
sâkihâtâhk

wi nanaskomatak
wî-nanâskomâtâhk

aci piko tapwetawatak
âci piko tâpwêtawâtâhk

naspic ka tipeyiciket.
nâspic kâ-tipêyihcikêt.

153

No. 15. Air : — *Nous vous invoquons tous.*

1

ᑭ ᓇᓇᐢᑯᒥᑎᐣ
ᐃᐢᐱ- ᐅᑌᐃᔭᐣ
ᓂ ᒪᓂᑐᐤ,
ᑭᑎᑕᓯᐍᐏᐣ
ᐁ ᑭ ᐯᑕᐏᔭᐣ,
ᐁ ᐍᐱᓂᓱᔭᐣ,
ᓂᔭ ᐅᒋ.

2

ᐏ ᓂᓱᑳᒪᐏᐣ
ᓂ ᑭᑎᒪᑭᓯᐣ,
ᓂ ᒪᓂᑐᐤ,
ᐏ ᐃᔨᓂᓯᐃᐣ
ᑭᒋ ᓇᐃᑕᑕᐣ
ᑭᒋ ᑕᐺᑕᒪᐣ
ᑭᑎᑘᐏᐣ.

3

ᑭ ᒪᐏᒧᐢᑕᑎᐣ,
ᐏ ᐃᑌᐦᑕᒪᐏᐣ,
ᑳᓇ- ᒪᕆ,
ᑭ ᓴᑭᐃᑯᓯᐣ
ᐁᑯᑌ ᑭᓯᑯᐠ,
ᑭ ᓇᐃᑕᐠ ᓴᓱᐢ
ᐍᑲᐏᒥᐟ.

No. 16. Air : — *Satkon.*

1

ᐊᐢᑕᐤ,
ᑭᔭ ᑲᐏ ᑫᒋᑯᓂᔭᐠ
ᐯᑕᑌᔨᑕᒥᐃᓇᐣ
ᐯᒋ ᐃᔭᓯᐢᑕᒪᐏᓇᐣ
ᐸᐸᐘᓂᓯᓄᐠ
ᑭᑐᓯᒋᑲᓇᐠ.

Refrain.

ᑫᒋᑯᓂᐟ
ᑲ ᑭ ᐅᑕᐏᒥᐢᑳᐤ,
ᑫᒋᑯᓂᐠ
ᓴᐍᔨᒥᐠ
ᐊᓄ- ᐁᑳ
ᑲ ᓇᓇᑐᒥᐢᑲᐠ.

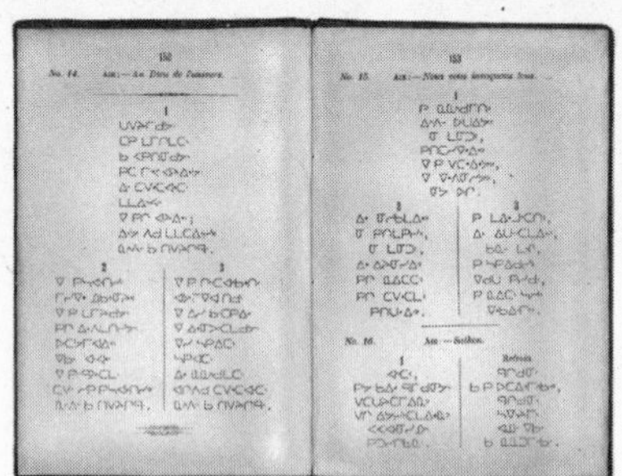

153 *No. 15.* Air: – *Nous vous invoquons tous.*
(We all call on You.)

1

I thank you
that You are there,
My God.
Through Your commandments
You heard me.
You gave Yourself
for me.

2

Work together with me.
I am poor in spirit,
my God.
Make me wise
to listen to You.
Help me to believe
Your word.

3

I pray to you.
Intercede for me,
oh, most pure Mary.
You are loved
above in Heaven.
Jesus listens to you,
the one He has for a mother.

No. 16. Air: – *Satkon. (Holy Spirit.)*

1

Come, Holy Spirit,
You are going to
renew us.
Come and change
our spirit.
Come to our aid.
Everywhere people
are lost, those that
You created.

Refrain.

Release my spirit.
They had taken You
as Father.
Take me away,

bless me
today and
when they invite You.

153 No. 15. Air: – Nous vous invoquons tous.
No. 15. Air: – Nous vous invoquons tous.

1

ki nanaskomitin
kinanâskomitin

ispic oteiyan
ispic otêhiyan

ni manitom,
nimanitôm,

kititasiwewin
kititasiwêwin

e ki petwawiyan,
ê-kî-pêhtwâwiyan,

e wepinisoyan,
ê-wêpinisoyân,

niya oci.
niya ohci.

2

wi nisokamawin
wî-nîsôhkamawin

ni kitimakisin,
nikitimâkisin,

ni manitom,
nimanitôm,

wi iyinisiin
wî-iyinîsihîn

kici naitatan
kici-nahîtâtân

kici tapwetaman
kici-tâpwêtamân

kititwewin.
kititwêwin.

3

ki mawimostatin,
kimawimôstâtin,

wi itwestamawin,
wî-itwêstamawin

kanac mari,
kanâc Mari,

ki sakiikosin
kisâkihikosin

ekote kisikok,
êkotê kîsikohk,

ki naitak sesos
kinahîhtâhk Sesos

wekawimisk.
wêkâwîmisk.

No. 16. Air: – Satkon.
No. 16. Air: – Satkon.

1

astam,
âstam,

kiya kawi kecikoniyak
kîya kâwî-kêcikoniyahk

petateyitamiinan
pêtatêyihtamihinân

peci iyasistamawinan
pêci-iyasistamawinân

papawanisinwok
papâwanisinwak

kitosicikanak.
kitosîhcikanak.

Refrain.

kecikonit
kêcikoniht

ka ki otawimiskwaw,
kâ-kî-otâwîmiskwâw,

kecikonik
kêcikonik

saweyimik
sawêyimik

anoc ekwa
anohc êkwa

ka nanatomiskwa.
kâ-nanâtomiskwâw.

154

2

ᓴᓴ+
ᑭ ᒍᓯᒥᐸᑎᓇᐤ ᐊᑕᐠ
ᐍᐱᓇᑳᑎᐠ ᑐᑕᐚᐤ:
ᐁ ᐃᔭᑭ ᐸᐸᒪᑘᒍᐟ
ᑭ ᐃ· ᑳᑭᒋᐊᐤ
ᐁ ᑭᑎᒪᑭᓯᐟ.

3

ᐅᓴᐨ
ᒪᔭᑕᑎᔫ ᐅᑎᑎᐏᐣ
ᐊᐏᔭᐠ ᐁ ᐊᑏᑕᐘᐟ
ᒪᑎᑐᐘ ᐁᓯ ᐃᑎᑯᐟ
ᐍᒋ ᒥᐢᑲᒪᓱᐟ
ᑭᒋ ᑳᑕᑭᐎᐟ.

4

ᓴᓱᐢ,
ᓇᒪ ᑫᑳ+ ᑭᐏᓴᑭᑕᐣ
ᑭ ᐸᑭᑌᓂᑌᐣ ᑭᔭᐤ
ᐃᐢᐱ ᐁ·ᑭᑎᒪᑫᓂᒪᐟ
ᑭ ᐃ· ᐯ ᐃᔭᓯᐣ
ᒋ ᑎᐳᐢᑕᒍᐘᐟ.

5

ᑭᔭ,
ᓇᐢᐱ ᐁᑭᓯᐘᑎᓯᔭᐣ
ᐁ ᑭᐘᑎᓯᐟ ᐃᔨᑎᐤ
ᐁ ᐅᑕᐘᓯᒥᓯᒪᐟ
ᐁ ᐃ· ᐱᒪᒋᐊᐟ
ᑳᑭᑫ ᑭᓱᑯᐠ.

No. 17. Air:—*A l'exemple des Anges.*

1

ᐃ·ᒪᒪᑕᑯᓯᑕᐠ
ᐅᑎᐱᐢᑳᐠ;
ᓴᓱᐢ ᑌᐯᔨᒥᑕᐠ
ᑎᑕᐃ·ᑭᐤ:
ᐁ ᐃ· ᑌᐱᔭᐍᔨᑕᐠ
ᑲ ᐃᑕᓯᔭᐠ
ᐁ ᐃᔨᑎᐃ·ᔭᐠ.
ᐃ·ᓇᑯᒪ. *(ter.)*

2

ᒥᓯᐍ ᒪᒪᑕᑳᐤ
ᐊᓄ ᒣᑳᐤ:
ᓴᓱᐢ ᐁ ᒪᒥᒋᒥᐟ
ᐃᔨᑎᓇᐠ
ᒪᒥᒋᒪᑕᐠ ᑭᐢᑕᓇᐤ:
ᑭᒋᑕᐃ·ᓯᐤ
ᐁ ᒪᑎᑐᐃ·ᐟ.
ᓴᑭᐊᑕᐠ. *(ter.)*

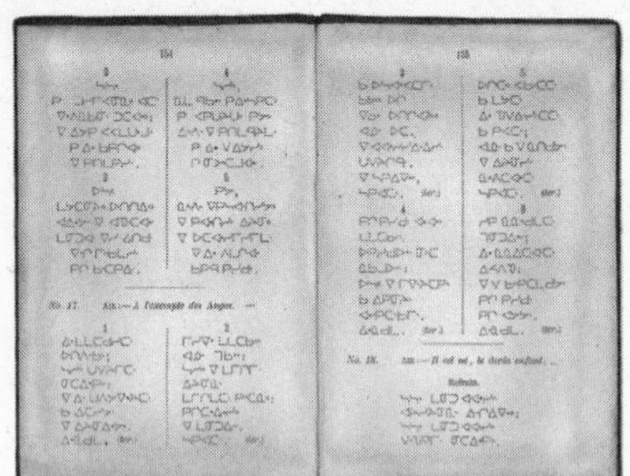

154

2

Already
our great grandfather
Adam
when he was cast out,
He went around crying
about it.
You are going to
console him
because he is pitiable.

3

Because
his words are bad,
he does not believe
what God said to him.
He had learned for
himself
how he would suffer.

4

Jesus,
You are never going
to be selfish;
You gave up Your body.
You are going to pity them.

You are going to descend

So that You die for them.

5

You, Lord,
forever You are kind.
A person who is an orphan,
You take as Your child.
You are going to give
them life
forever in Heaven.

No. 17. Air: – *A l'exemple des Anges.*
(By the example of the angels.)

1

Jesus gave us a gift
this night.
Jesus, we are satisfied.
He is born.
We are going to anger
You,
all of us,
because we are human.
Thank you. (*thrice.*)

2

He is divine.
Today, right now,
Jesus is praised
by the people.
Let us promise Him, too.

He is holy.
He is God.
Let us love Him. (*thrice.*)

154

2
sasay
sâsay

ki mosomipaninaw atak
kimosômipaninaw Atak

we-pinakanik totawaw:
wê-pinâkanik tôtawâw:

e iyaki papamatwemot
ê-iyâki-papâmatwêmot

ki wi kakiciaw
kiwî-kâkîcihâw

e kitimakisit.
ê-kitimâkisit.

3
osam
osâm

mayataniyiw otitiwin
mâyâtaniyiw otitiwin

awiyak e anwetawat
awiyak ê-ânwêhtawât

manitowa esi itikot
manitowa ê-isi-itikot

weci miskamasot
wêci-miskamâsot

kici kwatakiit.
kici-kwâtakihît.

4
sesos,
Sesos,

nama kekway kiwisakitan
namâ kîkway kiwîsâkihtân

ki pakiteyiten kiyaw
kî-pakiteyihtên kîyaw

ispic e kitimakeyimat
ispic ê-kitimâkêyimât

ki wi peiyasin
kiwî-pêyâsin

ci nipostamowat.
kici-nipôstamawât.

5
kiya,
kiya,

naspic ekisewatisiyan
nâspic ê-kisêwâtisiyan

e kiwatisit iyiniw
ê-kîwâtisit-iyiniw

e otawasimisimimat
ê-otawâsimisimimat

e wi pimaciat
ê-wî-pimâcihat

kakike kisikok.
kâkikê kîsikohk.

No. 17. Air: – A l'exemple des Anges.
No. 17. Air: – A l'exemple des Anges.

1
wi mamatakositak
wî-mamâhtâkosîtahk

otipiskak;
otipiskâk;

sesos tepeyimitak
Sesos (ê-)tipêyimitâhk

nitawikiw:
nihtâwikiw:

e wi tepiyaweyitak
ê-wî-têpiyawêyihtâhk

ka itasiyak
kâ-itasiyahk

e iyiniwiyak.
ê-iyiniwiyahk.

winakoma. (ter.)
wî-nakoma. (ter.)

2
misiwe mamatakwan
misiwê mamâtâkwan

anoc mekwac:
anohc mêkwâc:

sesos e mamicimit
Sesos ê-mamihcimiht

iyininak
iyinînak

mamicimatak kistanaw:
mamihcimâtâhk kîstanaw:

kicitawisiw
kihcitwâwisiw

e manitowit.
ê-manitowit.

sakiatak. (ter.)
sâkihâtâhk. (ter.)

155

3
ᑲ ᐅᓭᐊᐧᐸᑕᒥᐠ
ᑲᔭᐣ ᐅᒋ
ᐁᑯᐧ ᐅᒋᒋᐸᔦᐤ
ᐊᓇ ᐅᑕ.
ᐁ ᐊᐊᐧᔪᔪᐃᐧᐃᔪᐟ
ᑌᐯᔦᒋᑫᐟ,
ᐁ ᓭᑭᐃᐁᐧᐟ,
ᓭᑭᐊᑕᐠ. *(ter.)*

4
ᑭᒋ ᑭᔪᑯᐠ ᐊᐧᐊᐧ-
ᒪᒪᑕᑲᐧᐤ.
ᐅᑭᔪᑯᐅᐧᐠ ᓂᐣᑕ
ᓇᑲᒧᐅᐧᐠ;
ᐅᓭᐨ ᐁ ᒥᐁᐧᔦᑕᑭᐠ
ᑲ ᐃᑭᓂᔦᐠ
ᐊᐧᐣᑭᑕᐣᑲᒥᐠ.
ᐃᐧᓇᑯᒪ. *(ter.)*

5
ᐅᒋᑕᐤ ᐸᑲᐦᑕᑕᐠ
ᑲ ᒪᔭᑕᐠ
ᐃᐧ ᓃᐯᐃᐧᔪᐣᑕᑕᐠ
ᑲ ᑭᐸᑕᐠ;
ᐊᓇ ᑲ ᐯ ᓇᑎᑯᔭᐠ
ᐁ ᐃᔦᓂᔪᐟ
ᓇᐣᐱᑕᐊᐧᑕᐠ
ᓭᑭᐊᑕᐠ. *(ter.)*

6
ᔪᑭ ᓇᓈᐣᑯᒪᑕᐠ
ᒣᓃᑐᐃᐧᐟ;
ᐃᐧ ᓇᓇᐃᑕᐊᐧᑕᐠ
ᐃᓭᐱᓀ:
ᐁ ᐯ ᑲᐣᑭᑕᒪᑯᔭᐠ
ᑭᒋ ᑭᔪᑯᐠ
ᑭᒋ ᐊᔭᔭᐠ.
ᐃᐧᓇᑯᒪ. *(ter.)*

No. 18. Air:—*Il est né, le divin enfant.*

Refrain.

ᓭᓭᐩ ᒪᓂᑐ ᐊᐊᐧᔪᐣ
ᐊᔦᔪᔦᓂᓇᐠ ᐃᐧᒋᐃᐁᐧᐤ;
ᓭᓭᐩ ᒪᓂᑐ ᐊᐊᐧᔪᐣ
ᐯᐧᑑᐁᒥᐠ ᓂᑕᐃᐧᑭᐤ.

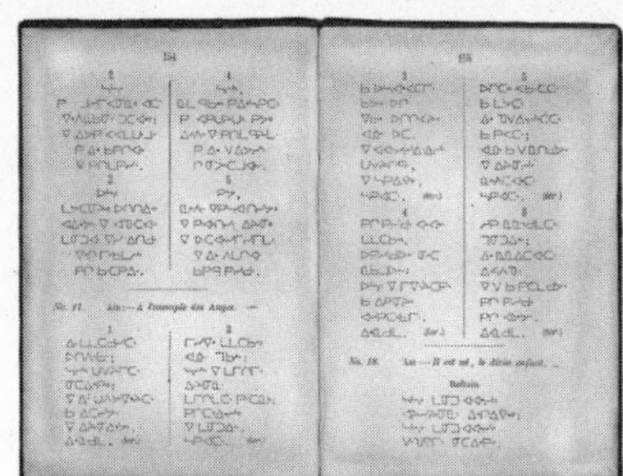

155

3
We have looked forward
to it
for a long time.
Now it is time,
here today
to rejoice.
The Lord owns
everything.
He loves me.
Let us love Him. (*thrice.*)

4
Above in Heaven
all is supernatural.
The angels too,
I thank them;
because they rejoice
that creation is
on earth.
Thank you. (*thrice.*)

5
With reason, let us despise
evilness.
We are ashamed of
the devil who imprisons us
in sin.
Today when He comes
for us,
let us be wise.
Let us be like the angels.
Let us love Him. (*thrice.*)

6
Let us thank Him very
much.
He is God.
Let us listen to Him,
Very closely.
He came to achieve
salvation for you
in Heaven,
for you to be there.
Thank you. (*thrice.*)

No. 18. Air: – *Il est né, le divin enfant.*
(The Holy Child is born.)

Refrain.
Already, God's child
journeys with His people.
Already God's child
in Bethlehem is born.

155

3

ka osawapatamik
kâ-osâwâpahtamihk

kayas oci
kayâs ohci

ekwa ocicipayiw
êkwa ocihcipayiw

anoc ota.
anohc ôta.

e awasisiwiisot
ê-awâsisiwihisot

tepeyiciket,
(ê-)tipêyihcikêt,

e sakiiwet,
ê-sâkihiwêt,

sakiatak. (ter.)
sâkihâtâhk. (ter.)

4

kici kisikok wawac
kihci-kîsikohk wâwâc

mamatakwan.
mamâhtâkwan.

okisikowok nista
okîsikowak nîsta

nakamowok;
nakamowak;

osam e miweyitakik
osâm ê-miywêyihtâhkik

ka ikiniyik
kâ-ikiniyik

waskitaskamik.
waskitaskamik.

winakoma. (ter.)
wînakoma. (ter.)

5

ocitaw pakwatatak
ohcitaw pakwâtâtâhk

ka mayatak
kâ-mâyâtahk

wi nepewisistatak
wî-nêpêwisîstâtâhk

ka kipatak;
kâ-kipahtâhk;

anoc ka pe natikoyak
anohc kâ-pê-nâtikoyahk

e iyinisit
ê-iyinîsit

naspitawatak
naspitawâtâhk

sakiatak. (ter.)
sâkihâtâhk. (ter.)

6

soki nanaskomatak
sôhki-nanâskomâtâhk

menitowit;
manitowit;

wi nanaitawatak
wî-nanahihtawâtâhk

iyepine:
iyêpinê:

e pe kaskitamakoyak
ê-pê-kaskîtamâkoyahk

kici kisikok
kihci-kîsikohk

kici ayayak.
kici-ayâyahk.

winakoma. (ter.)
wînakoma. (ter.)

No. 18. Air: – Il est né, le divin enfant.
No. 18. Air: – Il est né, le divin enfant.

Refrain.

sasay manito awasis
sâsay manitow-awâsis

ayisiyininak wiciiwew:
ayisiyinînak wîcihiwêw:

sasay manito awasis
sâsay manitow-awâsis

petleemik nitawikiw.
Petlehemihk nihtâwikiw.

156

1

ᑲᔾᐢ ᐅᒋ ᐅᑕᑎᒪ
ᑕᑭ ᐅᑐᓴᐊᐧᐸᒪᑕ+;
ᐁᑲᐧ ᐁ ᐅᑎᑎᑯᔾᐠ
ᒪᒪᐃᐧ ᒪᒥᒋᒪᑕᐠ.

2

ᐅᓴᶜ ᐁ ᑲᑕᐊᐧᓯᓯᐟ
ᓇᒪᐊᐧ- ᑭᑕ ᑭᐸᐢᑭᐊᐧ
ᓇᒪᐃᐧᑲ- ᐯᑕᑯᓯᐤ
ᐁ ᒥᔦ ᐊᐊᐧᓯᓯᐃᐧ.

3

ᒍᐢᑐᐢ ᐅᑲᒥᑯᐃᐧᑭᐤ
ᒪᐢᑯᓯᔾ ᐅᑏᐯᐃᐧᑏᐤ;
ᒍᐢᑐᐢ ᐅᑲᒥᑯᐃᐧᑭᐤ;
ᐅᓴᶜᑕᐯᐧ ᐱᐁᐧᔾᒧ.

4

ᑲ ᐣᑕᐁᐧᔾᑕᒪᑯᔾᐠ
ᐁᑲᐃᐧᔾ ᓴᑭᑐᐊᐧᑕᐠ
ᑭ ᑌᐃᓈᐊᐧ ᐃᐧ ᐊᔾᐤ
ᐃᐧ ᐸᑭᑎᓇᒧᐊᐧᑕᐠ.

5

ᑭᒋ ᐅᑭᒪᐅᐦ ᑏᐢᑐ
ᐊᐧᔾᐤ ᐅᒋ ᐯᐃᑐᑌᐅᐦ
ᐁ ᐃᐧᒥᔦ ᑐᑕᐊᐧᑕᐧᐤ
ᐁ ᒪᑏᑐᐁᐧᔾᒪᑕᐧᐤ.

6

ᑌᐯᔾᒋᑫᔾᐣ, ᓴᓱᐢ,
ᐁ ᐊᑕ ᐊᐊᐧᓯᓯᐃᐧᔾᐣ
ᑭ ᐯ ᐸᑯᓯᐃᑎᓇᐣ
ᐯᔾᑯᑌᐯᔾᒥᓇᐣ.

No. 19. Air—*Ça, bergers.*

1

ᐁ ᒣᑲᐧ ᑎᐱᐢᑲᔾᐠ
ᓴᓱᐢ ᑏᑕᐃᐧᑭᐤ:
ᐃᐧᔾ ᑲ ᐯ ᒥᐁᐧᐊᐧ
ᒣᒋ ᒪᑏᑐᐃᐧᔾᐟ.
ᐊᐤ ᐣᑕᐁᐧᐊᑕᒥᐢᑲᐊᐧᑕᐠ
ᐅᒧᑏᑐᒥᒪᑕᐠ.

2

ᐁ ᐊᑕ ᑲᓱᐢᑕᑫᐟ
ᑫᓯ ᑭᒋᑕᐧᐃᐧᓯᐟ,
ᐁᐅᑯ ᐊᑕᐃᐧᔾ
ᑲ ᐯ ᐱᑯᐃᐁᐧᐦ:
ᒪᓇᒋᐊᑕᐠ ᐁᑕᓯᔾᐠ,
ᐁ ᑭᓴ ᒧᑏᑐᐃᐧᐦ.

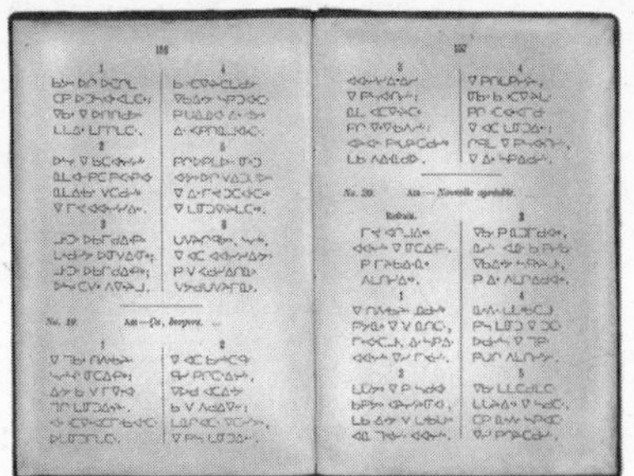

156

1

For a long time the
prophets
foretold His coming.
Now He has arrived
for us.
All together let us
praise Him.

2

Although He is beautiful,
His birth is hidden.
He is never heard.
He is a good child.

3

In a cow's stable

with grass as His bed,
in a cow's stable

because He is
considered lowly.

4

He wants life for us.

Let us not neglect Him.
Our hearts He is going to
have.
Let us allow Him to have
our hearts.

5

Three great kings
Came from far away.
They adore Him.
They know He is divine.

6

You own everything,
Jesus Lord.
Although You are a child,
we come and get hope
from You.
You alone are content
with us.

No. 19. Air: – *Ça, bergers. (Behold, shepherds.)*

1

While it is still night
Jesus Christ is born.
He comes and defeats
him,
the evil one.
Ah, let us greet Him;

let us accept Him as
our God.

2

Although He conceals
His divinity,
this Holy One

will come and deliver us.
Let us respect Him, all
of us.
He is God.

1

kayas oci otacima
kayâs ohci otâcimâ

taki otosawapamatay;
tâhki otosawâpamâtay;

ekwa e otitikoyak
êkwa ê-otîtikoyahk

mamawi mamicimatak.
mamâwi-mamihcimâtâhk.

2

osam e katawasisit
osâm ê-katawâsisit

namawac kita kipaskiat
namawâc kita-kipâskihât

namawikac petakosiw
namâwîhkâc pêhtâkosiw

e miyo awasisiwit.
ê-miyo-awâsisiwit.

3

mostos okamikowikiw
mostos okamikowikiw

maskosiya onipewiniw;
maskosiya onipêwiniw;

mostos okamikawikiw;
mostos okamikowikiw;

osam tapwe piweyimo.
osâm tâpwê pîwêyimo.

4

ka ntaweyitamakoyak
kâ-nitawêyihtamâkoyahk

ekawiya sakitowatak
êkâwiya sâkîtowâtâhk

kiteinowa wi ayaw
kitêhinowa wî-ayâw

wi pakitinamowatak.
wî-pakitinamawâtâhk.

5

kici okimawok nisto
kihci-okimâwak nisto

wayaw oci peitotewok
wâhyaw ohci pê-itohtêwak

e wi miyo totawatwaw
ê-wî-miyo-itôtawâtwâw

e manitoweyimatwaw.
ê-manitowêyimâtwâw.

6

tepeyicikeyan, sesos,
(ê-)tipêyihcikêyan, Sesos,

e ata awasisiwiyan
ê-âta-awâsisiwiyan

ki pe pakosiitinan
kipê-pakosihitinân

peyakotepeyiminan.
peyako-tipêyiminân.

No. 19. AIR: – Ça, bergers.
No. 19. AIR: – Ça, bergers.

1

e mekwa tipiskayik
ê-mêkwa-tipiskâyik

sesokri nitawikiw:
Sesokri nihtâwikiw:

wiya ka pe miweat
wîya kâ-pê-miwêhât

meci manitowiyit.
maci-manitowiyit.

aw ntaweatamiskawatak
aw nitawi-atamiskawâtâhk

omanitomimatak.
omanitômimâtâhk.

2

e ata kasostaket
ê-âta-kasôstâkêt

kesi kicitwawisit,
kêsi-kihcitwâwisit,

eoko atawiya
êwako atawîya

ka pe pikoiwet:
kâ-pê-pikohiwêt:

manaciatak etasiyak,
manâcihâtâhk ê-itasiyahk,

e kesi manitowit.
ê-kêsi-manitowit.

157

3

He makes Himself as
a child.
He is kind.
He does not resist
the way he is swaddled.
He is honourable
because He has a
lowly appearance.

4

He is pitiful.

At first people wanted
to go and see Him.
Although He is divine,
certainly He is kind.
He is loved.

No. 20. Air: – *Nouvelle agréable. (Good news.)*

Refrain.

It is a good story.
A child is born.
We are given life.
He gives you life.

1

At night He is born.
He comes to save you.
Be happy about it;
love Him
as a good child.

2

He has overpowered evil.
All of the people
He has surprised them,
that sweet child.

3

He comes and invites you.
Go to Him this day;
do not be discouraged.

4

Forever be surprised
at what God has done.
He gave us His Son

to have life from Him.

5

Let us see His cleverness.
He overpowers evil.
Forever, let us love Him.
He is honourable.

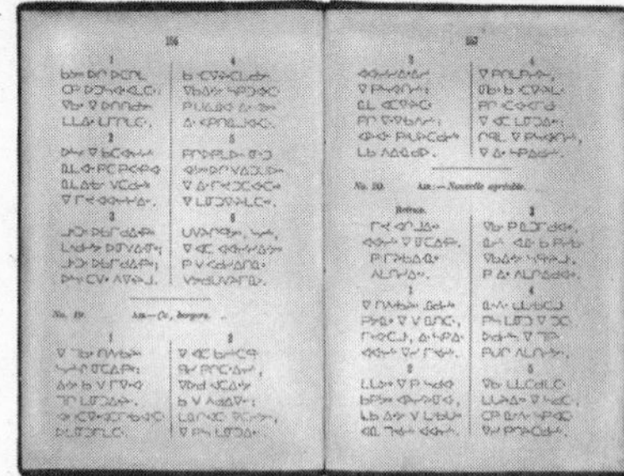

157

3

awasisiwiiso
awâsisiwihisow

e kisewatisit:
ê-kisêwâtisit:

nama ataweyitam
namâ âtawêyihtam

kici wewekapisot;
kici-wêwêkâpisot;

ayiwak kisteyitakosiw
ayiwâk kistêyihtâkosiw

maka piwinakoo.
mâka piwinâkohâw.

4

e kitimakisiyit,
ê-kitimâkisiyit,

nikan ka ntaweyimat
nîkân kâ-nitawêyimât

kici ntawapamikot
kici-nitawi-wâpamikot

e ata manitowit:
e-âta-manitôwit:

cikema e kisewatisit,
cikêmâ ê-kisêwâtisit,

e wi sakiikosit.
ê-wî-sâkihikosit.

2

macayaw e ki sakoat
macâyâw ê-kî-sâkohât

kakiyaw ayisiyiniwa,
kahkiyaw ayisiyiniwa,

maka wiya pe maskatwew
mâka wîya pê-maskâtwêw

ana meyosit awasis.
ana (ê-)miyosit awâsis.

5

ekwa mamatakomatak
êkwa mamâhtâkomâtâhk

macayiwin e sakotat,
macâyiwin ê-sâkôtât,

taki naspic sakiatak
tahki nâspic sâkîhâtâhk

esi kiceyitakosit.
(ê-)isi-kihceyihtâkosit.

No. 20. AIR: – Nouvelle agréable.
No. 20. AIR: – Nouvelle agréable.

Refrain.

miyo acimowin
miyo-âcimowin

awasis e nitawikit.
awâsis ê-nihtâwikit.

ki miyikawinaw
kimiyikawinaw

pimatisiwin.
pimâtisiwin.

1

e tipiskayik nokosiw
ê-tipiskâyik nôkosiw

kiyanaw e pe natitak,
kîyânaw ê-pê-nâtitâhk,

miywatamok, wi sakiik
miywâtamok, wî-sâkihihk

awasis esi miyosit.
awâsis (ê-)isi-miyosit.

3

ekwa ki natomikowaw,
êkwa kinatomikowâw,

nasik anoc ka kisikak
nâsik anohc kâ-kîsikâk

ekawiya sakweyimok,
êkâwiya sâkwêyimok,

ki wi pimaciikowaw.
kiwî-pimâcihikowâw.

4

naspic mamaskatamok
nâspic mâmaskâtamok

kise manito e totak
kisê-manitow ê-itôtahk

okosisa e mekit
okosisa ê-mêkit

kicoci pimatisiyak.
kicoci pimâtisiyahk.

158

No. 21. Air: — *Dans cette étable.*

1

ᑕᐯᐧ ᒪᒪᐣᑲ-
ᒧᐣᑐᐣ ᐅᑲᒥᑯᐧ
ᐊᐧᐸᒥᐠ ᓴᓱᐣ
ᓯᔭᑭᐃᑯᓯᐠ.

Refrain.

ᒪᓂᑐ ᐊᐊᐧᓯᐣ
ᑲ ᐱᒪᑎᐃᔭᐠ
ᑭᑕᑕᒥᐣᑲᑎᓇᐣ
ᐁ ᐃᐧ ᓇᑯᓯᔭᐣ
ᐃᐧ ᐱᑯᐃᓇᐣ.

2

ᒥᓯᐁᐧ ᐊᐣᑭᐠ
ᐁ ᑭ ᐊᐧᑎᐅᐠ
ᒪᑲᑎ ᐊᓇ-
ᐱᒪᑎᓯᓇᑎᐤ.

3

ᐊᔭᓯᔭᑎᐤ
ᐁᑲᐧ ᐊᑎᓯᐊᐤ,
ᐊᔭᒥᐊᐃᐧᐣ
ᐁ ᐯᑕᐧᑯᐃᐧᓯᐠ.

4

ᒪᓂ ᒪᓂᑐ
ᓇᐣᐱᑎ ᒥᐁᐧᐊᐤ
ᐁ ᑭ ᒪᐣᑲᒥᐠ
ᐅ ᒪᐣᑲᐃᐧᓯᐃᐧᐣ.

5

ᐊᐦ ᐃᐧ ᓇᑯᒪ
ᐃᐧ ᒪᒪᑕᑯᓯᐠ
ᐁ ᑎᑕᐃᐧᑭᐠ
ᒪᓂᑐ ᐊᐊᐧᓯᐣ.

No. 22. Air: — *Sortez de vos hameaux.*

1

ᒪᒪᐣᑲ- ᐃᑕᑲᒥᑲᐣ
ᐅᑕ ᐊᓇ- ᐊᐧᐣᑭᑕᐣᑲᒥᐠ
ᐁᑲᐧᔭᐠ ᐁ ᑎᑕᐃᐧᑭᐠ
ᑲ ᐃᐧ ᑭᑎᒪᑫᔭᒥᐁᐧᐠ.

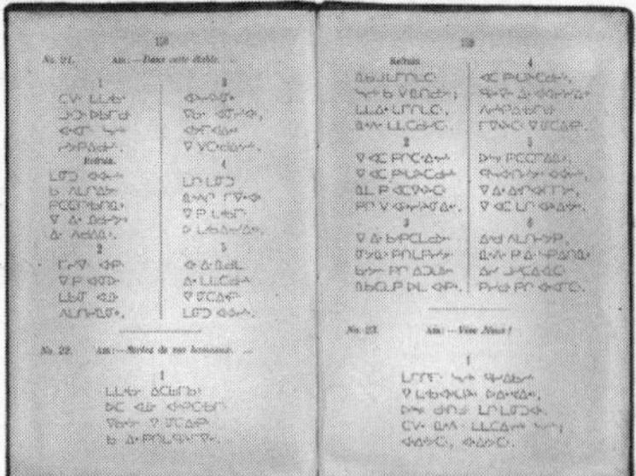

158 *No. 21.* Air: – *Dans cette étable. (In this stable.)*

1

Truly it is unbelievable
in a cow's stable
to see Jesus.
He is loved.

Refrain.

God's child
gave life to us.
We greet you.
You are visible.
Rescue us.

2

All over the land
we were lost.
With God today
everyone has life.

3

The people
and prophets,
their prayer
is heard.

4

The devil
runs away.
He has lost
his strength.

5

Thank you.
He is divine.
He is born,
God's child.

No. 22. Air: – *Sortez de vos hameaux.*
(Leave your villages.)

1

It is amazing: it is occurring
here today on earth.
He is now just born.
He is going to redeem us.

158

No. 21. Air: – Dans cette étable.
No. 21. Air: – Dans cette étable.

1

tapwe mamaskac
tâpwê mâmaskâc

mostos okamikok
mostos okamikohk

wapamik sesos
wâpamihk Sesos

siyakiikosit.
siyakihikosit.

Refrain.
manito awasis
manitow-awâsis

ka pimaciiyak
kâ-pimâcihiyahk

kitatamiskatinan
kitatamiskâtinân

e wi nokosiyan
ê-wî-nôkosiyan

wi pikoinan.
wî-pîkohinân.

2

misiwe askik
misiwê askîhk

e ki waniok
ê-kî-wanihok

makani anoc
mâkâni anohc

pimatisinaniw.
pimâtisinâniw.

3

ayisiyiniw
ayisiyiniw

ekwa anisiaw,
êkwa anisihâw,

ayamiawin
ayamihâwin

e petwakowisit.
ê-pêhtwâkowisit.

4

maci manito
maci-manitow

naspici miweaw
nâspici miwêhaw

e ki maskamit
ê-kî-maskamît

o maskawisiwin.
omaskawisiwin.

5

ay wi nakoma
ay wî-nakoma

wi mamatakosik
wî-mamâhtâkosik

e nitawikit
ê-nihtâwikit

manito awasis.
manitow-awâsis.

No. 22. Air: – Sortez de vos hameaux.
No. 22. Air: – Sortez de vos hameaux.

1

mamaskac itakamikan
mâmaskâc itâkamikan

ota anoc waskitaskamik
ôta anohc wạskitaskamik

ekwayak e nitawikit
êkwayak ê-nihtâwikit

ka wi kitimakeyimiwet.
kâ-wî-kitimâkêyimiwêt.

159

Refrain.

ᑎᑲᒧᒪᒥᒋᒪᑕᐠ
ᓴᓯᐢ ᑲ ᐯ ᑎᑎᑯᔮᐠ;
ᒪᒪᐃᐧ ᒪᒥᒋᒪᑕᐠ,
ᑎᐢᐱ- ᒪᒪᑕᑯᓯᑕᐠ.

2

ᐁ ᐊᑕ ᑭᒋᑕᐃᐧᓯᐟ
ᐁ ᐊᑕ ᑭᐢᑌᔨᑕᑯᓯᐟ
ᑎᒪ ᑭ ᐊᑕᐁᐧᔨᑕᐨ
ᑭᒋ ᐯ ᐊᔨᓯᔪᑎᐃᐧᐟ.

3

ᐁ ᐃᐧ ᑲᐢᑭᑕᒪᑯᔮᐠ
ᑑᔭᑖᐣ ᑭᑎᒪᑭᓯᔮᐠ
ᑲᐧᔭᐢ ᑭᒋ ᐃᑐᑌᔮᐠ
ᑎᑲᑕᒪᑭ ᐅᒪ ᐊᐢᑭᕀ.

4

ᐊᑕ ᑭᐢᑌᔨᑕᑯᓯᐤ,
ᑫᔮᐁᐧᐦ ᐃᐧ ᐊᐊᐧᓯᓯᐃᐧᐤ
ᐱᓯᐢᑭᐃᐧᑲᒥᑯᐟ
ᒥᐁᐧᔮᑕᐨ ᐁ ᑑᑕᐃᐧᑭᐟ.

5

ᐅᓴᐨ ᑭᑕᑕᒥᐃᑎᐣ,
ᑫᓴᐊᐧᑎᓯᔮᐣ ᐊᐊᐧᓯᐢ,
ᐁ ᐃᐧ ᐃᐧᒋᐊᐧᒥᒥᔮᐠ,
ᐁ ᐊᑕ ᒪᒋ ᐊᔮᐃᐧᔮᐠ.

6

ᐃᐢᑯ ᐱᒪᑎᓯᔮᑭ,
ᑎᐢᐱ- ᑭ ᐃᐧ ᓴᑭᐃᑎᑖᐣ
ᐃᔨ ᒍᔨᑕᐃᐧᑎᑕᐠ
ᑭᓯᑯᐧ ᑭᒋ ᐊᐧᐸᒥᑕᐠ.

No. 23. Air : — *Vive Jésus !*

1

ᒪᒥᒋᒥᐠ ᓴᓯᐢ ᑫᓯᐃᑲᓯᐟ
ᐁ ᒪᐢᑲᐊᐧᐢᑌᔮᐠ ᐅᐃᐧᔭᐃᐧᐣ,
ᐅᓴᐨ ᑯᐢᑎᑯᐟ ᒪᒋ ᒪᑑᑐᐊᐧ.
ᑕᐯᐧ ᑎᐢᐱ- ᒪᒪᑕᐃᐧᓯᐤ ᓴᓯᐢ;
ᐊᐃᐧᔮᑕᐠ, ᐊᐃᐧᔮᑕᐠ.

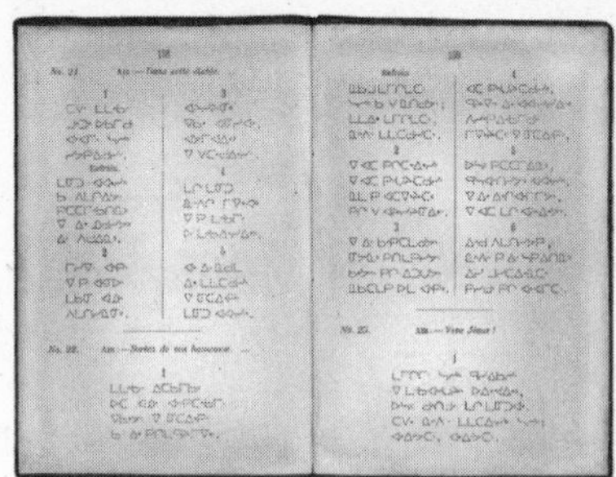

159

Refrain.

Let us give thanks.
When Jesus comes
to save us
let all of us praise Him;
forever let us be grateful.

2

Although He is holy,

although He is divine,

He humbled Himself
to become human.

3

He is going to win
salvation for us,
for us who are poor,
to go ahead properly
when we leave this earth.

4

Although He is divine,
He is also a child.

In an animal stable
He is happy to be born.

5

Because You have made
us grateful,
You are a compassionate
child.
You are going to save us,
although we are sinners.

6

As long as we live,

forever we will love You.
We live in hope
to see You in Heaven.

No. 23. AIR: – *Vive Jésus! (Long live Jesus!)*

1

Praise the One named Jesus.
His name is strong.
Because the devil is afraid of Him,
truly, forever He is divine, Jesus.
Glorify Him forever, Glorify Him forever.

159 Refrain.

nakamomamicimatak
nakamo-mamihcimâtâhk

sesos ka pe natikoyak;
Sesos kâ-pê-nâtikoyahk;

mamawi mamicimatak,
mâmawi-mamihcimâtâhk,

naspic mamatakositak.
nâspic mamâhtâkosîtâhk.

2

e ata kicitwawisit
ê-âta-kihcitwâwisit

e ata kisteyitakosit
ê-âta-kisteyihtâkosit

nama ki ataweyitam
namâ kî-atawêyihtam

kici pe ayisiyinwit.
kici-pê-ayisiyiniwit.

3

e wi kaskitamakoyak
ê-wî-kaskîtamâkoyâhk

niyanan kitimakisiyak
nîyanân kitimâkisiyâhk

kwayask kici itoteyak
kwayask kici-itohtêyahk

nakatamaki oma askiy.
nakatamâhki ôma askiy.

4

ata kisteyitakosiw,
âta kistêyihtâkosiw,

keyiwek wi awasisiwiw
kêyiwêk wî-awâsisîwiw

pisiskiwikamikok
pisiskiwikamikohk

miweyitam e nitawikit.
miywêyihtam ê-nihtâwikit.

5

osam kitatamiinan,
osâm kitatamihinân,

kesiwatisiyan awasis,
kisêwâtisiyan awâsis,

e wi wiciwamimiyak,
ê-wî-wîciwamimiyâhk,

e ata maci ayiwiyak.
ê-âta-maci-ayiwiyâhk.

6

isko pimatisiyaki,
isko pimâtisiyâhki,

naspic ki wi sakiitinan
nâspic ki-wî-sâkihitinân

isi mositawinatak
isi mositawinâtâhk

kisikok kici wapamitak.
kîsikohk kici-wâpamitâhk.

No. 23. Air: – Vive Jésus!
No. 23. Air: – Vive Jésus!

1

mamicimik sesos kesiikasot
mamihcimihk Sesos kâ-isiyihkâsot

e maskawasteyik owiyowin,
ê-maskawastêyik owîhowin,

osam kostikot maci manitowa.
osâm kostikot maci-manitowa.

tapwe naspic mamatawisiw sesos;
tâpwê nâspic mamâhtâwisiw Sesos;

wawiyatak, wawiyatak.
wawiyahtâhk, wawiyahtâhk.

160

2

ᒪᒥᒋᒥᐧ ᓭᓱᐣ ᐁᓯ ᒥᔦᓯᐧ
ᒪᒪᐃᐧᔦᐣ ᐁ ᑭᓭᐋᐧᑎᓯᐧ:
ᐅᐃᐧᔦᐃᐧᐣ ᓂ ᓯᑭᐅᑌᐣᑲᑯᐣ
ᐁᑯᓯ ᐁ ᓂᐣᑕᓯᐣᑲᑯᔅᐣ.
ᑕᑭ ᓭᓱᐣ ᒪᒥᒋᒥᐧ!

3

ᒪᒥᒋᒥᐧ ᓭᓱᐣ ᑌᐯᔨᒋᑫᐧ
ᑭ ᐃᐧ ᑭᑎᒪᑫᔨᒥᑯᓇᐤ:
ᓭᑭᐊᑕᐧ, ᑲᐧᔭᐣ ᐱᒪᑎᓯᑕᐧ
ᐃᐧᑭᐧ ᐅᑎ ᑭᑕᓯᑕᒪᑯᓇᐤ
ᓇᓇᐢᑯᒥᐧ, ᓇᓇᐢᑯᒥᐧ.

4

ᒪᒥᒋᒥᐧ ᒪᔨ ᑫᓯᐃᐧᑲᓯᐧ,
ᓭᓱᐢ ᐁ ᑭ ᐅᑲᐃᐧᒥᑯᐧ
ᑭᔮᓇᐤ ᒥᓇ ᐁ ᐅᑲᐃᐧᒪᔭᐧ
ᒥᐣᑕᐁ ᑭᓯᑯᐧ ᐊᔭᒥᐦᐊᒪᑫᐤ
ᑕᑭ ᒪᔨ ᒪᒥᒋᒥᐧ.

No. 24. AIR:—*Jesu dulcis memoria.*

1

ᓭᓱᐣ ᒣᔦᑭᐣᑭᓯᔭᐧ
ᐊᐧᐃᐧᐣ ᐁᓯ ᓭᑭᐊᑕᐧ
ᐱᑕᒋ ᐊᔭᐊᐧ ᒥᓇ
ᒋ ᒥᔦ ᐊᑕᒥᐊᑕᐧ.

2

ᓇᒪᐃᐧᔭᐧ ᑭᒋ ᐃᐧᑕᐧ
ᐁᓯ ᒥᔦᑕᑲᐧᑎᔭᐧ
ᑭ ᑭᒋ ᒥᔦ ᐃᐧᔦᐃᐧᐣ,
ᒥᔦ ᓭᓱᐣ ᐃᐧᓇᑯᒪ.

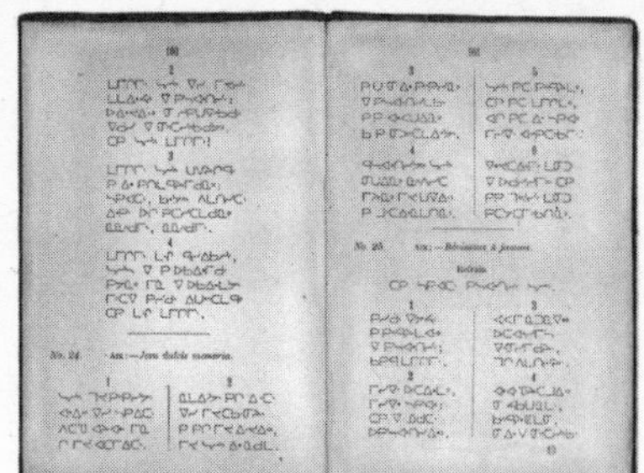

160

2

Let us praise Jesus as He is good.
Above all others He is compassionate.
His name strengthens me.
It comforts me.
All the time praise Jesus!

3

Praise Jesus, Lord of everything.
He is going to pity us.
Let us love Him; let us lead a good life.
He promises us eternal life.
Thank Him, thank Him.

4

Praise the one named Mary.
Jesus took her as His mother.
We also accept her as our mother.
She intercedes for us in Heaven.
Forever praise Mary.

No. 24. AIR: – *Jesu dulcis memoria.*
(Sweet memory of Jesus.)

1

Remember Jesus well,
especially the way in
which we love You.
So that we can
please You more.

2

Nobody tells about it
how good it sounds,

Your Holy Name.
Good Jesus, thank you.

2

mamicimik sesos esi miyosit
mamihcimihk Sesos (ê-)isi-miyosit

mamawiyes e kisewatisit:
mamawiyês ê-kisêwâtisit:

owiyowin ni sokiteskakon
owiyowin nisôhkitêhêskâkon

ekosi e nistosiskakoyan.
êkosi ê-nistasiskâkoyân.

ta ki sesos mamicimik!
tahki Sesos mamihcimihk!

3

mamicimik sesos tepeyiciket
mamihcimihk Sesos (ê-)tipêyihcikêt

ki wi kitimakeyimikonaw:
ki-wî-kitimâkêyimikonaw:

sakiatak, kwayask pimatisitak
sâkihâtâhk, kwayask pimâtisitâhk

wikik oci kitasotamakonaw
wîkihk ohci kitasotamâkonaw

nanaskomik, nanaskomik.
nanâskomihk, nanâskomihk.

4

mamicimik mari kesiikasot,
mamihcimihk Mari kâ-isiyihkâsot,

sesosa e ki okawimikot
Sesosa ê-kî-okâwîmikot

kiyanaw mina e okawimayak
kiyânaw mîna ê-okâwîmâyahk

mistae kisikok itwestamakew
mistahi kîsikohk itwêstamâkêw

No. 24. AIR: – Jesu dulcis memoria.
No. 24. AIR: – Jesu dulcis memoria.

1

sesos meyokiskisiyak
Sesos miyo-kiskisiyahk

wawis esi sakiitak
wâwîs ê-isi-sâkihâtâhk

pitone ayiwak mina
pitone ayiwâk mîna

ci miyo atamiitak.
kici-miyo-atamihitâhk.

2

namawiyak kici witak
namâwiyak kici-wîtak

esi miyotakwaniyik
(ê-)isi-miyotâkwaniyik

ki kici miyowiyowin,
ki-kihci-miyo-wîhyowin,

miyo sesos wi nakoma.
miyo-Sesos, wî-nakoma.

161

3

ᑭ ᑌ ᑎ ᐃᐧ ᑭᐢᑭᓯᓇᐣ
ᐁ ᑭᓴᐊᐧᑎᓯᒪᑳᐠ
ᑭ ᑭ ᐊᐧᐸᑌᐃᓇᐣ
ᑲ ᑭ ᓂᐳᐢᑕᒪᐃᐧᔮᐠ.

4

ᑫᓴᐊᐧᑎᓯᔮᐣ ᓴᓱᐢ
ᓂᑌᐃᓇᐣ ᓇᐢᐱᓯᑕ
ᒥᔭᓇᐣ ᒥᔪᑌᐁᐃᐧᐣ
ᑭ ᒍᐢᑕᐃᐧᓇᒪᑎᓇᐣ.

5

ᓴᓱᐢ ᑭᑕ ᑭᐢᑫᔮᒪᐤ,
ᑕᑮᐣ ᑭᑕ ᒪᒥᒋᒪᐤ,
ᐊᒋ ᑭᑕ ᐃᐧ ᓴᑭᐊᐤ
ᒥᓯᐁᐧ ᐊᐧᐢᑭᑕᐢᑲᒥᐠ.

6

ᐁᐧᔪᑕᐃᐧᒥᐟ ᒪᓂᑐ
ᐁ ᐅᑯᓯᓯᒥᐦ ᑕᑭ
ᑭᑭ ᒐᔪᐟ ᒪᓂᑐ
ᑭᑕᔅᑕᒥᐢᑳᑎᓇᐣ.

No. 25. Air: — *Bénissons à jamais.*

Refrain.

ᑕᑭ ᓴᑭᐊᑕᐠ ᑭᓴᐊᐧᑎᓯᐟ ᓴᓱᐢ.

1

ᑭᓯᑯᐧᐠ ᐁᔮᔦᐠ
ᑭ ᑭᐢᑫᔮᒪᐊᐧᐤ
ᐁ ᑭᓴᐊᐧᑎᓯᐟ;
ᑳᑭᑫ ᒪᒥᒋᒥᐠ.

2

ᒥᓯᐁᐧ ᐅᑕᐃᐧᒪᐤ,
ᒥᓯᐁᐧ ᓴᑭᐊᐤ:
ᑕᑭ ᐁ ᓇᑯᑕᐟ
ᐅᑭᓴᐊᐧᑎᓯᐃᐧᐣ.

3

ᐸᐸᒥ ᓇᑐᓇᐁᐧᐤ
ᐅᑕᐊᐧᓯᒥᓴ
ᐁᐧᑎᓯᒥᑯᔦᐟ,
ᒉᒋ ᐱᒪᑎᓯᔦᐟ.

4

ᐊᐧᐊᐧᑏᔦᑕᒧᐃᐧᐣ
ᑎ ᐊᐧᑲᑌᓇᒪᐠ,
ᑳᐢᑫᔦᑕᒪᑎ,
ᑎ ᐃᐧ ᐯ ᑎᐢᑕᓯᐢᑲᐠ

10

161

3

We must remember
the compassion
You showed us
when You died for us.

4

You are kind, Jesus.
In Your heart forever.
Give us a good spirit.
We ask this from You.

5

Jesus, He will be known.
Forever He will be praised.
More, you will love Him
all over the earth.

6

Our Father, God,
with Your eternal Son,
with the Holy Spirit,
we greet You.

No. 25. Air: – *Bénissons à jamais.*
(Let us bless forever.)

Refrain.

Let us love Him forever. Jesus is kind.

1

All you who are in
Heaven,
You all know Him.
He is kind.
Forever praise Him.

2

All over He is the Father.
All over He is loved:
Forever He shows
His kindness.

3

All over He looks for

His children.
He realizes
they are living badly.

4

Confusion
Remove it from us,
When I am lonely,
He will come and
comfort me.

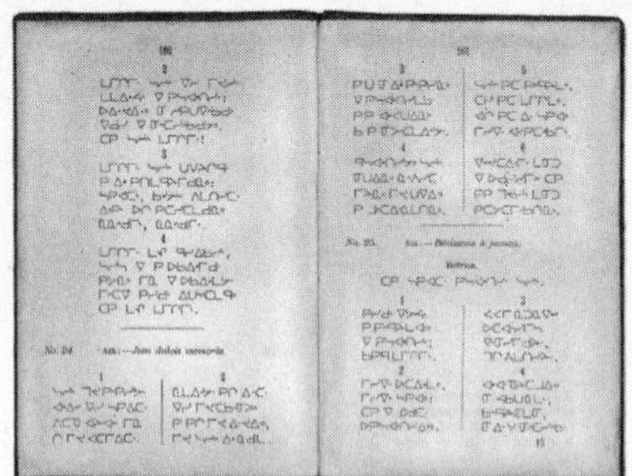

161

3

ki te ni wi kiskisinan
kitêh niwî-kiskisinân

e kisewatisimakak
ê-kisêwâtisimâhkak

ki ki wapateinan
kikî-wâpahtêhinân

ka ki nipostamawiyak.
kâ-kî-nipôstamawiyâhk.

4

kesewatisiyan sesos
(ê-)kisêwâtisiyan Sesos

niteina naspisita
nitêhinân nâspis ita

miyinan miyo teewin
miyinân miyo-têhêwin

ki mostawinamatinan.
kimostawinamâtinân.

5

sesos kita kiskeyimaw,
Sesos kita-kiskêyimâw,

taki kita mamicimaw,
tahki kita-mamihcimâw,

aci kita wi sakiaw
aci kita-wî-sâkihâw

misiwe waskitaskamik.
misiwê waskitaskamik.

6

weyotawimit manito
wiyôhtâwîmit manitow

e okosisimisk taki
ê-okosisimisk tahki

ki ki meyosit manito
kikî-miyosit manitow

kitayatamiskatinan.
kitayatamiskâtinân.

No. 25. AIR: – Bénissons à jamais.
No. 25. AIR: – Bénissons à jamais.

Refrain.

taki sakiatak kisewatisit sesos.
tahki sâkihâtâhk kisêwâtisit Sesos.

1

kisikok eyayek
kîsikohk (ê-)ayâyêk

ki kiskeyimawaw
kikiskêyimâwâw

e kisewatisit;
ê-kisêwâtisit;

kakike mamicimik.
kâkikê mamihcimihk.

2

misiwe otawimaw,
misiwê ohtâwîmâw,

misiwe sakiaw:
misiwê sâkihâw:

taki e nokotat
tahki ê-nôkôtât

okisewatisiwin.
okisêwâtisiwin.

3

papami natonawew
papâmi-nâtonawêw

otawasimisa
otawâsimisa

wenisimikoyit,
wênisimikoyit,

meci pimatisiyit.
maci-pimâtisiyit.

4

wawa-neyitamowin
wawa-nêyihtamowin

ni yekatenamak,
niyîkatênamâhk,

kaskeyitamani,
kaskêyihtamâni,

ni wi pe nistasiskak
niwî-pê-nistasiskâhk

162

5

7

6

8

No. 26. Air : — *Goûtez , âmes ferventes.*

Refrain.

(2)

1

3

2

4

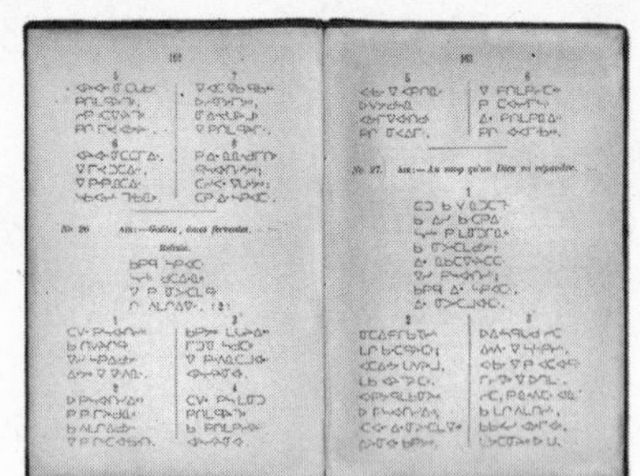

162

5

More so for spirit
He has pity on it.
He wants very much
for it to be well.

6

He pleases me more.
He does good for me.
He shows me the path,
the saving road.

7

Although I do not have
any money
or possessions,
He pities me.

8

I am going to thank You.
You are kind-hearted;
for that reason, I say
all the time, let us love
Him.

No. 26. Air: – *Goûtez, âmes ferventes.*
(Taste, ardent spirits.)

Refrain.

Let us love Him forever,
Jesus, our Father.
He died for others
So that they have life. (2)

1

Truly He is kind,
the One who owns
everything.
He shows He loves us
by giving up His body.

2

His kindness,
He gave it to us.
When He saved us,
He was nailed to a cross.

3

All sin,

He overpowers it.
He gains salvation
for the people.

4

Truly God
He had pity on them,
the poor
people.

5

ayiwak ni tacakwa
ayiwâk nitahcâhkwa

kitimakeyimew,
kitimâkêyimêw,

soki ntaweyimew
sôhki-nitawêyimêw

kici miyo ayayit.
kici-miyo-ayâyit.

6

ayiwak nitatamiik,
ayiwâk nitatamihik,

e miyo totawit,
ê-mîyo-tôtawit,

e kiskinotait
ê-kiskinôtahit

sekawasik meskanaw.
sêkawasik mêskanaw.

7

e ata eka kekway
ê-âta êkâ kîkway

o soniyamiyan,
osônîyâmiyân,

ni wiyoteyimon
niwiyotêyimon

e kitimakeyimit.
ê-kitimâkêyimit.

8

ki wi nanaskomitin
kiwî-nanâskomitin

kesewatisiyan;
(ê-)kisêwâtisiyan;

tasipwa etweyan:
tâsipwâ (ê-)itwêyân:

taki wi sakiatak.
tahki wî-sâkihâtâhk.

1

tapwe kisewatisiw
tâpwê kisêwâtisiw

ka tipeyiciket
kâ-tipêyihcikêt

esi sakiikoyak
(ê-)isi-sâkihikoyâhk

wiyaw e wepinak.
wîyaw ê-wêpinak.

2

o kisewatisiwin
okisêwâtisiwin

ki ki miyikonaw
kikî-miyikonaw

ka pimaciikoyak
kâ-pimâcihikoyâhk

e ki cistaaskwatit.
ê-kî-cîstahâskwâtît.

3

kakiyaw macayiwin
kahkiyaw macâyiwin

mitone sakotaw
mitonê sâkohtâw

e kispinatamowat
ê-kîspinatamôwât

ayisiyiniwa.
ayisiyiniwa.

4

tapwe kisemanito
tâpwê kisê-manitow

kitimakeyimew
kitimâkêyimêw

ka kitimakisiyit
kâ-kitimâkisiyit

ayisiyiniwa.
ayisiyiniwa.

No. 26. Air: – Goûtez, âmes ferventes.
No. 26. Air: – Goûtez, âmes ferventes.

Refrain.

kakike sakiatak
kâkikê sâkihâtâhk

sesos kotawinaw
Sesos kôhtâwînaw

e ki nipostamaket
ê-kî-nipôstamâkêt

ci pimaciiwet. (2)
kici-pimâcihiwêt. (2)

163

5

6

No. 27. Air:—*Au sang qu'un Dieu va répandre.*

1

2

3

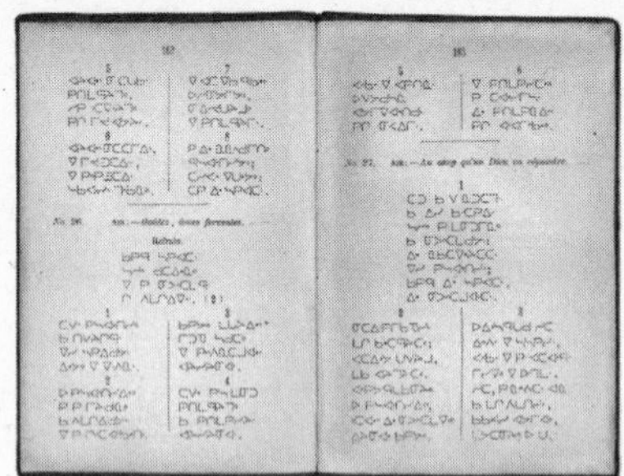

163

5
Even so He allowed
His only Son
on a cross
to be killed.

6
They are pitiful,
Your children.
Have pity on them.
Look with compassion
on them.

No. 27. Air: – *Au sang qu'un Dieu va répandre.*
(To the Sacred Blood outpoured.)

1
Each of you who comes to ask about
the way that He suffered,
Jesus, our Father.
He died for us.
Let us follow carefully
the way He is kind.
Let us love Him forever.
Let us die for Him.

2
In the garden
He begins to suffer in
His mind.
Still He is willing to die
but He finds it difficult.
It is a virtue,
His kindness.
Anyway He is going to
die for
all people.

3
The Jewish apostle
was poor in spirit.

He sold them Jesus.
All over he kissed Him.
He pretended to like Him.
Those who are deceitful
are not sincere when
they pray.
Their heart is evil.

163

5

paskac e pakitinat
paskac ê-pakitinât

o peyakosana
opêyakosâna

ayamiewatikok
ayamihêwâhtikohk

kici nipaimit.
kici-nipahimît.

6

e kitimakisitwaw
ê-kitimâkisihtwâw

ki tawasimisak
kitawâsimisak

wi kitimakinawik
wî-kitimâkinawik

kici wapamiskwaw.
kici-wâpamiskwâw.

No. 27. AIR: – Au sang qu'un Dieu va répandre.
No. 27. AIR: – Au sang qu'un Dieu va répandre.

1

tato ka pe natotamek
tahto kâ-pê-natotamêk

ka isi ka kwatakiit
kâ-isi-ka-kwâtakihiht

sesos ki manitominaw
Sesos kimanitôminaw

ka nipostamakoyak:
kâ-nipôstamâkoyahk:

wi nakataweyitatak
wî-nâkatawêyihtâtâhk

esi kisewatisit;
(ê-)isi-kisêwâtisit;

kakike wi sakiatak,
kâkikê wî-sâkihâtâhk,

wi nipostamowatak.
wî-nipôstamâwâtâhk.

2

nitawikicikanesik
nihtâwikihcikanisihk

maci kwatakeyitam;
mâci-kwâtakêyihtam;

atawiya tepeyimo,
âtawiya têpêyimow,

maka ayimeyitam.
mâka âyimêyihtam.

paskiyakemakaniyiw
paskiyâkêmakaniyiw

o kisewatisiwin,
okisêwâtisiwin,

nitawac wi nipostamawew
nitawâc wî-nipôstamawêw

iyiniwa kakiyaw.
iyiniwa kahkiyaw.

3

o wisakecako sota
owîsahkêcâhkow Sota

ispic e sasakisit,
ispic ê-sasâkisît,

paskac e ki atawaket
paskac ê-kî-atâwâkêt

misiwe e ocemat.
misiwê ê-ocêmât.

sota, ki naspitak ana
Sota, kinaspitahk ana

ka maci pimatisit,
kâ-maci-pimâtisit,

kakayesi ayamiaw,
kakayêsi ayamihâw,

mayataniyiw o te.
mâyâtaniyiw otêh.

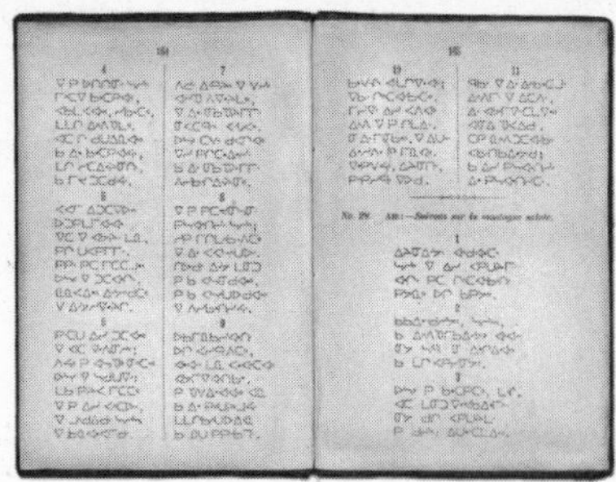

164

4

Jesus was assaulted.

He suffered greatly.

He was hit; He was
spit upon.
He was badly insulted.
Although you have hearts,

you have made Him
suffer
this torment
to do good for you all.

5

They rejected

their leader,
those who usually were
able to be counted on.
Also they denied
they were doing this
to Him.
Too late in exchange
when He comes in
judgement.

6

People do not know
how to react to Him.
He is offering a sacrifice.

Pierre rejected Him
three times
because he was a coward.
But quickly he regretted
the way he had sinned.
He was moved to tears
by Jesus.
He was watched by Him.

7

He is brought to Pilate's
house.
He is considered
worthless.
Who is thought of as
superior
is the murderer Barabbas.
Because truly He is
dominated,
He is holy.

Considered ahead of Him
is one that commits
murder.

8

Jesus's clothing was
removed,
yet He suffers.
He is bound tightly.
He is going to be scourged.
But He is God.
He takes away our sins.

He will punish us
if we commit serious sin.

9

At a thorny bush

He is scratched on
the face.
He is heavily burdened

by the cross.
You embarrassed Him,
you who are conceited.
You boast of your
tormenting power,
you who want to wear it.

164

4

e ki otitinit sesos
ê-kî-otîtiniht Sesos

mistae kwatakiaw,
mistahi kwâtakihâw,

pakamapawaw, sikwataw,
pakamapahwâw, sîkwâtâw,

mamaci ispinemaw.
mâmaci-ispinêmâw.

ata ci koteinawaw
âta kici-kotêhinâwâw

ka wi kwatakiayek,
kâ-wî-kwâtakihâyêk,

maci sotawiyinitik,
maci-Sotawiyinitik,

ka miyo totakoyek.
kâ-miyo-tohtakoyêk.

5

papami itotaewok
papâmi-itohtahêwak

o tokimamiwawa
otôhkimâmiwâwa

e ta e ayayit mana,
ê-âta ê-ayâyit mâna,

kici tepakimimik.
kici-têpakimimiht.

kikik kita mitatamwok
kikik kita-mihtâtamwak

osam e totawacik,
osâm ê-tôtawâcik,

nanapawis wiyaskotam
nânapawis wiyaskotam

pe wiyasoweyici.
pê-wiyasiwêyici.

7

pilat wikiyik e pesit
Pilat wîkiyik ê-pesît

asone piweyimaw,
âsone pîwêyimâw,

e wi nikaneyimimit
ê-wî-nîkânêyimimît

ni patakesk parapas.
nipahtâkêsk Parapas.

osam tapwe kopaciaw
osâm tâpwê kopacihâw

esi kicitawisit
(ê-)isi-kihcitwâwisit

ka wi nikaneyimimit
ka wî-nîkânêyimimît

pisikwaciwiyiniw.
pisikwâciwiyiniw.

8

e ki kitayonisenit
ê-kî-kêtayonisenît

kisewatisit sesos;
(e-)kisêwâtisit Sesos;

soki micimaskwapitaw
sohki-mihcimaskwâpitâw

e wi papasasteot.
ê-wî-pâpasastêhôt.

tiyakoc wiya manito
tiyakôc wiya manitow

ki ka asenikowaw,
kikâ-asênikowâw,

ki ka pasasteokowaw,
kikâ-pasastêhokowâw,

e pisikwatisiyek.
ê-pisikwâtisiyêk.

6

kwitate isi totawaw
kwitâtê isi tôtawâw

e ata wepinisot;
ê-âta-wêpinâsot;

piyer ki asenew nistwaw
Piyer kî-asênêw nîstwâw

osam e sakoteet:
osâm ê-sâkotêhêt:

maka kiyipa mitatam
mâka kiyipa-mîtahtam

e ki isi pastaot,
ê-kî-isi-pâstâhot,

e moskoikot sesosa
ê-môskohikot Sesosa

e kanawapamikot.
ê-kanawâpamikot.

9

okaminakasiwatik
okâminâkâsiwâhtik

oci pasikwepitaw,
ohci pasîhkwêpitâw,

wawac mana pwawataaw
wâwâc mâna pwawâtahâw

ayamiewatikwa.
ayamihêwâhtikwa.

ki nepewiawaw ana
kinêpêwihawâw ana

ka wi kisteyimoyek
kâ-wî-kistêyimoyêk

mamacikasteowina
mâ-macikastêhowina

ka note kikiskamek.
kâ-nohtê-kikiskamêk.

165

10	11
Jesus is going up on Calvary to be crucified. All over He is laughed at when He is made to suffer. "I am thirsty," He says. He is given gall to drink. People did this to Him. Remember that.	Just as He is going to breathe His last, He looks above. He is praying for those who killed Him. Continually we should imitate Him. When we are hated, We should imitate Him, and be kind like Him.

No. 28. Air: – *Suivons sur la montagne sainte.*
(Let us follow on the holy mountain.)

1

Let us people follow Jesus
in the way that He was given up on
the mountain, and crucified
for us all.

2

You who fall under the burden, Jesus.
You who are insulted,
I willingly go along,
when You start to fall.

3

Mary suffered.
God took you as mother.
For me you gave birth to Him,
your Son: speak to Him for me.

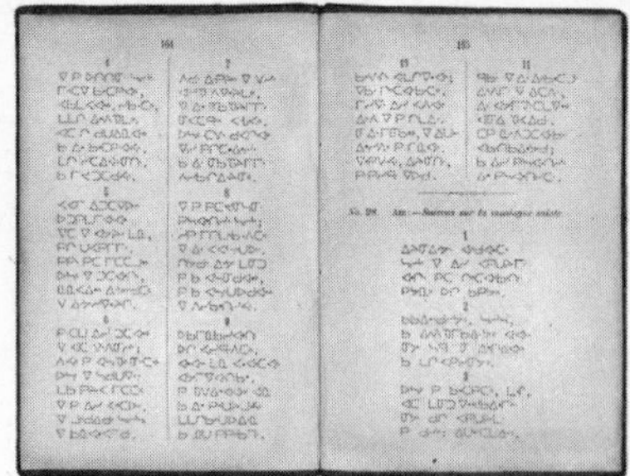

165

10

kalperik amaciweaw;
Kalperihk âmaciwêhâw;

ekwa cistaaskwaaw.
êkwa cîstahâskwâtâw.

misiwe isi papiaw
misiwê isi-pâhpihâw

ispi e ki cimait.
ispî ê-kicimahît.

ni wi minikwan, e itwet
niwî-minihkwân, ê-itwêt

wisopiy ki minaaw.
wisopiy kî-minahâw.

wekipeyek, iyinitik,
wî-kapêyîk, iyinitîk,

kiskisikek eoko.
kiskisîkêk êwako.

11

kekac e wi iskwatamot
kêkâc ê-wî-iskwatâmot

ispimik e itapit,
ispimihk ê-itâpit,

wi ayamiestamawew
wî-ayamihêstamawêw

anii nepaikot.
anihi nipahikot.

ta ki naspitotawakak
tahki-nâspitôtawakak

pakwatikawiyako;
pakwâtikawiyahko;

ka isi kisewatisit
ka-isi-kisêwâtisit

wi kisewatisitak.
wî-kisêwâtisîtahk.

No. 28. Air: – Suivons sur la montagne sainte.
No. 28. Air: – Suivons sur la montagne sainte.

1

iyiniwiyak askowatak
iyiniwiyak askôwâtâhk

sesos e isi pakiteyimit
Sesos ê-isi-pakitêyimit

wacik kita cistaaskwatit
wâcihk kita-cîstahâskwâtît

kiyanaw aci kakiyaw.
kiyânaw aci kahkiyaw.

2

kakawiskosoyan, sesose,
kâ-kawiskosoyan, Sesose,

ka ispinemikawiyan wawac
kâ-ispinêmikawiyan wâwâc

niya seki ni wiciiwan
niya sêhkê niwîcihiwân

ka maci pakisiniyan.
kâ-mâci-pahkisiniyan.

3

osam ki kwatakitam, mari,
osâm kî-kwâtakêyihtam, Mari,

ata manito weyokawimisk
âta manitow wêyokawîmisk

niya koci pakiteyimat
niya kôci-pakitêyimat

ki kosis: itwestamawin.
kikosis: itwêstamawin.

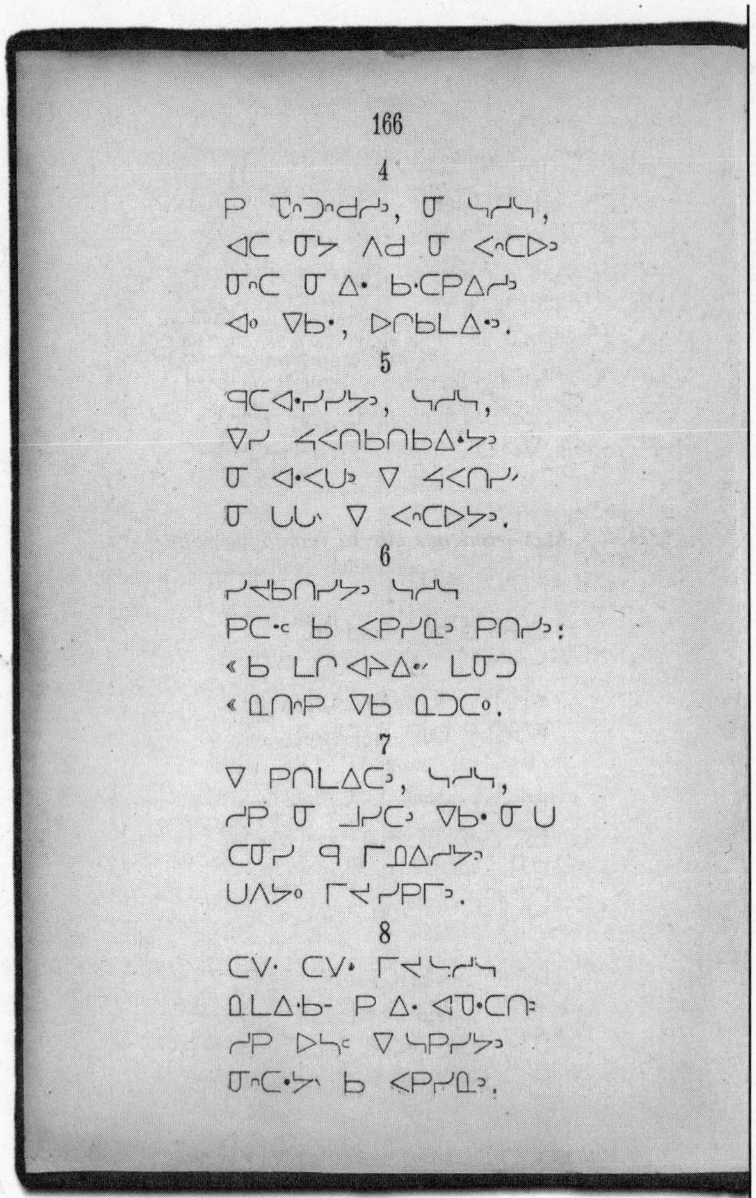

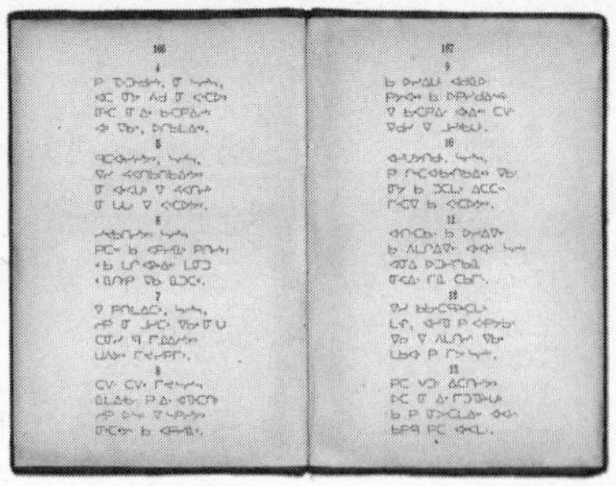

166

4

You are tired of the load, my Jesus.
Because I have sinned,
I, too, will suffer.
Ah, now help me.

5

Sweet Jesus
I see Your torment.
I see the dirt on Your face.
My spirit is sinning.

6

I am strong, Jesus.
Again I fall, and You say to me:
"It is the devil.
If he comes for you, do not listen to him."

7

I made You suffer, Jesus.
In my heart I feel very strongly
how to correct myself.
You give me good advice.

8

Truly, truly good Jesus
never will I reject You.
Because I am so weak
You fell down three times.

166

4

ki nestoskoson, ni sesose,
kinêstoskôson, niSesose,

ata niya piko ni pastaon
âta niya piko nipâstâhon

nista ni wi kwatakiison
nîsta niwî-kwâtakihison

aw ekwa, ocikamawin.
aw êkwa, ocikamâwin.

5

ketawasisiyan, sesose,
(ê-)kitawâsisiyan, Sesose,

esi yepatikatikawiyan
(ê-)isi-yêpatikatikawiyan

ni wapaten e yepatisit
niwâpahtên ê-yêpatisit

ni cacak e pastaoyan.
nitahcâhk ê-pâstâhoyân.

6

siyokatisiyan sesose
siyôkâtisiyân Sesose

kitwam ka pakisinan kitisin:
kîhtwâm ka-pahkisinan kitisin:

« ka maci ayiwit manito
"kâ-maci-ayiwit manitow

natiski eka natotaw. »
natiski êkâ natohtâw."

7

e kitimaitan, sesose,
ê-kitimahitân, Sesose,

so ki ni mositan ekwa ni te
sôhki nimôsîtân êkwa nitêh

tanisi ke minoisoyan
tânisi kî-minohisoyan

tepiyaw miyo sikimin.
tipiyaw miyo-sîhkimin.

8

tapwe tapwe miyo sesose
tâpwê tâpwê miyo Sesose

namawikac ki wi anwetatin
namâ wîhkâc kiwî-ânwêhtâtin

soki osam e sekisiyan
sôhki osâm ê-sêkisiyân

nistwayak ka pakisinan.
nistwayâk kâ-pahkisiniyan.

167

9

ᑲ ᐅᓯᐃᑌᐠ ᐊᑯᓇᐅᐠ
ᑭᔭᐋᐤ ᑲ ᐅᑭᓯᑯᐃᐧᔦᐠ
ᐁ ᑲᐧᑕᑭᐃᐟ ᐊᐧᐃᐧᐢ ᑕᐯᐧ
ᐁᑯᓯ ᐁ ᒍᓯᐢᑲᑌᐟ.

10

ᐊᓯᑌᔭᑎᑯᐠ, ᓴᓯᓴ,
ᑭ ᒋᐢᑕᐊᐢᑲᐧᑎᑲᐃᐧᐤ ᐁᑲᐧ
ᓂᔭ ᑲ ᑐᑕᒪᐤ ᐃᑕᑕᐤ
ᒥᐢᑕᐁ ᑲ ᐸᐢᑕᐅᔭᐤ.

11

ᐊᐧᒋᐢᑕᑲ- ᑲ ᐅᓯᐃᐁᐧᐟ
ᑲ ᐱᒪᒋᐃᐁᐧᐟ ᐊᐧᐊᐧ- ᓴᓯᐢ
ᐊᓂᐃ ᐅᑐᓯᒋᑲᓇ
ᓂᐸᐃᐠ ᒥᓇ ᑕᑲᒥᐠ.

12

ᐁᓯ ᑲᑲᐧᑕᑫᐳᑕᒪᐤ
ᒪᕆ, ᐊᓯᓃ ᑭ ᐸᐢᑭᔭᑲᐤ
ᐁᑯ ᐁ ᐱᒪᑎᓯᐟ ᐁᑲᐧ
ᒪᑲᐊᐧ ᑭ ᒥᔭ ᓴᓯᐢ.

13

ᑭᑕ ᐯᑐᐢ ᐃᑕᑎᓯᔭᐤ
ᐅᑕ ᓂ ᐃᐧ ᒥᑐᓃᐳᑌᐤ
ᑲ ᑭ ᓂᐳᐢᑕᒪᐃᐧᐟ ᐊᐧᐊᐧ-
ᑲᑭᑫ ᑭᑕ ᐊᐧᐸᒪᐠ.

167

9

Look away,
you all that are angels.
He is being made to suffer greatly,
when He is naked.

10

On a cross Jesus
You are crucified and
I nail You to it each time
I sin.

11

Consider that the One who made us,
Jesus who saved us,
by His own creatures
is being stabbed and killed.

12

The way that Mary suffered
humbles us very much.
Your Son has been killed,
Jesus, to whom you gave birth.

13

To behave differently
now, I am going to promise.
He died for me especially
to see Him forever.

167

9

ka osiitek akonaok
kâ-osîhtêk akonahok

kiyawaw ka okisikowiyek
kiyawâw kâ-okîsikôwiyêk

e kwatakiit wawis tapwe
ê-kwâtakihît wâwîs tâpwê

ekosi e mosiskatet.
êkosi ê-mosiskâkêt.

10

asiteyatikok, sesose,
asitêyahtikohk, Sesose,

ki cistaaskwatikawin ekwa
kicîstahâskwâtikawin êkwa

niya ka totaman itatwaw
niya kâ-itôtamân itahtwâw

mistae ka pastaoyan.
mistahi kâ-pâstâhoyân.

11

wacistakac ka osiiwet
wâcistakâc kâ-osihiwêt

ka pimaciiwet wawac sesos
kâ-pimâcihiwêt wâwâc Sesos

anii otosicikana
anihi otosîhcikana

nipaik mina takamik.
nipahîk mîna tahkamîk.

12

esi kakwatakeyitaman
(ê-)isi-kakwâtakêyihtamân

mari, asone ki paskiyakan
Mari, asônê kipaskiyâkan

eka e pimatisit ekwa
êkâ ê-pimâtisit ekwa

makawa ki miyo sesos.
makâwa kimiyo Sesos.

13

kita petos itatisiyan
kita-pîtos-itâtisiyan

ota ni wi mitoneyiten
ôta niwî-mitonêyihtên

ka ki nipostamawit wawac
kâ-kî-nipôstamawit wâwâc

kakike kita wapamak.
kâkikê kita-wâpamak.

168

14

ᐃ· ᒥᔨᐣ, ᓴᔨᓴ, ᓂ ᑌᐃᐠ
ᑕᑭ ᑭᑕ ᑳᓇᐁ·ᔨᑕᒪᐣ
ᑭ ᑳ·ᑕᕂᔨᑕᒧᐃ·ᓇ
ᑳ ᐅᒋ ᐅᔨᒧᐃᔭᐣ.

No. 29. AIR: — *Entends ma voix fidèle.*

1

ᑕᑭ ᓴᑭᐃᐠ ᑳ ᑎᐯᔨᒋᕂ
ᐊᔨᔨᔨᓂᐊ· ᑳ ᓂᐸᐃᑯ
ᑕᐯ· ᒥᓴᔨᐤ ᐅ ᓴᑭᐃᐁ·ᐃ·ᐣ
ᑳ ᓂᐳᐢᑕᒪᐊ·ᐧ ᑳ ᓂᐸᐃᑯ.

2

ᑳᓇᐊ·ᐸᒥᐠ ᑭ ᒪᓂᑐᒥᐊ·ᐤ
ᐊᔭᒥᐁᐊ·ᑎᑯᐠ ᐁ ᐊᑳ·ᒨ
ᐱᒪᑎᓯᐃ·ᐣ ᑭ ᐃ· ᒥᔨᑯᐊ·ᐤ
ᓇᑐᑕᐃ·ᐧ, ᐃ· ᑳᕂ· ᐱᒪᑎᓯᐠ.

3

ᐁᓯ ᒪᒪᑕᐃ·ᓯᐟ ᐊᑕ ᓂᐱ
ᐊᐢᑭᐠ ᑭ ᐊ·ᓂᑎᐱᐢᑳᐸᔨᐤ
ᐁ ᑭᐢᑕᐱᐢᑳᐠ ᑭ ᑕᑕᐢᑭᐸᔨᐤ
ᐁ ᓈᑯᑕᐟ ᐁ ᐃᓯ ᑭᔐᔨᐃ·ᐧ.

4

«ᓴᓴ⁺ ᒥᑐᑌ ᓂ ᑭᓯᑎᐸᐁᐣ,

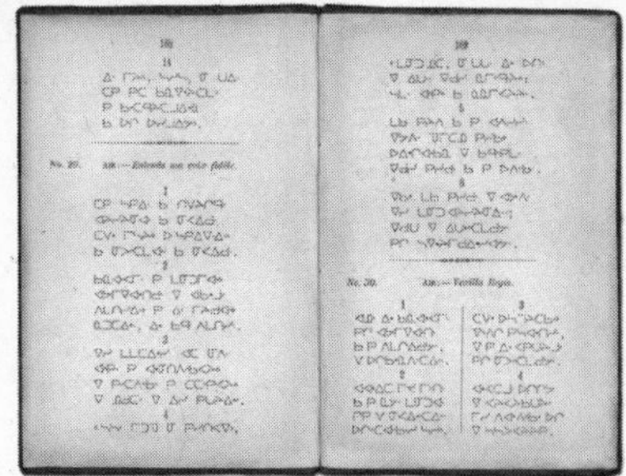

168

14

Let me have Jesus in my heart
all the time to look after it
your sorrows
you can escape them.

No. 29. AIR: – *Entends ma voix fidèle.*
(Listen to my faithful voice.)

1

The Lord loves forever
the people who killed Him.
Truly His love is great.
He died for those who killed Him.

2

Look at him Your God.
On a cross He is hanging.
He is giving you life.
Listen to Him to have life.

3

He is divine, although He is dead.
The earth got dark.
The rock of the temple split.
He showed that He is truly God.

4

"Already I have paid for sins.

14
wi miyin, sesose, ni teik
wî-miyin, Sesose, nitêhihk

taki kita kanaweyitaman
tahki kita-kanawêyihtaman

ki kwatakeyitamowina
kikwâtakêyihtamowina

ka oci osimoiyan.
kâ-ohci-osimohiyan.

No. 29. Air: – Entends ma voix fidèle.
No. 29. Air: – Entends ma voix fidèle.

1
taki sakiik ka tipeyiciket
tahki sâkihik kâ-tipêyihcikêt

ayisiyiniwa ka nipaikot
ayisiyiniwa kâ-nipâhikot

tapwe misayiw o sakiiwewin
tâpwê misayîw osâkihiwêwin

ka nipostamawat ka nipaikot.
kâ-nipôstamawât kâ-nipâhikot.

2
kanawapamik ki manitomiwaw
kanawâpamihk kimanitômiwâw

ayamiewatikok e akwamot
ayamihêwâhtikohk ê-akwamot

pimatisiwin ki wi miyikowaw
pimâtisiwin kiwî-miyikowâw

natotawik, wi kakwe pimatisik.
natohtawihk, wî-kâkwê-pimâtisik.

3
esi mamawawisit ata nipit
ê-isi-mamâhtâwisit âta nipit

askik ki wanitipiskapayiw
askîhk kî-wanitipiskapâyiw

e kistapiskak ki tataskipayiw
ê-kistapiskâk kî-tâtâskipâyiw

e nokotak e isi kicayiwit.
ê-nôkôtât ê-isi-kîcayiwît.

4
« sasay mitone ni kisitipaen,
"sâsay mitonê nikîsitipahên,

169

«ᒪᑌᑐᓇᑕ, ᑌ ᒐᒐᐠ ᐃᐧ ᐅᑎᐅ
ᐁ ᐃᑌᐧ ᐁᑯᓯ ᓇᑎᒥᐢᑫᐧᐦᐅ:
ᓴᒪᐠ ᐊᐢᑭ ᑲ ᓇᓇᒥᐸᔨᐠ.

5

ᒪᑲ ᑭᔦᐱ ᑲ ᑭ ᐊᐱᓯᓯᐠ
ᐁᔦᐱ- ᑌᒥᑕᓇ ᑭᓯᑳᐤ
ᐅᐃᐧᑎᐊᐧᑲᓇ ᐁ ᑲᑫᐢᑭᒪᐠ
ᐁᑯᓯ ᑭᓯᑯᐧ ᑲ ᑭ ᐅᐱᐢᑲᐠ.

6

ᐁᑳᐧ ᒪᑲ ᑭᓯᑯᐧ ᐁ ᐊᔦᐱᐠ
ᐁᓯ ᒪᑌᑐᐊᔨᓯᔨᑌᐃᐧᐟ;
ᐁᑯᑌ ᐁ ᐃᑌᐧᐢᑕᒪᑯᔦᐠ
ᑭᑎ ᓴᐁᐧᔨᒥᑯᐃᐧᓯᐊᐧᔦᐠ.

No. 30. AIR: — *Vexilla Regis.*

1

ᐊᓇ ᐃᐧ ᑲᓇᐊᐧᐸᒥᐠ
ᑭᑎ ᐊᔦᒥᐁᐊᐧᑎᐟ
ᑲ ᑭ ᐱᒪᑎᐊᑯᔦᐠ,
ᐯ ᐅᑎᑳᐧᓇᐱᐢᑕᐊᐧᐟ.

2

ᐊᐊᐧᐃᑕ ᒥᓴ ᒥᐢᑎᐟ
ᑲ ᑭ ᓇᔦᐠ ᒪᑌᑐᐊᐧ
ᑎᑭ ᐯ ᑌᐸᐃᐢᑕᐃᐧᐟ
ᐅᑎᐢᑕᐦᑳᐧᓯ ᓴᓯᐦ.

3

ᑕᐯᐧ ᐅᓴᒣᔦᑕᑳᐤ
ᐁᐧᐱᑎ ᑭᓴᐊᐧᑎᓯᐠ,
ᐁ ᑭ ᐃᐧᐸᑭᑌᔦᒧ
ᑭᑎ ᑌᔦᐢᑕᒪᑯᔦᐠ.

4

ᐊᐧᐸᑕᒧᐠ ᐅᒋᒋᔦ
ᐁ ᐸᐸᑭᔦᑲᑌᔦᐠ
ᒥᓯ ᐱᐊᐧᐱᐢᑳᐧ ᐅᑎ
ᐁ ᓴᓴᐸᐸᔦᑭ.

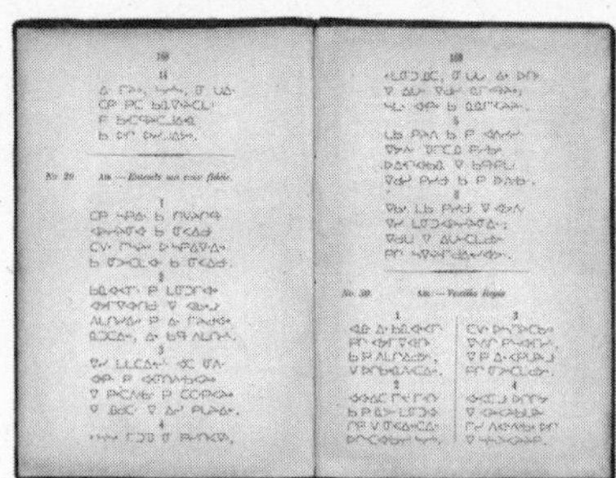

169

God, My Father, take My spirit,"
He said, and then He bowed His head.
Immediately the land trembled.

5

But quickly it was accomplished.
For forty days
He counselled His apostles.
And then He ascended to Heaven.

6

In Heaven, He is sitting.
He is God's Son.
He speaks for us,
how we are to be blessed.

No. 30. AIR: – *Vexilla Regis. (The standards of the King.)*

1

Today look at it,
the great crucifix
on which He saved us.
Come and kneel down
to Him.

2

Nevertheless, this cross
God carried on His back.
Come close, stand by
while Jesus is crucified.

3

Indeed it is humbling.
He has mercy within Him.
He surrendered
to die for us.

4

You see His hands.
They crucified Him.
With a big spike
they pierced right through.

169

manito nota, ni cacak wi otin »
manitow nohtâ, nicahcâhk wî-otin"

e itwet ekosi namiskweyiw:
ê-itwêt êkosi nâmiskwêyiw:

semak askiy ka nanamipayiyik.
sêmâk askiy kâ-nanamipayiyik.

5

maka kiyipi ka ki apisisik
mâka kiyipi kâ-kî-âpisisik

eyapic nemitano kisikaw
êyâpic nêmitanaw kîsikâw

owiciwakana e kakeskimat
owîciwâkana ê-kâkêskimât

ekosi kisikok ka ki opiskat.
êkosi kîsikôhk kâ-kî-ohpiskât.

6

ekwa maka kisikok e ayapit
êkwa mâka kîsikohk ê-ayapit

esi manito ayisiyiniwit;
ê-isi manitow ayisiyiniwit;

ekote e itwestamakoyak
êkotê ê-itwêstamâkoyahk

kici saweyimikowisiwayak.
kici-sawêyimikowisiwâyahk.

No. 30. AIR: – Vexilla Regis.
No. 30. AIR: – Vexilla Regis.

1

anoc wi kanawapamik
anohc wî-kanawâpamik

kici ayamiewatik
kici-ayamihêwâhtik

ka ki pimaciikoyak,
kâ-kî-pimâcihikoyahk,

pe ocikwanapistawik.
pê-ocihkwanâpîstawîk.

2

awa ita miyo mistik
awa ita miyo-mistik

ka ki nayat manitowa
kâ-kî-nayât manitowa

ciki pe nipawistawik
cîki pê-nîpawistawik

ocistaaskwaso sesos.
ocîstahâskâsow Sesos.

3

tapwe osameyitakwan
tâpwê osâmêyihtâkwan

es pici kisewatisit,
ês pîhci kisêwâtisit,

e ki wi pakiteyimot
ê-kî-wî-pakitêyimot

kici nipostamakoyak.
kici-nipôstamâkoyâhk.

4

wapatamok ociciya
wâpahtamok ohcihciya

e payipayikateyik
ê-payipayikâteyik

misi piwapiskwa oci
misi-pîwâpiskwa ohci

e sasapopayiyiki.
Ê-sâsâpopayiyiki.

170

5

Look at His feet. What!
Is it possible!
They are nailed.
His blood splashes up.

They were struck hard.

6

A sharp crown,
it is sharp;
they cruelly placed on
His head,
a crown of thorns.

7

Jesus, he took a breath

and His heart was stabbed.
Water and blood are
pouring out.
In this way it was going to
be finished.

8

And the cross
let us consider it all of us.
Let us repent

for we have sinned.

No. 31. Air: – *Stabat Mater. (The Mother stands.)*

1

Mary comes and stands close to where
her Son is being killed
on the cross.

2

She is exceedingly sad.
Grief is killing her.
He pities her.

3

She is even more
sorrowful.
She cries for Jesus.

who has died.

4

It is extraordinary.
His love is worth so much.
It looks out for people.

5

Mary goes about crying.

She longs for Him
completely,
the Son whom she loved.

5

osita nisi, wacistakac
osita nisi, wâcistakâc

sasakaikateyiwa!
sâsakahikâtêyiwa!

kwaskweciwaniyomiko
kwâskwêciwaniyo mihko

soki e pakamaamot.
sôhki ê-pakamâhamôt.

6

anakac ostikwan wawac
anakâc ostikwân wâwâc

e kasisiniyik oci
ê-kâsisiniyik ohci

soki postastotineaw
sôhki-postastotinêhâw

okaminakasiwatik.
okâminakasîwâhtik.

7

e ki iskwatamot sesos
ê-kî-iskwatamot Sesos

ekwa ote takatamwan
êkwa ôtêh tahkahtamwan

nipiy miko ocikawiyo
nipiy mihko ohcikawiyow

e wi isi kisiciket.
ê-wî-isi-kîsîcikêt.

8

ekwa ayamiewatik
êkwa ayamihêwâhtik

moskistawatak kakiyaw,
môskîstawahtâhk kahkiyaw,

kesinateyimisotak
kêsinateyimisotâhk

e ki maci pastaoyak.
ê-kî-maci-pâstâhoyahk.

2

e osami kaskeyitak,
e-osâmi-kaskêyihtahk,

naspic wi nipaeyitam
nâspic wî-nipahêyihtam

e kitimakinawat.
ê-kitimâkinawât.

3

wissakiteew ayiwak
wî-sâkitêhêw ayiwâk

e mawikatat sesosa
ê-mawîkâtât Sesosa

ka nakatikot sasay.
kâ-nakatikot sâsay.

4

ayiwakikin asone
ayiwâkîkin asônê

sokiteeyitakosiw
sôhkitêhêyihtâkosiw

esi kanawapaket.
ê-isi-kanawâpahkêt.

5

papami matwemo mari
papâmi-mâtwêmow Mari

naspic e kwitaweyimat
nâspic ê-kwitâwêyimât

ka waniat siyakiat.
kâ-wanihât siyâkihât.

No. 31. AIR: – Stabat Mater.
No. 31. AIR: – Stabat Mater.

1

mari onipawistawa
Mari onîpawîstawêw

okosisa nepaimit
okosisa nipahimiyit

ayamiewatikok.
ayamihêwâhtikohk.

171

6

“My Son, Jesus, my Son.”
“Why did you leave me?
Nevertheless, I will die.”

7

Who is not moved
to tears
when he sees Mary?
She thinks of her
Son sorrowfully.

8

You who have a heart,
let us go with our mother
in sorrow.

9

When we die,

and are able to be saved,
Mary, gain salvation
for me.

No. 32. AIR: – *Autour de nos sacrés autels.*
(Around our sacred altars.)

1

Let us praise Him always,
the One who died for us.
In the Heavenly kingdom,
He makes room for us.
Through His blood that
He came and poured for us
He is going to ransom us.
Truly, we are always sinners.
We are, in this way, poor in spirit.

2

Truly, He came and suffered.
He gave us life.
But He still loves us.
Our sins have held us back.

171

6

« ni kose sesos ni kose. »
"nikosê Sesos nikosê."

« taniki ko nakasiyan?
"tânêhki kô-nakasiyan?

aw! kiyam ni ka nipin. »
aw! kiyâm nika-nipin."

7

awena eka ke moskoit
awîna êkâ kê-môskohît

wiyapamaci mariwa
wiyâpamâci Mariwa

kekwatakeyimoyit?
kêkwatakêyimoyit?

8

kiyawaw ka oteiyek,
kiyawâw kâ-otehiyek,

wiciwatak kikawinaw
wîcêwâtâhk kikâwînaw

kaskeyitamowinik.
kaskêyihtamowinihk.

9

eyikok wi nipiyani,
iyikohk wî-nipiyani,

kici miyo pikooyan,
kici-mîyo-pîkohoyan,

mari, kaskitamawin.
Mari, kaskihtâmawin.

No. 32. AIR: – Autour de nos sacrés autels.
No. 32. AIR: – Autour de nos sacrés autels.

1

ekwa taki mamicimik
ekwa tahki mamihcimihk

ka ki nipostamakoyak
kâ-kî-nipôstamâkoyâhk

kisikok otenawiwin
kîsikohk ôtênâwiwin

ka ki tawinamakoyak
kâ-kî-tawinamâkoyâhk

omikom ka pe sikinak
omîhkom kâ-pê-sîkinak

kiyanaw e wi atawet
kîyânaw ê-wî-atâwêt

tapwe naspic wiyakio
tâpwê nâspic wiyakihow

e isi maci ayiwiyak.
ê-isi-maci-ayiwiyak.

2

tapwe ki pe kwatakitaw
tâpwê kî-pê-kwâtakihtâw

e wi pimaciikoyak
ê-wî-pimâcihikoyahk

maka kakiyaw sakotaw
mâka kahkiyaw sâkihtâw

ka ki micimiskakoyak.
kâ-kî-micimiskâkoyâhk.

172

ᐊᐅᓇ ᐁᑕᑯᑎᓯᐳᐠ
ᐃᐧᔭ ᐅᒪᒥ ᐃᑎᐃᐧᐣ
ᑕᐯᐧ ᒥᐢᑕᐁ ᓇᑯᑕᐤ
ᑭᑎ ᑭᓴᐊᐧᑎᓯᐃᐧᐣ.

3

ᑕᐯᐧ ᑫᑲᐧᕀ ᑭ ᐃᑕᑯᑊ
ᑭᑎ ᓱᑭ ᒥᑕᑕᒥᐠ
ᒪᑲ ᐁ ᑭ ᐊᐱᓯᓯᐠ
ᒉᐢᑯᐨ ᑭᑎ ᒥᐊᐧᑕᒥᐠ;
ᐁᑲᐧ ᒪᑲ ᒪᒥᑎᒥᐠ
ᐃᐧ ᑲᑭᓯᒧᑐᑕᐃᐧᐠ
ᐅ ᑭᓴᐊᐧᑎᓯᐃᐧᑎᐠ
ᑲ ᑭ ᐱᒪᒋᐃᑯᔭᐠ.

No. 33. Air: — *O Filii et Filiœ.*

Refrain.

ᐊᐱᓯᓯᐣ, ᐊᐱᓯᓯᐣ, ᐊᐱᓯᓯᐣ.

1

ᑕᐯᐧ ᓴᓯᐢ ᐊᐱᓯᓯᐣ,
ᑲᑭᔭᐤ ᒥᔭᐊᐧᑕᑕᐠ,
ᐁᑲᐃᐧᔭ ᑯᐢᑕᒧᑲᐠ,
ᐊᐱᓯᓯᐣ.

172

They exist,
our sins.
Truly He shows abundant
great kindness.

3

Truly it existed,
great and deep sorrow.
But He rises.
We will get some good of this,
and praise Him,
and pray to Him.
His compassion
gives us life.

No. 33. Air: – *O Filii et Filiae. (O sons and daughters.)*

Refrain.

He returns to life; He returns to life; He returns to life.

1

Truly, Jesus, you have returned to life.
Let us all be joyful.
Let us not fear.
You have returned to life.

172

apona etakoniyik
apôna ê-ihtakoniyik

wiya o maci itiwin
wiya omacihtiwin

tapwe mistae nokotaw
tâpwê mistahi nôkohtâw

kici kisewatisiwin.
kihci-kisêwâtisiwin.

3

tapwe kekway ki itakon
tâpwê kîkway kî-ihtakon

kihci soki mitatamik
kici-sôhki-mihtâtamihk

maka e ki apisisik
mâka ê-kî-apisisik

meskoc kici miwatamik;
mêskoc kici-mîwâtamihk;

ekwa maka mamicimik
êkwa mâka mamihcimihk

wi kakisi motatawik
wî-kâkîsi-mototawihk

o kisewatisiwinik
okisêwâtisiwinihk

ka ki pimaciikoyak.
kâ-kî-pimâcihikoyâhk.

No. 33. Air: – O Filii et Filiae
No. 33. Air: – O Filii et Filiae

Refrain.
apisisin, apisisin, apisisin.
âpisisin, âpisisin, âpisisin.

1

tapwe sesos apisisin,
tâpwê Sesos âpisisin,

kakiyaw miyowatatak,
kahkiyaw miyowâtâtâhk,

ekawiya kostamokak,
êkâwîya kostamohkêk,

apisisin.
âpisisin.

173

2
ᐅᓴᑦ ᑭ ᓴᑭᐃᑯᓇᐤ,
ᑭ ᑭᑎᒪᑭᓇᑯᓇᐤ,
ᐁ ᑭ ᓂᐳᐦᑕᒪᑯᔭᐠ.
ᐊᐱᓯᓯᐣ.

3
ᐐᔭᐤ ᐁ ᑭ ᐸᑭᑎᓇᐠ,
ᐁ ᑭ ᐎ ᒣᑎᑵᑲᐏᐟ
ᐐᑭᐠ ᑎ ᒥᔭᐘᑕᒥᐠ.
ᐊᐱᓯᓯᐣ.

4
ᑭ ᑕᑕᒥᐃᑯᐏᓯᐣ,
ᒪᕆ, ᑭ ᓴᑭᐃᑯᓯᐣ;
ᑭ ᑯᓯᐦ ᑲ ᑭ ᓂᐸᐏᐟ.
ᐊᐱᓯᓯᐣ.

5
ᒪᒧᔭᐌᐦᑕᒪᑯᓯᐤ,
ᑕᐍ ᓴᑭᐃᑯᐏᓯᐤ:
ᓇᒪ ᑭᑕᐧᐟ ᑭᑕ ᓂᐱᐤ.
ᐊᐱᓯᓯᐣ.

6
ᓴᓯᐦ ᓇᑐᑕᐘᑕᐠ,
ᑕᑭ ᓇᓇᐦᐱᑕᐘᑕᐠ,
ᐎ ᒥᔪ ᐱᒪᑎᓯᑕᐠ.
ᐊᐱᓯᓯᐣ.

7
ᓴᓯᐦ ᒧᓴᐠ ᑭᐦᑭᓯᑕᐠ
ᑭᓯᑯᐠ ᐊᐸᑕᐱᑕᐠ;
ᑲᑵ ᐱᒥᑎᓴᐘᑕᐠ.
ᐊᐱᓯᓯᐣ.

No. 34. Air:—*Je te salue, ô Pain de l'Ange.*

1
ᓴᓯᐠᕆ ᐁ ᑭ ᐊᐱᓯᓯᐠ
ᓀᒥᑕᓈ ᑭᓯᑲᐚ
ᐁ ᐸᐸᒥ ᑭᐦᑭᓈᐊᒪᑫ
ᑭ ᐊᔭᐤ ᐘᐦᑭᑕᑲᒥᐠ.

2
ᐅᑕᔭᒥᐁᐏᐹᑎᒪ
ᐁ ᐚᐎᑕᒪᐘᐟ ᒪᓈ
ᑕᑎᓯ ᑫ ᐊᐹᑐᑕᑫᐹᐟ
ᐁᐹᑯᐠ ᑭ ᓇᑲᑕᒋ.

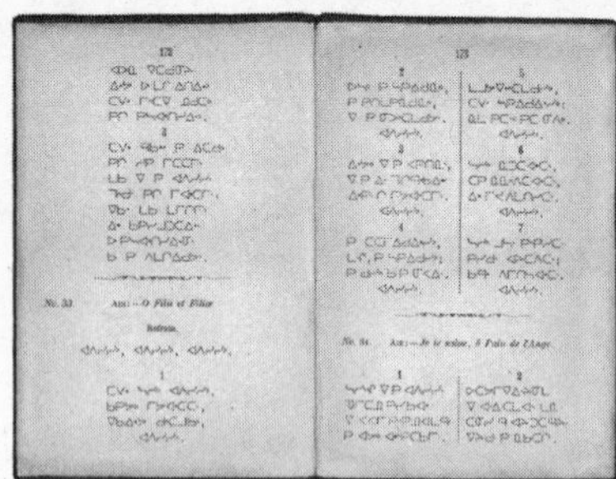

173

2
Because He loves us,
He looks at us with compassion.
He died for us.

He returns to the living.

3
He surrendered His body.
He shed all his blood

to glorify His name.
He returns to the living.

4
You are pleased,

Mary. Your loved Son,
the One who died,
returns to the living.

5
He returns.
Truly He is loved.

He will not die again like this.
He returns to the living.

6
Let us obey Jesus

and follow His example continuously.
Let us live a good life.
He returns to the living.

7
Let us always remember Jesus.
Let us look at Heaven.
Let us try to live like Him.
He returns to the living.

No. 34. Air: – *Je te salue, ô Pain de l'Ange.*
(I greet You, O Bread of the Angels.)

1
Jesus Christ, He came back to life.
For forty days,
He went around teaching,
while He was on earth.

2
His apostles

He counsels about
how to treat others,

until He leaves the earth.

173

2

osam ki sakiikonaw,
osâm kisâkihikonaw,

ki kitimakinakonaw,
kikitimâkinâkonaw,

e ki nipostamakoyak.
ê-kî-nipôstamâkoyahk.

apisisin.
âpisisin.

3

wiyaw e ki pakitinak,
wîyaw ê-kî-pakitinak,

e ki wi mecikwekawit
ê-kî-wî-mêscikwêkawit

wikik ci miyowatamik.
wîkihk kici-miyowâtamihk.

apisisin.
âpisisin.

4

ki tatamiikowisin,
kitatamihikowisin,

mari, ki sakiikosin;
Mari, kisâkihikosin;

ki kosis ka ki nipait.
kikosis kâ-kî-nipahît.

apisisin.
âpisisin.

5

mamoyawestamakosiw,
mamoyawêstamâkosiw,

tapwe sakiikowisiw:
tâpwê sâkihikowisiw:

nama kitwam kita nipiw.
namâ kîhtwâm kita-nipiw.

apisisin.
âpisisin.

6

sesos natotawatak,
Sesos nâtohtawâtâhk,

taki nanaspitawatak,
tahki nânaspihtawâtâhk,

wi miyo pimatisitak.
wî-miyo-pimâtisitâhk.

apisisin.
âpisisin.

7

sesos mosak kiskisitak
Sesos môsak kiskisitâhk

kisikok ayitapitak;
kîsikohk ayitâpitâhk;

kakwe pimitisawatak.
kâkwê-pimitisawâtâhk.

apisisin.
âpisisin.

No. 34. Air: – Je te salue, ô Pain de l'Ange.
No. 34. Air: – Je te salue, ô Pain de l'Ange.

1

sesokri e ki apisisik
Sesokri ê-kî-âpisisik

nemitano kisikawa
nêmitanaw kîsikâwa

e papami kiskinoamaket
ê-papâmi-kiskinohamâkêt

ki ayaw waskitakamik.
kî-ayâw waskitaskamik.

2

otayamiewiyinima
otayamihêwiyinîma

e wawitamawat mana
ê-wâwîtamawât mâna

tanisi ke ayitotakeyit
tânisi ka-ayitôtakêyit

eyikok ki nakataci.
iyikohk kî-nakatâci.

174

3
ᐊᐃᐧᔾ ᑲᓯᑎᒪᐧᐊᐧᔪ
ᐅ ᒪᓯ ᑐᑕᒧᐃᐧᓇ
ᑭᑕ ᑲᓯᑯᑲᐅᔨᐊᐧ
ᐁᑯᓯ ᑭᓯ ᑭᓯᑯᐧ.

4
ᐁᑲ ᑲᓯᓇᒪᐧᐊᐧᔪᑯ,
ᐁᑯᓯ ᑯᐦᑕ ᑭᓯᑯᐧ
ᓇᒪ ᑭᓯ ᑲᓯᓇᒪᐧᐊᐧᐣ,
ᑭᑎᓯ ᒥᔨᑎᓇᐊᐤ.

5
ᒣᔪᔨ ᒪᑯᑐᐊᐧ ᐅᓯ
ᐁᑲᐧ ᓯᑭᐅᐁᐧᐦᑲᐁᐧᐤ
ᑭᓯ ᒥᐦᑕᐁ ᓯᑲᐦᑕᐧᔨ
ᑲ ᐃᔨ ᒪᒪᑕᐃᐧᐊᐧ.

6
ᐁ ᑌᒥᑕᓇ ᑭᓯᑲᔨ
ᐁᑲᐧ ᓇᑐᐤ ᑲᑭᔪᐤ
ᐅ ᑭᐦᑭᓇᐊᒪᐊᐧᑲᓇ,
ᐁ ᐃᐧ ᐊᔨᒥᐁᐦᑕᒪᐊᐧᐣ.

7
ᓇᐦᐱᓯ ᐁᔨᑯᑫᐧᔨᒧ,
ᐊᐊᐧᐁᐧ, ᐃᐧ ᐸᐸᒧᑕᑕ
ᑯ ᑭᐦᑭᓄᐊᒪᑫᐃᐧᓇ
ᒥᓯᐁᐧ ᐊᐧᐦᑭᑕᐦᑲᒥᐠ.

8
ᐊᐃᐧᔾ ᓯᑲᓯᑲᓯᓯ
ᑎᔨᐯᐧᐅᐧᑫᐧᔨᑕᑭ
ᑭᑕ ᐅᑕᐊᐧᓯᒥᓯᒥᐠ
ᓴᓕ ᑭᓴ ᒪᑯᑐᐊᐧ.

9
ᑯ ᑲ ᑕᐯᐧᑕᑲᐃᐧᒼ ᒪᓇ
ᑎᔨᐯᐧᑕᑲᐃᐧᔪᑯ;
ᑯ ᑲᒥᔭᑐᑕ ᐊᐃᐧᔾ
ᐊᐧ ᒥᔭᑐᑕᑯᔪᑯ.

10
ᐁᑭ ᐸᑯ ᐱᑭᐦᑫᐧ ᓴᓯᐦ
ᐃᐦᑫᐧᔾ ᐃᐧ ᓴᐁᐧᔨᒣᐤ,
ᐁᑲᐧ ᑲ ᐅᐱᐦᑲᐧ ᑭᓯᑯ
ᑲᑫᔨᐤ ᐁ ᐊᐧᐸᒥᑯᐧ.

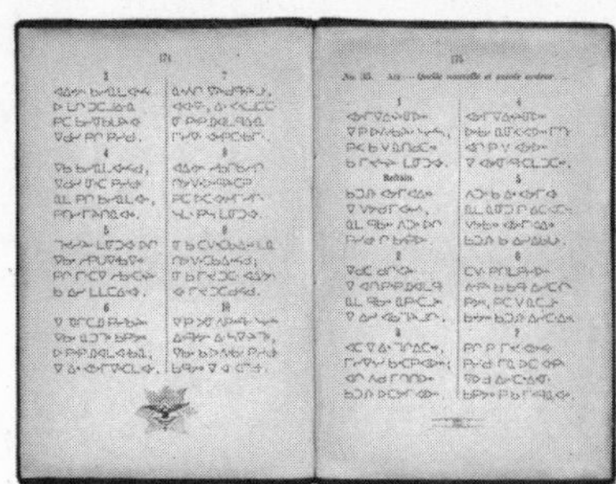

174

3
If someone forgives
his sins

And removes them,
So it is in Heaven.

4
If sins are not forgiven,

so I, too, in Heaven
Will not forgive them.
I give it to you this way.

5
Good God
gave His apostles a
strong heart,
to have great courage.

He gave them super-
natural power in
this way.

6
In forty days,
He calls everyone
together.
His apostles,

He is praying for them.

7
Forever are you enabled.
Now then who walk with
these words,
my teachings,
all over the earth.

8
When someone is
baptized,
if he believes in this grace,
he becomes a child
of God.

9
I will be believed usually,
if you are believed.

Someone will do good
for Me,
if he does something
good for you.

10
Jesus, He stopped talking.
At last, He is content.

And He ascends to
Heaven,
All see him.

[HOLY SPIRIT COPPERPLATE]

174

3

awiyak kasinamawayek
awiyak kâsînamawâyêk

o maci totamowina
omaci-tôtamowina

kita kasinikateyiwa
kita-kâsînikâtêyiwa

ekosi kici kisikok.
êkosi kihci-kîsikohk.

4

eka kasinamawayeko,
êkâ kâsînamawâyêko,

ekosi nista kisikok
êkosi nîsta kîsikohk

nama kici kasinamawak,
namâ kici-kâsînamawak,

kitisimiyitinawaw.
kitîsimiyitinâwâw.

5

meyosiyit manitowa oci
(ê-)miyosiyit manitowa ohci

ekwa sokiteeskawew
êkwa sôhkitêhêskawêw

kici mistae sokastwayit
kici-mistahi-sôhkastwâyit

ka isi mamatawiat.
ka-isi-mamâhtâwihât.

7

naspici eyikokweyimok,
nâspici iyikohkwêyimok,

awaek, wi papamotatak
awiyak, wî-papâmôtatak

ni kiskinoamakewina
nikiskinohamâkêwina

misiwe waskitaskamik.
misiwê waskitaskamik.

8

awiyak sikacikasoci
awiyak sîkâcikâsohci

tiyapwewokeyitaki
tiyapwêwakêyihtâhki

kita otawasimisimik
kita-otawâsimisimik

semak kise manitowa.
sêmâk kisê-manitowa.

9

ni ka tapwetakawin mana
nika-tâpwêtakawin mâna

tiyapwetakawiyeko;
tiyapwêtakawiyêko;

ni ka miyo totak awiyak
nika-miyo-tôtak awiyak

wa miyo totakoyeko.
wâ-miyo-tôtakoyêko.

6

e nemitano kisikayik
ê-nêmitanaw kîsikâyik

ekwa natomew kakiyaw
êkwa natomêw kahkiyaw

o kiskinoamawakana,
okiskinohamâwâkana,

e wi ayamiestamawat.
ê-wî-ayamihestamawât.

10

e ki poni pikiskwet sesos
ê-kî-pôni-pîkiskwêt Sesos

iskweyac wi saweyimew,
iskwêyac wî-sawêyimêw,

ekwa ka opiskat kisikok
êkwa kâ-ohpîskât kîsikohk

kakeyaw e wapamikot.
kahkiyaw ê-wâpamikot.

[HOLY SPIRIT COPPERPLATE]

175 No. 35. AIR: – *Quelle nouvelle et sainte ardeur.*
(What new and sacred force.)

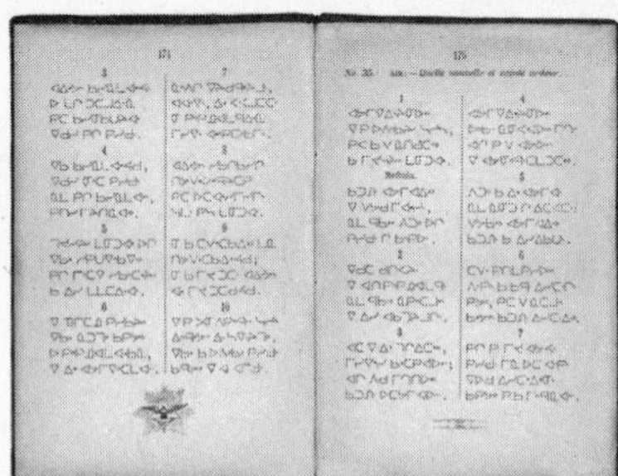

1

The apostles,
when Jesus had risen,

learned how

to speak to the good God.

Refrain.

Catholic prayer,

it alone is good.

You cannot do
anything differently
to make it to Heaven.

2

If the teaching comes
from God,
they begin to teach it.

They do not stop
for anything.
In this way they
persevere.

3

Nevertheless, there
are many
who are made to suffer.

More and more there
are many
Catholic martyrs.

4

Many priests
in the beginning were
killed.
More and more, they
gained
their inheritance.

5

If God is prayed to
differently,
it is all right to use one's
own mind.
The One universal religion

is called Catholic.

6

Truly, people are miserable

when they act separately,
on their own.
They will come and get

the way of Catholicism.

7

You will be well

in Heaven and here
on earth.
This one same religion

all of you will find it.

175 No. 35. Air: – Quelle nouvelle et sainte ardeur.
No. 35. Air: – Quelle nouvelle et sainte ardeur.

1

ayamiewiyiniwok
ayamihêwiyiniwak

e ki opiskayit sesosa,
ê-kî-ohpîskâyit Sesosa,

kipa ka pe natikotwaw
kîpa kâ-pê-nâtikotwâw

ka miyoseyit manitowa.
kâ-miyosiyit manitowa.

Refrain.

katolik ayamiawin
kâtolik ayamihâwin

e peyakomiwasik,
ê-peyako-miywâsik,

nama kekway pitos oci
namâ kîkwây pîtos ohci

kisikok ci kaskiok.
kîsikohk kici-kaskihok.

2

ekota kocipayik
êkota kôcipayik

e ati kiskinoamakek
ê-âta-kiskinohamâkêk

nama kekway nakistamwok
namâ kîkway nakîstamwak

e isi akameyimocik.
ê-isi-âhkamêyimocik.

4

ayamiewiyiniwok
ayamihêwiyiniwak

oskac nanipaawok micet
oskac nanipahâwak mihcêt

aci ki pe ayawok
âci kî-pê-ayâwak

e ayaniskestamatotwaw.
ê-ayaniskêstamâtotwâw.

5

pitos ka wi ayamiak
pîtos kâ-wî-ayamihâhk

nama manito ci itapatak:
nama manitow kici-itâpatâhk:

peyakwan ayamiawin
pêyakwan ayamihâwin

katolik ka isi ikatek.
kâtolik kâ-isiyihkâtêk.

6

tapwe kitimakisiwok
tâpwê kitimâkisiwak

piskis ka kakwe isitwacik
piskis kâ-kâkwê isîhtwâcik

kiyam, kita pe natamwok
kiyâm, kita-pê-natamwak

kwayask katolik isitawin.
kwayask kâtolik isîhtwâwin.

3

ata e wi meciitwaw,
âta ê-wî-mihcêtwâw,

misiwesi kwatakiawok;
misiwêsi kwâtakihâwak;

aci piko micetiwok
âci piko mihcêtiwak

katolik otayamiawok.
kâtolik otayamihâwak.

7

kici ki miyo ayayek
kici-kî-miyo-ayâyêk

kisikok mina ota askik
kîsikohk mîna ôta askîhk

eako isitwawinik
êwako isîhtwâwinihk

kakiyaw ki ka miskenawaw.
kahkiyaw ki-ka-miskênâwâw.

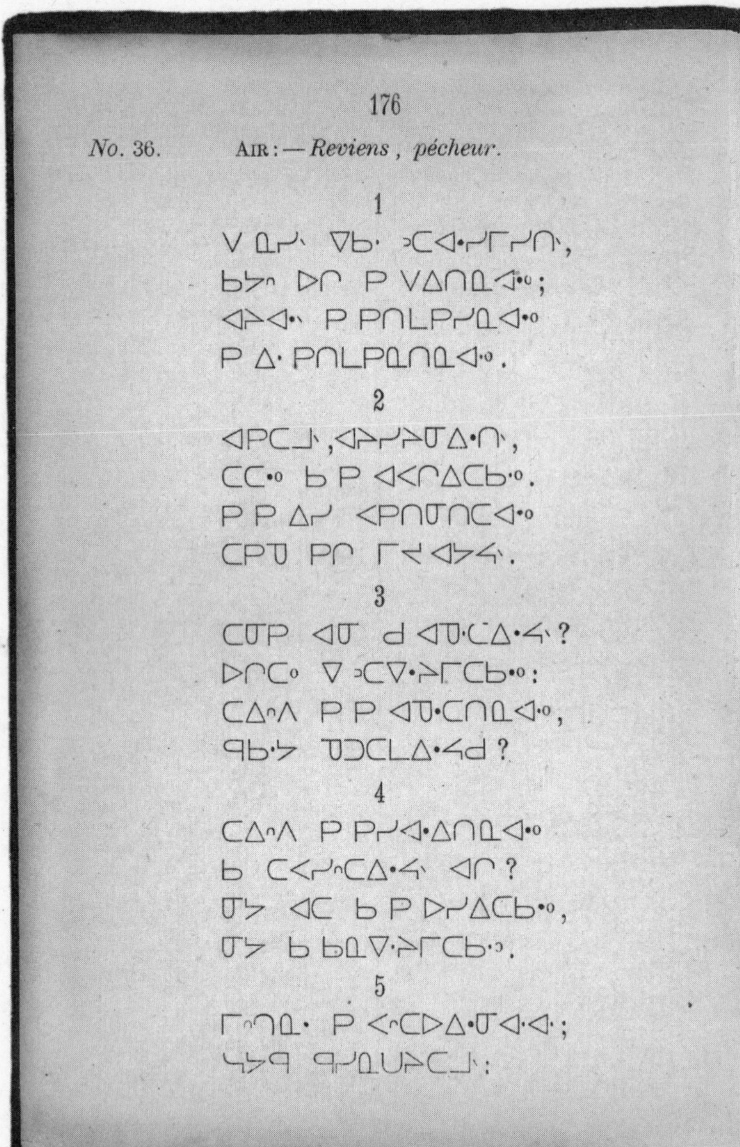

176

No. 36. Air: — *Reviens, pécheur.*

1

ᐯ ᓇᓯᐠ ᐁᑳᐧ ᐅᑕᐊᐧᓯᒥᓯᑎᐠ,
ᑲᔭᐢ ᐅᒋ ᑭ ᐯᐃᑎᓇᐚᐤ;
ᐊᐦᐊᐧᐠ ᑭ ᑭᑎᒪᑭᓯᓇᐚᐤ
ᑭ ᐃᐧ ᑭᑎᒪᑭᓇᑎᓇᐚᐤ.

2

ᐊᑭᑕᒧᐠ,ᐊᐦᓯᐦᑌᐃᐧᑎᐠ,
ᑕᑖᐤ ᑳ ᑭ ᐊᐸᒋᐃᑕᑳᐤ.
ᑭ ᑭ ᐃᓯ ᐸᑭᑎᑌᑎᑕᐚᐤ
ᑕᑭᑘ ᑭᒋ ᒥᔪ ᐊᔭᔦᐠ.

3

ᑕᑌᑭ ᐊᑌ ᑯ ᐊᑘᑖᐃᐧᔦᐠ?
ᐅᒋᑕᐤ ᐁ ᐅᑌᐃᐧᐦᔨᒥᑕᑳᐤ:
ᑕᐃᐢᐱ ᑭ ᑭ ᐊᑘᑕᑎᓇᐚᐤ,
ᑫᑳᐧᔭ ᑘᑐᑕᒪᐃᐧᔦᑯ?

4

ᑕᐃᐢᐱ ᑭ ᑭᓯᐘᐃᑎᓇᐚᐤ
ᑳ ᑕᐸᓯᐢᑕᐃᐧᔦᐠ ᐊᒋ?
ᑌᔭ ᐊᑕ ᑳ ᑭ ᐅᓯᐃᑕᑳᐤ,
ᑌᔭ ᑳ ᑳᓇᐁᐧᐦᔨᒥᑕᑳᐤ.

5

ᒥᐢᒐᓇᐧ ᑭ ᐸᐢᑕᐅᐃᐧᑌᐊᐧᐊᐧ;
ᓭᔭᑫ ᑫᓯᓇᑌᐦᔨᑕᒧᐠ:

 No. 36. Air: – *Reviens, pécheur. (Come back, sinner.)*

1

My children, come follow Me.
I have waited for you a long time.
You are poor in spirit.
I am going to have pity on you.

2

Count it, people,
each time you have used it.
In this way I have allowed it
so that your life will be good forever.

3

Why did you not believe in Me,
when, without fail, I desired you?
Why did you not believe in Me at that time,
when you asked for something?

4

When I anger you people,
why at that time do you flee from Me,
even though I made you
and sustained you?

5

Your sins are many.
At least you repent:

176 No. 36. AIR: – Reviens, pécheur.

No. 36. AIR: – Reviens, pécheur.

1

pe nasik ekwa ntawasimisitik,
pê-nâsik êkwa nitawâsimisitik,

kayas oci ki pe itinawaw;
kayâs ohci kî-pê-itinâwâw;

ayiwak ki kitimakisinawaw
ayiwâk kikitimâkisinâwâw

ki wi kitimakinatinawaw.
kiwî-kitimâkinatinâwâw.

2

akitamok, ayisiyiniwitik,
akihtamok, ayisiyiniwitik,

tatwaw ka ki apaciitakwaw.
tahtwâw kâ-kî-âpahcihitakwâw.

ki ki isi pakitinititawaw
kikî-isi-pakitinititâwâw

takine kici miyo ayayek.
tahkinê kici-miyo-ayâyêk.

3

taniki ani ko anwetawiyek?
tânêhki ani kô-ânwêhtawîyêk?

ocitaw e ntaweyimitakwaw:
ôhcitaw ê-nitawêyimîtakwâw:

taispi ki ki anwetatinawaw,
tânispî kikî-ânwêhtâtinâwâw,

kekwaya netotamawiyeko?
kîkwaya nêtotamawiyêko?

4

taispi ki kisiwaitinawaw
tânispî kikisiwahitinâwâw

ka tapasistawiyek aci?
kâ-tapasîstawiyêk âci?

niya ata ka ki osiitakwaw,
niya âta ka-kî-osîhtakwâw,

niya ka kanaweyimitakwaw.
niya kâ-kanawêyimitakwâw.

5

miscenwa ki pastaowiniwawa;
mihcênwa kipâstâhowiniwâwa;

seyake kesinateyitamok:
sêyâkê kêsînatêyihtamok:

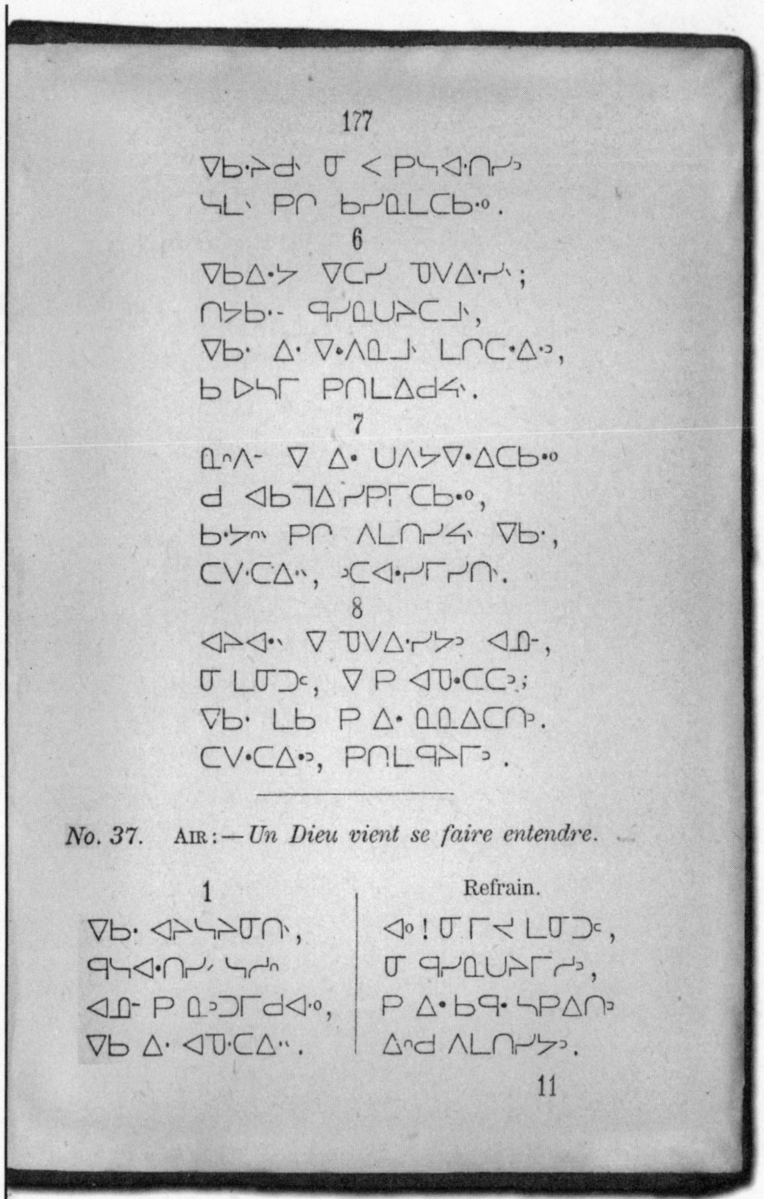

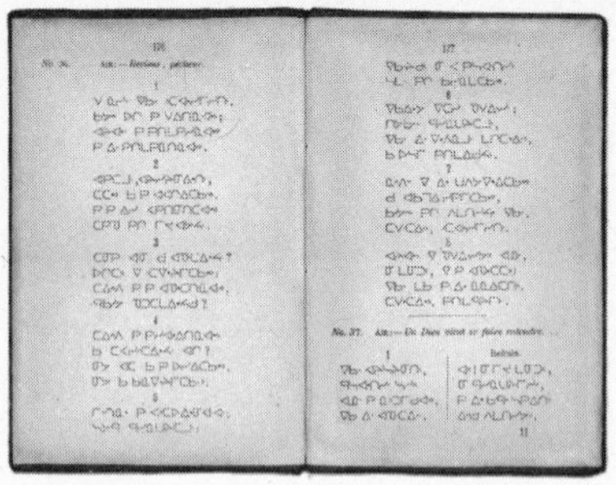

177 I am compassionate to that extent.
Right now I forgive you.

6

Do not then be ashamed;
on the contrary repent.
Others throw aside their sins,
which have made them miserable.

7

Forever I am content,
to encourage you untiringly.
Live a very good life, and
believe in Me, My children.

8

I am more ashamed today.
My God, I have been disobedient.
But I will obey You.
Believe me, have pity on me.

No. 37. AIR: – *Un Dieu vient se faire entendre.*
(God is heard.)

1

To the people
Jesus is merciful.
Today He invites you.
Do not disobey Him.

Refrain.

Oh, my God
I am sorry for myself.
I am trying to love You.
As long as I live.

177 ekwayikok ni pa kisewatisin
êkwayikohk nipa-kisêwâtisin

semak kici kasinamatakwaw.
sêmâk kici-kâsînamâtakwâw.

6

ekawiya etasi nepewisik;
êkâwîya êtasi nêpêwisik;

tiyakwac kesinateyitamok,
tiyakwâc kêsinatêyihtamok,

ekwa wi wepinamok macitwawin,
êkwa wî-wêpinamok macihtwâwin,

ka osami kitimaikoyek.
ka-osâmi-kitimahikoyêk.

7

naspic e wi tepiyaweitakwaw
nâspic ê-wî-têpiyawêhitakwâw

ko akamei sikimitakwaw,
ka-âhkami sîhkimitakwâw,

kwayask kici pimatisiyek ekwa,
kwayask kici-pimâtisiyêk êkwa,

tapwetawik, ntawasimisitik.
tâpwêtawik, nitawâsimisitik.

8

ayiwak e nepewisiyan anoc,
ayiwâk ê-nêpêwisiyân anohc,

ni manitom, e ki anwetatan;
nimanitôm, ê-kî-ânwêhtâtân;

ekwa maka ki wi nanaitatin.
êkwa mâka kiwî-nanahîhtâtin.

tapwetawin, kitimakeyimin.
tâpwêtawin, kitimâkêyimin.

No. 37. AIR: – Un Dieu vient se faire entendre.
No. 37. AIR: – Un Dieu vient se faire entendre.

1

ekwa ayiseyinitik,
êkwa ayisiyinitik,

kesewatisik sesos
kisêwâtisik Sesos

anoc ki nantomikowaw,
anohc kinanâtomikowâw,

eka wi anwetawik.
êkâ wî-ânwêhtawik.

Refrain.

aw! ni miyo manitom,
aw! nimiyo-manitôm,

ni kesinateyimison,
nikêsinâtêyimison,

ki wi kakwe sakiitiin
kiwî-kâkwê-sâkihitin

isko pimatisiyan.
isko-pimâtisiyan.

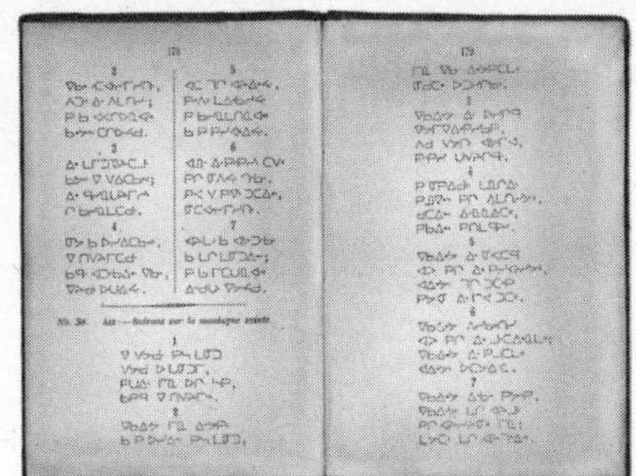

178

2

And My children
who live a contrary life,
it can benefit you
if you live a good life.

3

Go and reflect on this.
I have waited for you
for a long time.
You are going to regret
your actions
so that I will forgive you.

4

I am the One who
made you.
I satisfy you.

Try to work for Me and
have much courage.

5

Although you have sinned,
when you repent
I forgive you,
when you cried for Me.

6

Remember today, truly
to prepare for a good
death.
Come back to Me quickly,

My children.

7

It is hard when you work.

for the one who is the
devil.
You will grieve
when you are in the fire.

No. 38. Air: – *Suivons sur la montagne sainte.*
(Let us follow on the holy mountain.)

1

God alone, God is the One.
Have only one God.
Love Him from your heart also.
He satisfies you forever.

2

And never dare slander
the Creator God who made you.

178

2

ekwa ntawasimisitik,
êkwa nitawâsimisitik,

pitos wi pimatisik;
pîtos wî-pimâtisik;

ki ka apacionawaw
kikâ-âpacihonâwâw

kwayask tacioyeko.
kwayask itâcihoyêko.

3

wi mamitoneyitamok
wî-mâmitonêyihtamok

kayas e peitakwaw;
kayâs ê-pêhitakwâw;

wi kesinateyimisok
wî-kêsinâtêyimisok

ci kasinamatakok.
kici-kâsînamâtakok.

4

niya ka osiitakwaw,
niya kâ-osîhtâkwâw,

e tipeyimitakok
ê-tipêyimitakok

kakwe atoskawik ekwa,
kâkwê-atoskawik êkwa,

eyikok oteiyek.
iyikohk otêhiyêk.

5

ata meci ayiwiyek,
âta maci-ayiwiyêk,

kispin mawikasoyek
kîspin mâwîkâsoyêk

ki kasinamatinawaw
kikâsînamâtinâwâw

ka ki kisiwaiyek.
kâ-kî-kisiwâhiyêk.

6

anoc wi kiskisik tapwe
anohc wî-kiskisik tâpwê

kici ni piyek ceskwa.
kici-nipiyêk cêskwa.

kipa pe kiwe totawik,
kîpa pê-kîwê-tôtawik,

nitawasimisitik.
nitawâsimisitik.

7

ayiman ka ayatoskat
âyiman kâ-ayatoskât

ka maci manitowit;
kâ-maci-manitowit;

ki ka mitatenawaw
kika-mîtâtênâwâw

iskotek eyayeko.
iskotêhk ê-ayâyêko.

No. 38. Air: – Suivons sur la montagne sainte.
No. 38. Air: – Suivons sur la montagne sainte.

1

e peyakot kisemanito
ê-pêyakot kisê-manitow

peyako o manitomi,
peyako-omanitômi,

kiteik mina oci saki,
kitêhik mîna ohci sâkih,

kakike e tipeyimisk.
kâkikê ê-tipêyimisk.

2

ekawiya mina wiyakim
êkâwîya mîna wiyahkim

ka ki osiisk kisemanito,
kâ-kî-osîhisk kisê-manitow,

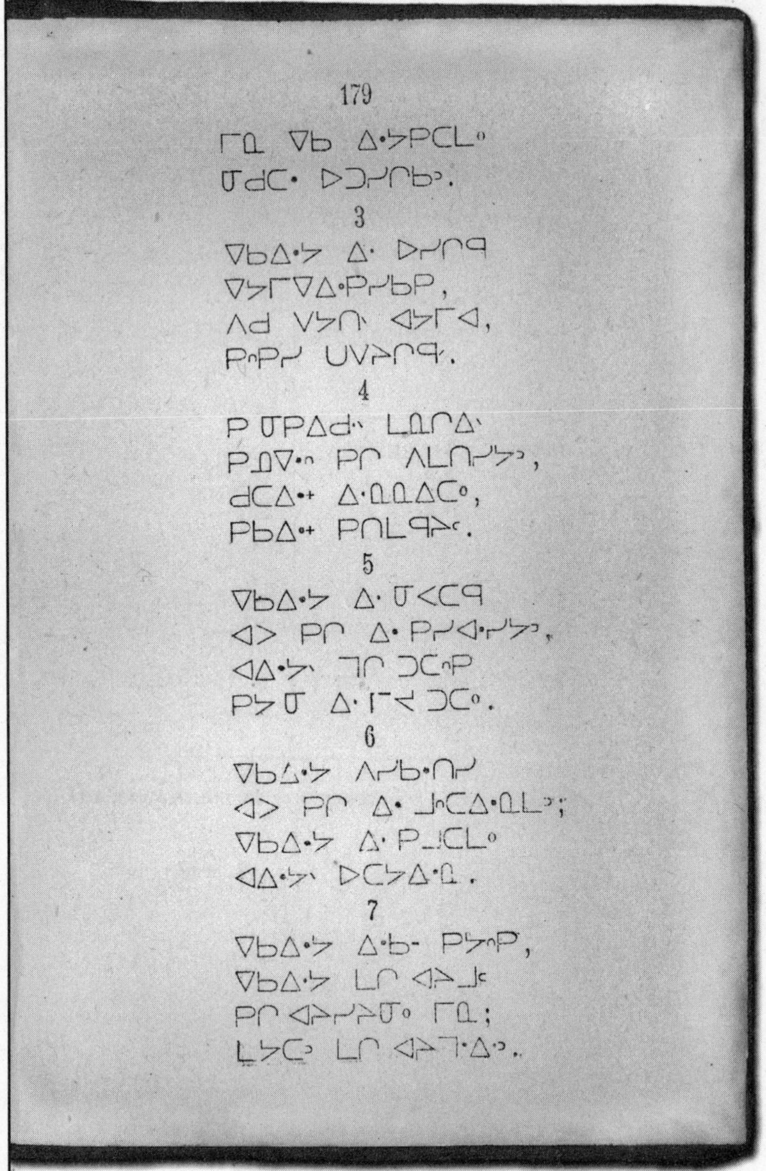

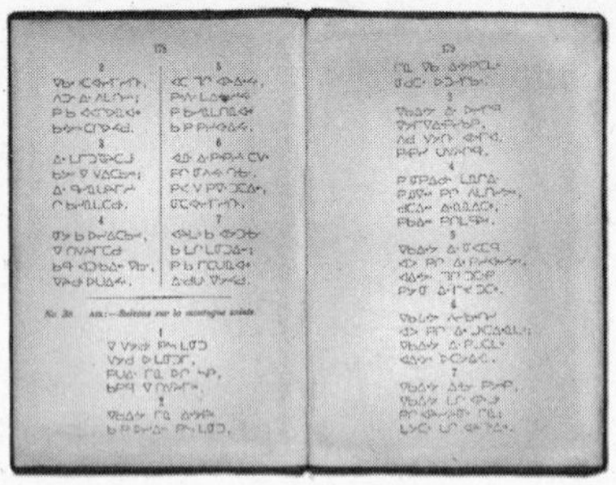

179

And never profane Him,
One or the other of His creatures.

3

Do not make anything on Sunday.
On Sunday
you must pray carefully.
Remember the Lord.

4

Respect your parents.
To have a good long life.
Listen to your father.
Be kind to your mother.

5

Never commit murder
or get into a rage.
When somebody does you wrong,
do good works for that person.

6

Never commit adultery
or covet another's partner.
Do not ever steal from
someone else's property.

7

Do not ever tell falsehoods.
Or ever use slander to
your neighbour for
slander is evil.

179

mina eka wiyakitamaw
mîna êkâ wiyahkîhtamaw

nikotwa otosicikan.
nikotwâw otosîhcikan.

3

ekawiya wi osicike
êkâwîya wî-osîhcikê

eyamiewikisikaki,
ayamihewi-kîsikâki,

piko peyatik ayamia,
piko pêyâhtik ayamihâ,

kiskisi tepeyiciket.
kiskisi (ê-)tipêyihcikêt.

4

ki nikiikwok manaciik
kinîkihikwâk manâcihik

kinowes kici pimatisiyan,
kinwês kici-pimâtisiyan,

kotawiy wi nanaitaw,
kôhtâwiy wî-nanahîtaw,

kikawiy kitimakeyim.
kikâwiy kitimâkêyim.

5

ekawiya wi nipatake
êkâwîya wî-nipahtâkê

apo kici wi kisiwasiyan,
ahpô kici-wî-kisiwâsiyan,

awiyak meci totaski
awiyak maci-tôtâski

kiyani wi miyo totaw.
kîyâni wî-miyo-tôtaw.

6

ekawiya pisikwatisi
êkâwîya pisikwâtisi

apo kici wi mostawinaman;
ahpo kici-wî-môstawinaman;

ekawiya wi kimotamaw
êkâwîya wî-kimotamaw

awiyak otayawina.
awiyak otayâwina.

7

ekawiya wikac kiyaski,
êkâwîya wîhkâc kiyâski,

ekawiya maci ayimom
êkâwîya maci-âyimôm

kici ayisiyiniw mina;
kihci ayisiyiniw mîna;

mayatan maci ayimwewin.
mayatân maci-âyimwêwin.

180

8

ᑳᑭᑫ ᐃᐧ ᐯᔭᑯᐃᑐᐠ,
ᑭᔭᐊᐧᐤ ᒪᓇ ᐃᐧᔦᑭᑐᔦᐠ.
ᐁᑳᐃᐧᔭ ᒥᓇ ᑳᑳᔦᐃᓯᐠ.
ᐁᐅᑯ ᑕᑭ ᑭᐢᑭᓯᐠ.

No. 39. AIR:—*Entends ma voix fidèle.*

1

ᓴᓯᐢ ᐅᑕᔭᒥᐁᐃᐧᓯᑕᐧᐃᐧᑎᐠ
ᑌᐸᑯᑊ ᐃᑕᑎᑎᔾᐊᐧ ᒪᓇ
ᐊᔭᒥᐁᓇᓇᑕᐃᐧᐅᐃᐧᓇ
ᐁ ᒥᓰ ᐃᔾᑎᑲᐃᑯᔭᑲᐧᐤ.

2

ᑎᐢᑕᐡ ᐊᔭᒥᐁᓯᑲᕆᑲᓱᐃᐧᐟ
ᑯᕆ ᐅᑕᐊᐧᓯᒥᓯᒥᑯᔭᐠ,
ᐁ ᑳᓯᓇᒪᑯᔭᐠ ᐸᐢᑕᐅᐃᐧᐟ
ᑳ ᑭ ᐯᕆ ᑭᑭᑎᑕᐃᐧᑭᔭᐠ.

3

ᐁᑲᐧ ᐊᔭᒥᐁᐊᐧᕆᒥᓱᐃᐧᐟ:
ᐁ ᐊᔭᒥᐁᓯᑳᕆᑲᓱᔭᐠ
ᒣᐧᐢᑕᐢ ᒣᕆ ᑐᑕᒪᑭ ᒪᓇ
ᐁᐅᑯ ᑭ ᑳᓯᓇᒪᑯᓇᐤ.

4

ᑭᕆᑕᐧᐤ ᐊᔭᒥᐁᓴᕐᑳᒐᐃᐧᐟ
ᒪᒫᐃᐧᔦᐢ ᑫᕆᑕᐁᐧᐃᐧᔾᑕᑲᐦ,
ᑯᕆ ᐃᐧ ᐊᓴᒥᑯᔭᐠ ᓴᓯᐢ

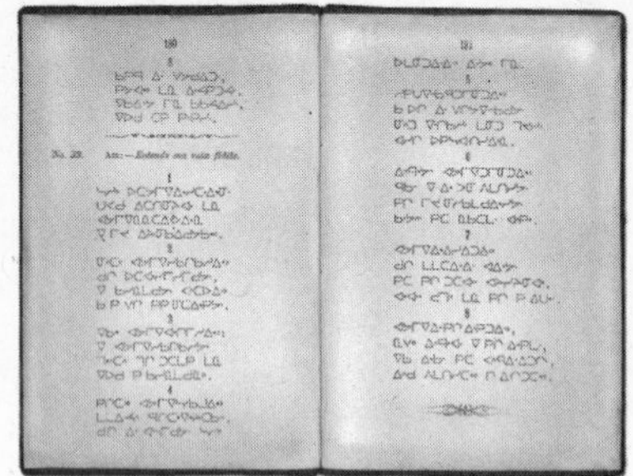

180

8

Try to remain together forever,
you who marry.
And do not ever cheat others.
This you should remember always.

No. 39. AIR: – *Entends ma voix fidèle.*
(Listen to my faithful voice.)

1

In Jesus's religion
there are seven
healing prayers
through which He heals you.

2

The first is baptism.
God takes us as His children.
He forgives us our sins
that we were born with.

3

And then, confession,
if we are baptized,
and if we do destructive things later,
then He forgives us our sins.

4

The Holy Communion is sacred and
The most important.
Jesus feeds us

8

kakike wi peyakoitok,
kâkikê wî-pêyakohitok,

kiyawaw mana wiyekitoyek.
kîyawâw mâna wiyêkihtoyêk.

ekawiya mina kakayeisik.
êkâwîya mîna kakayêhisik.

eoko taki kiskisik.
êwako tahki kiskisik.

No. 39. AIR: – Entends ma voix fidèle.
No. 39. AIR: – Entends ma voix fidèle.

1

sesos otayamiewisitwawinik
Sesos otayamihêwisîhtwâwinihk

tepakop itatiniyiwa mana
têpakohp itâtiniyiwa mâna

ayamienanatawiowina
ayamihênanâtawihowina

e miyo iyinikaikoyakwaw.
ê-miyo-iyinikahikoyahkwâw.

2

nistam ayamiesikacikasowin
nistam ayamihêsîkahâhcikâsowin

koci otawasimisimikoyak,
koci-otawâsimisimikoyahk,

e kasinamakoyak pastaowin
ê-kâsînamâkoyahk pâstâhowin

ka ki peci kikinitawikiyak.
kâ-kî-pêci-kiki-nihtâwikiyahk.

3

ekwa ayamiewacimisowin:
êkwa ayamihêwâcimisowin:

e ayamiesikacikasoyak
ê-ayamihêsîkahâhcikâsoyâhk

mwestas meci totamaki mana
mwêstas mêci-tôtamâhki mâna

eoko ki kasinamakonaw.
êwako ki-kâsînamâkonaw.

4

kicitwaw ayamiesaskamowin
kihcitwâw ayamihêsaskamowin

mamawiyes kecitwaweyitakwak,
mamawiyês kihcitwâwêyihtâkwak,

koci wi asamikoyak sesos
koci-wî-asamikoyahk Sesos

181

ᐅᒪᓀᑐᐃᐧᐃᐤ ᐃᐧᔦᐤ ᒥᓇ.

5

ᓯᑭᑌᐁᐦᑳᑫᑐᒥᓀᑐᐃᐧᐤ
ᑳ ᐅᒋ ᐃᐧ ᐯᒋᔦᐁᐧᐦᑳᑯᔦᐠ
ᓀᐦᑐ ᐁᐧᒋᑳᓯᐟ ᒪᓀᑐ ᒣᔪᓯᐟ
ᐊᓯᒋ ᐅᑭᓴᐊᐧᑎᓯᐃᐧᓇ.

6

ᐃᐦᑫᐧᔦ‐ ᐊᔦᒥᐁᑐᒥᓀᑐᐃᐧᐤ
ᑫᑳ‐ ᐁ ᐃᐧ ᐳᓀ ᐱᒪᑎᓯᔦᐠ
ᑭᒋ ᒥᔪ ᓀᓯᑳᒪᑯᐃᐧᓯᔦᐠ
ᑳᐧᔦᐦ ᑭᑕ ᓇᑳᑕᒪᐠ ᐊᐦᑭᐩ.

7

ᐊᔦᒥᐁᐃᐧᐃᓯᐃᑐᐃᐧᐤ
ᑯᒋ ᒪᒪᑕᐃᐧᐃᐟ ᐊᐃᐧᔦᐠ
ᑭᑕ ᑭᒋ ᑐᑕᐊᐧᐟ ᐊᐱᓯᐸᓀᐊᐧ,
ᐊᐧᐊᐧ‐ ᓱᒣᐦ ᒪᓇ ᑭᒋ ᑭ ᐃᑌᐧᐟ.

8

ᐊᔦᒥᐁᐃᐧᑭᒋ ᐃᐧᑭᑐᐃᐧᐤ,
ᓇᐯᐤ ᐃᐦᑫᐧᐊᐧ ᐁ ᑭᒋ ᐃᐧᑭᒪᐟ,
ᐁᑳ ᐃᐧᑳ‐ ᑭᑕ ᐸᐦᑫᐃᐧᐃᑐᒋᐠ,
ᐃᐦᑯ ᐱᒪᑎᓯᑕᐧᐤ ᒋ ᐃᐧᒋᑐᑕᐧᐤ.

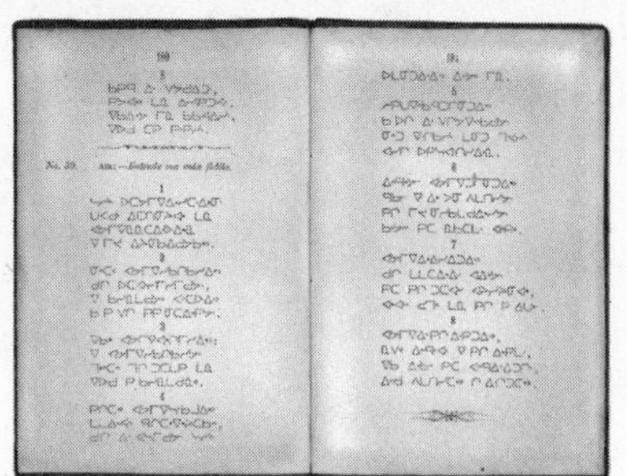

181

with His holy body also.

5

In Holy Communion,
God enters our body.
The Three-In-One God is good.
He is compassionate.

6

In the last sacrament
when we are going to stop living,
it strengthens us
so that we leave the world correctly.

7

Holy Orders is
for those who will gain spiritual power
to dedicate to the people
especially when they say the Mass.

8

In marriage according to Church law
the man marries the woman formally in church.
They should not ever divorce,
as long as they live together.

omanitowiwin wiyaw mina.
omanitowiwin wîyaw mîna.

5
sokiteeskaketominitowin
sôhkitêhêskakêtôminitowin

ka oci wi peciyaweskakoyak
kâ-ohci-wî-pêciyâwêskakoyâhk

nisto wecikasot manito meyosit
nisto-wîcikâsot manitow (ê-)miyosit

asici okisewatisiwina.
asici okisêwâtisiwina.

6
iskweyac ayamietominitowin
iskwêyac ayamihêtôminitowin

kekac e wi poni pimatisiyak
kêkâc ê-wî-pôni-pimâtisiyahk

kici miyo ni sokamakowisiyak
kici-miyo-nisôhkimâkowisiyahk

kwayask kita nakatamak askiy.
kwaywask kita-nakatamahk askîhk.

7
ayamiewiisiitowin
ayamihêwisîhtwâwin

koci mamatawiit awiyak
koci-mamâhtâwihît awiyak

kita kici totawat ayisiyiniwa,
kita-kici-tôtawât ayisiyiniwa,

wawac lames mana kici ki itwet.
wâwâc Lames mâna kici kî-itwêt.

8
ayamiewikiciwikitowin,
ayamihêwi-kihci-wîkihtowin,

napew iskwewa e kici wikimat,
nâpêw iskwêwa ê-kihci-wîkimât,

eka wikac kita paskewiitocik,
êkâ wîhkâc kita-paskêwihitocik,

isko pimatisitwaw ci wicitotwaw.
isko pimâtisitwâw kici-wîcêhtôtwâw.

182

No. 40. Air:—*Combien j'ai douce souvenance.*

1

ᓇᑕ, ᓇᑕ, ᑌᑕᑲᐊᐧᑌᐣ
ᒥᐢᑕᐁ ᑫ ᒥᐁᐧᔨᑕᒪᐣ
ᔦᔦᐢᑯᐯᔦᑌ ᑭᐢᐱᐣ,
ᓇᑕᓇᐣ,
ᑲ ᑭᑎᑕᐧᐁᐧᔨᑕᑲᐦ
ᑌᐱᐩ.

2

ᑳᔦᐢ ᐊᑕᐠ ᐁ ᐅᑎ ᑐᑕᐠ
ᐸᐢᑕᐅᐃᐤ ᓇᑎ ᑭᑭᐢᑫᐤ
ᑫᓴᐊᐧᑎᔨᔦᐣ ᐅᓴᐨ,
ᓇᑕᓇᐣ,
ᑌ ᑕᑕᐠ ᑲᔨᓇᒪᐃᐧᐤ
ᐁᑲᐧ.

3

ᑌᔦ ᑎᐱᔦᐤᑌ ᐸᐢᑕᐅᐣ
ᓇᒪ ᑌ ᑭ ᑳᓇᑎᐃᔨᐣ;
ᐱᑕᑌ ᑳᓇᑎᐃᔦᐣ,
ᓇᑕᓇᐣ,
ᑭ ᔨᑲᐊᑕᑫᐃᐧᑌᐠ
ᐅᑎ.

4

ᒪᑎ ᐸᐢᑕᐅᐃᐧᑌᐠ ᐅᑎ
ᑭᓴ ᒪᑌᑐ ᑌ ᐁᐧᐱᑌᐠ
ᓴᔨᐢ ᐅᔨᔨᒥᐟ ᑮᐢᐱᐣ,
ᓇᑕᓇᐣ,
ᑳᓇᑎᑕᒪᐃᐧᐤ ᐁᑲᐧ
ᑌ ᑌ.

5

ᐁᑭ ᐸᐢᑕᐃᔨᔦᐣ ᐅᑎ
ᑌ ᐸᑲᐧᑎᐠ ᑭᓴᒪᑌᑐ
ᐃᐧᐅᑯᔨᔨᒥᐣ ᑳᐃᐧ,
ᓇᑕᓇᐣ,
ᑌᑕᐃᐧᑭᐃᑯᔦᑌ
ᑌᐱᐩ.

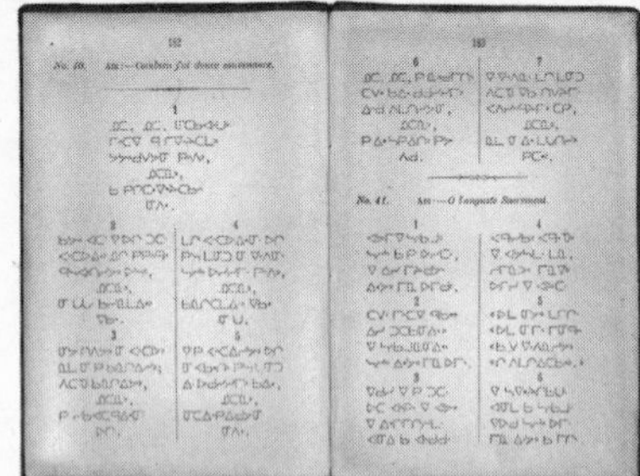

182 *No. 40.* Air: – *Combien j'ai douce souvenance.*
(How sweet is the memory.)

1

My Father, my Father,
I wish very much
to be happy.
For my sin against
our Father,
the One who is holy,
I repent.

2

A long time ago in the past I did
this evil sin of fornicating.
I regret this excess.

Our Father,
forgive my spirit.

And I admit

3

I bring evil upon myself.

I am not pure of heart.

I wish you to make me pure.

Our Father
You cleanse us through baptism.

Cleanse us.

4

From our sins.

God, You cast me aside because of sins.
If Jesus is risen,

our Father,
then cleanse

my heart.

5

I brought evil upon myself, for
the Creator does not accept me.
Please take me as Your son again.

You are our Father,
if I am born

in water.

No. 40. Air: – Combien j'ai douce souvenance.
No. 40. Air: – Combien j'ai douce souvenance.

1

nota, nota, nitakawaten
nôhta, nôhta, nitakâwâtên

mistae ke miweyitaman
mistahi ka-miywêyihtamân

yayaskopeyani kispin,
yayaskopêyani kîspin,

notanan,
nôhtânân,

ka kicitwaweyitakwak
kâ-kihcitwâwêyihtâkwak

nipiy.
nipiy.

2

kayas atak e oci totak
kayâs atak ê-ohci-tôtak

pastaowin noci kikisken
pâstâhowin nôci-kikiskên

kesewatisiyan osam,
(ê-)kisêwâtisiyân osâm,

notanan,
nôhtânân,

ni cacak kasinamawin
nicahcâhk kâsînamawin

ekwa
êkwa

3

niya tipiyaw ni pastaon
niya tipiyaw nipâstâhon

nama ni ki kanaciison;
nama nikî-kanâcihison;

pitane kanaciiyan,
pitanê kanâcihiyan,

notanan,
nôhtânân,

ki sikaotakewinik
kisîkahôtakêwinihk

oci.
ohci.

4

maci pastaowinik oci
maci-pâstâhowinihk ohci

kise manito ni we pinik
kisê-manitow niwê-pinik

sesos osisimit kispin,
Sesos osisimît kîspin,

notanan,
nôhtânân,

kanacitamawin ekwa
kanâcitamawin êkwa

nite.
nitêh.

5

e ki pastaisoyan oci
ê-kî-pâstâhisoyân ohci

ni pakwatik kise manito
nipakwâtik kisê-manitow

wi o kosisimin kawi,
wî-okosisimîn kâwî,

notanan,
nôhtânân,

nitawikiikoyani
nihtâwikihikoyâni

nipiy.
nipiy.

183

6

ᒍᑕ, ᒍᑕ, ᑭ ᓇᐢᑯᒥᑎᓐ
ᑕᐯ· ᑲᐃ· ᑯᑯᓯᓯᒥᑦ
ᐃᐢᑯ ᐱᒪᑎᓯᔪᐣ,
ᒍᑕᓇᑦ,
ᑭ ᐄᓴᑭᐦᐃᑎᑦ ᑭᔪ
ᐱᑯ.

7

ᐁ ᐁ·ᐱᓇᐤ ᒪᓯ ᒪᒋᑐ
ᐱᑕᒋ ᐁᑲ ᑎᐯᔨᒥᐤ
ᐸᐱᓯᐢᑫᔨᒥᑦ ᑕᑭ,
ᒍᑕᓇᑦ,
ᓇᒪ ᒋ ᐃ· ᒪᒋᑎᓯᑦ
ᑭᑖᐨ.

No. 41. Air:—*O l'auguste Sacrement.*

1

ᐊᔪᒥᐁ ᓴᐢᑲᒧᑦ
ᓴᓯᐢ ᑲ ᑭ ᐅᓯᑖᐤ,
ᐁ ᐃᓯ ᒥᔦᑯᔨᐤ
ᐄ·ᔪᐤ ᒥᓇ ᐅᒥᑯᕽ.

2

ᑕᐯ· ᒥᐢᑕᐁ ᑫᑳ·+
ᐃᓯ ᑐᑕᑲᒋᐃ·ᐤ
ᐁ ᓴᑲ ᒍᓇᒋᐃ·ᐢ
ᓴᓯᐢ ᐄ·ᔪᐤ ᒥᓇ ᐅᒥᐠ.

3

ᐁᑯᓯ ᐁ ᑭ ᑐᑕᐠ
ᐅᑕ ᐊᐢᑭᐠ ᐁ ᐊᔭᐤ
ᐁ ᐄ·ᑎᒥᑎᓯᒪᐤ
ᐊᒋᐊ ᑲ ᐊᐢᑯᑯᐤ

4

ᐸᑫ·ᓯᑳᐤ ᐸᑫ·ᒋᐤ
ᐁ ᐊᔪᓴᒪᐤ ᒪᓇ,
ᓯᒥᓇᐳ+ ᒥᓇᐁᐤ
ᐅᒥᓯ ᐁ ᐊᐱᑕᐤ

5

«ᐅᒪ ᒋᔪᐤ ᒪᒥᐢ
«ᐅᒪ ᒋᒥᐢ ᒥᒋᑫ·ᐢ
«ᑲ ᐯ ᐁ·ᐱᓇᓯᔭᐤ
«ᑎ ᐱᒪᑎᐊᑕᑳ·ᐤ. »

6

ᐁ ᓴᐁ·ᔭᑎᑲᐅᐤ
ᐊᒋᒪ ᑲ ᓴᐢᑲᒧᐤ
ᐁᐅᑯ ᓴᓯᐢ ᐅᒥᐠ
ᒥᓇ ᐄ·ᔪᐤ ᑲ ᒥᑎᐢ.

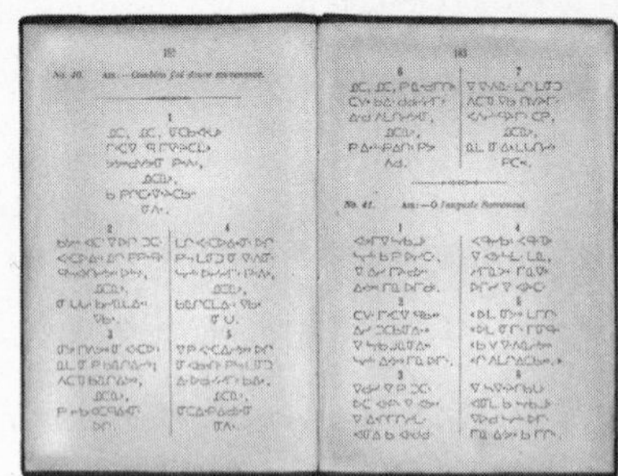

183

6

My Father, my Father,
I thank You.
Truly Your Son lives
again.
As long as I live,
our Father,
I am going to love You
alone.

7

I will cast aside the
evil one.
I wish that sin does not
govern me.
Look after me all the time.
Our Father,
I will not be a sinner
again.

No. 41. Air: – *O l'auguste Sacrement.*
(O Holy Sacrament.)

1

Holy Communion
Jesus prepared.
God blessed bread
this way
and also His blood.

2

This is a great gift
offered to everybody,
which He gives us in
Holy Communion.
Jesus offers His body
and blood.

3

He does it this way.
When He was here
on earth,
He eats with them,
Those apostles who
followed Him.

4

He broke the bread
and He fed them.
He gave them wine
to drink
and He said:

5

"This is my body. Eat it."
"This is My blood. Drink."
"I come to make an
offering
to save you."

6

It is a blessing
to receive Communion.

It is Jesus's blood,
and His body that is
broken.

183

6

nota, nota, ki naskomitin
nôhtâ, nôhtâ,
kinanâskomitin

tapwe kawi kokosisimin
tâpwê kâwî-kokosisimin

isko pimatisiyani,
isko pimâtisiyâni,

notanan,
nôhtânân,

ki wi sakiitin kiya
kiwî-sâkihitin kîya

piko.
piko.

7

e wepinak maci manito
ê-wêpinak maci-manitow

pitane eka tipeyimit
pitanê êkâ (ê-)tipêyimit

papisiskeyimin taki,
papisiskêyimin tahki,

notanan,
nôhtânân,

nama ni wi macatisin
nama niwî-macâtisin

kitwam
kîhtwâm

No. 41. Air: – O l'auguste Sacrement.
No. 41. Air: – O l'auguste Sacrement.

1

ayamiesaskamon
ayamihêsaskamon

sesos ka ki ositat,
Sesos kâ-kî-osîhtât,

e isi miyikoyak
ê-isi-miyikoyahk

wiyaw mina omikom.
wîyaw mîna omihkom.

2

tapwe mistae kekway
tâpwê mistahi kîkwây

isi totakaniwiw
isi tôtâkâniwiw

e saskamonaniwik
ê-saskamonaniwik

sesos wiya mina omik.
Sesos wîyaw mîna omihk.

3

ekosi e ki totak
êkosi ê-kî-tôtak

ota askik e ayat
ôta askihk ê-ayât

e wicimicisomat
ê-wîci-mîcisomât

anii ka askokot
anihi kâ-askôkot

4

pakwesikan pakwenew
pahkwêsikan pahkwênêw

e ayasamat mana,
ê-ayasamât mâna,

sominapoy minaew
sôminâpoy minahêw

omisi e ayitat
omisi ê-ayitât

5

« oma niyaw mamicik
"ôma nîyaw mamîcik

oma nimik minikwek
ôma nimihko minihkwêk

ka pe wepinasoyan
kâ-pê-wêpinâsoyan

ci pimaciitakwaw. »
kici-pimâcihitakwâw."

6

e saweyicikatek
ê-sawêyihcikatêk

anima ka saskamok
anima kâ-saskamok

eoko sesos omik
êwako Seso omihko

mina wiyaw ka micik.
mîna wîyaw ka-mîcik.

184

7
ᐊᔭᒥᐁᐃᐧᔨᒋᐤ
ᐃᐧᔭ ᑲ ᓴᐁᐧᔨᑕᐠ :
ᐁᑯᓯ ᑲ ᑫᐧᐢᑭᒥᐟ
ᒪᓂᑐ ᐸᑫᐧᓯᑲᐣ .

8
ᐁᑯᓯ ᑲ ᑐᑕᒉᐠ
ᒪᒥᑐᓀᔨᑕᒧᐠ ,
ᑲᑫᐧ ᑲᓇᑕᐗᑫᐧᐠ
ᑭᑎ ᐊᑕᒥᐊᔦᐠ .

9
ᑕᐯᐧ ᑭᓴᐊᐧᑎᓯᐤ
ᐃᐧᔮᐤ ᐁ ᐊᓴᑫᐠ
ᓇᐢᐱ- ᐁ ᑭᑎᑕᐧᔨᐠ
ᐅ ᑭᑎ ᐃᐧᑯᑫᐃᐧᐡ .

10
ᒉᔦᒪᓂᑐᐃᐧᔭᐣ
ᑭ ᒪᒨᔭᐁᐧᐢᑕᑎᐣ
ᑲ ᒥᔦ ᐊᓴᒥᔭᐣ
ᐊᔭᒥᐁᓴᐢᑳᒧᐣ .

No. 42. Air; — *Adorons tous.*

1
ᓴᓯᐢ ᐅᑕ ᐁ ᐃᑕᑌᔨᒥᑕᐣ ,
ᑯ ᐃᐧ ᐯ ᐅᑎᑎᑳᐧᓇᐱᐢᑕᑕᐣ ;
ᓇᒪᐃᐧᔭ ᑭ ᑲ ᐃᐧ ᐊᑕᐁᐧᔨᒥᐣ
ᐁ ᒪᐃᐧᒧᐢᑕᑕᐣ (ᑭᑎᒪᑭᑕᐃᐧᐣ . *bis.*)

2
ᐊᐳᐊᐧᐦ ᐁ ᑫᓯᓇᑌᔨᑕᒪᐣ
ᑲ ᑭ ᐃᓯ ᒪᒋᐱᒪᑎᓯᔭᐣ :
ᐁᑲᐃᐧᔭ ᐊᓀᐧᑕᐃᐧᐣ , ᓂ ᒪᓂᑐᐡ ,
ᑭᑭᓴᐊᐧᑎᓯᐣ (ᐃᐧ ᑲᓯᓇᒪᐃᐧᐣ . *bis.*)

3
ᐅᓴᐡ ᐁ ᒪᒋ ᐁᔨᑕᑯᓯᔭᐣ ,
ᒫᑲ ᓇᐢᐱ- ᐁ ᓇᐃᑕᑯᓯᒋᐠ ,
ᐁᑯᑌ ᑭᓯᑯᐠ ᑲ ᐃᐧᑕᐱᒥᐢᑭᐠ :

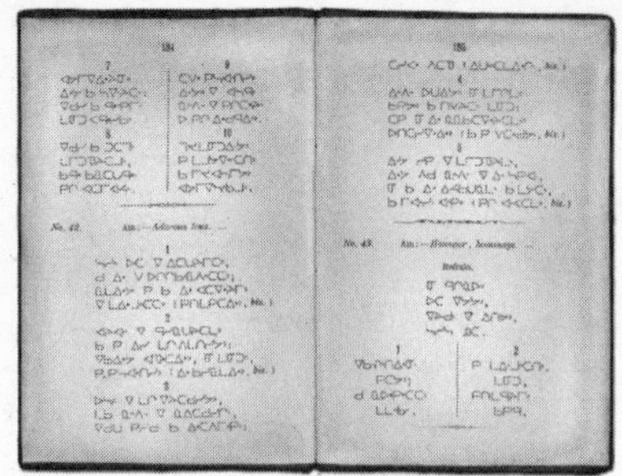

184

7
The priest,
he is the one who
blesses it,
and he changes it,
God's bread.

8
So then, you do it
this way.
You ponder this.
Try to be worthy
to please Him.

9
He is truly merciful.
He sustains us his with
His body.
It is forever holy
at His great feast.

10
You are a good God.

You invite us
to partake of
Holy Communion.

No. 42. Air: – *Adorons tous. (Let us worship.)*

1
Jesus, the One, I knew you would be there.
That is why I come and kneel to You.
No, you cannot refuse me.
I worship You; (have pity on me. *twice.*)

2
I regret truly
living a sinful life.
Do not deny me, my God.
You are merciful (You are going to
forgive me. *twice.*)

3
I am guilty.
But the saints are forever listened to,
there in Heaven where they sit with You.

184

7

ayamiewiyiniw
ayamihêwiyiniw

wiya ka saweyitak:
wiya kâ-sawêyihtahk:

ekosi ka kweskimit
êkosi kâ-kwêskîmît

manito pakwesikan.
manitow pahkwêsikan.

8

ekosi ka totamek
êkosi kâ-tôtamêk

mamitoneyitamok,
mâmitonêyihtamok,

kakwe kanatacakwek
kâkwê-kanâtahcâhkwêk

kici atamiayek.
kici-atamihâyêk.

9

tapwe kisewatisiw
tâpwê kisêwâtisiw

wiyaw e asaket
wîyaw ê-asâkêt

naspic e kicitwayik
nâspic ê-kihcitwâyik

o kici wikokewin.
okihci-wîhkohkêwin.

10

meyo manitowiyan
(ê-)miyo-manitowiyan

ki mamoyawestatin
kimamoyawêstâtin

ka miyo asamiyan
ka-miyo-asamiyan

ayamiesaskamon.
ayamihêsaskamon.

2

ayiwak e kesinateyitaman
ayiwâk ê-kêsinâtêyihtaman

ka ki isi maci pimatisiyan:
kâ-kî-isi-maci-pimâtisiyan:

ekawiya anwetawin, ni manitom,
êkâwîya ânwêhtawin,, nimanitôm,

ki kisewatisin (wi kasinamawin. *bis.*)
kikisêwâtisin (wî-kâsînamawin. bis.)

3

osam e maci eyitakosiyan,
osâm ê-maci-itêyihtâkosiyân,

maka naspic e naitakosicik,
mâka nâspic ê-nahitakosicik,

ekote kisikok ka witapimiskik:
êkotê kîsikohk kâ-wîtapimiskik:

No. 42. AIR: – Adorons tous.
No. 42. AIR: – Adorons tous.

1

sesos ota e itateyimitan,
Sesos ôta ê-itatêyimitân,

ko wi pe ocicikwanapistatan;
kô-wî-pê-ocihcihkwanapîstâtân;

namawiya ki ka wi ataweyimin
namâwiya kika-wî-atawêyimin

e mawimostatan (kitimakitawin. *bis.*)
ê-mawimostâtân (kitimâkihtwâwin. bis.)

185 For that reason (I wish them to intercede for me. *twice.*)

4

I have a good heart; I praise Him,
God who governs everything.
I am always going to follow Him,
His commandments (we will listen to them. *twice.*)

5

Very much I meditate on Him.
I will love Him forever.
Remove evil from the earth.
This good earth (the way you see it. *twice.*)

No. 43. AIR: – *Honneur, hommage. (Honour, worship.)*

Refrain.

I am certain
I am here,
as much as I know
Jesus is my Father.

1

In the Eucharist
we have faith.
The One I bow to
is marvelous.

2

I pray to You for help,
God.
Have pity on me
forever.

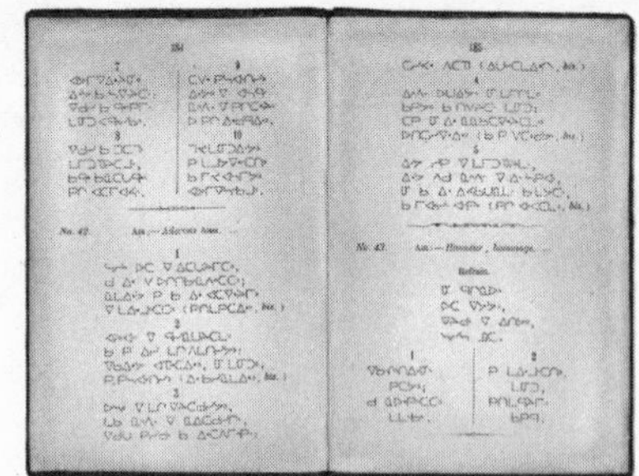

185 tasipwa pitane (itwestamawicik. *bis.*)
tâsipwâ pitanê (itwêstamawicik. bis.)

4

ispic oteiyan ni mamicimaw
ispic otêhiyan nimamihcimâw

kakiyaw ka tipeyitak manito:
kahkiyaw kâ-tipêyihtahk manitow:

taki ni wi nanakataweyitamwan
tahki niwî-nânâkatawêyihtamwân

otitasiwewin (ka ki petwakoyak. *bis.*)
otitâsiwêwin (kâ-kî-pêtwakoyâhk. bis.)

5

wiya soki e mamitoneyimak,
wiya sôhki ê-mâmitonêyimak,

wiya piko naspic e wi sakiak,
wiya piko nâspic ê-wî-sâkihak,

ni ka wi iyekatenamak ka mayatak,
nika-wî-iyîkatênamâhk kâ-mâyâtahk,

ka miwasik askiy (kici wapataman. *bis.*)
kâ-miywâsik askiy (kici-wâpahtamân. bis.)

No. 43. Air: – Honneur, hommage.
No. 43. Air: – Honneur, hommage.

Refrain.

ni kecinaon
nikêhcinâhon

ota eyayan,
ôta ê-ayâyân,

eyikok e itiyan,
iyikohk ê-itiyân,

Sesose nota.
Sesose nôhtâ.

1

ekaristiwinik
êkaristiwinihk

kitayan;
kitayân;

ko nawokistatan
kâ-nawokîstatân

mamaskac.
mâmaskâc.

2

ki mawimostatin,
kimawimôstâtin,

manito,
manitow,

kitimakeyimin
kitimâkêyimin

kakike.
kâkikê.

186

No. 44. Air:—*Élevez-vous, mon cœur.*

1

ᑎᑕᒐᑯᐨ ᒪᒪᑕᑯᓯ ᐊᑎ-
ᐁ ᐯᒋ ᐃᔭᓯᐢᑕᒪᐣ ᓴᓯᐢ;
ᐁᐧᐱᑌᓯᐃᐧᓇᑎᑯᐠ ᐁ ᐊᔭᐤ
ᐃᐧᔫ ᐁ ᐯ ᐁᐧᐱᑌᓱᐢᑕᑫᐤ.

2

ᐸᑫᐧᓯᑳᐤ ᓴᓴᐩ ᒣᐢᑯᒋᒍᐊᐤ
ᐁ ᐊᑕ ᐁᔭᐱ- ᐃᓯᓇᐅᐤ:
ᓯᒥᓈᐳᐩ ᒣᐢᑯᒋᒍᑕᑎᐃᐧᐤ,
ᐁ ᐊᑕ ᐁᔭᐱ- ᐃᓯᓈᒥᐠ.

3

ᑮᔭᐤ, ᑮ ᒥᐠ, ᒥᓯᐁᐧ ᑭᑎᓯᐃᐧᐤ
ᐅᑕ ᐊᐢᒍᐤ, ᑎ ᒪᑎᑐᐨ ᓴᓯᐢ,
ᑎ ᑕᐯᐧᒍᐤ ᑎ ᐃᐧ ᒪᑎᑐᑲᒍᐤ;
ᑕᓯᐸᐧ ᐁᐧᒋᑳᐧᓇᐱᐢᑕᒪᐤ.

4

ᐁᐧᑯᓯᓯᒥᑲᐃᐧᔫ ᒪᑎᑐ,
ᑮᔭ ᑲ ᑮ ᑎᐳᐢᑕᒪᐃᐧᔭᐠ,
ᑮᔭ ᑲ ᐯ ᐁᐧᐱᑎᓱᔫ ᐅᑕ,
ᑲᑮᑫ ᑮ ᐃᐧ ᓵᑭᐃᑎᓇᐤ.

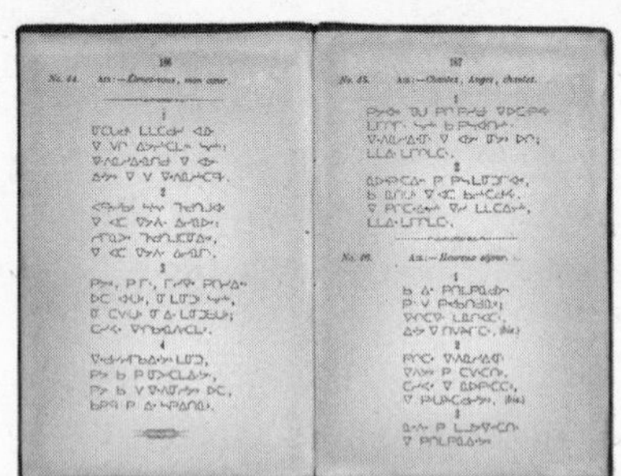

186 *No. 44.* Air: – *Élevez-vous, mon coeur. (Rise up, my heart.)*

1

My spirit be holy today.
Jesus entered your body.
He places it at the altar.
He comes to sacrifice Himself.

2

Already the bread is changed,
but it still appears as bread.
The wine takes the place of His blood,
but it is lifted in the chalice.

3

Your body You give me.
It is there Jesus, my Lord.
I believe in it. I will worship it.
For that reason I bow to it.

4

Your son, God,
You, the One who died for us,
You come to sacrifice Yourself here.
For all time we love You.

186 No. 44. Air: – Élevez-voux, mon cœur.
No. 44. Air: – Élevez-voux, mon cœur.

1

nitacakom mamatakosi anoc
nitahcâhkom mamâhtâkosiw anohc

e peci iyasistamask sesos:
ê-pêci-iyasîstamâsk Sesos:

wepinasowinatikok e ayat
wêpinâsowinahtikohk ê-ayât

wiyaw e pe wepinasostaket.
wiyaw ê-pê-wêpinâsôstâkêt.

2

pakwesikan sasay meskocemoaw
pahkwêsikan sâsay mêskocêmohâw

e ata eyapic isinaot:
ê-âta êyâpic isinahot:

sominapoy meskocemotaniwiw,
sôminâpoy mêskocêmôtâniwiw,

e ata eyapic isinamik.
ê-âta êyâpic-(it)isinamihk.

3

kiyaw, ki mik, misiwe kitisiwin
kiyaw, kimiyik, misiwê kîtîsiwin

ota astew, ni manitom sesos,
ôta astêw, nimanitom Sesos,

ni tapweten ni wi manitokaten;
nitâpwêtên niwî-manitokâtên;

tasipwa wecikwanapistaman.
tâsipwâ wêcihkwanapîstamân.

4

wekosisimikawiyan manito,
(ê-)wikosisimikawiyan manitow,

kiya ka ki nipostamawiyak,
kiya kâ-kî-nipôstamawiyâhk,

kiya ka pe wepinisoyan ota,
kiya kâ-pê-wêpinâsoyan ôta,

kakike ki wi sakiitinan.
kâkikê kiwî-sâkihitinân.

187

No. 45. Air :—*Chantez, Anges, chantez.*

1

ᑭᔭᐘᐤ ᑌᑌ ᑭᒋ ᑭᓯᑯᐠ ᐁᐅᑕᐧᑭᔦᐠ
ᒪᒥᑎᒥᐠ ᓭᓯᐣ ᑲ ᑭᓭᐘᑎᓯᐟ.
ᐍᐱᓇᓯᐑᑎᐠ ᐁ ᐊᔭᐟ ᑎᔭᐤ ᐅᒋ;
ᒪᒪᐑ ᒪᒥᑎᒪᑕᐠ.

2

ᓇᐆᑭᐣᑕᐄᐠ ᑭ ᑭᓭᒪᓂᑐᒥᐘᐤ,
ᑲ ᓇᑎᑌᐠ ᐁ ᐊᑕ ᑲᓯᐦᑕᑯᓭᐠ.
ᐁ ᑭᒋᑕᐃᐧᓯᐟ ᐁᓯ ᒪᒪᑕᐃᐧᓯᐟ,
ᒪᒪᐃᐧ ᒪᒥᑎᒪᑕᐠ.

No. 46. Air :—*Heureux séjour.*

1

ᑲ ᐃᐧ ᑭᑎᒪᑭᓇᑯᔭᐠ
ᑮ ᐯ ᑭᐸᐧᑲᑎᑯᓇᐤ;
ᐍᒋᑕᐍ ᒪᓇᒋᐊᑕᐠ,
ᐃᐧᔭ ᐁ ᑎᐯᔨᒥᑕᐠ. (*bis.*)

2

ᑭᒋᑖ ᐍᐱᓇᓯᐃᐧᑎᐠ
ᐁᐱᔭᐤ ᑭ ᑕᐯᐧᑕᑎᐣ,
ᑕᓯᐹ ᐁ ᓇᐅᑭᐣᑕᑕᐣ,
ᐁ ᑭᐣᑌᔨᑕᑯᓯᔭᐣ. (*bis.*)

3

ᓇᐣᐱ- ᑭ ᒪᒍᔭᐍᐣᑕᑎᐣ
ᐁ ᑭᑎᒪᑭᓇᐃᐧᔭᐣ

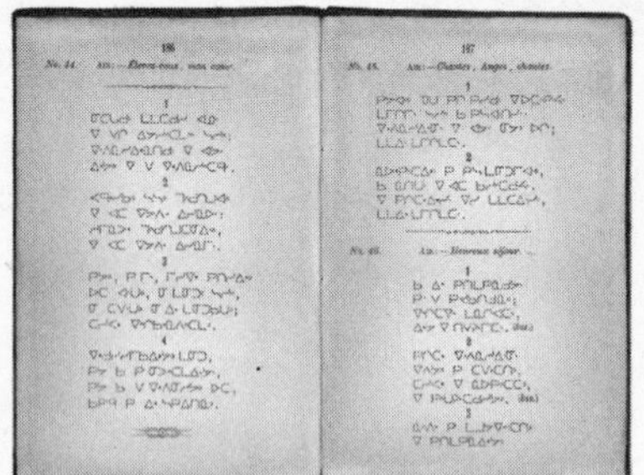

187 No. 45. Air: – *Chantez, Anges, chantez.*
(Sing, Angels, sing.)

1

You above in Heaven, where You are,
Praise Jesus, the One who is kind.
An offering He has for us.
All of us let us praise Him.

2

Bow down to Him, your Father.
Although He is not visible,
He is holy: He is supernatural.
All together, let us praise Him.

No. 46. Air: – *Heureux séjour. (O happy day.)*

1

He will have pity on us.
He comes to visit us.
Let us treat Him with great respect.
We are content. (*twice.*)

2

In holy offerings
Very much I believe in You.
For that reason I bow down to You.
You are adored. (*twice.*)

3

Forever I am guided by You
Have pity on me.

187 No. 45. AIR: – Chantez, Anges, chantez.
No. 45. AIR: – Chantez, Anges, chantez.

1

kiyawaw nete kici kisikok e otaskiyek
kiyawâw nêtê kihci-kîsikohk ê-otaskiyêk

mamicimik sesos ka kisewatisit
mamihcimihk Sesos kâ-kisêwâtisit

wepinasowinik e ayat niyan oci;
wêpinâsowinihk ê-ayât niyanân ohci;

mamawi mamicimatak.
mâmawi-mamihcimâtâhk.

2

nawokistawik ki kisemanitomiwaw,
nawokîstawik kikisê-manitomiwâw,

ka natitek e ata kasostakoyek.
ka-natitêk ê-âta-kasôstâkoyêk.

e kicitwawisit esi mamatawisit,
ê-kihcitwâwisit (ê-)isi-mamâhtâwisit,

mamawi mamicimatak.
mâmawi-mamihcimâtâhk.

No. 46. AIR: – Heureux séjour.
No. 46. AIR: – Heureux séjour.

1

ka wi kitimakinakoyak
kâ-wî-kitimâkinâkoyâhk

ki pe kiyokatikonaw;
kipê-kiyokâtikonaw;

wecitawe manaciatak,
wêcitawi manâcihâtâhk,

wiya e tipeyimitak. (*bis.*)
wiya ê-tipêyimitâhk. (bis.)

2

kicitwa wepinasowinik
kihcitwâw wêpinâsowinihk

epiyan ki tapwetatin,
ê-apiyan kitâpwêtâtin,

tasipwa e naokistatan,
tâsipwâ ê-nâwokîstâtân,

e kisteyitakosiyan. (*bis.*)
ê-kistêyihtâkosiyan. (bis.)

3

naspic ki mamoyawestatin
nâspic kimâmoyawêstâtin

e kitimakinawiyan
ê-kitimâkinawiyan

188

ᑲᑭᑫ ᐁ ᐃᐧ ᐃᐧᑭᒥᔭᐠ
ᒪᓂᑐ ᐸᑫᐧᓯᑲᓂᐠ. (*bis.*)

4

ᓂ ᒪᒋ ᐁᔮᑖᑯᓯᓇᐣ,
ᑭᔭ ᑭ ᑭᒋᑖᐧᐃᐧᓯᐣ;
ᐁᔮᐁᐧᐟ ᑭ ᐃᐧ ᐃᐧᑭᒥᓇᐣ,
ᐁᓯ ᑭᓴᐊᐧᑎᓯᔭᐣ. (*bis.*)

5

ᐊᔮᐊᐧᐟ ᓂ ᓴᑭᐃᑯᓯᔭᐣ
ᐃᐢᐱ ᑭᔭᐊᐧᐤ ᑲᑭᔭᐤ
ᐊᔭᒥᐁ ᓴᐢᑲᒧᔭᓂ.
ᐃᐧ ᒪᒨᔭᐁᐧᐢᑕᒪᐃᐧᐟ. (*bis.*)

No. 47. Air:—*Du Roi des rois.*

1

ᐁᑲᐧ ᑫᑳ ᐅᑎᐢᐸᒪᐤ ᓴᓯᐢ
ᓇᐢᐱ ᑲ ᑭ ᐯᒋᐊᑲᐊᐧᑕᐠ.

Refrain.

ᓂ ᒥᐁᐧᔮᑌᐣ,
ᐣᑕᑕᒥᓇᐣ:
ᐊᐢᑕᐦ, ᓴᓯᐢ, ᓯᔭᐁᐧᔮᒥᔭᐣ;
ᐊᐢᑕᐦ, ᓴᓯᐢ, ᒥᔭᒪᑕᑯᐃᔭᐣ.

2

ᓴᓴᐩ ᐁᓴ ᐱᑯ ᓃᑎᐢᐸᒪᐤ
ᐁᑲᐧ ᑲ ᐅᑎᑲᐧᓇᐱᐢᑕᐊᐧᐟ.

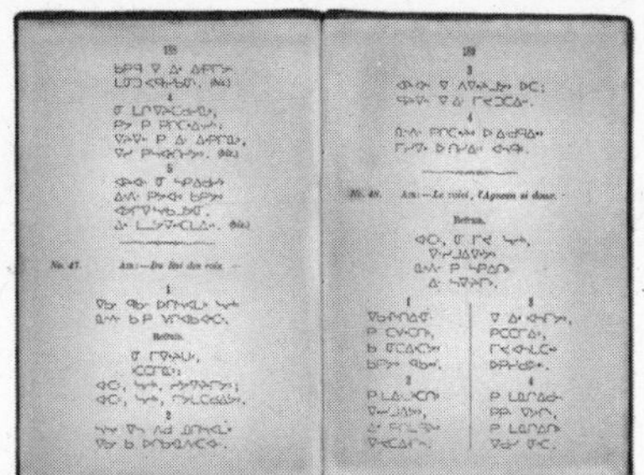

188

You are going to live with us forever
in God's bread (*twice.*)

4

We are sinful.
But You, You are holy;
nevertheless, You are going to live with us,
as You are kind. (*twice.*)

5

I am loved more
than all of you.
When I take Communion
I am guided by You. (*twice.*)

No. 47. Air: – *Du Roi des rois. (The King of kings.)*

1

Just about the time of seeing Jesus
completely the way He desired.

Refrain.

I am happy about it.
We are glad.
Come here, Jesus, take pity on me.
Come here, Jesus, strengthen me.

2

Already, I live to see Him.
And I bow for Him.

kakike e wi wikimiyak
kâkikê ê-wî-wîkimiyâhk

manito pakwesikanik. (*bis.*)
manitow pahkwêsikanihk. (bis.)

4

ni maci eyitakosinan,
nimaci-itêyihtâkosinân,

kiya ki kicitwawisin;
kiya kikihcitwâwisin;

eyiwek ki wi wikiminan,
êyiwêk kiwî-wîkiminân,

esi kisewatisiyan. (*bis.*)
ê-isi-kisêwâtisiyan. (bis.)

5

ayiwak ni sakiikosin
ayiwâk nisâkihikôsin

ispic kiyawaw kakiyaw
ispic kiyawâw kahkiyaw

ayamiesaskamoyani.
ayamihêsaskamoyâni.

wi mamoyawestamawik. (*bis.*)
wî-mâmoyawêstamawik. (bis.)

No. 47. Air: – Du Roi des rois.
No. 47. Air: – Du Roi des rois.

1

ekwa kekac otisapamaw sesos
êkwa kêkâc otisâpamâw Sesos

naspic ka ki peci akawatak.
nâspic kâ-kî-pêci-akâwâtâhk.

Refrain.

ni miweyiten,
nimiywêyihtên,

ntataminan:
nitataminân:

astam, sesos, siyaweyimiyan;
âstam, Sesos, siyawêyimiyan;

astam, sesos, miyo matakoiyan.
âstam, Sesos, miyo-mâtakohiyan.

2

sasay esi piko notisapamaw
sâsay êsi piko nôtisâpamâw

ekwa ka ocikwanapistawak.
êkwa kâ-ocihcihkwanapîstawak.

189

3

ᐊᐳᐊᐧᐠ ᐁ ᐱᐁᐧᐳᒧᔮᐣ ᐅᑕ;
ᑫᐳᐁᐧᐠ ᐁ ᐃᐧ ᒥᔦᑐᑕᐃᐧᐠ.

4

ᓇᐢᐱ- ᑭᑎᑕᐧᐳᐤ ᐅ ᐃᐧᑯᑫᐃᐧᐣ
ᒥᓯᐁᐧ ᐅᑎᓯᐃᐧᐣ ᐊᓴᑫᐤ.

No. 48. Air:—*Le voici, l'Agneau si doux.*

Refrain.

ᐊᐢᑕᐨ, ᓂ ᒥᔦ ᓴᓯᐢ,
ᐁᐧᓯᒧᐃᐁᐧᔦᐣ
ᓇᐢᐱ- ᑭ ᓴᑭᐃᑎᐣ
ᐃᐧ ᓴᐁᐧᐳᒥᐣ.

1

ᐁᑲᔑᐢᑎᐃᐧᓂᐠ
ᑭ ᑕᐯᐧᑕᑎᐣ,
ᑲ ᓂᑕᐃᐧᑕᔦᐣ
ᑲᑭᔦᐤ ᑫᑲᐧᐠ.

2

ᑭ ᒪᐃᐧᒪᐢᑕᑎᐣ
ᐁᐧᓯᒧᐃᔦᐣ,
ᐃᐧ ᑭᑎᒪᑫᐳᐨ
ᐁᐧᔦᑕᐃᐧᒥᐢ.

3

ᐁ ᐃᐧ ᐊᓴᒥᔦᐣ,
ᑭᑕᑕᒥᐃᐣ,
ᒥᔦ ᐊᓴᒪᑕᐧᐤ
ᐅᑭᓯᑯᐅᐧᐠ.

4

ᑭ ᒪᓇᒋᐃᑯᐧᐠ
ᑭᑭᐠ ᐁᔦᒋᐠ,
ᑭ ᒪᓇᒋᐃᑎᐣ
ᐁᑯᓯ ᓂᐢᑕ.

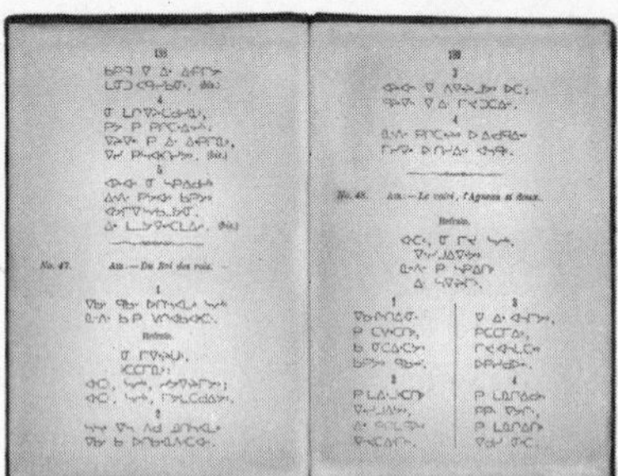

189

3

I am discouraged by myself here.
But He is going to strengthen me.

4

Forever His feast is holy.
All over He supplies grace.

No. 48. Air: – *Le voici, l'Agneau si doux.*
(Here He is, the gentle Lamb.)

Refrain.

Come, my good Jesus;
this is my plea.
Forever I love You.
You are going to bless me.

1

In the Eucharist
I believe in You
to bless
everything.

2

I pray to you.
In this way I implore
You.
I am pitiful.
I take you as my Father.

3

You are going to feed me.
You please me.
You feed us well
through Your angels.

4

The angels respected You.
They are in Your home.

I respect You
and me too.

3

ayiwak e piweyimoyan ota;
ayiwâk ê-piwêyimoyân ôta;

keyiwek e wi miyo totawit.
kêyiwêk ê-wî-miyo-tôtawit.

4

naspic kicitwayiw o wikokewin
nâspic kihcitwâyiw owîhkohkêwin

misiwe o tisiwin asakew.
misiwê otîsîwin asâkêw.

No. 48. AIR: – Le voici, l'Agneau si doux.
No. 48. AIR: – Le voici, l'Agneau si doux.

Refrain.

astam, ni miyo sesos,
âstam, nimîyo-Sesos,

wesimoiweyan
wêsimôhiwêyan

naspic ki sakiitin
nâspic kisâkihitin

wi saweyimin.
wî-sawêyimin.

1

ekaristiwinik
ekaristiwinihk

ki tapwetatin,
kitâpwêtâtin,

ka nitawitayan
ka-nitawîhtâyan

kakiyaw kekway.
kahkiyaw kîkway.

2

ki mawimostatin
kimawimôstâtin

wesimoiyan,
wêsimôhiyan,

wi kitimakeyim
wî-kitimâkeyim

weyotawimisk.
wiyôhtâwîmisk.

3

e wi asamiyan,
ê-wî-asamiyan,

kitatamiin,
kitatamihin,

miyo asamatwaw
miyo-asamâtwâw

okisikowok.
okîsikowak.

4

ki manaciikwok
kimanâcihikwak

kikik eyacik,
kîkik ê-ayâcik,

ki manaciitin
kimanâcihitin

ekosi nista.
êkosi nîsta.

190

5
ᐃᐢᐱ- ᒥᐋᓯᔮᐣ
ᑭ ᐁᐧᐱᓂᓰᐣ:
ᓂ ᑌ ᑭ ᒥᔦᑎᐣ
ᐯ ᑎᐯᔦᒥᐣ.

6
ᑳᐢᑫᔦᑕᒪᓂ,
ᑳᑭᒋᐃᑳᐣ,
ᐊᑳᐧᒥᓯᐃᑳᐣ,
ᐃᐧ ᓂᐱᔭᓂ.

7
ᑲ ᒪᒋ ᐊᔦᐃᐧᐟ
ᑭᑕᐠ ᓇᓯᒋ;
ᒋ ᐁᑲ ᓴᑯᐃᐤ
ᑳᐢᑭᑕᒪᐃᐧᐣ.

8
ᒣᐋᓯᔮᐣ ᒪᕆ,
ᐃᑌᐧᐢᑕᒪᐃᐧᐣ;
ᓇᐢᐱ- ᓂ ᓵᑭᐊᐤ
ᑭ ᑯᓯᐢ ᓴᓱᐢ.

9
ᓂᒋ ᐃᔦᓂᑎᐠ,
ᓇᐅᐧᑭᐢᑕᐃᐧᐠ.
ᓇᑲᒧᐢᑖᐧᑕᐠ
ᓴᓱᐢ ᒪᒪᐃᐧ.

10
ᐁᑳ ᑯᐢᑕᒨᑫᐠ
ᓂᐳᐃᐧᐣ ᐁᑳᐧ;
ᑲ ᐱᒪᒋᐃᐁᐧᐟ
ᐁ ᐯ ᓇᑎᑕᐠ.

11
ᒋ ᐱᒪᑎᓯᔪᐠ
ᑕᑭ ᑭᓯᑯᐠ
ᑭᑕᓴᒥᑯᐊᐤ
ᐁᑳᔑᐢᑎᐃᐧᐣ.

12
ᑭᑕᐋᐧᓯᒥᓴᐠ
ᐱᓯᐢᑫᔦᒥᐠ:
ᓴᐁᐧᔦᒥᐠ ᐁᑳᐧ
ᓯᔭᑭᐃᐢᑭᐠ.

No. 49. Air:—*Allons au banquet divin.*

Refrain.

ᐁᑳᐧ ᒥᔭᐋᐧᑕᑕᐠ
ᑌᐯᔦᒥᑕᐠ ᐃᐧᔪᒥᑕᐠ
ᐁᑳᐧ ᒥᔭᐋᐧᑕᑕᐠ
ᓴᓱᐢᑭᐢ ᑭ ᓇᐣᑐᒥᑯᓇᐤ

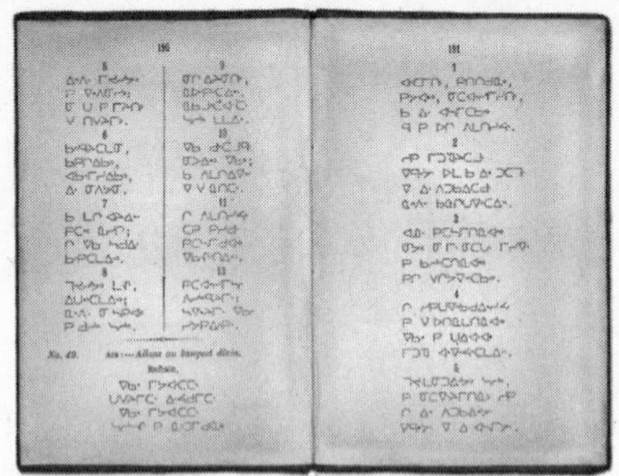

190

5
You are good.
Yet You gave Yourself
away.
I give you my heart.
Come and claim me.

6
When I am lonely,
Console me
With Your grace
When I die.

7
When the devil
comes and gets me
again,
so that he does not
overpower me,
rescue me.

8
Mary, you are wonderful.
You intercede for me.
Forever I love Him,

Your Son, Jesus.

9
My people,
bow to Me.

Let us sing for Him,
all together.

10
Do not be frightened
Of death.
The One who gives us life
Comes to claim us.

11
To live
forever in the Heavens,

He feeds you

with the Eucharist.

12
Your children,
Watch over them.
Bless them with Your
powers,
and they will love You.

No. 49. Air: – *Allons au banquet divin.*
(Let us go to the divine feast.)

Refrain.
And Let us glorify Him.
Let us be content when we follow Him.
And let us glorify Him,
as Jesus Christ invites us.

5

ispic miyosiyan
ispic (ê-)miyosiyan

ki wepinison:
kiwêpinison:

ni te ki miyitin
nitêh kimiyitin

pe tipeyimin.
pê-tipêyimin.

6

kaskeyitamani,
kaskêyihtamâni,

kakiciikan,
kâkîcihîkan,

akwamisiikan,
akwamisihikan,

wi nipiyani.
wî-nipiyâni.

7

ka maci ayiwit
kâ-maci-ayiwit

kitwam nasici;
kîhtwâm nâsici;

ci eka sakoit
kici êkâ sâkohit

kaskitamawin.
kaskîtamawin.

8

meyosiyan mari,
(ê-)miyosiyan Mari,

itwestamawin;
itwêstamawin;

naspic ni sakiaw
nâspic nisâkihâw

ki kosis sesos.
kikosis Sesos.

9

nici iyinitik,
nîci-iyinîtik,

nawokistawik.
nawokîstawik.

nakamostawatak
nakamôstawâtâhk

sesos mamawi.
Sesos mâmawi.

10

eka kostamokek
êkâ kostâmohkêk

nipowin ekwa;
nipiwin êkwa;

ka pimaciiwet
kâ-pimâcihiwêt

e pe natitak.
ê-pê-nâtitâhk.

11

ci pimatisiyek
kici-pimâtisiyêk

taki kisikok
tahki kîsikohk

kitasamikowaw
kitasamikowâw

ekaristiwin.
êkaristiwin.

12

kitawasimisak
kitawâsimisak

pisiskeyimik:
pisiskêyimihk:

saweyimik ekwa
sawêyimik êkwa

siyakiiskik.
siyakihiskik.

No. 49. AIR: – Allons au banquet divin.
No. 49. AIR: – Allons au banquet divin.

Refrain.

ekwa miyowatatak
êkwa miyowâtâtâhk

tepeyimitak wiyekomitak
têpêyimitâhk wiyêkômitâhk

kwa miyowatatak
êkwa miyowâtâtâhk

sesoskri ki nastomikonaw
Sesoskri kinatomikonaw.

191

1

ᐊᐢᑕᒥᑎᐠ, ᑭᑎᑎᑯᓇᐤ,
ᑭᔭᐊᐧᐤ, ᓂᑕᐊᐧᔨᒥᔨᑎᐠ,
ᑲ ᐃᐧ ᐊᓴᒥᑕᑲᐧᐤ
ᑫ ᑭ ᐅᒋ ᐱᒪᑎᓯᓭᐠ.

2

ᓯᑭ ᒥᑐᓃᐹᑕᒧᐠ
ᐁᑫᐧᔭᐠ ᐅᒪ ᑲ ᐃᐧ ᑐᑕᒉᐠ
ᐁ ᐃᐧ ᐱᑐᑲᐃᑕᑯᐠ
ᓇᐢᐱᐨ ᑲᓇᒋᑌᐁᐢᑕᐃᐦ.

3

ᐊᓅᐨ ᑭᑕᓴᒥᑎᓇᐊᐧᐤ
ᓂᔮᐤ ᓂ ᒥᐠ ᓂᑕᓚᐠ ᒥᔨᐁᐧ
ᑭ ᑲᓯᐢᑕᑎᓇᐊᐧᐤ
ᑭᒋ ᐯᑎᔮᐁᐧᐢᑕᑲᐧᐤ.

4

ᒋ ᓯᑭᑌᐁᐢᑲᑯᐃᐧᔨᓭᐠ
ᑭ ᐯ ᐅᑎᓇᒪᑎᓇᐊᐧᐤ
ᐁᑲᐧ ᑭ ᑌᐃᐊᐧᐊᐧ
ᒥᑐᓃ ᐊᐧᐁᐧᓭᐢᑕᒪᐃᐦ.

5

ᒉᓵᒪᓂᑐᐃᐧᔮᐣ ᓴᓯᐢ,
ᑭ ᓂᑕᐁᐧᔮᒥᑎᓇᐣ ᓯᑭ
ᒋ ᐃᐧ ᐱᑐᑲᐃᐧᔮᐠ
ᐁᑫᐧᔭᐠ ᐁ ᐃ ᐊᓴᒥᔮᐠ.

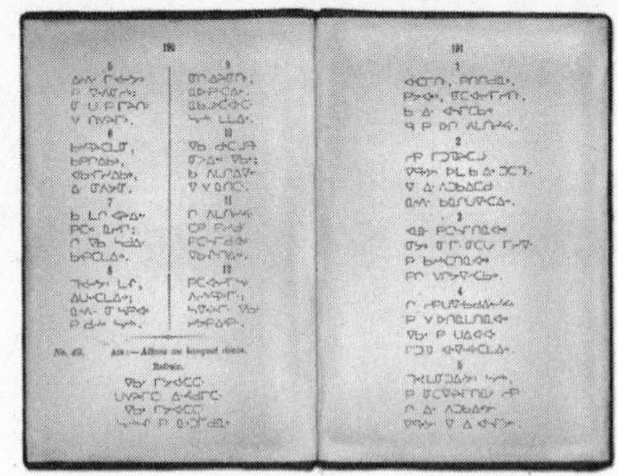

191

1

Come, He says to us.
You all are my little children.
I will feed you
and give you life.

2

Think hard over this.
At baptism I will do this for you.
I take you into My house.
Forever to purify you.

3

Today I will feed you,
He gives me the eternal Spirit.
I hide Myself from you all.
The Great One will come to you.

4

So that you all have strong hearts,
I come to give you new life.
And a renewed heart,
You will prepare for Me.

5

Jesus, You are a good God.
We want You very much.
So that You take us in,
only then will You feed us.

191

1

astamitik, kititikonaw,
âstamitik, kititikonaw,

kiyawaw, nitawasimisitik,
kiyawâw, nitawâsimisitik,

ka wi asamitakwaw
kâ-wî-asamitâkwâw

ke ki oci pimatisiyek.
kikî-ohci-pimâtisiyêk.

2

soki mitoneyitamok
sôhki-mitonêyihtamohk

ekweyak oma ka wi totamek
êkwêyâk ôma kâ-wî-tôtamêk

e wi pitokaitakok
ê-wî-pîhtokahitakok

naspic kanaciteestawik.
nâspic kanâcitêhêstawik.

3

anoc kitasamitinawaw
anohc kitasamitinâwâw

niyaw ni mik ni tacak misiwe
niyâw nimiyik nitahcâhk misiwê

ki kasostatinawaw
kikâsôstâtinâwâw

kici pe ciyawestakwaw.
kihci pê-ciyawêstâkwâw.

4

ci sokiteeskakowisiyek
kici-sôhkitêhêskakowisiyêk

ki pe otinamatinawaw
kipê-otinamâtinâwâw

ekwa ki teiwawa
êkwa kitêhiwâwâ

mitone waweyestamawik.
mitonê wawêyîstamawik.

5

meyo manitowiyan sesos,
(ê-)miyo-manitowiyan Sesos,

ki nitaweyimitinan soki
kinitawêyimitinân sôhki

ci wi pitokawiyak
kici-wî-pîhtokawiyâhk

ekweyak e i asamiyak.
êkwêyêk ê-i-asamiyâhk.

192

No. 50. *Même air.*

Refrain.

ᐁᑲᐧ ᒥᔭᐊᐧᑕᑕᐠ
ᓴᓱᐢᓯ ᐁ ᒥᔨᑯᔭᐠ ᐅ ᑌ
ᐁᑲᐧ ᒥᔭᐊᐧᑕᑕᐠ
ᐅᓴᒥ ᐁ ᓴᑭᐃᑯᔭᐠ.

1

ᐊᐢᑕᒥᑎᐠ ᑭ ᑎᑎᑯᓇᐤ
ᑭᔭᐊᐧᐤ ᓂᑕᐊᐧᔨᒥᔨᑎᐠ,
ᓂ ᑌᐃᐠ ᐯ ᐱᑐᑫᐠ
ᑭᑎ ᒥᔪ ᐱᒪᑎᓯᔪᐠ.

2

ᐊᐢᑕᒥᑎᐠ ᑮ ᑎᑎᑯᓇᐤ
ᑭᔭᐊᐧᐤ ᐁ ᑭᑎᒪᑭᓯᔪᐠ
ᐊᐧᐊᐧ ᑳᐧᑕᑭᑕᔪᐠ
ᐁ ᐃᐧ ᑌᐱᔭᐁᐧᐃᐧᑕᑲᐧᐤ.

3

ᐅᒪ ᓂ ᑌ ᐃᐧ ᐊᐧᐸᑕᒧᐠ
ᒥᐢᑕᐁ ᐁ ᐃᐧ ᓴᑭᐃᑕᑲᐧᐤ
ᒋᐢ! ᓂ ᓴᑭᐃᐁᐧᐁᐧᐤ
ᑲᐧᐢᑫᐧᑯᑌᐤ ᓂ ᑌᐃᐠ ᐅᒋ

4

ᐱᑯᓇᑕ ᑯ ᐸᑲᐧᓯᔪᐠ
ᑭᔭᐊᐤ ᐱᔭᐢᑕᐅᔪᐠ ᑕᑭ
ᑫᔦᐁᐧᐠ ᑕᐃᐧᐸᔦᐤ
ᓂ ᑌ ᑕᑭ ᒋ ᓴᑭᑕᔪᐠ.

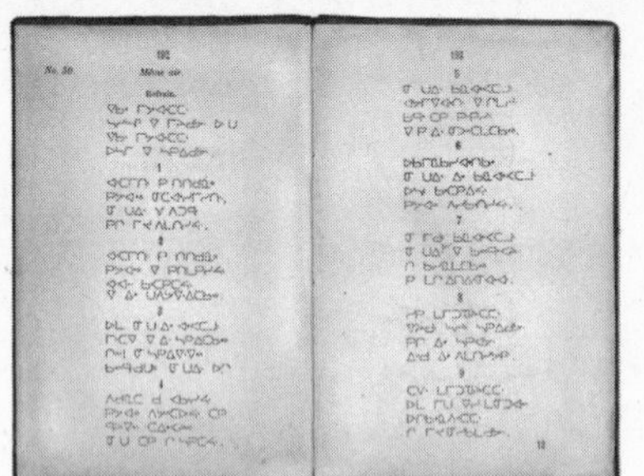

192 No. 50. *Même air. (Same air.)*

Refrain.

Let us rejoice.
Jesus Christ gives us His heart
Let us rejoice
because He loves us very much.

1

Come, He says to us.
You are all My little children.
Come into My heart
to live the good life.

2

Come He says to us all,
all you who are poor,
especially all who suffer,
I am going to make you content.

3

See My heart.
I love you tenderly.
Behold! My love for others
leaps from My heart.

4

For whatever reason, you hate Me.
You continuously sin.
There is room for you.
To love My heart forever.

192 No. 50.
No. 50.

Même air.
Même air.

Refrain.

ekwa miyawatatak
êkwa miyawâtâtâhk

sesoskri e miyikoyak o te
Sesoskri ê-miyikoyâhk otêh

ekwa miyawatatak
êkwa miyawâtâtâhk

osami e sakiikoyak.
osâmi ê-sâkihikoyahk.

1

astamitik ki titikonaw
âstamitik kititikonaw

kiyawaw nitawasimisitik,
kiyawâw nitawâsimisitik,

ni teik pe pitokek
nitêhik pê-pîhtokwêk

kici miyo pimatisiyek.
kici-miyo-pimâtisiyêk.

2

astamitik ki titikonaw
âstamitik kititikonaw

kiyawaw e kitimakisiyek
kiyawâw ê-kitimâkisiyêk

wawac kwatakitayek
wâwâc kwâtakihtâyêk

e wi tepiyaweitakwaw.
ê-wî-têpiyawêhitakwâw.

3

oma ni te wi wapatamok
ôma nitêh wî-wâpahtamok

mistae e wi sakiitakwaw
mistahi ê-wî-sâkihitakwâw

cist! ni sakiiwewen
cîst! nisâkihîwêwên

kwaskwekotew ni teik oci
kwâskwêkotêw nitêhik ohci

4

pikonata ko pakwasiyek
pikonata kâ-pakwâsiyêk

kiyawaw piyastaoyek taki
kiyawâw ê-pâstahoyêk tahki

keyiwek tawipayiw
kêyiwêk tawipayiw

ni te taki ci sakitayek.
nitêh tahki kici-sâkihtâyêk.

193

5

ᑍ ᑌᐃᐠ ᑳᑍᐘᐸᑕᒧᐠ
ᐊᔭᒥᐁᐘᑎᐠ ᐁ ᒋᒪᓯᐟ
ᑳᑫ ᑕᑭ ᑭᐢᑭᓯᐟ
ᐁ ᑭ ᐃᐧ ᑍᔓᐢᑕᒪᑕᑳᐤ.

6

ᐅᑳᒥᑍᑳᓯᐘᑎᑳᐧ
ᑍ ᑌᐃᐠ ᐃᐧ ᑳᑍᐘᐸᑕᒧᐠ
ᐅᓴᐨ ᑳᐧᑕᑭᐃᓭᐠ
ᑭᔭᐘᐤ ᐱᓯᑳᐧᑎᓯᓭᐠ.

7

ᑍ ᒥᑯᐨ ᑳᑍᐘᐸᑕᒧᐠ
ᑍ ᑌᐃᐠ ᐁ ᑳᐧᐢᑫᐧᐸᔾᐠ
ᑎ ᑳᓯᑍᒪᑕᑳᐤ
ᑭ ᒪᒋ ᐃᑎᐃᐧᑍᐘᐘᐧ.

8

ᓯᑭ ᒪᒥᑐᑑᔾᑕᑕᐠ
ᐁᔾᑯᐠ ᓴᓯᐢ ᓴᑭᐃᑯᔭᐠ
ᑭᒋ ᐃᐧ ᓴᑭᐊᔭᐠ
ᐃᐢᑯ ᐃᐧ ᐱᒪᑎᓯᔭᑭ.

9

ᑕᐯᐧ ᒪᒥᑐᑑᔾᑕᑕᐠ
ᐅᒪ ᒥᑌ ᐁᓯ ᒪᑍᑐᐘᐠ
ᐅᒋᑳᐧᑍᐱᐢᑕᑕᐠ
ᒋ ᒥᔕᑍᓯᑳᒪᑯᔭᐠ.

12

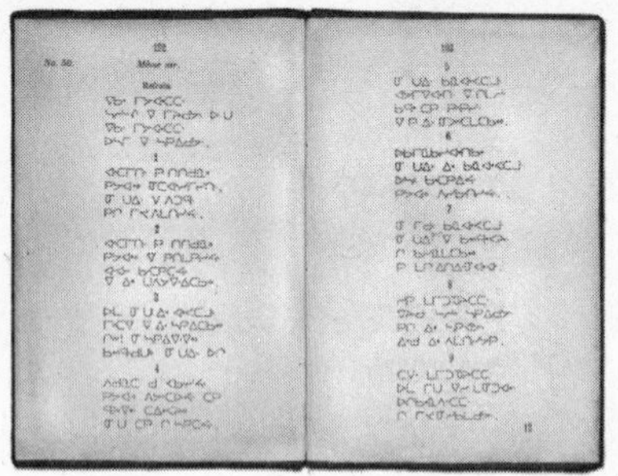

193

5

Look at My heart.
The cross was placed in the ground.
Try to remember always
I died for you.

6

Crowned with thorns
look at My heart.
Because you make Me suffer,
those of you who are committing adultery.

7

Look at My blood.
My heart leaps
to forgive you.
for your sins.

8

Meditate fervently about this.
Jesus loves us this much.
So that we will love Him
until we die.

9

Truly let us reflect on
this holy Heart.
Let us bow down to You.
So that He works together with us.

193

5

ni teik kanawapatamok
nitêhik kanawâpahtamok

ayamiewatik e cimasot
ayamihêwâhtik ê-cimasot

kakwe taki kiskisik
kâkwê tahki kiskisik

e ki wi nipostamatakwaw.
ê-kî-wî-nipôstamatakwâw.

6

okaminakasiwatikwa
okâminakasîwâhtikwa

ni teik wi kanawapatamok
nitêhik wî-kanawâpahtamok

osam kwatakiiyek
osâm ê-kwâtakihiyêk

kiyawaw pisikwatisiyek.
kiyawâw ê-pisikwâtisiyêk.

7

ni mikom kanawapatamok
nimihkom kanawâpahtamok

ni teik e kwaskwepayik
nitêhik ê-kwaskwêpayik

ci kasinamatakwaw
kici-kâsînamâtakwâw

ki maci itiwiniwawa.
kimacihtiwiniwâwa.

8

soki mamitoneyitatak
sôhki-mâmitonêyihtâtâhk

eyikok sesos sakiikoyak
iyikohk Sesos ê-sâkihikoyâhk

kici wi sakiayak
kici-wî-sâkihâyahk

isko wi pimatisiyaki.
isko wî-pimâtisiyâhki.

9

tapwe mamitoneyitatak
tâpwê mâmitonêyihtâtâhk

oma mite esi manitowak
ôma mitêh êsi manitowak

ocikwanapistatak
ocihcihkwanapîstâtâhk

ci miyo ni sokamakoyak.
kici-miyo-nîsôhkamâkoyahk.

194

10

ᑭᔮ ᔫᐢᐱᓯᔮᐤ ᓴᓯᐢᐟ
ᑭᐟ ᓂᑕᐍᔦᑕᒪᑎᓈᐤ
ᒋ ᔫᐢᐱᓯᑌᐃᔮᐠ
ᐁ ᐑ ᑎᐯᔨᑕᒪᐠ ᑭᑌ.

11

ᑭᐍ, ᑭᐍ ᒪᒋ ᒪᓂᑐ
ᓴᓯᐢ ᐅᑌ ᐁ ᐑᒋᐃᑯᔮᐠ
ᐁᑯᓯ ᓂ ᐑ ᑌᐹᐤ:
ᑕᑤᐤ ᐁ ᐑ ᒪᒋ ᓯᑭᒥᐟ.

12

ᒪᒥᔭᑕᐠ ᑭ ᑌᐃᓇᐘ
ᐅᓴᐨ ᓴᓯᐢᐟ ᐁ ᐅᑕᐍᔦᑕᐠ;
ᒥᔦᐤ ᑭᑌ, ᓂ ᑯᓴ,
ᑕᑭ ᐁᓯ ᐊᔨᑎᑯᔭᐠ

13

ᐁ ᐑ ᐊᑕᒥᐊᔭᐠ ᓴᓯᐢ
ᑳᑵ ᒥᐢᑕᑤᐤ ᒋ ᓴᐢᑲᒧᔭᐠ
ᐊᐤ! ᐸᑯᓭᔨᒪᑕᐠ,
ᐁᑯᓯ ᒪᓇᑐᑕᐚᑕᐠ.

14

ᐁᑯᓯ ᐃᓯ ᑎᓭᑕᒪᑭ
ᑭ ᑲ ᒥᓭᐱᒪᑎᓯᓇᓇᐤ
ᒥᓇ ᑭᒋᑭᓯᑯᐠ,
ᓴᓯᐢᐟ ᑭ ᑲ ᐚᐸᒪᓇᐤ.

R. P. Dupin.

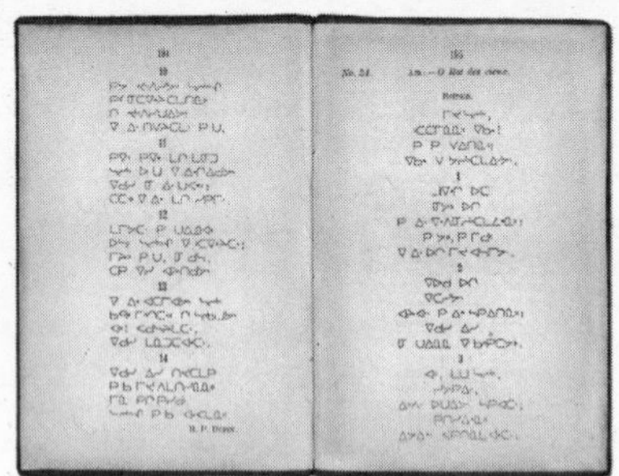

194

10

Jesus Christ, You are tender.
We want this for You
For us to be tender-hearted
when we are content with Your heart.

11

Go home! Go home, evil spirit.
Jesus here is helping us.
I will call out
every time he urges us to do wrong.

12

Let us give Him our hearts
because Jesus Christ wants us.
"Give Me your heart, My son."
He says this to us all the time.

13

You make us grateful.
Try many times to take Holy Communion.
Well! Let us wish for Him
to be our God.

14

If we do it this way,
we will live good lives,
And in Heaven
we will see Jesus Christ.

R. P. Dupin.

194

10

kiya yospisiyan sesoskri
kiya (ê-)yôspisiyan Sesoskri

ki nitaweyitamatinan
kinitawêyihtamâtinân

ci yospisiteiyak
kici-yôspisitêhiyâhk

e wi tipeyitamak ki te.
ê-wî-tipêyihtamâhk kitêh.

11

kiwe kiwe maci manito
kîwê kîwê maci-manitow

sesos o te e wiciikoyak
Sesos ôtê ê-wîcihikoyâhk

ekosi ni wi tepwan:
êkosi niwî-têpwân:

tatwaw e wi maci sikimit.
tahtwâw ê-wî-maci-sîhkimit.

12

mamiyatak ki teinowa
mâmiyâtâhk kitêhinowa

osam sesoskri e ntaweyitak;
osâm Sesoskri ê-nitawêyihtâhk;

miyin ki te, ni kose,
miyin kitêh, nikosê,

taki esi ayitikoyak
tahki (ê-)isi-ay-itikoyahk.

13

e wi atamiayak sesos
ê-wî-atamihayâhk Sesos

kakwe miscetwaw ci sakamoyak
kâkwê mihcêtwâw kici-saskamoyahk

aw! pakoseyimatak,
aw! pakosêyimâtâhk,

ekosi manatotawatak.
êkosi manitôtawâtâhk.

14

ekosi isi tiyotamaki
êkosi isi-tôtamâhki

ki ka miyo pimatisinanaw
kika-miyo-pimâtisinânâw

mina kici kisikok
mîna kihci-kîsikohk

sesoskri ki ka wapamanaw.
Sesoskri kika-wâpamânaw.

R. P. Dupin.

195

No. 51. Air: — *O Roi des cieux.*

Refrain.

ᒥᔪ ᓭᓱᐢ,
ᐣᑕᑕᒥᓇᓇᐣ ᐁᑲᐧ!
ᑭ ᑭ ᐯᐃᑎᓇᐣ:
ᐁᑲᐧ ᐯ ᔭᓯᐢᑕᒪᐃᐧᔭᐠ.

1

ᒧᐁᐧᒋ ᐅᑕ
ᓂᔭᐣ ᐅᒋ
ᑭ ᐃᐧ ᐁᐧᐱᓂᓯᐢᑕᒪᐃᐧᓇᐣ:
ᑭ ᔭᐤ, ᑭ ᒥᑯᐨ
ᐁ ᐃᐧ ᐅᒋ ᒥᔪ ᐊᓴᒥᔭᐠ.

2

ᐁᐅᑯ ᐅᒋ
ᐁᑕᓯᔭᐠ
ᐊᐳᐊᐦ ᑭ ᐃᐧ ᓴᑭᐃᑎᓇᐣ:
ᐁᑯᓯ ᐃᓯ
ᓂ ᑌᐃᓇᓇ ᐁ ᑲᐢᑭᑕᔭᐣ.

3

ᐊᐤ, ᒪᑌ ᓭᓱᐢ,
ᓯᔭᑭᐃᐟ,
ᐃᐢᐱ ᐅᑌᐃᔭᐠ ᓴᑭᐊᑕᐠ;
ᑭᑎᓯᐃᐧᓇᐤ
ᐃᔭᐃᐦ ᐸᑭᑎᓇᒪᐊᐧᑕᐠ.

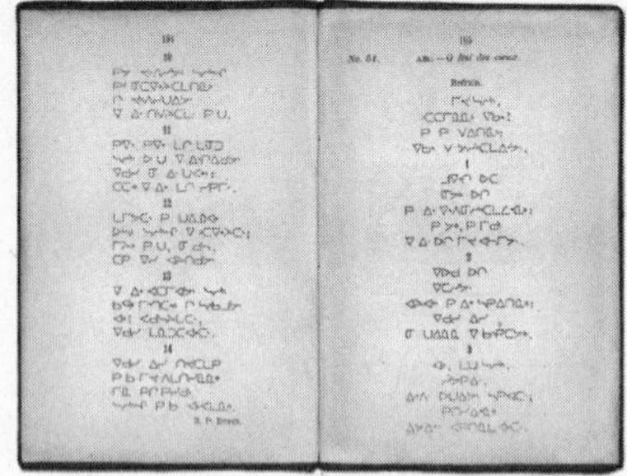

195 *No. 51.* Air: – *O Roi des cieux. (O King of Heaven.)*

Refrain.
Good Jesus,
We are grateful to Him.
We await You.
Now, come down to us.

1

Just as You are here for us
in Holy Communion,
You sacrifice Yourself for us.
Your body, Your blood
are going to feed us well.

2

That is why
all of us
love you more.
In this way
our hearts are able to love.

3

Oh let us see Jesus.
If He loves us
then from our heart Let us love Him.
Our behaviour,
let us offer it to Him.

195 No. 51. Air: – O Roi des cieux.

No. 51. Air: – O Roi des cieux.

Refrain.

miyo sesos,
miyo Sesos,

ntataminanan ekwa!
nitatamihânân ekwa!

ki ki pe itinan:
kikî-pê-itinân:

ekwa pe yasistamawiyak.
êkwa pê-yâsistamawiyâhk.

1

moweci ota
mowêci ôta

niyan oci
niyân ohci

ki wi wepinisostamawinan:
kiwî-wêpinâsôstamawinân:

ki yaw, ki mikom
kiyaw, kimihkom

e wi oci miyo asamiyak.
ê-wî-ohci-miyo-asamiyâhk.

2

eoko oci
êwako ohci

etasiyak
(ê-)itâsiyâhk

ayiwak ki wi sakiitinan:
ayiwâk kiwî-sâkihitinân:

ekosi isi
êkosi isi

ni teinana e kaskitayan.
nitêhinâna ê-kaskihtâyân.

3

aw, mate sesos,
aw, mahti Sesos,

siyakiit,
siyakihit,

ispic oteiyak sakiotak;
ispic otêhiyahk sâkihâtâhk;

kitisiwinaw
kitisiwinaw

iyawis pakitinamawatak.
iyawis pakitinamawâtâhk.

196

No. 52. AIR: — *Quelle nouvelle et sainte ardeur.*

Refrain.

ᑕᑭ ᐃᐢᑯ ᐱᒪᑎᓯᔪᓂ,
ᐃᐧ ᑳᓇ ᐁᐧᐹᒥᑳᐣ:
ᐊᐹᐊᐦ ᓂ ᐸ ᑭᑎᒪᑭᓰᐣ
ᐳᓂ ᐁᐧᑭᒥᔪᓂ.

1

ᐅᓴᐨ ᓂ ᒪᒪᑕᑯᓰᐣ
ᐊᓈ- ᐁ ᐯᒋᑌᐁᐢᑳᐃᐦ
ᑳ ᑎᐯᐹᒥᐧ ᒪᓂᑐ
ᑭᑕ ᐯ ᓯᑭᑌᐁᐢᑳᐃᐦ.

2

ᐃᐢᐱ- ᐁ ᑭᓴᐋᐧᑎᓯᐧ
ᐊᑕ ᐱᐁᐧᐹᑕᑯᓯᔪᐣ
ᐁᑲ ᐁ ᐊᑕᐁᐧᐹᒥᐧ
ᐁᐃᐧ ᐃᐧᒋᐁᐧᒥᐧ ᑳᑭᑫ.

3

ᐁᑳᐧ ᐁ ᐃᐧ ᐁᐧᐱᓇᒪᐣ
ᑳᑭᔪᐤ ᓂ ᒪᒋ ᐊᐹᐃᐧᐣ
ᑲ ᐯ ᑭᑎᒪᐃᑯᔪᐣ
ᐁ ᓴᑯᐃᑯᔪᐣ ᐊᐹᐊᐦ.

4

ᓇᐋᐧ- ᓂ ᑲ ᒥᐁᐧᐹᑑᐣ
ᐊᓈ- ᐳᓂ ᐱᒪᑎᓯᔪᐣ:
ᐃᐢᐱ- ᑭᑕ ᓇᑲᑎᑕᐣ,
ᐁ ᓴᑭᐃᑕᐣ ᐃᔦᐱᑑ.

No. 53. AIR: — *Te, Joseph, celebrent.*

1

ᒪᓂᑐ ᑭᓯᑳᐤ
ᐃᐧ ᒥᔪᐋᐧᑕᒧᐠ,
ᐅᑕᔪᒥᐊᑎᐠ,
ᐊᓈ- ᓇᓈᐢᑯᒧᐠ
ᑳ ᑎᐯᐹᒋᑫᐧ
ᐁ ᑭ ᒥᐹᑯᔦᐠ
ᐊᔪᒥᐁᐃᐧᑭᓯᑳᐤ.

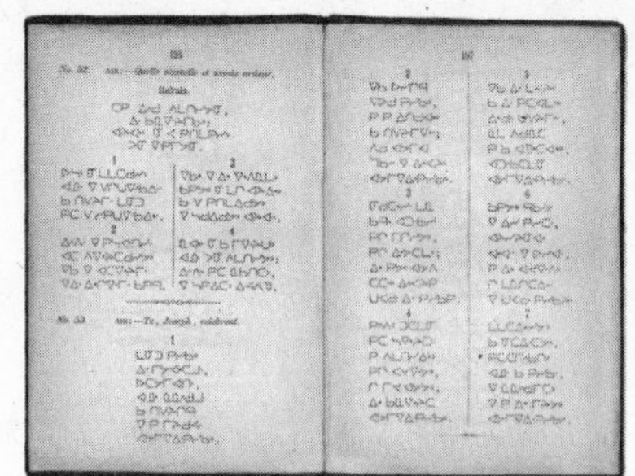

196 No. 52. AIR: – *Quelle nouvelle et sainte ardeur.*
(What new and holy force.)

Refrain.

Always, as long as I live
You are going to look after me.
I could not continue
if you stopped living with me.

1

Because I am gifted
with grace,
God enters my heart,
God, the One who
governs me,
the One who gives me
a strength.

2

For He is kind to me;
even though I am mortal
He does not refuse me.
He is going to
accompany me
forever.

3

I am renouncing
all my bad qualities.
He has shown pity to me
for the burden of my sins.

4

I will be happier than
before.
Today I stop living
(sinfully).
Instead of abandoning
You,
I love You absolutely.

No. 53. AIR: – *Te, Joseph, celebrent.*
(Celebrating you, Joseph.)

1

It is Christmas Day.
Let us be joyful.
The faithful
today are thankful.
The One who governs us
has given us everything
this praying day.

196 No. 52. Air: – Quelle nouvelle et sainte ardeur.

No. 52. Air: – Quelle nouvelle et sainte ardeur.

Refrain.

taki isko pimatisiyani,
tahki isko pimâtisiyâni,

wi kanaweyimikan:
wî-kanâwêyimîhkan:

ayiwak ni pa kitimakisin
ayiwâk nipa-kitimâkisin

poni wekimiyani.
pôni-wîkimiyani.

1

osam ni mamatakosin
osâm nimamâhtâkosin

anoc e peciteeskawit
anohc ê-pêcitêhêskawit

ka tipeyimit manito
kâ-tipêyimit manitow

kita pe sokiteeskawit.
kita-pê-sôhkitêhêskawit.

2

ispic e kisewatisit
ispic ê-kisêwâtisit

ata piweyitakosiyan
âta pîwêyihtâkosiyân

eka e ataweyimit
êkâ ê-âtawêyimit

e wi wiciwemit kakike.
ê-wî-wîcêwêmit kâkikê.

3

ekwa e wi wepinaman
êkwa ê-wî-wêpinamân

kakiyaw ni maci ayiwin
kahkiyaw nimaci-ayiwin

ka pe kitimaikoyan
ka-pê-kitimâhikoyân

e sakoikoyan ayiwak.
ê-sâkohikoyân ayiwâk.

4

nawac ni ka miweyiten
nâwâc nika-miywêyihtên

anoc poni pimatisiyan:
anohc pôni-pimâtisiyân:

ispic kita nakatitan,
ispic kita-nakatitân,

e sakiitan iyepine.
ê-sâkihitân iyêpinê.

No. 53. Air: – Te, Joseph, celebrent.

No. 53. Air: – Te, Joseph, celebrent.

1

manito kisikaw
manitow-kîsikâw

wi miyowatamok,
wî-miyowâtamok,

otayamiatik,
otayamihâtik,

anoc nanaskomok
anohc nanâskomok

ka tipeyiciket
kâ-tipêyihcikêt

e ki miyikoyek
ê-kî-miyikoyêk

ayamiewikisikaw.
ayamihewi-kîsikâw.

197

2

Do not make things
on this day.

He said this to you,
The One who
governs us.
Only pray
each hour
on Sunday.

3

But on the other six
days,
work for yourself
so that you can eat.
So that you hold
yourself holy
and sit quietly
each time it occurs,
the seventh day.

4

If you do this,
He will bless

your life.
So that you are fortunate,
so that you are in a
good place,
keep it holy,
Sunday.

5

Do not disobey God,
The One who preaches
to you;
He governs you.
Do not waste your effort.

You will reject Him,
if you work on something
on Sunday.

6

Everything

that He has finished,
all the people
whom God made

should rest.
So that they respect
the seventh day.

7

I will be blessed
by the One who gives
blessings.
I greet You.
On this day
I thank You.

You gave me
Sunday.

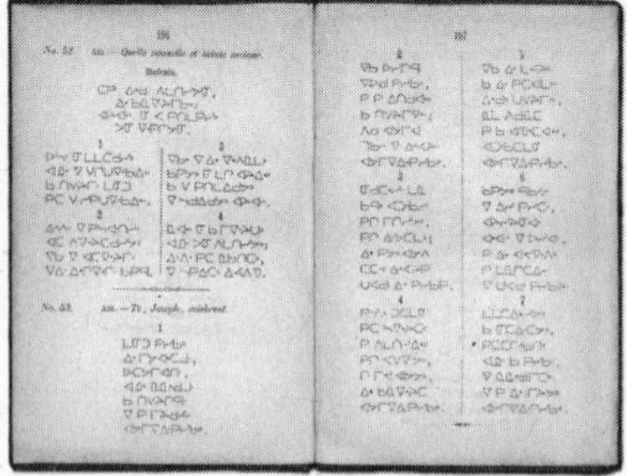

197

2

eka osicike
êkâ osîhcikê

eoko kisikaw,
êwako kîsikâw,

ki ki itikowaw
kikî-itikowâw

ka tipeyimiwet;
kâ-tipêyimiwêt;

piko ayamia
piko ayamihâ

mekwac e ispayik
mêkwâc ê-ispayik

ayamiewikisikaw.
ayamihêwi-kîsikâw.

3

nikotwasik mâna
nikotwâsik mâna

kakwe atoskaso
kâkwê atoskâso

kici micisoyan,
kici-mîcisoyan,

kici wiyataman;
kici-wiyâtaman;

wi kiyam ayapi
wî-kiyâm ayapi

tatwaw ispayiki
tahtwâw ispayiki

tepakok wi kisikaki.
têpahkohp wî-kîsikâki.

5

eka wi mayeyim
êkâ wî-mayêyim

ka wi kitaamask
kâ-wî-kitahamâsk

wikos tepeyimisk,
wikos ê-tipêyimisk,

nama pikonata
nama pikonata

ki ka anwetawaw,
kika-ânwêhtawâw,

atoskatamani
atoskâtamani

ayamiewikisikaw.
ayamihêwi-kîsikâw.

6

kakiyaw kekwaya
kahkiyaw kîkwaya

e isi kisitat,
ê-isi-kisîtât,

ayisiyiniwa
ayisiyiniwa

wawac e osiat,
wâwâc ê-osîhât,

ki wi ayowepiw
kiwî-ayowêpiw

ci manacitawit
kici-manâcihtâwit

e tepakok kisikayik.
ê-têpakohp kîsikâyik.

4

kispin totamani
kîspin tôtamani

kita saweyitam
kita-sawêyihtam

ki pimatisiwin
kipimâtisiwin

kici papeweyan,
kici-papêwêyan,

ci miyo ayayan,
kici-miyo-ayâyan,

wi kanaweyita
wî-kanawêyihta

ayamiewikisikaw.
ayamihêwi-kîsikâw.

7

mamatawisiyan
mamâhtâwisiyan

ka nitawitayan,
kâ-nihtâwihtâyan,

kitatamiskatin
kitatamiskâtin

anoc ka kisikak,
anohc kâ-kîsikâk,

e nanaskomitan
ê-nanâskomitân

e ki wi miyiyan
ê-kî-wî-miyiyan

ayamiewikisikaw.
ayamihêwi-kîsikâw.

198

No. 54. AIR:—*Je me croyais au milieu de ma course.*

198 *No. 54.* AIR: – *Je me croyais au milieu de ma course.*
(I see myself in the middle of my race.)

1

It is indeed good to deny yourself
through fasting.
When you fast,
Your purpose is to gain forgiveness.

2

Jesus teaches us.
For forty days.
He fasted in this way,
So that He teaches us in this way.

3

He teaches here on earth,
When He says: "this is the time."
Someone who will not do penance
will not go the right way.

4

Not with food only
should you deny yourself.
For those who have sinned,
you should abstain from wickedness.

5

Be honest people.
Be truthful in repenting,
and confess your sins.
So that you will surely go to the right place.

198 No. 54. Air: – Je me croyais au milieu de ma course.

No. 54. Air: – Je me croyais au milieu de ma course.

1

tapwe miwasin kwatakiisowin
tâpwê miywâsin kwâtakihisowin

wawac iyewanisiisowin
wâwâc iyêwanisihisowin

ocitaw e wi kwatakiisok,
ohcitaw ê-wî-kwâtakihisok,

ekosi e wi kasinamasok.
êkosi ê-wî-kâsînamâsok.

2

sesos e wi kiskinoomakoyak
Sesos ê-wî-kiskinohamâkoyâhk

nemitano kisikaw itato
nêmitanaw kîsikâw itahto

e ki isi iyewanisiisot
ê-kî-isi-iyêwanisihisot

ci isi kiskinoamakoyak.
kici-isi-kiskinohamâkoyâhk.

3

e kiskinoamaket ota askik
ê-kiskinohamâkêt ôta askihk

omisi itwew esa peyakwaw:
omisi itwêw êsa pêyakwâw:

awiyak eka kwatakiisoci
awiyak êkâ kwâtakihisoci

namawiya kwayask kita itotew.
namâwiya kwayask kita-itohtêw.

4

namawiya piko miciwin oci
namâwiya piko mîciwin ohci

koci kwatakiisonaniwik;
koci-kwâtakihisonâniwik;

awiyak wawac e macayiwit
awiyak wâwâc ê-macayiwit

kita ponitaw omacitwawin.
kita-pônîtaw omacihtwâwin.

5

ekwa tapwe, ayisiyiniwitik,
êkwa tâpwê, ayisiyiniwitik,

mitone kesinateyitamok;
mitonê kêsinâtêyihtamok;

ekwa wi iyewanisiisok
êkwa wî-iyêwanisihisok

kecina kwayask ci itoteyek.
kêhcinâ kwayask kici-itohtêyêk.

199

No. 55. Air:—*Jusques à quand, enfants des hommes.*

1

ᑲᑭᑫ ᑎ, ᐃᔨᒋᑎᐠ,
ᑫ ᐊᐊᐧᓯᓯᑎᓯᔦᐠ?
ᑕᑭ ᑎ ᐅᑕᒥᐅᔦᐠ
ᑎ ᒥᔭᐊᐧᑕᒣᐠ ᐱᑯ?
ᓇᒪ ᑎ ᑫᒋᓯᑐᑕᒣᐠ
ᐃᐧᐸ- ᑎ ᓇᑲᑕᐢᑫᔦᐠ ?
ᒪᔭᐤ ᐁ ᓇᑯᓯᐟ ᐃᔨᒋᐤ,
ᑭ ᑲ ᒋᐱᐣ ᓴᒪᐠ ᐃᑕᐤ.

Refrain.

ᑕᐯᐧ ᑯᐢᑕᑎᑲᐧᐣ
ᒥᐢᑕᐁ ᑯᐢᑕᑎᑲᐧᐣ.
ᒌᐱᔭᑭ, ᒪᒋᑐ
ᑫ ᐃᐧᔭᓯᐊᐧᑎᑯᔭᐠ.

2

ᓇᐢᐱ- ᑲ ᐃᐧᐘᑎᓯᑎᐠ
ᑲ ᑭᑎᐅᑭᒪᐃᐧᑎᐠ
ᒥᓯᐁᐧ ᐊᐢᑭᐠ ᐁᑯᐢᑎᑎᐠ;
ᑕ=ᑌ ᑲ ᐊᔭᑕᐧᐤ ᐊᓇ-?
ᐃᐧᐸ- ᑕᐯᐧ ᑭᐸᑭᓯᓇᐦ
ᒥᐢᑎᑯᐊᐧᑎᑲᒌᓯᐠ.
ᑕᒋᓯᐟ ᐁᑲᐧ ᐊᐸᑎᐅᐅᐧᐦ
ᑲ ᒪᒪᐢᑳᑌᔨᒥᑎᐠ?

3

ᑕᑐ ᑫᑲᐧᐦ ᓯᔭᑭᑕᔦᐠ
ᑭᑎ ᐃᐧᐘᑎᓯᐃᐧᓇ
ᒥᓇ ᒥᔭᐊᐧᑕᒧᐃᐧᓇ;
ᐊᐧᐢ ᑭᑲ ᓇᑲᑌᓇᐊᐧᐤ
ᓇᐢᐱ- ᑫ ᐊᔨᒣᔨᑕᒣᐠ
ᐁ ᐊᑕ ᒪᐃᐧᑲᑕᒣᐠ,
ᓇᒪ ᑭᑲ ᑕᑯᑌᓇᐊᐧᐤ.
ᐃᔨᒋᑎᐠ, ᐃᐧ ᑭᐢᑭᓯᐠ!

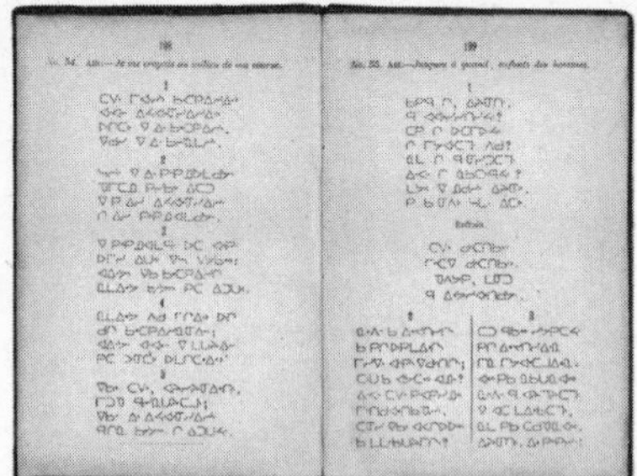

199 *No. 55.* Air: – *Jusques à quand, enfants des hommes.*
(Until when, children of mankind.)

1

Are you always wise
with your children?
Are you always busy
and joyful without fail?
Do you not understand
that you will die soon?
As soon as this person is born,
"You could die unexpectedly," I say to you.

Refrain.

It is frightful,
very dreadful,
that if we die in shame,
God will pass judgement on us.

2

For all time, there will
be rejoicing.
God will be King.
All over the earth,
all will fear Him.
Wherever they are today
they could indeed
fall soon
into the great pit.
And how will you fare
if you are in awe of God?

3

Everything that you love,

all your riches,
over which you are
rejoicing,
you will leave them all.
Even though you never
tire of them,
even if you cry about them,
you cannot carry them.
People, you are going to
remember this.

199 No. 55. AIR: – Jusques à quand, enfants des hommes.
No. 55. AIR: – Jusques à quand, enfants des hommes.

1

kakike ci, iyinitik,
kâkikê cî, iyinîtik,

ke awasisitisiyek?
kê-awâsisitisiyêk?

taki ci otamioyek
tahki cî otamihoyêk

ci miyowatamek piko?
cî miyowâtamêk piko?

nama ci ke ni sitotamek
nama cî nisitohtamêk

wipac ci nakataskeyek?
wîpac cî nakataskeyêk?

mayaw e nokosit iyiniw,
mayaw ê-nôkosit iyiniw,

ki ka nipin semak itaw.
kika-nipin sêmâk itâw.

Refrain.
tapwe kostatikwan
tâpwê kostâtikwan

mistae kostatikwan.
mistahi kostâtikwan.

nepiyaki, manito
nipiyâhki, manitow

ke wiyasowatikoyak.
kê-wiyasiwâtikoyahk.

2

naspic ka wiyotisicik
nâspic ka-wiyotisicik

ka kici okimawicik
ka-kihci-okimâwicik

misiwe askik ekosticik;
misiwê askihk ê-kostîcik;

tante ka ayatwaw anoc?
tânitê kâ-ayâtwaw anohc?

wipac tapwe ki pakisinwok
wîpac tâpwê kî-pâkisinwak

mistikowatikanesik.
mistikowâtikanêsik.

tanisi ekwa apaciowok
tânisi êkwa âpacihowak

ka mamaskateyimicik?
kâ-mâmaskâtêyimihcik?

3

tato kekway siyakitayek
tâhto kîkway sâkihtâyêk

kici wiyotisiwina
kihci-wîyotisiwina

mina miyawatamowina.
mîna miyawâtamowina.

ays kika nakatenawaw
ays kika-nakatênâwâw

naspic ke ayimeyitamok
nâspic kê-âyimêyihtamêk

e ata mawikatamek,
ê-âta-mawîhkâtamêk,

nama kika takonenawaw.
nama kika-takonênâwâw.

iyinitik, wikiskisik!
iyinîtik, wîkiskisik!

4

All your friends,
until your last breath,
God loves them all.
When they sit around
you in a circle,
God calls you
and He says to you
at one point they will cry,
even though all of you
will die.

5

Will you not forget
that you are mortal
people,
and that all will end in
a wooden box
on earth?
About the next life,
there are many false
gods,
that will make you
cry immediately
and will make you
long to see it,
when you turn to dust.

6

Come here and be
respectful,
especially you who
commit adultery.
look, please, into the box,
where you will stay.
Think about that.
It will help you out.
Many gain strength from
Those who are pure.

7

God will redeem you,
even though you ruin
yourselves.
In this way His creatures
are not abandoned.
Those that ask Him
for redemption
are going to please Him.
You will give it me if I
ask for it.

No. 56. AIR: – *Au fond des brûlants abîmes.*
(At the heart of the flaming abyss.)

I

You let us know it,
You who are rejected,
there in Hell
where you suffer.

Refrain.

You people,
do not imitate.
Do not enter here.

4

ki totemiwawok kakiyaw
kitôtêmiwâwak kahkiyaw

ati iskwatamoyeko,
ati iskwâtamoyêko,

tato kaki sakiikoyekwaw
tâhto ka-kî-sâkihikoyêkwâw

ke waskapistakoyekwaw.
ke wâskâpistâkoyêkwâw.

manito ni natomik ekwa
manitow ninâtomik êkwa

atiw atiw etayekwaw;
atiw atiw êtayêkwâw;

kita ati kici matowok
kita ati kihci-mâtowak

ata kika nipinawaw.
âta kika-nipinâwâw.

5

ekawiya we sakweyimok
êkâwîya wî-sâkwêyimok

ci petamek iyinitik,
kici-pêtamêk iyinîtik,

mistikowatikanik askik
mistikowâhtikanihk askîhk

tanisi kesi ayayek.
tânisi kê-isi-ayâyêk.

ekota miscet manicoksak
êkota mihcêt manicôksak

semak ke mawikoyekwaw:
sêmak kê-mawikoyêkwâw:

mina pikiskatitiyeko
mîna pikiskâtitiyêko

ki ka asiskiwinawaw.
kika-asiskîwinâwâw.

6

peitotek, kesteyimoyek
pe-itohtêk, kistêyimoyêk

wawac pesikwatisiyek,
wâwâc (ê-)pisikwâtisiyêk,

mate mistikowatikanik
mâhti mistikowâhtikanihk

itapik kesi ayayek.
itâpik kê-isi-ayâyêk.

eoko mitoneyitamok,
êwako mitonêyihtamok,

ki ka apacionawaw:
kika-âpacihonâwâw:

miscet kaskiowok oci
mihcêt kaskihowak ohci

kici miyo ayiwitwaw.
kihci-miyo-ayiwitwâw.

7

pemaciiweyan manito,
(ê-)pimâcihiwêyan manitow,

e ata kitimaatwaw
ê-âta-kitimahâtwâw

ekosi kitosicikanak
êkosi kitosîhcikanak

nama ki wi nakatawok.
namâ kiwî-nakatâwak.

tato ka natotaskik ota
tâhto kâ-natotaskik ôta

ki ka apisisimawok
ki-ka-apisisimâwak

e wi atameatwaw kikik.
ê-wî-atamêhatwâw kikik.

wi miyin ci natotatan.
wî-miyin kici-natotâtân.

No. 56. Air: – Au fond des brûlants abîmes.
No. 56. Air: – Au fond des brûlants abîmes.

1

wi kiskeyitamoinan,
wî-kiskêyihtamohinân,

wepinikowisiyek,
ê-wêpinikowisiyêk,

nete atamaskamikok
nêtê atamaskamikohk

ka kwatakeyitamek.
ka-kwâtakêyihtamêk.

Refrain.

iyinitik,
iyinîtik,

eka nanaspitawinan,
êkâ nanaspitawinân,

eka pitokek ota.
êkâ ê-pîhtokwêk ôta.

201

2

We are lonely here.

We are in the fire.
We pay greatly for
our bad deeds.

3

As soon as our
torment ends,
there will be rejoicing.
But it shall not cease,
the suffering here.

4

He makes us suffer
here in hell.
We will be angry all
the time.
We are pitiful.

5

Beyond all else it is
difficult
to have lost sight of God.
We will never see Him
over there in Heaven.

6

Even though we love Him,

and He created us,
we abandon Him,
and disobey Him all
the time.

7

At the moment
of our death,
He will either destroy us

or give us life.

No. 57. AIR: – *Digne objet de mes chants.*
(Worthy object of my songs.)

1

Although they are well,

all the people
here on earth, some

will not immediately
enter into Heaven,
where God is.

2

Those who do not have
a clean spirit
because of small sins
will not be completely
wiped clean.
Their way will be blocked.
He will forgive You
but first you must go to
purgatory.

2

ni kaskeyitenan ota
nikaskêyihtênân ôta

iskotek e ayayak;
iskotêhk ê-ayâyâhk;

mistae ni tipaenan
mistahi nitipahênân

ka ki maci totamak.
kâ-kî-maci-tôtamâhk.

3

wipac ki poni payiwa
wîpac kî-pôni-payiwa

miyawatamowina;
miyawâtamowina;

nama kita ponipayiw
nama kita-pônipayiw

kwatakitawin ota.
kwâtakîtawin ôta.

4

ni kwatakiikonan
nikwâtakihikonân

maci manito ota:
maci-manitow ôta:

taki e kisiwasiyak,
tahki ê-kisiwâsiyâhk,

ni kitimakisinan.
nikitimâkisinân.

5

mamawiyes ka ayimak
mamawiyês kâ-âyimak

manito e ki waniit,
manitow ê-kî-wanihît,

nama ni ka wapamanan
nama nika-wâpamânân

nete kici kisikok.
nêtê kihci-kîsikôhk.

6

ni wi sakianan ata,
niwî-sâkihânân âta,

e ki osiikoyak:
ê-kî-osîhikoyâhk:

maka e we pinikoyak
mâka ê-wêpinikoyâhk

taki ni pakwatanan.
tahki nipakwâtânân.

7

kita nikaneyitakwan
kita-nikânêyihtâkwan

poni pimatisiyak:
pôni-pimâtisiyâhk:

maka ketimaikoyak
mâka kêtimahikoyâhk

ni pimaciikonan.
nipimâcihikonân.

No. 57. AIR: – Digne objet de mes chants.
No. 57. AIR: – Digne objet de mes chants.

1

ata meyo ayiwik
âta miyo-ayiwik

tato ayisiyiniw
tâhto ayisiyiniw

ota askik ka nakatak
ôta askîhk kâ-nakatak

namawiya semak askaw
namâwîya sêmâk âskaw

pitokew kici kisikok
pîhtokwêw kihci-kîsikohk

manitowa ka ayayit.
manitowa kâ-ayâyit.

2

eka kenatacakwet,
êkâ kênatahcâhkwêt,

o pastaowinisa
opâstâhowinisa

iyawis eka kasinamot
iyawis êkâ kâsînamôt

eyapic ka kipiskakot
êyâpic ka-kipiskâkot

kasinamakewiskotek
kâsînamâkêw-iskotêhk

pita kita itotew.
pita kita-itohtêw.

202

3

ᐁᑯᑌ ᑭᑕ ᐊᔭᐤ
ᐃᐢᑯ ᐳᒋ ᐸᒥᔨᐦ
ᐅ ᑫᔨᓇᑌᔨ ᒧᐃᐧᐣ,
ᐁᑲ ᐁ ᑌᐱᐸᒥᔨᐦ
ᐅ ᒥᔕ ᑐᑕᒧᐃᐧᓇ
ᐅᑕ ᐊᐧᐢᑭᑕᐢᑲᒥᐠ.

4

ᐁᑯᑌ ᑲ ᐊᔭᒋᐠ
ᒉᐢᑯᐧ ᐊᐧᐢᑭᑕᐢᑲᒥᐠ
ᐊᔭᒥᐁᐢᑕᒪᐊᐧᐅᐧᐠ,
ᓇᐢᐱᐧ ᐁ ᓂᒋᐦᑲᒪᒋᐠ
ᑭᐸ ᑭᒋ ᑭᒋᑯᐠ
ᑭᒋ ᐃᐧ ᐱᑯᐅᑕᐤ.

5

ᓱᒉᐢ ᐅᒋ ᒥᐢᑕᐁ
ᑲ ᐊᐸᒋᐃᒋᐠ,
ᐁᑯᑕ ᐅᒋ ᐅᐢᓭ ᒪᓇ
ᑲ ᒥᓯᓂᒋᐦᑲᒪᑕᐤ.
ᐊᔭᒥᐁᐢᑕᒪᐃᐧᑯᐠ
ᑲ ᑭᒋᐊᐧᑎᒋᓴᐠ.

6

ᒪᐢᑯᐧ ᐊᐳ ᐁᑯᑌ
ᒉᑲᐧ ᐃᑕᒋ ᐊᔭᐤ
ᐯᔭᐠ ᑭᑐᑌᒥᐊᐧᐤ
ᐁ ᑭᒋ ᑲᒋᓇᒪᒋ;
ᑭ ᐸᑯᓭᔨᒥᑯᐊᐧᐤ
ᑭᒋ ᐊᐸᒋᐊᓴᐠ.

No. 58. Air: — *L'encens divin.*

1

ᑲ ᐃᐧᑭᓴᐠ ᑎᑌ ᑭᒋ ᑭᒋᑯᐠ,
ᒪᑌ ᐃᐧ ᑭᐢᑭᓄᐊᒪᐃᐧᓇᐣ
ᐊᓄ ᐁᑲᐧ ᑭᐢᑫᔨᑕᒧᐃᓇᐣ,
ᑲ ᐃᓯᓴᐠ ᑲ ᒥᔪᐊᐧᓯᐠ ᐊᐢᑭᐠ.

Refrain.

ᐊᐦ, ᐊᐦ, ᐃᔨᓂᑎᐠ,
ᒥᔪ ᐊᐢᑭᐦ ᐃᐧ ᑲᑫᐧ ᐅᑎᑕᒧᐠ
ᐊᐦ, ᐊᐦ, ᐃᔨᓂᑎᐠ,
ᐅᑕ ᐱᑯ ᐱᒪᑎᓯᓇᓂᐤ,
ᐅᒪ ᐊᐢᑭᐦ, ᐃᔨᓂᑎᐠ, ᐃᐧ ᑭᐢᑭᓯᐠ.

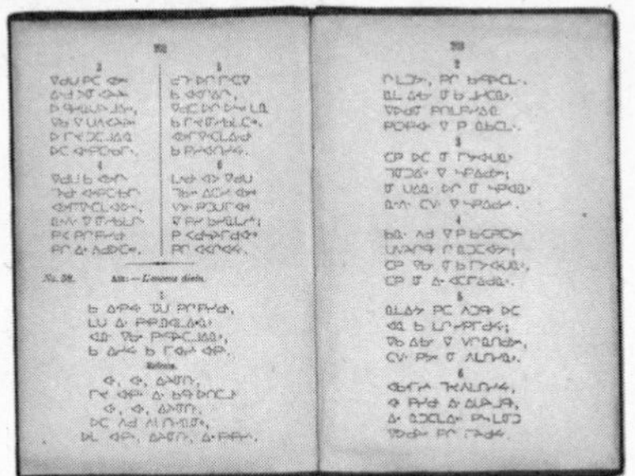

202

3

There you will be
as long as the world lasts.

His deep regretfulness
will not be enough
to make up for your sins
here on earth.

4

The ones who are
in purgatory,
instead of here on earth,
pray for them.
Forever help them
to gain Heaven quickly
so that they are saved.

5

At the High Mass
the One who is called
upon.
This is the source
of good help,
to pray for them,
those of you who are
compassionate.

6

Maybe

He is there
One of your friends.
He is completely Himself,
and hopes for you
to call on Him.

No. 58. Air: – *L'encens divin. (Holy incense.)*

1

You who live above in Heaven,
please come! Teach us
today and we will have spiritual knowledge.
You told us that the earth is good.

Refrain.

O people,
try to arrive at the good land.
O people,
only here there is life.
This land, people, remember it.

3

ekote kita ayaw
êkotê kita-ayâw

isko poni payiyik
isko pôni-payiyik

o kesinateyimowin,
okîsinâtêyimowin,

eka e tepipayiyik
êkâ ê-têpipayiyik

o miyo-totamowina
omiyo-tôtamowina

ota waskitaskamik.
ôta waskitaskamik.

4

ekote ka ayacik
êkotê kâ-ayâcik

meskoc waskitaskamik
mêskoc waskitaskamik

ayamiestamawawok,
ayamihêstamawâwak,

naspic e nisokamacik
nâspic ê-nîsôhkamâcik

kipa kici kisikok
kîpa kihci-kîsikohk

kici wi pikootwaw.
kici-wî-pikohotwâw.

5

lames oci mistae
Lames ohci mistahi

ka apaciicik,
kâ-âpacihicik,

ekota oci osam mana
êkota ohci osâm mâna

ka miyo nisokamatwaw.
ka-miyo-nîsôhkamawâw.

ayamiestamawikok
ayamihêstamawihkok

ka kisiwatisiyek.
kâ-kisêwâtisiyêk.

6

maskoc apo ekote
mâskôc ahpô êkotê

mekwac itasi ayaw
mêkwâc itasi ayâw

peyak kitotemiwaw
pêyak kitôtêmiwâw

e kisi kasinamasot;
ê-kîsi-kâsînamâsot;

ki pakoseyimikowaw
ki-pakosêyimikowâw

kici apaciayek.
kici-âpacihâyek.

No. 58. AIR: – L'encens divin.
No. 58. AIR: – L'encens divin.

1

ka wikiyek nete kici kisikok,
kâ-wîkiyêk nêtê kihci-kîsikohk,

mate wi kiskinoamawinan
mahti wî-kiskinohamâwinân

anoc ekwa kiskeyitamoinan,
anohc êkwa kiskêyihtamohinân,

ka isiyek ka miwasik askik.
kâ-isiyêk kâ-miywâsik askîhk.

Refrain.

ay, ay, iyinitik,
ay, ay, iyinîtik,

miyo askiy wi kakwe otitamok
miyo askiy wî-kâkwê-otîtamok

ay, ay, iyinitik,
ay, ay, iyinîtik,

ota piko pimatisinaniw,
ôta piko pimâtisinâniw,

oma askiy, iyinitik, wi kiskisik.
ôma askiy, iyinîtik, wî-kiskisik.

203

2

ᒋ ᒪᑐᔭᐠ, ᑭᒋ ᑲᐢᑫᔮᑕᒪᐠ,
ᓇᒪ ᐃᐧᑳ ᓂ ᑲ ᒧᔨᑕᓇᐤ.
ᐁᐅᑯᓂ ᑭᑎᒪᑭᓯᐃᐧᓇ
ᑭᑕᐢᑭᐊᐧ ᐁ ᑭ ᓇᑲᑕᒪᐠ.

3

ᑕᑭ ᐅᑕ ᓂ ᒥᔮᐊᐧᑌᓇᐤ
ᒣᓂᑐᐃᐧ ᐁ ᓴᑭᐃᐦᑯᔮᐠ;
ᓂ ᑌᐃᓇᐠ ᐅᒋ ᓂ ᓴᑭᐊᓇᐤ
ᓇᐢᐱᐨ ᑕᐯᐧ ᐁ ᓴᑭᐃᐦᑯᔨᐠ.

4

ᑳᓇᐠ ᐱᑯ ᐁ ᑭ ᑳᐧᑕᑭᑕᔮᐠ
ᑌᐯᔮᐦᒋᑫᐧ ᒋ ᓇᑐᑕᐋᐧᔮᐠ;
ᑕᑭ ᐁᑳᐧ ᓂ ᑲ ᒥᔮᐊᐧᑌᓇᐤ,
ᑕᑭ ᓂ ᐃᐧ ᐊᑕᒥᐃᑯᓇᐤ.

5

ᓇᒪᐃᐧᔮ ᑭᑕ ᐱᑐᑫᐤ ᐅᑕ
ᐊᓇ ᑲ ᒪᒋᔨᑭᒥᑯᓴᐠ;
ᐁᑳ ᐃᐧᑳ ᐁ ᐯᒋᓇᑎᑯᔮᐠ,
ᑕᐯᐧ ᑭᔮᐨ ᓂ ᐱᒪᑎᓯᓇᐤ.

6

ᐊᑳᐧᒥᓯᐠ ᒣᔪ ᐱᒪᑎᓯᓴᐠ,
ᐋ ᑭᓯᒍ ᐃᐧ ᐃᑌᔨᒧᑫᐠ,
ᐃᐧ ᓇᑐᑕᒪᐃᐧ ᑭᓴᒪᓂᑐ
ᐁᐅᑯᔨᐤ ᑭᒋ ᒥᔨᑯᓴᐠ.

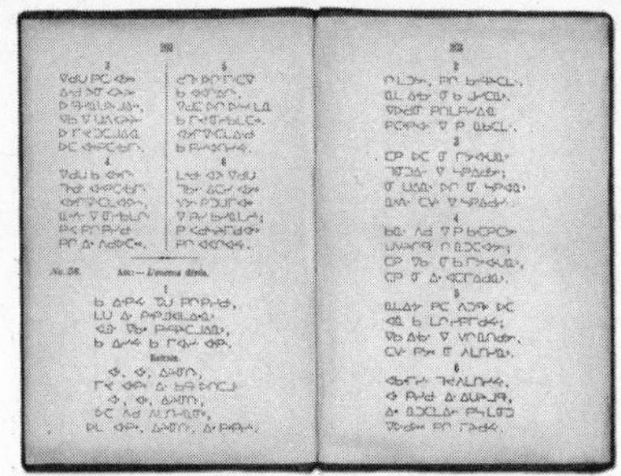

203

2

Because of the way we cry and are
  deeply lonely,
We will never feel God's presence.
We are the ones in poverty.
We left the earth.

3

We rejoice always here.
The One who is God loves us.
From our hearts, we love Him.
Forever, He loves us.

4

Only for a short time did we will suffer.
In order to listen to the Creator
and to rejoice forever,
He pleases us continuously.

5

No one can enter here.
The one who gives us evil commands,
He will never approach us.
Therefore, we live.

6

Be strong, all you, live well.
Be determined to reach Heaven.
Ask God
so that He will give you this.

2

ci matoyak, kici kaskeyitamak,
kici-mâtoyâhk, kici-kaskêyihtamâhk,

nama wikac ni ka mositanan.
nama wîhkâc nika-môsîhtânân.

eokoni kitimakisiwina
êwakoni kitimâkisiwina

kitaskiwak e ki nakatamak.
kitaskîwâk ê-kî-nakatâmahk.

3

taki ota ni miyawatenan
tahki ôta nimiyawâtênân

menitowit e sakiikoyak;
manitowit ê-sâkihikoyâhk;

ni teinak oci ni sakianan
nitêhinahk ohci nisâkihânân

naspic tapwe e sakiikosit.
nâspic tâpwê ê-sâkihikosit.

4

kanak piko e ki kwatakitayak
kanak piko ê-kî-kwâtakihtâyâhk

tepeyiciket ci natotawayak;
(ê-)tipêyihcikêt kici-natotawayâhk;

taki ekwa ni ka miyawatenan,
tahki êkwa nika-miyawâtênân,

taki ni wi atamiikonan.
tahki niwî-atamihikonân.

5

namawiya kita pitokew ota
namâwîya kita-pîhtokwêw ôta

ana ka maci sikimikoyek;
ana kâ-maci-sîhkimikoyêk;

eka wikac e pecinatikoyak,
êkâ wîhkâc ê-pêcinâtikoyâhk,

tapwe kiyam ni pimatisinan.
tâpwê kiyâm nipimâtisinân.

6

akwamisik meyo pimatisiyek,
akwâmisik miyo-pimâtisiyêk,

ay kisikok wi iteyimokek,
ay kîsikôhk wî-itêyimokêk,

wi natotamawik kise manito
wî-natotamawîk kisê-manitow

eokoyiw kici miyikoyek.
êwakoyiw kici-miyikoyêk.

204

No. 59. Air: — *Vole au plus tôt.*

1

ᑏᑕᑌᑯᐨ, ᑭᓯᑯᐧ ᐃᑌᐳᒧ,
ᐁᑯᑌ ᓴᓯᐢ ᑭ ᐣᑕᐁᐧᔨᒥᐠ;
ᑫᓯ ᐊᑕᒥᐊᐧ ᓯᐹᑭᐃᑯᐧ,
ᐁ ᐃᐧ ᐃᓯ ᐊᑕᒥᐃᐢᐠ ᑏᐢᑕ. (*bis.*)

CHŒUR

ᑭᑎᒪᑭᑕᐃᐧᓇᐣ,
ᑏ ᒪᑏᑐᐨ ᓴᓯᐢ;
ᑭ ᒪᐃᐧᒍᐢᑕᑎᓇᐣ
ᐃᐢᐱ- ᐅᑌᐃᔭᐠ.

SOLO

ᐅᓴᐨ ᒥᐊᐧᓯᐣ ᑭᑌ
ᑭᑕᐊᐧᓯᒥᓴᐠ.
ᑭᒋ ᐊᑗᐧᑕᐊᐧᑕᐤ
ᒣᐃᐧᒍᐢᑕᐢᑲᐧᐃᐧ.

2

ᓇᒪ ᑫᑲᐧ ᑭᒋ ᐊᐢᑕᐃᑯᔭᐣ,
ᑏᑕᑌᑯᐨ, ᑭ ᑲᐢᑭᐅᔭᑏ;
ᑭᔭᐨ ᐃᐧ ᑭᑎᒪᐃᑲᐃᐧᔭᑏ,
ᓇᒪᐃᐧᔭ ᑭᑕ ᑭ ᐃᐢᐸᔨᐤ. (*bis.*)

3

ᐁᑲᐃᐧᔭ ᐃᑕᓯ ᓴᑫᐧᔨᒨ
ᐁ ᐊᔨᒫᐠ ᐅᑕ ᑭ ᐊᐧᐸᑌᐣ;
ᑕᑭ ᐁ ᓴᑲᒧᑲᐢᑫᔨᑕᒪᐣ,
ᑐᑌ ᐱᑯ ᑭᔭᐨ ᑮ ᑲ ᐊᔭᐣ. (*bis.*)

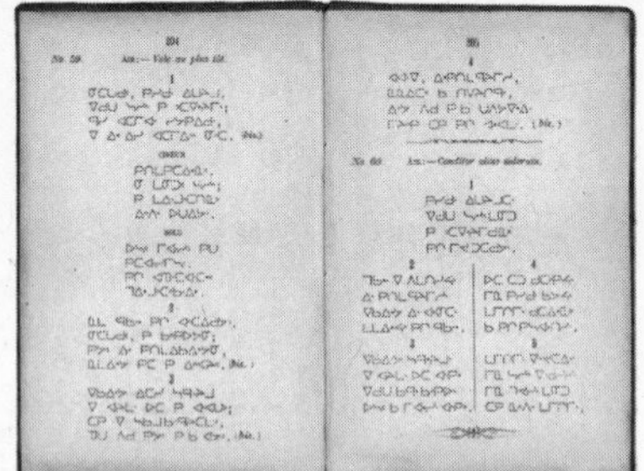

204 No. 59. Air: – *Vole au plus tôt. (Fly most quickly.)*

1

My spirit thinks of Heaven.
Over there Jesus wants you.
To please those who love Him,
in this way, He is going to please me too. (*twice.*)

CHŒUR

Have pity on us.
My God, Jesus,
We pray to You,
especially from our heart.

SOLO

Although Your heart is good,
your children
are terrible disbelievers,
if they speak without sincerity.

2

Nothing will terribly frighten us.
My spirit will protect me.
It matters not if I am oppressed by enemies.
Nothing will happen. (*twice.*)

3

Do not waste your time hesitating.
You saw that it was hard here.
You were always lonely.
Only over there will you be relieved. (*twice.*)

204 No. 59. Air: – Vole au plus tôt.
No. 59. Air: – Vole au plus tôt.

1

nitacakom, kisikok iteyimo,
nitahcâhkom, kîsikohk itêyimo,

ekote sesos ki ntaweyimik;
êkotê Sesos kinitawêyimik;

kesi atamiat siyakiikot,
kêsi atamihât siyakihikot,

e wi isi atamiisk nista. (*bis.*)
ê-wî-isi-atamihisk nîsta. (bis.)

CHŒUR

kitimakitawinan,
kitimâkihtawinân,

ni manitom sesos;
nimanitôm Sesos;

ki mawimostatinan
kimawimostâtinân

ispic oteiyak.
ispic otêhiyâhk.

SOLO

osam miwasin kite
osâm miywâsin kitêh

kitawasimisak.
kitawâsimisak.

kici anwetawatwaw
kici-ânwêhtawâtwâw

mewimostaskwawi.
mawimôstaskwâwi.

2

nama kekway kici astaikoyan,
nama kîkway kici-astahikoyan,

ni tacakom, ki kaskioyani;
nitahcâhkom, kî-kaskihoyâni;

kiyam wi kitimaikawiyani,
kiyâm wî-kitimâhikawiyâni,

namawiya kita ki ispayiw. (*bis.*)
namâwîya kita-kî-ispayiw. (bis.)

3

ekawiya itasi sakweyimo
êkâwîya itasi sakwêyimo

e ayimak ota ki wapaten;
ê-ayimak ôta kî-wâpahtên;

taki e sakamokaskeyitaman,
tahki ê-sakamow-kaskêyihtaman,

nete piko kiyam ki ka ayan. (*bis.*)
nêtê piko kiyâm kika-ayân. (bis.)

205

4

ᐊᐊᐧᐁ, ᐃᐧᑭᑎᒪᑫᔨᒥᓱ,
ᓇᓇᐃᑕᐤ ᑲ ᑎᐯᔨᒋᑫᐠ,
ᐃᐧᔭ ᐱᑯ ᑭ ᑲ ᑌᐱᔭᐁᐧᐃᐧ
ᒥᔨᐢᑭ ᑕᑭ ᑭᒋ ᐋᐧᐸᒪᐟ. (*bis.*)

No. 60. Air: —*Conditor alme siderum.*

1

ᑭᓯᑯᐠ ᐃᑌᔨᒍᑕᐠ
ᐁᑯᑌ ᓭᓱᐢ ᒪᓂᑐ
ᑭ ᐣᑕᐁᐧᔨᒥᑯᓇᐤ
ᑭᒋ ᒥᓭᑐᑕᑯᔭᐠ.

2

ᒉᑲᐧ ᐁ ᐱᒪᑎᓯᔦᐠ
ᐃᐧ ᑭᑎᒪᑫᔨᒥᓱᐠ
ᐁᑲᐃᐧᔭ ᐃᐧ ᐊᐧᓂᑕᐠ
ᒪᒪᐃᐧᔦᐢ ᑭᒋ ᑫᑲᐧᐦ.

3

ᐁᑲᐃᐧᔭ ᓴᑫᐧᔨᒧᐠ
ᐁ ᐊᔨᒪᐠ ᐅᑕ ᐊᐢᑭᐦ
ᐁᑯᑌ ᑲᑫᐧ ᑲᐢᑭᐅᐠ
ᐅᓴᐨ ᑲ ᒥᐊᐧᓯᐠ ᐊᐢᑭᐦ.

4

ᐅᑕ ᑕᑐ ᑯᑕᐢᑭᔦᐠ
ᒥᓇ ᑭᓯᑯᐠ ᑲᔭᔦᐠ
ᒪᒥᒋᒥᐠ ᑯᑕᐃᐧᓇᐤ
ᑲ ᑭᒋ ᑭᓴᐋᐧᑎᓯᐟ.

5

ᒪᒥᒋᒥᐠ ᐁᐧᔦᑕᐃᐧᐟ
ᒥᓇ ᓴᓱᐢ ᐁᐧᑯᓯᓯᐟ
ᒥᓇ ᒉᔦᓯᐟ ᒪᓂᑐ
ᑕᑭ ᓇᐢᐱᐟ ᒪᒥᒋᒥᐠ,

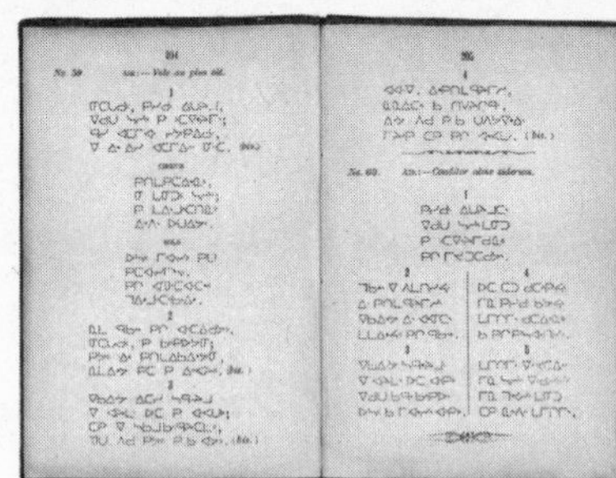

205

4

Now then, have pity on yourself.
Obey him, The One who is Lord.
He is the only One who can obtain salvation for you.
He will give it to you so that you will see Him forever.
(*twice.*)

No. 60. Air: – *Conditor alme siderum.*
(Founder of the lovely stars.)

1

Long for Heaven,
where our Lord, Jesus,
He wants to
be gracious to us.

2

Now as you live,
you are going to be blessed.
Do not renounce
all that is good.

3

Do not fear.
It is difficult here on earth.
Try to earn your salvation.
Know that the earth is good.

4

Many of you who take shelter on earth
and you in Heaven,
praise Him our Father,
the One who is merciful.

5

Praise Him, He is the Father
and Jesus the Son
and the Holy Spirit.
Praise Him forever.

4
awae, wikitimakeyimiso,
awiyak, wî-kitimâkêyimiso,

nanaitaw ka tipeyiciket,
nanahihtaw kâ-tipêyihcikêt,

wiya piko ki ka tepiyaweik
wiya piko ki-ka-têpiyawêhik

miyiski taki kici wapamat. (*bis.*)
miyiski tahki kici-wâpamat. (bis.)

3
ekawiya sakweyimok
êkâwîya sakwêyimok

e ayimak ota askiy
ê-âyimak ôta askiy

ekote kakwe kaskiok
êkotê kakwê-kaskihok

osam ka miwasik askiy.
ôsam kâ-miywâsik askiy.

5
mamicimik weyotawit
mamihcimihk wiyôhtâwit

mina sesos wekosisit
mîna Sesos wikosisit

mina meyosit manito
mîna (ê-)miyosit manitow

taki naspic mamicimik.
tahki nâspic mamihcimihk.

No. 60. Air: – Conditor alme siderum.
No. 60. Air: – Conditor alme siderum.

1
kisikok iteyimotak
kîsikohk itêyimotâhk

ekote sesos manito
êkotê Sesos manitow

ki nitaweyimikonaw
kinitawêyimikonaw

kici miyo totakoyak.
kici-miyo-tôtakoyâhk.

2
mekwac e pimatisiyek
mêkwâc ê-pimâtisiyêk

wi kitimakeyimisok
wî-kitimâkêyimisok

ekawiya wi wanitak
êkâwîya wî-wanîtâhk

mamawiyes kici kekway
mamawiyês kihci kîkway

4
ota tato kotaskiyek
ôta tahto kôtaskiyêk

mina kisikok kayayek
mîna kîsikohk kâyâyêk

mamicimik kotawinaw
mamihcimihk kôhtâwînaw

ka kici kisewatisit.
kâ-kihci-kisêwâtisit.

206

No. 61. Air:—*Je mets ma confiance.*

206 *No. 61.* Air: – *Je mets ma confiance.*
(I place my confidence.)

1

When earthly things
cease,
still, once again,
He shall come;
Jesus, the Lord,
to pass judgment on all.
It is His turn now
to judge all of them,
the people.

2

It is not known
which one
will see this,
when the earth ends.
Only God,
He knows
the way He plans it,
how it will happen.

3

All the people

will come back to life
when earthly things
cease;
so that He will judge
all people.
He will see all and it will
be frightful forever;
God is the One
who knows.

4

Do not run away from
Him
this day,
did God not
lose him.
Only then he will be afraid
if he sees this.
He makes them see this,
their deeds.

5

Today you rejoice.
But wait, you will cry.
You will be confused,
when you too die.
If you are a good person,
you should rejoice
forever in Heaven,
so that you will be in a
good place.

6

When our Lord stops
placing
judgement,
He will invite them,

to His home:

"Depart! All of you
with the evil spirit."
In this way He speaks to
the ones who are evil.

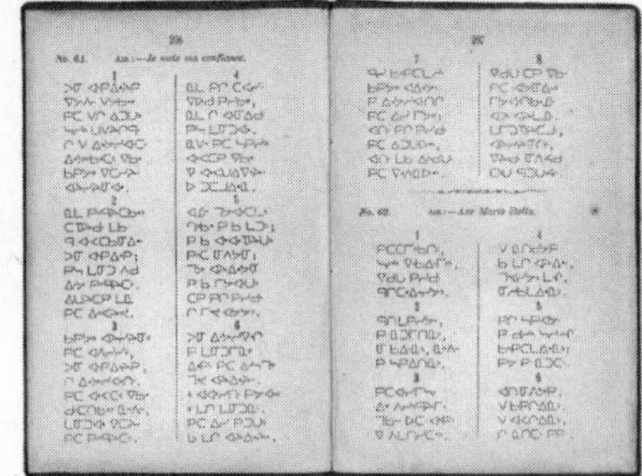

206 No. 61. Air: – Je mets ma confiance.
No. 61. Air: – Je mets ma confiance.

1

poni askiwiyiki
pôni-askiwiyiki

eyapic peyakwaw
êyâpic pêyakwâw

kita peci itotew
kîta-pêci-itohtêw

sesos tepeyiciket
Sesos (ê-)tipêyihcikêt

ci pe wiyasowatat
kici-pê-wiyasiwâtât

wiyaskwatam ekwa
wiyaskwatam êkwa

kakiyaw etasiyit
kahkiyaw (ê-)itâsiyit

ayisiyiniwa.
ayisiyiniwa.

2

nama kiskeyitakwan
nama kiskêyihtâkwan

taneyikok maka
tânêyikohk mâka

ke wapatakaniwik
kê-wâpahtakaniwik

poni askiwiki;
pôni-askiwiki;

kise manito piko
kisê-manitow piko

wiya kiskeyitam.
wîya kiskêyihtam.

iteyitaki mana
itêyihtâhki mâna

kita ispayiyo.
kita-ispayiyo.

4

nama kici tapasit
nama kihci-tapasît

eoko kisikaw,
êwako kîsikâw,

nama ci waniikot
nama kici-wanihikot

kise manitowa.
kisê-manitowa.

napec kita sekisiw
napêc kita-sêkisiw

wapataki ekwa
wâpahtahki êkwa

e wapateiweyit
ê-wâpahtêhiwêyit

o totamowina.
otôtamowina.

5

anoc meyawataman
anohc (ê-)miyawâtamân

ceskwa ki ka maton;
cêskwa kika-mâton;

ki ka wawaneyiten
kika-wawanêyihtên

kista nipiyani:
kîsta nipiyani:

meyo ayiwiyani
miyo-ayiwiyani

ki ka miyawaten
kika-miyawâtên

taki kici kisikok
tahki kihci-kîsikohk

ci miyo ayayan.
kici-miyo-ayâyan.

3

kakiyaw ayisiyiniw
kahkiyaw ayisiyiniw

kita apisisin,
kita-âpisisin,

poni askiwiyiki,
pôni-asikiwiyiki,

ci wiyasowatik.
kici-wiyasiwâtik.

kita wapatam ekwa
kita-wâpahtam êkwa

kostatikwan naspic,
kostâtikwan nâspic,

manitowa etayit
manitowa êtâyit

kita kiskeyitam.
kita kiskêyihtam.

6

poni wiyasoweci
pôni-wiyasiwêci

ki manitominaw
kimanitâminaw

wikik kita wisamew
wîkihk kita-wîsâmêw

meyo ayiwiyit.
(ê-)miyo-ayiwiyit.

« awasitik kiyawaw
"awasitik kîyawâw

maci manitonak. »
maci-manitônâhk"

kita isi kitotew
kita-isi-kitotêw

ka maci ayiwiyit.
kâ-maci-ayiwiyit.

207

7

ᑫᓱ ᑳᐢᑭᑕᒪᓱᐟ
ᑳᑭᔭᐤ ᐊᐃᐧᔭᐠ
ᑭ ᐃᐧᔭᓱᐊᐧᑎᒋ
ᑭᑕ ᐃᓱ ᒥᔭᐤ:
ᐊᑎᐟ ᑭᒋ ᑭᓯᒁᐟ
ᑭᑕ ᐃᑐᑌᐅᐦ,
ᐊᑎᐟ ᒪᑲ ᐃᐢᑯᑌᐠ
ᑭᑕ ᐁᐧᐱᓇᐅᐦ.

8

ᐁᑯᑌ ᑕᑭ ᐁᑲᐧ
ᑭᑕ ᐊᔭᒋᐃᐧᐤ
ᒥᔭᐊᐧᑎᑲᐧᓇᐠ
ᐊᐳ ᐊᐲᒪᓇᐠ.
ᒪᒥᑐᓀᐲᑕᒧᐠ,
ᐊᐲᓯᐹᒋᑎᐠ,
ᐁᐹᒁᐟ ᒋᐱᐦᑯ
ᑕᐣᑌ ᑫᑐᑌᐦᐠ.

No. 62. Air:—*Ave Maris Stella.*

1

ᑭᑕᑕᒥᐢᑳᑎᐣ,
ᓴᓯᐢ ᐁᐧᑳᐃᐧᒥᐦ,
ᐁᑯᑏ ᑭᓯᒁᐟ
ᑫᒋᑕᐧᐃᐧᓯᔭᐣ.

2

ᑫᑎᒫᑭᓯᔭᐠ,
ᑭ ᓇᑐᒥᑎᓇᐣ,
ᒋ ᑳᐃᐧᓇᐣ, ᓇᐢᐱ-
ᑭ ᓵᑭᐃᑎᓇᐣ.

3

ᑭᑕᐊᐧᓯᒥᓴᐠ
ᐃᐧ ᐱᓯᐢᑫᔨᒥᐠ
ᒣᑳᐧ- ᐅᑕ ᐊᐢᑭᐠ
ᐁ ᐱᒪᑎᓯᑕᐧᐤ.

4

ᐯ ᓇᑎᑰᔭᑭ
ᑲ ᒪᒋ ᐊᔨᐃᐧᐟ,
ᒣᔦᓯᔭᐣ ᒪᕆ,
ᒋᓯᑲᒪᐃᐧᓇᐣ.

5

ᑭᒋ ᓴᑭᐊᔭᐠ
ᑭ ᑯᓯᐢ ᓴᓯᐢᐦᑭ
ᑳᐢᑭᑕᒪᐃᐧᓇᐣ:
ᑭᔭ ᑭ ᓇᑐᑕᐠ.

6

ᐊᑎᒋᐱᔭᑭ,
ᐯ ᑳᑭᒋᐃᓇᐣ,
ᐯ ᐊᐸᒋᐃᓇᐣ,
ᒋ ᓇᑎᑕᐠ ᑭᑭᐠ.

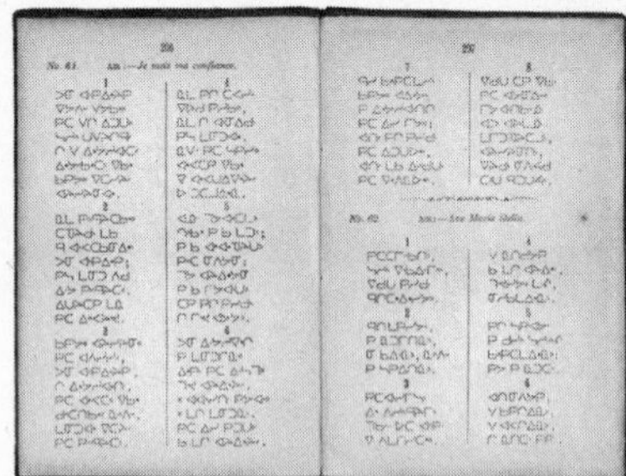

207

7

In this way He judges
all people.
When He judges you,
a decision will be made.
Some to Heaven
will go.
Some will go to hell.
They will be cast down.

8

Up above all the time
the people
will rejoice.
Even if it is hard,
meditate on this.
People,
when you die,
Where will you go?

No. 62. Air: – *Ave Maris Stella. (Hail, Star of the Sea.)*

1

I thank you.
You are the Mother of
Jesus.
in Heaven,
you are exalted.

2

When we are pitiful,
we call on you.
Our Mother, forever,
we will love you.

3

Your children
You pay attention to them
right now, here on earth,
as we are living.

4

When he approaches us,
the one who is evil,

Mary, you who are good,
Help us with this
temptation.

5

So that we love Him,
your Son, Jesus Christ.
Obtain this grace for us,
We beg you.

6

When we die,
come and comfort us.
Come and let us serve you
at your home.

7

kesi kaskitamasok
kêsi kaskitamâsok

kakiyaw awiyak
kahkiyaw awiyak

ki wiyasowatici
ki-wiyasiwâtici

kita isi miyaw:
kita-isi-miyâw:

atit kici kisikok
atiht kihci-kîsikohk

kita itotewok,
kita-itohtêwak,

atit maka iskotek
âtiht mâka iskotêhk

kita wepinawok.
kita-wêpinâwak.

8

ekote taki ekwa
êkotê tahki êkwa

kita ayaniwiw
kita-ayâniwiw

miyawatikwanok
miyawâtikwanohk

apo ayimanok.
ahpô âyimanohk.

mamitoneyitamok,
mâmitoneyihtamok,

ayisiyinitik,
ayisiyinitik,

eyikok nipiyeko
iyikohk nipiyêko

tante ketoteyek?
tânitê kî-itohtêyêk?

No. 62. Air: – Ave Maris Stella.
No. 62. Air: – Ave Maris Stella.

1

kitatamiskatin,
kitatamiskâtin,

sesos wekawimisk,
Sesos wêkâwîmisk,

ekote kisikok
êkotê kîsikohk

kecitwawisiyan.
(ê-)kihcitwâwisiyan.

2

ketimakisiyak,
(ê-)kitimâkisiyâhk,

ki natomitinan,
kinatomitinân,

ni kawinan, naspic
nikâwînân, nâspic

ki sakiitinan.
kisâkihitinân.

3

kitawasimisak
kitawâsimisak

wi pisiskeyimik
wî-pisiskêyimik

mekwac ota askik
mêkwâc ôta askîhk

e pimatisitwaw.
ê-pimâtisitwâw.

4

pe natikoyaki
pê-nâtikoyahki

ka maci ayiwit,
kâ-maci-ayiwit,

meyosiyan mari,
(ê-)miyosiyan Mari,

nisokamawinan.
nîsôhkamâwinân.

5

kici sakiayak
kici-sâkihâyahk

ki kosis sesoskri
kikosis Sesoskri

kaskitamawinan:
kaskîtamâwinân:

kiya ki natotak.
kiya kinatotâhk.

6

ati nipiyaki,
ati nîpiyâhki,

pe kakiciinan,
pê-kakihcihinân,

pe apaciinan,
pê-âpacihinân,

ci natitak kikik.
kici-nâtitâhk kîkik.

208

No. 63. Air: — *J'entends une voix attendrie.*

1

ᐅᑊᓓᑦ ᑕᕓ ᑭᓭᐚᑎᓯᐤ
ᑳ ᑳᓇᑕᑌᑫᐧ ᒪᕆ
ᑭ ᐃᐧ ᐅᑕᐚᓯᒥᒥᑎᐣ,
ᓂ ᑌᐃᐠ ᑭᒧ- ᐁ ᐃᓯᐟ.

Refrain.

ᑳᓇ- ᒪᕆᔦ,
ᓂᑕᑕᒥᓇᐣ,
ᐁ ᐅᑕᐚᓯᒥᒥᔦᐣ
ᑭ ᓴᑭᐃᑎᐣ,
ᑭ ᓇᐃᑕᑎᐣ
ᐃᐢᑯ ᐱᒪᑐᓯᔦᓂ.

2

ᑳ ᐃᓯ ᐃᐢᐱᑌᔨᒥᑕᐣ
ᐃᐢᐱᑌᔨᒥᑳᐣ ᑭᐢᑕ,
ᐣᑕᐚᓯᒥᐢ ᑭᑌᔨᒥᑎᐣ
ᓂᑳᐃᐧ ᐃᑌᔨᒥᑳᐣ.

3

ᑫᑕᑕᐍ ᐃᐧᓯᑭᒥᐢᑭ
ᐊᓇ ᑳ ᒪᒋ ᐊᔨᐃᐧ,
ᑭᑕ ᐃᐧ ᐯᓂ ᓴᑭᐃᔦᐣ
ᓂ ᑎᐯᔨᒥᐠ, ᐃᑕᑳᐣ.

4

ᐃᐧ ᐯᓂ ᐱᒪᑎᓯᔦᓂ
ᐁᑳᐃᐧᔦ ᑯᐢᑕᒧᑳᐣ
ᐁᑳ ᑭᑕ ᐸᑭᑎᐃᑕᐣ,
ᐁ ᑭᑎᒪᑫᔨᒥᑕᐣ.

5

ᑏᑌ ᑭᓯᑰ ᐊᔦᔦᓂ
ᓂᔦ ᐁ ᐃᑐᑕᐃᑕᐣ;
ᑭ ᑳ ᒫᒫ..ᑕᑯᓯᐣ ᑕᕓ
ᐁ ᑭ ᐅᑳᐃᐧᒪᐠ ᒪᕆ.

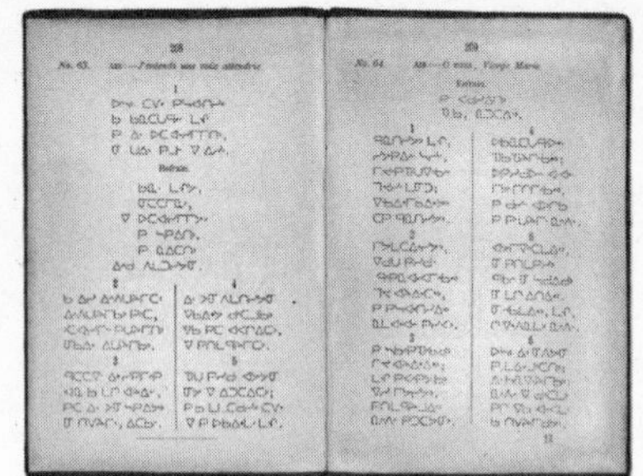

208 *No. 63.* Air: – *J'entends une voix attendrie.*
(I hear a compassionate voice.)

1

She is truly merciful,
Mary, the one whose soul is pure.
I am your child.
Guard my heart secretly.

Refrain.

For a short while, Mary.
We are grateful to you.
I am your child.
I will love you.
I will obey you
as long as I shall live.

2

In this way I consider you.
You too consider me.
Think of me as your little child.
I think of you as my Mother.

3

In the future,

if the one who is evil
governs me, then
You will stop loving me.

4

When you are going to die,

do not be afraid.
She will not leave you.

She will have mercy on you.

5

When you are there in Heaven.
I take you there.
You will be truly amazing
for Mary was your mother.

208 No. 63. AIR: – J'entends une voix attendrie.
No. 63. AIR: – J'entends une voix attendrie.

1

osam tapwe kisewatisiw
osâm tâpwê kisêwâtisiw

ka kanatacakwet mari
kâ-kanâtahcâhkwêt Mari

ki wi otawasimimitin,
kiwî-otawâsimimitin,

ni teik kimoc e isit.
nitêhik kîmôc ê-isit.

Refrain.

kanac mariya,
kanac Mariya,

nitataminan,
nitatamînân,

e otawasimimiyan
ê-otawâsimimiyan

ki sakiitin,
kisâkihitin,

ki naitatin
kinahihtâtin

isko pimatosiyani.
isko pimâtosiyâni.

2

ka isi ispiteyimitan
ka-isi-ispîhtêyimitân

ispiteyimikan kista,
ispîhtêyimihkan kîsta,

ntawasimis kiteyimitin
nitawâsimis kitêyimitin

nikawi iteyimikan.
nikâwiy itêyimihkan.

4

wi poni pimatisiyani
wî-pôni-pimâtisiyani

ekawiya kostamokan
êkâwîya kostamohkan

eka kita apaciitan,
êkâ kita-âpacihitân,

e kitimakeyimitan.
ê-kitimâkêyimitân.

3

ketatawe wi sikimiski
kêtahtawê wî-sîhkimiski

ana ka maci ayiwit,
ana kâ-maci-ayiwit,

kita wi poni sakiiyan
kita-wî-pôni sâkihiyan

ni tipeyimik, itakan.
nitipêyimik, itâhkan.

5

nete kisikok ayayani
nêtê kîsikôhk ayâyani

niya e itotaitan;
niya ê-itohtahitân;

ki ka mamatakosin tapwe
kika-mamâhtâkosin tâpwê

e ki okawimat mari.
ê-kî-okawîmat Mari.

209

No. 64. Air:—*O vous, Vierge Marie.*

Refrain.

ᑭ ᐸᑯᓯᐃᑎᐣ
ᑌ ᑲ, ᓇᑐᑕᐃᐤ.

1
ᑫᓇᑎᓯᔭᐣ ᒪᕆ,
ᓯᔭᑭᐃᐢ ᓭᓱᐢ,
ᒥᔦᐢᑭᑌᑌᐁᐢᑲᐢ
ᒣᔦᓯᐟ ᒪᓂᑐ;
ᐍᑳᐏᒥᑳᐏᔭᐣ
ᑕᑭ ᑫᓇᑎᓯᔭᐣ.

2
ᒥᔭᒪᑕᐏᓯᔭᐣ,
ᐁᑯᑌ ᑭᓯᑯᐠ
ᑫᐢᑭᓇᐚᐸᒥᐢᑳᐤ
ᒣᔦ ᐊᔨᐏᑖᐤ,
ᑭ ᑭᓴᐚᑎᓯᐃᐣ
ᓇᒪᐚᐋ ᑭᓯᐸᐣ.

3
ᑭ ᓴᑲᐢᑭᑌᐢᑲᑯᐣ
ᒥᔦ ᐊᔨᐃᐏᐃᐣ;
ᒪᕆ ᑭᐸᐢᑭᔅᑲᐣ
ᐁᓯ ᒥᔭᓯᔭᐣ.
ᑭᑎᒪᑫᔨᒧᐃᐣ
ᓇᐢᐱ ᑭᑐᑕᔭᓂᐣ.

4
ᐅᑲᓇᑕᓗᑫᐅᐤ
ᑌᑲᑌᔨᒥᐢᑳᐤ;
ᐅᑭᓯᑯᐅᐢ ᐊᐚ-
ᒥᔭ ᒥᑎᒥᐢᑳᐤ,
ᑭ ᑯᓯᐢ ᐊᐳᑎᑲ
ᑭ ᑭᐢᑌᔨᒥᐟ ᓇᐢᐱ.

5
ᐊᔭᒥᐁᐢᑕᒪᐃᐣ,
ᓂ ᑭᑎᒪᑭᓯᐣ
ᑫᑲ ᓂ ᓴᑯᐃᑰ
ᓂ ᒪᒋ ᐃᑎᐃᐣ.
ᓂᐦᑲᒪᐃᐣ, ᒪᕆ,
ᒋ ᐍᐱᓇᒪᐣ ᓇᐢᐱ.

6
ᐅᓴᐢ ᐃᐧ ᓂᐱᔭᓂ
ᑭ ᒪᐃᐧᒧᐢᑕᑎᐣ;
ᐃᐧ ᑲᓇᐍᔨᒥᑳᐣ:
ᓇᐢᐱ ᐁ ᑯᐢᑕᒪᐣ
ᑭᒋ ᐁᑲ ᐋᐸᒪᐟ
ᑲ ᑎᐯᔨᒥᑯᔭᐟ.

13

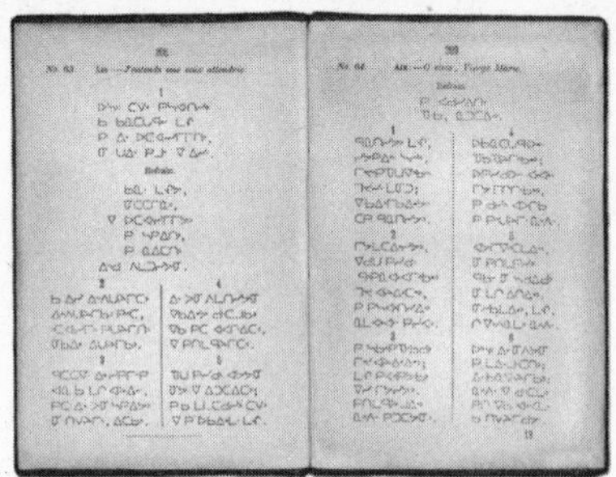

209 *No. 64.* Air: – *O vous, Vierge Marie. (O Virgin Mary.)*

Refrain.
I beg you
Mother, Oh hear me!

1
You are pure, Mary.
Jesus loves you.
You have a good heart
from Almighty God.
You understand as
Mother.
You are always pure.

2
You are supernatural
above in Heaven.
You will show us
that we are good.
You are merciful.
Your mercy has no end.

3
You fill me
with goodness;
Mary you prevail.
Clearly, you are good.
Have pity on me.
Forever intercede
for me.

4
You, whose spirit is pure,
we see you as our superior.
The angels
praise you.
Your Son

will praise you forever.

5
Pray for me.
I am in need.
I am nearly defeated.
I am sinful.
Help me, Mary,
So that I reject sin forever.

6
When I die,
I will pray to you for help;
Watch over me;
I am forever fearful
of the God I do not see,
The One who rules
over us.

209 No. 64. AIR: – O vous, Vierge Marie.
No. 64. AIR: – O vous, Vierge Marie.

Refrain.
ki pakosiitin
kipakosîhitin

ne ka, natotawin.
nêkâ, natôtawin.

1
kenatisiyan mari,
(ê-)kanâtisiyan Mari,

siyakiisk sesos,
siyâkihisk Sesos,

miyoskineteeskask
miyoskinêtêhêskâsk

meyosit manito;
(ê-)miyosit manitow;

wekawimikawiyan
(ê-)wêkawîmikawiyan

taki kenatisiyan.
tahki (ê-)kanâtisiyan.

2
miyamatawisiyan,
(ê-)miyamatawisiyan,

ekote kiskikok
êkotê kîsikohk

keskinawapamiskwaw
kêskinawâpamiskwâw

meyo ayiwitwaw,
miyo-ayiwitwâw,

ki kisewatisiwin
kikisêwâtisiwin

nama wawac kisipan.
nama wâwâc kisipan.

4
okanatacakwewok
okanâtahcâhkwêwak

nekaneyimiskwaw;
nîkânêyimiskwâw;

okisikowok wawac
okîsikowak wâwâc

miyamicimiskwaw,
miyamihcimiskwâw,

ki kosis apocika
kikosis aphô cika

ki kisteyimik naspic.
kikistêyimik nâspic.

5
ayamiestamawin,
ayamihêstamawin,

ni kitimakisin
nikitimâkisin

kekac ni sakoikon
kêkâc nisâkohikon

ni maci itiwin.
nimacihtiwin.

nisokamawin, mari,
nîsôhkamawin, Mari,

ci wepinaman naspic.
kici-wêpinamân nâspic.

3
ki sakaskineskakon
kisâkaskinêskâkon

miyo ayiwiwin;
miyo-ayiwiwin;

mari kipaskiyakan
Mari kipaskiyâkan

esi miyasiyan.
(ê-)isi-miywâsiyan.

kitimakeyimowin
kitimâkeyimowin

naspic kitotayanin.
nâspic kitotayanin.

6
osam wi nipiyani
osâm wî-nipiyâni

ki mawimostatin;
kimawimostâtin;

wi kanaweyimikan:
wî-kanawêyimîkan:

naspic e kostaman
nâspic ê-kostamân

kici eka wapamak
kici êkâ wâpamak

ka tipeyimikoyak.
kâ-tipêyimikoyâhk.

210

No. 65. AIR: — *Bénissons à jamais.*

Refrain.

1 · 4 · 2 · 5 · 3 · 6

No. 66. AIR: — *D'être enfant de Marie.*

1 · Refrain.

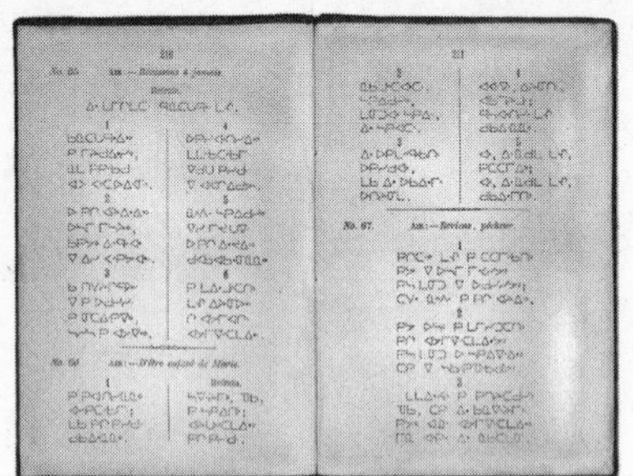

210 *No. 65.* AIR: – *Bénissons à jamais. (Let us bless forever.)*

Refrain.

Let us praise Mary, the one whose soul is pure.

1

Purity of soul
She receives from God.
She does not bear
any sin.

2

Greatness
is hers.
Over all women
she reigns supreme.

3

The One who is ruler
of all
is her Son.
She gave birth to Him,
Jesus.

4

Compassion
is a wonderful virtue.
Above in Heaven
it serves us well.

5

She is forever amiable.
She has a good heart.
Her name is great:
advocate for us all.

6

I pray to you for help,

Mary's people,
so that they pray.
Pray for them.

No. 66. AIR: – *D'être enfant de Marie. (To be the child of Mary.)*

1

We were orphaned
here on earth.
But in Heaven
we will have a mother.

Refrain.

Mother, bless us.
We love you.
Intercede for us
in Heaven.

No. 65. AIR: – Bénissons à jamais.
No. 65. AIR: – Bénissons à jamais.

Refrain.
wi mamicimatak kenatacakwet mari.
wî-mamihcimâhtâhk (ê-)kanâtahcâhkwêt Mari.

1

kanatacakwewin
kanâtahcâhkwêwin

ki miyikowisiw,
kimiyikowisiw,

nama kikiskako
nama kikiskâko

apo pastaowinis.
ahpô pâstâhowinis.

2

o kici ayiwiwin
okihci-ayiwiwin

osami misayiw,
osâmi-misâyiw,

kakiyaw iskwewa
kahkiyaw iskwêwa

e isi paskiyawat.
ê-isi-paskiyawât.

3

ka tipeyicikeyit
kâ-tipêyihcikêyit

e ki okosisit
ê-kî-okosisit

ki nitawikiew,
kî-nihtâwikihêw,

sesosa ki ayawew.
Sesosa kî-ayâwêw.

4

okisiwatisiwin
okisêwâtisiwin

mamaskataskamik
mâmaskâtaskamik

ekote kisikok
êkotê kîsikôhk

e apaciikoyak.
ê-âpacihikoyâhk.

5

naspic sakiikosiw
nâspic sâkihikosiw

esi miyo teet
(ê-)isi miyo-têhêt

o kici wiyowin
okihci-wihowin

kopakaakwaninanaw.
kopakahakwaninânâw.

6

ki mawimostatin
kimawimostâtin

mari iyiniwok
Mari iyiniwak

ci ayamiacik
kici-ayamihâcik

ayamiestamawik.
ayamihêstamawik.

No. 66. AIR: – D'être enfant de Marie.
No. 66. AIR: – D'être enfant de Marie.

1

ki kiwatisinanaw
kikîwâtisinânâw

waskitaskamik;
waskitaskamik;

maka kici kisikok
mâka kihci-kîsikôhk

kokawinanaw.
kôkâwînânâw.

Refrain.

saweyimin, neka,
sawêyimin, neka,

ki sakiitin;
kisâkihitin;

ayitwestamawin
ayitwêstamawin

kici kisikok.
kihci-kîsikôhk.

211

2

ᑎᑲᒧᑕᐊᐧᑕᐠ,
ᓴᑭᐃᑯᓯᐤ,
ᒪᓂᑐᐊᐧ ᓴᑭᐃᐠ,
ᐃᐧ ᓴᑭᐊᑕᐠ.

3

ᐃᐧ ᐅᑭᒪᐢᑫᐧᑲᓂᐠ
ᐅᑭᓯᑯᐊᐧ,
ᒪᑲ ᐃᐧ ᐅᑲᐃᐧᒥᐠ
ᐅᑎᐸᑎᒪ.

4

ᐊᐊᐧᐁᐧᐠ, ᐃᐸᑎᓂᐠ,
ᐊᑲᒣᐸᒧ;
ᑫᓴᐊᐧᓂᐸᐢ ᒪᕆ
ᑯᑲᐃᐧᓇᓇᐤ.

5

ᐊ+, ᐃᐧᓇᑯᒪ ᒪᕆ,
ᑭᑕᑕᒥᐃᐣ;
ᐊ+, ᐃᐧᓇᑯᒪ ᒪᕆ,
ᑯᑲᐃᐧᒥᓂᐠ.

No. 67. Air:—*Reviens, pécheur.*

1

ᑭᑎᑕᐤ ᒪᕆ ᑭ ᑕᑕᒥᐢᑲᓂᐣ
ᑭᔭ ᐁ ᐅᓴᒥ ᒥᔪᔭᐣ
ᑭᓴ ᒪᓂᑐ ᐁ ᐅᑯᓯᓯᔭᐣ;
ᑕᐯᐧ ᓇᐢᐱᐨ ᑭ ᑮᐱᑎ ᐊᔨᐃᐤ.

2

ᑭᔭ ᐅᓴᐟ ᑭ ᒪᒥᓯᑐᑕᐣ
ᑭᑎ ᐊᔭᒥᐁᐧᑕᒪᐃᐧᔭᐣ
ᑭᓴ ᒪᓂᑐ ᐅ ᓴᑭᐃᐁᐧᐃᐧᐣ
ᑕᑭ ᐁ ᓴᑲᐢᑭᑌᐢᑲᑯᔭᐣ.

3

ᒪᒪᐃᐧᓭᐢ ᑭ ᑭᑐᔭᑕᑯᓯᐣ
ᑌᑲ, ᑕᑭ ᐃᐧ ᑲᓇᐁᐧᔨᒥᐣ
ᑭᔭᐨ ᐊᓇ ᐊᔭᒥᐁᐧᑕᒪᐃᐧᐣ
ᒥᓇ ᐊᐢᑭ ᐃᐧ ᓇᑲᑕᒪᐣ.

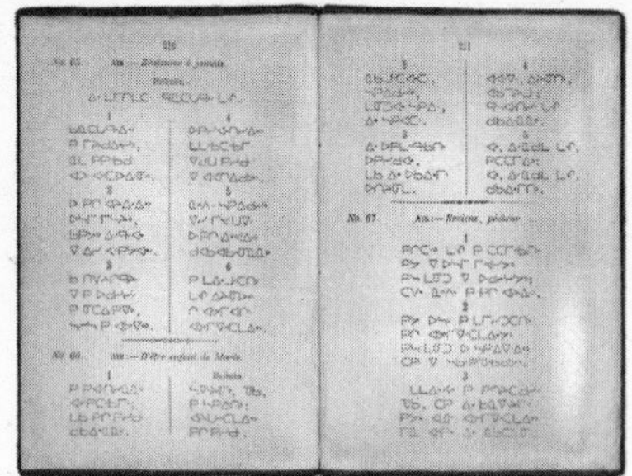

211

2

Let us sing for her.
She is loved.
She is loved by God.
We are going to love her.

3

The angels treat her
As a Queen.
We, His people, take
her as our Mother.

4

You people
persevere.
Mary is merciful.
We will have a mother.

5

I sing to Mary.
I am thankful to you.
Mary, I sing to you.
I take you as my Mother.

No. 67. Air: – *Reviens, pécheur. (Come back, sinner.)*

1

Holy Mary, I am grateful to you.
You are far too good.
The compassionate God is your Son.
You are truly and forever exalted.

2

I pray to you for help
To pray for me.
Kind God, His love,
continuously fills my heart.

3

Above all others, you are the greatest.
Mother! Take care of me always.
Let it be; pray for me today,
and when I die.

2

nakamostawatak,
nakamostâwâtâhk,

sakiikosiw,
sâkihikosiw,

manitowa sakiik,
manitowa sâkihik,

wi sakiatak.
wî-sâkihâtâhk.

3

wi okimaskwekatik
wî-okimâskwêkahtik

okisikowa,
okîsikowa,

maka wi okawimik
mâka wî-okâwîmik

otiyinima.
otiyinîma.

4

awaek, iyinitik,
awiyak, iyinîtik,

akameyimok;
âhkamêyimok;

kesewatisit mari
(ê-)kisêwâtisit Mari

kokawinanaw.
kôkâwînânâw.

5

ay, wi nakoma mari,
ay, wî-nakoma Mari,

kitatamiin;
kitatamihin;

ay, wi nakoma mari,
ay, wî-nakoma Mari,

kokawimitin.
kôkâwîmitin.

No. 67. Air: – Reviens, pécheur.
No. 67. Air: – Reviens, pécheur.

1

kicitwaw mari ki tatamiskatin
kihcitwâw Mari kitatamiskâtin

kiya e osami miyosiyan
kiya ê-osâmi-miyosiyan

kise manito e okosisiyan;
kisê-manitow ê-okosisiyan;

tapwe naspic ki kici ayiwin.
tâpwê nâspic kikihci-ayiwin.

2

kiya osam ki mamisitotatin
kiya osâm kimamisîtôtâtin

kici ayamiestamawiyan
kici-ayamihêstamawiyan

kise manito o sakiiwewin
kisê-manitow osâkihiwewin

taki e sakaskineskakoyan.
tahki ê-sakâskinêskâkoyan.

3

mamawiyes ki kiceyitakosin
mamawiyês kikihceyihtâkosin

neka, taki wi kanaweyimin
nêka, tahki wî-kanawêyimin

kiyam anoc ayamiestamawin
kiyâm anohc ayamihêstamawin

mina askiy wi nakatamani.
mîna askiy wî-nakatamâni.

212

No. 68. Air:—*Je te salue, ô Pain de l'Ange.*

1

ᑫᓇᑕᑌᑫᐧᔭᐣ ᒪᕆᔭ,
ᑭᑐᒋᑲᐧᓇᐱᐢᑕᑎᐣ
ᑭᔭ ᐁ ᒥᔮᑯᐃᐧᓯᔭᐣ
ᑭᑎ ᓴᐁᐧᔮᑎᑫᐃᐧᐣ,

2

ᓇᐊᐧ- ᑭᒥᐁᐧᔮᑕᑯᓯᐣ
ᐃᐢᑫᐧᐅᐧ ᑲ ᐃᑕᓯᑕᐧᐤ
ᐁ ᓴᐁᐧᔮᒥᑯᐃᐧᓯᔭᐣ
ᑭᔭᐠ ᓴᓱᐢ ᐁᑭ ᐅᑎᐟ.

3

ᓴᓱᐢ ᑲ ᐅᓯᒧᐃᑯᔭᐠ
ᑭᔭ ᑲᑭ ᐅᑲᐃᐧᒥᐢᐠ,
ᐃᐧ ᐊᔭᒥᐁᐧᐢᑕᒪᐃᐧᓇᐣ
ᐊᓈ- ᒥᓇ ᑌᐱᔭᑭ.

No. 69. Air:—*A servir le Seigneur.*

1

ᑎᓯᑲᒪᐃᐧᓇᐣ
ᑭᑎᑕᐧ ᒪᕆ ᑌᑲ,
ᑭᑎ ᑭᐢᑫᔮᑕᒪᐠ
ᓴᓱᐢ ᐅᑎᑌᐃᐧᐤ,
ᑎᓯᑲᒪᐃᐧᓇᐣ.

2

ᐊᔭᒥᑎᑫᐃᐧᐤ
ᑲ ᐯᔭᑯᒥᐊᐧᓯᐠ
ᑭᑎ ᐃᐧ ᑕᐯᐧᑕᒪᐠ,
ᑭᑎ ᓴᑭᑕᔭᐠ
ᐊᔭᒥᑎᑫᐃᐧᐤ.

3

ᐊᐩ ᐊᐩ, ᐃᐧ ᓇᑯᒪ !
ᑕᑭᐧ ᑎ ᐃᐧ ᓇᑲᒧᐣ
ᐁᓯ ᐊᑕᒥᓇᔭᐣ
ᐁ ᐅᑲᐃᐧᒥᑕᐣ.
ᐊᐩ ᐊᐩ, ᐃᐧ ᓇᑯᒪ !

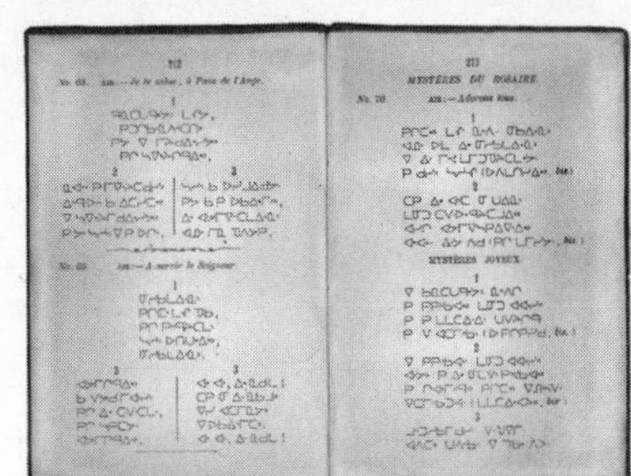

212 *No. 68.* Air: – *Je te salue, ô Pain de l'Ange. (I greet You, O Bread of the Angels.)*

1

Your soul is pure Mary.
I kneel before you.
You have received God's spirits.
The greatest blessing.

2

You are, by comparison,
more appreciated
than the women are.
You are blessed by God.
Jesus came from you.

3

Jesus, the One who is our
brother,
You were His mother.
You are going to pray
for us,
today and when we die.

No. 69. Air: – *A servir le Seigneur. (To serve the Lord.)*

1

Work together with us,
Holy Mother Mary,
for us to know His words,
Jesus's sayings.
Help us with them.

2

The Bible,
it alone is good.
We believe it the most.
We love it the most,
the Bible.

3

Thank you, we sing!
We will sing forever
You are glad for us.
We have you as a mother.
Thank you, we sing!

No. 68. AIR: – Je te salue, ô Pain de l'Ange.
No. 68. AIR: – Je te salue, ô Pain de l'Ange.

1

kenatacakweyan mariya,
(ê-)kanâtahcâhkwêyan Mariya,

kitocikwanapistatin
kitocihkwanapîstâtin

kiya e miyikowisiyan
kiya ê-miyikowisiyan

kici saweyicikewin,
kihci-sawêyihcikêwin,

2

nawac kimiweyitakosin
nawac kimiywêyihtâkosin

iskwewok ka itasitwaw
iskwêwak kâ-ihtasitwâw

e saweyimikowisiyan
ê-sawêyimikowisiyan

kiyak sesos e ki ocit.
kiyak Sesos ê-kî-ohcît.

3

sesos ka osimoikoyak
Sesos kâ-osîmohikoyahk

kiya ka ki okawimisk,
kiya kâ-kî-okâwîmisk,

wi ayamiestamawinan
wî-ayamihêstamawinân

anoc mina nepiyaki.
anohc mîna nipiyâhki.

No. 69. AIR: – A servir le Seigneur.
No. 69. AIR: – A servir le Seigneur.

1

nisokamawinan
nîsôhkamawinân

kicitwa mari neka,
kihcitwa Mari nêkâ,

kici kiskeyitamak
kici-kiskêyihtamahk

sesos otitwewin,
Sesos otitwêwin,

nisokamawinan.
nîsôhkamawinân.

2

ayamicikewin
ayamihcikêwin

ka peyakomiwasik
kâ-pêyako-miywâsik

kici wi tapwetamak,
kihci-wî-tâpwêtamâhk,

kici sakitayak
kihci-sâkihtâyâhk

ayamicikewin.
ayamihcikewin.

3

ay ay, wi nakoma!
ay ay, wî-nakoma!

taki ni winakamon
tahki niwî-nakamon

esi ataminayan
(ê-)isi-ataminayan

e okawimitan.
â-okawîmitân.

ay ay, wi nakoma!
ay ay, wî-nakoma!

213

MYSTÈRES DU ROSAIRE.

No. 70. Air ; — *Adorons tous.*

1

ᑭᑎᑕ·ᐤ ᒪᕆ ᑎᐢᐱ- ᑌᑲᐃ·ᑎᐣ
ᐊᑎ- ᐅᒪ ᐃ· ᑌᓯᑲᒪᐃ·ᑎᐣ
ᐁ ᐃ· ᒥᕙᒪᒥᑐᑌᔦᑕᒪ·ᔦᐠ
ᑭ ᑯᓯᐢ ᓴᓯᕆ (ᐅᐱᒪᑎᓯᐃ·ᐣ, *bis.*)

2

ᑕᑭ ᐃ· ᐊᐢᑕ ᑌ ᐅᐃᑎᐠ
ᒪᑌᑐ ᑕᐯ·ᐅ·ᕃᔦᑕᒨᐃ·ᐣ
ᐊᓯᕆ ᐊᔦᒥᐁᓴᑭᐃᐁ·ᐃ·ᐣ
ᐊ·ᐊ·- ᐃ·ᔦ ᐱᑯ (ᑭᕆ ᒪᒥᓯᔦᐠ, *bis.*)

MYSTÈRES JOYEUX.

1

ᐁ ᑳᑎᑕᓭᕃ·ᔦᐣ ᑎᐢᐱᕆ
ᑭ ᑭᑭᐢᑳᐊ·ᐤ ᒪᑌᑐ ᐊᐊ·ᓯᐢ
ᑭ ᑭ ᒪᒪᑕᐃ·ᐃ·ᐠ ᐅᐯᔦᕆᕃ
ᑭ ᐯ ᐊᑕᒥᐢᑳᐠ (ᐅᑭᕆᑭᓯᑯ, *bis.*)

2

ᐁ ᑭᑭᐢᑳᐊ·ᐠ ᒪᑌᑐ ᐊᐊ·ᓯᐢ
ᐊ·ᔦᐤ ᑭ ᐃ· ᑌᑕᐁ·ᑭᕙᑳᐊ·ᐤ
ᑭ ᕆᐊ·ᒥᐢᕃ·ᐤ ᑭᕆᑕ·ᐤ ᐁᑎᓴᐯ·
ᐁᑕᒥᐢᑳᑐᕂᐠ (ᒪᒪᑕᐃ·ᐸᔦᐤ, *bis*)

3

ᒨᐢᑐᓯᑳᒥᑯᓯᐠ ᐯ·ᑌᐁᒥᐠ
ᐊᐱᑕᐤ ᑌᐱᐢᑳᐠ ᐁ ᒉᑳ· ᐱᐳᐠ

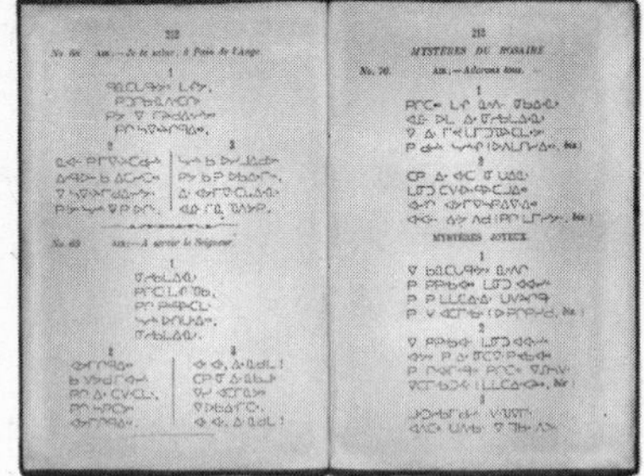

213

MYSTÈRES DU ROSAIRE.

(MYSTERIES OF THE ROSARY.)

No. 70. Air: – *Adorons tous. (Let us all adore.)*

1

Holy Mary, you are our greatest mother.
On this day you are going to help us.
We are going to reflect on Him,
Your Son, Jesus (His life. *twice.*)

2

We are always going to put in our hearts
God's faith.
Also with loving prayer
especially her (in this way we depend on her. *twice.*)

MYSTÈRES JOYEUX.

(JOYFUL MYSTERIES.)

1

Your soul is forever pure.
You are pregnant with God's child.
He gave you supernatural powers, the Creator.
He comes to greet you (in Heaven. *twice.*)

2

You are pregnant with God's child
You are going to visit.
Your cousin, the holy Elizabeth.
You embrace each other; (it is amazing. *twice.*)

3

In the manger at Bethlehem
At midnight during the winter

213

MYSTÈRES DU ROSAIRE.
MYSTÈRES DU ROSAIRE.

No. 70. AIR: – Adorons tous.
No. 70. AIR: – Adorons tous.

1

kicitwaw mari naspic nikawinan
kihcitwâw Mari nâspic nikâwînân

anoc oma wi nisokamawinan
anohc ôma wî-nîsôhkamawinân

e wi miyo mamitoneyitamwayak
ê-wî-miyo-mâmitonêyihtamwâyâhk

ki kosis sesokri (opimatisiwin. *bis.*)
kikosis Sesokri (opimâtisiwin. bis.)

2

taki wi asta ni teinak
tahki wî-astâ nitêhinahk

manito tapwewokeyitamowin
manitow tâpwêwakêyihtamowin

asici ayamiesakiiwewin
asici ayamihêsâkihiwêwin

wawac wiya piko (kici mamisiyak. *bis.*)
wâwâc wîya piko (kici-mamisîyâhk. bis.)

MYSTÈRES JOYEUX.
MYSTÈRES JOYEUX.

1

e kanatacakweyan naspici
ê-kanâtahcâhkwêyan nâspici

ki kikiskawaw manito awasis
kikikiskawâw manitow awâsis

ki ki mamatawiwik tepeyiciket
kikî-mamâhtâwiwik (ê-)tipêyihcikêt

ki pe atamiskak (o kicikisiko. *bis.*)
ki-pê-atamiskâhk (okihci-kîsikohk. bis.)

2

e kikiskawat manito awasis
ê-kikiskawât manitow awâsis

wayaw ki wi nitawekiyokawaw
wâyaw kiwî-nitawi-kiyokawâw

ki ciwamiskwew kicitwaw elisapet
kiciwâmiskwêw kihcitwâw Elisapet

etamiskatoyek (mamatawipayiw. *bis.*)
ê-atamiskâtoyek (mamatawipayiw. bis.)

3

mostosokamikosik petleemik
mostosokamikosihk Petlehemihk

apitaw tepiskak e mekwa pipok
âpihtaw-tipiskâhk ê-mêkwâ-pipok

214

ᒪᓂᑐᑯᓯᓴᐣ ᑭ ᓂᑕᐏᑭᐊᐤ
ᐁ ᐸᑭᑎᓂᓯᐟ (ᒋ ᐱᒪᒋᐃᐍᐟ, *bis.*)

4

ᐯᒋ ᓇᑲᒧᐗᐠ ᐅᑭᓯᑯᐗᐠ
ᒥᓇ ᐅᑲᓇᐍᐱᓯᐢᑭᐍᐗᐠ
ᐃᔭᔭᐤ ᓴᒪᐠ ᐯᒪᓂᑐᐍᔭᒣᐗᐠ
ᐊᐘ ᐊᐚᐤ ᐅᒋ (ᓂᐢᑐᐅᑭᒪᐗᐠ, *bis.*)

5

ᐊᒋᔭᐤ ᐁ ᑭ ᐘᓂᐊᐟ ᑭ ᑯᓯᐢ
ᒥᐢᑕᐃ ᑭ ᐸᐸᒥ ᑳᐢᑫᔦᑌᐣ
ᑭ ᒥᐢᑳᐘᐤ ᑌᐯᔨᒋᑫᐏᑲᒥᑯᐠ
ᐁ ᐊᑕᒥᓇᔭᐣ (ᒥᓇ ᑭ ᐏᒋᐘᐤ, *bis.*)

MYSTÈRES DOULOUREUX.

1

ᐁ ᐃ· ᑳᑳᐧᑕᑭᐁᐢᑕᒪᑯᔭᐠ
ᓂᑕᐏᑭᒋᑳᓂᓯᐠ ᐃᑐᑌᐤ
ᐁᑯᑌ ᐁ ᑳᑳᐧᑕᑫᔨᒧᐟ ᓇᐢᐱ-
ᒪᒋ ᐃᑎᐍᓇ (ᐃ· ᓂᐸᐁᔨᑕᐢ *bis.*)

2

ᐅᑳᒥᓇᑳᓯᐘᐦᑎᑳᐤ ᐅᒋ
ᐸᓯᑫᐱᑕᐤ ᑭ ᒪᓂᑐᒥᓇᐤ
ᐅᐢᑎᑲᐧᐣ ᒥᐢᑕᐃ ᑭ ᑳᐧᑕᑭᐘᐤ
ᐃ· ᒪᐏᑳᑎᓯᐟ (ᑳ ᒪᒋᑳᐢᑌᔨᐟ, *bis.*)

3

ᓴᓯᐢ ᐁ ᑭ ᑫᑕᔪᓂᓴᐱᑎᐟ
ᒥᒋᒪᐢᑳᐱᑕᐤ ᐸᐸᓴᐢᑌᐘᐤ

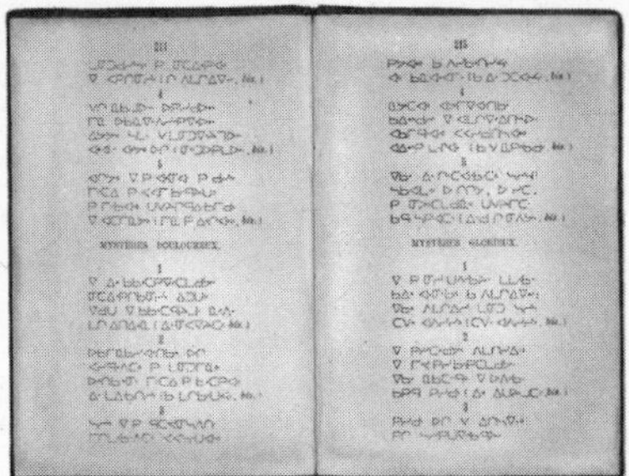

214 God's Son was born.
He surrendered Himself (to give people life.
twice.)

4

Angels approach singing.
So do the shepherds.
Preferring to come and worship Him as soon as possible,
especially from far away (the three kings. *twice.*)

5

For a little while your Son was lost.
You were very lonely for Him
until you found Him in the temple.
You make me grateful (and you help Him. *twice.*)

MYSTÈRES DOULOUREUX.
(SORROWFUL MYSTERIES.)

1

He is going to suffer for us.
He goes to the small garden.
He is distressed beyond measure.
The sins (they are going to agonize Him. *twice.*)

2

The thorn bush
scratches our God's head.
He was greatly distressed.
You will cry for yourselves (you who are proud.
twice.)

3

They remove His clothes.
He is tied down and whipped.

manitokosisan ki nitawikiaw
manitokosisân kî-nihtâwikihâw

e pakitinisot (ci pimaciiwet. *bis.*)
ê-pakitinisot (kici-pimâcihiwêt. bis.)

4

peci nakamowok okisikowok
pêci-nakamowak okîsikowak

mina okanawepisiskiwewok
mîna okanawêpisiskiwêwak

iyayaw semak pe manitoweyimewok
iyâyaw sêmâk pê-manitowêyimêwak

wawac wayaw oci (nistookimawok. *bis.*)
wâwâc wahyaw ohci (nistohokimâwak. bis.)

5

aciyaw e ki waniat ki kosis
aciyaw ê-kî-wanihat kikosis

mistae ki papami kaskeyiten
mistahi kipapâmi-kaskêyihtên

ki miskawaw tepeyicikewikamikok
kimiskawâw têpêyihcikêwikamikohk

e ataminayan (mina ki wiciwaw. *bis.*)
ê-ataminâyan (mîna ki-wîcihâw. bis.)

MYSTÈRES DOULOUREUX.

MYSTÈRES DOULOUREUX.

1

e wi kakwatakiestamakoyak
ê-wî-kakwâtakihêstamâkoyahk

nitawikicikanisik itotew
nihtâwikihcikanisihk itohtêw

ekote e kakwatakeyimot naspic
êkotê ê-kakwâtakêyimot nâspic

maci itiwina (wi ni paeyitam *bis.*)
macihtiwina (wî-nipahêyihtam bis.)

2

okaminakasiwatikwa oci
okâminakasîwâhtikwa ohci

pasikwepitaw ki manitominaw
pasîhkwêpitêw kimanitôminâw

ostikwanik mistai ki kwatakiaw
ostikwânihk mistahi kikwâtakihâw

wi mawikatisok (ka macikasteyek. *bis.*)
wî-mawîkâtisok (kâ-macikastêyêk. bis.)

3

sesos e ki ketayonisepitik
Sesos ê-kî-kêtayonisêpitik

micimaskwapitaw papasastewaw
mihcimêskwâhpitaw pâpâsastêhwâw

215

ᑭᔭᐚᐤ ᑳ ᐱᓯᑳᐧᑎᓯᔦᐠ
ᐋᐤ ᑳᓇᐋᐧᐸᒥᐟ (ᑳ ᐃᐧ ᑐᑕᐋᐧᔦᐠ, *bis.*)

4

ᓇᔭᑕᐤ ᐊᔭᒥᐁᐋᐧᑎᑳᐧ
ᑳᐃᐧᐦᑯᓯᐟ ᐁ ᐊᒪᒋᐁᐧᐃᑎᓴᐅᐟ
ᐸᑲᒥᑫᐋᐧᐤ ᐸᐸᓯᑯᑎᐢᐊᐧᐤ
ᐊᐃᐧᐦᑭ ᒪᕆᐊᐧ (ᑳ ᐯ ᓇᑭᐢᑳᑯᐟ, *bis.*)

5

ᐁᑳᐧ ᐃᐧ ᒋᐢᑕᐊᐦᑳᐧᑖᐤ ᓴᓗᕆ
ᓴᑳᐊᒪᐤ ᐅ ᒋᒋᔭ, ᐅ ᓯᑕ.
ᑭ ᓂᐳᐢᑕᒪᑯᓇᐤ ᑌᐯᔨᒥᑕᐠ
ᑳᑫᐧ ᓴᑭᐊᐦᑕᐠ (ᐃᐢᑯ ᒋ ᓂᐱᔭᐠ, *bis.*)

MYSTÈRES GLORIEUX.

1

ᐁ ᑭ ᓂᓱ ᑌᐱᐢᑳᔭᐠ ᒪᒪᐢᑳ
ᑳᐃᐧ ᐊᐧᓂᐢᑳᐤ ᑳ ᐱᒪᒋᐃᐁᐧ:
ᐁᑳᐧ ᐱᒪᒋᐃᓯ ᒪᓂᑐ ᓴᓯᐣ
ᑕᐯᐧ ᐊᐱᓯᓯᐤ (ᑕᐯᐧ ᐊᐱᓯᓯᐤ, *bis.*)

2

ᐁ ᑭᓯᑖᐧᑯᔭᐠ ᐱᒪᑎᓯᐃᐧᐣ
ᐁ ᒥᓴ ᑭᓯ ᑳᐦᑭᑕᒪᑯᔭᐠ
ᐁᑳᐧ ᓇᑲᑕᐦᑫᐤ ᐁ ᐅᐱᐦᑳᐟ
ᑳᑭᑫ ᑭᓯᑯᐠ (ᐃᐧ ᐃᑌᔨᒧᑕᐤ, *bis.*)

3

ᑭᓯᑯᐠ ᐅᒋ ᐯ ᐃᑎᓴᐁᐤ
ᑭᒋ ᓴᓯᑭᑌᐁᐦᑳᑫᔭᐟ

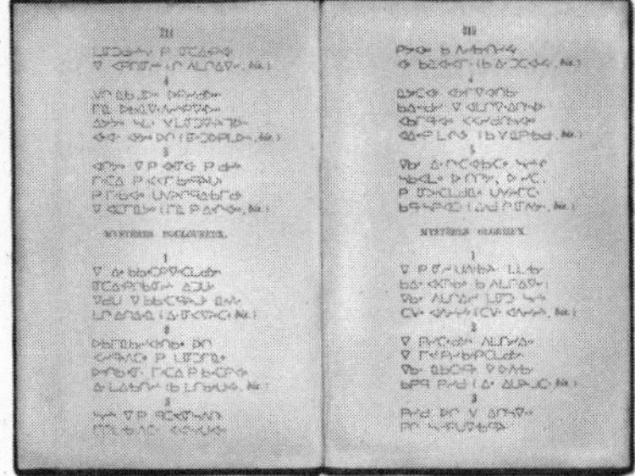

215 You, the ones who are adulterers,
look at Him (see what you have done to Him. *twice.*)

4

He is heavily burdened by the cross.
He falls under the burden but they pull Him uphill.
They strike Him in the face; He is made to get up.
Suddenly, Mary is here (she comes to meet Him. *twice.*)

5

Jesus Christ is going to be nailed to the cross.
They prepare to drive the nails through His hands, His feet.
He dies for us; be content with Him.
Try to love him (in this way until you die. *twice.*)

MYSTÈRES GLORIEUX.
(GLORIOUS MYSTERIES.)

1

Amazingly He was absent for two nights.
He rose up again, to resurrect.
He lives, the Lord Jesus.
Truly, He returns to life! (Truly He returns to life. *twice.*)

2

He gave us life.
He gains this reward for us.
He leaves the earth and He ascends.
Forever in Heaven (let us hope to get there. *twice.*)

3

From Heaven He sends Him,
to come and strengthen their hearts.

215 kiyawaw ka pisikwatisiyek
kiyawâw kâ-pisikwâtisiyêk

aw kanawapamik (ka wi totawayek. *bis.*)
âw kanawâpamîk (kâ-wî-tôtawâyêk. bis.)

4

nayataaw ayamiewatikwa
nayatahaw ayamihêwâhtikwa

kawiskoso e amaciweitisaot
kawiskoso ê-âmaciwêhitisahot

pakamikwewaw papasikotisawaw
pakamikwêhwâw papasîkotisahwâw

awiski mariwa (ka pe nakiskakot. *bis.*)
awiski Mariwa (ka-pê-nakiskâkot. bis.)

5

ekwa wi cistaaskwataw sesokri
êkwa wî-cîstahâskwatâw Sesokri

sakaamwan o ciciya, o sita.
sakahamwân ocihciya, osita.

ki nipostamakonaw tepeyimitak
kinipôstamâkonaw têpêyimitâhk

kakwe sakiatak (isko ci nipiyak. *bis.*)
kâkwê-sâkihatâhk (isko kici-nipiyâhk. bis.)

MYSTÈRES GLORIEUX.

MYSTÈRES GLORIEUX.

1

e ki niso tepiskayik mamaskac
ê-kî-nîso-tipiskâyik mâmaskâc

kawi waniskaw ka pimaciiwet:
kâwi-waniskâw kâ-pimâcihiwêt:

ekwa pimaciiso manito sesos
êkwa pimâcihisow manitow Sesos

tapwe apisisin (tapwe apisisin. *bis.*)
tâpwê âpisisin (tâpwê apisisin. bis.)

2

e kisitwakoyak pimatisiwin
ê-kisitwâkoyahk pimâtisiwin

e miyokisikaskitamakoyak
ê-miyo-kisikaskitamâkoyahk

ekwa nakataskew e opiskat
êkwa nakataskêw ê-ohpîskât

kakike kisikok (wi iteyimotan. *bis.*)
kâkikê kîsikôhk (wî-itêyimotân. bis.)

3

kisikok oci pe itisawew
kîsikôhk ohci pê-itisahwêw

kici sasokiteeskakeyit
kici-sasôhkitêhêskâkêyit

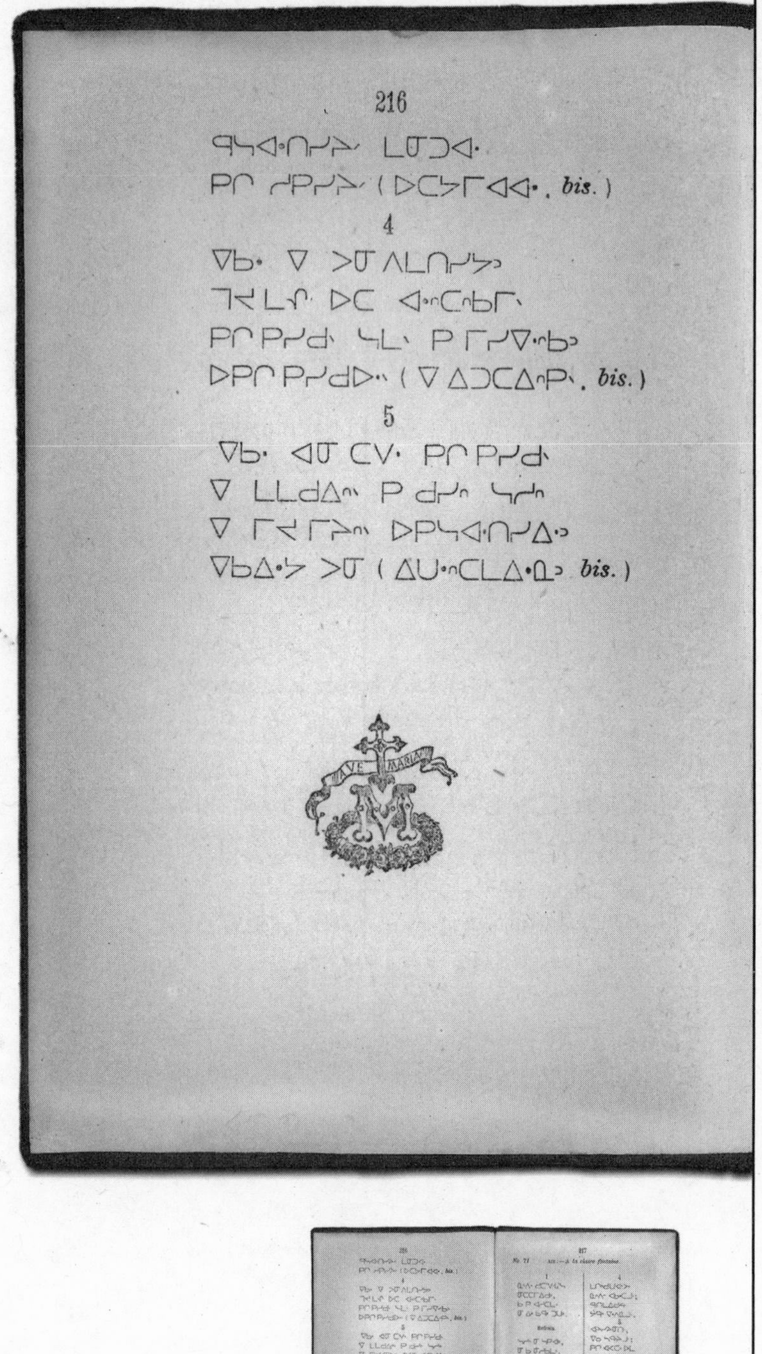
216

ᑫᓴᐚᑎᓯᓰᐟ ᒪᓂᑐᐚ
ᑭᒋ ᓲᑭᓯᓰᐟ (ᐅᑕᔮᒥᐊᐚ, *bis.*)

4

ᐁᑳ ᐁ ᐹᒋ ᐱᒪᑎᓯᔮᐣ
ᒣᕁᒪᕒ ᐅᑕ ᐋᐢᑕᐢᑲᒥᐠ
ᑭᒋ ᑭᓯᑳᐟ ᓴᒪᐠ ᑭ ᒥᓯᐍᐢᑳᐤ
ᐅᑭᒋ ᑭᓯᑯᐅᐦ (ᐁ ᐃᑐᑕᐃᐢᑭᐠ, *bis.*)

5

ᐁᑳ ᐊᑎ ᑕᐺ ᑭᒋ ᑭᓯᑳᐟ
ᐁ ᒪᒪᑯᐃᐦ ᑭ ᑯᓯᐢ ᓴᓯᐢ
ᐁ ᒥᔦ ᒥᔩᐦ ᐅᑭᓴᐚᑎᓯᐃᐤ
ᐁᑲᐑᔮ ᐹᒋ (ᐄᑌᐢᑕᒪᐑᑏᐤ *bis.*)

216 God is merciful,
so that they are strong (the ones who pray. *twice.*)

4

When you stopped living,
Holy Mary, here on the face of the earth,
you immediately went all over into Heaven.
His angels (they took you there. *twice.*)

5

Truly in Heaven
Your Son Jesus crowns you.
His greatest gift to you is His compassion.
Do not stop (interceding on our behalf. *twice.*)

[HAIL MARY COPPERPLATE]

216

kesiwatisiyit manitowa
(ê-)kisêwâtisiyit manitowa

kici sokisiyit (otayamiawa. *bis.*)
kici-sôhkisiyit (otayamihâwa. bis.)

4

ekwa e poni pimatisiyan
êkwa ê-pôni-pimâtisiyan

meyo mari ota wastaskamik
miyo Mari ôta wastaskamik

kici kisikok semak ki misiweskan
kihci-kîsikôhk sêmâk kimisiwêskên

okici kisikowok (e itotaiskik. *bis.*)
okihci-kîsikôwak (ê-itohtahiskik. bis.)

5

ekwa ani tapwe kici kisikok
êkwa ani tâpwê kihci-kîsikôhk

e mamakoisk ki kosis sesos
ê-mamakohisk kikosis Sesos

e miyo miyisk okisewatisiwin
ê-miyo-miyisk okisêwâtisiwin

ekawiya poni (itwestamawinan. *bis.*)
êkâwiya pôni- (itwêstamawinân. bis.)

[HAIL MARY COPPERPLATE]

217

No. 71. Air: — A la claire fontaine.

1

ᑶᐢᐱ- ᑯᑖᐯᕍᐢᓴ
ᓂᑕᑕᒥᐃᑰ,
ᑲ ᑭ ᐊᓯᑕᒪᐣ
ᓂ ᐃᐧ ᑲᑫᐧ ᑐᑌᐣ.

Refrain.

ᓴᓯᐢ ᓂ ᓴᑭᐊᐤ,
ᓂ ᑲ ᓂᓯᑲᒪᐠ.

2

ᑕᐯᐧ ᑯᑖᐯᕍᐢᓴ
ᐅᓴᒥ ᒥᐊᐧᓯᐣ,
ᐊᐃᐧᔦᐠ ᐁ ᑐᑖᐠ
ᒪᓂᑐᐊᐧ ᐅᒋ.

3

ᑕᑭ ᑯᑖᐯᕍᐢᓴ
ᑲᓇᐁᐧᔨᑕᒧᐠ,
ᐃᐧ ᐊᐸᒋᐃᓯᐠ,
ᐊᒋ ᐃᐧ ᓇᑲᒧᐠ:

4

ᒪᒋᐢᑯᑌᐊᐧᐳᐩ
ᑶᐢᐱ- ᐸᑲᐧᑕᒧᐠ;
ᑫᑎᒪᐃᑯᔦᐠ
ᔦᑫᐢ ᐁᐧᐱᓇᒧᐠ.

5

ᐊᔨᓰᔨᓂᑎᐠ,
ᐁᑲ ᓴᑫᐧᔨᒧᐠ;
ᑭᒋ ᐊᐸᑖᐣ ᐅᒪ
ᑯᒋ ᐃᔨᓂᓯᐠ.

6

ᐃᐧ ᐅᒋᑲᒪᑐᐠ
ᐊᔦᒥᐊᐃᐧᓂᐠ,
ᑭᓯᑰᐠ ᐃᑕᐱᐠ,
ᐃᐧ ᐊᑲᒁᔨᓯᐠ.

7

ᑲ ᑎᐯᔨᒥᔨᐣ
ᑭᑎᒪᑫᔨᒥᐣ,
ᑲ ᑭ ᐊᓯᑕᒪᐣ
ᑭᒋ ᐊᑕᒥᐃᑖᐣ.

ᑭ ᒪᐃᐧᒧᐢᑕᑎᐣ,
ᐃᐧ ᓂᓯᑲᒪᐃᐧᐤ.

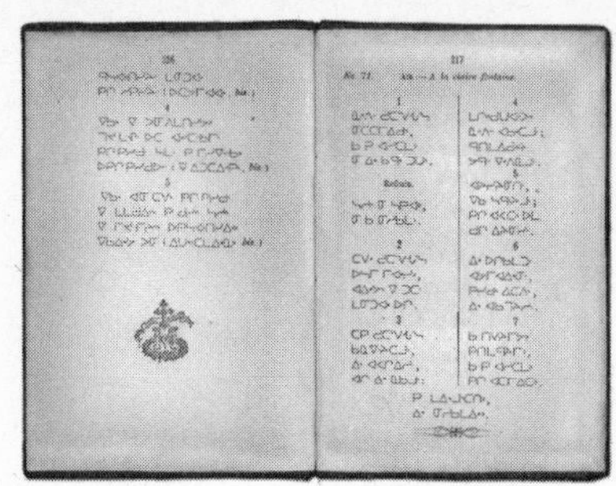

217 *No. 71.* Air: – *À la claire fontaine. (At the clear springs.)*

1

Forever the practice
of living
makes us grateful.
What I promised,
I fulfilled.

Refrain.

I love Jesus,
He will help me.

2

Truly the practice of
living,
it is too good.
God did this
for us.

3

Forever, the practice
of living,
look after it.
Use it for yourselves.
Sing more and more.

4

Bad liquor

God disapproves of it.
It will harm you.
Throw it away.

5

Be wise people.
Do not be afraid.
It is very useful
to follow those who
are wise.

6

Help one another

in prayer.
Look to Heaven.
Be courageous.

7

You govern me.

Have pity on me.
For what you promise
so that I am grateful to
You.

I worship You.
You are going to help me.

217 No. 71. Air: – À la claire fontaine.
No. 71. Air: – À la claire fontaine.

1

naspic latakperakse
nâspic Latakperakse

nitatamiikon,
nitatamihikonân,

ka ki asotaman
kâ-kî-asotaman

ni wi kakwe toten.
niwî-kakwe-tôtên.

Refrain.

sesos ni sakiaw,
Sesos nisâkihâw,

ni ka nisokamak.
nika-nîsôhkamâhk.

2

tapwe latakperakse
tâpwê Latakperakse

osami miwasin,
osâmi-miywâsin,

awiyak e totak
awiyak ê-tôtak

manitowa oci
manitowa ohci

4

maciskotewapoy
maci-iskotêwâpoy

naspic pakwatamok;
nâspic pakwâtamok;

ketimaikoyek
(ê-)kitimahikoyêk

yakes wepinamok.
yakês wêpinamok.

5

ayisiyinitik,
ayisiyinitik,

eka sakweyimok;
êkâ sakwêyimok;

kici apatan oma
kihci-âpatan ôma

koci iyinisik.
koci-iyinîsik.

6

wi ocikamatok
wî-ohcikamâtok

ayamiawinik,
ayamihâwinik,

kisikok itapik,
kîsikôhk itâpik,

wi akameyisok.
wî-âhkamêyisok.

3

ta ki latakperakse
tahki Latakperakse

kanaweyitamok,
kanawêyihtamok,

wi apaciisok,
wî-âpacihisok,

aci wi nakamok:
âci wî-nakamok:

7

ka tipeyimiyan
kâ-tipêyimiyan

kitimakeyimin,
kitimâkêyimin,

ka ki asotaman
kâ-kî asotaman

kici atamiitan.
kici-atamihitân.

ki mawimostatin,
kimâwimostâtin,

wi nisokamawin.
wî-nîsôhkamawin.

218 [MARY AND INFANT JESUS COPPERPLATE]

Holy Mary, God takes you as His mother.
You pray for us sinners.

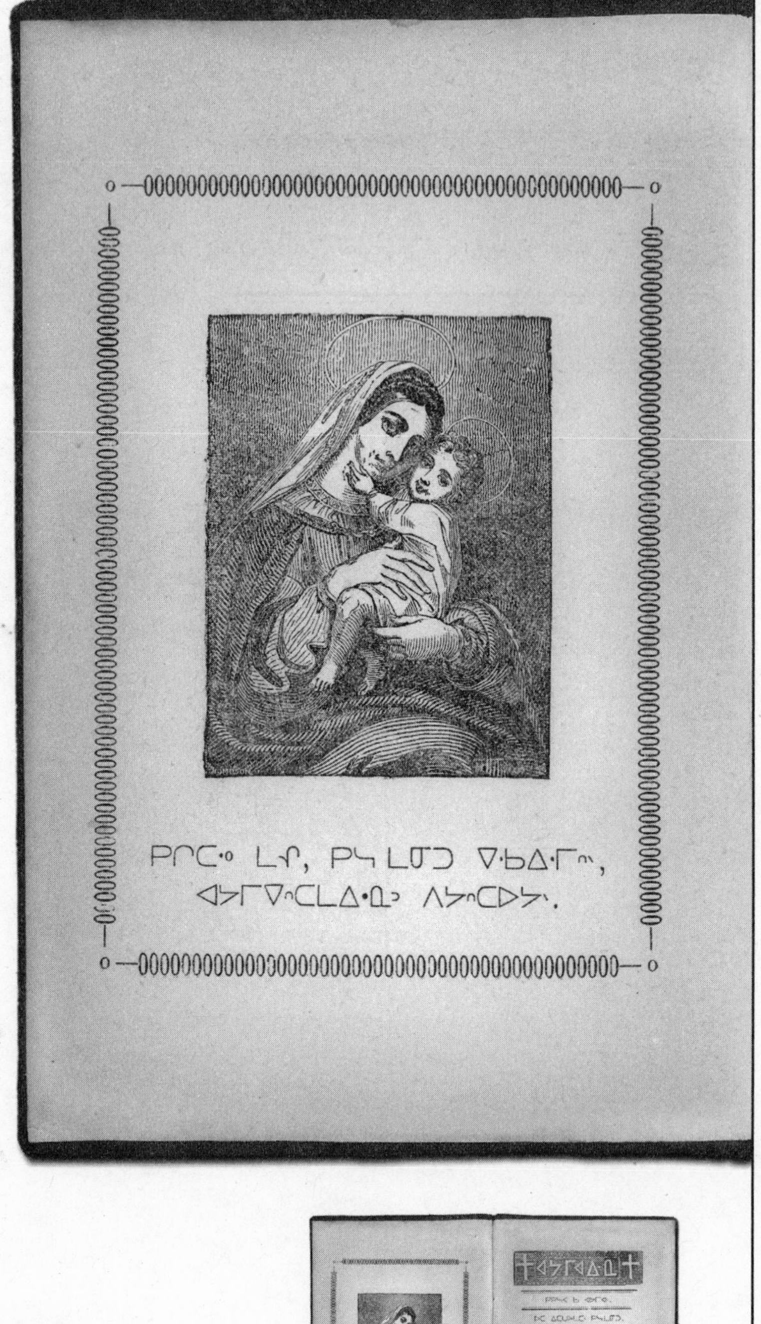

kicitwaw mari, kise manito wekawimisk,
kihcitwâw Mari, kisê-manitow wêkâwîmisk,

ayamiestamawinan piyastaoyak.
ayamihêstamawinân (ê-)piyâstahoyâhk.

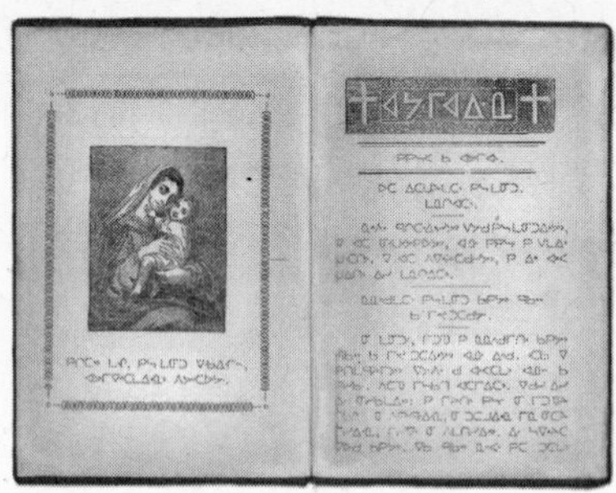

OUR PRAYERS

to pray in the morning.

We believe You are here God.
Let us respect You.

Forever You are the supreme and only God. Nevertheless You are made in three ways. This morning I worship You even though I am pitiful. I am going to show my respect for You in this way.

Let us thank the Lord for everything,
the One who is generous to us.

Truly my God I thank You for everything, for being so generous today. You take pity on me. Everyday I wish to thank You in this way. You are going to help me. I offer to You my thoughts, my words, my actions, my hardships, and all my life. Bless it all. All these things I will do for You.

219

AYAMIAWINA

AYAMIHÂWINA

kikisepa ka ayamiak.
kîkisêpa kâ-ayamihâk.

ota itateyimatak kise manito.
ôta itateyimâtâhk kisê-manitow.

manaciatak.
manâcihâtâhk.

---

naspic kecitwawisiyan peyako kise manitowiyan,
nâspic (ê-)kihcitwâwisiyan (ê-)pêyako-kisê-manitowiyan,

e ata nistweyakioyan, anoc kikisep ki pemawimostatin.
ê-âta-nistwêyakihoyan, anohc kîkisêp kipê-mawimostâtin.

e ata piweyitakosiyan, ki wi wapateitin isi
ê-âta-pîwêyihtâkosiyân, kiwî-wâpahtêhitin (ê-)isi-

manaciitan.
manâcihitân.

---

nanaskomatak kise manito kakiyiaw kekway
nanâskomâtâhk kisê-manitow kahkiyaw kîkway

ka miyototakoyak.
kâ-miyo-tôtakoyâhk.

---

ni manitom, mitone ki nanaskomitin kakiyaw kekway
nimanitôm, mitonê kinanâskomitin kahkiyaw kîkway

ka miyo totawiyan anoc isko. ntaka e kitimakeyimiyan
kâ-miyo-tôtawiyan anohc isko. nitaka ê-kitimâkêyimiyan

eyapic ko wapataman anoc ka kisikak. pitane misakame
êyâpic kô-wâpahtamân anohc kâ-kîsikâk. pitanê misakamê

atamiitan. ekosi isi wi nisokamawin: ki miyitin kisac
atamihitân. êkosi isi-wî-nîsôhkamawin: kimiyitin kisâc

ni mitoneyicikana, ni pikiskwewina, ni totamowina mina
nimitonêyihcikana, nipîkiskwêwina, nitôtamowina mîna

nitayimisiwina, misiwe ni pimatisiwin. wi saweyita eoko
nitayimisiwina, misiwê nipimâtiswin. wi-sawêyihta êwako

kakiyaw. ekwa kekway naspic kita totaman
kahkiyaw. êkwa kîkway nâspic kita-tôtamân

220 Today I hope to live the way You wanted. So let it be.

Try to be content. Do not again
live a bad life.

You are good, Jesus. You came to teach me the good life. I will try to do this. I will copy You. I wish never again to anger You with my evil life and envy. In this way I pray to You for help to please You.

Let us pray to God, to help us.

My God, You know from experience that I am weak. But it does not matter. I will try to follow you well and not shun Your help. You do not love evil. Make me courageous to be good at escaping it, as You have counselled me to do. You have taught me to pray

Our Father you are in Heaven &.....
I greet you Mary &.....
I trust you God &.....

Holy Mary, let us place our trust in you.

Holy Mary, compassionate God took you as His mother.

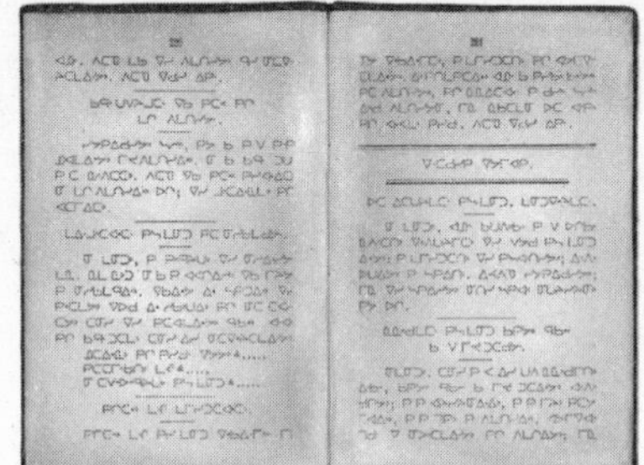

220 anoc. pitane maka esi pimatisiyan kesi
anohc. pitanê mâka (ê-)isi-pimâtisiyan kê-isi-

nitaweyitamawiyan. pitane ekosi ikik.
nitawêyihtamawiyan. pitanê êkosi ihkik.

---

kakwe tepeyimotak eka kitwam kici
kakwê têpêyimotâhk êkâ kîhtwâm kici-

maci pimatisiyak.
maci-pimâtisiyahk.

---

siyakiikosiyan sesos, kiya ka ki pe kiskinoamawiyan
(ê-)siyakihikosiyan Sesos, kiya kâ-kî-pê-kiskinohamâwiyan

miyo pimatisiwin. ni ka kakwe toten ki ta naspitatan.
miyo-pimâtisiwin. nika-kakwê-tôtên ki-ta-naspitâtân.

pitane eka kitwam kisiwaitan ni maci pimatisiwin oci:
pitanê êkâ kîhtwâm kisiwahitân nimaci-pimâtisiwin ohci:

esi mostawinaman kici atamiitan.
(ê-)isi-mostawinamân kici-atamihitân.

---

mawimostawatak kise manito kita nisokamakoyak.
mawimostawâtâhk kisê-manitow kita-nîsôhkamâkoyahk.

---

ni manitom, ki kiskeyiten esi nisowisiyan mana.
nimanitôm, kikiskêyihtên (ê-)isi-nîsowisiyân mâna.

nama nanto ni ka ki apaciison eka miyiyan
namanânitaw nikâ-kî-âpacihison ekâ miyiyan

ki nisokamakewin. ekawiya wi sakitowin esi kwitamayan
kinîsôhkamâkewin. êkâwiya wi-sâkitowin (ê-)isi-kwitamayan

eoko wi sokastein kici nita tapasitayan tanisi esi
êwako wî-sôhkâstêhin kici-nihtâ-tapasîhtâyân tânisi (ê-)isi-

kitaamawiyan kekway wawac kici kakwetotaman tanisi
kitahamawiyan kîkway wâwâc kici-kakwê-tôtaman tânisi

isi nitaweyitamawiyan.
(ê-)isi-nitawêyihtamawiyan.

notawinan kici kisikok eyayan &.....
nôhtâwînan kihci-kîsikôhk (ê-)ayâyan &.....

kitatamiskatin mari &.....
kitatamiskâtin Mari &.....

ni tapwewokeyimaw kise manito &.....
nitâpwêwakêyimâw kisê-manitow &.....

---

kicitwaw mari mamisitotawatak.
kihcitwâw Mari mamisîtotawâtâhk.

---

kicitwaw mari kisi manito wekawimisk mina
kihcitwâw Mari kisê-manitow wêkâwîmisik mîna

221 I take you as my mother. I trust you to pray for me. Have pity on me. Today, I will live properly this day. I will obey your Son Jesus, as long as I live and until I leave this earth. I wish to see Him in Heaven. So let it be.

WHEN HE ARRIVES, ALL WILL PRAY.

Let us believe that You are here, God.
Let us worship You as our God.

On this day, my God, I come to kneel before You. I consider You as the only God. I trust You for You are merciful. You have a good heart. You are loved more than anyone. And in this way You are love. In this way I love my neighbour for You.

Let us thank You God for everything
that has been good for us.

My God, I come to thank you. Through all things You are bounteous. You taught the human race how to pray Your prayer. You gave Your life on the cross. You died for me to give me life.

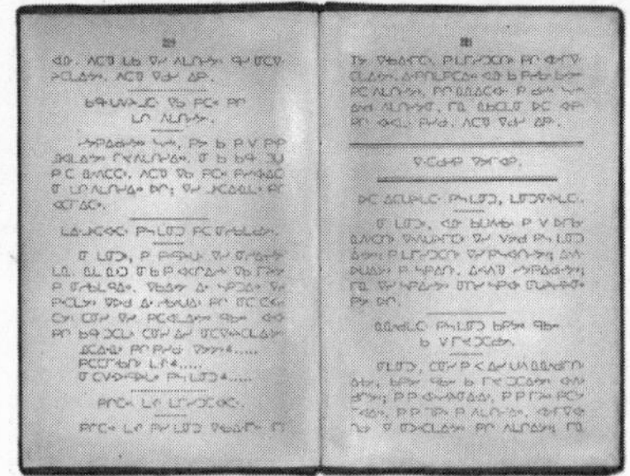

221 niya wekawimitan, ki mamisitotatin kici
niya wêkâwîmitân, kimamisîtotâtin

ayamiestamawiyan. wi kitimakitawin anoc ka
kici-ayamihêstamawiyan. wî-kitimâkihtawin anohc kâ-

kisikak kwayask kita pimatisiyan, kici nanaitawak ki kosis
kîsikâk kwayask kita-pimâtisiyan, kici-nanahihtawak kikosis

sesos isko pimatisiyani, mina nakatamani ota askik kici
Sesos isko pimâtisiyani, mîna nakatamani ôta askîhk kici-

wapamak kisikok. pitane ekosi ikik.
wâpamak kîsikôhk. pitanê êkosi ihkik.

---

wetakosiki eyamiaki.
wêtakosiki ayamihâki.

---

ota itateyimatak kise manito, manitoweyimatak.
ôta itatêyimâtâhk kisê-manitow, manitowêyimâtâhk.

---

ni manitom, anoc katepiskak ki pe ocikwanapistatin
nimanitôm, anohc kâ-tipiskâk kipê-ocihkwanapîstâtin

espiteyimitan esi peyako kise manitowiyan:
(ê-)ispîhtêyimitân (ê-)isi-pêyako-kisê-manitowiyan:

ki mamisitotatin esi kisewatisiyan; ispic oteiyan
kimamisîtotâtin (ê-)isi-kisêwâtisiyan; ispic otêhiyan

ki sakiitin. iyepine siyakiikosiyan; mina esi
kisâkihitin. iyêpinê (ê-)siyakihikosiyan; mîna (ê-)isi-

sakiisoyan nitisi sakiaw nicayisiyiniw kiya oci.
sâkihisoyan nitisi-sâkihâw nîcâyisiyiniw kiya ohci.

---

nanaskomatak kise manito kakiyaw kekway
nanâskomatâhk kisê-manitow kahkiyaw kîkway

ka pe miyototakoyak.
kâ-pe-miyo-tôtâkoyâhk.

---

ni manitom, tanisi ki pa isi tepinanaskomitin wikac,
nimanitôm, tânisi kipê-isi-têpinanâskomitin wîhkâc,

kakiyaw kekway ka miyo totawiyan aspin kociyan; ki ki
kahkiyaw kîkway kâ-miyo-tôtawiyan aspin (ê-)kocîyan; kikî-

ayisiyiniwiwin, ki ki miyin kitayamiawin, ki ki mekin
ayisiyiniwiwin, kikî-miyin kitayamihâwin, kikî-mêkin

ki pimatisiwin, ayamiewatikok e nipostamawiyan kici
kipimâtisiwin, ayamihêwâhtikohk ê-nipôstamawiyan kici-

pimaciiyan; mina
pimâcihiyan; mîna

222 Still each day I doubt even though You do good for me. How much have I sinned. I thank You so much for Your compassion.

Those who are in Heaven help. All together we praise You. God is so kind. So let it be.

Let us ask God to let us know
our evil deeds.

You are a good God in every way. You are all-knowing. Let me be aware of all my sins. Make me powerful to have great disdain for the wicked life. I am greatly afraid that I will anger You again. What I have done over and over, let me remember this.

We obey You, God, the One who knows all about
our transgressions:
to confess our bad thoughts, bad words, and bad deeds.

You govern all. I am ashamed for my evil ways. Although I truly regret that way that I did not believe in You, You still love me and You are compassionate. Even so, You died for me. Is this the way I can repay You for the good You have done for me? By being selfish I angered You. I pray to You to take away my sins.

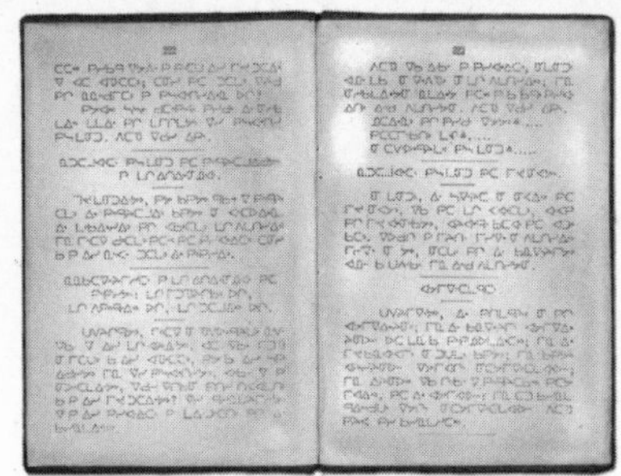

222 tatwaw kisikake eyapic ki kwitate isi miyototawin e ata
tâhtwâw kîsikâki êyâpic kikwitatê isi-miyo-tôtawin ê-âta-

anwetatan; tanisi kita totaman eyikok kici nanaskomitan
ânwêhtâtân; tânisi kita-tôtaman iyikohk kihci-nanâskomitin

ki kisewatisiwina oci?
kikisêwâtisiwina ohci?

kiyawaw sasay kotaskiyek kisikok wi ni sokamawik
kiyawâw sâsay ê-kôtaskiyêk kîsikôhk wî-nîsôhkamawik

mamawi kici mamicimayak esi kisewatisit kise
mâmawi-kici-mamihcimayâhk (ê-)isi-kisêwâtisit kisê-

manito. pitane ekosi ikik.
manitow. pitanê êkosi ihkik.

---

natotamowatak kise manito kita kiskeyitamoikoyak
natotamowâtâhk kisê-manitow kita-kiskêyihtamohikoyâhk

ki maci itiwininowa.
kimacihtiwininâwa.

---

meyo manitowiyan, kiya kakiyaw kekway
(ê-)miyo-manitowiyan, kiya kahkiyaw kîkway

e kiskeyitaman wi kiskeyitamoin kakiyaw
ê-kiskêyihtaman wî-kiskêyihtamowin kahkiyaw

ni pastaowina wi maskawisiin kici pakwataman
nipâstâhowina wî-maskawisîhin kici-pakwâtaman

maci pimatisiwin mina mistae kostaman kitwam kita
maci-pimâtisiwin mîna mistahi (ê-)kostaman kîhtwâm kita-

kisiwaitan tanisi ka ki isi naspac totaman wi kiskisoin.
kisiwâhitân tânisi kâ-kî-isi-nâspic-tôtamân wî-kiskisohin.

---

nanakataweyimisotak ki maci itiwininowa kita
nânâkatawêyimisotâhk kimacihtiwininâwa kita-

kiskisiyak: maci mitoneyicikan oci,
kiskisiyâhk: maci-mitonêyihcikan ohci,

maci pikiskwewin oci, maci totamowin oci.
maci-pîkiskwêwin ohci, maci-tôtamowin ohci.

---

tepeyicikeyan, mistae ni nepewokeyiten napec ekwa
(ê-)tipêyihcikêyan, mistahi ninêpêwikêyihtên napêc êkwa

e isi maci ayiwiyan. ata ekwa mitone ni mitaten ka isi
ê-isi-maci-ayiwiyan. âta êkwa mitonê nimihtâtên ka-isi-

anwetatan, kiya ka isi sakiikosiyan mina esi
ânwêhtâtân, kiya ka-isi-sâkihikosiyan mîna (ê-)isi-

kisewatisiyan, paskac e ki nipostamawiyan, ekosi ecikani
kisêwâtisiyan, pâskac ê-kî-nipôstamawiyan, êkosi êcikani

kitisi tipaamatin ka ki isi miyototawiyan? esi
kitisi-tipahamâtin kâ-kî-isi-miyo-tôtawiyan? (ê-)isi-

kesinateyimisoyan e ki isi kisiwaitan ki mawimostatin kici
kêsinâtêyimisoyan ê-kî-isi-kisiwâhitân kimawimôstâtin kici-

wi kasinamawiyan.
wî-kâsînamawiyan.

223 I wish that I will no more anger You, my God. Today I abandon my evil life and ask You to help me. I will try not to anger You again. For as long as I live I wish this to be so.

Our Father, the One in Heaven &.....
I greet you Mary &.....
Glory be to God &.....

Let us ask God, that we should sleep well.

My God, You are going to bless my sleep so that I sleep well and not dream bad things. In the morning so that I will have a proper awakening. I will work for You. That is why I give You my entire life, my whole body, my spirit, so that You are going to watch over me, today and in the future for as long as I live.

Let us pray for all people.

You are content with me; I know You will have pity on them. The priest will watch over them. As You taught them, He will watch over all my friends carefully and all people who are thankful to Him. I will pray for them all. And people, Indians, who do not know Him from their own experience, they should learn Your religion. Even if they go to purgatory, I will still pray for them. I wish You to be quick to forgive them.

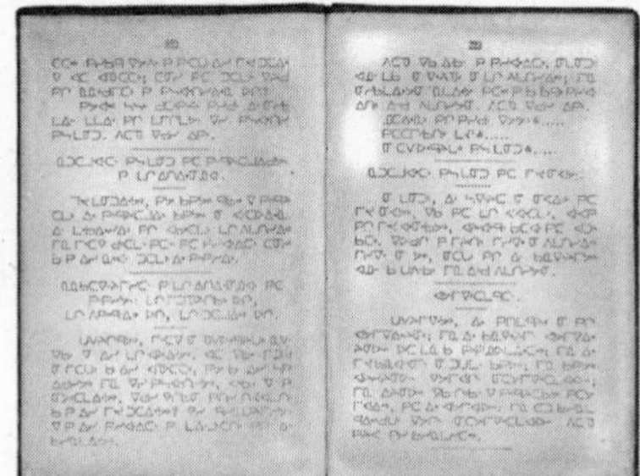

223 pitane eka wikac ki kisiwaitan, nimanitom anoc maka
pitanê êkâ wîhkâc kikisiwâhitân, nimanitôm anohc mâka

ni wepinen ni maci pimatisiwin; mina nisokamawiyani
niwêpinên nimaci-pimâtisiwin; mîna nîsôhkamawiyani

namawiya kitwam ki ka kakwekisiwaitin isko pimatisiyani.
namâwiya kîhtwâm kika-kakwê-kisiwâhitin isko pimâtisiyani.

pitane ekosi ikik.
pitanê êkosi ihkik.

notawinan kici kisikok eyayan &.....
nôhtâwînân kihci-kîsikôhk (ê-)ayâyan &.....

kitatamiskatin mari &.....
kitatamiskâtin Mari &.....

ni tapwewokeyimaw kise manito &.....
nitâpwêwakêyimâw kisê-manitow &.....

---

natotamowatak kise manito kita miyonipayak.
natotamowâtâhk kisê-manitow kita-mîyo-nipâyâhk.

---

ni manitom, wi saweyita ni nipawin kita miyo nipayan,
nimanitôm, wî-sawêyihta ninipâwin kita-miyo-nipâyân,

eka kita maci pawataman, wapaki kici miyo waniskayan,
êkâ kita-maci-pawâtaman, wâpahki kici-miyo-waniskâyân,

ayiwakes katawa kita atoskatan. eokoci ki miyitin misiwe
ayiwakês katawa kita-atoskâtân. êwakohci kimiyitin misiwê

ni pimatisiwin misiwe ni yaw, nitacak kici wi
nipimâtisiwin misiwê niyaw, nitahcâhk kici-wî-

kanaweyimiyan anoc ka tepiskak mina isko pimatisiyani.
kanawêyimiyan anohc kâ-tipiskâk mîna isko pimâtisiyani.

---

ayamiestamaketak.
ayamihêstamakêtâhk.

---

tepeyimiweyan, wi kitimakeyim ni kici
(ê-)tipêyimiwêyan, wî-kitimâkêyim nikihci-

ayamiewiyinim; mina wi kanaweyimik ayamiewiyiniwok
ayamihêwiyinîm; mîna wî-kanawêyimik ayamihêwiyiniwak

ota mana ka kiskinoomawitwaw; mina wi
ôta mâna ka-kiskinohamawitwâw; mîna wî-

miyokanawapamik ni totemak kakiyaw; mina kakiyaw
miyo-kanawâpamik nitôtêmak kahkiyaw; mîna kahkiyaw

ayisiyiniwok eyamiacik nitayamiestamawawok; mina
ayisiyiniwak (ê-)ayamihâcik nitayamihêstamâwak; mîna

iyiniwok eka ciskwa e kiskeyitakwaw kitayamiawin, kita
iyiniwak êkâ cêskwa ê-kiskêyihtakwâw kitayamihâwin, kita-

wi ayamiawok: mina tato kasinamakewiskotek
wî-ayamihâwak: mîna tâhto kâsînamâkêw-iskotêhk

eyacik ni tayamiestamawawok pitane kiyipa kisi-
(ê-)ayâcik nitayamihêstamâwak pitanê kiyipa kisi-

kasinamasotwaw.
kâsînamâsotwâw.

224

ᑕᑐᑕᒪᕋᑦ ᑭᓴᒪᑎᑐ ᑭᑕ ᒥᔦᑎᐱᐊᐧᔦᐠ.

ᑎ ᒪᑎᑐᑦ, ᑎ ᑭᐢᑫᔦᐦᑌᐣ ᑭᑎ ᑎᐱᔦᐣ ᑕᑎ ᐊᑎᑕ, ᒪᑲ ᑕᒪᐃᐧᔦ ᑎ ᑭᐢᑫᔦᐦᑌᐣ ᑕᑎᔦᐊ ᑫ ᔦᑎ ᐊᐊᔦᐣ; ᐁᐅᐊᑎ ᒥᐢᑕᐁ ᑎ ᓴᑭᔦᐣ ᑭᑎ ᑕᐣᑐ ᒥᔦᐣ ᑫᑕᑕᐁᐧ ᐁᑲ ᐊᓴᐧᔦᑕᒪᑎ. ᐊᐅ ᐊᑕ- ᑲ ᑎᐱᐢᑲᐠ ᑕᒪᐃᐧᔦ ᑎ ᑫᑎᑕᐅᐣ ᑭᑕᐠ ᑭᑕ ᐊᐧᑎᐢ ᑲᔦᐣ ᐁᐅᐊᑎ ᐱᑕᑌ ᐁᑲᐃᐧᑲ- ᑭᑭᐢᑲᐊᔦᐣ ᒪᑎ ᐸᐢᑕᐅᐃᐧᐣ ᐁᑲ ᑭᑕ ᒪᑎ ᑎᐱᔦᐣ. ᑭᔦᑦ, ᑎᒪᑎᑐᑦ ᐱᐊ ᐁᔦᐊᐠ ᐃᑌᔦᑕᒪᑎ ᑭ ᑲ ᐅᑎᑌᐣ ᑎ ᐱᒪᑎ ᔦᐃᐧᐣ. ᑭ ᑎᑎᐠ ᑎ ᐸᑭᑎᑕᐤ ᑎ ᓚᓚᐠ ᐅᒪ ᑲᐃᐧ ᑎᐸᔦᐣ, ᒥᑕ ᐃᐧ ᑎᐱᔦᑎ ᐃᐧ ᐅᑎᑏᑲᐣ ᑫᓴᐊᐧᑎ ᔦᔦᐣ ᓴᔦᐢ: ᒥᑕ ᒪᑎ ᑌᑲ, ᑭᑕᐊᐧᔦᒥᐢ ᐃᐧᑲᑕ ᐁᐧᔦᐠ ᐊᑕ- ᒥᑕ ᑲᑭᑫ ᐅᑕ ᐊᐢᑭᐠ.

ᒣᒧᓴᔦ.

ᑕᐢᐱ- ᐁᔦᒥᐁᐊᐧᑎᔦᔦᐣ ᒪᑎ, ᐃᐧ ᑭᐢᑭᔦ ᐁᑲᐃᐧᑲ- ᑫᐢᑲᐧ ᐁ ᐯᑕᑲᐧ ᑭᑎ ᐁᑲ ᑭᑎᒪᑭᑕᐊᐧ ᐊᐃᐧᔦᐠ ᒣᐃᐧᒧᑕᐢᑭ, ᐁᐅᐊᑎ ᑎᐢᑕ ᐁ ᑫᑎᑕ ᐅᔦᐣ, ᑭᔦ ᐁ ᐸᐢᑭᔦᑫᔦᐣ ᐁᔦ ᑲᑕᑕᓗᑫᔦᐣ, ᑭ ᒪᒥᔦᑐᑕᐣ, ᑭ ᑕᑕᒧᑐᑕᐣ; ᐁ ᑫᔦᑕᐅᐣ ᒥᔦᐣ ᐁᔦ ᒪᑎ ᐊᐣᐃᐧᔦᐣ, ᑭ ᐯ ᒪᐃᐧᒧᑕᐣ ᑭᑎ ᐊᔦᒥᐁᐢᑕᒪᐃᐧᔦᐣ. ᐁᑲᐃᐧᔦ ᐃᐧ ᐊᑕᐁᐧᐣᒥᐣ ᐁᑲᐃᐧᔦ ᒥᑕ ᐃᐧ ᓴᑭᑐᐃᐧᐣ ᑲ ᐃᔦ ᑕᐣᑐᑕᒪᑫᐣ.
ᐱᑕᑌ ᐁᐊᔦ ᐃᑭᐠ.

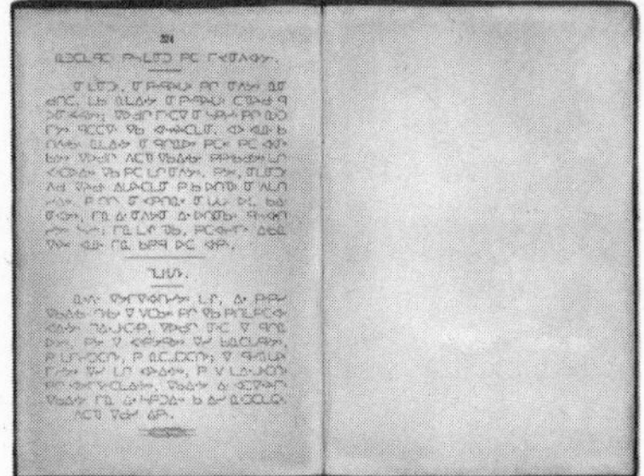

224 Let us ask this of God, that we have a good death.

My God, I know from experience how to die. A day will come when I will know no one. That is when I am not here. That is why I am very afraid when You ask for me suddenly and unexpectedly even today. At night I am certain of no one. That is why I wish never to commit any evil sin or to have a bad death. My God, it does not matter how much I think about it. You will take my life. In Heaven I will surrender my spirit. Here when I die and when I am about to die, take me. You are compassionate, Jesus. Mother Mary, watch over your child today and always here on earth.

Memorare.

I am a worshipper. Remember Mary, who has always heard and had pity when someone implores you. For that reason I am certain you will protect my soul. Your soul is pure. I place my spiritual hope in you. You will defend me; I am certain you are good in this way. I will come to worship you so that you will intercede for me, never reject me. Your love will never forget me.
So let it be.

natotamaketak kise manito kita miyonipiwayak.
natotamakêtâhk kisê-manitow kita-miyo-nipiwayahk.

---

ni manitom, ni kiskeyiten kici nipiyan nanikotita,
nimanitôm, nikiskêyihtên kici-nipiyan nani-kotita,

maka namawiya ni-kiskeyihten taneyikok ke poni
mâka namâwiya nikiskêyihtên tânêyikohk kê-pôni

eyeyan; eokoci mistae ni sekisin kici kici nantomiyan
(ê-)ayâyân; êwakohci mistahi nisêkisin kici-nantomiyan

ketatawe eka asweyitamani. apo anoc ka tipiskak
kêtahtawê êkâ aswêyihtamâni. ahpô anohc kâ-tipiskâk

namawiya ni kecinaon kitwam kita waniskayan eokoci
namâwiya nikêhcinâhon kîhtwâm kita-waniskâyan êwakohci

pitane ekawikac kikiskakoyan maci pastaowin eka kita
pitanê êkâ wîhkâc kikiskâkoyân maci-pâstâhowin êkâ kita-

maci nipiyan. kiyam, ni manitom piko eyikok iteyitamani
maci-nipiyan. kiyâm, nimanitôm piko iyikôhk itêyihtamani

ki ka otinen ni pimatisiwin. ki cicik ni pakitinaw
kika-otinên nipimâtisiwin. kicicik nipakitinaw

ni cacak oma kawi nipayan, mina wi nipiyani wi
nicahcâhk ôma kawî-nipâyân, mîna wî-nipiyani wî-

otinikan kesewatisiyan sesos: mina mari neka,
otinihkan (ê-)kisêwâtisiyan Sesos: mîna Mari nêka,

kitawasimis wi kanaweyim anoc mina kakike ota askik.
kitawâsimis wî-kanawêyim anohc mîna kâkikê ôta askîhk.

---

memorare.
memorare.

---

naspic eyamiewatisiyan mari, wi kiskisi eka wikac
nâspic (ê-)ayamihêwâtisiyan Mari, wî-kiskisi êkâ wîhkâc

ceskwa e petakwak kici eka kitimakitawot awiyak
cêskwa ê-pêhtakwahk kici êkâ kitimâkîhtawat awiyak

mewimostaski, eokoci nista e kecinaoyan, kiya
mawimostâski, êwakohci nîsta ê-kêhcinâhoyân, kiya

e paskiyakeyan esi kanatacakweyan, ki mamisitotatin,
ê-paskiyakêyan (ê-)isi-kanâtahcâhkwêyan, kimamisîtotâtin,

ki natamototatin; e kesinateyimisoyan esi maci ayiwiyan,
kinâtamototâtin; ê-kêsinatêyimisoyan (ê-)isi maci-ayiwiyan,

ki pe mawimostatin kici ayamiestamawiyan. ekawiya
ki-pê-mawimostâtin kici-ayamihêstamawiyan. êkâwiya

wi ataweyimin ekawiya mina wi sakitowin ka isi
wî-atawêyimin êkâwiya mîna wî-sâkihitowin ka-isi-

nastotamatan.
nastotamâtân.

pitane ekosi ikik.
pitanê êkosi ihkik.

225

AFTERWORD

Language and Devotion: A Missionary's Use of Cree Syllabics

by Patricia Demers, Naomi McIlwraith, and Dorothy Thunder

An unexpected symmetry and a good modicum of luck have propelled this project. With the benefit of networks, strategic introductions, and friendly help, it turned out that three University of Alberta colleagues—a professor and native speaker of Cree, a poet who is an advanced student of Cree, and an English professor—came together to collaborate in translating Grouard's three-part text: prayer book, catechism, and hymnal. But, as with any translating project, the work did not fit into tidy compartments. There was a lot of conversation and negotiation, overlap and exchange, when we met often to talk about the accretive nature of Cree, the liturgy of the Mass, and ways of accommodating, interleaving the rhythms of a people with the fervour of a catechizing missionary. What continues to buoy our confidence in this project is the realization that our efforts are actually pioneering: there is no comparable examination and reconstructive translation of a mission press imprint in the language of the people being catechized.

One of the first agreements we reached concerned our role as translators. We knew we were entering relatively uncharted territory, both in grappling with and making available a nineteenth-century catechetical text and in positioning ourselves at the interface of oral culture and textual representation. We recognized that fidelity to this untranslated, largely forgotten text would mean we would have to make a whole series of adjustments. In respecting the textual archive and trying to convey its conversational cadences, we had to allow for what seemed at first glance unorthodox or unconventional syntax. Very soon, however, we understood the regularity and pedagogical reinforcement of reversed sentence order, rapid changes of person and tense, and the accumulation of compound but unpunctuated sentences. We realized the emphatic underscoring of such declarations of the penitent as "Me, I did it. Me, I did it. Me truly, I did it" (Prayer Book [PB] 15). Rote learning and examination of conscience intertwined in this exercise so dedicated to the principle of repetition, of sounding again, as the etymology of *catechesis* (from the Greek κατηκειν: to sound or ring thoroughly) implies. Our own comments on this text, its language and theology, take their cue from Grouard himself. We attend, in the first instance, to the complexity of the language and syntax, and then we turn to the message this language conveys.

Cree functions polysynthetically: several and sometimes all of the syntactic elements required for constructing the full meaning of a sentence can be contained in one word. Peter Bakker explains that, "Cree is a typical polysynthetic language in the sense that almost all of the grammatical information is given in the verb, and very little in the noun. This means that verbs are frequent and morphologically complex."[1] Two orthographies are available for writing the Plains Cree language: Cree Syllabics and Standard Roman Orthography. As a writing system that illustrates the single spoken beats or pulses that are most often one vowel or a composite of one vowel and one consonant,[2] Cree Syllabics offer the modern reader one way of perceiving the world as Grouard and the Cree people he worked with did.

The alphabetic Standard Roman Orthography (SRO), by comparison, is a phonemic writing system that uses hyphenation and other indicators to provide phonological (sound) and morphological (word structure) information that cannot be found in early Syllabics or early Cree writing that uses Roman letters. Although the understanding and representation of Syllabics are still issues of variability for researchers, our project benefited from the path-breaking work of Cree scholars and their collaborators. Among these, we acknowledge the scholarship of Freda Ahenakew, H. Christoph Wolfart, et al. at the University of Manitoba; Jean Okimâsis, Arok Wolvengrey, et al. from the First Nations University of Canada in Saskatchewan; and the inestimable contributions of members of the Cree speech community. While Cree linguists and scholars have in recent decades achieved much in developing and refining SRO as a modern method of signifying the phonological and morphological workings of *nêhiyawêwin*, SRO users understandably struggle when transliterating from Syllabics to SRO mainly because early Cree Syllabics writers did not use enough detail to enable modern readers to differentiate the finest of sounds. For example, the preverbs /maci / and /maci / do not, in fact, mean the same thing even though in early Cree writing with Syllabics or Roman letters their different meanings are not evident. SRO represents the first as */maci-/*, meaning "bad, evil, or ugly" and the second as */mâci-/*, complete with diacritical marking to delineate the long "â" vowel and meaning "to begin or start something." Such imprecise representation in early Cree Syllabics renders the task of transliterating and translating exceptionally complex.

Although Cree Syllabics do not mark the boundaries of words and morphemes, Grouard frequently denotes these boundaries with spaces, affording us a measure of confidence in understanding his intentions. We have chosen to provide both a complete, straight transcription—that is, an alphabetic equivalent—of Grouard's rendition of Syllabics in the first line *and* in the second italicized line a thorough transliteration in contemporary SRO that signals not only Cree sounds but Cree word structure, as well. Understanding the missionary's every thought, however, has occasionally eluded us, and in a number of cases we have had to infer his meaning. Furthermore, Grouard certainly worked with greater technological limitations than we do now, and for this reason, the reader will notice differences—some significant and some slight—between the straight transcription and the SRO transliteration.

One area of particular difficulty for us was with Grouard's frequent and able use of "initial change." Where we thought Grouard exhibited a number of mistakes, such as transposing te–ᑌ for ti–ᑎ, we now see more clearly, with Arok Wolvengrey's generous assistance, that Grouard did not err as often as we initially supposed. We find the most enlightening example of this in the various conjugations of the stems *têpêyim* and *tipêyim*. *Têpêyimêw* is a transitive animate verb meaning "s/he is content with someone." *Tipêyimêw* is another transitive animate verb and, by comparison, means "s/he owns someone, s/he possesses someone, s/he is in charge of someone, s/he controls someone, s/he rules over someone, s/he governs someone."[3]

As Wolvengrey has clarified for us, the process of initial change was especially productive at Grouard's time, where short vowels such as /i/ and /a/ become [e]. The stem *tipêyim*, as seen frequently in *kâtolik ayamihêwi-masinahikan*, modifies to *têpêyim* as a result of initial change. The difference in meaning between *têpêyim* and *tipêyim* (sometimes represented as tepeyim) is significant enough to have caused us considerable confusion. We owe Wolvengrey and C. Douglas Ellis a sincere thank you for elucidating this for us. As Ellis explains:

> Certain conjunct forms display so-called INITIAL CHANGE, a systematic modification of the structure of the first syllable of the forms concerned. The patterns (where "C" stands for any consonant or for none) are:

UNCHANGED FORM	CHANGED FORM
Ci-	Cē-
Ca-	Cē-
Co-	Cwē-
Cī-	Cā-
Cē-	Ciyē-
Cā-	Ciyā-, Cēyā-
Cō-	Cwā-

Two forms differing only in this way are said to be of the same mode (and tense), but of different submodes, the CHANGED and UNCHANGED, respectively. The changed neutral indicative is often used as a participle, the changed subjunctive as an ITERATIVE:

	UNCHANGED FORM	CHANGED FORM
INDIC.	tipēlihcikēt *that he rule, govern*	tēpēlihcikēt *ruling one, governor, lord*
SUBJ.	tipēlihcikētē *if he rules, governs*	tēpēlihcikēcih *whenever he rules, governs*[4]

We could not have found a more appropriate example to illuminate this phenomenon. Where modern Plains Cree speakers use the /ê-/ preverb in the conjunct mode and say *ê-tipêyimiyâhk* to mean, "You govern us all," and *ê-têpêyimiyâhk* to connote "You are content with us all," we discover that during the nineteenth century the initial /i/ of tipeyim modifies to /e/ as a result of initial change. This means that while speakers of Cree in the twenty-first century will also prefer *ê-miyosit*, meaning "He is good," because changes in the language have led to a reduction in the prevalence of initial change, Cree speakers in Grouard's time would have approved of meyosit, also meaning "He is good." Grouard uses both forms in *kâtolik ayamihêwi-masinahikan*. Imagine the confusion for a modern reader of Cree. The following legend illustrates how we came to resolve this issue. Table 1 provides a straight transcription of Grouard's Syllabics in the first column, an alphabetic equivalent in the second column, a transliteration into contemporary Standard Roman Orthography in italics in the third column, and a translation into English in the fourth column. Page numbers refer to Grouard's original.

LEGEND

1s First person singular (the speaker)—I, Me
2s Second person singular (the listener)—You
1p First person plural (excluding the listener)—We, Us
21p First person plural (including the listener)—We, Us
2p Second person plural (more than one listener to whom someone speaks)—You, You All
3s Third person singular (not a part of the conversation)—She/He
3p Third person plural (not a part of the conversation)—They, Them
3' Third person obviative (one step further away than 3s or 3p)—His Sister, Her Brother[5]

TABLE I

PB PAGE	CREE SYLLABICS	TRANSLITERATION	SRO	
17	ᑌᐯᔨᒥᔭᐠ	tepeyimiyak	*(ê-)tipêyimiyâhk*	You (2s) govern us all (1p).
20	ᑌᐯᔨᒥᔭᐣ	tepeyimiyan	*(ê-)tipêyimiyan*	You (2s) govern me (1s).
38	ᑌᐯᔨᒥᔭᐠ	tepeyimiyak	*(ê-)tipêyimiyâhk*	You (2s) govern us all (1p).
183	ᑎᐯᔨᒥᐟ	tipeyimit	*(ê-)tipêyimit*	He (3s) governs me (1s).
197	ᑌᐯᔨᒥᐢᐠ	tepeyimisk	*(ê-)tipêyimisk*	He (3s, 3') governs you (2s).
223	ᑌᐯᔨᒥᐍᔭᐣ	tepeyimiweyan	*(ê-)tipêyimiwêyan*	You (2s) govern me (1s).

TABLE 2

PB PAGE	CREE SYLLABICS	TRANSLITERATION	SRO	
9	ᐁ ᑎᐯᔨᒥᔭᐣ	e tipeyimiyan	*ê-tipêyimiyan*	You (2s) govern me (1s).
20	ᐏ ᐯᔭᑯ ᑎᐯᔨᒥᐣ	wi peyako tipeyimin	*wî-pêyako-tipêyimin*	You (2s) alone will govern me.
137	ᑲ ᑎᐯᔨᒥᐍᐟ	ka tipeyimiwet	*kâ-tipêyimiwêt*	God (3s) who governs all.
178	ᐁ ᑎᐯᔨᒥᑕᑯᐠ	e tipeyimitakok	*ê-tipêyimitakok*	I (1s) govern you all (2s).
	ᐁ ᑎᐯᔨᒥᐢᐠ	e tipeyimisk	*ê-tipêyimisk*	He (3s, 3') governs you (2s).
197	ᑲ ᑎᐯᔨᒥᐍᐟ	ka tipeyimiwet	*kâ-tipêyimiwêt*	The One who governs all.
209	ᑲ ᑎᐯᔨᒥᑯᔭᐟ	ka tipeyimikoyak	*kâ-tipêyimikoyâhk*	The One (3s, 3') who governs us all (1s).
217	ᑲ ᑎᐯᔨᒥᔭᐢ	ka tipeyimiyan	*kâ-tipêyimiyan*	You (2s), the One who governs me (1s).

ABBREVIATIONS

VAI *animate intransitive verb*
VII *inanimate intransitive verb*
VTA *transitive animate verb*
VTI *transitive inanimate verb (following Wolvengrey et al., vi)*

Now consider Grouard's spelling on the above pages. Notice that in Table 1, Grouard chooses not to use the /e / preverb, but that in Table 2 he does.

Originally, we perceived Grouard to have simply erred in inverting ᑎ /ti/ for ᑌ /te/. Now, however, we see (and hear) tepeyimiyak for what it really meant in Grouard's time and for what it still means to a modern Cree speaker: *ê-tipêyimiyâhk*—"You (2s) govern us all (1p)." Just as we write how a modern Cree speaker will understand and voice this utterance with the preverb */ê-/* included in this sentence, we choose to include this preverb in our contemporary SRO, showing the modern Plains Cree reader the process of initial change at work. On the other hand, ki nipostamakonaw tepeyimitak—*kinipôstamâkonaw têpêyimitâhk*, does not demonstrate initial change because it is an imperative construction that does not require any preverb: "He dies for us, let us be content with Him" (PB 216). These examples surely confirm both the intricacies of translating *kâtolik ayamihêwi-masinahikan* and the need for an orthography that will alleviate some of these difficulties. Our provision of a second line of text with a transliteration into contemporary Standard Roman Orthography, to reflect Grouard's alphabetic equivalent in line one, is in no way a "correction" of his work; neither is our decision to indicate the */ê-/* where he does not an effort to adjust his intentions or change his language. While Grouard would have spoken a northern variation of the Plains Cree dialect, he would not have spoken a different language. He spoke Plains Cree and he wrote Plains Cree. We honour Grouard's representation of Plains Cree in our transcription of an alphabetic equivalent in line one of our text, as he learned it from the speakers he lived and worked amongst. Nevertheless, we also recognize that Plains Cree, like all languages, has changed and will continue to change over time: accordingly, we indicate these language changes in the SRO.

We have seen widespread critical disagreement about the role of initial change in relative and subjunctive clauses. For example, some readers speculate that for the first two forms listed in Table 1, from pages 17 and 20, it is possible that Grouard uses initial change to construct relative clauses that might be translated respectively as, "You (2s) who govern us" and "You (2s) who govern me," a slightly different interpretation from ours. As well, it is possible that the forms from Table 2, complete with the /e / preverb and with no initial change, might be understood as complements supporting main verbs in their particular sentences. These suggestions are plausible, though we are not fully convinced of their definitiveness. Why would Grouard construct relative clauses with initial change as shown in Table 1, but choose the /ka /— */kâ-/* prefix to signal relative clauses as we see in Table 2? Although we recognize and respect other opinions, we have kept our original analysis because of the difficulty in achieving absolute certainty about Grouard's every meaning. Another possibility for why Grouard would have included the /e / prefix in some cases and not in others can perhaps be best explained by surmising that the language was changing as he learned to speak and write it, and that some words would have been voiced with the prefix while others were not. One such example occurs when Grouard writes e iteyimiyan (PB 23), complete with a space between preverb and verb, but without initial change. We follow Grouard's lead: *ê-itêyimiyan*—"You (2s) think thus about me."

Almost every time he invokes "Our Father, You are there in Heaven": ᓄᑕᐃᐧᓇᐣ ᑭᒋ ᑭᓯᑯᐠ ᐁᔭᔭᐣ: notawinan kici kisikok eyayan—*nôhtâwînân kihci-kîsikohk (ê-)ayâyan*, Grouard writes ᐁᔭᔭᐣ—eyayan: *(ê-)ayâyan*—"You are there" (PB 34), and we witness another example of initial change. Again, we include the *(ê-)* preverb for the modern reader to discern here in this sentence *and* in the manuscript, as well. We recognize that this is a controversial issue since some prefer the preverb */ê-/* to be written in its changed form, to show the mutation in the first syllable, rather than in parentheses. For consistency, however, we signal to the modern reader the process of initial change by including the preverb: *(ê-)ayâyan*. Although we have received the suggestion to leave meyosit as *mêyosit*, as Grouard writes it, we have chosen—again for consistency—to include the */ê-/* preverb and demonstrate to the modern reader that initial change occurs here as well: *(ê-)miyosit*. Again, we are not attempting to show errors where Grouard has not erred; rather, we are illustrating the sheer complexity of editing this text and revealing to the modern Cree reader Grouard's intentions in the alphabetic equivalent of line one and using SRO in line two to demonstrate how subtly Plains Cree works in constructing meaning and how the language has changed.

There are other places, however, where Grouard does not include the /e / prefix, and the reason cannot be explained by initial change. For example, when he writes maci mamitoneyitamak a modern speaker will want to insert the preverb */ê-/* and say *ê-maci-mâmitonêyihtamâhk*—"As we (first person plural excluding the listener) have evil thoughts" (PB 5). And yet, in other places the missionary includes the /e / prefix, as in e pimatisiyit (PB 6): *ê-pimâtisiyit*—"As they live," and e ki iteyimiyan (PB 10): *ê-kî-itêyimiyan*—"As he thought thus of someone." According to Ellis, initial change occurs in "certain conjunct forms," and Grouard does conjugate these examples in the conjunct order. His reasons for not including the /e / prefix in maci mamitoneyitamak are clearly not because of initial change, because even without the preverb /maci /, the verb begins with a consonant, not a vowel. We believe that real certainty on these matters is not possible because we cannot now ask Grouard himself or the speakers of Plains Cree during his time.

Sandhi, another morphophonological process that occurs regularly in Cree, is worth considering at this juncture, because it functions quite differently from initial change. Western Canadian Cree scholars describe sandhi as the coalescence of the final vowel of one word with a vowel at the start of the next word. Okimāsis and Wolvengrey agree with this explanation, though they are more specific in their description:

> The process of sandhi refers to a contraction of vowels across word or word formation boundaries. This means that when two words or parts of words occur next to each other, placing two vowels adjacent to one another, these two vowels, under certain conditions, may contract together. This is very common in Cree speech.[6]

Grouard also demonstrates sandhi in *kâtolik ayamihêwi-masinahikan*, and its presence provides a good example for contrast to initial change. For example, he writes e ki macitotaman—*ê-kî-maci-itôtaman*—"As you (2s) do something thus" (PB 7). Here is another instance where the advantages of Standard Roman Orthography clearly help modern readers and Cree learners to discern the meaning in a text such as Grouard's. The preverbal particle /maci /, without any long vowels, means "bad, evil, or ugly." When Grouard affixes it to the stem itotam we can see how the final /i-/ of maci and the initial /i-/ of itotam merge into one vowel /i-/. SRO provides important information with the hyphen to show that */maci-/* and */itôtam/* are indeed two different and separate morphemes. Even though Grouard does not signal his recognition of the two morphemes by placing a space between the preverb and the verb, in the very next sentence he tells us exactly this by placing a space between the preverb /ka / and the verb itotaman: niya ka totaman, niya ka totaman, niya tipiyaw ka totaman—*niya kâ-itôtaman, niya kâ-itôtaman, niya tipiyâw kâ-itôtaman*—"Me I did it, Me I did it, Me truly I did it" (PB 15). His elision of the initial "i-" in itotaman signifies his understanding of the process of vowel contraction at word and morpheme boundaries in operation. Much later in the manuscript, Grouard writes ka isi miyo totat—*ka-isi-miyo-itôtât*, revealing sandhi at the boundary between /miyo-/ and /itotat-/ (PB 92). The preverbal particle /miyo-/ ends with a vowel, and the verb stem /itotat-/ begins with a vowel; hence they merge into a single vowel "o-." Two examples where Grouard tells us he recognizes the boundary by placing a space between preverb and verb and opting to retain both vowels are e nita atoskatak—*ê-nihtâ-atoskâtahk*—"he works well at something" (PB 75), and poni askiwiki—*pôni-askîwiki*—"the earth will cease to be" (PB 76).

In addition to indicating word and morpheme boundaries with hyphens, other refinements to the Standard Roman Orthography that assist modern readers include marking pre-aspirated aitches and long vowels. Grouard indicates neither the aitch nor the long vowel and this, too, has important implications for our ability to understand his intended meaning. Grouard writes ᐁ ᐃᐧ ᑎᐯᔾᑕᒪᐠ—e wi tipeyitamak (PB 194), which in modern SRO is either *ê-wî-tipêyihtamâhk* or *ê-wî-tipêyihtamahk*. The VTI stem *tipêyihta* means "to own or rule something inanimate." The suffix / mak/ that Grouard provides could be either */-mahk/* (21p, denoting first person plural including the listener) or */-mâhk/* (1p, signifying the first person plural excluding the listener). Think about a straight transliteration of verse 10 (PB 194) and then a more complete transliteration into SRO:

CREE SYLLABICS	TRANSLITERATION	SRO
ᑭᔭ ᔪᐢᐱᓯᔭᐣ ᓭᓱᐢᑯᕆ	kiya yospisiyan sesoskri	*kiya yôspisiyan Sesoskri*
ᑭ ᓂᑕᐍᔾᑕᒪᑎᓇᐣ	ki nitaweyitamatinan	*kinitawêyihtamâtinân*
ᒋ ᔪᐢᐱᓯᑌᐃᔭᐠ	ci yospisiteiyak	*kici-yôspitêhêhiyâhk*
ᐁ ᐃᐧ ᑎᐯᔾᑕᒪᐠ ᑭ ᑌ.	e wi tipeyitamak ki te.	*ê-wî-tipêyihtamâhk kitêh.*

You are gentle, Jesus
We want it for You
So that we (all of us) have a soft heart
We are going to rule Your heart.

Given the initial three lines, it seems that in the fourth Grouard intends not that we will control Jesus's heart, but that we will be content with it: *ê-wî-têpêyihtamâhk kitêh:* "We will be content with Your heart." Both possibilities of */-mâhk/* or */-mahk/* tell us that this is not a 2s verb conjugation in the conjunct order, which would be */-man/*. There is also a slight ambiguity in whether Grouard means 1p—the first person plural excluding the listener—or 21p—the first person plural including the listener—though a fluent speaker will hear the long vowel in the correct construction.

The third line also stumped us, but once again we credit Wolvengrey for helping us understand Grouard's intentions. Wolvengrey suggests that possibly Grouard did not mean yospisitehe, a VAI stem meaning to "have a soft heart," but *yôspitêhêh*, a VTA stem meaning to "soften someone's heart" resulting in *kici-yôspitêhêhiyâhk*, meaning "for you to soften our hearts." This seems to agree with a possible reading of line four as: "We are going to be content with Your heart"—*ê-wî-têpêyihtamâhk kitêh*, instead of e wi tipeyihtamak ki te. Observe our representation as including the full form of */kici-/* instead of the contracted /ci /.

We see another example where Grouard writes in verse 2 (PB 165):

CREE SYLLABICS	TRANSLITERATION	SRO
ᑲᑲᐏᐢᑯᓱᔪᐣ, ᓭᓱᓭ,	kakawiskosoyan, sesose	*kâ-kawiskôsoyan, Sesose*
ᑲ ᐃᐢᐱᓀᒥᑲᐏᔭᐣ ᐘᐘ	ka ispinemikawiyan wawac	*kâ-ispinêmikawiyan wâwâc*
ᓂᔭ ᓭᑫ ᓂ ᐏᒋᐃᐘᐣ	niya seke ni wiciiwan	*niya sêhkê niwîcihiwân*
ᑲ ᒪᒋ ᐸᑭᓯᓂᔭᐣ.	ka maci pakisiniyan.	*kâ-mâci-pahkisiniyan.*

Grouard does not place a space between the preverb /ka / and the verb kawiskoso, but he indicates very clearly the preverb /ka / before ispinemikawiyan and pakisiniyan with a large space. We conclude that this is what he means:

> You, who fall under the burden, Jesus.
> You, who are insulted.
> I willingly go along,
> when You start to fall.

While early Cree Syllabics do not denote the long vowels in the prefixes of relative clauses, subjunctive clauses, and reduplicatives, modern SRO differentiates these from their short vowel counterparts with diacritical markings. In lines one, two, and four, Grouard denotes the /ka / prefix, though in line one he does not separate it from the verb stem with a space. We believe lines one, two, and four are all relative clauses and that even though Grouard indicates no space between the morpheme boundary in line one, it is unlikely a reduplicative prefix, the */kâ-/* specifying, rather, that "You, Jesus" is the One to whom the narrator speaks and that the */kâ-/* in line four indicates a relative clause, "when You start to fall." The underspecification in early Syllabics contributes to current difficulties in ascertaining an early Syllabics writer's intentions. We insert a long *â* in the preverb */mâci-/* in line four to indicate an action that someone starts to do, rather than our earlier assumption of */maci-/*, a preverb without a long vowel meaning that something is bad, evil, or ugly. This decision corrects our earlier supposition that lines three and four read, "I willingly accompany you,/ you who fall badly" a less likely reading than "I willingly go along,/ when You start to fall." Furthermore, the verb *pahkisiniyan*, as written in contemporary SRO, provides more information than Grouard could have. First, the placement of the aitch before the k—*/hk-/*—in *pahkisiniyan* is an instance of pre-aspiration not delineated in early Cree Syllabics. Second, the verb is conjugated with a short final */a-/* agreeing with this fourth line as a second person singular construction.

Long vowels present certain challenges to scholars producing texts in the Plains Cree language. The practice in Alberta is to leave the long */e-/* unmarked because it has no short counterpart. Although we work in Alberta, we mark the long */ê-/* throughout this manuscript, following the example of scholars, such as those working at First Nations University of Canada in Regina and the University of Manitoba in Winnipeg, because of the difficulties English speakers have in letting go of their sense of the vowel "e-" as sounding like that of "beet" or "seat." Okimāsis and Wolvengrey provide a most convincing argument for demarcating the long */ê-/*:

> ē sounds like the English "ay" in "hay" or "ai" in "main." This sound has no short counterpart. It is always long, and therefore it is always marked as long (with the macron (ē) or circumflex (ê)) just as the other long vowels are. Sometimes, as has been common in Alberta, this vowel is written without the length mark. However, this leaves a bare "e" symbol, which can be quite misleading, often resulting in confusion over its use between the ē and ī sounds. Spelling it with the macron or circumflex not only marks this vowel as long, but sets it apart as if to say: This is *not* the English "e"![7]

We demonstrate this standard throughout *kâtolik ayamihêwi-masinahikan*, with thanks to those leading the way east of us.

The Standard Roman Orthography provides even more important information with the letter aitch to mark aspiration, and modernized Cree Syllabics uses two, tiny, elevated, vertical lines, ᐦ, to indicate the same. Unfortunately this denotation was unavailable to Grouard, and its absence in his texts makes it difficult for modern readers to discern between preverbs, such as kici (*kici-*), meaning "so that," and kici (*kihci-*), meaning "great, big, or important."[8] Modern Syllabics signifies *kici-* as ᑭᒋ and *kihci-* as ᑭᐦᒋ.

Just as Grouard signifies the kind and compassionate God with ᑭᓭᒪᓂᑐ and then ᑭᓭ ᒪᓂᑐ (PB 6), the former with no space and the latter with a space throughout *kâtolik ayamihêwi-masinahikan* without consistency, we recognize the limited technology he worked with and the difficult conditions he laboured under. Equally important, we acknowledge our own struggles to achieve a measure of accuracy in our use of Standard Roman Orthography, a critically needed writing system that contributes to standardizing the written form of *nêhiyawêwin*. Despite his challenges, in other places Grouard exemplifies remarkable understanding of word boundaries in the way he places spaces between nimitasi and piciwok (PB 119). Contemporary SRO illustrates these as two potential verbs:

nimitâsiw—"s/he moves camp to the open country," and *piciw*—"s/he moves camp, s/he moves his/her belongings and family."[9] Grouard unmistakably appreciates the rules of agglutination and compounding, though a modern Cree scholar would not place *ni* on the previous line as he has done.

There are other more complex ambiguities in Grouard's text: ᐊᓯᑎᑫᐧᔭᑲᑐᓯ—asitikweyakatoso (PB 45). We cannot discern a space between what appears to be the particle */asici-/* and the verb. We infer that Grouard possibly mistakes ᑎ for ᒋ but intends the preverb */asici-/*—"with, together with, along with."[10] Unfortunately, however, the remainder of the word eludes our understanding: kweyakatoso. Wolvengrey has suggested the possibility that Grouard intends the meaning of the preverb */kakwâyaki-/*—"greatly or extremely." Earle Waugh et al. gloss a number of verbs that could serve as possibilities: *kwayakitâw*—VTA—"s/he betrays something," *kwayakihiwêw*—VTA—"s/he betrays others," or *kwayakihêw*—VTA "s/he betrays him/her."[11] Could Grouard possibly intend to say "to betray each other, along with each other," in a reflexive construction that involves changing a VTA to a VAI and then conjugating the resulting verb according to the VAI paradigm: *asici-kwayak-âtisow*, the /iso/ element serving to signify the reflexive action and the /w/ indicating a 3s conjugation?

Grouard writes
ᑕᑕᐢᑕᐁᐧᔭᑲᐢᑭᒋᒐᓂᐢᑕᐊᐧᐤ ᒥᓇ ᑕᑕᐢᑕᐁᐧᔭᑲᐢᑭᓯᑌᓂᐢᑕᐊᐧᐤ (PB 46), which in a straight transliteration appears as:

tatastaweyakaskicinestawaw mina
tatastaweyakaskisitenestawaw.

With Wolvengrey's assistance we represent this in SRO as:

tâ-tastawêya-kaskicihcânêstawâw mîna
tâ-tastawêya-kaskisitânêstawâw,

placing hyphens between the particle and the following verbs. We also signify the reduplicative prefix */tâ-/*. The particle */tastawêyas-/* means "in between, in the place between."[12] This is another example of the importance of contemporary SRO in assisting us analyze such verbal constructions to arrive at a correct recognition of the author's intended meaning. Again, we are indebted to Wolvengrey in helping us determine that the more likely meaning of these words is that "He (Jesus) had (between) his fingers broken" and "He (Jesus) had (between) his toes broken" in the crucifixion, a much more likely reading than our earlier theory that a completely different verb indicated that Jesus was tired.

Another word almost defeated us until we discovered Grouard's knowledge of agglutination as the process of aggregating grammatical elements to express compound ideas. Grouard writes ᑲ ᑭ ᐸᓯᑫᐧᐱᑎᐟ—ka ki pasikwepitit: *kâ-kî-pasîhkwêpitit* (PB 35). *pasîhkwêtahwêw* is a VTA meaning "s/he slaps someone on the face,"[13] but it is different enough from Grouard's expression that it concerned us. Later, Grouard writes ᐸᓯᑫᐧᐱᑕᐤ—pasikwepitaw—*pasîhkwêpitâw* (PB 164). Some linguists might see Grouard and his informants building beginning, middle, and end sequences to form words. For example, elements from both of *pasîhkwêtahwêw* and *cîstikwêpitêw*—a VTA meaning "s/he chokes someone, s/he pinches someone's neck (pulling),"[14] convey that Jesus was scratched on the face. While modern Plains Cree speakers hear such constructions as unusual, Grouard demonstrates considerable knowledge in combining verbal elements in this way. Unfortunately, his not marking pre-aspiration does lead to some confusion as to how he conjugates this verb.

Grouard writes ᑲ ᐃᓯ ᑲᓯᓇᒪᐊᐧᑭᑕᐧᐤ—ka isi kasinamawakitwaw—*kâ-isi-kâsînamawakihtwâw* (PB 5), demonstrating the archaic suffix, */-akihtwâw/*, that the western Cree dialects no longer use. *kâ-isi-kâsînamawâyâhkik* and *kâ-isi-kâsînamawâyâhkwâw* illustrate the modern way to voice and write this construction, meaning "we forgive them"; the first person plural excluding the speaker does the action on the third person plural. Wolvengrey has suggested to us that there are two possibilities for why Grouard used this archaic suffix. Perhaps Cree speakers from whom Grouard learned to speak *nêhiyawêwin* in the Lac La Biche area could have still been using the */-akihtwâw/* suffix, or Grouard may have borrowed from Cree materials published in Manitoba, in particular the first Cree Syllabics text of the Old Testament that was produced in 1861.

At every turn we encountered linguistic and cultural traces of French, Cree, and Latin influences. Grouard's dedication to the *Amen* formula of *ainsi soit-il* (so be it) emerges in "Pitane ekosi ikik" or "So let it be." He demonstrates a sort of playful experimentation with language when he "Creeizes" the Kyrie and Gloria (PB 16–17), and uses Cree Syllabics to illustrate the Greek and Roman sounds. His presentation of the liturgical prayers of the Mass is one of the most sustained examples of intermingled Cree and Catholic locutions: "nitacakonanak wesi" or "*Kyrie eleison*: Lord have mercy" (PB 16), "okisiko nakamowin" or "*Gloria in excelsis Deo:* Glory to God in the highest" (PB 16–17), "tapwewokeyitamawin" or "*Credo in unum Deum*: I believe in one God" (PB 18–20), "kicitwaw, kicitwaw, kicitwaw" or "*Sanctus, sanctus, sanctus*: Holy, holy, holy" (PB 21–22), and "kiaseamowatwaw" or "*Agnus Dei*: Lamb of God" (PB 23–24). We were struck by his innovative, phonetic rendering of the Latin in Cree Syllabics, *cahkipêhikanak*, as in "Kiriyi eleison itweki" (PB 16), "Kloria in ekselsis/tewo" (PB 16), "krito in onom teom" (PB 18), "Saktos, saktos, saktos" (PB 21), and "Aknos tei kwitol lis/pekatamoktimiserere nopis" (PB 23). He is compelled to sway from the usual convention of Cree Syllabics to illustrate both the vowel and consonant that typically make up a Syllabic by combining consonants in such words as ekselsis, poloktatin, propter, and maknamkloriam. As an Oblate missionary, he uses symbols in the Roman Catholic variant of the Western Cree Syllabary to illustrate the / l / and / r / sounds.[15] Okimāsis and Wolvengrey explain that SRO uses these sounds only for "borrowed words which retain them,"[16] such as in the names of persons or places. Whereas Okimāsis and Wolvengrey use ≲ for */-l-/* and ≳ for */-r-/* in their Syllabics, Grouard depicts the various combinations of l and r with vowels this way:

re	ᕃ	le	ᓓ
ri	ᕆ	li	ᓕ
ro	ᕈ	lo	ᓗ
ra	ᕋ	la	ᓚ

We also found ourselves fascinated by his adaptations. One, in particular, was his use of the root "-iyiniw" to describe the Egyptians, Palestinians, and other Near Eastern peoples. Because the Cree use the same root to designate Upstream People, "*Natimiyiniwak*," Downstream People, "*Mâmihkiyiniwak*," and Prairie People, "*Paskwâwiyiniwak*," Grouard's use of "Sotawiyiniwak" for the Jews, "Esiptiwiyiniwak" for the Egyptians, "Israeliyiniwak" for the Israelites, and "Eprewiyiniwak" for Abraham's people seems to us especially insightful.

Since Cree is an accretive language, we noticed the constructive principles at work in words now rarely heard in casual conversation or popular usage, such as "ayamiewinanatawiowin—*ayamihêwi-nanâtawihowin*," a sacrament, "maci itiwina—*macihtiwina*," sins, "meyosit manito—*ê-miyosit manitow*," Holy Spirit, "wekosisimit—*wêkosisimit*," Son of God, "ayamietapwewokeyitamowin—*ayamihêwi-tâpwêwakêyihtamowin*," faith, "pakitinasiwin—*pakitinâsowin*," sacrifice, and "kasinamakewiskotek—*kâsînamâkêw-iskotêhk*," Purgatory. The compounding of these words allows for the layering of concept on concept to expand upon meaning. The following derivations illustrate these linguistic strategies.

ayamihêwi-nanâtawihowin:
ayamihêwi—preverb, of the Christian Church, of church;
nanâtawih—transitive animate verb, to treat someone (medically), to doctor someone, to heal someone;
o—consonant joiner;
win—nominalizer suffix changes a verb into a noun;
Derivation: A Christian ceremony to heal people.

macihtiwina:
maci—preverb, bad, evil, wrong, wicked, ill;
macihti—animate intransitive verb, to sin;
win—nominalizer suffix;
a—pluralizer suffix;
Derivation: Evil deeds.

miyosit manitow:
(ê-)miyosi—animate intransitive verb, to be good, nice, pretty, handsome, beautiful;
t—third person singular inflection in the conjunct order without the */ê-/* preverb;
manitow—an animate noun, spirit, spirit being, God;
Derivation: He is a good God.

wêkosisimit:
kosis—dependent animate noun, son;
wê—third person singular variant possessive prefix;
im—noun possession element affixed to regular animate dependent nouns;
i—suffix found on some animate intransitive verbs derived from transitive animate verbs;
t—third person singular inflection in the conjunct order;
Derivation: He is God's Son.

ayamihêwi-tâpwêwakêyihtamowin:
ayamihêwi—preverb, of the Christian religion, of church;
tâpwêwakêyihtam—transitive inanimate verb, conjugated third person singular, independent order; s/he believes in something, regards something positively, to hold something to be true;
o—consonant joiner;
win—nominalizer suffix;
Derivation: Christian faith.

pakitinâsowin:
pakitinâso—animate intransitive verb, to give an offering (in a collection plate), to tithe;
win—nominalizer suffix;
Derivation: A sacrifice or a letting go.

kâsînamâkêw-iskotêhk:
kâsînamawêw—transitive animate verb, conjugated third person singular in the independent order; s/he wipes (it/him) off for someone; [Christian]: s/he forgives someone;
-ikê—suffix deriving an animate intransitive verb from a transitive animate verb, thus *kâsînamaw* becomes *kâsînamâkê*;[17]
iskotêw—inanimate noun; fire;
hk—locative suffix, in, on, under, over;
Derivation: At a fiery place for cleansing, in Purgatory.[18]

We grappled not only with adaptations and variants but also with unique terms. One seemingly insurmountable challenge was a word that could not be located in any dictionary or grammar; it appeared to stump every Elder and language expert we consulted. "Latakperakse" (PB 217) in SRO, found in the first lines of stanzas one, two, and three of Hymn 71, prompted hours of debate. Because it occurs close to the end of the text, we agreed that it was designed to convey a summative, affirming statement. Our first conjecture, which Cree Elders endorsed, "the belief of this faith," still sounded obscure and difficult to justify. We searched for clues in the word itself, since by that point we had acquired some familiarity with Grouard's hybridized, blended terms. Could there be a derivative in French or Latin, or another classical language, we wondered. Then, through splitting the term in two and repeating its components endlessly, the moment of illumination occurred. Might "latak" be a Cree representation of *la tâche* (task, work, or responsibility)? Could "perakse" be a form of *praxis* / πραξις (action, or practice)? By assembling the conjectural clues from these two parts, we arrived at the understanding of "the practice of living," which nicely complements and illustrates "the belief of this faith."

As we continued to pore over Grouard's work, we grew more and more impressed by his agility and deep understanding. We discovered his knack for fashioning Cree Syllabics to convey biblical discourse. The descent of the Son of God to earth to save His creatures is a fundamental portion of the Christian salvation account. Yet we struggled to find a Cree equivalent for "descend." Undaunted, Grouard uses two verbs to express this concept. On page 154 he writes ᑭ ᐃᐧ ᐯ ᐃᔭᓯᓐ—ki wi pe iyasin. We represent this in SRO as *kiwî-pêyâsin*—"You are going to come down through the air." Later, on page 195, Grouard writes ᐯ ᔭᓯᐢᑕᒪᐃᐧᔭᐠ—pe yasistamawiyak, which we write as *pê-yâsêstamawiyâhk*. In the first instance Grouard uses *pêyâsi-*, an animate intransitive verb stem meaning "to come down through the air,"[19] conjugated for a second person singular. The missionary chooses *yâsêstaw-* in the second example, a transitive animate verb stem meaning "to slide down to them,"[20] thus leaving us with the fanciful but fitting image of Jesus tobogganing down a great hill to earth. Another instance of his adaptability, this time as a hybridist, occurs in his forceful pastoral admonitions about the avoidance of sin. When Grouard catechizes about fleeing sin and thinking of the future, he skilfully combines one verb stem with a different verb final and warns against the lure of sin: ᐊᑲᒣᔨᑕᐸᓯᑕᐠ—akameyitapasitak (PB 130)—*âhkamêyihtapasîhtâhk*—"we must continuously flee sin and think of the future." He derives this particular verb by combining the VTI stem *âhkamêyihta*—"s/he continues to think of future deeds or tasks," with the VAIt final *-apasîht*—"s/he flees with something."[21]

These discoveries and challenges, which have enriched our experience with *kâtolik ayamihêwi-masinahikan*, stimulated meaningful discussions confirming that Grouard's text engages important and intriguing concerns. While transcription and transliteration are very manageable tasks, translation proves an extraordinarily more complex effort. Whereas it is relatively straightforward to translate nouns from Cree to English, such as in *masinahikan* (book) or *pahkwêsikan* (bread), translating verbs and whole sentences word for word from Cree to English is not possible because of the intricate word formation processes characteristic of *nêhiyawêwin*. For those who do not speak Cree, the practice of agglutination can bewilder us. Not only do Cree speakers compound words, they also inflect a multitude of prefixes and suffixes onto words to communicate an abundance of grammatical information, such as subject, verb, object/goal, possession, independent, conjunct, and subjunctive moods, as well as many others. Polysynthesis is another example of how Cree operates very differently from English; just as English follows rules of syntax within the sentence, word order is more fluid in Cree. This is not to say that *nêhiyawêwin* is any less developed a language than English, but the making of meaning in a Cree utterance, that is syntax, tends to occur in the sequencing of inflections in single words that may by themselves encompass a whole sentence. Where an English sentence might contain fifteen words, its translation in Cree might comprise only five or six words. Grouard understood these rules and how to make meaning in Cree. He has also given us a book of consequence that offers considerable clarification on the relationship between the missionary's message and the medium through which he delivered that teaching, a northern Indigenous language that showed remarkable adaptability to conveying new and different concepts.

What could arguably be more foreign to some readers today than the accretivism of Cree is the cast of the religious instruction in this text. Grouard does not palliate or mitigate. Expressing the urgency and commitment of a pastor, he recognizes but refuses to sugarcoat moral fallibility. Neither does he resort to finger-pointing or constantly threaten fire and brimstone. Yet we read this engrossing text as more than a study of tough love. Searchingly, Grouard plumbs the reality of the catechist's role: to inform and change lives. In the idiom and phraseology of his audience and readers, he presents accessible versions of standard prayers: the Our Father, Hail Mary, and the Creed (PB 6), and later the Rosary (PB 17–26) and the Angelus (PB 29). He catalogues and explains the Ten Commandments and seven Precepts of the Church (PB 7–9), interspersing brief, aphoristic observations about the need of "clean spirits" and the release of "bad words." His progress through the stages of the Mass (PB 15–24) emphasizes mercy, love, and forgiveness available from the divine source. Even as the communicant recognizes his unworthiness, he also acknowledges that "You thought of me as worthy" (PB 14). The sinner is encouraged to petition the Creator to "take me into Your home where they are happy" (PB 23).

A salient feature of Grouard's instruction is the humanizing links he draws between biblical narratives and lived experience. In the third Joyful Mystery of the Rosary, Jesus's being "born in poverty" is the cue that "we should not hate" this state (PB 27). In the third Station of the Way of the Cross, Jesus's falling the first time prompts the admission that "many times I have fallen down badly" and the realization that "that is why You are going to fall under the burden, so that my sins are forgiven" (PB 35). The catechism (PB 52–87), which rehearses the foregoing prayers and precepts, interprets their teachings through question and answer. Although our postmodern and post-Darwinian sensibilities might be mildly amused by the quaint cosmology of Grouard's biblical narratives (PB 55–73; 109–29), he drives home the point of the Eden story and Adam and Eve's eating of the forbidden "berries" (PB 59) as forcefully as he relates the mounting sin that occasioned the Flood (PB 60). The rapid summary of the exile of Israel in Egypt, the wandering in the desert, the reigns of David and Solomon, and the burning of the Temple in Jerusalem (PB 109–29) is suitably bookended by a meditation on the Beatitudes (PB 108) and a direction to "live well and humbly" (PB 129).

The moods of praise, thanksgiving, and petition in the concluding hymnal (PB 137–224) reinforce the previous lessons. The pithy but unrhymed lines bear little relation to the original Latin or French texts cited in their titles, but it is likely that the settings of these old hymns supplied the melodies with which they were sung. In many ways, this appropriation and re-fashioning are indicators of the earnestly purposive recycling of the whole *kâtolik ayamihêwi-masinahikan* project. Grouard used the melodies and lessons he knew and internalized so well to communicate with and evangelize the Cree. He was offering a teaching about evil to defeat evil, and an acknowledgement that we must forgive others before we can expect to be forgiven. For Grouard, the mission did not involve distancing himself from the Cree but leading them to share the zeal with which he was imbued.

NOTES TO AFTERWORD

1. Peter Bakker, "Algonquian Verb Structure: Plains Cree," *What's in a verb? Studies in the verbal morphology of the language of the Americas*. LOT. (Utrecht: Netherlands Graduate School of Linguistics, 2006): 3–27.
2. Arok Wolvengrey, compiler, and Freda Ahenakew, editor, et al., *nēhiyawēwin: itwēwina*, 2 vols (Regina: Canadian Plains Research Center, University of Regina, 2001), I: xx.
3. Wolvengrey and Ahenakew, *nēhiyawēwin: itwēwina*, I: 222, 225.
4. C. Douglas Ellis, "Cree Verb Paradigms," *International Journal of American Linguistics* 37.2 (1971): 76–95.
5. Emily Hunter and Betty Karpinski, *Plains Cree Grammar Guide and Glossary* (Edmonton: School of Native Studies, University of Alberta, 2001), 31.
6. Jean Okimāsis and Arok Wolvengrey, *How to Spell it in Cree (The Standard Roman Orthography) (oskana kâ-asastêki* [Regina]: *miywāsin ink*, 2008): 24.
7. *How to Spell it in Cree*, 8.
8. Wolvengrey and Ahenakew, *nēhiyawēwin: itwēwina*, I: 59.
9. Wolvengrey and Ahenakew, *nēhiyawēwin: itwēwina*, I: 134, 180.
10. Wolvengrey and Ahenakew, *nēhiyawēwin: itwēwina*, I: 8.
11. Earle Waugh, editor, Nancy LeClaire, George Cardinal, et al., *Alberta Elders' Cree Dictionary: alperta ohci kehtehayak nehiyaw otwestamâkewasinahikan* (Edmonton: University of Alberta Press and Duval House Publishing, 1998), 63.
12. Wolvengrey and Ahenakew, *nēhiyawēwin: itwēwina*, I: 217.
13. Wolvengrey and Ahenakew, *nēhiyawēwin: itwēwina*, I: 170.
14. Wolvengrey and Ahenakew, *nēhiyawēwin: itwēwina*, I: 32.
15. John D. Nichols, "The Cree Syllabary," In *The World's Writing Systems*, Peter T. Daniels and William Bright, eds. (New York: Oxford University Press, 1996): 601–602.
16. Jean Okimāsis and Arok Wolvengrey, "Cree Spelling: The Standard Roman Orthography" (Saskatoon: Cree Language Retention Committee, November 2002): 1.
17. Wolvengrey and Ahenakew, *nēhiyawēwin: itwēwina*, I: li.
18. Wolvengrey and Ahenakew, *nēhiyawēwin: itwēwina*, I: 16, 39, 56, 83, 84, 87, 110, 116, 122, 220.
19. Wolvengrey and Ahenakew, *nēhiyawēwin: itwēwina*, I: 180.
20. Waugh et al., *Alberta Elders' Cree Dictionary*, 235.
21. Wolvengrey and Ahenakew, *nēhiyawēwin: itwēwina*, I: 20, 216.

WORKS CITED AND CONSULTED

Abel, Kerry. *Drum Songs: Glimpses of Dene History*. Second Edition. Montreal: McGill-Queen's University Press, 2005.

Axtell, James. "Some Thoughts on the Ethnohistory of Missions." *Ethnohistory* 29.1 (1982): 35–41.

Banks, Joyce. "The Church Missionary Society and the Rossville Mission Press." *Papers of the Bibliographical Society of Canada* 32.1 (1994): 31–44.

Beaudet, Rev. Gérard. *Cree-English, English-Cree Dictionary*. Winnipeg: Wuerz Publishing, 1985.

Blaeser, Kimberly. "Writing Voices Speaking: Native Authors and an Oral Aesthetic." *Talking on the Page: Editing Aboriginal Oral Texts*. Ed. Laura J. Murray and Keren Rice. Toronto: University of Toronto Press, 1999; 53–68.

Boon, T.C.B. *The Anglican Church from the Bay to the Rockies*. Toronto: The Ryerson Press, 1962.

———. "The Use of Catechisms and Syllabics by the Early Missionaries of Rupert's Land," *The Bulletin* 13 (1960): 8–17.

Bruno-Jofré, Rosa. *The Missionary Oblate Sisters: Vision and Mission*. Montreal: McGill-Queen's University Press, 2005.

Canada. Dept. of the Interior. "General map of the northwestern part of the Dominion of Canada." Ottawa, Mortimer & Co. Lith., 1898. Map from William C. Wonders Map Collection, University of Alberta Libraries.

Castonguay, Thérèse, sgm. *A Leap of Faith: The Grey Nuns Ministries in Western and Northern Canada*. 2 vols. Edmonton: The Grey Nuns of Alberta, 1999.

Chroniques historiques de la mission du Lac La Biche. Unpublished typescript. Grey Nuns Regional Centre Archives, Edmonton, Alberta.

Daniels, Peter T. and William Bright, eds. *The World's Writing Systems*. New York: Oxford University Press, 1996.

Dickason, Olive Patricia. *Canada's First Nations: A History of Founding Peoples from Earliest Times*. Toronto: McClelland & Stewart, 1992.

Distad, Merrill. "Newspapers and Magazines," "Print and the Settlement of the West." *History of the Book in Canada, 1849–1914*. Ed. Yvan Lamonde, Patricia Lockhart Fleming, Fiona A. Black. Toronto: University of Toronto Press, 2005; 293–303, 62–71.

Duchassois, Rev. Father P., OMI. *The Grey Nuns in the Far North (1867–1917)*. Toronto: McClelland & Stewart, 1919.

Dusenberry, Verne. *The Montana Cree: A Study in Religious Persistence*. Stockholm: Almquist & Wiksells, 1962; rpt, Norman: University of Oklahoma Press, 1998.

Ellis, C. Douglas. "Cree Verb Paradigms." *International Journal of American Linguistics* 37.2 (1971): 76–95.

Evans, James. *Cree Syllabic Hymn Book* [Norway House, 1841]. *Bibliographical Society of Canada*, Facsimile Series No. 4, Publication 8. Toronto, 1954

Faraud, Monsignor Henri. *Dix-Huit Ans Chez les Sauvages*. Paris: Régis Ruffet & Cie, Successeurs, 1866.

Faries, Ven. R.A. *A Dictionary of the Cree Language. Based upon the Foundation Laid by Rev. E.A. Watkins, 1865, CMS Missionary*. Toronto: The General Synod of the Church of England in Canada, 1938.

Fauteux, Aegidius. *The Introduction of Printing into Canada*. Montreal: Rolland Paper Co., 1930.

Gingell, Susan. "Teaching the Talk That Walks on Paper: Oral Traditions and Textualized Orature in the Canadian Literature Classroom." *Home-Work: Postcolonialism, Pedagogy, and Canadian Literature*. Ed. Cynthia Sugars. Ottawa: University of Ottawa Press, 2004. 285–300.

Grouard, Monsignor. *Souvenirs de mes Soixante ans d'Apostolat dans l'Athabaska-Mackenzie*. Lyon: Œuvre Apostolique, de M.I., 1923.

Hanley, Philip M. *History of the Catholic Ladder*. Ed. Edward J. Kowrach. Fairfield, Washington: Ye Galleon Press, 1993.

Hengstler, Paul. "A Winter's Research and Invention: Reverend James Evans's Exploration of Indigenous Language and the Development of Syllabics, 1838–1839." MA Thesis, Department of History and Classics, University of Alberta. 2003.

Hospice Saint-Joseph Lac La Biche: Mémoire sur les 20 premières années de son histoire 1862–1882. Unpublished typescript. Grey Nuns Regional Centre Archives, Edmonton, Alberta.

Huel, Raymond. *Proclaiming the Gospel to the Indians and the Métis*. Edmonton: University of Alberta Press, Western Canadian Publishers, 1996.

Hulan, Renée and Renate Eigenbrod, eds. *Aboriginal Oral Traditions: Theory, Practice, Ethics*. Halifax and Winnipeg: Fernwood Publishing with the Gorsebrook Research Institute, 2008.

Hunter, Emily and Betty Karpinski. *Plains Cree Grammar Guide and Glossary*. Edmonton: Faculty of Native Studies, University of Alberta. 2001.

Hutcheon, Linda. *A Theory of Adaptation*. New York: Routledge, 2006.

Ingles, Ernie E. and N. Merrill Distad, eds. *Peel's Bibliography of the Canadian Prairies to 1953*. Revised and enlarged. Toronto: University of Toronto Press, 2003.

Levasseur, Donat, OMI. *Les Oblats de Marie Immaculée dans l'Ouest et le Nord du Canada, 1845–1967*. Edmonton: University of Alberta Press, Western Canadian Publishers, 1995.

Maccagno, Mike. *Rendezvous Notre-Dame des Victoires*. Lac La Biche: Mission Historical Preservation Society, 1988.

MacLean, John. *James Evans, Inventor of the Syllabic System of the Cree Language*. Toronto: William Briggs, 1890.

McCarthy, Martha. *From the Great River to the Ends of the Earth: Oblate Missions to the Dene, 1847–1921*. Edmonton: University of Alberta Press, Western Canadian Publishers, 1995.

McCullough , Edward J. and Michael Maccagno. *Lac La Biche and the Early Fur Traders*. Lac La Biche: Canadian Circumpolar Institute, Alberta Vocational College, 1991.

McKenzie, D.F. "Print and Publishing 1557–1700: constraints on the London book trade." *The Cambridge History of the Book in Britain*. Vol. IV. 1557–1695. Ed. J. Barnard and D.F. McKenzie. Cambridge: Cambridge University Press, 2002.

McNally, Vincent J. *The Lord's Distant Vineyard: A History of the Oblates and the Catholic Community in British Columbia*. Edmonton: University of Alberta Press, Western Canadian Publishers, 2000.

Mihesuah, Devon Abbott. *Indigenous American Women: Decolonization, Empowerment, Activism*. Lincoln: University of Nebraska Press, 2003.

Miller, J.R. *Lethal Legacy: Current Native Controversies in Canada*. Toronto: McClelland & Stewart, 2004.

———. *Shingwauk's Vision: A History of Native Residential Schools*. Toronto: University of Toronto Press, 1996.

Missions de la Congrégation des Oblats de Marie Immaculée. Paris: A. Hennuyer, 1875–1900.

Nichols, John D. "The Cree Syllabary." *The World's Writing Systems*. Ed. Peter T. Daniels and William Bright. New York: Oxford University Press, 1996; 599–611.

Okimāsis, Jean and Arok Wolvengrey. "Cree Spelling: The Standard Roman Orthography." Saskatoon, SK: Cree Language Retention Committee, 2002.

Ondaatje, Michael. *Divisadero*. Toronto: McClelland & Stewart, 2007.

Ong, Walter, SJ. *Orality and Literacy*. London: Methuen, 1982.

Peel, Bruce. "Rossville Mission Press: Press, Prints and Translators." *Papers of the Bibliographical Society of Canada* 1 (1960): 28–43.

Petitot, Émile. *Traditions Indiennes du Canada Nord-Ouest*. Paris: G.P. Maisonneuve & Larose, 1886.

———. *Travels around Great Slave and Great Bear Lakes 1862–1882*. Trans. Paul Laverdure, Jacqueline Moir, and John S. Moir. Toronto: The Champlain Society, 2005.

Ruffo, Armand Garnet. *(Ad)dressing Our Words: Aboriginal Perspectives on Aboriginal Literatures*. Penticton, BC: Theytus, 2001.

Sanneh, Lamin. *Translating the Message: The Missionary Impact on Culture*. New York: Orbis Books, 1984.

Shipley, Nan. *The James Evans Story*. Toronto: The Ryerson Press, 1966.

Stevenson, Winona. "Calling Badger and the Symbols of the Spirit Languages: The Cree Origins of the Syllabic System." *Oral History Forum* 19–20 (1999–2000): 19–24.

———. "The Journals and Voices of a Church of England Native Catechist: Askenootow (Charles Pratt), 1851–1884." *Reading Beyond Words: Contexts for Native History*. Ed. Jennifer Brown and Elizabeth Vibert. Peterborough, ON: Broadview Press, 1996; 305–29.

"Syllabics" www.tiro.com/syllabics/index.html (accessed 30 June 2008).

Warkentin, Germaine. "In Search of 'The Word of the Other': Aboriginal Sign Systems and the History of the Book in Canada." *Book History* 2 (1999): 1–27.

Waugh, Earle, ed. *Alberta Elders' Cree Dictionary*. Edmonton: University of Alberta Press, 1998.

Wolfart, H.C. and Freda Ahenakew. *The Student's Dictionary of Literary Plains Cree*. Winnipeg: Algonquian and Iroquoian Linguistics, 1998.

Wolvengrey, Arok, compiler. *nēhiyawēwin: itwēwina Cree: Words*. 2 vols. Regina: Canadian Plains Research Center, University of Regina, 2001.

Wolf, Maryanne. *Proust and the Squid: The Story and Science of the Reading Brain*. New York: Harper Perennial, 2007.

MANUSCRIPT SOURCES

Archives Deschâtelets, l'Université Saint-Paul, Ottawa, Ontario

Centre du Patrimoine de la Société Historique de Saint-Boniface, Manitoba

Grey Nuns Regional Centre, Edmonton, Alberta

Hudson's Bay Company Archives, Winnipeg, Manitoba

Oblate Collection, Provincial Archives of Alberta, Edmonton, Alberta